The Miracle of the Met

Books by QUAINTANCE EATON

Opera Caravan
Opera Production: A Handbook
The Boston Opera Company
Music and Recordings (*with Fred Grunfeld*)
Musical U.S.A. (*editor*)
The World of Music: An Encyclopedia (*editor*)
The Miracle of the Met

The
MIRACLE *of the* MET

An Informal History of the Metropolitan Opera

1883 – 1967

by

QUAINTANCE EATON

MEREDITH PRESS   NEW YORK

First edition

917224

To G. L. G. and T. M. P.

CONTENTS

ACKNOWLEDGMENTS

Research for such a project as this involves innumerable details to be found in the printed (and out-of-print) word and in conversations with people—such a quantity that the mention of all is difficult if not impossible. The earlier part of the Met's history required delving into old newspaper files, a fascinating job when there were a dozen morning and seven evening New York dailies, ten semiweeklies, and two hundred weeklies—not all pertinent of course. It was enjoyable unearthing treasurable bits from the critics less quoted by current historians: James G. Huneker (in the *Musical Courier, Recorder, Town Topics, New York Sun, Times,* and *World*), Henry T. Finck (*Evening Post*), Reginald de Koven (*World*), and various other gentlemen, mostly anonymous, on the *American, World, Herald, Brooklyn Eagle,* and others, instead of cleaving exclusively to the giants on the *Times* (W. J. Henderson and Richard Aldrich) and the *Tribune* (Henry E. Krehbiel), although both of course had pride of place. For Huneker quotes, the great man's son Erik spent a great many hours culling trenchant paragraphs to pass along. *Town Topics* and its busy editor Colonel Mann, winnowed with glee by Bill Cunningham, provided many delicious items in a society context. These and the musical journals were the publications most consulted in the New York Public Library central branch, newspaper division, and music division at Lincoln Center (where Sirvart Poladian gave assistance). In Newport's illustrious Redwood Library, Richard Champlin was helpful.

In order to keep the text as smoothly readable as possible, the author decided to forgo the impediments of notes and full pedigrees of books. Most volumes are specified by title as they occur, but to complete the record, a selected bibliography is appended (many of these books obtained from the comprehensive catalogue of the Mercantile Library in New York City). First and foremost, two impressive tomes must be credited: William Seltsam's *Metropolitan Opera Annals* and Supplement, and Irving Kolodin's *The Story of the Metropolitan Opera* (carried to 1950; the later edition of 1966 was not available when this manuscript was handed in). Mr. Kolodin's exhaustive chronicle is indispensable for factual material, a companion piece to Seltsam's, the two twin bibles of the Metropolitan.

Personal interviews were productive of much new material. The author is particularly grateful to two former Met administrators, Frank St. Leger and Max Rudolf. In a weekend at Indiana University, where Dean Wilfred Bain was most hospitable, prolonged conversations were possible with St. Leger, Tibor Kozma, and the numerous singers who have gravitated there from the Met. A side trip to Cincinnati yielded an hour with Rudolf, who also gave some of his valuable time in New York when he came on for the Farewell Gala. In the present administration unfailingly courteous were Rudolf Bing himself (his interview with this author provided a dress rehearsal for his radio broadcast soon after and, therefore, cannot be considered exactly exclusive, but many years of observation also served), John Gutman, Reginald Allen, Robert Herman, and Francis Robinson (as well as the press department's invaluable Anne Gordon, Dale Heapps, and Jean Thomas), Paul Jaretzki, Frank Paola, Glen Sauls, and Alfred F. Hubay. Herman Krawitz' department, especially Charles Riecker, supplied many facts. The incredibly efficient and charming secretaries of these gentlemen, beginning with Florence Guarino, deserve medals.

Talks with the outgoing and incoming presidents of the Association, Anthony A. Bliss and George S. Moore, provided background and current estimations of financial matters and artistic hopes; G. Lauder Greenway, a pillar of strength, supplied both history and anecdote; Howard Hook discussed the new plan for the Auditions. William Schuman gave pointers on Lincoln Center, of which he is president.

Many new insights into old regimes came out in conversations with Mrs. Herbert Witherspoon, Mrs. Charles Gleaves (daughter of Edward Ziegler), Helen Worden Cranmer (widow of John Erskine), Mrs. John Bingham (formerly Mrs. Lawrence Tibbett), Bruno Zirato (former secretary to Enrico Caruso), and Hy Faine (national executive secretary of AGMA). Lillian Gish shared her memories of Maurel; Edward Steichen, his of Morgan; Peggy Wood communicated her emotion about the Old

House. New light was shed on the Vanderbilts by a collateral, Mrs. Vanderbilt Webb; Mrs. Lytle Hull talked of early days; George Henry Warren recalled the first of his name who was so influential in the Met's genesis. A contemporary member of the Whitney family, Mrs. Flora Whitney Miller, reported that she is still faithful, and will watch performances from Box 25 in the New House. Max de Schauensee, critic and friend, disclosed some of his recollections of famous songbirds.

In the Metropolitan Archives, Mrs. John De Witt Peltz and Miss Marietta Fuller were patiently helpful, especially in the matter of photographs. *Opera News* was, of course, the invaluable source of photographic material (as well as offering an Aladdin's cave in its own bound volumes), and special thanks are owed to the editor Frank Merkling and to those who helped sift out the photographic selection that eventually became honed to a fine edge—Jean Uppman and Peggy Thomas. Gerald Fitzgerald read galleys and gave the benefit of his unparalleled knowledge of the current scene. The remainder of the staff provided genuine interest and moral support.

Once more, gratitude is owed to the best of editors, Theodore M. Purdy, who possesses ineffable knowledge and enthusiasm far beyond the call of duty. It has become a habit to finish the labors on bookish offspring at Theodore Erickson's Point View in Jamestown, R. I., and is very pleasant not to have to break that habit, especially as the summer retreat provided the ideal springboard for the Met's Verdi Festival at Newport 'cross the bay, where Dale Heapps and Eileen O'Brien labored valiantly, solving everyone's problems.

Q. E.

The Miracle of the Met

1

THE MEN

This was the day of Coal Barons, Merchant Princes, Tin-Plate Kings, and Monarchs of Finance. Bigness was synonymous with greatness, and expensiveness with worth. Although dynasties were often short—"three generations from shirtsleeves to shirtsleeves," as Oliver Wendell Holmes remarked—they sought to be as gloriously baroque as the brief reign of Heliogabalus. A château by Hunt, a box at the Metropolitan and a pair of opera glasses made by Lemaire [at a cost of $75,000], a C-spring carriage and a pair of spanking bays to drive through Central Park, and a yacht with rosewood panelling and marble pilasters in the saloon were the dream of every young accountant and bond-salesman. To own them was to belong to Society.

—DIXON WECTER, *The Saga of American Society*

Although there was hardly a true music lover in the lot, the men who lined the Golden Horseshoe at the opening of the Metropolitan Opera in New York represented all the royalty America could hope for— the royalty that Henry Clews, self-appointed historian of Wall Street, declared "springs from success in business." The opera was the first visible guerdon of the new Society's collective triumph.

From Ogden Goelet in Box 1, commanding the stage on the left, through Parterre cubicles containing Vanderbilts, Warrens, Astors, rival Goelets, Wetmores, a Rockefeller, a Clews, and a Field, on to Box 2 at the right, where Jay Gould could be seen to applaud frequently; from the First Tier just above, which swept around to contain J. P. Morgan and a substantial sampling of his complaisant partners, as well as James A. Roosevelt, James Gordon Bennett, D. Ogden Mills, and Adrian Iselin, over to Joseph W. Drexel at the right side of the proscenium arch, the current ran hot, swift, exhilarating—the power and wealth of the New World compressed and glittering within a few hundred cubic feet. That several older names should creep in—a Rhinelander and a Knickerbocker among them—only added the finial to the pinnacle. Eight years hence, nine of the upper-tier patrons, spearheaded by Morgan, would descend to the choicer regions below, but at this breathless, ineffable moment, the golden lyre rang out sweetly and completely. New York's capital-S

1

Society was alchemized into pure metal for three decades, to be dissolved only by a world upheaval and a government jealous of its worldly goods and aghast at their ruthless exploitation.

The men really started the new opera, however much prompting may have been applied in the boudoir. Their pride and their standing in the community of wealth had been challenged when the Academy of Music on East Fourteenth Street could not accommodate them with proper boxes. It was even rumored that William K. Vanderbilt had offered $30,000 for precious space, but had been politely rejected. The Academy's entrenched patrons, many of them bearing the "old Knickerbocker society" brand—Cuttings, Bayards, Lorillards, Van Hoffmans, Leavitts, Jaffrays, Beekmans, Van Rensselaers, Schuylers, and Sewards (August Belmont and Mrs. William Backhouse Astor should possibly not be included in this category), would move over only a mere trifle for the upstarts, and grudgingly at that. Robert Cutting, who refused to attend even a Metropolitan dress rehearsal for fear he would be taken for one of "them," expressed the Academy sentiments: "The new crowd could have been satisfied in time."

But there was no time. The new crowd was not willing to wait. So they built their own. Retaliation of this sort has been common to rich men always, and to Americans as wealth and capriciousness overtook them. One can still look to Texans for comparative flamboyance, while out in Colorado, the miner Spencer Penrose, an offshoot from a conventional Philadelphia family, was banished from Colorado Springs's superior hotel, The Antlers, and ran off in pique to erect the Broadmoor for his own use. When a guest of James Gordon Bennett, Jr., rode his polo pony into the sacrosanct Newport Reading Room, bringing down censure on Bennett, that unforgiving gentleman built a club of his own opposite his own house on Bellevue Avenue. This was the Casino, hallowed in tennis fame. In reprisal for the New York Union Club's blackballing of a business associate in 1891, J. P. Morgan founded the Metropolitan Club, which soon came to be known as the Millionaire's Retreat.

Rumblings of discontent in New York's opera world boiled to the surface early in 1880, when the *New York Times* reported on April 7 that $600,000 had been guaranteed by "sixty gentlemen of wealth and influence" (at various times this number would fluctuate) to build a new opera house. "The location will be near Fifth Avenue and Thirty-seventh Street." The next news proved the *Times* wrong, for the site proposed was the square block bounded by Vanderbilt and Madison avenues, Forty-third and Forty-fourth streets. A meeting on April 28 at Delmonico's (the famous restaurant that had moved from Fourteenth Street and Fifth Avenue to an elegant new location on Twenty-sixth, running through from Broadway to Fifth Avenue) brought out the information that J. N. A. Griswold had been elected president of the board (he gave way to James A. Roosevelt after a year); George Henry Warren, vice-president; and Egisto P. Fabbri, treasurer. Fabbri, a member of an old shipping firm and one of Morgan's first partners, would retire in 1884 because of a breakdown in health. Several directors fell by the wayside before the next year, among them a Livingston and a Winthrop.

The chosen site was owned, as could easily be discerned, by Vanderbilts. It was offered at $300,000; the building would cost $450,000. This block would undoubtedly have become a straitjacket as confining as the Metropolitan's eventual site, and been subject as well to the subterranean shakes from railroad trains' arrivals and departures. These fiery demons (just so many "iron horses in a china shop," remarked Louis B. Schlivek in *Man in Metropolis*) ran from the Grand Central Depot just across the street all the way in their smoky inferno under Park Avenue up to the Annexed District, which would later be incorporated into the city and become known as the Bronx.

But the Vanderbilts themselves had unwittingly stymied their project. Original owners of the New York and Harlem Railroad depot on the site (the first railroad in Manhattan, which had fallen into Vanderbilt hands) had protected themselves from the possibility of a freight or express depot as neighbor with a clause excluding any but residential structures in the vicinity. This was of course overcome, but not in time for the opera committee, which might have put up the $65,000 thought to be necessary to evade the restriction, since William H. Vanderbilt showed no intention of doing so himself.

Perhaps William H. was secretly relieved that the opera didn't stand there. It would, after all, have taken up the empty lot he had had fenced in for the sole occupancy of his prize trotter, Maud S., whose exercises he could watch fondly from his office window in Grand Central.

Another Vanderbilt property, on Thirty-fourth Street and Fourth Avenue, was considered. Then on Christmas Eve, William H. sent the following letter to Roosevelt:

DEAR SIR:

I am in receipt of yours of the 20th Inst. In naming the price to the Opera House Company I was largely influenced by the benefit which might ultimately accrue to the Railroad company from its successful operation. There was, therefore, a concession made to you of not less than twenty percent from its fair market value.

Having offered the property at a sacrifice it is impossible for me acting for the Company to contribute towards the removal of the restrictions as suggested by you and even if the whole amount was paid by you the property would still be cheap.

I am personally as desirous of facilitating in every way this enterprise as any other of the shareholders but in the present matter I necessarily act as an officer of the Company and can only convey as originally proposed the title we have at the price named.

The 34th St. property—200 feet on Park Avenue by 250 feet on 34th St. we will sell for $300,000, the Opera House Co. agreeing not to interfere with our City Line Railroad or its facilities.

Very truly yours,

WM. H. VANDERBILT

The Thirty-fourth Street lot was found to be subject to the same restrictions. Both East Side properties were abandoned. The Biltmore Hotel eventually occupied the first; the Vanderbilt Hotel the second. On January 10, 1881, the board reported that a possible site had been located. It could be bought for $450,000 from Roger Monoghan, and comprised the southwest corner of Thirty-ninth and Broadway, running through to Seventh Avenue, with 145 feet on the latter. Roosevelt discovered that the rest of the block could also be bought (part owner was said to be Jeremiah Johnson, Jr., one of the owners of the Knickerbocker Line and the Twenty-third Street Stage Line, son of General Johnson, mayor of Brooklyn in 1837–38). The complete parcel would cost $605,000. Estimate of the undertaking now rose to $1,050,000, and the capital stock was increased to that amount after forty-five stockholders had indicated on February 21 their willingness to go along. Of the 10,500 shares involved, William H. and William K. Vanderbilt each took 300, Cornelius 150.

The chosen architect, Josiah Cleaveland Cady, hoped to complete the building by October 22. One holdout in the dispossess proceedings having been dealt with for $3,010 plus lawyer's fee, the road seemed clear.

But by March 1882, abandonment of the entire project loomed. Roosevelt, speaking for the stockholders, told the newspapers: "The company will probably build an apartment house on the land." The inevitable had happened: building costs had zoomed. The total would be $1,525,000; individual assessments more than $23,000.

✗ How might the opera house be saved? Three plans had been proposed on March 7: to sell the land and divide the loss; to hold the land and let it lie unimproved; or to go ahead and meet the cost by mortgaging the superfluous land at the corners. The stockholders met on March 27. How they settled the troublesome matter of the "superfluous" corners soon same to light. Tailoring them to the opera's use for reception and supper rooms, with the possibility of earning rent as the Academy had done with extra space, would cost $370,000. George Kemp demurred: it would *not* be profitable. R. T. Wilson (whose somewhat opportunistic record of selling blankets to the Confederate Army had to be ignored in the light of his children's fortunate marriages) and G. G. Haven (partner of J. P. Morgan's closest friend and destined to endure long in the Metropolitan hierarchy) argued: "Yes, it would." The "ayes" carried. The Metropolitan Improvement Company was formed on the spot, capitalized at $350,000, to which many subscribed $5,000 each at once. Others were urged to consider the extra burden as an assessment. Roosevelt was reelected president; Warren, vice-president; Luther Kountze, banker, became treasurer. Board members also included Adrian Iselin (already considered among the Old Guard), W. H. Vanderbilt, W. H. Tillinghast, Robert Goelet, J. W. Drexel, T. A. Havemeyer, George Peabody Wetmore (distinguished Rhode Island politician and a Morgan associate), W. C. Whitney, and Edward Cooper (Vanderbilt connections). Edmund C. Stanton, a relative of one of these and destined for even greater authority, was chosen as secretary.

✗ The acquisition of a home for what Henry James had called the "great vessel of social salvation" was now assured. James Roosevelt helped with a bit of philosophy that did not entirely jibe with his fellow stockholders' opinions: "We never expected it to pay. No opera house ever has. It is simply for the enjoyment of first-class opera." But after all he

[handwritten margin note:] they abandoned 2 sites by this time because of certain restrictions

represented what might be called the patrician element of the group, minuscule as it was.

To a writer for *Harper's Weekly,* the agonies of this group of patrons were completely discounted. What other cause, he wondered, could so briefly and easily induce seventy men of business to subscribe more than $20,000 each for an opera house? "Compare this with the struggle of the Metropolitan Museum (which had moved into its huge new building on upper Fifth Avenue in 1880) to raise money, or the languishing condition of the project to erect a Protestant cathedral." Opera must exert a powerful attraction, he concluded, with possibly conscious naïveté.

The date of completion was pushed forward a year. Then, after inspecting the unfinished house on May 23, 1883, the stockholders repaired to the foyer of the Casino across the street to participate in the solemn ceremony of drawing for boxes. They persisted in the charming fiction that it was all a gamble, pure chance, and so democratic! Of course, anyone could change afterward if he wished (and could persuade another to bend to his wishes). At the end, three boxes remained unclaimed in the Parterre: numbers 9 and 24, snapped up by the Astors (who gave up 30 to W. K. Vanderbilt, already in 28, and Number 34, which W. H. Vanderbilt was happy to add to his adjoining 35. That the gods could permit a Vanderbilt or Astor or Morgan such evil luck as to pull out an upper-tier number seems unlikely, yet W. K. Vanderbilt was handed numbers 54 and 58 as well as 28. Incredible as it may be, Morgan gave up Number 7 to William C. Whitney, of the Standard Oil fortune, whose faultless Yankee pedigree equaled Morgan's own, and whose son Harry Payne clinched a fifty-million-dollar dowry by marrying Gertrude Vanderbilt, daughter of Cornelius II. (For his infrequent incursions into musical society, Morgan would perch in Number 56 until 1891, when he outdrew the Vanderbilts for Number 35 at the very heart of the horseshoe.) Robert Goelet managed to trade his upper 47 to Edward Lockmayer for 18, so that the Goelets already in 20 could spread over a double dominion. Presumably happy in their higher perches were George F. Baker, James A. Roosevelt, R. T. Wilson, D. O. Mills, G. G. Haven, L. P. Morton, J. W. Drexel, J. G. Bennett, and William Rhinelander.

No one seemed to blame any initial ill luck on Miss Warren (George's daughter), who drew envelopes with names enclosed, and a Miss Townsend, who matched them with numbers selected by chance. G. G. Haven called out the results and R. T. Wilson presided over the animated scene.

Of the seventy-three boxes, two in the First Tier were left for the use of the impresario, who invited his second prima donna, Mme. Marcella Sembrich, to the opening. The top tier showed no social distinction whatever, having been auctioned off for opening night only. In Box 102 sat William Steinway, the piano manufacturer, who because of his familiarity with transportation to and from his factory on Long Island, would be appointed the first Rapid Transit Commissioner in the city.

Before the positions had hardened irrevocably, relationship with the Academy of Music came up for serious discussion. The correspondence for the past three years between the warring factions passed around the circle; soberly it was proposed that once again a reconciliation be attempted. As late as the twin opening nights of the Met and the Academy, the *Tribune* put forth the unrealistic suggestion that the two camps might hold forth alternately.

The Academy impresario, the intransigent Col. James H. Mapleson, answered all this nonsense with a florid negative. He had, he said, been offered all concessions from his own board and preferred to remain exclusive. This sanguinity did not entirely match the report that Academy stockholders had expressed anger at the possibility of an assessment of $130 per share to make up Mapleson's deficit. But the manager, turning his back to the wall on which dim writing was already beginning to appear, dismissed the whole Metropolitan venture as a plaything of "a number of rich persons."

Rivalry between the old and new houses showed plainly on opening night. "The social power of each audience was exerted to the utmost to give prestige and success to its house," commented the *Tribune,* although to be truthful, the Academy gathering did not quite measure up to previous brilliance. Perhaps this was because Mrs. William Astor had not even come into town, although her satellite Ward McAllister was seen at both openings. Adrian Iselin, descended from a distinguished Swiss banking family, and S. L. M. Barlow were the only open defectors from the Academy.

It was not impossible to find, in the Golden Horseshoe's round, personages unattached by marriage or money to the Triple Entente—Astor, Vanderbilt, Morgan. The Roosevelts moved in their own orbit. Whatever their origins in "trade," this family, particularly Franklin Delano's branch, had become aristocrats. Franklin's father, the James A. Roosevelt of the Metropolitan's first governing board, was by now the Squire of Hyde Park and immune to mere moneymaking. The Cutting family— Robert soon joined the Metropolitan's inner circle—had a real estate background. George H. Warren's ancestors had come over on the boat "just after the *Mayflower,* the second section," according to his grandson, the present George Henry. He moved from Connecticut to Troy, New York (a favorite birthplace of many eminent persons) and thence to the metropolis. A favorite with his contemporaries for his wit and perennial good nature, the lawyer and banker was the ideal emissary to the Academy for the "new crowd," although he eventually had to admit defeat.

As for the Goelets, they wielded their own sceptres. Robert and his younger brother Ogden each inherited fifty million from their father Peter, who forsook *his* father Peter's modest musical instrument business for ironmongery and soon realized the value of the land on which he trod. He bought "a few acres to the north." Robert was married to George Warren's sister, Harriet Louise, who matched her brother as a wit. Mrs. Ogden Goelet was one of the rather "pushy" Wilson girls. Her sister Grace did even better, winning Cornelius Vanderbilt III, while her brother Orme married Carrie Astor. Robert and Ogden drew abreast in the matter of yachts and Newport cottages, entertaining royalty, and just entertaining, but Mrs. Ogden scored by drawing Box 1 at the Metropolitan (as well as an upper-tier box). Mrs. Robert professed to be content with numbers 18 and 20.

Directly across from Mrs. Ogden, in Box 2, brooded the powerful, shrunken, ugly Jay Gould. He was forty-seven that first night at the opera, and worth $100 million. He had just relinquished to Joseph Pulitzer his four-year hold on the New York *World,* which promptly turned against him. He had used the newspaper to threaten Western Union, largest of telegraph companies, with lower-priced competition, and when its stock plummeted, promptly acquired control. He had performed the same service for the Manhattan Elevated Railway Company.

Gould died "the most hated man in the United States," wrote the indignant Gustavus Myers in his *History of the Great American Fortunes.* At his death, newspapers which had "bootlicked" in his life, now "belched forth vituperation and rehearsed his odious deeds." These, too many to be catalogued, included looting of the railroads—even Vanderbilts smarted under his tactics and his association with the notorious James Fisk and Daniel Drew. The most famous of his infamies was the attempt to corner gold, which led to the Black Friday of 1869, and brought Morgan in as "the great sublime patriot" to save the country by persuading the President to sell gold.

"If any man ever called Jay Gould friend, the record of it is lost," remarked Stewart H. Holbrook in *The Age of the Moguls*. What could be seen above a gray-streaked heavy beard reminded Holbrook of a frustrated poet, although his other detractor, Myers, detected no frustration in his "swarthy, bilious, glowering face, rigid with hard, deep lines." He seldom left his opera box during the rare performances he attended.

A complete contrast was his crony, Russell Sage, tall, with light skin and gray eyes, resembling in those surroundings a country gentleman seeing the sights, as Henry Clews described him. Partly because his fortune amounted to only about one fifth of his mentor's, and also because of his own nature, Sage thought twice before spending two pennies apiece for his daily lunch apples when his favorite apple seller confessed that the price of apples had doubled. Sage made do with a single apple thereafter except for the days when he walked many blocks to the Western Union Building, where free lunch was served to the stockholders. Practicing this and other personal economies, Sage ran his fortune up two and one-half times, and probably would have turned over in his grave to see what his widow did with it. The Russell Sage Foundation, which aims to improve social (not "Social") conditions in the United States, and the Emma Willard School and other worthy institutions sprang from the second Mrs. Sage, not from the parsimonious old capitalist who died at ninety in 1906.

If either Gould or Sage could have been suspected of delicacy, one might believe that they remained in their opera snuggery on opening night in order to avoid the gentleman who sat in Box 8, just two removed. They could hardly be seen for the dividing walls, but it is possible that Cyrus West Field cast some sorrowful glances their way. They had barely finished ruining him. The distinguished inventor of the ocean cable, which had been laid successfully in 1858 after several disappointments, had gone in over his depth with Gould and Sage in controlling the Manhattan Elevated Railway. He put himself in exceedingly bad graces with his partners by reducing the "El" fare to five cents and they decided to do without him. They urged him to buy more stock, "watered" it, and let him drown. Mrs. J. Borden Harriman's grandfather told her that J. P. Morgan "gave an income" to Field anonymously when he was ruined and ill. Neither Field nor Gould lived to join in the next opera-box drawing.

Probably Gould looked indifferently at Box 29 across the way, where sat José F. de Navarro, an official of the Metropolitan Elevated Railway, which had been investigated on charges of bribery in 1879.

It might have amused Gould in a ghoulish sort of way to know that Henry Clews, in his rambling reminiscences of Wall Street, would attribute pure motives to him in trying to corner gold—originally, at least—and place the blame on his "erratic" associate, Jim Fisk. But then the bright-eyed Clews, who sat in Box 14 beyond Field, always saw the gold lining. He set the tone for generations to come when he wrote: "The very magnitude of Wall Street is living proof of its moral stamina."

Directly across the brilliantly lit chasm in Box 11 was another Wall Street operator, a "great bear," whom Clews accounted a bold iconoclast. Charles T. Woerishoffer, light in weight and slight in stature, did not look the part, but he had snarled at the heels of Gould and Sage in one railroad battle already and was presently involved with the Titan of them all, William H. Vanderbilt, whom he could see at the center of the horseshoe. His West Shore Railroad, built in direct competition to the Vanderbilt's New York Central, and for which he got money even from Astors and D. O. Mills, would soon meet the fate of all who braved the colossus, but not before it figured ingloriously in the second of the Metropolitan's ventures out of town.

Three California plutocrats aroused excited interest. Charles Crocker's bushy beard could be seen in Box 31. The western railroad manipulator, born in Troy, New York, and beginning as a blacksmith, would see the consolidation of his Central Pacific and Southern Pacific railroads in 1884 and find California scenery more agreeable than New York's from then on. A fall from his carriage in 1886 resulted in injuries which carrried him off two years later. The huge Collis Potter Huntington, who physically did resemble a bear but was often compared to a shark or a crocodile in business dealings, was gentled down to fairly steady opera patronage only after he acquired a socially ambitious second wife in 1884. Born in the East, he stayed when Crocker went back west.

Darius Ogden Mills lingered longest in the East where he was born. His sagacity in banking and mining stock brought the means to decorate a mansion opposite St. Patrick's Cathedral at slightly less than half a million—which frankly he thought too high once it was done—and to acquire the niceties of life in European capitals. Delighted at the marriage of his son Ogden to one of the revered Livingstons a year before the Metropolitan opening, Mills was equally gratified at the joining of his name to the aristocratic Whitelaw Reid's, and bought his daughter the Villard palace on Madison Avenue, not blinking this time at the price of $400,000. Mills's cup remained comfortably full and would have spilled over generously had he known that his daughter would be a devoted Red Cross official and a sincere philanthropist, his son-in-law Ambassador to the Court of St. James and a distinguished journalist, one grandson (Ogden Mills Reid) the editor of the New York *Tribune* (which his mother owned and his father had edited), and another (Ogden Livingston Mills) Secretary of the Treasury (if only for a fleeting year to fill out the term of Andrew Mellon, who was sent to the Court of St. James). D. O. Mills might have protested as excessive the claim of the Reverend Charles Wilbur de Lyon Nichols in an exquisitely serious tract, *The Ultra-Fashionable Peerage of America,* that his son "descended gracefully from kings." Although Mills suffered bad luck in drawing an upper-tier box, his son and daughter were invited to Cornelius Vanderbilt's Number 17 for the opening and he himself got Number 20 the next go-around, his family holding it for four dozen years.

Another "new" fortune, not so large but speaking boldly through the pranks of its flamboyant owner, bought an upper-tier box, Number 60. James Gordon Bennett, Jr., believed fervently in the power and grace of Society with a capital S, utterly reversing the stand of his fiercely independent sire, who peppered the columns of his New York *Herald* with many "saucy" remarks about the institution. Happy in the sporting set, Bennett Junior introduced polo to America, gloried in coaching parades, and made himself—as well as a cow and an electric milker—at home on a succession of magnificent yachts. New York could not quite accustom itself to his wild, nocturnal—and often naked—drives down the avenues, alternating with determined sorties on a bicycle while his butler waited on the sidewalk with a decanter of brandy to be nipped between laps. It was hard to forgive his insulting behavior to a genteel young lady (he is said to have used a fireplace for unsuitable purposes), which got him a horsewhipping from the girl's brother in front of the Union Club and a farcical duel. The ensuing ridicule drove Bennett to Paris except for flying visits. Several of these must have found him in his Metropolitan box, although his fondness for opera never was demonstrated except as a place to exhibit his pronounced dandyism. Yet Dixon Wecter implies that he liked the theatre to the extent of kidnaping an entire company in Amsterdam for a few days' performances at sea. Gould would remember him with no pleasure as the destroyer of his monopoly of the transatlantic cable, in which enterprise his partner was John W. Mackay (whose descendants became opera-minded). American expatriates like himself remember him with gratitude for founding their bible, the Paris edition of the *Herald*. And the general public might like to thank him for making possible the greeting that became a catchword: "Dr. Livingstone, I presume?" as he financed Stanley's pilgrimage to Africa.

Everybody, or almost everybody, liked the occupant of Box 32. William Rockefeller, the "nice" brother of John, inherited a slice of the temperament if not of the moral code of his patent-medicine-man father, "Big Bill." William's elder brother, John Davison, it is safe to say, cared little for opera or for the social whirl that encompassed it. A certain dutiful attitude would animate his son, John Davison, Jr., into offering the opera a new home in what came to be known, almost five decades later, as Rockefeller Center; one of *his* sons, John Davison III, belongs to today's Lincoln Center hierarchy. Another, Nelson, as Governor of New York, instituted an Arts Council that has been the prototype for such governmental sponsors of the arts. But for the moment William carried the musical—or rather, social—amenities alone. In fact, he was "not averse to a little innocent social climbing," said Wecter, and was happy to be associated with Roosevelts and Astors in the new Metropolitan. Yet in business he remained "sharp as they came, usually sharper," commented Holbrook. J. P. Morgan, who professed himself chilled by the cold money lust of the first John D., was one of those who liked William, inviting him to join the exclusive Corsair Club, inner circle of yachtsmen. William did not endure past the great reshuffle of 1891, but he enlivened the scene of the Metropolitan's first years.

With a few exceptions, the remainder of the Golden Horseshoe turned like flowers to one of three golden suns that outshone the magnificent gas chandelier and left an afterimage on the retina when the lights lowered. Astor, Vanderbilt, Morgan—which is the greatest, most dazzling, most magnetic? Whether to genuflect most deeply before the nobility of real estate, railroads, or just plain money? This was the modern nobility that had sprung from success in business, as defined by Henry Clews, himself the son of an uneducated English potter, now risen to a point where his wife met Newport cottagers on their own ground (by the direct partisanship of Mrs. Belmont).

The John Jacob Astor who sat in Box 24 had come a long way up Fifth Avenue since his grandfather, whose name he had inherited, had to a considerable extent fulfilled his ambition to buy every square foot on the Island of Manhattan. "The Landlord of New York" was excoriated only slightly less than Jay Gould for his methods of trade with the Indians for furs and for his seeming callousness to the fate of those who dwelt in his slums.

John Jacob III was accounted the first to receive an infusion of blue blood; his mother, Rebecca Armstrong, was a member of the "most aristocratic family in New York." His own son would forswear the America for which John Jacob himself professed contempt and become more English than the English. At the time of the Metropolitan's inauguration, John Jacob III was six feet tall, with ruddy face, thick moustache, and side-whiskers. His biographer, Harvey O'Connor, stamped him as "a symbol of masterful wealth, aloof and austere as Jove, imperial in his style of living, generous in charities (as his progenitors had not been), rock-ribbed in High Church and Republican orthodoxy"—altogether a forbidding character. The Civil War came as a blessed channel for his energies.

Brother William was accounted the first "decadent" Astor, retreating from outward social life as well as business. Both men were treasured targets of that malicious dart-thrower, Col. William d'Alton Mann of *Town Topics,* the gossip magazine that titillated and infuriated New York's Fifth and Newport's Bellevue avenues. Typical was: "If an Astor were to be reminded that he owes something to his community, he would immediately have a bilious attack and order the curtailment of his house expenditures. As for utilizing any portion of his fortune to improve the intellectual or artistic status of his fellow countrymen, that would be an eccentricity in an Astor that would move the remainder of his family to put him in seclusion."

Both brothers married girls with wills as strong as the whalebones in their bodices: John Jacob a Southern belle, Charlotte Augusta Gibbes, fragile and charming, who felt she was entitled to live on Fifth Avenue, own a villa at Newport, entertain lavishly, buy paintings, and show herself at the opera. Her father had founded the Union Club.

William's wife, Caroline, was another story, as will be seen.

The example *in excelsis* of the American plutocrat was John Pierpont Morgan. Character was Morgan's watchword; he confounded a Congressional investigation into the "money trusts" by naming "character" as virtually a sole criterion for trusting a man in business—which usually meant lending money—above wealth or property. Other symbols that could have emblazoned Morgan's shield might have been a sleek black ship, the *Corsair* ("If you have to ask the cost of a yacht, you cannot afford one"); prancing horses pulling his carriage onto a sidewalk at his orders ("I owe the public nothing!"); and a monstrous complex of steel threatened by a man who carried a big stick ("Theodore Roosevelt was a gentleman gone wrong!"). The President of the United States had publicly avowed his disrespect for mere wealth, naming Morgan specifically. There would scarcely have been room in a Morgan coat of arms for his mountainous acquisitions—paintings, statues, manuscripts, miniatures, and thousands of other art objects, bought "by the ton" and housed (the choicest items) in the beautiful marble library built by Charles McKim adjoining the Morgan brownstone at Thirty-sixth and Madison; for the dogs—his gift of a collie to a promising young man indicated the first step up the Morgan ladder; for the Morgan partners—called a "partner-killer," he himself came through the grind "as impregnable as a force of nature."

Hewing to religion and public morality to an extreme the opera would later feel, he exempted himself from censure and shrugged off the jests that attended his founding of a Society for the Prevention of Vice on the one hand and a lying-in hospital on the other. When Charles M. Schwab, the steel magnate, had been skylarking all over Europe but gave the excuse that it was done openly, not behind closed doors, Morgan remarked dryly, "That's what doors are for!"

Historians of various stamp reserve contrasting words for Morgan's "singlehanded" rescue of the American nation on two occasions, in panics of 1893 and 1907. He showed himself to be a kind of supergovernment, one biographer, John K. Winkler, observed. "Part poet, part pirate, almost God in his own and others' estimation, he ruled the pitiless, predatory world of cash. He did things that today could not be defended in law or morals, but for his time, he played the game fairly" —by rules he largely set up himself.

"Under present-day rules," Stewart Holbrook remarked in *The Age of Moguls*, "almost every man in the book would face a good hundred years in prison."

Morgan's personality, which could only be termed overwhelming, made up of "audacity, sublime self-confidence, unequalled courage and amazing virility of mind and body," dominated the Metropolitan's inner circles as surely as his banking house came to represent all their fortunes, no matter how diverse, no matter what clashes of temperament between the central figure and a Vanderbilt, a Gould, a Drexel, a Ryan, a Field. A good hater, Morgan reserved the depths of this emotion for Jews and certain vigorous dissidents from his position—E. H. Harriman, Andrew Carnegie, John ("Bet-you-a-million") Gates, and the older Rockefeller.

Morgan had not been elevated to the higher realms of the new opera coterie because of his musical appreciation or taste. A strong and indefatigable hymn singer, who could wear out his friends by his energy and roaring voice—not always immaculately in tune—he also, with that ambivalence notable in his private life, collected and relished sprightly ditties in English, German, and French. Bored except for a few tune-saturated operas such as *Il Trovatore*, he would doze off in the box salon during his infrequent visits. Still, a work of art could kindle in him an extraordinary emotion. The man of steel and iron "became putty before the brush of Raphael or the melody of Mozart." There is little evidence that this composer really awoke such sentiments, but Morgan's bondage to the visual arts was genuine. Aline Saarinen insists that he was not the "checkbook collector," nor megalomaniac like William Randolph Hearst, but a "true patrician, to the art-manner born; he collected because he enjoyed shopping; collected art because he was truly moved by beauty." The Morgan collections, she concludes, represent "the most grandiose gesture of *noblesse oblige* the world has ever known." The Metropolitan Museum (of which he was president from 1904 to his death) drew infinitely more response from him than the Metropolitan Opera.

Everyone mentioned his eyes first in describing him. Really dark blue, said Winkler, they were awful in anger, they blazed and seemed to change color. "They came at you like locomotive headlights," said the famed photographer Edward Steichen. These spectacular orbs would ignite the more fiercely if they caught others dropping ever so slightly to the nose between them. This nose, horribly enlarged and suffused with purple veins through a mysterious and unrelenting disease, gave Morgan his sole excuse for personal unhappiness. Like Cyrano, he would jest to forestall comment, but it remained perpetually a sore point.

Morgan satellites revolved around their sun in opera circles, well content that they had been allowed to "buy in." George F. Baker loomed among them, that sphinx of the First National Bank, who belonged to the dazzling group that made financial history a decade later—James Stillman, Henry Clay Frick, Henry H. Rogers of Standard Oil, Levi P. Morton, James J. Hill, Jacob H. Schiff, and Edward H. Harriman— the "malignant magnates," as a detractor was to call them. Baker was accounted Morgan's closest friend as well as business associate. He came into the Metropolitan at upper-box level, and in 1891 moved to the consolidated ring below. J. Hood Wright, one of Morgan's first partners, occupied Box 23 in 1883 and Box 21 in 1892. An incorporator of the Edison Electric Illumination Company in 1882, he had been largely responsible for Morgan's venturesome installation of the new lighting in his Madison Avenue house in the summer of 1883—the first private residence to boast it.

George Peabody Wetmore, holding boxes 3 and 4 in 1883 and Box 5 in 1892, came under Morgan's wing. Both Senator from and Governor of Rhode Island, Wetmore and his family attained such distinction in Newport that they could afford to ignore a snub from King Edward VII. The only other politician in the circle—which considered politicians pawns to be moved across the board of their own interests—was Levi Parsons Morton, a Congressman in 1879, Minister to France in 1881, and destined to be the United States Vice President in 1889 and Governor of New York in 1895. A lovable personality, Chauncey Depew said of him—that Chauncey Depew who was master of the afterdinner speech, publicist for the Vanderbilts, and author of a book that shows not a whit of the sparkle attributed to his verbal utterances.

Morgan's flock contained more business associates than blood relatives. His son, John Pierpont Morgan, Jr., and three daughters, Mrs. Paul Pennoyer, Mrs. George Nichols, and Mrs. Herbert L. Satterlee (Satterlee wrote a cordial biography of his father-in-law), were more often seen than the titan himself. This was in sharp contrast to the second vital arc of the circle—the Vanderbilts.

The Vanderbilts seemed to be all family. What Morgan conferred by partnership, this dynasty conferred by marriage, embracing, though not always willingly, grit along with diamond dust—Wilsons with Whitneys, Sloans with Twomblys, Gwynns and (Southern) Smiths and even lesser lights with Webbs, striking a generally favorable balance, however, and often adding social luster with each generation. Since dowries did not invariably accompany brides, while grooms were not always stable (in fact, one couldn't really make up his mind, so he married two Vanderbilt girls—in tandem of course), the Founding Father would not have approved each and every addition. Profane, audacious, hot-tempered; the parsimonious householder who nevertheless equipped the costliest yacht for a braggadocio trip to England; the ruthless husband who imprisoned his wife for nagging; the indulgent father who incarcerated his epileptic son—in short, "Commodore" Cornelius Vanderbilt was the very heart of the flame of the growing spirit of materialism. He had "discovered and taken the then new way of imperialism and monopoly," wrote Holbrook. He pyramided ten million to a hundred within twelve years after the Civil War and could then be reckoned the richest man in America.

At his death in 1877, the Commodore was sung out by his family intoning with perfect irony the hymn "Come, Ye Sinners, Poor and Needy." His son William Henry and two grandsons, Cornelius II and William Kissam, turned their minds to higher musical plateaus a few years later. William H. had blossomed surprisingly as a businessman, perhaps because of the nature of his first coup, a sharp deal in manure from the family horsecar stables. His slowly budding concern with culture manifested itself in purchases of large, sentimental paintings (horses on canvas fascinated him as in the flesh, so that Rosa Bonheur inevitably dominated his $11½ million collection); in the spectacular gesture of bringing Cleopatra's Needle from Egypt to Central Park at the cost of $100,000; in building twin mansions for himself and his daughters on Fifth Avenue between Fifty-first and Fifty-second streets; and in the opera box. Henry Clews generously attributed to him "a refined taste for music, especially opera music."

Only the last two years of his life enabled him to display that taste; he died in 1885, leaving the field, along with the fortune he had doubled, to Cornelius II and William K. A passion for horses may have contributed to William Henry's death at only sixty-four. Just four days before the opera opening, he had been thrown from his wagon, driving the cup races of the Gentlemen's Driving Association Club up at Fleetwood Park in the north end of the city. He "fell in a heap, as the expressive phrase is," reported the *Tribune,* but seemed fully recovered almost immediately. He had retired from active railroad business in May, almost premonitorily, then had gone through painful days in October refuting rumors that his son William K. was bankrupt. "Why, W. K. was worth at least eight million above his engagements," fumed William's father. "He could buy 'em all up. A damnable outrage!" he concluded.

At the opera opening, W. H. was thought by the *Times* to have developed an unusual degree of sociability, "occupying two of the three boxes at different times, visiting friends in their boxes and chatting freely in the lobby, apparently in good spirits, but growing round-shouldered."

He had never lived down the unfortunate remark that his apologists never tired of trying to explain away. How extenuating were the circumstances, one may judge from Henry Clews's account Vanderbilt wanted to take off the fast mail train to Chicago because it was losing money. A reporter protested that the public found it convenient and useful. "If so, why don't they patronize it?" demanded the magnate. The reporter countered (foolishly, one would think): "Are you working for the public or for your stockholders?" "The public be damned!" Vanderbilt exploded, placing himself and his four words forever enshrined alongside Marie Antoinette's own four: "Let them eat cake!"

The young Vanderbilts seemed to Clews "remarkable for their intellectual power as well as a high degree of refinement, showing how fast human evolution under favorable circumstances progresses in this country." Cornelius II became head of the clan; he was considered more "serious" than William K. Both remained close in the councils of the opera, while their wives fought out the battle in the other two corners of the triangle—Fifth Avenue and Newport. The most formidable adversary had already been met at the time of the Metropolitan's opening: the lady known simply as Mrs. Astor.

2

THE WOMEN

It is the women who regulate the style of living, dispense hospitalities, exclusively manage society, control clergy, men, and churches, regulate the schemes of benevolence, patronize and influence the arts, and pronounce upon Operas and foreign novelties.

—N. P. WILLIS

Her name was Caroline Webster Schermerhorn; she was born in 1831. Her father, Abraham, descendant of a Revolutionary ship chandler, was said to be worth half a million in 1845. Her brother Bruce left her all his property in 1862. By that time she could be said not to need it, for in 1853 she had married William Backhouse Astor, grandson of John Jacob—then the richest man in America—and brother of John Jacob III. Although deploring her husband's relatively inferior blood (somewhat purified by his mother, an Armstrong), she did not disdain the name of the founder and called her son John Jacob IV (the founder's namesake, John Jacob II, had been rendered mentally incompetent by a childhood fall).

For two decades William, who had shared his father's residuary estate with John Jacob III (now designated head of the House of Astor with certain real estate perquisites over William) had found his wife to be an ideal housewife and mother. But greater ambitions stirred within her. After she had brought up her son and three daughters (not uniformly attractive) to marriageable age, she, with the generosity Ward McAllister appreciated so deeply, "gave herself to society."

In a fatuous book entitled *Society As I Have Found It*, McAllister, the Grand Arbiter, had written:

The mistake made by the world at large is that fashionable people are selfish, frivolous and indifferent to the welfare of their fellow creatures . . . [they] nourish and benefit art and artists; they cause the expenditure of money and its distribution; and they really prevent our people and country from settling down into a humdrum rut and becoming merely a money-making and

20

money-saving people, with nothing to brighten up and enliven life. . . . I have found as warm, loving hearts in the garb of fashion as out of it . . . [one woman] having great fortune, had the ability to conceive and carry out social projects. Above all, she is a true and loyal friend in sunshine and shower.

Displaying a generalship worthy of her grandfather-in-law, McAllister's true and loyal friend proceeded, according to Harvey O'Connor, to rival the great "consolidators"—Vanderbilt, Gould, Harriman, and Hill in railroads, Morgan in industry—by creating in society "the community of interests, the perfect harmony and centralization of control that marked the emergence of modern America." In short, a monopoly.

Over this realm Caroline Astor reigned supreme, the dictator without rival. Nowhere else in American history is there recorded an instance of equal social power in the hands of one woman. It was a time of concentration of wealth that invariably spilled over into excess. The men, gamblers all, with batteries of lawyers to keep them out of jail, played at putting industries together, forming corporations and holding companies with capital of staggering size—coal, oil, gold, silver, copper, tobacco, wool, cotton, transportation, utilities, banks—and they all gravitated to New York.

Their women considered it a duty as well as a privilege to assist them in spending their incomes. The fifty or more who rounded out the opera's golden circle were motivated by the necessity to justify their husbands' investments as well as by social obligation, although the opera represented only a tiny portion of actual outlay. The thousands invested in an opera box fell low in the scale beside the millions spent on Fifth Avenue mansions by Vanderbilts, on the art collection in Morgan's marble library, on the Astors' twin house at 840-842 Fifth Avenue, on the country homes and blooded horses and elegant carriages that were necessary to a full life, not to mention the furnishings that filled every inch of the Louis XV or XIV drawing rooms, the Japanese, Turkish, and Chinese rooms that gratified a deep and tasteless desire for the exotic.

Incredible sums vanished into decorations for Arabian Nights feasts and for the viands consumed at them. McAllister admiringly described a banquet at which the entire room, with space only for diners' chairs and servants behind them, was filled with a huge table on—or in—which a real lake had been constructed, where swans floated majestically, only now and then reaching across the flowery border to try to snare a morsel from a guest's golden plate.

During the days of Mrs. Astor's hibernation, New York Society was, by the account of a contemporary quoted in Cleveland Amory's *Who Killed Society?* divided into three classes: "first, the rich; second, the 'good old families'; third, a group made up of sundry French tailors, bootmakers, dancing masters and Mr. Brown." Isaac Hull Brown, McAllister's predecessor, was a resourceful character (only incidentally a sexton at Grace Church) who solved the ever-present problem of "extra" young men by organizing a hundred or so eligibles, promptly named "Brown's Brigade." Few owned carriages; society rented them from Brown. He handled all the carriage calls at the Academy of Music, calling everyone by name and shouting out the addresses for the coachmen. Even before Brown's death in 1880, McAllister had adopted and refined his methods, organizing in 1872 a ball committee called "the Patriarchs," a group of twenty-five men who were permitted to invite to each ball four ladies and five gentlemen and were put on their honor to select the "right" guests. On the Patriarchs' list were John Jacob Astor as well as his brother William (and only one other future Metropolitan boxholder, George Henry Warren). By consent that may or may not have been unanimous, McAllister asked his "Mystic Rose" to be a general adviser. This was, of course, Caroline Astor, whose name would be successively cropped from Mrs. William Backhouse Astor to Mrs. William Astor to *the* Mrs. Astor.

In the decade between her emergence and the opening of the Metropolitan, Mrs. Astor had claimed the title of "Queen of Society" over all opposition. McAllister expounded on the attributes that made her ascent possible:

It was not long before circumstances [the debutante daughters? Or the necessity to assert authority over Mrs. John Jacob III?] forced her to assume the leadership she has held with marked ability ever since, having all the qualities necessary—good judgment and a great power of analysis of men and women, a thorough knowledge of their surroundings, a just appreciation of the rights of others—a good appreciation of the value of ancestry; always keeping it near her, and bringing it in in all social matters; but also understanding the importance and power of the new element.

By the "new" element, the apologist must really have meant the next most powerful lady in the Golden Horseshoe, who had been ruing bitterly the railroad fight that had given Vanderbilts a victory over Astors and led to a feud that naturally penetrated into the respective battlers' homes. The energetic Alva Smith, having married her Vanderbilt, determined to push him and herself into upper echelons at all cost. Frank Crowninshield wrote in *Vogue* magazine more than a half century later that the Vanderbilts coveted so little a career in the fashionable world that they employed elaborate means of avoiding it, but that their good intentions were completely annihilated by Alva's advent. (Crowninshield's latterday portrait of the Vanderbilt clan as "people of the greatest cultivation," and their progenitor the Commodore as an exclusive clubman, serves mainly to reinforce Robert Benchley's description of this last of the society arbiters, the powerful editor of *Vanity Fair* from 1914 to 1935, as "broadminded.")

In March 1883, William K. and his wife established themselves in the Fifth Avenue château that Richard Morris Hunt had built for them. Quickly the rumor spread that the redoubtable Hunt had perpetrated a joke on his patron by copying exactly the castle of a notorious French scoundrel of the Middle Ages, Jacques Coeur of Bourges. William K. paid no attention. The house was beautiful, to his mind. He could not in all honesty be modest about its glories, hiring Edward Strahan to write and publish fifteen volumes of elephant folio (two and one half by four feet) to describe and picture its entrancing details. Now it stood ready to launch. Invitations went out for a costume ball. Alva, deep in preparations, learned that young Caroline Astor had been rehearsing a special cotillion with a group of her friends. She pounced.

Mrs. Astor had not even called on her, was the burden of her threnody; how could Miss Astor be expected to receive a Vanderbilt invitation?

To her everlasting fame, the proud Caroline donned her best street costume, ordered her carriage, and drove up Fifth from Thirty-fourth to Fifty-first to drop a card at Mrs. Vanderbilt's. The proper invitations were sent by hand and Mrs. Astor even consented to lead a quadrille herself. She could not disappoint her daughter.

"An Event Never Equalled in the Social Annals of the Metropolis," trumpeted the *World* on March 28, 1883. More than 800 thronged the beautifully decorated rooms, yet it never seemed crowded. The house, commented the reporter defensively, "is not—as it has been described—a reproduction of a French Renaissance château, but a new development under new conditions of the French transition style in domestic architecture, treated in a freedom and boldness and originality that gives it an unique character. . . . Features borrowed from a score of architectural schools have been successfully utilized and harmonized," a tribute which cannot have entirely pleased architect or owner. Still, no one cherished grudges, and Hunt became the favorite society architect, strewing his extravagant ideas over the Avenue and Newport.

On that splendid night, the gaily caparisoned guests passed between rows of curious spectators to an entrance hall sixty-five by twenty feet, with polished stone floor and paneled oak ceiling, the walls, over a high wainscoting of Caen stone richly carved, hung with antique Italian tapestries. The grand stairway led up from the right, "climbing by ample easy stages to a height of fifty feet, ending in a pendentive dome. A second stairway seen through a rampart arch recalls the unique and glorious Château of Chambord."

Further architectural notes concerned Mrs. Vanderbilt's bathroom, "the most exquisite ever built in this country—a beautiful Renaissance chamber on the Fifth Avenue frontage."

Six elaborate quadrilles were danced in the "gymnasium" on the third floor, fifty by thirty feet. The "Hobby Horse," in which the gentlemen wore elaborately constructed "horses," led off, followed by the "Opéra Bouffe," organized by Mrs. Vanderbilt's sister, Mrs. Fernando Yznaga, and the "Go-as-you-please," led by Mrs. Cornelius Vanderbilt, who "pleased" to be the spirit of the electric light, with a magnificent diamond headdress. Her husband was satisfied to appear as Louis XVI. The hostess emulated a Venetian princess, her costume a blend of gold, white, orange, and red, shining with iridescent beads and embroideries. Her cap glittered with jewels, most notably a many-colored peacock. Lady Mandeville received with her, in contrasting black satin embroidered with jet, a train of black velvet, an immense Venetian lace collar and black Van Dyck hat with drooping plumes. "Nothing could have been more becoming to her blonde, *spirituelle* and piquant beauty than this magnificent and sombre dress," breathed the worshipful *World*. The host stood beside her as the Duke de Guise in yellow silk tights and black-and-yellow doublet. His cloak was embroidered in gold, with the Order of St. Michael suspended on a black ribbon. Orme Wilson, who would marry young Caroline Astor, assumed the role of Le Petit Duc. Mrs. Seward Webb, a Vanderbilt sister, portrayed a hornet, with brilliant yellow satin waist, brown velvet skirt and gauze wings.

The dancers all joined in a colorful parade through the new mansion, then settled down for supper at one o'clock, content that the party had been "unquestionably the most brilliant and picturesque entertainment ever given in New York"—until the next one came along.

Mrs. Astor's balls, on the third Monday of each January, and the Monday night Patriarchs' balls, as well as Assembly Balls and the Family Circle Dancing Classes (organized for the junior *haut ton*), firmly established this early week night as *the* night. Opera fitted neatly into the pattern: "Society hears music Monday nights as methodically as prayers at church, as religiously as it cuts coupons on Tuesday," wrote Ralph Pulitzer (in a bitterly satirical little book, *New York Society on Parade,* that echoed his famous publisher-father Joseph's disdain of the *haute monde* rather strangely, considering that Ralph had married a Vanderbilt girl himself). It supplied that crucial interval between the absolutely essential formal dinner (American society's very existence depended on functions because of its nature as "a whirlpool of tentative novices, with a sediment of permanent members") and the affair to "go on to," which at last allowed the glorious fulfillment of display of gowns—full-length— and jewels against richly ornamented backgrounds. The opera box unfortunately cut off much of the view. But it had to be tolerated, because, as Pulitzer put it, "Exclusive society, to have any reason to exist, must exclude. . . . The reunion in the midst of its foes gives an *esprit de corps,* a solidarity never secured or maintained by uninterrupted aloofness. If not for the many called, the few chosen would not experience any peculiar gratification."

On Sunday, October 21, 1883, the day before the opening of the Metropolitan, the society columns of the *Tribune* made this observation: "No one has better learned the motto, 'In time of peace, prepare for war,' than the women of fashion. [For weeks now] carriages have been grouped around favorite dressmakers' doors." Although Henry Eugene Abbey had ordered his opera costumes, bonnets to buttons, from the famous French couturier Worth, most of the women in his audience still preferred to entrust their *couture* to artisans not so *haute,* and to employ home talent.

Only two dresses from Paris were listed by the *World*'s society columnist reporting on the opera (fashion experts per se on the dailies would come later; for the moment, this vital aspect of opera-going was left to the magazines, which, oddly enough, paid no attention to this particular occasion). These—from Worth—were worn by the Matthews girls, Louise and Florence, guests in S. L. M. Barlow's Box 36. Louise's was white satin under gauze, looped up with blue bows and water lilies. Florence's, also white, was tulle and gauze over silk.

All gowns bore a family resemblance to each other, counting for variety on materials, draping, and trimmings. Bodices uniformly took the shape of quite stiff corselets, extending over the waist to a point in front, and to an even deeper point at the back, anchoring draperies that often became quite elaborate, particularly at the back. Avalanches of artificial flowers, row after row of fringe, or deep ruffles of priceless lace added individuality. Short trains adorned many. Bodices were draped softly with tulle, gauze, or lace, trimmed with flowers or bows, here lightly sleeved, there more daringly dropped a bit off the shoulder. The hair was dressed relatively simply, the fringes, bangs, or curls mounting only to moderate height, with flowers tucked in coyly when tiaras were absent. A lady carried either a fan or a nosegay in filigree gold, silver, or enamel holder. Over immaculate long white kid gloves, bracelets could be worn —a fashion that later was thought vulgar. With these guidelines, one can understand the cryptic codes of the time-and-space-pressed reporter.

White was easily winner in the color scheme. Mrs. W. K. Vanderbilt's brocade satin boasted a front (top) of pearls. Mrs. Warren's was also brocade; Mrs. Wetmore's was trimmed with velvet flowers. Mrs. Cornelius Vanderbilt boasted a silk sleeveless décolletage, edged with folds of tulle; her skirt front was exquisitely embroidered. Mrs. Robert Goelet's satin was draped in tulle. Colors that broke the white spell were often pale, such as Mrs. W. H. Vanderbilt's blue brocaded satin with its front (skirt) covered with point lace flounces, and an unusual square décolletage; or Mrs. Henry Knickerbocker's pink brocade satin trimmed with pendant jets, and quite low-cut. Here and there appeared a vivid splash of green velvet (Mrs. Buchanan Winthrop) or ruby velvet (Mrs. Lawrence Turnure). Diamonds in almost every case could be taken for granted as the touchstone of the occasion.

"Toilets" at the Academy of Music were not described. And Mrs.

Astor's costumes would have to wait for analysis until one grand occasion or another. (A later benefit ball at the Metropolitan seemed to some observers to be merely a catchall for the lesser ranks of society, 3,500 of whom could gaze in awe at Mrs. Astor's emerald velvet robe embroidered in silver flowers set with rhinestones—by Worth, of course—as she sat on a throne under a gas-jet display spelling "Charity.")

While the opera house lights were up, curious peeks could be taken by the ladies at the salons of other boxes, barely visible through parted curtains. (One never left one's own box, of course.) Each boxholder followed his whim in decoration. J. P. Morgan used quiet but rich taste, as was to be expected. But many ladies thought Lily Hamersley, the sensation of coaching parades, with her tiny feet in French shoes (she was later to become the Duchess of Marlborough after Consuelo Vanderbilt had at last shed the duke), had gone a trifle far in festooning the walls and ceiling of her salon in Box 33 just next to Morgan's with fresh orchids each time she appeared at the opera.

Mrs. Paran Stevens, widow of the hotel magnate, engaged in a little marathon of her own. First to appear at the Academy, to Mapleson's expressed satisfaction, she ducked out at the first intermission, to show up at the Met in Box 14 with Mr. and Mrs. Henry Clews. By next intermission she was absent, completing her round by gracing the Horse Show at Madison Square Garden, the first of the annual rivals to the opera which persisted long after the Academy. In a way, it seemed rather a pity that she never actually owned a box, although she was frequently seen with the Clewses and for some years shared (on a rental basis, no doubt) Number 26 with Luther Kountze. Some of the ladies who never quite accorded her the exalted position she claimed for herself opined that her decor would not have been in her husband's taste but as "thrifty" as the musicales that made her famous. "She had her peculiarities of temper and mind," said the *Tribune* cautiously; the more outspoken accused her of skimping both on the food and music. Mrs. Stevens, whose father had been the richest grocer in Lowell, Massachusetts, fought her way into society, grimly overcoming by sheer persistence the canard that she was "low born" and had been a chambermaid in one of Paran's hotels. The self-made Stevens, who acquired hotels much as Commodore Vanderbilt acquired railroads, impressed the *Tribune* with "refined taste, delicate and equitable both in sentiments and everyday feelings." He had astonished New York by offering, at his Fifth Avenue Hotel in Madison Square, an American-plan rate of three meals and bed for $2.50, then throwing in a fourth meal. Just before his death in 1872, he had built a "monster apartment house, the finest in the world," the Neo Grec at Fifth Avenue and Twenty-seventh Street (later rebuilt as the Hotel Victoria).

Although Mrs. Stevens' power increased, a sense of uneasiness drove her and her marriageable daughter Minnie frequently to London, where any American woman was appreciated if she was pretty and rich and her man merely rich. But the Stevenses couldn't afford the duke they wanted, and finally attached young and untitled Arthur Paget, who proved a bargain, as he later gained a knighthood.

Whether Mrs. Astor ever really accepted Mrs. Stevens is a moot point. Caroline's exclusiveness, recognized as inescapable by both the excluders and the rejected, became further refined just after the fifth opera season and crystallized to glittering perfection four years later. These two dates mark the conception of "The Four Hundred" and its emergence as an entity. It may have been sheer whimsey, one of those airy asides McAllister loved to toss off. But the beginnings of immortality were plain on that March 25, 1888, when the *Tribune* printed this paragraph in unmistakable McAllister style:

Why, there are only about 400 people in fashionable New York Society. If you go outside that number you strike people who are either not at ease in a ballroom or else make other people not at ease. See the point? When we give a large ball like the last New Year's ball for 800 guests, we go outside of the exclusive fashionable set, and invite professional men, doctors, lawyers, editors, artists and the like.

This acknowledgment of the low caste of professional men marked a hundred years' decline since the days of Mrs. John Jay, wife of the Secretary for Foreign Affairs when New York was the United States capital, and her "Dinner and Supper List for 1787 and 1788" which included all these professions and more—clergymen, statesmen, politicians, and scholars.

The public was at once aroused—to malice, amusement, and curiosity. Hardly a month passed without its quota of quips, cartoons, and barbs. Charles Dana Gibson, the unremitting satirist of the day, depicted

McAllister in *Life* (then a magazine devoted to humor) as a goosegirl leading his flock. *Life* later announced that the 400 had risen to 1,500 because Wall Street had watered the stock. When Mrs. Astor's arbiter finally allowed the list to be published on the occasion of her great ball in 1892, it was seen to be a fraud—barely 300 names (of which, alas, only some two dozen were opera boxholders!). These were, it was quickly ascertained, nothing but the Patriarchs' lists with a few current visitors. But "The Four Hundred" never died; any description of Society anywhere will evoke it.

McAllister himself was on his way out. His all-too-revealing book disgusted or infuriated the very people he hoped to flatter and placate. He had written: "If you want to be fashionable, be always in the company of fashionable people." Soon after Mrs. Astor moved from her Thirty-fourth Street mansion (she could not, of course, go on living next door to a hotel, even if her own nephew, William Waldorf, of the English immigrant branch, had built it) to the great double house on the Avenue at Sixty-fourth which she would share with her son, John Jacob IV, McAllister's Mystic Rose turned her face away from her majordomo of two decades. The qualities that had recommended him—taste and authority—now appeared to be mere gourmandizing and finicky attention to dress (at least to fancy ball costumes, since in *propria persona* he seemed rather unprepossessing, with straggling hair and beard) while his leadership became assumption of the divine right of an arbiter to be arbitrary. "The Autocrat of the Drawing Room," a title he had been pleased to accept, was no longer an intimate of either "nobs" or "swells" —his divisions of society. Nobs, it seems, were born to their position, good to be "in" with, but the support of swells was more advantageous. Society was really carried on by swells, while nobs looked on. Nobs could be swells if they wanted to spend the money, but it wasn't necessary for their social existence.

Curiously enough, this "Shepherd of the Four Hundred" won a tribute from his successor's wife, Elizabeth Drexel Lehr. In *King Lehr and the Gilded Age,* she wrote:

I rather liked this . . . most complete dandy in America, his pleasant, lazy drawl, his hearty laugh, but Mother [Mrs. Joseph W. Drexel] used to raise her eyebrows at many of the things he said. . . . "I cannot admire a man who spends all his time pushing some people into society and pushing others out of it," she would say.

He took his responsibilities very seriously. Knowing that his decision was regarded as the verdict of the Supreme Court of Appeal where manners or etiquette were under discussion, he devoted his whole life to compiling his famous set of rules for the guidance of social New York. He read books on heraldry and precedence, studied the customs of every court of Europe. He revelled in forms and ceremonies, his cult of snobbishness was so ardent, so sincere, that it acquired dignity; it became almost a religion. No devout parish priest ever visited his flock with more loyal devotion to duty than did Ward McAllister make his rounds of the opera-boxes on Monday evenings. . . . He would spend ten minutes discussing the wording of an invitation, the color of a sheet of notepaper. And all the while his watchful eyes would be observing the neighboring boxes, noting the newcomers, whom they were talking to, "who was taking them up." . . . "You can never be absolutely certain whether people are in society or not until you see them at four or five of the best houses. Then you make advances to them without the danger of making a mistake."

When at last he disappeared in disgrace, even his severest detractor, *Town Topics,* admitted that the scene was duller for his absence. The zest went out of things. *Town Topics* was the weekly that most socialites for almost two decades trembled to see on their breakfast trays unless they had become partners in its editor's widespread affairs to the extent of subscribing—minimum $1,500—to a book of "puff" biographies called *Fads and Fancies.* This character, Col. William d'Alton Mann, with his flowing white moustaches, red bow tie, and clerical frock coat, began his career as society's scourge in 1891, when he took over the magazine from his brother. Many a magnate paid to keep his name out of these closely written columns; his eventual list of "sacred cows" included Morgan, W. K. Vanderbilt, George Gould, Perry Belmont, James R. Keene, Stuyvesant Fish, Chauncey Depew, William C. Whitney, and a dozen others more or less closely connected with the Metropolitan.

If McAllister had been Prime Minister, Harry Lehr became Court Jester. His Queen was the same. "Mrs. Astor made Harry Lehr," his wife wrote. "She liked him the moment she met him at the Elisha Dyers' house in Newport, invited him to lead the cotillion at her next ball, and ever afterwards her loyalty was unswerving. She always saved him a place in her Metropolitan box. She was naturally sincere and gracious."

As for the Queen's tolerance, *Town Topics* once quoted her as saying: "My dear, we have no right to exclude those whom the growth of this

great country has brought forward, provided they are not vulgar in
speech and appearance."

If the affairs on the Metropolitan Opera stage underwent a radical
change for the better at the advent of Giulio Gatti-Casazza's new management in 1908, society in boxdom now began that long slide leading
to the loss of the capital letter S. The traditional exclusiveness of the
famed Diamond Horseshoe had been shattered, mourned—or gloated—
the vigilant *Town Topics*. More than forty changes had occurred, half
of them surprising, "almost sensational." The game of musical chairs, or
"who's got the box," had begun.

Most disconcerting, of course, at the opening *Aida* on November 16,
1908, was the aspect of Box 7. For the first time since the fire in 1892,
when they changed from Box 9, the Astors were absent. The dowager
had died on October 30. Even Mrs. Philip Lydig, in an Empire gown
of black velvet trimmed with Venetian point and a diamond plastron
narrowing from her shoulders to her waist (or a long diamond chain with
pendants, depending on which paper you read) and Mrs. Clarence
Mackay, in cloth of silver with a pearl-and-diamond necklace and a
diamond bandeau, offered insufficient grandeur in Box 7. Mrs. Lydig
had taken the box for Mondays, said the *Times*. A different disposition
of the choice site appeared in *Town Topics*: the Pembroke Joneses on
Mondays, the Smith Hollins McKims on Wednesdays, the Alford Chapins
and Charlie Sampson, the ex-Boston bachelor, dividing Fridays and
Seth Barton French (who appeared in the *Times* list as in Box 21) taking
Saturday matinees.

This was typical of the carving up of the carcass. Oh, it was a proper
mess! Only three boxes still remained for the whole season in one name:
No. 19 (originally Knickerbocker), purchased a year ago by Henry C.
Frick and, incidentally, said the waspish *Town Topics* observer, holding
no distinguished guest since then; No. 6, the W. K. Vanderbilts', not
even split with W. K., Junior, though of course available when wanted;
and No. 35 in the very center of the horseshoe, which J. P. Morgan
vowed would never be sublet during his lifetime. (The Vanderbilts' No.
6, by the way, is credited by the *Times* to Frederick Havemeyer, another
instance of the existing confusion.)

New names to the Parterre listed by *Town Topics* crowded in, including "some of the Brooklyn Pratts" in No. 15; John T. Pratt (Standard Oil) in No. 33 and "more Pratts" (this was a far-flung clan); two brothers Guggenheim; William Willis Reese, "who married the wealthy daughter of Mrs. George Bliss"; and Mr. and Mrs. James Brown, "who are pushing forward by way of Newport and have a debutante daughter," in No. 25. In the Charles B. Alexander box (No. 18), in addition to Reids, Bryces, and Pulitzers (Ralph and his wife, the Seward Webbs's daughter, Frederica Vanderbilt), were found Mr. and Mrs. Herbert Terrell and the Moses Taylor Pyneses, "who, I believe, came in for a share of the George Taylor millions, although they didn't really need it to rent an opera box."

This chatty, if not always accurate account—if compared with the *Times*—concluded with a note of malice: "Mrs. William Everard Strong will doubtless use No. 34 in a final effort to capture a man for the handsome Alice." (No. 34 had been purchased from Heber R. Bishop by James B. Haggin in 1903 for a reputed price of $100,000 and retained by him until the bitter end in 1940. Mrs. Strong obviously rented it.)

Although it was "a great relief to the opera patron to see a new face occasionally in a parterre box," this was carrying it rather far. The "honored squatters," minus Astors, Wilsons, and two Vanderbilts (Mrs. Cornelius was still abroad and Mrs. William K. was in mourning), as well as the staunch old-timers Mrs. Thomas Hitchcock, Mrs. Henry Clews (Henry was there, with the George Goulds, who shared Box 12 as usual), were forced to wage a battle of tiaras to get proper attention. The contestants were few but impressive: Mrs. Harry Payne Whitney, Mrs. H. McK. Twombly, Mrs. W. D. Sloane, and Mrs. Reginald Vanderbilt from that clan; Mrs. Robert Goelet, Mrs. George Gould (who also sported her $500,000 famous loops of pearls), and Mrs. Ogden Mills, with assorted chokers, necklaces, stomachers, and aigrettes to match. It was difficult to know how to classify the crowned Mrs. Craig Biddle and Mrs. Perry Belmont, or the bandeau-ed Mrs. Mackay, while Mrs. Payne Whitney, who belonged in the Vanderbilt group, wore merely a wreath of tiny green leaves in her low coiffure.

The auditorium buzzed, the jewels glittered, *Aida* was thrilling, but the Queen had departed. Society, as Mrs. Astor knew it, had shown signs of incipient decay long before, but she had shored it up with her own rectitude and leadership, rejecting what seemed meretricious, accepting certain inevitabilities. Her remark quoted above referred to the admission of the Vanderbilts to her charmed circle, and was made on the occasion of her capitulation, the Vanderbilt ball of 1883. "It was the result of reflection and not the glamour or wealth of the hostess," added *Town Topics* defensively. Mrs. Astor had given in to the new, but would continue for two decades more to "wield the only sceptre possible in a democratic country: womanly kindliness, refinement, discretion and tact," said the *Times* in a rare tribute.

For the past few years, her flag had been dipping, chiefly because of her own physical inability to hold its standard upright. For the first time in years, January Mondays of 1904 slipped by without an Astor ball. She rallied in 1905, but it was the swan song for the pivotal event of New York society. The balls bore, in addition to the family stamp of decorum and richness, such a sameness that descriptions of one would fit all: the massed American Beauty roses that were an Astor guerdon; the supper, which *Town Topics* delighted to report as "piping hot" each year; the unchanged ballroom with its solemn ranks of heavy paintings; and the lady herself, dressed perhaps in a green gown instead of "sable hue or dead white." But then Mrs. Astor was approaching fourscore and saw no reason to alter her routine. Her taste, Frank Crowninshield said, was always "for old families, old ways, old servants, old operas and old friends." *Town Topics* reported in 1903 that she had found a becoming new coiffure, with a small Venetian cap atop it, trimmed with one superb diamond and a high-rising aigrette. This is the style shown (minus aigrette) in the famous Carolus Duran portrait, one of only two likenesses the camera-shy lady ever permitted to be shown. The writer did not mention (either through kindness, which seems incredible, unless the Astors had joined Colonel Mann's expensive publishing business and thus had become immune to his particular form of blackmail, or through ignorance, which seems equally impossible for this supersnoop) that the *doyenne* had long hidden her own head-covering under a jet-black wig. Under it, in 1905, her face showed her seventy-five years but the expression as always was serene—or haughty, as some preferred to describe it.

This was the last time that a fierce, though superficially dignified, struggle would be necessary to get, somehow, on the list of those who attended the ball, even if one had not been invited. *Town Topics* had exposed the cunning method. It was suggested to the "outsiders" by the habit of the daily papers to send several reporters to the opera, one to review the performance itself, one to concoct a "news" story, and one or more to deal with society. They seldom got their heads and notes together, but wrote separate columns. An ambitious lady would see to it that her gown offered newsworthy interest and that her jewels shone competitively; it would be assumed by the reporter that she would not have got herself up thus unless she were "going on." Her name would appear in the Astor guest list next day. *Town Topics* went so far as to mention one of these "list-crashers." It seemed that the entire Vanderbilt clan had not been admitted to the holy of holies, for quite definitely, the magazine stated, Mrs. W. D. Sloane (née Emily Vanderbilt, daughter of William H. and sister of Cornelius and Willie K.) did not receive Mrs. Astor's invitations.

One startling departure in 1905 attracted universal attention: Mrs. Astor did not receive alone. By her side stood Miss Constance Knower, the fiancée of Mrs. Astor's favorite grandson, Henry Coleman Drayton. But for that engagement, it is probable there would have been no ball. Those with long memories gossiped a little in corners away from the hostess; they remembered another occasion when Mrs. Astor received with a Drayton—or at least an ex-Drayton. This was the celebrated reception in 1898, when all Society was agog: would Mrs. Astor *dare* to stand by her disgraced daughter, Charlotte Augusta? This luckless one had married James Coleman Drayton in 1879 and proceeded to raise four children. Then she flung all caution to the winds and "went astray," as the saying goes, with Hallett Alsop Borrowe, son of a vice-president of Equitable Life (which would later experience other troubles with another official, James Hazen Hyde). Borrowe indiscreetly allowed certain of her letters to be published (one story held that he had himself sold them to the newspaper). Drayton sued for divorce and also challenged Borrowe to a duel, not once but many times. As fast as Borrowe accepted, Drayton was somewhere else; at last both crossed the Atlantic on the same steamer but carefully avoided each other. Borrowe eventually dueled—not with Drayton, but with his own second for making the whole mess public. This bit of gallantry hardly jibes with his alleged treachery in selling Augusta's letters. However, it added to the arsenal of gossip to be fired behind the fans in opera boxes on the boring nights when Melba or the De Reszkes weren't singing.

Once before a duel in the William and Caroline Astor orbit had threatened: when the eldest daughter, Emily, had wished to marry James Van Alen, her father had objected in offensive terms and had the gauntlet thrown down by Jimmy's father. This time, too, the fireworks fizzled out. Eventually Charlotte got the divorce herself, and married a young Scotsman, Col. George Haig Ogilvy, whose wealth derived from the national beverage. It was under his name that she stood by her mother's side on the fateful day that New York's royal lady made an exception to her own rules for her own family. She had given no outward sign that public attacks on her attitude might have wounded her. The most vicious, written by the son of the author of *The Scarlet Letter,* showed no mercy.

Thundered Julian Hawthorne in the *Journal,* as quoted by Elizabeth Eliot in *Heiresses and Coronets*:

Let us have no illusions, it does not excuse this lady to plead that the culprit was her own daughter; nor that she believed her innocence. By virtue of her position she was bound to fulfill the utmost letter of the day. For her, there should have been no daughter; no innocence; nothing but a woman who had so far forgotten her social duty as to let herself be accused and never have disproved the accusation. Human nature, maternal sentiments, have no place in the case; she must remember only the obligations of the throne and condemn without mercy or reprieve.

In this hour of trial, Mrs. Astor turned gratefully to one of her guests, the famous and social (perhaps on this occasion even a bit cynical) Bishop Henry Codman Potter, a man of broad sympathies and great deeds. His obligations to the Queen of Society may be said to have extended even to the choice of his date of death—the same year as hers.

Years after the scandal, Borrowe wrote a poem which was published in *Harper's Weekly*: "Money that you cried for and lied for and died for/ Money that you died for yet could not take away/ On your coffin lid the rattle/ Of the gravel calls to battle/ And your heirs-at-law are off to start the fray."

No one has ever discovered if Mrs. Astor repented her earlier ostracizing of the most prominent of all social divorcées, Mrs. William Kissam Vanderbilt, the very lady who had first broken the ice between the two families. Alva Smith, the willful Alabama belle, had boasted of being the first of her set to marry a Vanderbilt, then of being the first to divorce one. That her object was to marry Oliver Hazard Perry Belmont, with whom she was often seen on coaching parties, did not diminish her popularity in New York and Newport, once the shock had worn off, except with Mrs. Astor, who never felt the same for her, although her former husband still received invitations. The vigorous Alva lived on to Do Good in many ways, including a fiery campaign for women's suffrage, and to be one of the unquestioned Newport leaders. But she wore out Belmont, another to die in the same year as Mrs. Astor.

Some of these thoughts might have passed through the minds of the older guests at Mrs. Astor's 1905 ball, "her last offering on the altar of hospitality to the select and exclusive society of her native city," wrote *Town Topics,* for once in sober vein. There she stood, "regal in a magnificent Marie Antoinette costume of the deepest shade of purple velvet, both the skirt and bodice trimmed with a rich shade of pale-blue satin embroidered with gold paillettes. Her jewels were superb—a massive tiara that seemed a burden upon her head, and she was further weighted down by an enormous dog collar of pearls with diamond pendant attachments. She wore also the celebrated Marie Antoinette stomacher of diamonds and a huge diamond corsage ornament. Diamonds and pearls were pinned here and there about the bodice."

Truly, for this portentous occasion, the Queen decked herself in her best, a "dozen Tiffany showcases personified."

Then, after the cotillion, Mrs. Astor slipped quietly away and retired, "while less than fifty feet from her boudoir, New York society danced."

As a footnote to this extraordinary performance, *Town Topics* noted that in spite of the long dinners preceding the ball (two of which probably cost more than the dance itself), society made a good showing at the opera to hear the "heavy" *Die Meistersinger* with Ackté, Homer, Knote, and Van Rooy. Manager Heinrich Conried made good his promise to give Wagner on not more than four Monday nights—this year only *Lohengrin* further bored the boxholders.

In the spring of 1906, Mrs. Astor suffered a fall in her house at 840 Fifth Avenue and never really recovered. In the first year of her long illness, she continued to attend the opera faithfully, appearing on the stroke of nine, but never staying very long. Then the shadows gathered around her active mind.

Although it is fictional, Edith Wharton's description of a demented old lady's entertainment in *After Holbein* is more real and poignant than reality. The eternal diner-out, himself near the border of sanity, stumbles into the Fifth Avenue mansion that is prepared each evening for ghostly guests and joins his raddled hostess in the macabre travesty of a formal dinner. Mrs. Wharton wrote:

> The big house had been an entertaining machine. She had lived, breathed, invested and reinvested her millions to no other end [and] in that vast pompous dining room which one had only to close one's eyes to transform into a railway buffet for millionaires. . . . There was no reason why that kind of standardized entertaining should ever cease . . . all the dinners she had given merging into one Gargantuan pyramid of food and drink, with the same faces, perpetually the same faces, gathered stolidly about the same gold plate.

Who wanted to admit that it was all very dull and boring? That one asked too much of one's digestive juices and too little of one's brain? That perching a moment on the "Throne" beside the hostess (a bench at the head of the art-gallery ballroom) did not after all mean perfect achievement? That while cotillion favors changed from gold cases to jeweled fans, all remained the same? That the opera required more fortitude than it rendered enjoyment? In short, that *plus ça change, plus c'est la même chose?*

Now that the Queen was dead, who would succeed her? For some time the contest had been waged subterraneously, several prospective Crown Princesses vying in the excellence of their entertaining, the brilliance of their wardrobe and jewels, the acquisition of titled friends or sons-in-law. Speculation rested on Mrs. John Jacob IV, for, after all, she was the dowager's daughter-in-law, the well-born Ava Willing, and, as Elizabeth Drexel Lehr wrote, possessed "that quality of insolence that either repelled or attracted: *'nonchalante et froide,'* Comte Robert de Montesquiou [himself a decadent French flower called "His Arrogance"] had described her." But she preferred Bohemian company to high society. And only a year later she would be divorced from Astor in a secret foray to New City, Pennsylvania, that cheated the infuriated New York papers. Jack's subsequent marriage to eighteen-year-old Madeleine Force (whose mother thereupon became known as *La Force Majeure*) antagonized a great part of what friends he had left. No social leader was to be found among the Astors.

Two other contenders quickly were rejected. Mrs. Ogden Mills might have seemed a natural, the aristocratic descendant of the formidable Livingstons. But along with her supremacy went a cold sarcasm and an overweening rudeness that repelled acquaintances and kept friends uneasy. One of the most elegant women in New York, she owned a set of jewels for every color of her rich gowns: at this year's opera (1908) it was the emeralds and diamonds with a dark-green brocade. She had reduced the Four Hundred by half and claimed that only twenty families were worth knowing. Having narrowed her circle to the vanishing point, she could hardly claim leadership on a broad scale.

If Mrs. Mills had too few friends, Mrs. O. H. P. Belmont had too many enemies. The ruthless Alva had alienated many, if not by her divorce and remarriage, certainly by her treatment of her own daughter, forcing her into a loveless marriage with the Duke of Marlborough and otherwise hewing about her with vigor and unconcern, letting hurt feelings fall where they might.

Still another possibility loomed, although greeted with horror by matrons in their Fifth Avenue parlors and Newport cottages. Mrs. Stuyvesant Fish had all the qualifications of ancestry: on her own side as a collateral of the Stuyvesants, who had once been mountaintop but now were sliding down to the valley; on her husband's the real American autocracy that arrived in 1635 aboard the appropriately named *Increase*. But Mrs. Fish was a "sport," a real rebel who had the grace not to repent any of her backslidings. She could show up at the opera with Mrs. Orme Wilson (that same Caroline Astor who had unwittingly precipitated her mother into the Vanderbilt camp) and start teeth gritting all around the circle at "one of those wonderful gunmetal gowns which every other smart woman finds impossible to imitate," or, as *Town Topics* insisted, drape on her slender person the only jewels Mrs. Astor need envy: a spray of diamonds instead of a tiara, a veritable bandage of pearls three inches deep around her neck, from which hung by a diamond chain four inches long a cluster that "glowed like a sixteen-candle electric lamp." This looked like a single stone, a triumphal *trompe l'oeil*. Then, extending diagonally down her corsage was a row of buttons composed of diamonds set around sapphires, each as large as a fingernail; a festoon of diamonds hung from her left shoulder. "Wearing this new outfit, Mrs.

Fish would be safe collateral for the salary of the President of the United States for his full term and a holdover," Colonel Mann ended maliciously.

But all her display and all her wit could not make Mrs. Fish anything more than the leader of a "set" that delighted in high carnival rather than high society. It was she who, according to Frank Crowninshield, decreed that one wine should replace five; that cigarettes might be smoked with the soup; that string orchestras must give way to jazz; and that any way to kill time was more endurable than an opera at the Metropolitan. She frequented the opera, spasmodically, to be sure, but such orthodoxy did not excuse the pranks of this *enfant terrible,* who, teamed with Harry Lehr, committed mischief after mischief. What came to be called the "Monkey Dinner" perhaps led in outrageousness. Invited to meet "Prince del Drago," Newport's finest discovered themselves expected to kowtow to a monkey attired in full dress. Or to bend the knee to Harry Lehr, costumed as the Russian Tsar on an occasion when the rival Mrs. Ogden Goelet had refused to allow her pet lion, the Grand Duke, to attend Mrs. Fish's Yacht Week ball. This was the era of bizarre entertainment—a gala feast for dogs only; a "Horseback" dinner at Sherry's, where the guests consumed delicacies from the backs of their favorite mounts; James Hazen Hyde's ball, which transformed Sherry's into the Versailles Hall of Mirrors at a cost of $200,000, set investigators at the books of his Equitable Life Assurance Company and forced the elegant bachelor's expatriation to France.

Mrs. Fish had learned not to cross a Wilson in her brush with Mrs. Goelet. "The Wilsons are deadly opponents, their minds work like oiled steel," Harry Lehr had warned her. Now it was another Wilson girl who contended for—and won—the place of Mrs. Astor as avowed Queen of Society. Grace Wilson—slim, girlish, sixteen, radiant—so captivated Cornelius Vanderbilt III that he dared his family's united opposition to their marriage. Never was it so much as hinted that her fascination extended to Cornelius II, prompting the understandable coldness of Grace's mother-in-law, the former Alice Gwynne. The rift was complete when Cornelius II died in 1899, cutting his son Neily off with a tiny million. The second son, Alfred Gwynne (an earlier-born William Henry II had died very young) thus became head of the family, and proved his magnanimity by giving Cornelius III a tidy six million. Grace was thus able to fulfill her destiny in style. As early as 1901 she proved her divine right by a dinner at Sherry's for 166, at which a mountain of food and the presence of Mrs. Astor in spangled purple velvet and diamonds guaranteed success. She imported an entire Broadway show to Beaulieu, her Newport villa, for a "Fete of Roses" in the summer of 1902, to which she invited only 200—"nobody was there who ought not to be," wrote her admiring son. The opera posed no problem; if she was not always welcome in her in-laws' box, she could occupy her father's Number 3, which, indeed, she inherited. But perhaps the clincher for Grace Vanderbilt was her triumph over both Mrs. Astor and Mrs. Goelet in the matter of Prince Henry's visit. The brother of Kaiser Wilhelm II had decided to honor America in February 1902. The Metropolitan Opera immediately arranged a benefit performance for him, when tickets went to an unprecedented high of $30 and great stretches of empty space upstairs spoiled the effect. Although Prince Henry seemed to care little for the music, it was noted that he paid marked attention to Mrs. Cornelius, visiting her in her box, the *Times* remarked next day. Mrs. Vanderbilt had indeed scored a *coup d'état,* crowed *Town Topics.* "Mrs. Astor had aspired [to the honor of entertaining the Prince] and postponed going abroad, never dreaming she would be euchred by the Wilsons." Mrs. Vanderbilt's ploy had been to write a sweet letter to the German ambassador, asking his advice, and recalling that she had been kindly treated at Potsdam when visiting her sister, Belle Goelet. The Kaiser remembered, and sent Grace a cable, requesting her to ask the Prince to dinner, "representing American families." No bigger plum could be picked from the pie. Even Mrs. Ogden Mills's immediate countermove, letting the Kaiser know that to single out one woman might bring unpleasant complications, and thereby securing the royal personage for a breakfast the day before Grace's dinner, didn't matter, much less the business luncheon of J. P. Morgan, when captains of industry consumed terrapin and champagne for three hours. The opera gala, hastily organized as a retaliation for Morgan's snub to many a millionaire, gratified society but upset the opera house routine not a little, causing skimpy rehearsals for a previous day's *Rheingold* and forcing several singers to shift schedules.

As for Mrs. Astor, she sailed as planned, *before* the dinner, commented *Town Topics.* The Vanderbilt dinner was as posh as expected. Not one other Vanderbilt was invited. Cornelius himself waited outside to greet the Prince. They had been fellow auto and yacht fans. It was a pity, Neily thought, that Henry was only a second son; he was as urbane and charming as his elder brother, the Kaiser, was arrogant and overbearing.

Neily's wife, on the contrary, had thought the Kaiser delightful, if only for his admiration of her. This vain and shallow woman could write revealingly of her own character and her son, Cornelius IV, did not hesitate to quote her in his biography, *Queen of the Golden Age*. Her meetings with royalty conveyed nothing more to her than their reaction to her beauty and attire. "The King . . . said how charming I was," she gushed. "And they all said I had the most beautiful jewels . . . the King of England had told them . . . that I had looked so lovely at the opera! Is it not kind of him to recommend me to the Italian King and Queen?"

So insensitive was she to the world about her that after World War I had begun, she entertained Count von Bernstorff, the German ambassador, at Newport. Her entire staff departed before dinner, the butler leaving a note that they refused to serve an enemy.

No matter what her qualities as a human being (and Frank Crowninshield, the eternal apologist, counted among them a great heart that "more than made up for her preoccupation with ceremony"), Grace ruled Society rigidly, with a gold-headed cane for a sceptre and her famous headbands (of which she had thousands) as crowns. Her husband tired early of her preoccupations, and gave himself to business and the National Guard. He was called "General" because of service in World War I. His wife bought at the sacrifice of his love and his millions the title of *the* Mrs. Vanderbilt.

Several of Grace's in-laws commanded affection and even respect from the public and the great world outside their corral of wealth. Sister Gertrude, a sculptress, married Harry Payne Whitney and founded the Whitney Museum of American Art, which flourishes today. Brother Alfred Gwynne, who had so generously shared with Neily, died a hero in the *Lusitania* disaster. He had been ideally happy with his second wife, Margaret Emerson McKim, a remarkable and popular woman. Brother Reginald was less sterling but more spectacular, giving his merry life to wine, wagers, and motors. Sister Gladys married Count László Széchenyi and is warmly remembered "as one of the nicest of that generation" by a collateral, Mrs. Vanderbilt Webb, the former Aileen Osborn, whose husband was the son of Eliza Osgood Vanderbilt, sister of Cornelius II, and William Seward Webb, and who thus was a cousin-in-law of Grace's. Gladys bequeathed her father's mansion, The Breakers, to the Society for the Preservation of Newport, and lived modestly there on the top floor until her death. Harold, son of William Kissam and brother of Willie K., distinguished himself as a sportsman and the inventor of contract bridge. There was indeed no lack of talent in this clan. But they possessed no clan feeling, said Mrs. Webb. The only time they ever met was at funerals. At the death of Mrs. Frederick (a cousin who had married the only son of William H. with a college education), Vanderbilts met Vanderbilts whom they had never seen before.

The habit of going to the opera persisted with several members of the family, notably Mrs. H. McKown Twombly of the rainbow stable of Rolls Royces, whom Lucius Beebe apostrophizes so charmingly in *The Big Spenders,* and, more recently, Gloria Vanderbilt, whose early marriage to Leopold Stokowski may have given her an inspiration that has endured through subsequent bridegrooms.

But as *the* grande dame, it is *the* Mrs. Cornelius who is remembered even past the shifting of gears in 1940 that brought "democracy" to the Diamond Horseshoe. Brandishing her cane fiercely at a photographer (her aversion to publicity of this sort having arrived only as her beauty faded), her emeralds gleaming under a wattled chin, her headband firmly in place over whitened locks, Mrs. Vanderbilt symbolized Grand Opera in its most autocratic aspect until her death in 1953 at the age of eighty-three.

3

CADY'S LYRE

There is emphatically no place like New York. Here are some of the finest stores in the world and mansions of which a Doge of Venice or a Lorenzo de Medici might have been proud. Here are the most beautiful ladies in the world, as well as the most refined and cultivated; here are the finest theatres and art galleries, *and the true home of opera is in this country*; here is the glitter of peerless fashion, the ceaseless roll of splendid equipages, and the Bois de Boulogne of America, the Central Park; here there is a constant round of brilliant banquets, afternoon teas and receptions, the germans of the elite, the grand balls with their more formal pomp and splendid circumstance; glowing pictures of beautiful women and brave men threading the mazes of the dance; scenes of revelry by night in an atmosphere loaded with the perfume of rare exotics, to the swell of sensuous music. It does not take much of this new kind of life to make enthusiastic New Yorkers of the wives of Western millionaires and then nothing remains but to purchase a brown stone mansion and swing into the tide of fashion, with receptions, balls and kettle drums, elegant equipages with coachmen in bright-buttoned livery, footmen in top boots, maid-servants and man-servants, including a butler and all the other adjuncts of fashionable life in the great metropolis.

—HENRY CLEWS, *Twenty-Eight Years in Wall Street*

"It was such a fine night!" the man from the *Times* exclaimed thankfully. "The roofs over the porte-cocheres were not missed." If rain had fallen that night of October 22, 1883, when the new Metropolitan Opera House opened its doors for the first time, one shudders to think of the misery and confusion added to the already pandemoniac scene. Carriages —whether rented or the proud adjunct of the wealthy man—with their steeds excited to the point of rolling eyes and high-lifted hoofs, pounded down the cobblestone street, bouncing and tossing as if on a rocky fastness instead of the chief thoroughfare of the nation's largest and finest metropolis, New York City on the Island of Manhattan. Smoother streets, paved in "scrimshaw," wood blocks covered with tar, existed in patches farther south and in a long stretch on upper Eighth Avenue, where the Vanderbilts and other sport lovers raced their harness rigs. Asphalt would come still later.

43

Broadway reached five miles "from the Bowling Green to the Central Park, lined with stately edifices and thronged with an endless crowd of busy workers and restless pleasure seekers, good and bad, grave and gay. There is no more wonderful sight," added a contemporary admirer, "than this grand street at high noon." Unless it were Broadway on this fine night, at "the frontier of theatre-land and the end of the uptown cocktail route," described by Henry Collins Brown in one of his chatty manuals on the vagaries and vicissitudes of New York. Of the 1,200,000 who already held the island in an atmosphere "half camp, half Mayfair," 30,000 were on hand to see in a new era of culture.

One by one the carriages rounded the corner into Thirty-ninth Street, coming to a restless halt under the unroofed iron marquee in the midst of a milling throng unprotected by so much as a railing. A few hundred of the menaced pedestrians finally managed to stumble into a doorway and up the long steep stairway that would lead them to their haven, the Balcony or the Gallery. The others, pushed and tormented by the notoriously rough police, held their ground as best they could. Among them, so novel as to provoke jeering comment, bobbed the black-glazed sailor hats of the new "stenographers" in their severe daytime clothes, greatly daring to stay out by themselves after dark. The invention of the typewriter had created a whole new female profession. To them and to the more conventional feminine watchers, it was worth the discomfort and danger to see the swells alight from their frail equipages, ladies in furs and satins and feathers and diamonds handed tenderly to the newly swept pavement by liveried footmen or by their top-hatted escorts.

Broadway itself presented an equally fierce aspect, with the carriage line clotted all the way past the new Gedney Hotel on the northwest corner at Fortieth, the Metropolitan Concert Hall (later to be replaced by the Broadway Theatre) on the southwest corner of Forty-first, and the Rossmore Hotel at Forty-second, where an occasional cross-town conveyance had to give way to the Broadway trolley, both horse-drawn.

"But this traffic congestion is nothing new; it has been with us always," remarked a philosopher of the eighties.

On Fortieth Street, the serpentine line struggling to gain the door which, like its counterpart on Thirty-ninth, led to the upper reaches of the House, registered periodic seismic upheavals accompanied by spirited exchanges of oaths and threats of violence to the jostlers' persons.

Scalpers' cries rose shrill above all other human utterance: "Get yer tickets here—choice seats fifteen dollars—yes, sir, it's in the Parquet. Balcony first row, eight dollars—no, sir, you have to pay five dollars to get in." This last to the man from the *Times,* who yelled: "But I want standing room!" He had promised his editor an "experience" story. "No standing room sold," rejoined the scalper contemptuously, readjusting his nickel badge and turning away to flirt the bank bills twined between his fingers as he resumed his noisy search for easier marks. The newspaperman forced his way through the Broadway lobby to the ticket office, where we lose him temporarily.

The $2 and $3 tickets for the Gallery (Family Circle) had long gone. Hoping to get in, many individuals claimed acquaintance with Henry E. Abbey, the impresario of the new company, or with Captain Williams of the police. Both gentlemen professed astonishment at the number, but were not swayed to issue passes to their new friends.

Atop poles at each corner the glass flames stirred, stretched, and crouched in their globes, flickering impartially on the animated scene below and the warp of telegraph and telephone wires above, a canopy that oppressed those main streets not already cowering under the three elevated railroad systems built in 1876. In a year or two this overhead thicket would be driven underground; that very December of 1883 the alderman's committee would threaten: "Wires must go!" The mayor himself had to hack down a pole at Twenty-third and Broadway before the point was taken by the utilities companies, the thriving Western Union among them. Widespread use of Bell's telephone was just beginning. Two of the conveniences had been installed in the new opera house.

One of the new electrical lamps had appeared on a tall mast in Madison Square only recently, but the opera still relied on gas. The restless beams dimly showed the Casino at Thirty-ninth, a Moorish palace managed by Rudolph Aronson, which regularly drew celebrities of the opera, Wall Street, and the *jeunesse d'orée* to its first nights. In the Hotel Vendome at Fortieth an elaborate bar was being readied for the after-opera crush.

The opera building still presented a raw, unfinished look. Its yellow brick, designed to mellow to an ivory tint, seemed ochre-harsh. Few took time to inspect the Italian Renaissance style of the exterior, or the design of the Broadway portico, which one writer later praised for "notable refinement of detail," with terra-cotta panels depicting graceful dancing and singing figures. No one had been able to decide what to do with the corners—whether to incorporate them into the House proper as lounges and use the upper stories as select bachelor apartments, or to rent them out to business concessionaires. Brick walls blocked them off now. As late as three o'clock in the afternoon, a *World* reporter vowed he saw 20,000 square feet of plaster, shavings, whitewash, and dirt mingled with lumber and paintpots littering the house, while 700 women scrubbed floors and doorways.

By 6:30 the scaffolding had disappeared and no barrier save the human conglomeration separated the rightful ticket holders from their temple. Boxholders, fashionably late as was to be expected, turned into their special stairways from the foyers on either side of the House and were thus spared prolonged contact with the general public, though they missed the spectacle of the huge marble staircase with massive gilded railings that sent divided wings to their aerie from the Broadway vestibule.

The commotion seemed to mount as minutes passed: ticket takers straining to keep cool with the outside temperature mounting to 45 degrees; ticket holders bewildered at the unaccustomed paths to be trodden to get anywhere, and ushers bedeviled by their bewilderment; gasmen flying up and down stairs to make sure their lights were all ablaze. Denizens of the Orchestra, or Parquet, squeezed through a marbled-floored passage, "very narrow," commented the *Times*. Corridors, only nine feet wide and claustrophobically low-ceilinged, paved with artificial stone and uncarpeted ("not like the Academy"), and painted a "hot orange," became overheated and for lack of ventilation quickly grew oppressive. Entrances were spacious enough if one exercised care not to crowd—but drafty. It had not occurred to anyone to call the exits *vomitoria,* the Roman term, said *Harper's Weekly* whimsically, "even if modern notions of verbal propriety did not restrain."

Once inside the audience chamber, the initial impression was of size—the largest in the world, with 3,045 seats. Then the overpowering aura of gold struck the eye: literally, because of the yellow-painted walls and the upholstery of the boxes; figuratively, because the lower tier of boxes represented $450 million. This favored circle "might be called a 'golden horseshoe,' " wrote the *Tribune,* uttering the phrase that became inseparably attached to opera royalty. *Harper's* disputed the conception, saying that the auditorium approximated more nearly the form of a lyre than "glittering horseshoe's ample round." Indeed, "Lyre" had been the code name for the winning architect's drawing.

Josiah Cleaveland Cady's astonishingly long-lived anachronism (the Metropolitan certainly deserves to be called "anything incongruous in point of time with its surroundings") was for more than half a century in thrall to the power of gold, personified by its boxholders. The architect and his assistant, Louis de Coppet Bergh, provided lavishly for his patrons with 122 boxes, all but twelve in three solid tiers. The extra dozen, known as *baignoires* because of their bathtub shape, sat six to a side at the very front of the House, Orchestra level. Cady, whose forte was college buildings in early Renaissance style, modeled his first experiment —and his last—chiefly after London's Covent Garden. He could not know that his beautiful auditorium (later redecorated) would continue to be the delight of all operagoers except those 700 or so who could not see very well, and the despair mounting to frenzy of those who worked in any other part of the oddly shaped building.

Cady's lyre had been originally planned for the 200-foot square block bounded by Madison and Vanderbilt avenues and Forty-third and Forty-fourth streets. He did not see any necessity to alter the plans in essence for the final location. Because of Broadway's oblique slash across otherwise checkerboard streets, the Metropolitan occupied what the *Tribune* called one-and-a-quarter city blocks. Geographically wrong, this had relative truth, as the block is larger than the usual square or rectangle. Foot measurements are: Broadway, 205; Seventh Avenue, 197; Thirty-ninth, 284; Fortieth, 229. Imprisoned in these off-balance dimensions, the opera house could never be enlarged except by adding to its height; never be reformed or remodeled except by substituting one functional space for another.

Patrons on that warm October night possessed no gift of clairvoyance; their contentment or irritation arose from personal, immediate circumstances. From bottom to top, these varied widely. In the Parquet, even the most corpulent Italian (the symbol for the "true" opera lover then as now) could sit in his chair without feeling his neighbors' elbows in his ribs. Under his seat (which folded back, a reasonably new invention) a cunningly designed wire frame would hold his hat. In each box were six slender black chairs, seated and backed with rattan, seeming too fragile to bear the weight of heavy fabrics and jewels placed upon them. The fashionable women whose husbands had built this showcase for them were disturbed by the unflattering background for their display. The rich brocade, warm and golden close to, faded to a dirty brown when seen from afar. The irreverent John C. Freund in his early publication, *Music and Drama* (his chief chalice for crusading would later be *Musical America*), advised the ladies, who "looked like prisoners in their cells who cultivated flowers and didn't wash their faces," to go to Myers, the wig man, and get made up in a deep Indian-red color in order to look healthy against the deadening background. Cady had copied the box dividers, curved back and upward from the rail, almost exactly from the Paris Opéra. While they allowed privacy, they did restrict the view, and their edges, of metal painted white, added an incongruous raw touch. The entire color scheme, as a matter of fact, seemed ill considered —the prevailing yellow broken by the peculiar shade of crimson silk upholstery for parquet seats (woven by the Cheney Mills in South Manchester, Connecticut) and the curtain to be dropped between acts, a lightblue plush, embroidered with a seventeen-foot border showing a life-size Greek chorus. The ceiling above the blazing gas chandelier was finished in white, gold, and pale pink.

Each box fronted on a spacious "saloon" (the term used in the official diagram), useful as a cloakroom, a place to receive guests (usually eligible young men on the prowl), and even a peaceful corner where the host might sneak a nap, worn out as he was from his business day, the necessity to change into tailcoat, and a dinner of noble proportions. Two steps led down into the box, so the unwary suffered the humiliation of tripping awkwardly into the scene.

As the usher unlocked the box door appreciable moments after the performance had begun, a maid sprang to help with ladies' cloaks and fur overshoes, so that the little room became "the scene of bewildered confusion, a powdered medley of writhing arms, contorted backs and heaving bosoms." The men waited stoically in the stifling corridor, then followed the women. The hostess pulled aside the curtain dividing the box proper from the saloon with a rattle "that the music almost drowns," continued this account, "then she settles in comfort with a few wiggles." This scene comes from the acid pen of Ralph Pulitzer.

Furthermore, boxholders not yet familiar with the right thing to do kept their boxes locked, reported the *World* the following day, so that visiting gentlemen were forced to hop up and down to peek in the tiny transom almost six feet from the floor. Finally, timid knocks brought the host with apologies. The more forethoughted William H. and William K. Vanderbilt, as well as Jay Gould and others, "had valets stationed before their doors."

Corridors bounding the boxes were thought to be of insufficient width, but as *Harper's* jested: "The maximum number of box occupants in any one tier was 222, and only the male half was liable to engagements between the acts." It was unthinkable that a lady should leave her box.

Although seating six, boxes were occupied by from two to eight persons. Many of the *baignoires* were edified by the presence of members of the Union Club, New York's finest. This ultraselect body currently seethed under a scandal that resulted in expulsion of one of its members and a long-drawn-out legal battle known inevitably as the Union Suit.

Above the triple-layer cake of boxdom, joy was relatively confined. The first two rows in the Balcony and Gallery could not complain, but only these few among the former's 735 and the latter's 978 could see the full stage. The *Times* reporter, by now installed at the extreme end of the back row (Balcony or Gallery not specified), had attained his perch by the expedient of climbing over the back, because others in the row left no room to pass. His view encompassed the upper half of the other side of the auditorium. By stretching, he could glimpse a quarter of the orchestra. The only animated thing in sight was the conductor's cranium. No one at all could see more than ten feet of the stage. What was almost worse, sounds reached them only fitfully. A high voice came over, but the men were muffled in a manner extremely irritating except for their loftiest notes. So much for the tender matter of acoustics, which, however, the *Tribune* critic pronounced admirable. But then, he was sitting comfortably in the Parquet. Beneath the orchestra floor an oval-shaped brick chamber was supposed to enhance the sound, a device copied from La Scala in Milan, which had already proved successful in Philadelphia's Academy of Music, built in 1857. The *Tribune* man had a few more prophetic words to say on the subject: "All authorities on acoustics from Pythagoras to John Tyndall [British physicist] failed to lay down a rule that might insure to designers . . . even an average or moderate degree of success."

As for the sight, it was perfect from his vantage point and "even from the utmost corners of the boxes! Furthermore, the worst seats in the corners of the Gallery command more than one half of the stage." One wonders if he had personally investigated, or had merely taken Cady's word. There is irony in his defense of Cady, who had executed more than 700 drawings to test sight lines, seeing that his industry produced almost exactly that number of seats that had to be marked "obstructed view." *Harper's* writer joined his newspaper colleague in remarking complacently that no theatre existed in which fewer bad seats were to be found.

There was still more to observe before the performance could be properly attended to. Abbey allowed a breathing space before his an-nounced curtain time, 6:45, when he saw yawning gaps in the horseshoe. Without programs, for the printer was also a late-comer, those already seated had to guess who was who in the trickle of fashionable entrants. When the programs did arrive, the desired information was not to be found. Until 1886, when diagrams and names of boxholders first ap-peared, the curious could often be observed consulting daily newspapers like scorecards.

The lavishness of the decor drew all eyes at one time or another. E. P. Treadwill was responsible for it, a Bostonian who "went with Cady along the path of honesty and consistency, omitting all garishness and avoiding every tawdry effect," wrote that man of goodwill, the *Tribune* critic, already discovered to be Henry E. Krehbiel, although his name did not appear. Others, however, were not so generous. The lack of a proscenium was felt to be a drawback by Pulitzer's *World* and James Gordon Bennett's *Herald,* who missed comparable boxes close to the stage that held the Academy of Music *haut monde.* The square opening of the stage seemed graceless, the decoration surrounding it tame and conventional. Apollo and his Muses provided suitable material, but the four panels on either side of the kneeling god and two attendants, painted by Francis Lathrop on zinc, omitted the ninth Muse, who was kept "forever waiting for a call boy who never calls," added the *World*. Furthermore, the two rectangular panels at the ends of the arch seemed decidedly out of drawing and superficial. However, some good figures by George W. Maynard, emblematic of Song and Dance, and much delicate and decorative effect by Theodore Robinson, in cartouches one above the other, won favor.

When the time came, patrons at Parquet level could congregate in the south (Thirty-ninth Street) foyer, forty-three by eighty-five feet, brilliantly lighted by gas jets on fixtures of novel patterns, or a similar space on the north, thirty-three by forty-eight. Or they could climb two flights of stairs to a spacious lounge, thirty-three by eighty-two feet, with music gallery, or visit a reception room overlooking Broadway. One feature that might have proved charming in less urban surroundings was the plan for open-air promenades for Balcony patrons on the flat roofs over the side wings, between the front towers and the stage house. As the dirt potential rose in the growing city, balconyites had to be satisfied to remain indoors.

Boxholders in the very nature of their hegemony had inspected the unfinished premises as early as May, but it is doubtful that they penetrated very far into the fastnesses beyond the great hall where lay their concern. Reporters, however, had ranged over the building. Now, perhaps wearing Dr. Coppelius' magic spectacles, at least one writer proclaimed all was well, even going to the extreme of pronouncing the artists' dressing rooms as being on a "liberal scale." The prima donna boasted a door directly to the stage. This *Herald* arbiter noted "every mechanical improvement," including gas effects, a paint bridge wide enough for a coach-and-four, and novel arrangements of footlights with colored globes, which allowed the banishment of red fire on the stage, so objectionable to artists and audience alike. No necessity existed for the calcium lights in the gallery that had so annoyed patrons in other theatres with their fizzing and endangered with their casual explosions.

The reporter was much struck with the ingenuity of a thunder machine. Immense cannonballs dropped onto plates of sheet iron and ran around the flies on a track of iron to produce realistic storms. The magnificent organ, built by Hilbourne L. Roosevelt, had previously been used in Chicago as well as in the elegant Seventh Regiment Armory at Sixty-sixth Street and Park Avenue. The keyboard in the orchestra pit was electrically connected to the pipes; similar wires between various spots for summoning personnel ensured smooth functioning.

The stage itself owed precedence in size to only two theatres—the Paris Opéra and the Imperial Opera in St. Petersburg—being 91 feet high, 101 wide, and 86 deep, and with 30 feet below (the Academy made do with only 9). The curtain opening measured 50 by 50 feet.

Dressing rooms and a green room equipped with settees and a drinking fountain for chorus and ballet seemed ample, and the wardrobe chamber on Fortieth Street, fourth floor, was the pride and delight of William Parry, the neat English stage manager whom Abbey had stolen from the Academy. The management even found room (temporarily at least) for a wine cellar on the Thirty-ninth Street side.

No one at first, least of all Cady, realized that storage in the basement of more than one or possibly two sets of scenery would be forbidden by fire laws. Fireproofing had been a prime concern with the architects. Everyone congratulated everybody else that in the Metropolitan the acme of safety had been attained. Not only one of the first new asbestos curtains separated stage from auditorium, but a tank of water fed a sprinkler system of sorts and the substructure of the stage was metal. The *Tribune* seized the occasion for a little digression into the subject of theatre fires, quoting a German author's catalogue of 516 entirely destroyed, 400 within the past century. Abbey's own Park Theatre was a case in point. And the state legislature only the other day had defeated a building law that contained some wise provisions. There had been no advance in fireproofing materials for the past 250 years, it was claimed, for although wooden walls were pretty generally abolished in the seventeenth century, light timber, canvas, and equally flammable stuff in proscenium and on stage had continued to the present. The gas jets bake and char walls so that they become tinder. Still, "Melpomene and Thalia lure their devotees into the arms of the terrible Moloch," the writer mused, unknowingly prophetic. This very temple of the Muses would yield to Loki, a god in another mythology, within a single decade.

Cady, although he knew his patrons would not stand for the open, fan-shaped auditorium of the Bayreuth Festspielhaus, with its boxes at the back, yet tried with that honesty attributed to him to incorporate at least one feature of Wagner's domain: the concealed orchestra. Unfortunately, the conductor objected, both for himself and his band, and persuaded Abbey to raise the floor, so that the orchestra was "sprawled between audience and performers in the old-fashioned manner. Musicians," continued the complaining *Tribune*, "are not as a rule beautiful. Miss Maud Morgan in a Grecian robe and fillet, plucking the strings of a harp, is a picture to delight the soul of the classical lover; but not so Herr Bassgeige, engaged in a desperate wrestle, catch-as-catch-can, with his double bass." Then drums and brass instruments had to be placed outside the orchestra railing, ruining the view from the *baignoires*.

Although the programs were late, everyone knew, from frequent accounts of the "opera war" in the newspapers, that the cast for Gounod's *Faust* had been pirated almost *in toto* from Col. James Mapleson. The loquacious Englishman had had opera all his own way until now, with proprietary interest in the Academy of Music down on Fourteenth Street and Irving Place and annual tours around the country since 1878–79. Mapleson, whose "Colonel" was purely *soi-disant,* called Abbey's move a *razzia* (raid) and dubbed the other impresario a *guastamestieri* (spoiler), "causing him to consult his solicitor."

"Abbey took all the old ones," he said of pilfered chorus members. Even the subscription secretary and the callboy were on the list. "I am keeping quiet now," he told the *Tribune,* "but when the time comes, I will spring my mine suddenly under the feet of my rival." Mapleson's hold on Adelina Patti (whose fee Abbey had previously bid up to $5,000 per performance) and the well-loved Etelka Gerster provided a certain justification for real confidence. "Poor old Campanini," Mapleson continued. "I suppose he feels hurt," inferring that the tenor, assigned by Abbey to the role of Faust and indubitably ready to tip over the great divide of his prime, had been on the Academy discard list. "Now the men *I* have got are fine-looking fellows, gentlemanly, you know, and all that sort of thing. Women rave about them and then men go to see what the women rave about."

Abbey's *prima donna assoluta,* the stately Christine Nilsson, had flown Mapleson's banner since 1867 in London, but had toured America with Maurice Strakosch in 1870–72. She would sing a favorite role, Marguerite, which she had created in Gounod's revision for the Paris Opéra in 1869. Since 1868 the Colonel had managed Sofia Scalchi, whose irresistible good nature and shapely nether limbs (often visible as Siébel and in other "trouser" parts) went with a bewitching voice to make her the most popular contralto on the stage. Giuseppe del Puente, an ideal Escamillo in *Carmen* and scheduled for Abbey's Valentin, and Emily Lablache, an expansive personality who was to sing Marthe, were the only two on whom Mapleson could get a legal hold. Del Puente preferred new pastures and was allowed to buy his contract for 15,000 francs (about $3,000), but Mme. Lablache had to obey a restraining injunction at least until November 5, when she was free to sing at the Metropolitan. Her daughter, Louise, substituted on opening night, quite creditably.

"They will all be back with me next season after Abbey has failed," Mapleson said airily. "Parry and the chorus people come now." He added, "New York cannot support two opera houses." He was right on both counts.

The only new face and voice of consequence for the Metropolitan audience belonged to Franco Novara, the Méphistophélès, who as an Englishman signed his business papers "Frank Nash."

The performance finally got under way at 7:15. Not until five hours later did the conductor, perfectly visible by his own request, lay down his baton. Naturalized in France so that his name read Auguste Charles Leonard François Vianesi, he was never called anything but the original Augusto at the Metropolitan.

Once curiosity had been sated, apathy set in. Campanini's *Salve dimora,* saluting the house of his beloved, should have been repeated, scolded the *Times* critic, concurring in the pestilent habit of encores that plagued opera for many years to come. And any Devil who could not wring an encore to his "Calf of Gold" aria must be accounted inefficient indeed. But then, Vianesi for some reason never seemed prepared for encores, the *World* remarked later. "A singer has to come down to the footlights and hold animated conversation with him."

The *Times* found young Lablache feeble and Del Puente overcome by the newness of the scene or just plain indisposed (possibly mourning his 15,000 francs). To rouse the spectators, it took the presentation of a chaplet of gold leaves to Nilsson, who first showed the wreath to the audience in its crimson casket, then placed it on a chair as the object of adoration in the repetition of the "Jewel Song." The "wreath," described by the omnipresent *Music and Drama,* was an exact reproduction of a spray of bay leaves and berries on a movable stalk. Two circular brooches were supplied so that the spray, spread out, could be attached to one shoulder and at the waist on the other side.

Slovenly stage management disturbed the *Herald,* which noted a crash and curses behind the scene as a piano fell during Scalchi's second-act aria—though Siébel showed not a tremor. Flower beds somehow strayed into street scenes and Gothic pillars into the dungeon. The pro-fusion of floral tributes invariably heaped on the favorites prompted the critic of the *Nation* and the *Evening Post* to remark testily that the opera house is not a flower mart, nor the tenor a dray horse. This seer added: "Only the strongest voices have any opportunity of asserting themselves, and will have to make a constant effort, in the long run detrimental."

Still, the rosy haze persisted over the *Tribune,* which found nothing but praise for the stage pictures, of "fascinating beauty and almost per-fect allusion."

Abbey professed himself satisfied. There was $9,000 in the box office and he could have taken in $3,000 more. Early in the evening he was observed, hands in his pockets, smiling almost imperceptibly under the droop of his thick moustache. His clear-cut, rather pale features and pene-trating eyes, together with a temperament even and reserved, stamped him to a Western admirer as a New Yorker, although he hailed from Akron, Ohio. Because his father was a jeweler, Abbey always wore a beau-tiful piece, often an emerald tiepin or ring. Though his opera experience amounted to exactly zero, he had owned and managed theatres in New York and Boston, where he had played such great stars as Irving and Booth, as well as handling their profitable tours. Mrs. Langtry flaunted her beauty under his banner; later Lillian Russell would tour in light operas. He had piloted Patti about the country in 1881–82 and would lure her away from Mapleson in 1889–90.

Abbey was no novice, although he overplayed his operatic hand the first trip out. The wisdom of his partners, the old trouper Maurice Grau and the practically invisible John B. Schoeffel ("the hyphen between Abbey and Grau," according to the young German musician, Walter Damrosch, who watched the scene with more than indifference), did not save him from a temporary setback. One of the most potent forces arrayed against success for a manager who acted merely as an employe of the stockholders (read "boxholders"), who put up a mere $1,000 per performance for him to work with, was the House they built without consulting him or any of his kind.

The man in the *Nation* and *Evening Post* put his finger on it right away. This was the perspicacious Henry Theophilus Finck, who followed the Metropolitan's fortunes from the beginning until 1924. In all its implications, he said somberly: "There are too many boxes."

Manhattan's gilded gentlemen and ladies filled their golden horseshoe to the brim—at least for a while.

4

MAGNIFICENT GAMBLE

An impresario is a person who has paid all his money for the pleasure of being blackguarded by everybody.

—*Harper's Weekly,* November 1883

Although the social side of the Metropolitan Opera suffered a decrescendo immediately after the gala opening, the musical values rose sharply with the second performance, on October 24. Henry E. Abbey had been forced to allot half of his $60,000 guarantee for the entire season to one prima donna's demands. Fortunately for the impresario's reputation, if not necessarily his bankroll, Praxede Marcelline Kochanska almost immediately became the toast of musical New York. Equally fortunate for the toasters, who presumably did not know how to capture a Polish accent, the little lady had simplified her name and as Marcella Sembrich started on the long road which ascended to highest triumphs.

It began with Donizetti's *Lucia di Lammermoor.* "Before the crisis of the 'Mad Scene,'" reported the *World,* "it was conceded that as vocalist she had few peers and no superiors this side of the Atlantic. Still, such is the perversity of the stockholders, a great many chose to stay away." Wednesday with a new prima donna evidently was considered an off-night. Ten boxes yawned empty in the Parterre: eight in the First Tier, fourteen in the Second, leaving "a sort of cream-colored vacancy with its hollow reproach." The vaunted lovers of music who gravitate to higher levels also missed a treat; only four rows in the Balcony were occupied.

At first, merely the condescending patter of gloves could be heard, for "nothing is so fatal as to concede the possession of genius before it has asserted itself." But after Sembrich's *"Quando rapito"* and the E in alt, it began to dawn on the listeners that here indeed was a rare voice, superbly used. The ushers rushed forward with a monster violin made of roses from generous Christine Nilsson, who returned Sembrich's opening-night courtesy by appearing in one of the boxes. The petite singer then repeated the aria ad lib, with variations of her own, chromatic scales and a cadenza which revealed all the attributes of her voice. "It is pure, without a weak spot," the reviewer conceded. "It does not preserve its color in the high register as does Patti's, yet it is fresher, and of equal if not greater compass."

Abbey had augmented the audience by inviting the great actors under his management, so that Helen (*sic*) Terry and Edwin Booth could be spotted in a *baignoire*. Sir Henry Irving was rehearsing for his October 29 debut in *The Bells,* adapted from Erckmann-Chatrian's *Le Juif Polonais.* Ellen Terry would appear the following night in W. G. Wills's *Charles I.*

The news spread quickly, and by Sembrich's next appearance, as Elvira in Bellini's *I Puritani* the second Monday, and at her later assumption of the leading roles in *La Traviata, La Sonnambula, Rigoletto, Il Barbiere di Siviglia, Don Giovanni,* and in the spring season, Thomas' *Hamlet,* Flotow's *Martha,* and as Marguerite in Meyerbeer's *Huguenots,* no doubt remained about whose head wore the crown for vocalism. Her acting had not always shown a "natural abandon," and the *Herald* thought her display of petulance in *Les Huguenots* to be in very bad taste—she was seen to shake her fan at the conductor and speak to him with great displeasure. Other occasional gusts of temperament could perhaps be laid at the door of her solicitous husband, Wilhelm Stengel, who had been her piano teacher. Still, she won all hearts by her triple-threat performance at the benefit for Abbey on April 21—revealing herself as a schooled violinist in the De Bériot Concerto, then as an excellent pianist in an encore, a Chopin mazurka, and of course the darling of the evening for her singing.

Nilsson continued to show "her usual dignity and sweetness" (sometimes reversed as "sweetness and dignity"), as Mignon, Donna Elvira in *Don Giovanni,* Margherita and Elena in *Mefistofele,* and Valentine in *Les Huguenots.* The Swedish diva had been a favorite in America since the seventies, when she had toured with Maurice Strakosch. Not only was she revered by the musical public, but the ladies sympathized with her, since her first husband, Auguste Rouzaud, had died only a year or so before. Furthermore, she was one of the rare singers, a "genteel female," who could be received socially in Victorian America. Mrs. and Miss DeHone entertained her at a large reception on November 15. "Nilsson always appears to great advantage in society with her gracious manner and charming conversation," remarked the *World* admiringly. She would further entrench herself in high circles by marrying the Spanish Count Angel Vallejo y Miranda in 1887, but by then her American career had waned.

Upon her arrival on October 2, she received the press in her suite at the Hotel Windsor, the elegant hostelry on Fifth Avenue between Forty-sixth and Forty-seventh streets that had been known for the past decade as "largely patronized by foreigners," and would go down in flames in 1899 in the worst hotel fire in New York's history.

At first seriously: "How disgracefully Mapleson behaved to me last season, did he not? After all I have done to help him retrieve his sinking fortunes!" (Mapleson, of course, told a diametrically different story.) She had visited the Metropolitan and professed herself glad to see no heavy hangings to deaden the sound. Then, disposed to light conversation, she admitted to bringing twenty-nine "boxes" of raiment. Her favorite dresses were cut after the Venetian pattern—by Worth, of course—from the time of the Inquisitors: "Those pleasant days when someone wrote your name on a piece of paper and stuck it in the lion's mouth and good-bye to you," she added, consciously or not advertising Abbey's new opera, *La Gioconda,* in which she would star.

In the American premiere of Ponchielli's opera, the Swedish soprano was overshadowed, however, by the Laura of Emmy Fursch-Madi. Although musically unsatisfactory to the purists, the large and resplendent cast, the scenic effects of sheer magnificence, and the stunning "Dance of the Hours" with Malvina Cavalazzi roused the house to stormy applause, in which calls for Abbey were mingled. The impresario finally appeared, holding Nilsson's hand. One of those minor contretemps that lend a certain liveliness to opera's serious progress occurred in the second act. Roberto Stagno, a self-conscious tenor whose be-all and end-all were notes above the staff, had hardly embarked on his romanza, *"Cielo e mar,"* when a curious black cat decided to investigate. The animal made the rounds of the scene behind the tenor, who had naturally gravitated to the footlights. "The good taste of the audience allowed it to break out in laughter," said the *World* reporter, which perplexed the singer but did not really embarrass him.

In spite of its tortuous and occasionally incomprehensible plot, *Gioconda* was to prove one of the most durable of new entries, returning at intervals throughout the years. *Mefistofele* has not been so fortunate. "Purely dramatic operas are no longer written," mourned a critic after witnessing Boito's opera, a complaint that has often been echoed about this monumental work. *Don Giovanni,* Abbey's laudable attempt to strike either high seriousness or high comedy (many in the audience weren't sure and reacted coldly), admitted an odd bit of casting in a late performance when Sembrich was ill. Scalchi, the buxom mezzo-soprano, portrayed the pert Zerlina. Giuseppe Kaschmann, who divided the chief baritone roles with Giuseppe Del Puente, looked the part of the amorous Don perfectly, thought one reviewer, although another found his lungs satisfactory but his legs unattractive, and still another believed him to be the dullest lady-killer extant. Del Puente was at his best—as New York already knew him—in the role of Escamillo in a January performance of *Carmen* that found no empty seats in the House and made a heroine out of Zelia Trebelli. The slim, dark—and, it must be confessed—veteran of several Mapleson campaigns had previously found little outlet except an early Azucena, the double mezzo roles in *Mefistofele,* and a couple of Sunday night concerts. She was a heroine, that is, to the audience and to the *World,* which attributed to her a "marvelous vocal method," if not to the *Tribune's* Krehbiel, who declared that she threw "a lurid light over [Carmen's] wickedness, but found neither tones nor actions for those amiable qualities in which most of the artistic force of the character lies," a surprising judgment from this highly moral scribe.

The vocal success, to Krehbiel's mind, was that of Alwina Valleria as Micaela. A Baltimore girl, née Schoening, she had sung with Mapleson in London ten years previously and had toured with him in America. Abbey's audiences had also liked her as Philine in *Mignon* and as Leonora in *Il Trovatore* on October 26, her debut as the first American to sing on the Metropolitan stage.

The season had been labeled "Italian" without reservation, which meant that nine of Abbey's repertory of nineteen operas suffered from translation. Meyerbeer's great sprawling scores, which should thus be listed as *Gli Ugonotti, Il Profeta,* and *Roberto il Diavolo,* seemed less affected than Flotow's *Martha* and Thomas' *Hamlet,* and the trio of decided Gallic stamp, *Faust, Carmen,* and *Mignon,* but of the entire list, Wagner's *Lohengrin* was most distorted. *Traduction,* the French word with its English overtones of betrayal, would be used for a good many years before the adoption of the original language in the House.

Seldom through the season did Abbey's orchestra pit live up to what might be expected as a standard for good orchestral playing. Only occasionally the Italian imports rose to excellence, and at worst produced some ragged tatters of tone. Persuaded by his leading tenor, Abbey had engaged young Cleofonte Campanini to relieve Vianesi; some of the qualities of greatness that were to lead him to Oscar Hammerstein's service and then to domination in Chicago appeared in this rudimentary season. Italo always sang more freely with his brother in the pit, it was believed. This collaboration was accomplished in *La Sonnambula, Mefistofele,* and *Carmen.*

Henry Abbey was hero or villain according to the observer. It was said of him and his two partners that Maurice Grau provided the successes, Abbey provided the losses, and John B. Schoeffel did the grumbling. Walter Damrosch called Abbey a magnificent and honorable gambler in "stars," whom he paid so liberally that, while he sometimes gained large profits, he many times lost more heavily. "It was too much like the roulette tables at Monte Carlo, with the odds in favor of the stars."

At one time *Music and Drama* cited Abbey's "large purposes and princely generosity," at another boldly declared that his plan for settling any grave difficulty "is to disappear and drink brandy and soda." Both the difficulty and the brandy would vanish in due time. *Keynote* preached that Abbey must learn "other qualities besides oversmartness to cope successfully with so experienced and fully equipped a campaigner as Mapleson."

Grau, who developed into a first-class manager according to Damrosch, was at first accused by *Keynote* of being merely a graduate in French *opéra bouffe*. He had, indeed, busily traversed the country in the wake of his Uncle Julius and had made such songstresses as Aimée deservedly popular. A businessman rather than one of artistic sensibilities, he yet possessed a real flair, and dealt honorably with his singers, who displayed a grudging liking for him. "He used to sit like a spider in his office from morning till night," said Damrosch, "working out repertories, quarreling with the singers or placating them."

Examining the books at the beginning of the year, Abbey must have felt the chill of panic. The box office through Christmas Eve amounted to $159,063.75, or an average of about $3,615 for each of forty-four performances, not nearly enough to cover the costly mountings and star salaries. Ahead lay a fortnight in Boston, three operas in Brooklyn across the new bridge, and a concert at home, then the wide tour that seemed to promise the pot of gold. Abbey's motto had always been: "When in doubt, take to the road." His bankroll had fattened through his tours during the past three years with Sarah Bernhardt, Edwin Booth, Christine Nilsson, and Lily Langtry, and the concurrent appearances of Henry Irving, as well as stands in Boston and New York in his own theatres. So, with a sigh of relief, he turned his face south and west and prepared to recoup. With solid bookings in Philadelphia (the clockwork regularity of Tuesday visits was not established until later), Chicago, Cincinnati, Washington, and Baltimore, the prospects seemed bright. But Abbey had not reckoned with Mapleson's fierce competition in almost every city and the popularity of his rival's twin stars, Patti and Etelka Gerster; nor could he anticipate the *force majeure* of a crippling flood in Cincinnati. Furthermore, he found no stages but Cincinnati's Music Hall that could accommodate his brave and beautiful new scenery, so that makeshifts lessened the attractiveness of his productions all along the way. He limped home in March to put on a spring season of twenty performances, including a sacred concert on Good Friday. The illness of the usually reliable Sembrich forced postponement twice and final abandonment of Gounod's *Roméo et Juliette,* which was later seen in Philadelphia as a part of an afterthought allotment of seven performances. Nilsson was taken ill suddenly so that only one act of *Les Huguenots* could be put on and Sembrich stepped in to finish up with two acts of *Lucia.* Trebelli's indisposition before the *Carmen* that was to conclude the series on April 12 proved the next-to-last straw; the final impetus to despair was Sofia Scalchi's refusal to sing in the substitute *Prophète,* her excuse being that she had not been informed until noon, and her late breakfast lay too heavily on her diaphragm. This marked one of the few complete cancellations of a performance in the Metropolitan's entire history.

In January the directors had been quite sanguine, expressing their satisfaction that "the acoustic properties of the new house are of the finest, that the ventilation is as perfect as that of any public building, and that for safety, commodiousness and comfort and in general effect it compares favorably with any house in the world . . . and has already grown into great popularity. The very best test of this is the fact that the stock of the company commands a premium of as high as fifty percent, as shown by the most recent sales of boxes [to whom is not specified]."

But in the matters of "commodiousness and comfort," a certain amount of dissension had already been registered. As early as October 31, the *World* reporter had discovered drawbacks: "With the larger crowd [for *Mignon*] more painfully apparent becomes the wretched plan of the building. The miserable little cafe on the ground floor (no larger than a bedroom) is the only place where men can smoke and exchange opinions. One hundred men were all very uncomfortable. The great barren vestibules are a waste of space. The upper foyers, like hotel parlors, are shunned by men and ladies alike. Dissatisfaction is loud."

The financial statement issued in January showed discomfort of another sort, in what had become known in some quarters as the "uptown folly." The actual cost of the real estate was $622,191.44; and the building $951,322.41, of which the largest factors were masonry and ironwork. The architects' fees amounted to $44,690.58. Other items, to which scenery, costumes, properties, and music library added $142,500, brought the total to $1,835,833.

Then the stockholders had disbursed $76,445 for taxes, interest, legal fees, and insurance. Estimates for future costs included $5,200 for carpets in corridors (remedying a raw note in the decor). Abbey's stipend was said to be $53,000. Grand total: $2,019,478. Truly, if the gentlemen had known who Molière was, they might have groaned with him: "Of all the noises known to man, opera is the most expensive."

Their receipts, counting capital stock, two assessments of stockholders and rentals, totaled $1,781,000. The deficit: $238,478.

Whereas seventy men might absorb this loss with little distress (although it was certain that their screams of rage and pain would penetrate even the thickest board-room walls), Abbey's plight was his own and a desperate one. Box office receipts at home and on the road ($500,565) brought the average for 140 performances (sixty at home, eighty on the tour) to about $3,500, apparently far too little. The gossip ran that Abbey had dropped half a million. This would seem to indicate that each performance had cost him about $7,000. Sometime later, Schoeffel told

Henry Krehbiel that the amount was closer to $600,000. (Contemporary research is afoot to disprove the size of this amount.) Abbey was left with the bare armature of his fortune, to flesh out arduously once again by booking his actors and actresses, among them Mary Anderson, Mme. Helena Modjeska, and Coquelin, as well as Irving and Terry.

The directors allowed him a benefit before slamming the door. The singers and Irving and Terry contributed their services (except Scalchi, who sent money, which Abbey promptly returned, the coolness between them, probably because of her refusal on the twelfth, not having abated). The intake was $34,544.50, of which Abbey's profit was about half—a rill in an ocean.

What really had happened? One freethinking dissenter tried to get back to root causes:

"To expend two million on a theatre on an unfavorable site, a failure from an acoustical point of view, deficient in architectural beauty either of form or design, and then to lose steadily during the first season $1,700 at each performance is a method of procedure scarcely in accordance with sound business policy."

Sound business policy might have been expected to be the criterion of the group of men who engaged in this speculative venture. But "the party of gentlemen utterly ignorant of the important features to be considered in the construction of an opera house selected a church architect whose experience equalled their own. The impresario had never before managed Italian opera and placed himself in the hands of two deputy assistant managers . . . [he paid] exorbitant fees for singers and engaged too many."

One prominent cause of the fiasco was "the retention of two tiers of boxes by the stockholders to the entire exclusion of the paying public in order to enable the monopolists to enjoy their private privilege at the expense of the public."

Furthermore, a less antagonistic attitude toward the Academy should have been adopted. Taxes alone could run the older house, this writer pointed out.

There hadn't been a brilliant audience since Lent began, which accounted for the poorest intake of the season: a mere $937 for the March 31 La Traviata with Sembrich, Del Puente, and Victor Capoul (who no longer, it seemed, wore the wreath of the adored matinee idol, the "perfect lover" of other years). Anyway, at the best of times "the house is so cheerless, so ill-adapted to the wants of American audiences, so barn-like and badly constructed that none but 'deadheads' or unfortunate stockholders care to go."

The dilemma was put up to the stockholders in a way that left them little choice. They were offered two plans: one to raise $245,000 by a second mortgage; the other to ask each stockholder to subscribe an additional $3,500. The officers professed to feel delicately about asking, but still they felt the money should be raised by subscription. Krehbiel insisted they paid their losses "cheerfully."

With Abbey out of the running, the choice turned to Ernest Gye of London's Covent Garden. But Gye had suffered his own losses and, as Krehbiel pointed out, looked to New York with an attitude "something like that which the Germans describe as a cat walking about a dish of hot porridge." On the Metropolitan's side, a great uneasiness persisted because of Gye's marriage to Emma Albani, the Canadian-American who had triumphed in Europe and had appeared with Strakosch at the Academy in 1874. It was hardly beyond possibility that Gye might wish to put Mme. Albani in place of Mme. Nilsson, whom the directors staunchly admired—it appeared, in fact, that they had been the donors of the gold wreath-*cum*-sash at the opening. Maurice Grau, Mapleson himself, and Italo Campanini were advocated in some quarters. One adviser flippantly nominated variety-house manager Tony Pastor. But serious consideration rested solely on Gye. Then, at some moment in late summer, negotiations were broken off for good.

How the means of salvation came to hand is explained in three different ways. One faction maintained that young Edmund Stanton, the board's secretary, suggested that he knew a man who could put on good opera very cheaply. Walter Damrosch wrote that Hilborn Roosevelt, nephew of James and president of the New York Symphony Association, was responsible. Krehbiel states that Leopold Damrosch himself came forward with the proposition to give a season entirely of German opera with himself as impresario-conductor.

And thus did the complexion of New York's new opera change so drastically that the effects were profound and lasting. So did German opera find a home in America.

5

RHINE MAIDENS CROSS THE ATLANTIC

The [Metropolitan] stockholders created an art spirit which was big
with promise while rich in fulfilment, and then killed it because its
manifestation bored them.

—HENRY E. KREHBIEL, *Chapters of Opera*

Leopold Damrosch looked like a saint and labored like a longshore-
man. Grappling with the Metropolitan Opera became literally a life-and-
death matter for this conscientious musician. The eleventh-hour basis on
which the season was organized brought a sense of strain from the first;
sailing in August for Europe to select appropriate singers, he had concluded arrangements within a month and announced a complete season
at the end of September. To the Italian-oriented public of New York,
the details came as a shock. Everyone knew Amalia Materna, who had
sung with Theodore Thomas in his festival of 1882, but who in the world
were Kemlitz, Kögel, Staudigl, Tiferro, Totzech, Udvardy, Gutjar, Schröder-Hanfstängl and Slach? You couldn't even pronounce them, much less
recognize them! Grudgingly it was admitted that one had possibly heard
of Anton Schott, the burly tenor, and Adolf Robinson, the baritone, and
among the women Marianne Brandt.

Of course, to the large segment of the German-born, who had hitherto played little part in the management's thoughts, the change-over
brought unalloyed delight. They were fully determined to alter the
complexion of the Metropolitan audience.

"Ah, well!" sighed the bored boxholders, "it might do for a time;
after all, we must retrench." Polite attention turned to the new shepherd
of the Metropolitan flock. The fleece might not be golden, but at least
it would be warm and serviceable—and cheap. Leopold Damrosch, practicing physician, had turned to music professionally after only a brief
time in medicine, concertizing as a violinist, then obtaining positions in
the theatres of Posen and Breslau. While conducting the orchestra in the
latter city, he received a call from New York in 1871 to found a singing
society, the Arion. Two years later he helped into existence the organiza-

tion that provided bedrock *réclame* for him—the Oratorio Society of New York. Braving the wrath and probable retribution of Theodore Thomas, who considered the realm of the symphony orchestra his own, Damrosch founded the New York Symphony Society in 1878. Damrosch's son Walter quotes Thomas as threatening: "Whoever crosses my path I crush." Whatever the truth of this, the two conductors played at orchestral rivalry for a decade or so. But Damrosch beat Thomas to the opera world. The latter had hankered after an opera season and had thought to introduce the idea with a magnificent festival in the Seventh Regiment Armory in May 1882, when Amalia Materna, revered for her association with Bayreuth from the beginning in 1876, was the bright particular star. She had gone back to the Festspielhaus after the New York Festival to create the role of Kundry in the master's *Parsifal.* Damrosch persuaded her to head his Metropolitan casts in the second half of the season, when she shone as Elisabeth, Valentine, Rachel in *Die Jüdin,* and finally the *Walküre* Brünnhilde. Her appearances were considered to be "most significant in their bearing upon the operatic problems which the Metropolitan management this season is engaged with," in Krehbiel's words, although her fee of $1,000 per performance approached dangerously near the extravagance that had ruined Abbey.

Most problems seemed on the way to being solved by the time Materna arrived in January. What had been a painful transition for the stockholders, who never would give more than lip service to the "new" music—and this literally, as the conversation level in the boxes crescendoed through the years—and at first had been greeted with more curiosity than affection by everyone else, soon exerted a new magic over the Parquet, the Balcony, and the Family Circle. When in the second season the third tier of boxes was sensibly remodeled into the "paying" seats of a Dress Circle, and two *baignoires* on each side gave way to standing room, even more of the populace could partake of the new sacrament. Still, it is difficult to see how the 5,000 cited as the number admitted to the House on one occasion could have been accommodated.

Not everyone's taste could turn so quickly from wine to beer. Much of the first night's *Tannhäuser,* virtually a novelty, must have been inexplicable; some of it (especially the singing of Herr Anton Schott) little short of monstrous, the *Tribune* sage thought. But to a smaller portion of the audience, it brought "a vivid realization of what Wagner could mean in terms of music drama, and opened a door to an entirely new world."

Although Wagner claimed only one quarter of the repertoire with *Tannhäuser, Lohengrin,* and *Die Walküre,* it was soon realized that "the music of the future" carried the only real meaning in the unfamiliar bill of fare, and that the time was ripe for it to become "the music of today." To Teutonize *Les Huguenots, Don Giovanni, Le Prophète, La Juive,* and, even more incongruously, *Rigoletto* and *Guillaume Tell,* forced a suspension of disbelief greater than the across-the-board Italianization of the year before. Merely faint interest could be summoned up for Auber's quaint *Muette de Portici,* in which the heroine is not even a singer, but only a dancer. Then to expect an American audience to sit still for great chunks of spoken dialogue in German (in the *Singspiel* of Weber's *Der Freischütz* and Beethoven's *Fidelio*) presupposed a type of sophistication not yet imported (and indeed hardly accepted in the opera house in years to come, with the possible exception of *The Bartered Bride,* although Americans grew used to dialogue in operetta and in the form of musical comedy brought to perfection on the American stage). Furthermore, these singers had a declamatory style that could explode a melodic line into fragments. Meyerbeer, Verdi, Mozart, and Rossini came through severely scathed.

The stockholders, having paid Abbey (to the tune of some $80,000) for the scenic and costume investiture of his twenty operas, naturally retained ownership. But only five of these works could be used by the Germans. Of the seven new mountings in 1884–85, the largest budget item was $4,000, and the average $3,500. Congratulating themselves on the economy of their protégé, the stockholders failed to realize that Abbey's average had been but $4,000. The new stage decorations, commented Krehbiel, were all much finer than those of the "hurdy-gurdy Italian list," a gibe which hardly seems fair considering Abbey's taste and largess.

Of the lineup of singers, only a half dozen would remain beyond this year or return for a season or two. Among these Marianne Brandt towered, "the most thrilling Ortrud in the world," Henry T. Finck avowed. In the days when German morals paralleled Anglo-Saxon Victorianism, Maria Anna Bischof had violated all polite canons by going on the stage and tempted hellfire and her brothers' denunciation by appearing in trousers no less. The part was Romeo in Bellini's *I Capu-*

letti ed i Montecchi, favorite of both contraltos and mezzos as well as of powerful sopranos. It went without saying, both from the artistic and family points of view, that she had to change her name. Although the odor of brimstone faded during her substantial career, by her own confession "the theatre can suffice those only who are born comedians; to me it brought more pain than joy, although, on the other side, I must value it as the only place where I could fully develop my artistic individuality."

Brandt had shared the role of Kundry with Materna at Bayreuth in spite of her plain face and figure. Kundry is described by the Master as "a young woman of the greatest beauty." Neither Brandt nor Materna could fulfill that prescription, but Finck states that Wagner called the former a clever actress, saying that "cosmetics could make up the rest," while Materna radiated *Gemütlichkeit* that compensated for good looks. In fact, the opera-oriented author, William Armstrong, maintained that "homeliness is a help to success; it compels more than ever to a developing of the beauty that is within, the only source of reliance when it comes to a final decision."

As the season progressed, one virtue outshone all others. It was apparent that Damrosch believed to the highest degree in what was called ensemble, that interplay of parts and attention to the smallest detail as well as matters of greater import that welded together a production into a homogeneity never before experienced on the American operatic stage. Effectiveness of staging added to the good impression. Damrosch had imported Wilhelm Hock, who had a genius for handling crowds on stage and whose direction in *Lohengrin, La Muette de Portici,* and *Le Prophète* astonished Metropolitan audiences, accustomed to stiff and stationary groupings. This was to whet a minority appetite that never dulled, although it might be distracted in periods of star supremacy. As a further blessing, the highly trained New York Symphony played in the pit, producing beautiful sounds.

From the beginning of the year all efforts were bent toward what Damrosch meant to be at once the climax of his stewardship and the earnest of a new opera life—the production of Wagner's *Die Walküre,* the first "day" of the great *Ring* trilogy. New York had heard the music in what amounted to a travesty under the well-meaning Adolf Neuendorff at the Academy of Music in 1877, and excerpts had invaded the concert halls on numerous occasions. But the full impact of the music drama came at the performance of January 30, 1885. Materna's Brünnhilde, which she had created at Bayreuth, Brandt's equally impressive Fricka, Auguste Kraus's "refined" yet highly dramatic Sieglinde, and Josef Staudigl's Wotan shared in the achievement. Even Anton Schott—the pet aversion of Hans von Bülow, who called him a *Schwein* (Swine) rather than a *Schwanenritter* (Swan Knight) and who had to resign from the Hanover Opera in a losing dispute with the pompous tenor— surprisingly exhibited some agreeable traits, at least to W. J. Henderson of the *Times,* who noticed "a hundred dainty touches of tenderness in his scenes with Sieglinde."

Damrosch had proceeded at his own peril. Conducting every performance—four a week—with day-long rehearsals in between, and rehearsals and performances of the Oratorio Society mounted up to a schedule that not even his almost superhuman dedication could meet without penalty. His son Walter watched with increasing disquiet as the pressure increased. At last, at one of the Thursday evening chorus rehearsals, Damrosch collapsed. His resistance had so weakened that pneumonia found him an easy victim, and he died on February 15.

Not much of the season remained. Walter had conducted performances of February 11, 12, and 14, and the young chorus master, John Lund, got his first pit assignment on the very evening of Damrosch's death, a Sunday concert. Three performances under Lund rounded out the cycle in an atmosphere of dismay and uncertainty.

Shortly before his death, Damrosch had received the stockholders' blessing in the form of a contract that raised his salary from $10,000 to $14,000. In the reassuring warmth and luxury of George Henry Warren's home, after a bounteous dinner and fat cigars, the impresario-conductor also learned that in addition to the fixed sum, his expenses to Europe would be paid.

Thinking to emulate Abbey's—or perhaps Theodore Thomas'— example, Leopold had contracted on his own to visit three cities immediately after the New York season. With no other alternative, because his father's practically nonexistent estate fell liable, young Damrosch took over. He was of course blamed for the gesture toward economy that prompted the use of the West Shore Railroad, which he later categorized as "a rather lame rival of the New York Central," but arrangements had doubtless been concluded months before, and Damrosch was but an innocent bystander in the fierce railroad wars of the day. Although two hours late into Chicago because of disasters both natural and mechanical, he saved the situation with that bonhomie which in later life became a trademark, taking Materna by the hand and proceeding *en train* down the aisle to the stage, giving the patient audience an early version of the "personal appearance." Damrosch even managed to perform on the road two operas his father had hoped for but not realized at home, Gluck's *Orfeo ed Euridice* (with Brandt) and Boieldieu's *Dame Blanche*—both in German guise, of course.

The younger Damrosch's transfer to full-time operations with the Metropolitan had not been unaccompanied by quiet rejoicing on the part of an organization which thus lost his services. On February 16, the *Tribune* published a statement from the Plymouth Church, expressing the general sentiment to be of satisfaction. "There was a feeling that Mr. Damrosch was not adapted to lead devotional music, and his chorus was not a success." The next day, the paper expounded its own opinions on the young man, saying that an "emotional nature is less helpful in the work of orchestra and opera conducting, and sometimes marred the precision, firmness and intelligibility of his time-beating. He frequently became excited and manifested it much in the way that most composers do when directing their own works."

In the midst of the confusion and grief, a decision had to be made. The stockholders barricaded themselves against the assault of Schott, not the first tenor to aspire to management, nor the last. Unfortunately the powerful-lunged Anton forgot all those "dainty" touches that might have served his cause. Proceeding almost immediately from Damrosch's impressive funeral at the opera house, Schott turned his artillery on the Thirty-ninth Street House, conveying the threat that if they did not accept, the Academy would. Fourteenth Street indignantly denied the liaison, whereupon Schott was dismissed. Several features of his plan, however, were adopted, most notably the choice of a chief conductor as apart from a manager. The latter position fell to Edmund C. Stanton, who had already appeared as the board's secretary. Walter was retained as assistant conductor; with Stanton, he sailed to Germany to try to engage the best possible man, Anton Seidl, for the advancement of the German cause, more especially Wagner's operas.

Seidl, then thirty-four, had been for six years an intimate member

of Wagner's household, serving as secretary, copyist, and assistant conductor. The Master had already introduced him publicly as "the young
artist whom I have brought up, and who is now accomplishing astound-
ing things."

Furthermore, Wagner had jocularly inscribed in a *Rheingold* score
a poetic effusion which sounded hardly more elegant in German than
in English:

> Everything in life is hollow
> Surely it must therefore follow
> When no bottle can be had
> You must take a mug instead
> Anton has alone succeeded
> Everything he does is needed
> He has entered to the core
> Of the Nibelungen score.

Seidl had already conducted the complete *Ring* in many cities in
Germany and in London in 1882. After Wagner's death in 1883, he took
a post in Bremen, from which he was fetched to America. New York's
first *Ring* was to wait until 1888–89 (when five cities outside the metropolis shared the exalting experience), although *Das Rheingold* was the
only unfamiliar segment by then, *Walküre* having persisted and *Siegfried* and *Götterdämmerung* added in 1887.

Seidl was a known and already revered quantity; the other star
destined to rise high and remain fixed for what to a singer represents
eternity came well advertised but not for the qualities that were later
to set her apart from lesser mortals. Lilli Lehmann cherished no delu-
sions about herself. "Rarely are so many desirable and necessary ante-
cedents united as in my case," she admitted. Of impeccable musical
background, the Bavarian proved her mettle as early as her first operatic
experience in Prague, when she went on as Pamina in *The Magic Flute*
with no other preparation than having observed this leading role from
a minor one. Wagner himself coached her in Bayreuth, but for lesser
characters: she was kept up in a tree as the Forest Bird in *Siegfried* or
in the depths as a Rhine Maiden. With the exception of an Isolde in
London, her extraordinary capacities had hardly been plumbed; still,
the coloratura roles such as *Violetta* which were her portion, laid a

foundation of *bel canto* that few dramatic singers can boast—she was, as Finck said, a model to modern Italian singers in the lost art of singing florid music dramatically.

This paragon burst with a rather dull concussion on the American public. Who chose Carmen for her? Stanton? Seidl, who conducted? Critics politely waited.

The revelation came with her Brünnhilde five nights later. "Her voice glorified the music!" exclaimed Krehbiel. "Her cries were brimming with eager, happy vitality." The queen among dramatic sopranos, Finck was to proclaim her. It was the first time she had ever sung the part. The year held many lesser triumphs for her, with Sulamith in *The Queen of Sheba,* Bertha in *Le Prophète,* Irene in *Rienzi,* and Venus in *Tannhäuser,* and an occasional reversion to the lyric realms as Marguerite in *Faust.* Her taste of the Wagnerian waters acted like Isolde's love potion, instilling a passion that never waned. To escape being thrust back exclusively into the shallows of Gounod, Bizet, and the lighter Verdi, she bought off her contract with the Berlin Opera, allowing a festival in Milwaukee to pay her fine by asking the same amount for a fee.

From her first step on the Metropolitan stage, Lehmann was partnered often by the German equivalent of a matinee idol, the imperious Max Alvary, whose handsome features and long legs encased in tights threw many a feminine heart into palpitations. Not only were the usually awkward fur jerkins and rough gaiters that denoted the high-style Wagnerian becoming to him, but he dressed impeccably offstage. Such a combination of virtues far overshadowed the other two tenors who struggled for position: the robust Eloi Sylva and the more lyric Albert Stritt.

Lehmann began to feel that she was being pushed into the shade as well, or that two suns on one stage may scorch each other. Still, their abrasive relations might not have reached a painful point had not the goddess, wise enough in Valhalla, developed a fatal human weakness— she fell in love with another tenor, Paul Kalisch. He was almost as handsome as Alvary, with a jaunty moustache and yearning eyes, but his worshiping *Frau* tended to overvalue his artistic stature. In earlier days it was said of Patti that she accepted a lower fee when her tenor-husband Nicolini sang beside her; such a canard never was whispered of the righteous Lilli, yet it became a matter of knowledge that the world's greatest female Wagnerian was happier when her own Siegfried or Tristan appeared in the cast listing.

They were married in the briskest, most businesslike manner imaginable. The bride sent a message to the Reverend Bartholomew Krusi of the German Presbyterian Church at 296 Madison, stating simply that she wished to be married "this evening" (February 24, 1888) between four and five and that the ceremony was to be private. In a furious rainstorm, they arrived at the church, Lehmann in a black silk frock, Kalisch in full evening dress. The *Lohengrin* march was played by the minister's daughter Minnie on the organ; a choir of church-school children had hastily been assembled. The couple spent the first day of their honeymoon sequestered on the fifth floor of the Hotel Normandie on Broadway, close to the opera house, where streams of callers and even notes and cards were turned back. One newspaper mentioned that the groom was twenty-eight; the bride one year younger than Patti—who he neglected to say was born in 1843. (This does not quite jibe with Lehmann's birthdate of 1848 or Kalisch's of 1855 but it makes a point.)

The rivalry between tenors emitted sparks in Chicago the following year. Public and critical sentiment was obviously in favor of Alvary. (One columnist had described Kalisch backstage as "mild, trivial . . . his rosy face beamed with good nature . . . he pulled his mustaches and skipped airily across to the Rhinemaidens, laid a detaining hand on the waist of one and passed a caressing hand over the hair of another. What a comedian!")

One wonders that the marriage lasted as long as it did (some years later they were legally separated though never divorced) when the fair Lilli's prescription for her new young (and, it is to be suspected, more than a trifle frivolous) husband is studied: "It was not to be exclusively a life of idleness or pleasure. I proposed [it should be] one of strong cooperation in the development of ourselves and our art that should lead our united lives to a single lofty goal."

Hearing that the dissension between the tenors had become public with Alvary's declaration that Kalisch could not sing, Lehmann demanded with wounded dignity that audiences judge for themselves. "I never quarrel before *mit* no one," the Chicago *Tribune* gave as her exit line.

6

"SEVEN LONG YEARS HAVE FLOWN"*

There in the darkness, the first phrases caught me like a small wave and washed me into an opening sea of sound. Up to the crests and into the shallows of the sea I was tossed and buffeted, and for over four hours it seemed as if there would come no moment of rest. My blood flowed with the tide. When, in the orchestra, the painful seconds pressed one another, I felt it in my wrists. It was as if there were wounds there and fingers that pinched back the flowing blood. And when the harmonies widened, then the fingers relaxed and the blood flowed out. The wound was eased and became a flower and one flower grew out of another. These flowers had a dark, luminous texture. They were huge and palpitant; they bore up little human beings in their hot, velvet depths. I was tossed in warm scented flowers up and down with the tumult of the sea.

—JEAN STARR UNTERMEYER, *Private Collection*

The impact of *Tristan* upon an unexperienced audience must have been breathtaking. Columns were written, of course, by those who professed to be the Master's disciples, and knowing ones spoke of "chromaticism" and "leitmotifs," yet what the public actually felt was more difficult to discern. Mrs. Untermeyer's emotional response is probably typical of the more rapturous reactions. James Huneker, like a Teutonic Colline, pawned his overcoat to hear the first performance from a top-gallery seat, although his friend Maurice Egan warned him that "people don't do such things, even for art." Huneker never quite recovered, and wrote later, refuting a charge that Wagner's music was indecently sensual: "Oh, you people who are so nasty nice that Goethe is coarse, Shakespeare shocking and Wagner sensual. . . . The man whose pulses do not quiver during the second act of *Tristan* is as bloodless as a turnip."

At that historical performance on December 1, 1886, Lilli Lehmann's Tristan was the aging but puissant Albert Niemann, while Max Alvary, her *bête noire,* had been assigned the tiny role of the Sailor's Voice off-stage, probably in line with the German regime's insistence on "ensemble" (he was later to sing Melot, hardly more important except that he could at least appear in the flesh).

* *Der Fliegende Holländer.*

Although Lehmann rather contemptuously dismissed Niemann as "just good enough for such a susceptible public as New York's," she later was to write that "nothing set free greater emotion than these *Tristan* performances," when the audience "sat still for minutes, silent, motionless."

Niemann had conquered in spite of his age (fifty-five) and the obviously threadbare quality of his voice. He had forged his acting personality in three dozen years of steady advancement. Wagner had chosen him for the Tannhäuser of the Paris revision in 1861, and for Siegmund at Bayreuth in 1876. It was as the young hero in *Die Walküre* that he made his Metropolitan debut on November 10, 1886, taking possession of the stage "like an elemental force," according to Krehbiel. Although he appeared rather more grandfatherly than boyish, still "the colossal figure, the head like 'the front of Jove himself,' the eyes large and full of luminous light that seems to dart through the tangled and matted hair that concealed the greater portion of his face" made an indelible impression upon the *Tribune* critic. Wagner had joked with Niemann, so recounted Walter Damrosch, because he would not dispense with the thicket of his beard for Parsifal. The tenor is supposed to have answered aggrievedly, "I would cut off my nose if it were necessary to sing one of your roles properly." Both nose and beard were flourishing during his two New York seasons. He had not been allowed to sing Siegfried in Bayreuth because the Master did not wish the same man to interpret both young heroes, Siegmund and Siegfried, but Seidl gave him the chance at the elder Siegfried the following year. He also re-created Lohengrin and Tannhäuser, as well as ennobling Florestan in *Fidelio,* John in *Le Prophète,* Eléazar in *La Juive,* and Cortez in Spontini's opera.

Tristan und Isolde excited more comment, more abuse, and more admiration than any other work, the *Herald* reported. Many regarded its production as hazardous, but a more emphatic, even unqualified, success could not be imagined. All during the first act the audience sat in breathless suspense, and at the curtain a scene of enthusiasm the like of which had rarely been witnessed greeted the principals and the conductor. The score was probably the most perfect thing Wagner had ever written, opined this observer, "a constant passage from beauty to beauty." First place had to be accorded to Anton Seidl, for his achievement with the orchestra—"an orchestra with a soul, a chief actor in the tragedy."

Lilli Lehmann showed at last what a really magnificent dramatic singer she was. Even her Brünnhilde had not prepared New York for this blazing glory; singing of beauty, strength, and intensity, acting full of intelligence, grace, and imagination. Niemann looked "every inch" the legendary hero, which, considering his huge, heavy-boned frame, encompassed a goodly number of inches. He husbanded his vocal resources, as the reviewers were fond of saying, until the last act, which makes cruel demands upon the tenor both as singer and as actor. Pruning pages from Wagner's score, considered by some to be judicious, by others sacrilege, became the accepted procedure in the New World, but on this occasion Krehbiel maintained that if anything justified retention of all of *Tristan's* third-act music it was "the perfection of Niemann, the equal of which for forcefulness and truthfulness we have never witnessed on the lyric stage."

Still, Krehbiel wished that the tenor had followed Wagner's directions a little less realistically, and "stopped short of the exposure of the sword wound—it was shocking, and sent a thrill of horror through the audience." The writer prudishly recalled afterward that "an experienced actress at my elbow in a *baignoire* grew faint and almost swooned." The titillating gesture was banned thereafter.

Wagner's music led all others in popular acceptance during those seven "German" years, and of his masterpieces, *Tristan* continued to hold the fascinated attention of the Metropolitan Parquet, Dress Circle, and Balcony, even when toward the last other lovers succeeded Lehmann and Niemann. Heinrich Vogl, who had created Loge and Siegmund and was considered for years a model Tristan, took over in 1890–91, his Isolde Antonia Mielke, who followed Lehmann in all the great dramatic roles.

Lohengrin and *Tannhäuser* naturally remained staples. *Die Meistersinger* had been received cordially in the second season, introducing the lovable Hans Sachs of Emil Fischer, and eliciting the remark from Henry T. Finck (for which he apologized but not sufficiently) that the baritone "could have toured for years as a Sachsophone." Fischer indeed did remain on the scene for a number of years as a teacher.

It was more difficult for the public to accept *Siegfried* at its American premiere on November 9, 1887, because no woman appears until the third act; instead, said Krehbiel, "[we have] a bear, a dragon and a bird;

a sublimely solemn peripatetic god who asks riddles and laughs once, and two dwarfs, repulsive of mind and hideous of body—plus all of the mechanical devices." Still, the audience overcame its confusion and admired the work, if not extravagantly. At least it had been reduced from its original four hours and thirty minutes to three hours and forty minutes. Siegfried was Max Alvary's real specialty, but unfortunately for his niche in Valhalla, his good looks were not matched by good sense. "A matinee idol at thirty, he was dead and gone at forty," mourned Henry Sherman Adams, a loving chronicler of the times, inaccurate in the interests of round numbers to the extent of two years chopped from the tenor's actual forty-two.

Götterdämmerung, the last of the trilogy (*Das Rheingold* waited a year to make the *Ring* complete), was rendered more "human" by Seidl's cuts, which were warmly excused by Krehbiel on this account. The excised scenes—the Prologue with the Norns and Brünnhilde's colloquy with Waltraute—did not catch up with the body of the work until 1898, and the Norns were often omitted thereafter.

Fidelio ran *Tristan* a close race in popularity for a few seasons, and led all operas in average receipts one year. Stanton had been reluctant to mount Beethoven's only opera because of the presence on his roster of two famous Leonores, and "they mustn't quarrel." His premonitions were justified, and even more drastically than he had feared, because the public was let in on what the *Herald* called "a most painful incident." It occurred in the second act. Marianne Brandt was singing the faithful wife who is about to rescue her imprisoned husband. What she uttered (*"Nichts, nichts, mein Florestan!"*), the *Herald* noted, was perhaps "in a somewhat exaggerated and declamatory fashion, but no reason for the burst of laughter from one of the boxes. The singer was so staggered by the insult that her voice failed her, and her memory as well. Herr Geidl [*sic*] was obliged to stop the orchestra and look at the offender." The performance finally resumed, and "a wild demonstration ensued. Brandt and Niemann [Florestan] were recalled four times after the duet. There were hisses too and justly so" for the laugher.

Lilli Lehmann's guilt of this breach of colleaguery was never firmly established, but Brandt believed it. Her ravaged feelings were not soothed by Lehmann's appearance five nights later in the role, which Lilli loftily said was hers by right anyway. Krehbiel had found Brandt thrillingly effective on its musical side and "rising to grandeur on its histrionic." But Leonore never reverted to Brandt until, with a motivation that seems plain, she chose it for her farewell at an extra matinee on March 17, 1888. Wagner's *Rienzi* brought the two women together for four out of five performances soon after the fateful *Fidelio,* but without any fireworks other than those necessary to consume the scenery and protagonists as demanded by the plot.

Other female singers throughout several seasons appear to have associated peacefully with one another, but this may have been because they were not on a collision course. Marie Schröder-Hanfstängl, the coloratura from Frankfort and Paris, had things pretty much her own way in 1884–85, taking roles first in *Don Giovanni, Les Huguenots,* and others ranging from Elisabeth to Gilda. When she returned in 1888–89, she added Aida and Leonora in *Il Trovatore* (in German, of course). Her voice was considered to combine the grace and beauty of the Italian with the sincerity and accent of the German. She was, in two words, described as a "finished songstress."

Auguste Kraus had been married to Anton Seidl about a year when she joined Damrosch's company to sing Elisabeth, Marzelline, Elsa, Sieglinde, Bertha (*Le Prophète*), and Ännchen (*Der Freischütz*). When she returned the next year, it was to sing under her husband's baton, her fresh and lovely voice and forceful acting winning many friends in additional roles—notably Eva, Gutrune, and Micaela. Her Elsa was considered at this time an almost complete realization of Wagner's ideal. Remaining until the spring of 1888, she hyphenated her name with her husband's, a contemporary habit adopted also by Marie Krämer-Weidl, the first Queen of Sheba, whose husband, August Krämer, was the Met's first David in *Die Meistersinger.* Another married couple belonged to the roster in 1886–88, although while Theresa Herbert-Förster sang Aida, Elsa, Irene (*Rienzi*), and Elisabeth, her husband played cello in the pit. His name: Victor Herbert.

Stanton and Seidl—the former bearing most of the responsibility, it is to be feared—infested the Metropolitan corpus with a virus that has periodically recurred to undermine the health of the institution— the novelty-of-no-return. Neither Abbey nor Damrosch had attempted wide deviations from the conventional, considering the habits of the day.

Out of Stanton's six-year crop of nine works new to America, only three outlived his regime, and at that only once apiece: Goldmark's *Königin von Saba* (which returned in 1905), Cornelius' *Barbier von Bagdad* (heard in 1925–26), and Weber's *Euryanthe* (which Toscanini revived in 1914–15). With the laudable intent of presenting a complete Wagnerian canvas, Stanton had played *Rienzi* (previously heard at the Academy of Music in 1878) and *Der Fliegende Holländer* (given in Philadelphia in 1876 and New York in 1877 and subject to periodic Metropolitan revival—*vide* annals even unto 1964). But Goldmark's *Merlin* in 1886–87 could not compare to his sumptuous *Queen*. "The old saying that what is good is old and what is new is not good applies more to *Merlin* than any other work heard in a long time," commented the *Herald* acidly. "Cribbing (if things are called by their proper names) was noticeable throughout. Indeed, the second act was a sort of illegitimate offspring of the love scene in *Tristan*." Still, the critic noted one improvement over *The Queen of Sheba*: *Merlin* was not weighted down by an Oriental whine—perhaps referring to the very music in the former that Krehbiel said "rushes along like a lava stream, every measure throbbing with eager, excited and exciting life." Even a fashionable opening-night audience succumbed perforce to the *Queen*'s charms, which the *World* defined as "one pageant hurled upon another, successfully preventing silence from healing the blows of sound." Unlike many great spectacles, the writer concluded, Goldmark's had not been "rehearsed in life to be hearsed to death the first night." The *Tribune* man complimented Goldmark curiously by saying that not every Jew could thus handle a Jewish subject—"compare Halévy, Meyerbeer, and Rubinstein."

The Cornelius *Barbier* also aroused Krehbiel's admiration, but suffered postponement through illness of tenor and conductor, and was given only four times in 1889–90, though repeated another season. Bracketing the little opera with a ballet provided the second of those double bills (occasionally triple) which were to stud the Metropolitan repertoire with incongruities both laughable and atrocious. The first had been in 1886–87, when Brüll's *Goldene Kreutz* ("The Golden Cross") was followed by a ballet called simply Vienna Waltzes. The opera inspired the word "pretty" in practically all its aspects. The rather artificial plot was resolved in what the *Herald* called "a startling amount of embracing."

Two additional new spectacles were set before the long-suffering stockholders, both with indifferent success. Nessler's *Trompeter von Säkkingen,* which Krehbiel said had fairly devastated German audiences with its charms for nearly five years, had the same effect on this 1887 American one, but in an entirely opposite way. Reviving it after one season brought no radical change in opinion. Spontini's *Fernand Cortez,* heard for the first time on January 6, 1888 (in translation from the French), added to the devastation. "It was a good deal like trying to revive a mummy," said Krehbiel.

The *World* found its music a mixture of "puerile Italian melody and German noise." Still, Niemann was at his best, "an edifying spectacle on a white horse," the *Times* chortled, dressed in an ermine-lined cloak and cavalier hat. He took his curtain calls on foot, however. In Hanover, where the tenor had sung the role three years previously, according to Maria Jeritza, he had insisted on riding King Ernst's horse, and in order to break it in, had stipulated that he should ride it through the town in advance, to the amazement of the populace. But the King happened to be an ardent music patron as well as an accomplished equestrian. Krehbiel thought that giving the stage Cortez only three horses less than the real conqueror had taken to Mexico carried realism pretty close to historical veracity. And this elaborate fiasco ate up $19,727.27, more than half of the total set aside for new productions.

Worse was still to come. Stanton took judgment perilously in hand when he produced for his last opening night (1890) Alberto Franchetti's *Asrael,* static, oratoriolike, and an utter failure in the voice parts, not helped by its translation from Italian. The composer, wrote the *World* slyly, was that *rara avis,* a very, very rich man—a nephew of the Roth-schilds, no less, "about thirty, dark, handsome, over six feet in stocking feet," though how this last measurement was discovered by the newspaper Peeping Tom was not made clear. He had written some attractive measures for the orchestra, about the only favorable thing that could be said for him. The scenery came in for a few sarcastic words as well, heaven and hell being "cheap lithographs like a child's story book."

The manager lost even more self-confidence after December 12, when another novelty, *Der Vasall von Szigeth* by Antonio Smareglia, which had aroused considerable affection in European centers, confounded and antagonized New York. One might listen to the opinion of the noted critic, Eduard Hanslick, that "the music was Italian soul and melody wedded to German science and precision," but New York found it simply Hungarian, and goulash at that. In revenge for the theft of his wife, a vassal drives the wife of one of his master's sons into the other son's arms by magic, and poisons her. The betrayed husband kills his brother. This libretto, said Krehbiel, "offered such a sup of horrors as had never been seen on an operatic stage before."

The third and wildest lapse in judgment occurred on January 9, 1891. No possible excuse could have been found for putting on the boards a creation such as *Diana von Solange* except that someone (Stanton was strongly hinted) was mightily desirous of a *quid pro quo.* "A Duke's Grand Opera," read the headline in the *World,* after which all of the titles of the gentleman were strung out imposingly—his *nom de compositeur* appearing as the Duke of Saxe-Coburg-Gotha. Both the dilettante Duke's propensity to scatter decorations indiscriminately and the antiquity (premiere, 1858) of his pretentious work (which, incidentally, possessed what the *World* thought a marvelous ballet) were aired by newspapers. *Diana* of course suffered corruption to *"Solang-weilig"* among other even more uncomplimentary terms. When it was learned that the management intended a third performance, three hundred irate subscribers got up a petition and *Fidelio* was hastily substituted.

In addition to their dismal character, the three novelties shared another and more prepossessing common denominator—the leading tenor, Andreas Dippel, thrust into a trio of unpleasant situations, nevertheless began to attract favorable attention and revealed further charm as Lohengrin, Walther (*Die Meistersinger*), Nureddin (*Barbier*), and in the (Teutonized) French spectrum as José and Vasco da Gama. Eventually to earn the label "Old Reliable," Dippel joined Lehmann, Kalisch, and Seidl as the only quartet to remain in the new day that was to dawn all too soon.

The German company never ventured very far afield. Stanton lost $15,000 in a Philadelphia fortnight that ruined the Christmas holidays of 1885–86 and brought him further anguish when a Quaker City newspaper quoted him as saying that he "did not know one side of the stage from another, or a wing from a fly." He listened reluctantly to a proposition by Herman Grau, brother of the J. Grau who piloted French operetta troupes about the country, and uncle of the Maurice Grau more closely associated with the Metropolitan. Grau outlined a tour as far-flung as one of Mapleson's—to the West Coast and back. Stanton agreed, but never really was reconciled, and is alleged to have let slip many spiteful remarks about the whole affair. In spite of this and of the absence of Lehmann, Stritt, and Seidl, Grau got together a reputable troupe but eventually showed them off to but four cities—Chicago, St. Louis, Cincinnati, and Cleveland. Whatever the defects of the mission, it paved the way for Seidl's tour in 1888–89, when the *Ring* enchanted five cities in varying degrees, critics struggling manfully with what one called "lieb" motives and chromatic sequences, marveling at the aquatic achievements of the Rhine Maidens and the other magical manifestations of the *Rhinegold* scenery.

Yet Wagner in anticipation held greater lure than in realization; the country's music lovers reacted more sluggishly than had been anticipated. Stanton, reconfirmed in his distrust of the road, agreed only after considerable pressure from the eager Damrosch to let the younger man take a troupe to Chicago and Boston in the spring of 1889–90. By the following January the blow had fallen. Between two *Meistersingers* the public learned that German opera as an exclusive way of life would be no more after the close of the season.

In immediate reaction, Stanton hastily revised the repertoire to cram as much Wagner into the few remaining weeks as possible. The public let the opera know in rousing terms that its adoration belonged chiefly to *Tristan* and to *Meistersinger,* and to the singers involved in these two favorites—as well as to the conductor. The final *Tristan* on March 20 brought the most brilliant audience of the season—one of the finest ever in the House. Wreaths, innumerable curtain calls, and a *Tusch* for Seidl (highest compliment an orchestra can pay its leader) glorified the night hours. The final matinee surpassed the evening, if possible. *Meistersinger,* the Sachs of Fischer, the revered conductor, and even the manager, Stanton, came in for tributes not often accorded before or since. With such proofs of affection, it was cruelly hard to believe that the honeymoon was over.

In retrospect, those halcyon days had lasted longer than might have been expected, considering that each season was negotiated separately, so that no continuity was possible. The papers generally ranked themselves on the side of the management and performance, one of them citing Stanton (who had already been called "the most gentlemanly manager in the world" by Lilli Lehmann) as the "sagacious, prudent, methodical lieutenant with the broad view, level head and firm grip, so different from the Italians who bought and begged for a season." A word of praise dropped from the *World* also for the stockholders who could stomach it all—"patience and fortitude shone on the forehead of wealth"—at least for a while. Through the German tenure, they continued to fulfill their duties of appearing on opening nights at least.

In 1885, the boxes were full, from *baignoire* to upper tier, "all in full dress," the first opportunity to "exhibit winter costumes and diamonds" (presumably their summer diamonds had been stored away in safety vaults). A procession of young men was noted, although debutantes were few. The "public" responded too, "whelmed the big parquet, stood up in the side pens and sat packed in the new dress circle." The new conductor, Seidl, was greeted by "the mellow sound of gratulation by kid gloves," which swelled to "sharp applause" as bare hands got into the act.

Society might be growing cooler to its central showcase, but its journalistic admirers waxed more lyrical year by year. The opening of 1886–87 found the House "brilliant in soft lights (still gas, although some new electric lights had been brought over from Dresden) flooding the great expanse of white and gold," gushed the *Herald*. "And the ladies! The flowers, the diamonds and the toilets! They paralyzed the senses and seduced the reason. Glorious radiancy!"

Then in 1887, with the announcement that the old rival, the Academy of Music, had been sold to E. G. Gilmore of Niblo's Garden and Eugene Tompkins of the Boston Theatre and would soon be giving opera at low prices, rumblings of dissatisfaction began to appear among the stockholders. Even German opera cost too much, they grumbled. They were losing about $800 every time the curtain went up. To continue would mean assessments of $3,200 per box. But—if they closed the House, it would still mean $1,000 out of each pocket just to pay fixed costs. The controversy reached the *Times,* which laid it forth judiciously for all to see.

Assessments had risen from $700 the first year to the present $2,500. Was opera worth it? Especially German opera. True, a good deal of

Wagner's music is unsingable, they mused, but that is not a sufficient reason why the singable parts should not be sung!

Among opinions expressed by the powers who allowed themselves to be quoted in January 1888, hardly one touched on artistic matters more deeply. An exception was Luther Kountze, who professed himself as heartily in favor of the regime, and entirely satisfied with its progress, while some weight might be given to the words of the California tycoon, C. P. Huntington, who confessed: "I can't read a note, but something in those German operas agrees with my constitution."

Joseph W. Drexel came right out with it and accused the public of the sins attributed to the stockholders: of being satiated and weary of Wagner. "Let's take a rest from it," he urged. "It *is* heavy," agreed Elbridge T. Gerry, who vowed himself in favor of paying the $1,000, closing up, and then reverting to Italian opera next season. Adrian Iselin thought it too expensive to close. Henry Clews, with his usual brightness, offered several trenchant proposals: "Let the operas be cut so we can get out at eleven; introduce something in a lighter vein; get exemption from taxes; let management show more enterprise, using the house for entertainments and so on. Get Ward McAllister," he concluded, "he'll stir things up—put some new blood in!"

But the loudest dissident was Washington E. Connor, who had just gone through a stormy shipwreck with the too-ambitious American (National) Opera Company, of which he was accounted an "angel," at least to the extent of providing the necessities for an ill-advised production of Rubinstein's *Nero* in their one tenancy of the Met. The company, founded in innocent good faith by Jeannette Thurber (who was also responsible for the National Conservatory of Music to which Anton Dvořak was imported), had bickered and broken on the road after only two seasons. Theodore Thomas' yearnings for an opera of his own went with it, as did the fortunes of many well-known singers. Connor switched his allegiance to the Metropolitan.

"German opera is a dismal failure!" he howled. "We shall go into bankruptcy!"

But George G. Haven of the executive committee and the more moderate views prevailed. At the meeting on January 27, only Connor and James Harriman voted positively No.

German opera was saved, but only for the moment. The stockholders had but voted themselves into a mood of temporary quiescence, observed Krehbiel ominously.

Unpleasant incidents multiplied until it became open war between the golden circles and the "masses" nine feet below. Upstairs they complained it was too gloomy to see each other during performances. Stanton heeded and left the lights up in *Fidelio*. When Florestan in his dank prison exclaimed: *"Gott, welch' Dunkel hier!"* downstairs, consisting three quarters of Germans, murmured or laughed contemptuously. Dark it wasn't. When upstairs suggested that the last act of *Meistersinger* be put ahead as it contained the only music worth listening to, Stanton turned a deaf ear, and downstairs didn't even get to know about the sacrilegious request. Then upstairs grew so unruly that it was forced to chastise itself. On January 1, 1891, a neat white sign appeared in each box:

Many complaints having been made to the directors of the Opera House of the annoyance produced by the talking in the boxes during the performances, the board requests that it be discontinued.

BY ORDER OF THE BOARD OF DIRECTORS

It is to be feared that the buzz upstairs grew fiercer, at least for a few evenings. Stanton is even supposed to have come before the curtain one night to request silence. One director asserted arrogantly that paying his $3,200 had given him the right to talk if he wanted to. While these arrant bad manners abated, the conversational habits of the aristocracy were ingrained and very difficult to uproot. Lady Susan Townley, in a visit after the turn of the century to New York from Washington, where her husband was counselor at the British Embassy, remarked on the curious toleration of talking all through the performance.

By a stroke of irony, the notices were posted in the boxes on the same day that the directors signed a contract with Henry E. Abbey to return and bring Italian opera with him.

Metropolitan eyes had turned toward Abbey as long before as his marathon tour with Adelina Patti, Emma Albani, Lillian Nordica, and Francesco Tamagno in 1889–90. He had opened the magnificent Chicago Auditorium (when Patti made each golden note of "Home, Sweet Home" and Eckert's "Echo Song" count to a total of $5,000), conquered Mexico

City, San Francisco, and other points west and east, and showed once again the daring spirit that was never quenched. When he announced that the new Metropolitan family would include such illustrious members as the De Reszke brothers, Emma Eames, Jean Lasalle, Emma Albani, Sofia Scalchi, and Marie Van Zandt, as well as Lilli Lehmann and Seidl himself, even the stoutest Teuton began to wonder if life might not be worth living once again.

7

GOLD AND SMOKE

The world's great age begins anew, the golden years return.

—Percy Bysshe Shelley

It is always easier to determine the end of a golden age than to fix the exact beginning of one. The decade that in retrospect was accounted the Metropolitan's finest began with an uncertain alchemy. Even the glorious Jean de Reszke (Jean, as, kinglike, he preferred to be called) did not step onto a ready-made throne. Only much later Henry T. Finck wrote: "He enjoys the consciousness of being the greatest tenor that ever lived; he loves the roles he impersonates incomparably; and he must be royally happy in knowing that he does everything for art's sake and nothing for effect or applause."

But at the moment of Jean's first appearance in New York, as Roméo to Emma Eames's Juliette and brother Edouard's Friar Laurence on December 14, 1891, the *Evening Post* critic jested: "Jean de Reszke is said to be higher priced, but we would not be surprised if Edouard proved to be more highly prized."

Jean's voice lacked *schmaltz,* Finck continued, and in a later *Huguenots* seemed singularly unsympathetic in quality, often fuzzy, and worse, curiously uneven in timbre in the different registers, as if the tones "came from different throats."

This opinion was virtually unanimous. While paying attention to Jean's generous equipment, Henry Krehbiel admitted in the *Tribune* that his voice could scarcely be described as sensuously beautiful. W. J. Henderson in the *Times* thought the organ agreeable though not surprising. The *World* joined the chorus in voting Edouard an even more exceptional artist than Jean. And the *Herald* added an ironic touch: Jean went unrecognized at his entrance with Mercutio. But the writer gave the singer full marks for artistic aplomb. At the end of the second act, the curtain began to fall too soon, whereupon the tenor stepped hastily in front of it and finished his aria on the stage apron.

The same reluctance to admit Jean fully to his rightful kingdom had been evinced in the real American debut of the brothers and Eames. Henry Abbey, possibly sensing a probationary attitude on the part of his New York employers, had settled on an out-of-town tryout period, taking the company to Chicago for five weeks. *Lohengrin* had launched his new bark on November 5. Everyone agreed that no such performance of one of Chicago's favorite operas had ever been heard, but it was only a minority spokesman who wrote about Jean: "He swept into view in a swan-drawn boat, tall and fair as a Viking, the light playing on his shining armor . . . with a rarely fine physique, broadshouldered and commanding, and a face strong, yet fair, manly yet mild." But his crown was yet to be safely won. Brother Edouard stole the show, as later he would in New York.

Had these scribes all applied themselves to the writings of George Bernard Shaw, who for a year or two committed one act of *lèse majesté* after another as the new critic for the London *World*? G.B.S. regretted, in the first place, that Jean had ever turned from baritone to tenor. Then, in his eagerness to see and hear the later Wagner roles from Jean, he poked and prodded at the "half gods," scolding Jean for not fulfilling his promise as an actor, citing his interesting Otello and Don José as results of "the rivalry of younger men and the decay of his old superficial charm, which, with advancing years, forced him to make the most of all his powers." Shaw's chiding was "like that of the Lord, who chasteneth whom He loveth," commented Clara Leiser, Jean's biographer. He wanted Siegfried and Tristan, or at least Tannhäuser.

Shaw's gibes at Edouard were more genuinely deflationary, a sting of truth within the bouquet. The bass's beloved Méphistophélès showed "a smile that would make the most timid child climb straight up on his lap." As for intellect or the absence of it, "he has found his voice and his musical instinct so entirely adequate to his modest needs, that he never thinks about his work and never makes any point that is not a purely musical one." But what about singing? "He no longer sings; he bawls, reveling in the stunning sound with a prodigality which comes of knowing that he has so much voice to draw on that no extravagance can exhaust it."

America was, of course, left to find its own estimate of these two giants and the third one, Jean Lassalle, who soon joined them, as well as the bevy of *prime donne* who revolved about them as triple suns.

Hysterical fandom was ignited almost immediately, and its roar and gusty consumption of all subtlety in its path sometimes obscured real values; but the artistic dignity of the two Polish brothers never wavered once the pattern was set and accepted. As Jean grew more sensitive to the stages and audiences of vast America and his critical listeners accustomed themselves to his individual qualities, it is possible that both the artist and his audiences improved.

It took a little while, however. Probably Abbey's peculiar ideas about repertoire and casting were more responsible than any other factor. For New York, Gounod's Shakespearean opera was not the strongest vehicle to support these heavyweights, in spite of Jean's reputation as the "perfect" Roméo; yet four times again Abbey or Grau chose to open with it to show off what became known as "ideal casts." The nucleus for one of these "ideals" was of course the De Reszkes; when Jean gave way to Alvarez and Saléza the ideal perhaps tarnished a little. Eames or Melba completed the trio, with Frances Saville once succeeding to the high place when Eames was absent and Melba came late. Gounod's somewhat less favored work thus led his *Faust* as an opener, although during these "ideal" days the latter was given so often that W. J. Henderson coined his unforgettable epithet for the Metropolitan as the *"Faustspielhaus."*

The De Reszkes' first *Faust* together in New York did not occur until February 1 and had meaning chiefly because of Edouard's first Méphistophélès. Jean's interpretation of the hero had already come as a Christmas present to his audience; he received in return a gift from the *World* critic, who deemed him the most satisfactory Faust on the stage, an artist of commanding powers and attainments. Other blessings were few for Jean. Edouard had been judged the better artist once again in *Les Huguenots*; Jean had not obliterated Finck's memories of Niemann in *Le Prophète*—and he seemed "unable to sing a low note loudly or a high one softly"; and because of abominable stage management no one even looked in his direction when as Lohengrin he arrived by swan on January 4. Still, he sang well as the Grail Knight, Finck thought, but dramatically he should have read Wagner's letter to Liszt, which insisted that if singers want to solve the purely lyric problems, they must first grasp the dramatic essence of their parts. *Otello* on January 11 also suffered from a dire confusion in chorus and ensemble, while the orchestra (no longer the New York Symphony, it must be remembered) helped the cacophony materially. The truth seemed to be that after experiencing the fine ensembles of the German company, the more discerning were not willing to revert to the star system, especially in "modern" operas like *Otello*. Jean had one of his better evenings, though, more resonant and charged with feeling than usual. Shaw had found him at first uncertain, halfheartedly attempting to attain the savagery of Tamagno (who virtually owned the part because he had been chosen by Verdi to create it), and only making the role his own by investing it with the chivalry and romance that Tamagno had plowed under. Jean had confessed in Chicago that the blood and thunder of Verdi's and Shakespeare's Moor had little appeal for him, saying, "Naturalism is disagreeable to me. To die spluttering and spitting—oh no! It is the stage, not the hospital, where I work." Furthermore (including Don José), he was reluctant to act a murderer's role.

He appeared less frequently in Bizet's opera, although at first Finck bracketed it with Walther as his best role and practically every Carmen longed passionately for his partnership. Zélie de Lussan, one of the best known, said that she had sung the role 789 times to 49 Josés, that Jean was the thirteenth and the best. An even more famous gypsy wrote him: "I feel just like jumping on your neck to embrace you and thank you for being willing to sing Don José," and signed herself Emma Calvé. He was willing seven times out of fourteen her first season, 1893–94, but became wary as Calvé's capriciousness grew and extremely reluctant after she had popped a rose (thorns and all?) into his mouth just as he was beginning his tender aria. *"Cette fleur"* wasn't cherished very long. *Carmen* is a breeding ground for tall stage tales, so the one originating in California is no doubt apocryphal. Calvé is supposed to have stalked off stage immediately after being stabbed; Jean, no longer either the polite gentleman or the contrite lover, rushed after her, brought her back and tossed her on the floor. But she literally had the last word, singing his heartbroken cries along with him.

In the middle of this first season for the De Reszkes at the Metropolitan, the whole town was talking, said Finck, about the smallness of the Met's attendance. Jean was alleged to have complained that audiences needed education, probably merely a way of expressing his chagrin at his unexpectedly ragged reception.

A catalyst arrived on January 15 in the person of the 250-pound, six-foot-four French baritone Jean Lassalle, usually inseparable from the brothers. He had delighted Chicago with Valentin, Don Giovanni, and an Italian but "artistic" Sachs, as well as Telramund. The impressionable Chicago audiences had gasped at his "tawny-tinted physique," revealed in the scanty costume of Nelusko in *L'Africana*. This was his introductory role in New York; the Metropolitan audience rose to him in fascination. Such animal attraction, coupled with a sonorous and passionate voice and zeal and intelligence in acting—the combination proved irresistible. A few days later he sparked the younger De Reszke in *Don Giovanni* (although Edouard's Leporello was not very funny, said Finck) and inspired the older Jean in *Meistersinger,* while both brothers reacted to his presence in *Huguenots* and *Faust.* Furthermore, he bolstered the sagging Franco-Italian wing, singing with Marie Van Zandt in *Dinorah* and with another American, Margaret Reid, who had a small triumph as Ophelia, in Thomas' *Hamlet.*

"To see three such splendid representations of physical and artistic manhood on the stage was in itself a unique sensation," admitted the hitherto lukewarm Henry E. Krehbiel at Lassalle's debut.

It was like the old home weeks in Paris, London, and Chicago to reunite the trio of huge men. Edouard, the "Singing Cannon," reached two inches over six feet; Jean fell slightly under. Lassalle's chest measured fifty and one half inches. It was Edouard's custom, in the playful romps that would have crushed lesser men's bones, to invite Lassalle to clasp hands around his neck, then, by merely inclining his head, to lift the other eighth-of-a-ton giant from the floor. Clara Leiser credits Edouard with twisting a horseshoe out of shape with one hand. With this trio, moments of ease took on a larger-than-life character, as described by James G. Huneker in the *Musical Courier*:

Someone hums, and instantly the room is flooded with tone, the Great Trio from *William Tell,* perhaps. Jean sings C-sharp without effort [though Shaw maintained he could only touch C, and was afraid of that]. Then that rapturous breakdown known as the can-can is indulged in and suddenly a fierce dispute about the psychic possibilities of Hamlet arises and is ended only by a call for fresh beverages. These big fellows are men, men. They play billiards, run, wrestle [Lassalle was even proficient in that murderous French version of boxing called *savate*], smoke [Jean gave up cigars but enjoyed a mild cigarette named after him] and possibly swear, too.

The brothers' gift of mimicry was a sidesplitting delight to the rare hostess who could lure them within her portals socially; treasured forever would be the portraits in caricature of their colleagues and their imitations of musical instruments. From Jean's wicked talent no one was safe, neither conductor's eccentricities nor performers' vanities. Miss Leiser tells of Jean's habit of calling to his dressing room the great Pol Plançon just as the latter was ready to make his entrance on stage in Massenet's *Manon,* and to utter the elder Des Grieux's line, *"Elle est vraiment fort belle,"* in precisely Plançon's manner, so that the bass, convulsed with laughter, could hardly go on. It speaks for Jean's kingship that it was he who summoned Plançon.

The feminine roster selected by Abbey *redivivus* did not coalesce so readily and his repertoire resembled a patchwork quilt rather than an organism. Those who called loudest for the return to the cradle of opera stayed away in discontent from what they got—*Rigoletto, Aida, Dinorah,* and *Norma*—in spite of the bait held out in the shape of the respected Emma Albani and Lillian Nordica, the beloved Lilli Lehmann and the young Marie Van Zandt. Giulia and Sophia Ravogli, famous for their sister act in Gluck's *Orfeo,* fizzled rather damply in that and other operas. Maria Pettigiani won only a small place with her nimble coloratura and Sofia Scalchi alternately pleased and infuriated with her familiar charms. As for Van Zandt, this American was put through a round of Aminas, Harriets (*Martha*), Mignons, and Dinorahs before the more desirable Lakmé was allowed her on February 22. Why defer, even to Washington's birthday, the role that Delibes had written for her? subscribers wondered. Marie, the daughter of Jennie Van Zandt, a former popular concert and opera singer, and the granddaughter of the noted magician Signor Blitz, had been completely vindicated of the Paris charge of appearing on the stage when tipsy. Although Huneker, for one, found her wholly charming as Lakmé, and the purity of her voice in the "Bell Song" earned her two repetitions in which her E in alt was invariably faultless, New York never took to her as heartily as did Chicago or Boston, and she returned to recapture her Paris public and end her days as a Russian countess.

It seemed heartless of Abbey to place her slender figure as Mignon against the stout Lehmann as Philine, but this oddity of casting amused several tour cities, one of them likening the combination to "a steam locomotive drawing a horsecar." By hiring Lehmann and Paul Kalisch,

Abbey had hoped to retain the loyalty of the German sympathizers. But as they sang in Italian, many were alienated. Kalisch became the victim of Vianesi's persecution; the conductor, heartily disliking both the soprano and the foppish tenor, but finding Lilli too big to handle, took it out on the latter, dragged his accompaniments and otherwise bedeviled him. Huneker described with glee one occasion when Kalisch, after struggling through Ottavio's *"Il mio tesoro,"* stepped to the footlights and shook his fist at Vianesi.

Lehmann was truly spreading her powers this season, gradually finding her way to that level of versatility that was to set her apart from all other Olympian beings of her time. She plunged into the Italian language the second night as Leonora in *Il Trovatore,* and followed with Norma, Aida, Donna Anna, Bertha, and even the translated *Fidelio.* But her stout heart and devoted artistry cracked under Abbey's demand that she learn Selika in a hurry to replace Nordica.

"Lehmann is working too hard," commented Huneker on February 27, 1892. In fact, she had suffered "an attack of heart failure a week ago Sunday," just two days before she took the new role on February 15. But what a contrast to Patti, the critic scoffed. "Imagine Lehmann giving a farewell!" Lehmann, who always sang through Isolde in full voice on the morning of a performance! Still, she sang Selika only once—appeared no more at the Metropolitan, in fact, until 1898, when Grau lured her back to make one season—her last—memorable with the three Brünnhildes, Donna Anna, Isolde, Sieglinde, Venus, Bertha, and Valentine. She shared many of these roles with Nordica, but it was the American who assumed sole right to Selika after the first venture, and good riddance, thought Lehmann. The stately Lilli could never quite recover from her initial chilliness to the young American, who had ventured on the same stage at her own peril to sing Elsa, which Lehmann considered her role in spite of the fact that Lilli was embarking on a try at Ortrud with Walter Damrosch's company. Lilli took it out in considering Nordica a sybarite because she ordered a cab on a rainy day. "*I* valk!" snorted the elder goddess, picking up her heavy skirts and setting out in her sensible boots.

Lehmann plucked one unexpected posy out of her luxuriant bouquet of mature gifts in 1899, stepping in at five hours' notice to sing the *Rheingold* Fricka, a part she had never done before.

In all fitness, her last utterance on the Metropolitan stage should have been Brünnhilde's tremendous Immolation Scene, which ended the testimonial on March 23, 1899, for Anton Seidl, who had died on March 28, 1898. But life is not so tidy nor opera schedule so accommodating to coincidence. A *Huguenots* enlisted her two days later.

Ever just to the point of severity, this sterling artist had estimated the two De Reszkes and Lassalle rather reticently at first, remarking that they might be as fine artists as men, "if they would only work." But by the time of her last Metropolitan days, Jean and Edouard had already made that amazing leap into the Wagnerian realm which signaled one of the great artistic feats of all time, and Lehmann revised her opinion sharply upward. She remembered one Saturday matinee with Jean (it must have been on January 7, 1899) as the ideal *Tristan* of her life. Jean had thought her Isolde superb.

From the *Lohengrin* that marked their mutual debut in Chicago to a *Faust* in Boston on April 1, 1899, Jean's first American leading lady, Emma Eames, always pleased him by "the smell of violets about her." She did not return the compliment. Jean always reeked of the iodoform and ether with which he sprayed his throat, she said. Like the brothers, Eames did not receive her full due at first, but before the end of 1892 she could claim to be as well loved in America as in London, where no other celebrity had been feted so royally. If all other criteria failed, she could claim prima donna-ism by virtue of having suffered a jewel robbery, said the sly "Raconteur" (Huneker) of the *Musical Courier*. She eventually grew quite annoyed at being inevitably called "cool," maintaining that this was only during the days when she was not sure of herself. But this serene beauty, with the clear, pure voice, the proud carriage, and the lake-blue eyes appealed to that portion of the public that liked its sopranos to be ladylike. She spread a dainty calm over the most rowdy *Carmen* when she entered as the simple country girl Micaela, and her distaste for the slightest hint of vulgarity extended to the most famous protagonist of the gypsy, Emma Calvé. Antagonism between the two enlivened many a performance, until in the spring season, on April 17, 1894, the fireworks erupted in a curtain call, Calvé snatching her hand from Eames's and beginning to "moult" combs, scarves, and so on until the poor tenor, Fernando de Lucia, was hard put to retrieve them all, and when he handed her a scarf "received such a fierce glance that he dropped it and ran as if pursued by the bull."

Eames was perhaps the first "artist" who was invited by Mrs. Astor to one of her "dull and stupid dinners," as noted in the gossip sheet *Town Topics*. The soprano described the Thirty-fourth Street mansion as a "miracle of richness and hideousness." The Bradley-Martins also asked her and her husband to listen to their "commonplace talk of gowns and petty personalities." Eames's manners were doubtless superior to her hosts', the writer fancied.

After her first year, she went out socially very seldom and remained aloof from gossip, not touched by a scandal in Chicago that drew her livelier sisters, Calvé and Melba, into a newspaper wrangle, and not even censured for her divorce from the painter Julian Story (he had remarked caustically that she had the artistic temperament "hugely") and remarriage to the cultivated baritone Emilio de Gogorza. The girlish chatter attributed to her in a Louisville interview seemed unlikely, yet her championship of the De Reszkes had the proper ring: she had been sure America would adore them, she said, and she liked Jean's acting.

"Spine *glacé* could be a delightful beverage in its way," mused Huneker. "Not that I felt superior," said the lovely lady, "but I believed sincerity and personal worth should hold their own without the aids of cunning and intrigue."

What Eames seemed to achieve without apparent effort (although she maintained that she never passed a day without pain), Lillian Nordica had to fight for every step of the way. Most of her triumphs had come "through the back door." Her brilliant debut as Violetta at Covent Garden had been a last-minute substitution. Abbey had introduced her to the Metropolitan only as a member of his Patti company in a rented season—and Tamagno got the most attention for his high C's in *Trovatore*. Now she was called in from a concert tour to take the place of Emma Albani at the third of Abbey's performances in 1891. The important thing about Nordica was that she always managed to be there when wanted, even though she had not been wanted at first. It had been Albani who had sung the *Huguenots* Valentine in Abbey's tour of 1889–90, but Lillian knew the role from London. She made a memorable entrance, wrote her biographer Ira Glackens, in a riding gown of pale-green velvet over a brocaded skirt, a Henry II hat of black velvet with a plume, and carrying a crimson rose. She skipped a few bars in the third act, what Krehbiel called "a disaster of a lesser sort," but was in excellent voice and acted with great spirit. Then, when Abbey scheduled

L'Africaine for Lassalle's debut, Nordica was summoned again on January 15 and 25, departing soon after for London, and leaving Selika temporarily to the reluctant Lehmann.

Nordica, the New Englander, had followed Polonius' precept to the letter. She knew herself, perhaps better than anyone, recognized her shortcomings as well as her virtues. She told her assisting artist: "It has been a long, hard climb, and I have seen others pass me on the road to fame with seeming ease, but I was content to keep on plodding, and I made it in the end." She knew that others possessed equal voice and equal talent, "but I have worked," Ira Glackens, her biographer quoted her as saying.

Her first position as a regular member of the Metropolitan came in 1893–94, when once again her sterling contributions were overshadowed by the scintillant presence of Calvé and Melba—Nordica even had to share *Lohengrin* and *Faust* with both Melba and Eames. Susanna in *Le Nozze di Figaro* seemed not quite to display her best qualities, although there was considerable pleased comment on the way her voice blended with Eames's in the letter duet. Furthermore, she had been bitten with the Wagnerian bug and the urge to release the Master from Italian bondage, while reasonably rapturous response to her Aida had confirmed her aspirations to the dramatic realms. A letter from Bayreuth settled it—at Cosima Wagner's bidding, Nordica would create Elsa at Bayreuth, where *Lohengrin* had never been heard before. As for the grueling work such an adventure would entail, hard labor was Nordica's forte. She triumphed. The Bayreuth stamp of approval immediately enhanced her reputation in America—for everyone except the captious Boston critic Philip Hale. This arbiter of culture in the Hub called her "a cardboard figure," and never relented in his peevishness toward "the Maine singer" until after the turn of the century, when he admitted her Isolde to possess taste, brilliance, emotion, and power—and also to represent a creature of flesh and blood. Her appearance with the Boston Opera Company on March 26, 1913, that invited these remarks was her last on an operatic stage.

Companioned by Jean de Reszke, Nordica saw her fondest wish fulfilled in the *Tristan* of November 27, 1895, that marked a wholly new and liberal policy of Abbey and Grau. Having already introduced French opera in French, the managers at last acceded to pressure from without and within (the De Reszkes had never ceased to exert their influence) and allowed German opera to be sung in German. This was the beginning of the "international" policy that chiefly London and New York established and that led to the formation of "wings," French, Italian, and German. Most other opera houses in the world laid down a carpet of their own languages and forced every singer to walk on it. The Metropolitan reformation was not quite complete, however, for while one *Lohengrin* reverted to German, others stayed in Italian in 1895–96 (most with Nordica and Jean). German productions of *Die Walküre* and *Fidelio* might have been in Choctaw, so badly were they sung, and *Tannhäuser* was listed as in French in 1896–97 but also boasted several Italian singers who clung to their native tongue. *Die Meistersinger* remained in Italian as *I Maestri Cantori* until 1899.

All this time, Abbey and Grau had been building up their star system to a point where it no longer sufficed to include one (or two, according to the contract with the boxholders) in every cast, but three at least and, in the case of *Huguenots* or *Don Giovanni,* six or seven. Furthermore, casting a houseful of prima donnas of both sexes called for diplomacy, firmness, and patience of a high order. In their first season, 1891–92, the dangers had not been so apparent, for only Eames and Albani needed to be juggled, Lehmann filled her niche, while the De Reszkes and Lassalle had everything their own way. But came the day when to Eames were added Calvé, Nordica, and Melba, and Grau worked overtime to fit together his brilliantly colored bits and pieces into a repertoire that should satisfy everyone, not the least the quartet of thoroughbreds on which his premises were built. Meanwhile, the manly trio was employed as often as possible, and even returned for a spring season that saw Edouard and Lassalle in an Italian *Flying Dutchman.* Several guest appearances of Adelina Patti (in her succession of "farewells") brought the season to a close. Before another could open, the forces of nature—and man—took a hand. As early as March 2, 1892, Grau was quoted in the *Musical Courier* as saying that Abbey was disgusted. Whether he would return, no one knew. Already at the sign of dissolution, the birds of prey hovered: Henry Mapleson (the Colonel's son) advanced a proposition for Covent Garden's Augustus Harris, but the idea of paying him the fee per performance of £1,000 he demanded chilled Roosevelt, Vanderbilt, and Morgan, even though he promised a marvelous company. There were even rumors of a return to German opera with Jean de Reszke. But by March 23, the worst news possible (according to Huneker) issued from the Metropolitan's stronghold. Abbey and Grau had received a three-year contract, with the per-performance price raised to $2,000 and all rentals of the building their perquisites. The directors would be assessed $3,000, said Roosevelt, Whitney, Haven, Wetmore, Iselin, Goelet, Curtis, and Kountze.

Yet by the following September, their plans lay, like the opera house interior, in ruins.

Shortly after 9 A.M. on Saturday, August 27, 1892, passersby spotted plumes of smoke arising from the Seventh Avenue side of the opera house and gathered on the sidewalks to watch the clanging fire engines and pounding hoofs of Fire Chief Benner's horses bringing hoses and water carts until Police Chief McAvoy and a hundred of his men forced them behind hastily assembled barricades. The crowd grew to 10,000, among whom the rumor passed that the opera house was done with. The *Times* headline next morning rather overplayed the situation: "A Great Playhouse Gone," with the subhead: "The Metropolitan Opera House Wrecked by Fire." Reading a little farther, one could discover that the damage was not likely to exceed $100,000, and that, indeed, only the interior had been destroyed. What had happened?

There were very few people in the building that hot morning, the *Times* noted in a typically circumstantial account. The first to arrive was Harry Collins, day watchman, who was not obligated to make hourly rounds as his opposite number, the night watchman, had done. Next came Cornelius Hogan, a young assistant to the scene painters, followed shortly by the scenic artist Operti, who stood near the doorway for a few minutes, talking to another arrival. Engineer Walter Scattergood, a carpenter named Brown, George Baxter, boss "fly" man for scenery, two firemen, and a scrubwoman completed the list.

Hogan was observed busy about the scene frames, getting material ready for the painters. He made several trips to the paint room on the third tier high above the stage on the Thirty-ninth Street side, and it was from there that his sudden cry came—"Fire!" Almost before its echoes died away, flames rushed along the scenery on stage. Scattergood turned in an alarm from the opera's special box. Simultaneously, a saloonkeeper across the street noticed smoke seeping from the building and rang a second alarm from the regular box.

Firemen arrived in less than two minutes, but had to break down the doors in the vestibules to get into the building. The stage was already an inferno. After two more alarms, twelve engines, four hook-and-ladder trucks, and a water tower appeared. One engine lost a wheel at Broadway and Thirty-third Street and so remained out of action.

The first men in saw what they called a "grand sight." The auditorium, practically untouched, was filling with smoke, while the tall proscenium arch framed a great wall of flame. Immediately "the fiery breath of the dragon," as the *World* picturesquely recounted, licked out into the hall, past the walls whose scorched paint and plaster hurried it on, catching draperies and upholstery, and in moments enveloping the chamber.

The firemen retreated, until suddenly a crash signaled the fall of the glass roof. Flames leaped through the roof fifty feet into the sky, then retreated, causing such suction that the whole body of fire swept back onto the stage. Firemen immediately took positions in the Parterre boxes, a sight that would have horrified the boxholders, and played streams of water into the fiery cavern. It was all over within the hour.

By noon, officials could walk into the shambles and try to estimate the damage. First glimpse was discouraging. In the deep pit where the stage had been lay the huge water tank and the iron girders that had supported it. Nothing remained in the auditorium but the skeletons of the rising tiers of seating space. But soon favorable facts emerged. Neither wing had suffered more than trifling harm, which meant that all offices, and even more important, $200,000 worth of costumes, were untouched. The false floor that was laid over orchestra chairs to join with the stage for balls and other nonoperatic functions was in place, though no one said why this should be so. It was suspected that the vast space had been used for spreading out scenes to paint. This floor held, catching all the debris from above and protecting the orchestra seats and floor.

No weakness was found in the structure itself, except for a portion of the Seventh Avenue wall, which was removed and replaced. The lobbies, except for the broken-down doors, remained intact. So did the

Broadway front, fortunately for the fifty "finely furnished" apartments (whose tenants remained calm after an initial fright), the Metropolitan's Assembly Rooms, the Amsterdam Bank, and Broadway Cafe.

To calculate the scenery loss proved more difficult. About two hundred pieces were presumed to have been on the stage, while considerable was stored below. Marcus Mayer, Abbey's touring associate, was said to own most of it. A rumor that Designer Hoyt had been working on scenes for a Daly production of *The Scarlet Letter*, as well as some investiture for the Casino and the Brooklyn Academy of Music, was later denied. It caused some heartburning among the directors. Hoyt, at first in despair because of the likely loss of his collection of books of design, worth thousands of dollars, was jubilant to find them still tucked away in a closet.

How did it start? everyone wondered. Spontaneous combustion was suggested, but the *Times* grimly remarked: "As Spontaneous Combustion did not seem the least affected by countless charges of arson preferred against him, perhaps it is just as well to attribute the Opera House fire to him." A hint at a possible breach of discipline in the touchy matter of cigarettes and matches was appended. The man who might have acknowledged guilt, however, was unable to speak. Hogan, after his warning cry, had lost his head and his footing, and had fallen through a trap more than forty feet to the stage floor. Firemen got him out and to Bellevue Hospital, where, after uttering only incoherences, he died that night. He was the only casualty, although Baxter had a narrow escape, foolishly pausing to collect his coat under the stage. Through thick smoke, he crawled to Fortieth Street, where a barred window confronted him. Suddenly beside him an iron weight fell from a burned rope. Using this as a lever, he pried open the bars and climbed to safety.

Adrian Iselin, the only director on the spot, posed the question that lurked in all the directors' minds: Where was the vaunted fireproofing that Cady had installed? The tank above the stage had been drained because it froze in winter. Iron struts below the stage had been replaced by wood because they had proved an impediment to the moving and storage of scenery. Worst of all, the asbestos curtain that might have confined the fire to the stage house had been looped up permanently, useless. These sins sat on the management's doorstep. Further cause for consternation came in the realization that so firmly had the directors relied on Cady's safeguards that insurance would amount to only $60,000.

Hastily, directors were summoned from Newport, where, as the *Times* assured readers the next day, as "gay, pleasure-loving people," they had been in the midst of festivities; and from Bar Harbor, where it had been a season of "revels and robberies." The Vanderbilt house in Bar Harbor had suffered depredations amounting to $20,000. By the middle of the week, ten men had gathered, to issue a report that the opera house would be rebuilt, although James Roosevelt contradicted Edmund Stanton by declaring that it was out of the question that restoration could be completed in time for the November opening. Abbey's contract had been canceled automatically, he added. Abbey and Grau were both on the Continent, leaving John B. Schoeffel to deal with the emergency. This usually silent partner was quoted in one of his rare utterances, popping into the opera office and saying jocularly, "I smell smoke!"

Behind the closed doors of the stockholders' meeting on September 9, a new conflagration raged. Enough leaked out to reveal a deep schism between those who wanted to rebuild and those who merely wanted out. Ten of the original stockholders must be considered delinquent, having refused for several years to accept assessment. They were legally correct, George L. Rives, lawyer for the group, admitted reluctantly, but that fact didn't add to their popularity. Most prominent among them were Jay Gould and E. H. Harriman, who were called "musical welchers" by their fellows, according to the *World*. They had highhandedly used their boxes whenever they felt like it, while others paid their share. The general fund recovered only the amount of rentals on these delinquent boxes. The sixty faithful had grown understandably weary of the situation.

Oddly enough, Harriman made a suggestion that carried the ring of prophecy, but which was immediately rejected as utterly foolish and impractical. Why not make the company a National Metropolitan? he offered. Subscribers all over the country would be interested. He personally knew of men in the South and West who would gladly join. Then when they were out of town, their boxes would be rented for general profit.

The only other details that came out of the meeting concerned the probable assessment of $10,000 each, and Abbey's recommendation that the orchestra seats be made smaller to leave room for more standees.

A week later, the news burst on an unbelieving public. "Will Sell Opera Temple," the *World* headline read. It appeared that the rebuilders had been defeated in a surprise rally. No one was more taken aback than Schoeffel, who had shown up with plans by Architect J. B. McElpatrick for restoration. The management firm had agreed to assume the cost, which was estimated at $150,000 plus $60,000 for scenery and stage (nearer the *Times* figure of $100,000 than the *World's* million). A review of the financial position of the company revealed a $600,000 first mortgage on the entire block and a second of $210,000 on the opera house proper, excluding the front apartments, which had been sold the first year to the Metropolitan Improvement Company (a group mainly within the stockholders' body). A floating debt of $101,000 existed.

Schoeffel joined the public in mourning. "It was a pity," he said, "and such fine artists engaged," among them Nellie Melba. He added as an inducement that she had just been divorced from Capt. Charles Armstrong and that it was said in Europe that the Duc d'Orléans admired her very much.

Behind the scenes, several of the stauncher boxholders worked quietly, gathering support for a countermove. But as late as October 16, "not an operatic leaf was stirring," wrote Reginald de Koven, the operetta composer who had been a critic in Chicago and would join first *Harper's Weekly* and then the *World,* still later the *Herald.* It was Pulitzer's rambunctious sheet that carried his plea for a leader to bring the public out of its apathy, now that it was evident private citizens could not be expected to carry the burden again.

He was answered, ironically, by the announcement that indeed the opera house would be sold, but not to a strange faction that might want to tear it down for the sheer value of the land (which, according to Henry Clews, had increased to two million), but to the Old Guard, the triumvirate Astor-Morgan-Vanderbilt, who would assume tighter control than ever.

Had a social conscience or love of opera or civic pride prompted this action? The statement of a boxholder "who preferred to remain anonymous" clarifies the overwhelming motive: "Socially the best people are behind [the rebuilding]. They couldn't afford to let [the opera house] be rebuilt by any Tom, Dick or Harry and the best boxes be occupied by parvenus and nobodies—to get into the hands of the Philistines!"

Against a few mutterings of "good money after bad," a nucleus of stockholders closed ranks and prepared to go ahead. This prompted a jeering comment from *Town Topics*. Colonel Mann wrote: "New York's enthusiastic love for culture, amounting to a positive madness to possess a temple devoted to music, is a marvel to Europe." The admirable generosity of rich and intelligent men to support opera is commented on repeatedly by visitors, he added. "Our Astors, Vanderbilts and Goulds are great men. If they do not subscribe to the new opera house, it is sure that their children will toss pennies to the man with the piano organ."

A new group was formed, the Metropolitan Opera and Real Estate Company, composed of exactly half the number of former stockholders: thirty-five. By an odd coincidence, this was the exact number of boxes they planned to fill (one was lopped off in the Parterre Circle, which henceforth would be the only citadel of exclusivity). They paid themselves $1,425,000 for the privilege, a neat profit if Clews's estimate was correct, not to mention the building. When the smoke of this fire behind the scenes had cleared, it could be seen that a good deal of dross had been shed. Delinquent shareholders had been dropped entirely. Others were glad to give up the pretense of being opera lovers, and took their $20,000 share and retired. Among them was Jay Gould, who in any event died in December of that year. His son George would share a box from time to time with Clews to show off his actress-wife, Edith, in her famous pearls (said to be valued by Tiffany at half a million). Cyrus Field also died in 1892. Other names missing were J. H. Woershoffer, James R. Keene, H. Knickerbocker, the Westerners Crocker and Huntington, Gordon Hamersley, A. W. Sherman, C. J. Osborne, Jeremiah Milbank, Henry and Matthew Morgan, S. L. M. Barlow (whose Box 36 had been sheared away), William Rockefeller, and J. F. Navarro, who had died earlier, as well as a couple of dozen from the Grand Tier. Those who moved down from upstairs to join the hard core were George F. Baker, R. T. Wilson, D. Ogden Mills, George G. Haven, Edward Cooper, H. T. Sloane, Levi P. Morton, Adrian Iselin, S. O. Babcock, and, of course, J. P. Morgan. Was it fate that allowed Morgan to draw first choice in the new deal? He naturally chose Box 35 at the very center of the ring.

The newcomers into the charmed circle needed little screening; a few were former Academy boxholders who enjoyed seniority in social position: Perry Belmont, A. T. Van Nest, Mrs. H. I. Barbey, and W. Bayard Cutting; the wealthy textile man, A. D. Juilliard; Morgan associates Cornelius Bliss, C. T. Barney, Calvin S. Brice, and Thomas Hitchcock.

This left Astors with but one box while Vanderbilts had three, but Mrs. Astor continued to be a power within herself, while the Vanderbilt family tentacles multiplied.

From now on, no matter how wealthy, charming, or persuasive the applicant for the rare vacancies in the Parterre, he or she would be subject to the vote of the thirty-five and, more often than not, found wanting.

It all alchemized to the fact of ownership, as Ralph Pulitzer carefully explained. Then you had a brass plate on your box door. When guests sat there, they felt a twinge of veneration that their host owned a number of square feet of music, actually owned a proportion of the tenors, sopranos, baritones, brass, strings, and woodwinds, and the passion and beauty—and boredom—of the music.

But if snobbery came intact from the crucible, artistry likewise arose ennobled and refined. The fire had indeed forged precious metal behind the footlights.

8

ALL THAT GLITTERS IS DIAMONDS

Truly opera returned to her home last night, the Queen of a Titanic and glorious pageant, the ruler of the divine revel.

—*New York Times,* November 28, 1893

The nineties in America have most often been called gay, but for that "happy breed of men," that "little world" of Metropolitan Opera box-holders, the word was "diamantine."

New York itself had gained a new, fresh, glittering look. Even the lights hardened; the lambent radiance of the gas jet gave way to the concentrated power of the electric-light globe. Hotels discontinued posting notices warning guests not to blow out the gas. Thomas Alva Edison, inventor of the incandescent lamp, had already gone on to new pastures, inventing the Kinetoscope, which projected moving pictures on a screen.

Fifth Avenue stretched, a line of brownstone stoops and gardens, from Washington Square to the Park, broken only by an occasional Renaissance-style mansion. Then an official discovered a flaw in the zoning and widened the avenue several feet on each side. The first touch of commercialism crept in with the invasion by Franklin Simon of Thirty-eighth Street, fought vainly by Vanderbilt and Rockefeller.

In ladies' fashions, bustles waxed and waned, leg-of-mutton sleeves took up a good deal of room; heavy corsets presented a straight, unyielding front. The inexorable rise in hemlines began daringly with a young woman named Daisy Miller whose shoetops were exposed by the costume, Rainy Daisy, she devised, ostensibly for wet weather. Men became seriously and publicly interested in style; should the ascot be worn before six P.M.? The correct answer: No. Shirts became lighter, were not always boiled stiff; suspenders went out, belts came in. Tan or russet shoes began to appear; previously the only alternative to black was the tennis shoe. A very few oxfords made their appearance, but only in summer.

Bicycles scorched the roadways in upper Manhattan; the most distinguished violator of the speed law was the Duke of Marlborough, in town to marry (against her will) Consuelo Vanderbilt. Bicycling became the vogue among fashionable women, who revived those laughable "bloomers" *pour le sport*. Even prima donnas such as Nordica and Scalchi took it up. Bicycles hastened the paving of streets, and new asphalt replaced the granite blocks.

By 1896, a hundred golf courses flourished. Tennis was the sport for "dudes" of both sexes; fencing enlisted a sprinkling of "the upper classes." New trolleys, powered by electricity, drove horsecars off the streets, except for cross-town routes. Cable cars had their day, but so dangerous was the corner at Broadway and Fourteenth that it became known as Dead Man's Curve. Around the opera house, these "clanging Polyphemuses, each with its ugly blazing eye, gliding up or down with a hideous and alarming velocity, menaced and disturbed the well-bred and supersensitive horses," bleated the *Times*.

Automobiles had not yet become a hazard to the pedestrian. While a good many were being tried out, among them Henry Ford's, the machine was something one read about rather than saw with one's own eyes. Millionaires began to collect them, of course.

Pay stations, not in booths but in the open, sprang up all over for the use of the telephone. A Kodak craze developed; with the perfection of photoengraving, newspapers could at last publish photographs instead of line etchings. The *World* progressively installed the first halftone equipment. Cyrus H. K. Curtis of the *Ladies' Home Journal* and George H. Hazen of *Century Magazine* sensed the importance of advertising and Madison Avenue's mission was launched.

Clamor for cleaner streets spawned Col. George F. Waring's White Wings with their carts and brushes and immaculate uniforms. At first the butt of constant jokes, they won their way to universal approval. "Eatin' " tobacco lost out as manners improved, so that filthy sidewalks became a thing of the past, and ladies' sweeping dresses were spared. It was noted that the Prince of Wales never used a toothpick; handkerchiefs became the genteel thing for nose-blowing. With the advent of porcelain tubs, bathing invaded the entire week instead of being merely a Saturday night ritual.

Victorianism died hard. Cincinnati still draped nude statues in calico blouses and canton flannel drawers; but in New York, the ladies' entrance to the Waldorf-Astoria was abolished, marking the end of an era. The new hostelry also helped to toll the knell of private entertaining. Even Mrs. Astor succumbed, giving a few small functions outside her home.

Few opera boxholders displayed civic minds or public spirit; an exception was John Jacob Astor IV, the first millionaire to serve on a jury. He was also the first blueblood to write a book (*Journey in Other Worlds,* a piece of veritable science fiction), anticipating another scion, Cornelius Vanderbilt IV, who wrote sixteen.

A two-year depression that began in 1893 brought strikes and other labor unrest, but the mentors of the Metropolitan sailed through the turbulence with impunity; their entrenchment in mountainous wealth became even more secure as the Supreme Court declared unconstitutional a law to tax incomes, passed by Congress in 1895.

Where did the term "Diamond Horseshoe" originate? One cannot be sure. Its appositeness leaps to the eye. At the Metropolitan Opera opening, the dazzle of the 10,000 electric lights in the auditorium, reflecting from tiaras, earrings, chokers, necklaces, and stomachers—"incessantly quivering like the play of summer lightning, flashing, gleaming, flickering, blazing," said the *Times*—could have inspired no more fitting appellation. Even aside from the stage with its 5,000 globes, the scene was worth traveling miles to see, remarked James G. Huneker in the *Recorder.* The house itself showed scarcely a reminder of the old interior, the *Times* reported. Its colors were now a marvel of ivory, white, and gold, while the orchestra seats (obviously new although the old ones had been spared) showed dull red with embroidered figures, the carpets generally the same hue. By taking out the *baignoires* and installing several rows of seats almost all around the orchestra, the capacity had been increased to 3,400 —all occupied, needless to say. And, as a concession to the populace, more than a thousand could now stand.

Other improvements included the welcome two elevators to hoist thirty Balcony and Family Circle patrons each from the Fortieth Street lobby; the lowering of main floor and stage by three and one half feet; and the installation of five chandeliers, four grouped about a large central fixture. Over the proscenium arch now presided a painting of "Melody," while the ceiling boasted a series of pictured allegories.

In a confused outpouring of language that clearly hastened the promulgation of the *Times*'s literary style manual, that sheet saw fit to print an unrivaled description of the opening.

The social pomp and ceremony at which the fashionable *monde* of New York appeared as if under a silent spell of some mysterious compulsion, mixed with splendid figures of the social show and infused with enthusiasm of a vivacity both spiritual and intellectual was a dense, wholesome, luxurious yet unpretending crowd of Americans who only found amusement in the dainty foreign affectations of their neighbors. . . . There was nothing gaudy or meretricious in the decor to vie impertinently or incongruously with the toilets expected to vivify the audience and fill the boxes with colors like so many caskets in which fresh-gathered orchids found their dainty beds.

A huge breastwork of roses was the only "artificial" decor [surely not fake posies?]. All the rest was the fine flower of the women of the American metropolis and the splendor of their attire. [This in spite of the absence of Mrs. Astor, in mourning for her daughter, Mrs. Roosevelt Roosevelt, the Goelets, and the W. K. Vanderbilts, who were still in Europe.] The background should be such a rebuke to vulgarity that it would hang its head and go. The atmosphere was for orchids, not poppies [why poppies?].

New York had lost out to Chicago as the host to a World's Fair that year. Our narrator deduced that the "immense number of foreign folk were probably the lingering of visitors" to the fair, adding a somewhat patronizing ethnic note:

New York's cosmopolitan character is no longer sustained by peanut vendors, sellers of bananas, dealers in cheap flowers, pastry cooks and waiters alone . . . [but is now] varied by Italians, Germans, French, Spanish and even Greeks of higher class.
    [Then rising to a poetic peroration]: The stately muse of opera is to be happily married to the frisky harlequin of spectacle. . . . What a constellation of tint and form it made! The pearly flesh tones that lurked in rich measures of arms and shoulders and bosoms; the exquisite convolutions of silken hair . . . the faces set as flowers upon their stalks . . . while the huge orchestra sustained a mighty ocean of harmonies.

The music critic W. J. Henderson, whose style dried off the page somewhat, welcomed the old and valued friends, Eames, the De Reszkes, Lassalle, and the indispensable comprimaria, Mathilde Bauermeister;

dismissed the newcomer, Olimpia Guercia, who substituted for Scalchi, with a "Wait and see"; noted that the chorus and orchestra functioned admirably under the new conductor, Luigi Mancinelli; approved the new scenery and costumes, and concluded that "fire is sometimes a blessing in disguise."

A few nights later, the ineffable Nellie Melba stepped onto an American stage for the first time, as Lucia. The Australian diva came closer than any other so far in winning instantaneous glory. She "Came, sang and conquered," wrote Huneker in the *Recorder*. "Her voice is remarkable in power, compass and brilliance, the tones solid and well-packed, the quality absolutely crystalline." Then came reservations. While she would not efface memories of Gerster or Patti—the "warm and peachy bloom which made Patti's voice so luscious in coloring Melba has not . . . nor the charm that thralls us to Calvé, nor yet a dramatic instinct"—and the Mad Scene had been sung with greater virtuosity by Ilma di Murska (the stormy Croat who had blazed through America fifteen years previously), still her "extreme purity in tone and a surety that denotes great art" showed her to be patterned after the prima donnas of yore. "She comes to the footlights," he continued, "and hurls aloft an astonishing volume of tone . . . what freshness, what elasticity, what endurance!" Her high tones floated over the orchestra "like silver threads in a breeze," opined another.

After the Mad Scene, there was a perfect tumult in the house, so she repeated the cadenza. Truly, Melba "at once gained the suffrages of her audience."

Another Mad Scene, this time from Thomas' *Hamlet* two nights later, found her irreproachable, a virtuoso par excellence, partnered brilliantly by the "melodramatic prince who storms heaven" of Jean Lassalle and the finished artist, Pol Plançon, who had made his debut earlier in Gounod's little opera, *Philémon et Baucis*.

Henry Krehbiel of the *Tribune* admitted to not a single reservation, not even an exception in favor of Patti, naming Melba's the finest voice since Sembrich. W. J. Henderson of the *Times* called hers "the unique voice of the world." While never abrogating a judicial sense, other high priests of the musical columns acknowledged a "Queen of Song" had come to her rightful throne. There she reigned until 1897, then for single seasons at intervals until 1911. Meanwhile, it pleased her to bestow her art also upon Oscar Hammerstein at his Manhattan Opera in New York, after that intrepid impresario had got down on his knees to carpet her floor with bank notes; and to visit the Boston Opera Company several times at the invitation of her friend-antagonist, Henry Russell, who arranged sparkling seasons there between 1909 and 1914.

If Emma Eames had to endure the charge of being "cold" most of her singing life, Melba was pursued by the accusation of pale histrionics. Oddly enough, she had previously appeared on the stage only once before, when she was hailed for good acting in London; then after some European experiences (perhaps association with her French duke), which were supposed to have loosened her Anglo-Saxon inhibitions, London insisted that she "overacted." America never saw a great deal of what had prompted this English charge, but still found very affecting the wild figure, white robes flowing, hair streaming, eyes focused on some point in infinity, who would materialize as Lucia, after having completed a beautifully sung but emotionally cool *La Bohème,* and go through the tremendous *bel canto* feat of Donizetti's Mad Scene. These encores out of context, inappropriate as purists considered them, commanded public adoration for years.

As Eames's beauty formed a potent element in her success, Melba's own particular brand brought its worshipers. The description of the Brussels historian Jacques Isnardon dwells lovingly on her best points: "The nose is straight, long and delicate; the neck is exquisite, superbly set; . . . the mouth is frank and loving. The build of head, neck and shoulders reveals the thoroughbred." With small and beautifully shaped ears, hands, and feet, long, curling eyelashes over strangely colored red-brown eyes, and the carriage of a princess, "a true prima donna stands before you. On the stage this is poetized," added the Belgian.

Melba was a woman of the world by the time of her arrival in America. Already at her Brussels debut she had encountered her first queen. She always filled a special place in the affections of royalty and nobility, and command performances clustered thick and fast from many countries. Because the King of Sweden sent for her, she begged an extra week from Grau before her debut and was granted it. Not only did the Duc d'Orléans "admire her," as Schoeffel had revealed, but loved her many years. Most of her fabulous pearls were his gift, Henry Russell's wife said. Russell, who entertained her many times in Monte Carlo, believed that hers was the greatest voice of all time.

When she came to America, she was feted by Boston's Mrs. Jack Gardner (who gave her a precious yellow diamond "coveted by the King of Cambodia"), and was even received later by the New York hostesses who at first clamored for her vocal services at exclusive receptions. Frank St. Leger, her accompanist of many years, told of a skating party in Ottawa at which the Duke and Duchess of Connaught entertained Melba and Mrs. John Jacob Astor. A newspaper described the latter, her hair perfectly white, looking stunning in black velvet and chinchilla. Melba did not skate; she was to sing that night.

Rarely one prima donna may confer public accolade upon another: Calvé wrote to Melba, *"Comme une ange vous chantez avec votre voix divine,"* and as Melba said of Calvé's Carmen, on the occasion when the usually unbending soprano "graciously at the behest of the management" sang Micaela at a command performance, "It will be known in the history of music as an incomparable performance." But the two were not genuine rivals, sharing only—in America, at least—a few roles, such as Marguerite and Ophelia, and the latter for only a brief period.

The American Emma Eames was a different story. She openly referred to her "enemy," who "as a lifelong instructress in operatic intrigue" tried to ruin her at every turn—no names mentioned, of course. Although Eames reached into dramatic realms where Melba could not follow, innumerable Marguerites and Juliettes lay divided between them, with the additional irritation of rivalry for the affection and esteem of the De Reszkes. Eames must have smoldered when Jean was quoted as saying that Melba was his "pet Marguerite"—although she claimed never to read criticisms, this bit of journalistic endeavor must have reached her ears if only through loving friends. Perhaps she burst into flame privately at Melba's chilly, "I do not know Madame Eames," when a reporter asked if the quarrel between Eames and Calvé had been patched up. Calvé and Melba closed ranks against their mutual antagonist when Eames sang Charlotte in the American premiere of Massenet's *Werther* in Chicago in March 1894. The two sat prominently in a box, following a vocal score and giggling frequently. What matter that the score was held upside down? Revenge was accomplished to their own satisfaction.

It is always the prerogative of a prima donna to believe that her reign ends the golden age and that all subsequent claimants flounder in the deluge. Eames as *doyenne* could say to Max de Schauensee, after a *Don Giovanni* production that engaged a Metropolitan star cast in the forties: "But of course, my dear, none of them knows how to sing."

In her own dowager period, Melba was persuaded to attend a performance and send backstage a luxuriant posy to a coloratura who by all accounts was fast rising to stardom. The poor young lady did not live up to her reputation that evening, although she was to climb to heights indeed. Melba, muttering for several moments to herself, finally turned to Frank St. Leger in the box beside her and whispered fiercely: "Go take my card off those flowers this instant." St. Leger could but obey, and to the day of her death the other singer never guessed her anonymous admirer.

Accused of jealous bias toward this very soprano, Melba is supposed to have snapped, "Why? I know I have the most beautiful voice in the world, and as long as I know that, I shall continue to sing." Arrogance was hers, but not fatuousness, as has been attributed to her in a London incident. After a performance of *La Bohème* with Giovanni Martinelli at Covent Garden, the audience called insistently for "Martinelli, Martinelli!" Melba is supposed to have said, "Listen! They still want their Auntie Nellie!"

The nickname had been given to Melba in Australia, where among the troops she often sang for were her nephews, Douglas and Gordon Patterson. The remark was actually made at a supper party after the opera by a lady who misunderstood the audience's shouts and who gushed: "Isn't it sweet how the dear English public still knows Melba as 'Auntie Nellie!'" When St. Leger told her about the incident, Melba exclaimed with her usual force: "Damn fool!"

She also had an expletive for Charles Spalding, Manager Charles Ellis' representative, who hired a car in an emergency to get her to a train during a fierce storm. She rewarded the chauffeur with a two-dollar tip because of his careful driving, not knowing that the vehicle was a funeral equipage. When St. Leger dared reveal the circumstance to her, she snorted: "You think that's so bloody funny?"

Still, she claimed to possess no natural superstition, and only cultivated one foible because it seemed required of a diva: She always refused to be photographed in costume before a performance, which would have created some little difficulty with publicity machinery today.

Auction bridge was a favorite pasttime in moments of waiting to rehearse, to go on stage, or merely to pass an hour or two. She played as seriously as she worked. With her fingers tapping impatiently on the table, she would reprimand her companions, who liked a little shoptalk along with their cards. "You think only of music," she scolded. "Play bridge!"

With all the prickliness of temperament that seems built into a prima donna's constitution, she yet dealt fairly with her associates, St. Leger insisted, and was invariably his champion. He cited a typical letter from her explaining a previous gift of money for a private concert that the host had not thought to pay him for, addressing it "Dear Cherub," her name for the fresh-faced, snub-nosed young pianist. "The twenty pounds of yesterday will be your fee for last Sunday. I am very upset. I simply hate it! I am very angry."

Partnership with Jean de Reszke brought particular delight to Melba, who called him "so perfect, so gallant!" Never had there been an artist like him. He was credited with teaching her the Italian way of breathing —he himself was not provided by nature or study with a long breath and had camouflaged the lack by what the baritone Emilio de Gogorza called a remarkably quick intake of breath. "The greatest artistic emotion of my life," Melba described her first Juliette to his Roméo. They shared many odd experiences in this opera. Juliette's false curls fell at her swain's feet one night; he promptly stepped on them until he could unobtrusively kick them into the wings. Another time the tenor went on stage to speak to Melba as the Tomb Scene was being set. The curtain found him still there, though not yet due. He quickly improvised some dialogue to change the plot.

With the Met in Chicago, as Jean was singing his aria in the Balcony Scene, a man rushed down the aisle, threw his hat and coat over the footlights, and clambered after them onto the stage, "his face twitching and his eyes blazing," so one observer noticed. Quick-wittedly Jean drew his sword and threatened the interloper, who turned to face the stunned audience.

"You may think I'm crazy, but I will make a speech to prove I am not," he shouted hoarsely.

Stage Manager William Parry now entered, disliking to intrude on the stage, but knowing that spoken dialogue did not belong in Gounod's opera. De Reszke called for the curtain, hoping to trap the miscreant behind it. But he was too late: the "lunatic" had reached the footlights. Two stage hands in shirtsleeves made the final capture.

The unexpected star of the evening confessed that he was Robert Richard Rothman, a printer who believed himself to possess the biggest brain in the world, to be a Messiah who would be crucified at three P.M. the next day. He subsided behind bars in the Harrison Street police station.

At the opera house, hysteria still quivered in the air. Women fainted and remained shuddering in the ladies' lounge. Behind scenes, Melba was persuaded to retain her self-possession by Jean. "He caught my hands tight and said everything would be all right."

Enrico Bevignani, the conductor, said testily that such a thing had never happened in Europe, even in Russia, for when the lunatics came on stage there it was during curtain calls, hoping to embrace some of the singers. At last, the curtain rose again and Roméo began exactly where he had left off.

Melba continued to reign as queen in the realm of pure song; one devotee thought it a pity that "these wonderful notes cannot be bottled for future enjoyment!" She also retained the admiration and affection of Jean, who wrote: *"La nature vous a doué d'une voix d'or, positivement la plus belle de notre temps; vous êtes musicienne, vous êtes femme charmante. Toutes ces qualités peuvent être appréciées par le public, mais ce que je sais, moi, c'est que vous êtes la meilleure des camarades, et que je garderai un éternal souvenir de nos rélations artistiques et amicales."*

This "artistic and friendly relationship" would be temporarily interrupted in the season of 1896–97, at the height of the De Reszkes, pursuit of ideal Wagnerian opera. Whether Jean actually suggested Brünnhilde to Melba or meant only the Forest Bird when he urged her to join him in *Siegfried* and even recommended the casting to Grau has never been settled. Melba had already scored some success with Elsa and Elisabeth, but now she reached for something way beyond her grasp. The Brünnhilde on December 30, 1896, was a dismal failure in spite of certain polite critics and loyal friends. "You cannot use a rose bush for the same purposes as an oak," declared Henry T. Finck. The prima donna admitted afterward that her "appetite exceeded capacity." Various biographers describe the occurrence differently; the adulatory Agnes Murphy claims that Melba had not recovered from an attack of blood poisoning. The nervous strain was bad enough, but apparently her vocal mechanism also suffered, for she sang only one Juliette in early 1897.

The effect on Nordica was equally serious. Because Melba had secured sole right to the *Siegfried* heroine, Nordica left the company. Grau thus lost two prima donnas and must have rued his capitulation to the powerful tenor. The quick substitution of Félia Litvinne, an enormous woman who was privileged to be the sister of Edouard de Reszke's wife, further alienated Nordica, who now berated Jean even more heatedly.

Henceforth, both Melba and Nordica dashed off periodically to individual pursuits, Melba forming her own company with the aid of the formidable concert manager, Charles Ellis of Boston, who "handled" only the best. Rachmaninoff, Kreisler, and Geraldine Farrar, among others, later chose him as pilot. Melba's Italianate wing joined with Walter Damrosch and his German company in several tours. Nordica, the independent, had already organized her own concert tour with Ellis as manager during the season of the Met's discontent, featuring as a climax the duet from the last act of *Siegfried*. In a pinwheel of letters returned unopened, apologies demanded and rejected, the word "gentlemen" evoked when it should not have been, and press reports of stiffening attitudes in both camps, the Nordica-Jean feud had been fanned to a flame. Nordica refused to bail Grau out even when he lost both Eames and Calvé through indisposition. She promptly joined Damrosch's troupe and at last sang in *Siegfried* on the Metropolitan stage (rented by the conductor in 1897–98) to raised prices and an overflow house.

All the pieces in Grau's jigsaw did not return to their proper places until 1898–99, when Melba finally played a *Faust* with Jean, who had been gallantly piloting Eames, the young American, Suzanne Adams, and the triumphantly returning Marcella Sembrich through the Gounod operas. Nordica too was back in the fold and with Jean sang in *Lohengrin, Tristan, L'Africaine* (now in French), and *Götterdämmerung*, but Andreas Dippel was her Young Siegfried. Jean (pointedly?) did not include *Siegfried* in his duties.

In 1899–1900 Jean was absent, so that by the time he returned for his finale to America in 1900–1901, all disaffection had vanished among his garland of prima donnas. Melba enjoyed a *Faust*, Massenet's *Le Cid*, a

Roméo and one *Huguenots* with the peerless hero (though her *Traviata* tenor was Dippel, and in *Bohème, Rigoletto,* and *Lucia* she appeared with Albert Saléza).

Nordica had the deep satisfaction of being Jean's first heroine as he returned on New Year's Eve for this portentous season, sharing the agony of suspense on the crowded stage as Lohengrin dismissed his *lieber Schwan* and uttered his first words. Henderson warned that anyone who knew De Reszke's singing need not be told that his first measures "are no demonstration of the state of his voice on any occasion." But no one need have worried. The incomparable Jean was in their midst again—ideal in every role. But now Nordica had to share him in all but *Les Huguenots.* An alternative Elsa, Isolde, and Brünnhilde had appeared—even for *Siegfried* as well as *Götterdämmerung.* Milka Ternina, the tall and majestic Croat, had sung with Walter Damrosch in 1896, and had entered the Metropolitan during Jean's absence. She was his first Isolde of that fateful season, and his final Elsa in New York. He bracketed her with Lehmann as "superb" in *Tristan,* further confessing that while he usually remained objective enough to watch other singers' methods (having learned a good deal about taking high notes from observing Lehmann's uvula at close range), he was completely swept away during the love duet with Ternina, to the conductor's consternation. Ternina returned the compliment by saying that as Tristan the lover he never had an equal. This *Tristan* on January 25, 1901, was hailed as "the greatest ever known," a writer explaining that it was a night to fill the critic with despair. So glowing were the accounts of this and subsequent performances that Henderson felt called upon to deny that any cabal existed among the newspaper writers to boost De Reszke to the skies undeservingly.

Jean, always careful of his health to the point of mania (Eames said his eyes were full of terror as he sang, although others maintained that he cast aside worry the moment he stepped on stage), neglected his usual custom to place the couch in the third act of *Tristan* on February 11 so that drafts would not reach him as he lay exposed. He always shuddered at the remembrance that the first Tristan, Ludwig Schnorr von Carolsfeld, had died from that exposure. On this occasion Jean did catch cold. But he made a magnificent comeback to complete the marathon season with a parade of his greatest roles. The single performance as the Young Siegfried found him with a moustache. He had agonized deeply over the propriety of retaining the adornment—to beard or not to beard had been a burning question throughout the past decade, baritones and basses usually hiding under their hirsute decorations, while tenors varied in their approach. Jean had exposed his "large, sensuous mouth" for his first Siegfried in 1896 (the one with Melba), but considered it not worth the single showing in 1901.

Other lucky ladies sang with Jean that year. The young Johanna Gadski, who had been introduced by Damrosch, portrayed Elsa and also Eva on the single occasion that Jean and Edouard sang *Die Meistersinger* in German together. With her, Jean sang an *Aida* that confounded any possible leftover criticism. He had been guilty on previous occasions of omitting the *"Celeste Aida,"* but this time he sang it—"celestially." Gadski would go on to a distinguished American career, shortened by some differences of opinion about proper patriotism in 1917.

Jean's Eva in Pittsburgh brought the prediction that she would one day outstrip Aimée, the rage of the operetta circuit. Seemingly incongruous as a companion for the dignified Polish Walther, yet attractive as Musetta, Papagena, and other charming roles, Miss Fritzi Scheff did indeed live up to the prophecy. At that very moment, Victor Herbert, the conductor of the Pittsburgh Symphony since he had left the Metropolitan's cello ranks some time before, was also writing light operas, one of which would enhance Scheff's fame as Fifi—*Mlle. Modiste.*

Lucienne Bréval, the handsome French soprano for whom Grau had introduced the unappreciated *Salammbô* by Ernest Reyer, assumed the roles of Selika (*L'Africaine*) and Chimène (*Le Cid*) in New York and Philadelphia, giving Jean yet another change in partners. But Nordica had the last word—or rather the last note—with the transcendent singer on an American stage. Ternina had watched Lohengrin sail away in New York, but Nordica was by his side in Chicago, where he had first loomed on the operatic consciousness of this country. Ternina again had one Isolde on the road, but Nordica claimed two. And it was his first Isolde who sang the *"Liebestod"* over his body at the farewell gala in the house on April 29, an evening that marked the beginning of the end of the golden years.

One of those bookmarks in the annals of time that can be seen in retrospect to have closed off an era gave opera boxholders a chance to dress up even more elaborately than the opera stars. This was the Bradley-

Martin ball, which became the symbol of the sins of the idle rich, condemned from pulpits, fulminated against in newspaper editorials, damned by social historians, lampooned by satirists. How it came about was related by Frederick Townsend Martin, brother of Bradley (the hyphen came along with social aspirations) in a genteel little book called *Things I Remember.*

One morning at breakfast, in 1897, when the country was suffering a severe depression, Bradley Martin remarked that it would be a good thing to "get up something" to relieve the situation in trade. A concert, he suggested. His wife objected: it would only benefit foreigners. Why not a fancy-dress ball? With short notice, no one could order costumes from Paris.

It was true that local trade greatly enjoyed the rush of orders for a thousand or so costumes that would appear at home in a French court, but the accusations of callousness and arrogance outshouted the sycophantic praise, and the Bradley-Martins were forced by public opinion to migrate to England—where they were happier anyway. The sore memories of the gentlemen who found their swords an awkward third in the close contact of a waltz were swallowed up in grimmer tidings the morning after. Most of the Metropolitan boxholders had been unwillingly absent, by reason of their gaudy getups, from an opera they would have loved to see, Flotow's sentimental *Martha.* Armand Castelmary, an oldtime buffo favorite, still full of admirable fire and force, collapsed on the stage at the end of the second-act roughhouse called for in his role as Lord Tristan. The audience applauded heartily, believing it a realistic part of his performance. Jean de Reszke, a close friend, had been watching from the wings. He burst into tears, and helped carry the portly old man to his dressing room, where Dr. F. H. Bosworth, a member of the Opera Club who was hastily summoned, pronounced him dead. A substitute went on to finish the opera; the audience learned of the death only as they departed. Unfortunately the opera tragedy aroused less attention than the social triumph. Even Frederick Townsend Martin turned against his brother's lavish display in later years, excoriating him and his kind with unconcealed bitterness in a passionate tirade titled *The Passing of the Idle Rich,* a true harbinger of the young century.

9

THE CENTURY TURNS

Things have become too easy; it is time to make them difficult again.
—KIERKEGAARD

Four years after his fresh start in a redecorated opera house, Maurice Grau could have claimed that the Danish philosopher had pointed directly at him and his enterprises. After two seasons of relative prosperity, in which the road tours provided a fair profit, Henry E. Abbey had failed noticeably in health. Grau became increasingly responsible for their business. The suave little manager developed a set of vertical lines between his scanty eyebrows, while his moustache hid the fact that he smiled less often than before. Usually such glamorous stage personalities as Lillian Russell, Réjane, Irving, Terry, and Bernhardt could be counted on to make up any opera deficit. But in 1895–96 one theatrical company after another turned in a poor score, dissolving the fat that had accumulated in previous years. The final straw was laid on by a French comedian, Mounet-Sully, who provided "a frost seldom equalled."

While Grau was still in Paris, scouting for new talent, Abbey died on October 17, 1896, in the Osborne Apartments on West Fifty-seventh Street. To his cumulative misfortunes in health and finances had been added a sensational divorce suit. The bride who had charmed the Luigi Arditis as "the life and soul" of the 1890 tour with Patti had soon tired of her marriage. She was an English actress, a clever pantomimist named Florence Gerard. The divorce decree awarded her a third of Abbey's salary (about $10,000); then, in spite of his claim to the furniture and bric-a-brac in her residence at 160 West Fifty-ninth Street (valued at $25,000), she quickly put it all in storage and sailed for Europe.

Grau's first season on his own, clouded by the death of his partner, bedeviled by the loss of Melba and Nordica, and skimpily rewarded by a spring tour, ended on April 20, 1897, with a benefit for Abbey's daughter. Previously he must have wished that he could join the ranks of the "Poor of New York," for whom a great benefit had been held on February 9.

Grau decided to lie fallow for a season while reorganizing. The House did not remain wholly dark, however. German opera returned briefly. Each time the Italians fell into trouble, the rumors would rise up that the Germans were returning. Walter Damrosch had done his best to keep the idea alive, with his traveling group that came into New York each year. Engaging Rosa Sucher, Gadski, Fischer, Alvary, and Marie Brema, he had revived memories in 1895, further spurring the De Reszkes to action. Grau had refused him a lease in 1896, possibly fearing competition with the House's own budding attempts at Wagner in its original language, whereupon the wily Walter took to the inferior but still viable Academy of Music, inciting the public to petition and a few passionate critics to demand more German opera. Now, with an empty house and no company of his own, Grau, whose contract had just been renewed for three years, felt safe in allowing Damrosch to enter once more. Lilli Lehmann, who had waxed as fat as Materna, still sang gloriously, and Nordica's *Siegfried* Brünnhilde provided the soprano with the sweet taste of revenge.

The respect in which Grau was held by the profession showed in that year of his distress, when even his singers came to his aid. Jean de Reszke contributed $4,000, his brother $2,000, Calvé $3,000, Lassalle $2,000. This was in every case a sum higher than the fee for a performance. When the disgruntled stockholders complained in 1892 that exorbitant fees and managerial salaries (the $15,000 paid to Edmund Stanton seemed to stick most peskily in the craws of the millionaires) had ruined the company or were about to, they cited figures that would indeed seem high to later generations. But at the very outset of his Metropolitan engagement Abbey had proclaimed the pattern.

"Money is a power and with that power talent can be secured," he stated bluntly. "The market value of a singer is at once increased from fifty to 100 percent—or even more—when he is engaged for America."

Jean's first American stipend was $10,000 per month for eight performances, plus 25 percent of the gross over $5,000. This average of $1,250 per performance was later raised to $1,500 and in 1901 was said to be $2,500, although Jean claimed that he had never asked for a raise. In fact, when Grau fell into trouble, Jean reduced his percentage to 25 percent of gross over $5,500. The eminent tenor made out a good case for a singer's high fee, describing the difficulties of an uncertain profession and its short span. His brother Edouard always commanded less: $500 or $600 plus 10 percent over $5,000. Neither did feminine stars of the time quite scale Jean's heights. Nellie Melba, beginning at $1,000, rose to match Jean but without percentage. Emma Eames started with less but rose to $1,000. Emma Calvé also began more modestly, but by 1896 her popularity ensured a cachet of $1,500. It should be remembered that America demanded no taxes on these fees.

No one need pity Grau, Jean thought. In those halcyon years when stars carted away loads of bank notes, the manager slipped more than a comparable amount into his own tin box, and retired with a fortune. (What Jean's biographer did not add was that Grau, in addition to shrewdness in choosing stars, knew his way around the stock market.)

When Grau reorganized in 1898, he chose as backers his own personal friends rather than any member of the Wall Street circle. These included Henry Dazian, the costumer; Frederick Rullman, ticket broker and founder of the Metropolitan's libretto concession; Charles Frazier, banker: Edward Lauterbach; Roland F. Knoedler; Frank W. Sanger, Grau's first business manager; and John William Mackay, Sr., the colorful Irishman who, after making his money in the spectacular Comstock lode, formed the Commercial Cable Company and the Postal Telegraph Cable Company, and succeeded in breaking Jay Gould's Western Union monopoly. His son Clarence was to cut an important Metropolitan figure as well. Grau also depended heavily on the Tysons, who bought many thousands of tickets at a slight discount and resold them in their agencies in the Fifth Avenue Hotel and the Gilsey House. Even when his subscriptions began to go at a premium, Grau never refused tickets to Tyson, claimed Aimé Gerber, paymaster, who began in the House as Grau's office boy, responding "to summonses in four languages" and watching the "making of musical history."

In his entertaining book, *Backstage at the Opera,* Gerber maintains that Grau took infinite pride in his casts, quite apart from their business value. "They were, in a sense, his form of personal expression." He actually reveled in difficulties and delighted in fitting together engagements for his artists in concerts and opera, wrote the American baritone David Bispham in *A Quaker Singer's Recollections.* "He viewed the profession of an impresario in the light of a complicated and highly interesting game in which, when his partners did not upset his calculations, he was usually successful." Bispham adds a picture of Grau at work:

In the midst of a discussion of the most intricate nature, arising out of the illness of several of his principals and the need of filling their places in compliance with their contracts, taking into account the probable effect upon the public of the changes in the casts. At the same time he was hearing a complicated report from the managers of the company; discussing the terms of his written agreement with an artist without referring to the document, except to prove the artist wrong; speaking as many as three foreign languages in rotation with men of as many nationalities; calling up his broker in Wall Street to give him orders to buy and sell, and evidently calculating the possible gains and losses mentally as he spoke.

In 1897, Jean de Reszke had used his influence to secure the managership of Covent Garden for Grau; he ran both "monster companies . . . in addition to many other theatrical and musical ventures, making for himself a name that will go down in history."

Large in large affairs, Grau was small in little ones. To Jean is attributed the remark: "Grau would give a man a fine cigar but would not offer him a match to light it unless such generosity had been nominated in the bond."

His tact, equal to a woman's, one observer noted, was reserved for occasions when it was needed. Behind scenes, he occasionally expressed a more cynical view, as when he asked the stage manager William Parry: "How is Madame X today?"

"Oh, Madame is alive," answered Parry.

"Then I'll bet she's kicking."

As the successor to James G. Huneker on the *Musical Courier* remarked that he would fill Huneker's space, not his place, so a half dozen tenors in one year or another assumed the names if not always the characters of Jean's roles. Saléza, Ernst Van Dyck (whose silvery, pliable voice had turned to yelps and gurgles through Bayreuth's influence), Alvarez, Carlo Dani (small but sweet voice), Alois Burgstaller (who would sing the first Parsifal outside of Bayreuth), all passed in review. Even little Thomas Salignac, who most often appeared merely in the list of those who "also sang," had his uses; he cheerfully confessed that they probably kept him around because he could bear with Calvé's tantrums and ever-growing capriciousness. That adorable creature continued to astonish the public and exacerbate her colleagues and manager for as long as she pleased, which was exactly one year after Grau's departure. Grau had coped with her as best he could, but there were occasions, especially on the road, when her sudden illness (or whim) brought disappointment to the customers and box office alike. On Grau's longest tour (1901–1902) the trouble began in Toronto, where, in a concert to honor the future King George V and Queen Mary, Calvé was forced to wait for the long-delayed entrance of the royal party, then to sing against a din compounded of brass band, fish horns (particularly noisy and irritating instruments), a procession of fire engines, and a band of pipers. From then on, the country's most demanded prima donna became the least predictable. The climax came in Nashville, when she positively refused to sing.

Her substitute, Camille Seygard, was forced to compete not only with the audience's letdown in expectations but also with the builder of the Ryman Tabernacle, one T. G. Ryman, a retired riverboat captain, who had caught religion rather severely a few years before. The evangelist for whom Captain Ryman erected his temple never saw it until he preached Ryman's funeral service. Meanwhile, the revival business slackening, the Captain was forced to admit crassly commercial rentals, among whom Grau's troupe signalized the first opera company to tread the hallowed boards. So fearful of a rain of brimstone on this sacrilegious intruder was the Captain that he stood below stage and prayed at the top of his voice during the whole performance, his powerful vocalism occasionally penetrating the lyric outpourings and heel tappings from the gypsies above.

Calvé's real gamut was never experienced in America, which type-cast her as Carmen, with an occasional venture into an equally violent impersonation as Santuzza or the heroine of *La Navarraise*. Marguerite or a rare Mignon were the only "conventional" ladies allowed her. Part of her endless fascination consisted in her individualizing of every role. She put her stamp on Leïla in *Pearl Fishers* in the single season Bizet's tuneful opera appeared, and as Ophélie proved herself to be in actuality a high soprano. Her explicit performance in Isidore de Lara's *Messaline,* a small-scale scandal in the rising tide of moral display among press and patrons alike, is said to have resulted in a personal visit from one or two box-holders, who begged her to leave something to the imagination.

With her restless and volatile temperament, the Carmen became more and more Calvé's, less and less Bizet's, until one critic could sadly remark in 1904, "The star has risen above the work." "The lines had deepened, perhaps coarsened, like an engraving that has been worked over too much," Huneker judged. "For me the old charm has vanished . . . hers was ever a *beauté du diable,* and the devil we know has a dislike for a woman past her youth." The final seal: "Mme. Calvé's Carmen is a thing of the past."

Calvé's fight with Alvarez before one *Carmen* and her mischievous flitting around the stage with José in hot pursuit led Bispham to be much relieved that the tenor had not actually planted his dagger between her shoulder blades when he finally caught her. But she took her curtain call, smiling and beautiful as usual.

Bispham considered Nordica "one of the most beautiful and obliging" prima donnas, deeply admiring her pluck and generosity in going on for Sembrich in Washington as Violetta, a lyric-coloratura role the Wagnerian had left far behind her. Lehmann, too, he revered, for her superb art and the self-confidence that banished a prompter. He cherished sentiments not quite so warm for Melba, however. Watching the ill-fated *Siegfried,* after finishing his stint as Alberich, the baritone thought the lady forgetful of Wagnerian tradition to remain within the scene, and commiserated with the fur-clad Jean, who was kept busy "patrolling the forward part of the stage" to prevent Brünnhilde "from rushing to the footlights, over which she had so many times sung to delighted audiences." Bispham went on naughtily to compare her to a white calf who was trying in great excitement to get too close to a fire in a stable he had once witnessed. "The field between the young animal and the conflagration was in this instance patrolled by the mother cow."

Striding through the annals of the golden age just before the turn of the century, perhaps the only male who showed no fear—nor needed to— of the De Reszkes, or even of Jean Lassalle, Victor Maurel "touched nothing he did not adorn." Debutantes whose mothers had sighed over his lithe figure, handsome face, and compelling artistry two decades before now found in him the perfect matinee idol and swooned at his masterful Iago, his dangerously alluring Don Giovanni, his sinister yet pitiful Rigoletto. This privileged being, to whom "all baritones owed something," as one of them (Bispham) admitted, appeared to another (Emilio de Gogorza) as the marvelous actor whose skill made up for the loss of his voice.

Both his Iago and his Falstaff were new to America in 1894–95. Italo

Campanini had employed another baritone in his introduction of *Otello* at the Academy of Music in 1888; Del Puente had sung the role in Abbey's 1889–90 tour, while Eduardo Camera was the soon-to-be-forgotten Iago in Jean de Reszke's single performance each in Chicago and New York in 1891, the only Metropolitan hearings of Verdi's towering work until Maurel made his Metropolitan debut on December 3, 1894. Maurel was at once "a revelation to the public of the resources that go to make the art of a truly great singing actor," said W. J. Henderson. This sensation was followed two months later by the first *Falstaff* in America, which Henry Krehbiel likened to a "perfect sea of melodic champagne," and named Maurel's role one of the great creations of the lyric stage that, De Gogorza added, would never be effaced from the memories of the *cognoscenti* who heard it. Truly, Verdi had chosen wisely when he created both Iago and Falstaff for this artist after hearing Maurel's Simon Boccanegra in the revised form of the earlier opera.

One triumph followed another in Maurel's Indian summer—a Rigoletto which he lived, emphasized De Gogorza, in which the intensity of *"Si vendetta,"* capped by an A-flat that was as unexpected as it was effective, "left you limp and wondering how the worn voice could so respond and electrify the public through art and magnetism that actually mesmerized." His Amonasro, another Verdi role he had introduced to America in 1873, his Figaro, De Nevers, Escamillo, Lescaut, and Nelusko enraptured his admirers, while his Valentin in *Faust* recalled to the more knowledgeable that he had also sung the Méphistophélès in the original bass version.

Jean de Reszke remembered that Maurel, with the help of Brother Edouard and Massenet, had literally wrestled him onto the stage as a tenor in Massenet's *Hérodiade* in 1883, overcoming his timidity by locking him in, forcing him into costume, and escorting him to the stage. Meaner spirits credited Maurel with an easy disposal of a baritone rival, for people—notably George Bernard Shaw—had begun to make unflattering comparisons about Valentin and even Don Giovanni, which the younger man had attempted. One effective way to remove competition is to raise or lower one's voice into an entirely different set of roles. Whatever the motive, the change enabled Maurel to sing alongside of Jean in *Manon* as Lescaut and *Faust* as Valentin, and in the latter, as well as *L'Africaine,* with Edouard joining in, to weld a male trio as powerful as

New York could wish to see and hear. The three formed the core of one of Grau's priceless casts for *Les Huguenots* as well, including also Nordica or Lehmann, Melba or Sembrich, Scalchi or Mantelli, and Plançon. Lehmann remembered that Maurel's portrayal of Valentin's death moved her so profoundly that she kept silence for hours afterward. Much later, she confessed that recollections of the whole period completely spoiled her taste for everything she was doing at the time.

And yet, offstage—at least to De Gogorza—this paragon shone with a somewhat diminished light: for all his handsomeness "inarticulate, nebulous, commonplace." Distaff opinion apparently differed violently; his amorous adventures were said to be patterned after his favorite Mozart character's. Lilli Lehmann, impervious to any such importunities —if, indeed, Maurel had ever thought to approach the formidable lady thus, which is doubtful (Bispham found her mending Maurel's socks in motherly fashion one day)—believed him to be the first singer and artist she had met who could talk well about singing and art. "We did not neglect a moment when we could instruct each other mutually on these subjects," she explained loftily. She even took criticism from him, always with this preamble: "Listen, Madame Lehmann, we are too great as artists to pay each other compliments; let us try to correct each other's faults!" Geraldine Farrar was witness to one such encounter. Maurel did begin this time with compliments, very fulsome ones for Lehmann's superb Donna Anna. Then, after he had reduced her to blushes and smiles, he added: "But for God's sake, burn those costumes!"

In his old age, teaching in New York, the gallantry and the grand manner remained. Lillian Gish, just beginning the career that would spin its fine threads into the rewarding future, studied with him under an arrangement that gave him a half hour of her posing for his painting —undimmed in energy, Maurel had turned to a sister art—and in return a halfhour study for her. "This was very kind to a struggling youngster," Miss Gish remembers. Mme. Maurel, thirty years Victor's junior, became greatly attached to the fragile and beautiful girl and gave her the opal necklace and bracelets she still wears—her own birthstone.

In the two Verdi operas which headed Abbey's and Grau's "novelties" during two seasons, Maurel's companion was the other whom Verdi had chosen—Francesco Tamagno. The trumpet voice, which was said to bring shivers to human spines as well as crystal chandeliers, had ranged over its own repertoire in Abbey's 1889–90 tour, and had soared through the Metropolitan's reaches in his rented spring weeks, but official recognition came only on the second night of the 1894–95 season, with his Arnold in *William Tell*. Henderson dampened his spirits by comparing the 1890 Otello to the present, with the devastating remark that Tamagno owed more to Verdi's training than to natural ability. His Samson, too, was faulted, his clarion tones not leading themselves readily to the "accents of love." Still, nine years later, the critic recalled his Otello as "great," and when *Simon Boccanegra* came along in 1932, Henderson remembered the original La Scala cast of 1881 with Edouard de Reszke and Tamagno, and murmured, "We are not doing quite as well as that, but may survive." Thus are golden ages formed out of the veils drawn over intervening years.

De Gogorza spoke of one of Tamagno's tenorisms. He was perhaps the first to transpose the high B-flats of *"Di quella pira"* in *Il Trovatore* a half tone up to C—"it comes easier," was his explanation—and sang it that way in Barcelona. The *aficionados,* not expecting the note, blew on pitch pipes and banged on tuning forks (presumably always a part of theatre equipment), whereupon the general audience booed the dissenters and Tamagno, encouraged by the multitude, repeated the aria with its controversial notes three times.

The masculine contingent of the Grau years was further strengthened by the inimitable Plançon, who possessed a voice of dark velvet with the execution of a *prima donna assoluta,* as well as the distinction of being the only person who dared interrupt Grau when the managerial door was closed. David Bispham, to whom we are indebted for several slightly malicious stories about his confreres (and who possibly acquired a critical faculty from absorption in his most famous role, Beckmesser, as he "became almost a living embodiment" of whatever character he studied), paints Plançon as a quivering mass of nerves before a Sunday night concert, "weeping violently, mopping from his cheeks and beard the tears that continued to flow, until the moment for him to walk upon the platform."

The only American male in the company, Bispham arrived on the Metropolitan scene in 1896, already famous for the *Meistersinger* town clerk as well as Kurvenal in *Tristan,* two roles in which he himself admitted he had no rival. As a Quaker, it seems rather astonishing that he should accept the advice to study them, as well as Amonasro and Wolfram, from planchette, the little platform on an Ouija board, but he could disarm criticism by pointing to the correctness of planchette's prophecy. He was ready when Manager Harris, in London, asked him unexpectedly to do Kurvenal. The whole thing was in a class with the miracle at Lourdes, he thought.

Whatever his beliefs, Bispham became a warmly admired member of Grau's troupe, for his Alberich and Hunding and Iago, among other roles. A note of bitterness crept in when, after his own rather casual attempt to take Grau's place ("I had the temerity to offer myself"), a new impresario brought in "a deluge of talent unknown to New York [including a certain Italian tenor who might have claimed that the deluge came, in fact, after him] while a dozen of us who were still prime favorites with the public were not reengaged."

It was naïve for a man of Bispham's intelligence not to realize that a manager cannot abide in the neighborhood a potential or putative rival. The dozen "dismissals" included several of the brightest stars indeed, as we shall see, but among those not returning was Albert Alvarez, who had nearly thrown Bispham off balance when he pushed Iago's foot off his chest in the former's moment of triumph at the end of the third act of *Otello*. Neither would Georg Anthes return, the luckless Lohengrin who had fallen overboard from the swan boat, and whose *Siegfried* anvil split before he even touched it with the newly forged Nothung.

Another baritone, the tiny Mario Ancona, occasionally played Escamillo in earliest days, then added to the respect and even affection audiences felt for him by turning in excellent Tonios, Valentins, Rigolettos, Lescauts, and even Telramunds (in Italian). Plump, with quivering moustaches and a merry look in his eyes, the dapper little baritone carried on respectably for four seasons. Soon he began to notice that one role after another was being whittled away from him. Most notably, the encroachment was accomplished by Giuseppe Campanari, an expert musician (he had played the cello with the Boston Symphony), a charming personality, and a thoroughgoing artist. His second major assignment was one that thirty years later brought fame to another baritone—Ford in *Falstaff,* although under differing circumstances. Lawrence Tibbett's success was as a dark horse; Campanari merely added the role to a growing series that encompassed a tidy repertoire by the end of his fourteen seasons with the

Metropolitan. Spanning four managerial tenures, he stood alone at the end with only four other singers who had experienced service in the nineties.

In this foursome was a baritone destined to long life and high repute with the company in a span of thirty-three years. He made his debut as De Nevers in *Les Huguenots* on November 15, 1899, in Chicago, during the long preseason tour Grau favored in four of his five seasons. "A newcomer with the suggestive name of Scotti," Huneker described this baritone in *Town Topics* after he had sung Don Giovanni in January. "He is an Italian, however, of good presence, good voice and an actor of ease if not distinction." Antonio Scotti waited practically no time for critical appreciation of his powers: Krehbiel found him an artist "in the highest sense of the word"; Henderson declared his success to be immediate. By the end of the year he was "popular"; in two seasons, "infallible." Another quick victory awaited him in February, 1901, when he put his stamp on the role that was to be exclusive to him until 1910, and which he virtually monopolized even after. His Scarpia, said Huneker with purposeful alliteration, was "vengeful, vile and full of malevolent vitality." With fewer flourishes, the important critics agreed.

Antonio Pini-Corsi, the genial buffo bass-baritone, was the second of "Campanari's Quartet." The remaining two were women: the young Gadski and the contralto, who, considering her longevity and stature, both physically and artistically, it is difficult to picture as ever having been young. Ernestine Schumann-Heink, at the time of her American debut in Chicago with Grau, November 7, 1898, was in fact thirty-seven, had divorced her first husband, Ernst Heink, married her second, Paul Schumann, and taken both their names. The family that was to make her as famous for a motherly image as for her tremendously wide-compassed, equal, beautiful, and powerful voice and her juggernaut figure already consisted of four little Heinks, a couple of little Schumanns, and another on the way. Schumann brought one of his own to the marriage, which lasted until his death in 1904. Dale Warren, Boston editor and author, draws the parallel with Erda, the Earth Mother, whom Schumann-Heink portrayed magnificently even to her farewell in 1932. A life of hardship had prepared her for almost any contingency; giving birth between a season in Chicago that had her singing Fricka as late as November 23 and a New York debut as Ortrud on January 9 became merely an incident in a fruitful life. She was bracketed immediately with Brandt and Lehmann and shared with both the best of both the Italian and German styles; the artistic *cachet* led quickly to financial comfort. Henry T. Finck relates that Grau, having engaged her at $6,500 a year, tore up this contract, paid her full salary for a third of a season's work, and raised her fee to $12,000. Her Azucena and Brangäne proved unforgettable, the first for its dramatic impact *à l'allemand,* the second for the incredible outpouring of beautiful tone *à l'italien,* "rolling forth in an ever-increasing crescendo," wrote John Alan Haughton in *Musical America.* Ortrud's invocation to the pagan gods made the listener shiver. So perfect was the control of her voice that she "could have sung a good Marguerite or a capable Wotan." She did accomplish one piece of technique that was rare even then for heavy voices and seemingly became impossible later—a trill above the staff, notable in the coloratura music of the *"Brindisi"* from *Lucrezia Borgia*—or at least her recording of it. The only Metropolitan performance of this Donizetti work occurred in one of the seasons when Mme. Schumann-Heink absented herself for one reason or another, as will be seen. Perhaps her potential virtuosity should not have been tested so far as assigning her to sing the Shepherd in *Tannhäuser* in Pittsburgh. She overwhelmed the tiny part as well as the boy's costume, which was mildly criticized as "not becoming." Nor was she happy as a Rhine Maiden, for the swimming harness struck her as undignified for the mother of eight and dizziness from the swooping and swaying disconcerted her.

Several other singers entered Grau's portals to remain in subsequent managers' lists, notably the comely American contralto Louise Homer; the versatile tenor Albert Reiss; the skilled baritone of the "declamatory school," Anton Van Rooy; and the enduring and reliable French bass Marcel Journet. In San Francisco, where Homer made her debut as Amneris on November 14, 1900, a critic wrote of her: "Remember her name—it is going to spell something big." New York did not obey immediately, but Homer came to occupy a specially warm place in her countrymen's affections after a year or so. Journet played King to her Princess Amneris on the West Coast, having made his bow previously in Los Angeles as Colline in the Metropolitan's first *La Bohème* on November 9, 1900, with his fellow debutants Fritzi Scheff as Musetta and the enormously talented bass-baritone Charles Gilibert as Schaunard. Assuming bass parts in French, Italian, and even German to the total of almost three dozen (eventually more than a hundred), the personable Journet remained a stalwart of the Metropolitan until 1908, then returned to Europe, journeying back to Chicago after World War I. He sang in France and Italy until his death in 1933.

Van Rooy (who was christened Antonius Maria Josephus in Rotterdam) resembled an ultraconventional businessman more than the average idea of an opera star, with pince-nez and a stiff moustache. Perhaps it was his Bayreuth experience, immediately preceding his American debut in 1898, that inflicted a sorrowing mien upon him. His voice would be gone within ten years, he was quoted as saying in *Musical America*. Every time he sang Wotan, he felt a heartstring snap. Those who aren't worn out don't sing with the soul, was his conclusion. Amfortas must have deepened his woe, for his Amfortas in Chicago "never forgot his wound and the ceaseless pain." Fortunately for his public, the impressive Wagnerian came safely through Metropolitan seasons until 1908, pulled out a good many of his heartstrings as a regular member of the Frankfort Opera thereafter, and joined the Boston Opera as Hans Sachs on their Paris visit in the summer of 1914.

The diminutive tenor Albert Reiss, who revealed his true humorous spirit by seizing every opportunity to be photographed with the tallest members of the company, filled comic and character roles with distinction for twenty years—the valued Mime, Alfred (*Fledermaus*), Wenzel (*Bartered Bride*), and Monostatos. He was also an admirable David in *Meistersinger*. But he could claim two other distinctions, one comparatively unknown. He was the Beppe for whom Caruso sang the little serenade in *Pagliacci* behind the scenes, raising hardly a ripple of applause and proving an audience's lack of discrimination. He was also the only tenor, so far as is known—certainly at the Met—to sing the part of the Witch in *Hänsel und Gretel*.

Of lighter weight but more immediate sensation, the presence of Sybil Sanderson in the company on the first of two separate occasions aroused a small tempest among those who delved into foreign society and intrigue. News had leaked across the cables that the expatriate Californian was the pet of Paris, courted and bejeweled by royalty, the cause of a Belgian prince's suicide, and, most astonishing of all, the inspiration of two composers. Massenet wrote three operas for her: *Le Mage, Esclar-*

monde, and, more importantly, *Thaïs* (which Huneker liked to call *"Thighs"*). Saint-Saëns's *Phryné* was likewise dedicated to her. Her love life occupied equal space in the press with her art, which consisted of notes so high (G in alt) that they were, of course, compared with the Eiffel Tower, which was erected in the year of her debut; she had a chic that few could equal, and a doll-like prettiness.

Alas for her homecoming, her exoticism did not transplant very well. Other cities, dazzled by her elegance and reputation, treated her with *éclat,* and she came away with a genuine prize: Philip Hale's estimation of her as "easily the first actress in the company, a charming apparition." But New York turned a chilly shoulder with the exception of Huneker, who had boasted (according to H. L. Mencken) of carrying on a love affair with Sanderson at the very time the young Mary Garden was a protégée of the American. The tale, probably apocryphal, is in any case not mentioned by Garden, although she herself, Sanderson, and Olive Fremstad were undoubtedly the sources of a character in one of Huneker's novels.

Sanderson sang but two *Manons* (the first French production of Massenet's opera) in New York, where Krehbiel greeted her with "kindly recognition if not enthusiasm." When she returned in 1901 to traipse over the countryside with Grau, substitutes had to be found more often than not for her Manon and Juliette, and even the citizens of her home town, Sacramento, considered their pilgrimage to San Francisco a sorry waste. Ill and lonely, she returned to Paris to follow her wealthy Cuban husband, Antonio Terry, to death two years later. Her elegant ghost joined those of Diane de Poitiers and Catherine de Médicis in the Château of Chenonceaux, her wedding gift, which had rung to the sounds of the entire Opéra Comique troupe playing *Esclarmonde* as another *petit cadeau* to his exquisite wife from Terry.

Grau's choice of repertoire, largely fortuitous, was tailored to the singers he had to sing it. His novelties, with the exception of *Cavalleria, Pagliacci, Bohème,* and *Tosca,* which were catapulted into the Met's lists by sheer propulsion of notoriety, generally bore a tag reading "Property of———." For Jean de Reszke, Bemberg's *Elaine,* Massenet's *Werther* and *Le Cid* (the latter revived one season for Lucienne Bréval after Jean's departure); again for Bréval, the highly expensive *Salammbô;* for Tamagno, *Samson et Dalila* (the first New York performance in operatic form) and *Guillaume Tell* (a revival from the German years); for Melba,

Semiramide and other war horses in revival; for Sembrich, *La Fille du Régiment* (considered too short without the appendage of either *Cavalleria* or *Pagliacci*); for Calvé, *Hamlet, Messaline,* and *La Navarraise.* Sembrich, whose star had risen and remained fixed while Calvé's sank, was the darling of the critics. Huneker wrote in *Town Topics*: "She is, with the possible exception of Melba, the greatest vocalist alive—for Patti is petrified—and if Melba had Sembrich's musical temperament she would be put under glass and preserved as the most wonderful singer of the age. But," he added, "she has not."

To honor the great Paderewski, who had been commanding feverish concert audiences since his appearance as the first recitalist in the new Music Hall built by Andrew Carnegie in 1891, Grau valiantly gave his *Manru.* And also as a gesture to a composer, *Ero e Leandro* had a place in two seasons, conducted by Luigi Mancinelli, who happened to be the chief Italian conductor during most of Grau's years. Mancinelli thus became the first to conduct his own work at the Metropolitan. At least the score was in authoritative hands.

The only woman composer ever to be accepted within the sanctuary arrived in 1903 by Grau's invitation. Ethel Smyth (later Dame Ethel) came over from England to witness two showings of her short opera *Der Wald.* Henderson paid it an infuriating compliment: "No one would ever suspect that this score was the work of a woman."

Grau confessed to a contemporary that he would never by choice have allowed so much prominence to Wagner if it had not been the wish of the powerful De Reszkes and Nordica and because pressure was exerted by the remnant of Stanton's German audiences. But he made an honest attempt to stabilize the reputation of Mozart by giving *Figaro* almost every season, omitting *Don Giovanni* only once, and adding *Magic Flute* three times. Cynics might note that Grau's favorite method of "casting" played a large part in these three masterpieces, for he could throw into all of them a half dozen of his luminaries. "A retrospect to boast of," Huneker wrote later of a *Giovanni* cast that included Maurel, Edouard de Reszke, Lehmann, Nordica, and Sembrich. Unfortunately another definition of the word "cast" did not always apply, as no sooner would one "particular shape" become hardened into a mold than a component of it would drop out. For Nordica read Susan Strong (who gave up opera to become a fashionable laundress in London), for Edouard de Reszke,

Pini-Corsi. But few could quarrel with the *Flute's* makeup: Sembrich, De Lussan, Eames, Dippel, Campanari, Plançon, with the mighty Ternina as one of the three ladies. The one surprise would be the bass-baritone Pini-Corsi doing the buffo tenor part of Monostatos, later taken over by Reiss. (A comprimario tenor named Gaetano Pini-Corsi did show up in the Boston Opera in 1913–14, singing, for example, the four buffo roles in *Tales of Hoffmann,* but Antonio is the only one mentioned in New York annals.)

Grau further made a gesture toward the mountain peaks by arranging a little Verdi cycle in his last season. To *Aida, Rigoletto, Traviata, Trovatore,* and *Otello* were added *Ernani* and *Masked Ball.* Still, although he secured the distinction of an American premiere for *Tosca* only, it was the four *verismo* innovations that Grau could claim as solid achievements in progressiveness. Not that all were immediately taken to critical and lay bosoms. So much brouhaha preceded the advent of *Cavalleria Rusticana* that the warm-blooded little melodrama came as no great surprise to the Metropolitan audience, further cooled off as it was by the something less than white-hot leading lady. Emma Eames related that she had studied the part in the gorgeous, monumental marble ballroom of a Venetian palace, which may have had something to do with it. Far more interest was shown in Gluck's *Orfeo,* also receiving its Metropolitan baptism on that December 30, 1891. But when Calvé took over in 1893, Santuzza came into her own torrid kingdom. This same season welcomed Leoncavallo's *Pagliacci* to the Met (like *Cavalleria,* it had been hustled into an American premiere by the alert Gustav Hinrichs in Philadelphia), offering a steppingstone to Melba in her rapidly ascending career as well as the perfect partner for Mascagni's piece. The "ham and eggs" of opera, known thereafter as "Cav-Pag," was first served to eager consumers on December 22, 1893.

It was Puccini's two operas, introduced in a single season, 1900–01, that provided one of the most typical instances of the critics' clouded crystal ball. Krehbiel's invective lived to haunt him. *Bohème,* he said, "is foul in subject and fulminant but futile in its music." The story held "silly and inconsequential incidents and dialogues designed to show the devil-may-care life of artistic Bohemia." Murger's book for some reason had had a great vogue among addlepated persons, he added, and decadent French writers had impotently attempted to ape its spirit ever since. This story was "daubed over with splotches of instrumental color without reason and without effect except the creation of a sense of boisterous excitement and confusion." Other adjectives picked up along the way were "superficial" and strident." If the opera secured a vogue, he concluded, it would be because of the tenor. Melba's beautiful voice and placid style hardly carried the day. On the contrary, Huneker thought, Melba made the success of her life in the part, really *acting* Mimi, while her voice was "so luscious in color, so silvery, so ductile, you could have eaten it without sugar."

This was December 26, 1900. When *Tosca* came along on February 4, the *Tribune* critic summoned up new ammunition for his blunderbuss. The "melodramatic music upon which Sardou's play floats? Much of it is shreds and patches of many things with which the operatic stage has long been familiar. . . . Phrases of real pith and moment are mixed with phrases of indescribable balderdash." But Krehbiel had a good word to say for Puccini's fluency, as well as for the heroine of the evening in a left-handed sort of fashion, expressing amazement at the "tragic power disclosed by Mme. Ternina, which in its most hideous moment has had no companion on the local operatic stage since Mme. Calvé created nightmares with her impersonation of 'La Navarraise.'"

Eames soon conceived a desire to sing Tosca as she had craved Aida a few years previously. Grau tried to discourage her about Verdi's role, giving the reason that the opera had never drawn in America. (*"Aida?"* one gasps!) When she asked for Tosca, he demanded to know why she wanted another failure. It could be possible that he was remembering Huneker's criticism of the charming Emma's first Ethiopian princess: "There was skating on the Nile last night." Eames got her way, however, as she had once before. She took over Puccini's Roman singer from Ternina in 1902. She did not hesitate to reveal that she "went down into her soul for each character," which perhaps accounts for the aloofness of many of her portrayals. "I am no prude," she confessed, "but was brought up to be both fastidious and chaste."

Krehbiel's vitriol may have eclipsed the milder outpourings of others, among them Henderson, who, while blaming the subject for the lack of opportunity to write "winning" music, nevertheless conceded individuality, picturesqueness, ingenuity, and occasional grace and sweetness to this talented dramatic composer. Huneker, although he never strongly supported Puccini, vowed that both the opera and the heroine made an impression; in fact, that Ternina offered a sensation. She acted with "a sureness of touch, a psychological insight and a brilliancy of style which left little doubt as to her versatility." The "sex duel" with Scarpia was "most moving, most thrilling and technically perfect." This singer had seemed ready for the most elevated plateau of artistry in her four seasons in America, but was struck down with a facial paralysis supposed to have been the result of a cold caught while mountain climbing, and was seen no more after 1904.

Krehbiel never fully recovered from the double dose of *verismo*. Even after seventeen years of perspective, he was viewing it "through a vista which looks like a valley of moral and physical death through which there flows a sluggish stream thick with filth and red with blood." The music thus fructified "rasps the nerves, even as the dramas revolt the moral stomach."

Since the advent of *Cavalleria,* he continued, "piquancy has been the cry; the piquant contemplation of adultery, seduction, and murder amid the reek and stench of the Italian barnyard."

To close off Grau's short term of five years, it might be well to remember with some sense of balance that *La Traviata* and *Carmen* had also come into the world with the stigma of failure. Perhaps their "real" people, as opposed to gods, goddesses, kings, and queens, hit too close to home, even though, as W. H. Auden has pointed out, the courtesans, gypsies, and bullfighters, the diva and the Bohemian artists are social types "every bit as unfamiliar to the average operagoer." The poet concludes that "every encounter with a work of art is a personal encounter; what it *says* is not information but a revelation of itself which is simultaneously a revelation of ourselves."

At the very beginning of the twentieth century, it seemed Americans were not yet quite prepared to reveal themselves in terms of *verismo* opera.

10

ENTER MELODRAMA WITH CONRIED

Only a fool or a madman will take up where I leave off.

—Maurice Grau

Heinrich Conried, resembling the culprit in a whodunit, was the most unlikely person to succeed to the leadership of America's only steadily functioning opera house. He had been brought to New York in 1877 by Adolph Neuendorff, an energetic conductor whose name never appeared in the Metropolitan Opera roster, but who had conducted the "unauthorized" tour of the German company in 1886, and whose wife, Georgine von Januschowsky, sang at the Met several seasons thereafter. Neuendorff had just gone into partnership with Oscar Hammerstein to produce plays in the Germania Theatre on East Fourteenth Street. Conried soon left Neuendorff for the Thalia Theatre, which he bought and ran for some years, producing several operettas which were considered successful. A later association with Rudolph Aronson at the Casino involved Conried in the presentation of Strauss's *Gypsy Baron,* which he remembered to restore at the Metropolitan for his own benefit in 1905–6. At some time in the early eighties, he became the partner in a firm of playbrokers, cornering the rights to many Viennese operettas. While with Aronson, he even contemplated hiring the Metropolitan for seasons of comic operas on a grand scale, but the scheme did not meet Stanton's favor. What appealed to the Metropolitan's profit-oriented board was the success that accrued to the German actor-manager at the Irving Place Theatre, which he leased from William Steinway in 1892. Conried's brilliant staging and diversification of repertoire brought the theatre five years of ever-mounting acclaim.

Although he had been associated with musicians and felt entirely at home in the operetta world, Conried possessed "little distinctive musical taste," his biographer was forced to admit. Lamely, Montrose J. Moses added that nevertheless Conried "often exhibited a natural ear for music." As an illustration, Conried is supposed to have corrected the tempo of a Strauss (Johann?) march when an orchestra leader conducted it like a dirge.

Even Abbey had managed grand opera singers on concert tours and had piloted Lillian Russell's popular company in earlier days. Abbey, furthermore, was never without Grau's counsel; Conried asked no one for advice. As was to be expected, his judgment did not always prove infallible. To invite Geraldine Farrar to sing Salome and Emma Eames to investigate Selika *in L'Africaine* showed something less than a complete grasp of the potentialities of the younger singer and the limitations of the elder. Also, his early ignorance of Caruso's rising fame and his subsequent negotiations with the tenor betrayed inexperience that amounted to an almost irretrievable fumble.

But he learned on the job. By bold and original strokes he laid up several treasures in the Metropolitan's annals. And his emphasis on stagecraft and discipline accomplished near miracles in those departments, which had hitherto received skimpy attention. Still, like other impresarios after him, he lost his fiercest battle: to put down the "star" system.

The very day his appointment was announced, on February 14, 1903, Conried presented a valentine to his directors and company in the form of a proclamation which bore undertones of a ukase. First, he would engage the best singers that money could buy, new ones among them—but he would subordinate stars to ensemble. "I warrant I can put a star on one night and an ensemble opera the next and draw as great a crowd."

Novelties there would be, new and entertaining works, he promised, but no more trips to Philadelphia nor one-night stands in Brooklyn. "The time spent catching cold on the cars and on extra work in public in the neighboring cities will be given to rehearsal."

Discipline, discipline, and yet more discipline. The ironfisted theatre monarch intended to wear no velvet glove to greet his prima donnas, threatening, "I am afraid the artists don't realize what downright rehearsals mean. . . . No one is absolutely necessary to success," he concluded. "If I felt dependent on any one person I should seek another as alternate or close up my theatre."

His firm outline wavered even before the first season had ended, and he was forced to eat many of his fine words. The regular visits to

Philadelphia were not abandoned, although reduced to twelve from twenty-one. Brooklyn automatically relieved his problem when its Academy of Music was destroyed by fire on November 30, 1903. As for the iron rod of discipline, Calvé and Gadski endured it for a season only, the Frenchwoman having become virtually her own law and the German grumbling: "Vocal artists cannot be bullied, driven or whipped into getting around for eight A.M. rehearsals like the little German actors of Conried's little German theatre." Eames could hardly expect to be among those present, as she had personally begged J. P. Morgan to keep the ideals of Grau alive. Nordica, led by the presence of Ternina for *Parsifal* to think that Conried did not need her, went off to tour with Damrosch, and again competed with the House by singing some of Kundry's music. Schumann-Heink had departed for similar reasons to Scheff's—a flier into musical comedy. The portly matron had recently acquired a coquettish way of singing that was hardly suitable to her voice, physique, or personality, commented *Musical America.* Too easy conquests of a public on tour led her to dreams of glamour; she joined a light opera called *Love's Lottery,* in which she played a charming young laundress, singing a saccharine ballad, "Sweet Thoughts of Home." Soberer thoughts of her proper place in the operatic scheme of things brought her back shortly to the Met. Gadski, Nordica, and Eames likewise eventually rejoined the faithful. Eames even succeeded in Conried's last season in securing a novelty of her own. Yearning to appear in Japanese garb and finding Madama Butterfly's kimono already occupied, Eames persuaded Conried to give her Mascagni's *Iris,* a bizarre Oriental story the composer had introduced to America in Philadelphia in 1902. (One of her quarrels subsequently with General Director Giulio Gatti-Casazza concerned his refusal to revive *Iris* for her, although he found it possible for Bori and Toscanini in 1914–15.) Scheff, having found her true kingdom, never returned. Others missing from Conried's initial lineup were Suzanne Adams, Eugenia Mantelli, Charles Gilibert, and the tiring Edouard de Reszke.

Irony of ironies, Conried became so dependent upon one single star that the promise to "get the best" was broken. In a reflection of his biases and temperament, he neglected the entire French gamut and some notable Italians, opening a large vacuum for the entrance of Oscar Hammerstein. This was perhaps Conried's most grievous mistake. Hammerstein would undoubtedly have pushed his way into the arena, but if Conried had taken advantage of all his opportunities, Oscar might have been denied the services of Mary Garden, Mario Sammarco, Charles Dalmorès, Hector Dufranne, Clotilde Bressler-Gianoli, Jeanne Gerville-Réache, and Giovanni Zenatello, while those who appeared later at the Met—Maurice Renaud, John McCormack, Luisa Tetrazzini, Maria Gay, Alessandro Bonci, Adamo Didur, and Amadeo Bassi—might have owed their first loyalty to Conried.

Conried's novelties numbered thirteen during his five years. To include *La Dame Blanche* (given as *Die weisse Dame*) would ruin the magic of the number thirteen, so Boieldieu's work may be omitted on a technicality: It had been performed by Walter Damrosch and the German company on tour in 1885.

Only thirteen members of the Metropolitan board were on hand in President George G. Haven's office on that Friday the thirteenth that settled Conried's fate. Seven of them were said to be for him; the other six were presumably fixed on Walter Damrosch.

As far as New York knew, all other contenders had dropped out. The list had been long and shifting in importance from day to day, one or more favorite sons occupying the limelight temporarily. Charles A. Ellis seemed to have a good chance—at least in Boston. Frederick Charles of the New Orleans French Opera commanded a Southern following. Theatrical personalities Daniel and Charles Frohman were mentioned. David Bispham cherished a momentary ambition, as we have seen. It was rumored that Henry Russell, who was just beginning to sniff around the edges of the operatic catnip in London, would enjoy the climate at Broadway and Thirty-ninth. (He later founded the Boston Opera Company and still aspired to the Metropolitan all the days of his life.) John Duss, a band leader who seems to have gained control over the Metropolitan orchestra and several singers, threatened through his manager, R. E. Johnson, to draw out these forces if he didn't get the job. Though Duss was never taken seriously, Henry W. Savage, who had been allowed to use the Metropolitan in 1901 with the only English-language company ever to grace its portals, gradually assumed the position of a real competitor.

And then there was George W. Wilson of Pittsburgh, who worked fiercely for the job, but who never stood a chance, even with the backing of seventy-six millionaires recruited by Andrew Carnegie. The object was to raise $150,000 capital for the new regime by March 1. Damrosch had already managed this with the help of Samuel Untermeyer, the eminent lawyer, and Jacob Schiff, a member of Kuhn, Loeb and Company, the latter, however, pledged to Damrosch only if Conried failed.

In a squeeze play possibly designed to eliminate Wilson—he could not help considering it as such—Haven got the Pittsburghian out of a sickbed on Lincoln's Birthday and informed him the capital was due the next day, when the board was to meet. In twenty-four feverish hours Wilson—and on a legal holiday at that—raised $200,000, cabling Charles M. Schwab, who was lazing at Cannes, and rallying a few other backers.

It seems obvious that New York plutocrats had no intention whatsoever of allowing Pittsburgh to encroach on their playground. One look at Conried's backers should have discouraged Wilson. Henry Morgenthau, Sr., headed the group, having been a patron at Conried's Irving Place Theatre. It was his sure knowledge that saved Conried from proposing as sole fellow backers the names of Thalman, Guggenheim, Guggenheimer, and Ickelheimer—"a wine list," derided the worldly lawyer, and one sure to antagonize most of the directors who were only just beginning to accept the Belmonts, originally Schönbergs, and the Morgenthaus, and would have balked at exclusively Jewish names. He suggested the sweetening of James Hazen Hyde, vice-president of the Equitable Life Assurance Company, Eliot Gregory, Henry Rogers Winthrop, George J. Gould (son of Jay), J. Henry Smith, William McIntyre, and Clarence H. Mackay. Among them were persons, as Haven admitted, who could not be ignored, proving Morgenthau right. To them were added three incumbent boxholders, Alfred G. Vanderbilt (who had become "head of the family" at Cornelius' death in 1899), Harry Payne Whitney, and Robert Goelet, who risked $10,000 each on the assurance that the opera was now entering a profit-making phase. Conried was their man. "We knew we were dealing with an assured success," is the way they put it.

Regardless of this tremendous accumulation of power and wealth, one New York critic always maintained that it was he who had tipped the balance in Conried's favor, Henry T. Finck boasted about it afterward. Not one to shy away from performers or public figures for fear that he might be considered prejudiced or even suborned, Finck made friends with his favorites.

"How would you like to be manager of the Metropolitan?" he is supposed to have asked Conried. Conried murmured something to the effect that he had never thought of it. (Whether this was early days or a mere show of modesty, Finck does not make clear.)

"Would you accept?" the critic pursued.

"Certainly!" answered the Irving Place Theatre manager.

"Then read the *Evening Post* tonight."

Finck did come out with editorials touting Conried for the position, maintaining that he would not sacrifice artistic to financial considerations (lip service that the directors were always pleased to echo, although they privately retained their conviction that opera should pay its way), and predicting that long tours for extra gain would be eschewed (a prophecy completely false, as Conried gave 275 performances out of town in his five years and would have racked up more had it not been for the San Francisco earthquake).

Conried's backers remained the core of the boxholders' group, to which was added a representative of Jacob Schiff, who pleaded the press of business as an excuse and sent along his junior partner by the name of Otto Hermann Kahn, later shortened to Otto H. Kahn, and even later to O. K.

It remains fascinating to speculate on the fate of the Metropolitan had the leadership fallen to Wilson and Carnegie or Damrosch and Untermeyer instead of Conried and Kahn. German opera would certainly have taken a front position and maintained it, for Carnegie adored Wagner, although his taste otherwise dropped to his native Scottish ballads and he attended opera performances in any language only spasmodically. As for Damrosch, Finck feared that he might produce a new work of his own almost every season and personally conduct all important performances, a prospect that did not fill the critic's soul with unmitigated joy.

Damrosch could not have foreseen doom as inevitable: his backing was good but his luck phenomenally bad. Shortly after the Metropolitan fiasco, he was turned down by the Pittsburgh Symphony in favor of Emil Paur. Wilson had apparently proposed his fellow Metropolitan contender for the job, but Pittsburgh rankled under Damrosch's aggressiveness and at least one faction, spearheaded by the Pittsburgh *Times,* had grown tired of Wilsoniana.

"Damrosch jumped at the hook before it was properly baited," is the way the *Times* described it, "and was lacerated in the effort to get away, meanwhile upsetting a whole kettle of fish."

Wilson, bitterly disappointed, as indignant and almost illegible scrawls about the unfavorable sector of the press in his scrapbook reveal, nevertheless went quietly back to the orchestra, but relinquished local management of the opera.

Damrosch continued his tangential course, after yielding his German chores to Alfred Hertz in 1902. He was never invited back to a regular season of the Metropolitan, although he presided at the premiere of his *Man Without a Country* in the Spring Season of 1937. Hertz had led Damrosch's earlier opera, *Cyrano de Bergerac,* in 1912–13. Damrosch's lasting fame came as conductor of the New York Symphony and the radio concerts for children he founded in later years.

At first, after the Conried victory, a rumor gained strong currency that because Damrosch's minority vote had loomed so large, he would be allowed to work in harness with Conried. Those who believed it didn't appreciate their new leader. That one immediately caused it to be known that his was a single-seated throne.

From the first days when he took over a theatre in Bremen, he had recognized no one above him, his biographer stated, and from then on "adopted an imperious manner which instilled confidence into those under him, but which gained him many enemies." The cloak of the cult of personality, which Grau had always avoided, fitted Conried's heavy shoulders snugly; his chest expanded proudly to show a cluster of decorations; he wore his hair thick, pompadoured and long, his heels high.

Because of the alterations to the stage made necessary by the *Parsifal* production, Conried has always received credit for these and for the redecoration accomplished in 1903, although Grau had had many of them in mind. Improvements to the stage included counterweights to fly scenery and a new floor with traps. A foyer was redone on the Grand Tier floor to accommodate those who did not occupy boxes. At the same time, the interior of the auditorium assumed the guise it has worn ever since—the lustrous gilding of tier façades molded in baroque plaster shapes, the wafflelike ceiling with the sunburst chandelier, the deep maroon of hangings and upholstery. A different proscenium arch greeted the first audience of 1903: The little doors on either side used for curtain calls had been closed up, the plaster molding became ornate, the corners were softly rounded and panels inserted which bore the proud names of Mozart, Verdi, Wagner, Gounod, and (rather oddly, considering their slight contribution to the operatic life of the House) Beethoven and Gluck. Historians have pointed out that only three seasons in the Met's history have included works by all six—1891–92, 1895–96, and 1940–41. The *Musical Courier* remarked that the new curtain opened sideways instead of being raised.

The authors of this fresh elegance were John M. Carrère and Thomas Hastings, who had been influenced by apprenticeship to the noblest of architects, McKim, Mead and White, creators of many new Renaissance façades throughout the city. Carrère and Hastings helped to remake the New York scene with the Public Library to replace the reservoir at Forty-second and Fifth Avenue, the New Theatre, which was to involve Metropolitan fortunes, and the Frick mansion, later to become a museum, as well as notable contributions to other cities, including the Senate and House office buildings in Washington. Their choice of the Vanderbilt colors for the opera house did not necessarily reflect slavish imitation, for appropriateness to opera of red and gold has seldom been questioned.

With its usual waspishness, the *Musical Courier* added a few details: the ushers had new uniforms but no idea of the location of seats; there was a fresh cake of ice in the cooler on the main floor and the dents had been smoothed out of the near silver cups (this was long before the age of paper); and the boxes were still numbered on the side toward the audience, like so many horse stalls. This bit of convenience seems never to have been mentioned before or since.

If another of Conried's innovations had survived him the Metropolitan would have had its opera school all along, a kind of farm system as in baseball, to train young people for the big leagues. Several of the fifty gifted girls (few men enrolled) later graduated into the House roster, among them Henriette Wakefield, Jeanne Jomelli, Lucy Call, and Jane Freund, a protégée of Felix Mottl. *Parsifal's* Flower Maidens, various relatives of Madama Butterfly, and sundry bit parts came their way. Conried's brand of discipline prevailed. At least one neophyte agreed wholeheartedly; when to Blanche Yurka fell the part of the Grail-bearer in *Parsifal*, the aspiring singer and future well-known actress fasted all day before her holy duty.

If Pittsburgh could not furnish a manager, at least it spawned a press agent for the Metropolitan. Gustave Schlotterbeck, who had taken over the opera's visits from Wilson and whose effusions in the *Post* had delighted or disgusted Pittsburgh readers, brought a new purple hue to the doings at the Met that matched—even surpassed—Conried's flamboyance, though he valued his own efforts merely as "vigorous, intelligent and absolutely truthful." Conried admired his bustling energy and could not have been displeased at being described as "Rejuvenator of the Opera," who had swept aside all obstacles, "striving sleeplessly for *Ideality of Performance* [his italics]."

New York had reveled in his involved, inverted, and infinitely ornamental language at least once before, when the *Sun* picked up one of his reviews: "Nervously, even violently intent all day yesterday were the heartstrings of nearly 10,000 opera patrons. . . . Quickened was the flow of blood by the thrill of heaven-scaling ensembles and of solo performances that were spangled with the diamond light of pristine brilliance. High were [*sic*] the beating of the waves of enthusiasm which washed from the auditorium across the footlights and immersed soloists, orchestra and chorus. . . ." The *Sun* commented wryly: "In the waves, what happened to the footlights?"

For Sembrich, the "seven-mooned coloratura," the very air was drunken—"it staggered, heaved, reeled and rolled . . . from her throat issued such tones as put the flush of deep-seated envy upon the rich limpidezza of the mellow-voiced flute."

Though he was soon succeeded by Charles Henry Meltzer as publicity man for the House, Schlotterbeck's own effervescence enveloped the opera company for as long as the 100,000 booklets he prepared for the *Parsifal* tour remained cherished bits of memorabilia. Their sixty-four pages were almost equally divided between the spiritual (the story of the consecrated play, of Conried and his new Opera School, and sketches of the artists and personnel) and the crassly material (a lady in camisole and petticoat demonstrating C. B. foundation garments or the display of an elegantly appointed bathroom by the Standard Sanitary Mfg. Co. of Pittsburgh among the more modest pianos, autos, and champagne advertised for sale). Its cover displayed a luscious nymph with flowing golden hair and artfully careless drapery, holding aloft a gold trumpet twice as tall as she. Down a shaft of light floated a bird which combined the best features of a dove (white feathers and a gentle expression) and a swan (longish neck). At the bottom of the cone of light rested a ruby-red urn.

The "Rape of Parsifal," as Finck unblushingly called it, occupied the entire country for two years. When Conried announced that he would perform the *Bühnenweihfestspiel* ("Stage Dedication Festival Play") against the expressed interdiction of Cosima Wagner, who had fiercely guarded the Master's last work as exclusive to Bayreuth, a storm broke out that has never been equaled in intensity and duration in the musical world. Two opposing camps at once threw up bastions labeled, respectively, "Religion" and "Law." Ministers took to their pulpits to denounce the "sacrilege"; attorneys prepared to defend Cosima against this "audacious [German] Barnum"; critics took sides, for and against, on both religious and musical grounds; Finck fought valiantly for what he called the "liberation" of the opera, which he considered purely as opera, and not a churchly mumbo jumbo.

To its new American audiences, *Parsifal* held the further attraction of inspiring in others, while embodying in itself, a curious ambivalence. It represented good and evil; the act of performing it placated Mammon while the trumpets sounded to call the faithful. Because of its complications and mystic overtones, its employment of the leitmotif and the symbolical, *Parsifal* cried out for more preparation of the lay mind than any work before it—even Wagner's *Ring* dramas. Not that many knew what they were arguing about; ignorance and misapprehension appeared even in the highest places. Bishop Frederick Burgess of the Episcopal Diocese of Long Island carried the banner for the church without ever mentioning the offending name of the opera:

Old stories of the Holy Grail sprang up in an age full of childlike yet sincere faith. . . . [Now they are] introduced by men who declare themselves pagans to make a background for magnificent stage scenes. . . . The stage today has proclaimed itself a substitute for the pulpit . . . no fine acting can blot out the undertone of sacrilege. Surely this is blasphemy against the Holy Ghost!

Another Protestant dignitary was revolted by the idea that Christ's person, as well as the blood, would be shown. Both Conried and William J. Henderson sprang to answer this, pointing to the absence of any such scenes in the opera. Conried added testily that he wished the attackers would pay Wagner the civility of reading the text before girding their loins for battle. Furthermore, although one Catholic authority also thought Christ actually appeared as Parsifal and decided not to "take our ideas of what is sacred and what is not from these Protestant clergymen," another brought comparative comfort to Conried by asserting that the church "never thinks of confounding a series of medieval legends, no matter how close the verisimilitude, with the sacrifice of the mass instituted by Christ."

The *Musical Courier,* from which Huneker had recently departed, was carrying on a running campaign against Conried and all his works, rising to its highest pitch of righteous indignation at the "piracy." When at last Conried's legal position was upheld, the courts judging that because the opera score had been published and sold, even in America, and because no copyright agreement existed between Germany and the United States, it could not be restricted, the *Courier* loftily retreated into a moral stronghold, asking, "Has the ethical problem been met?" and deciding that there was "no way to escape from the offense committed against morality and ethics. Punishment is bound to come," the oracle concluded darkly.

Conried felt no pangs of conscience; retribution did not arrive from that source—or any other. As for the "first class American commercial venture" the *Courier* accused him of conducting, the $183,608 said to have accrued from the eleven sold-out nonsubscription performances in the House at prices raised to $10 and the $167,000 from sixteen cities on the road were sweet punishment indeed—not to mention the extra performance that Conried designated as his own benefit and from which he pocketed the entire proceeds.

Aimé Gerber relates how Conried locked him up in a special room to handle the mail orders which swamped the regular box office. His sole duty was "to take the money from one envelope and put it into another," with an apology from the management. Conried came in from time to time to show some friend just how much money he was obliged to return. He was also proud of the swollen payroll occasioned by *Parsifal,* and would spread out the long sheets of extra wages on his office floor to show the visitor.

Cosima never relented; her bile extended to the singers who had shared in the rapine. They would never be allowed in Bayreuth again.

This hit hard at Alois Burgstaller, Conried's Parsifal, who had been cherished at the Master's shrine. Olive Fremstad too felt the bane of the "Bayreuth curse," while Lillian Nordica, already under the displeasure of the chatelaine, had sworn never to go back anyway. Milka Ternina, the Met's first Kundry, was not affected, as she retired soon after. Others in that first cast were Anton Van Rooy as Amfortas, Robert Blass as Gurnemanz, Otto Goritz as Klingsor, and Marcel Journet as Titurel. Alfred Hertz conducted.

Underneath the raging controversy over rights and rites, another dilemma occupied the average operagoer. The *Times* labeled it "Question of Attire." What to wear to a performance that began at five P.M., suspended for a dinner period of an hour and a half, and resumed at 8:45? Evening dress? "Yes," said Conried. "No," protested tailors and dressmakers. There was endless speculation whether King Edward VII had ever dressed for so early a performance. Some tailors advised renting hotel rooms in which to change and catch a bite of supper. One seamstress vowed that an evening gown would be positively indecent at that daylight hour. She nearly fainted at the "awful nudity of it, the blazing impropriety."

As for dining, "Take a bar of chocolate and eat it in the theatre," one suggested, "as *Parsifal* is religious anyway, and fasting is appropriate." To avoid picnicking basket parties in the House, tables were set up in one foyer "like a railroad lunch counter," was the derogatory comment, where a selection of delicacies could be purchased a la carte. (When the time came, only a few daringly brought their lunch and ate it in their seats, a practice from then till now deplored by the management.)

After the week of anxiety, curiosity, and preparation (Walter Damrosch led the bank of proselyters who lectured far and wide, endeavoring to lighten the mysteries and probe the esoterics), Christmas Eve morning, 1903, dawned fair in spite of the curses of those who saw the ultimate in sacrilege at Conried's unfeeling choice of this day of days.

When the performance had ended, close to midnight, *Parsifal* was an established fact of musical life, never again to rouse quite so great a commotion. It would be judged now on its musical and dramatic merits as one of the masterpieces of all time. Excerpts had been familiar for quite a while, and the *cognoscenti* had heard concert performances, but the impact of the total production impressed deeply all those who experienced it. It was, as the *Times* admitted, "in many aspects one of the most important and significant" events, stirring the imagination of the whole musical world. Its artistic value was judged to be the highest; equality with Bayreuth not an impossibility. This went far to justify Conried's boldness, and nobly crowned many months' work.

As for that perplexing matter of dress, society settled it in many ways. Mrs. Astor simply did not show up; nor did E. T. Gerry and R. T. Wilson; still in the country were W. K. Vanderbilt, the Webbs and Whitneys. Mrs. Warren and several other women without their husbands wore street dress but did not return in the evening. Among those who carried through in the same costumes were Mrs. Cornelius Vanderbilt in black velvet with a silk beaver hat, Mrs. Baylies in black lace pailletted in gold (rich but not too gaudy for the occasion) and a small black hat with long white plume. Many merely removed their hats as a token of the shades of evening, but Mrs. Ogden Mills made a complete change. So did those men who possessed a good valet and a motorcar or fast horses.

Although the Germans sat in glory, a sprinkling of black-moustached Italians could be seen in the galleries. When several started to applaud in contradiction to the request to refrain, three quarters of the balcony rose and glared. Even when the wild Kundry, clad in skins and with disheveled hair, came galloping madly in, silence was as of the grave, a paper reported.

Conried had justified himself to the directors, who promptly sent him a special resolution of appreciation and admiration, said Finck, who always seemed to know these inner workings of the management.

The ultimate accolade descended on Wagner's consecrational work when many of the newborn that winter were named Parsifal. An usher called McGillicuddy, whose wife gave birth on December 23, provided the most irresistible combination.

One generation's shock becomes humdrum to another. *Parsifal* has come to be routine, though given on Good Friday, whether as religious or theatrical tradition it would not always be easy to say. A reverent atmosphere still surrounds the Festival Play (music drama?), and applause is discouraged except after the second act's decidedly worldly caperings.

But if Wagner's last work came to be accepted with no aftermath of scandal, Richard Strauss's early opus immediately ran aground on the shoals of piety. Conried had counted on *Salome* to rank with *Parsifal* as profitable sensations. With a showman's instinct and an eye to the box office, he had wanted to remove the scheduled performances from the subscription, giving to the directors the tactful reason that he wished "to avoid imposing [the work] on any unwilling listener, and to present it only to those purposely going to hear it." Also, the prevailing winds told him of possible objections to some of the more explicit details of Wilde's libretto. He had ignored warnings from the pulpit about *Parsifal*; perhaps he should have realized the difference in the present case. Audiences that still had difficulty in accepting *La Bohème* and *La Traviata* might not be prepared to go many steps farther into morbidity. Furthermore, his usual bad sense of timing, which had led him to throw *Parsifal* into the holy atmosphere of Christmas Eve, prompted him to hold a dress rehearsal on Sunday, January 20, 1907, allowing his directors to proceed to Herod's degenerate court directly from church. He showed still another error in judgment by making his first-night audience wait for its titillation until anticipation dwindled, by prefacing the *pièce de résistance* with a "miscellaneous" concert that dragged on and on, involving a quartet from *Fidelio*, Farrar and Scotti in a duet from *Don Giovanni*, Homer and Louise Kirkby-Lunn in the "Barcarolle" from *Tales of Hoffmann*, Celestina Boninsegna and Riccardo Stracciari in a duet from *Rigoletto*, Caruso, Marie Rappold, and Lina Cavalieri in arias, and the final trio from *Faust* sung by Bessie Abott, Charles Rousselière, and Marcel Journet. The only near approach to appropriateness was a brace of Strauss songs by Sembrich.

Still unconscious of the tidal wave building up in his board of directors, Conried announced additional showings after the first and proceeded to sell a good many tickets to the curious. Three days after the January 22 premiere, the ax fell. *Salome* must be withdrawn. Even the prospect of repaying more than $25,000 costs did not deter the moralists. J. P. Morgan, whose daughter, Mrs. Herbert Satterlee, has always been credited with the instigation of the successful interdict, offered to pay for his family's prejudices out of his own pocket, but Conried (and the ones who took his side, notably Otto Kahn, Robert Goelet, R. L. Cottenet, James Speyer, and Henry Rogers Winthrop) preferred full martyrdom. Herodias' wayward daughter was seen no more at the Metropolitan for twenty-seven years, although patrons and papers could transfer outrage if they so desired to Oscar Hammerstein, who introduced Mary Garden in ten unforgettable performances a bare two years later. New York soon began to take the horror piece in stride although the sign "Banned in Boston" was slapped on it by Mayor "Honey Fitz" Fitzgerald (grandfather of President John F. Kennedy).

The lurid premiere of the opera cannot be said to have scored exactly a critical success. The words "degeneracy," "moral stench," "repulsive," "gruesome," "abhorrent," "diseased and polluted," "bestially perverted" splattered from various pens to describe the story, virtually blotting out what appreciation existed for the music. Even Finck, generally Conried's champion, was one of the most violent assailants of this "operatic monstrosity." Krehbiel found three moments of beauty, two purely instrumental, the third the finale, "in which an impulse, which can only be conceived as rising from the utmost pit of degradation, is beatified." Olive Fremstad, who had been one of Conried's shining acquisitions from the start, gave up the part of Isolde to study Salome so that this season she did not add that impersonation in which she became supreme to the Sieglinde, Venus, Fricka (*Rheingold*), Kundry, and Brünnhilde (*Siegfried*) that had already ranked her high in Wagnerian rolls. Salome's music, she thought, made Wagner sound like Mozart. She confessed to her biographer, Mary Watkins, that her amorous approach to the severed head of John the Baptist gave her some trouble, for the prepared head looked exactly like her father's. When she carried the "silver salver" with its grisly burden, she staggered a little, because, she explained, a human head is very heavy. She had gone to the morgue to find out for herself.

One bit of realism Fremstad could not inject was the dance itself. No matter how thick the seven veils, Salome's writhings were not for the substantial soprano. The prima ballerina, Bianca Froelich, took over, while Herodias' daughter temporarily retired to the sidelines.

It remains for one final barb to be thrown from across the seas. Ernest Newman, writing in the Birmingham *Daily Post,* was quoted in the *Musical Courier*:

> It is only to be expected that the immaculate moral instincts of New York, city of Mr. Hearst and the yellow press and Tammany, and the gentle art of Congress lobbying and decorous criminal courts . . . where Mr. Rockefeller just invited Mr. Aked to preach denunciation of those who rob the widow and orphan and grind the faces of the poor—would revolt against *Salome.*

In addition to all the moral stewing over *Salome,* Conried had revealed what some called bad taste and others sheer greed by marking the premiere for his annual "benefit," as he had done with *Parsifal* in his first season. Because he personally owned their contracts, Conried requested his artists to appear once a season for his own profit. With *Fledermaus* and *Gypsy Baron,* the former operetta producer had simply gone too far. Critical judgment might not have fallen so heavily on *Fledermaus* had it not been for the air of extortion that hung over Prince Orlovsky's salon, with a "vaudeville turn," in which even the most dignified members of the company joined in entertaining the nobleman's guests. The presentation was "inflated beyond the market value of operetta," remarked Henderson sarcastically. Three subscription performances were added at regular prices and without trimmings. *Gypsy Baron* showed its comic face but once. A later manager would dare equally in introducing these two lilting pieces to Metropolitan audiences, even with saucy interpolations, but at least the artists got—and the manager too—their regular money.

11

Curtains for Conried

It has been remarked that a spirit of commercialism has prevailed here during the present regime. This criticism is unjust and foolish. I shared in the profits of the company more than any other person; so, if I had run this opera house in such a way as to make the financial results as large as possible, if I had managed it with primary regard for the dollars, I assure you that I could have made a fortune by my share of its profits and salary.

—Heinrich Conried,
quoted by his biographer, Montrose J. Moses

If Conried is remembered for his daring in introducing *Parsifal* and *Salome,* those two German operas of such different aspect, he found an even more prominent niche in the musical hall of fame for an accomplishment he had not intended—the acquisition of the most famous and beloved opera star ever to glorify the Metropolitan's annals.

The Metropolitan almost missed Enrico Caruso. A contract he had signed with Grau—after a good many misunderstandings and on Caruso's part a reluctance to transact business through an agent—lay on Conried's desk when he took over. But as Conried's biographer admitted, "when he became Impresario [Conried] was ignorant of most musical matters and had never heard of the great Italian tenor." Alessandro Bonci was his objective. Then he heard one of Caruso's recordings in Europe. The negotiations from then on resembled a spider web of cables, conversations with intermediaries (notably one Pasquale Simonelli, an Italian banker in New York, who eventually received a 3 percent commission and other profits, only to become estranged from and much later reconciled with the tenor), and indecisions on both parts. At last an agreement was reached, giving Caruso twenty-five performances (instead of the forty Grau had promised), with the proviso that there would be more if the public liked him.

This vital question, as well as the attitude of the critics, was not resolved at first. It may seem astonishing in retrospect that Caruso's career did not begin with a bolt of lightning. After his debut as the Duke in *Rigoletto* on November 23, 1903, the stars did not reel from their

154

orbits, the sun came up precisely as scheduled. And the daily papers also came out cool and unscorched.

The figure they had seen on the stage was, as P. V. R. Key wrote in Caruso's biography, "undeniably fat." His appearance was "decidedly plebeian; his manners had not in them anything to commend." Nervousness beset him in the realization that his crucial test before the first opera house in the world lay ahead; "an indifferent reception, regardless of other fields which still called him, could not be set imperialistically aside." Fortunately, the pendulum was swinging "across a propitious arc"— America was ready for just such a tenor. The shades of Jean de Reszke, though still hovering, would be dissipated very soon.

It took a week and five days. The "indisposition" that attacked Caruso for a week after his debut could well have been induced by Krehbiel's patronizing lines:

Signor Caruso has many of the tiresome Italian vocal affectations, and when he neglects to cover his tones, as he always does when he becomes strenuous, his voice becomes pallid. But he is generally a manly singer, with a voice that is true, of fine quality and marvelous endurance.

On the other hand, Caruso may have been slightly encouraged by W. J. Henderson in the *Sun,* who gave him full marks for vocal qualities but faint praise for acting. Richard Aldrich, who had succeeded Henderson on the *Times* in 1902, may be pursued from his first estimate of the new voice as "of large power but inclined to take on the 'white' quality in its upper register," to the judgment, after an *Aida* a week later, that he showed remarkable mastery over the voice, skill of technique and manifold resources, flexibility and expressiveness, and authoritative marks of the adept in stagecraft. His Cavaradossi moved both audience and critics greatly. Aldrich eventually capitulated after the *Bohème* of December 5: "For the first time he showed supreme beauty of a voice and perfection of style. Now we know what Mr. Caruso's voice really is." The King had mounted his throne, never to depart until summoned by a higher power. Finck undignified the opera house as a "Carusel" during the tenor's long reign. How ignominiously the impresario had retreated from his early emulation of Louis XV, when he had cried: "Formerly it was the star who managed the opera house; now it is I!"

Bound to the chariot wheels of stardom, not only by the natural phenomenon of public craving, but also by his own agreement with the board of directors, which went even further than Grau's by committing him to two favorites in each subscription performance and no more than four performances of Wagner on Monday nights, Conried perforce continued to search for new singers who would add the element later known as personality to their artistic qualifications. He did not find it in Aino Acté, an Eva and Micaela for two seasons, nor in Bella Alten, who lingered on usefully in lyric roles, however, until the First World War. Nor was Maria de Macchi exciting in the only Metropolitan performance ever of Donizetti's *Lucrezia Borgia*. Ernest Kraus, an excellent singer, nevertheless looked to one observer like a huge armadillo in his vast Siegfried armor. However, Otto Goritz, the dramatic German baritone, the first Klingsor out of Bayreuth, gave outstanding value to Conried, and to Gatti-Casazza after him, until the war. Heinrich Knote (whose only peculiarity seemed to be his extreme formality; he was wont to address everyone by both name and title) embodied Tristan and an occasional Lohengrin and Walther admirably for three seasons; and Carl Burrian would persist as *Heldentenor* until 1913 in what amounted to a virtual galaxy of this species.

Four American girls won distinct places. Bessie Abott, who was hailed as Jean de Reszke's pupil, sang the Micaela in the portentous San Francisco *Carmen* and made a slender and appealing Marguerite. Edyth Walker, a splendid Amneris, Ortrud, Brangäne, and Erda, earned a tribute to her voice from Schlotterbeck: "Pass your hand over a strip of heavy Wilton velvet until neither wrinkle nor fold is left, and it lies before you, soft and lovely to the touch as pigeon wings. Polish a tube of heavy crystal glass [etc., etc.], and fill it with fluid of deep, rich lilac hue. . . ." For her, Conried revived Donizetti's *La Favorita* in 1905 with Caruso and Scotti, and she sang in one season's revival of *La Gioconda* with Nordica, Homer, Caruso, and Plançon.

Marion Weed, who had studied with Lilli Lehmann and sung in three Bayreuth festivals, made her debut in 1903 as the Brünnhilde in *Walküre,* played Herodias in the short-lived *Salome,* flouted Cosima Wagner by singing Kundry, and was the first Gertrude in Humperdinck's *Hänsel und Gretel,* with the composer present.

Edyth Walker left Conried in 1906 because he would not allow her to sing soprano roles; the Hamburg Opera did, and she had the satisfaction of doing both Salome and Elektra, as well as Octavian and Kly-temnestra (creating the latter at Covent Garden), Ortrud, Kundry, Isolde, and the three Brünnhildes, a record that should have borne a New York stamp. She would have gone to the Chicago Opera but for the war; later she lived in New York and filled out a useful life as a revered teacher.

Marie Rappold, who became an American by virtue of moving to Brooklyn from London, still showed her native German talent in several of the oddities that Conried and Gatti-Casazza designated as "novel." She divorced Dr. Julius Rappold in 1913 and married the *Heldentenor* Rudolf Berger, who, with Alois Burgstaller, Jacques Urlus, and Carl Jörn or Johannes Sembach, gave Wagnerian casts a high polish for two seasons. Berger's heart failed in his own personal *Götterdämmerung* ten days after a performance as Siegfried on February 18, 1915. Rappold stayed on with the company until 1920, then went guesting, and settled in California, where she died in 1957.

Conried's true exotic, the ravishing beauty who troubled the very air with her passage, came as a curiosity and remained as an irritant. Lina Cavalieri had sold flowers on street corners in Rome, sung in cafés, and reached the Folies Bergère as a pinnacle, meanwhile accumulating a trail of Russian princes whose only objective in life seemed to be to set her down on a fine cushion and admire her. Her operatic reputation also trailed through cities in Italy, Poland, and Russia. When she arrived in New York in 1906, along with her first objectives of making sure that her costumes were in good repair and that Conried properly appreciated her repertoire, she scouted the eligibles of American royalty—the merchant princes—and soon lighted on a collateral of the Astor clan, who proved fatally susceptible. Robert Astor Chanler married her in Paris in 1908. The Chanlers were all eccentrics. A few showed the only touch of genius since Founding Father John Jacob I. Their oddness stretched to studying Buddhism and Bahai, establishing prizes for young Americans to study in Paris, running safaris, marrying actresses and princesses (one Chanler girl went so far as to wed the *Times* music critic, Richard Aldrich), entering politics, becoming pacifists and vegetarians, and entering a thousand other colorful avenues of escape from the ordinary. John Armstrong Chanler even landed in Bloomingdale (the current retreat from reality several times employed by New York millionaires to be rid

of a troublesome scion), but escaped to write sonnets against the split
skirt and brutality to English suffragettes and a canto to the cockroaches
which protected him against bedbugs at Bloomingdale. He was a close
friend of Architect Stanford White, so that when he shot a man in what
was considered "justifiable homicide," the *Evening Post* was reminded of
White's death at the hands of Harry Thaw. But the paper was unwise to
remark that "the latest prominent assassin had the rare foresight to have
himself declared insane before he shot his man." Chaloner (as he called
himself by then) sued and got $175,000, according to Wayne Andrews in
The Vanderbilt Legend.

Why should any of the Chanler clan cavil at Bob's marriage? The
jeering question, "Who's looney now?" which has passed into public
domain, was attributed both to Harry Thaw and John A. Chanler; it is
certainly apposite to the latter's view of Bob's liaison. Lina demanded
Bob's entire fortune; when the family rallied and stiffened her bride-
groom's spine, she left him after one week. Bob forlornly took to painting
and became fashionable for bizarre creations.

Than the Chanlers, the biographer summed up, could be found no
finer specimens of blooded, moneyed aristocracy, "each a classic example
of energetic idleness, high-spirited with nothing important to do," so that
their talent was "twisted into fantasy."

The Met board's feeling of repugnance to Lina was further heightened by the rumor that a young Vanderbilt also cherished fond ambitions
for her. Oscar Hammerstein took her on his list for the express purpose
of infuriating the rival company, after she had served two terms with
Conried. The latter brought three novelties for her: Puccini's *Manon
Lescaut,* which fulfilled critics' prophecies as being the only likely contender for steady repetition; Giordano's *Fedora,* in which she made her
debut on December 5, 1906, and which even in its later revival for
Jeritza still was associated in Krehbiel's mind with Cavalieri's "Hogar-
thian curves"; and Cilea's *Adriana Lecouvreur,* which opened the 1907–8
season. In all three she was surrounded with prime casts headed by
Caruso and Scotti. She also sang an occasional Mimi and Nedda. She had
never even rehearsed Tosca when Conried threw her in for Eames a month
or so after her debut. But realizing the effectiveness of the role, she
polished it until Hammerstein later allowed her to show her gifts as the

Roman singer she aspired to be. Andrés de Segurola describes the scene in his unpublished manuscript, "Through My Monocle":

In the second act, [she appeared] in a long cape of the bestest snow-white Caucasian ermine artistically wrapped around her body, neck to feet. . . . For a few moments she stood motionless against the frame of the door. But when in a graceful motion she nonchalantly let the cloak slip on a nearby chair, 3,000 persons in the audience saw that vision of glowing white satin and luscious flesh, topped by deep green emeralds of her tiara, necklace and brooch, a wave of exclamations, gasps and interjections roared over, completely disregarding the orchestral perorations.

Her voice seems not to have been important one way or the other. It was described as light, lyric, pretty in quality, but not rich or vibrant— serviceable enough for Oscar Hammerstein, who used her as a pawn in his battle with Conried. He also set her off against Mary Garden, promising her publicly a share in the role of Thaïs, which Mary considered her own property, and thus "opening another chapter in New York's Operatic Book of Scandal," wrote Krehbiel. The *Tribune* critic described Mary's reaction, hiring a lawyer "to protect her monopoly of the privilege of displaying her physical charms with the scantiest garments allowable to the public gaze." The case became in a double sense *nudum pactum,* he added. And Miss Garden, who "always informed Oscar Hammerstein through that favorite medium of communication between artists and managers, the newspapers,"—won her point and continued to be the only Thaïs (with one important exception) until Geraldine Farrar "threw her garments into the ring at the Metropolitan in 1917." America saw Cavalieri again as the second wife of the exquisite tenor, Lucien Muratore, not singing but watching her husband jealously from a Boston Opera stage box as he made love in *Monna Vanna* to his first wife, Marguerite Bériza, who had gleefully substituted for Mary Garden. Muratore went the way of the divorce court in 1927; Cavalieri married once again, but lived in retirement in Paris, then Florence, retaining her beauty far into age. She was crushed to death in the rubble of an air raid in 1944, a tragic end to her flamboyant passage through the operatic and society worlds.

A jewel destined to be firmly fixed in the Metropolitan's crown found its place on the opening night of November 26, 1906, when Geraldine Farrar of Melrose, Massachusetts, returned to her native land after captivating European centers, notably the Court in Berlin. This saucy lass had everything in her favor—a youthful beauty that delighted the eye, a voice "curiously rich in what sound experts call 'color,' " the allure of a graceful and winning personality, and the will of a Cleopatra. To this was added a Yankee shrewdness that she attributed to her mother, allowing that matron in later years to take over (by remote control after her death) the touchy parts in an autobiography, entitled *Such Sweet Compulsion,* that purported to tell all. Framing this enticing picture were the ill-concealed rumors of the press, which went as far as they dared in suggesting that she had been the intimate of the German Crown Prince. Actually she had been a favorite with the Kaiser and a frequent visitor to Potsdam, even after the Crown Prince married Kronprinzessin Cäcilie of Brunswick. The Kaiser had made her a *Kammersängerin,* which strengthened the rumors; "Mother" admitted that Geraldine was an audacious flirt. When the two arrived in New York aboard the liner *Kaiser Wilhelm II* to the accompaniment of a press furore, Geraldine smiled at everything, admitted nothing. The groundwork could not have been better laid for her debut.

For once, a star *was* born on an opening night. Henry T. Finck insisted three years later in his book *Success in Music and How It Is Won* that his review (in the *Evening Post*) was almost the only favorable one of her Juliette, but the facts belie him. Aldrich in the *Times* mentioned her youthful charm, skill, and resource in stagecraft and full, rich soprano, "lyric in its nature and flexibility." Krehbiel came to terms at once, stating flatly that she achieved a place "among those whom a Metropolitan audience recognizes as in the forefront of the world's operatic artists," and added the words "beautiful," "exquisite quality," "vibrant," "eager" in the right places. Even Henderson, perhaps because as Finck says he loved to ruffle or pull out her beautiful feathers, admitted her impact, and questioned: "What may this girl not do?" Such serpentine grace had not been observed, he added, since Mrs. Leslie Carter and Bernhardt; such lovemaking since the age of Calvé. In a jest more worthy of Finck he concluded: "She might go Farrar and fare worse." It seems impossible to believe Finck's assertion that if Conried had not sided with him, Farrar's contract might have been canceled after her fourth performance.

Farrar's first contract with Conried fulfilled most of her terms, but only after a lengthy struggle. "I could take some things on faith," she said, "but not assertions where rival sopranos had prior claims. . . . It matters little if a board member favors a pretty singer, a critic is enamored of an artist's special interpretation or a social hostess pushes a protégé toward the limelight. In the end, willy-nilly, the public decides." So Geraldine worked toward being presented to the public in the light she considered best. Her first season produced the Butterfly and Marguerite that would endure, Mimi and Nedda that would appear occasionally, but only one Elisabeth in New York (several on the road) in the *Tannhäuser* that she favored above all. Her teacher Lilli Lehmann had coached her in the Wagner role and set it for her permanently. The grand old lady had also forced restraint on Farrar's too-generous gestures by tying her hands behind her back hours on end.

It was not until a change of regime that the determined young American wrested certain privileges from the management—to secure prior rights to roles on subscription nights; to pay no agent's commissions whatever for recordings or tours; to refuse at her own option to go on spring tours so as to be able to fulfill her Berlin obligations; and a crowning triumph that no one before her—and only Kirsten Flagstad afterward—clinched: her own dressing room with its key. This was an airless cubicle, Number 17, on the women's side, which had previously been a storeroom. Here at least she could store her priceless costumes and install all the comforts of a boudoir, and go away and lock it up!

Charles Rousselière played her Roméo at that first night and later companioned her in Gounod's *Faust* and Berlioz' *Damnation of Faust* (which persisted exactly as long as the tenor—one season). She did not join the partnership that was to spell sold-out houses and frantic demonstrations thereafter until the *Madama Butterfly* premiere of February 11, 1907. Caruso was her Pinkerton. Already in the niche from which nothing and no one could dislodge him, the tenor had yielded to Farrar the opening night in 1906, the only one of his Metropolitan career on which he did not appear. She had met him first when they both were to make debuts in *Bohème* at Monte Carlo in March 1904. An apparition walked into the first rehearsal, she wrote, "clad in shrieking checks, topped by a grey fedora, yellow gloves grasping a gold-headed cane. A happy smile illumined a jolly face, which was punctuated by the two largest black eyes I had ever seen. Fresh from South American triumphs, this young phenomenon was affable and pleasant to us all." She almost forgot to sing, so mesmerized was she by that thrilling voice. They became almost invariably good colleagues, with only a rare falling-out. Finck denies that Farrar once slapped "King Enrico," but the chastisement is confirmed by a present-day patron, Walter Sands Marvin, who delighted in playing super in his young days and who witnessed the *lèse-majesté* from the stage. Caruso, it seems, had an uncontrollable need to expectorate and proceeded to this routine measure, but over the soprano's shoulder in the midst of a loving embrace. The offended Geraldine hauled off and whacked her lover with a certain amount of understandable passion. But they remained friends, although the handsome woman must have chafed at Caruso's cartoons which usually showed her with ugly, open mouth and horrendous teeth.

In her second season with Conried, Farrar added another Marguerite, that of Boito's *Mefistofele,* thus becoming the only soprano in the House to sing all three heroines, *Mefistofele* was given chiefly to show off Feodor Chaliapin, but probably the management did not expect as much of him as appeared. Audiences gasped at the sight of the basso's huge frame, stripped—"to the rump," said Krehbiel—except for a loincloth and painted gray. A "raree" show Krehbiel thought it, drawing on the Savoyards' use of the Hindu term for a cheap street exhibition. When he sang in Philadelphia, a newspaper aptly called the performance the "naked truth." New York also dismissed as vulgar the Russian's habit of hawking and spewing as Don Basilio in *Barber,* and professed to find his Leporello very low comedy indeed. America evidently was not ready for Chaliapin.

As his success did not measure up to the usual European hysteria, Farrar says, he "dissolved in a huge Russian pout all winter." The complete capitulation to his Boris had to wait a baker's dozen of years.

Geraldine was the Zerlina in one 1908 *Don Giovanni* made touch and go by the Russian's pranks and his mischievous habit of reverting to his Slavic language for Leporello's recitatives. Scotti, the Don, and Gadski, the Donna Elvira, showed understandable irritation. The rest of the cast (which bore the unmistakable stamp of latter-day Golden Age) were not affected—Eames, Bonci, Baracchi and Blass. The burden lay heaviest on Gustav Mahler, already doomed by the illness that encroached rapidly, and sensitive, irascible, and difficult, says the soprano.

The acquisition in 1907 of Mahler, one of the true twinklers in Conried's chaplet, marked a new and glistening aura of beauty and authority from the orchestra pit, one, alas! in which he shared only briefly after he inaugurated it. Alfred Hertz still exhorted the brass wildly in the German repertoire, but to Mahler he yielded the *Tristan, Walküre, Siegfried,* and *Fidelio* for one season only. *Don Giovanni* rejoined in a rebirth under this magician, all the more extraordinary for its brevity— incredibly Mozart's masterpiece was not heard again at the Metropolitan until 1929.

Mahler had felt a great release of spirit in his first contacts with the Metropolitan. He had left a hidebound Vienna Opera, where every cor- ridor wall bristled with official memos, and found the New York House, orchestra, and singers marvelous. So testified his wife, Alma, in two sub- sequent books, one about him, the other mostly about her and her famous unconventional loves and marriages, of which Mahler was the first.

Fortunately the conductor did not have to worry about the staging (which was "often though not always abominable," and only amused him in any case), and he reveled in the stars assigned for every role. For *The Bartered Bride,* which he introduced the following year, he was allowed to import six pairs of native dancers from Prague. In Vienna he had opened up every cut in performances that thus lasted from five to six hours; here he cheerfully agreed to the old cuts and even more. He no longer wheeled furiously to stare through gleaming spectacles at late- comers (a practice Alma Mahler insists Toscanini adopted from Mahler). This had disconcerted even the Austrian Emperor, who inquired plain- tively, "Should the theatre not be a pleasure?"

Mahler, periodically ill and always depressed outside the theatre, had to contend with yet another ailing man—Heinrich Conried. At first he and Alma saw only the comic side of the bulky impresario, reclining on a divan under a baldachin with convoluted pillars. The room was darkened by draperies, lit by glaring colored globes. The Mahlers laughed over the suit of armor, illuminated by red lights from within, and commented cruelly that the impresario already showed signs of megalomania. They further jeered at his "utter innocence of culture," and his artistic blunders. Once he proposed a tenor for a bass part and even suggested to Caruso that as the tenor had so little to sing in *La Traviata* he interpolate some melodious bars. Mahler remained impervious to these gaucheries, preferring them to the implacable misunderstanding of the more distinguished man who followed. Tired of fighting, the towering leader finally gave way to one even more imperious when he acceded wearily to the loss of *Tristan* to Toscanini, but only in 1909–10, and not the previous season, as Mrs. Mahler recounts. Mahler had the 1908–9 *Tristan,* but lost the other Wagner works to Hertz or Toscanini, his portion consisting only of *The Bartered Bride, Le Nozze di Figaro,* which suffered the same fate as *Don Giovanni* in not being revived for a long period afterward, and *Fidelio,* for which Mahler was content to import the Vienna scenery. With Toscanini firmly in the saddle in 1909–10, and Hertz claiming even *The Bartered Bride,* Mahler came late and conducted only four performances—in German—of Tchaikovsky's *Pique Dame,* a conspicuous waste of his great talent. He did not return to the opera at all the following season, but confined himself to the New York symphonic world for the brief time remaining to him.

Another conductor had been flung to the wolves in Conried's first year, or rather to the vixenish Calvé, who returned after a year's absence. Felix Mottl, highly respected in Europe, came to Conried under a former contract with Grau which named him *Generalmusikdirektor,* the first time that title appears. Mottl bore most of the German repertoire (incurring favorable comparisons with Seidl), including a *Magic Flute* for the first time in that language with a cast that included Sembrich, Gadski, Dippel, Goritz, and Ternina as the First Lady. Then the *Flute* was Italianized in midstream, and though it gained Plançon in place of a lesser Sarastro, Mottl was unhappy. His woes became further compounded with Calvé's Carmen; he endured her willful pranks in the House as well as on the road. Long before she laughed openly at him when she missed a high note in the quintet, Mottl began to wonder why he had been chosen to pilot this wayward temperament along her erratic paths. He was spared a performance in New Haven (taken over by Gustav Hinrichs, another one-season tenant of the podium) because he conducted *Siegfried* in New York, but a few days later found him in the usual altercation with the soprano at a final postseason concert. When he refused to transpose for her at a moment's notice, she waved good-bye to him—and the Metropolitan. This was his finale also.

Conried grew steadily more ill, eventually not showing up on Thirty-ninth Street for weeks at a time. His troubles had begun in earnest as early as 1906, when the San Francisco earthquake wiped out the physical properties of his company and shook the nerve and health of many of his singers.

Far from drawing in his horns in the contentious matter of touring, Conried had caught the virus of empire building that had infected Grau and would break out thrice again in the Met's history. The flag had already been planted in the Golden Gate the year before, where Grau had pioneered in 1900 and 1901. Omens hovered fair above Conried's second Western pilgrimage. For a fortnight's season, $120,000 already lay in the bank and San Franciscans prepared themselves to converge in force upon the old Mission Street Opera House. Within its flimsy shell were stacked flat after flat, prop after prop, costumes in ranks and trunks—all the investiture for the nineteen operas of the repertoire. Ferrying one setting a day back and forth from the railroad terminal in Oakland was considered impractical as well as overcostly. Larger orchestral instruments also found sanctuary backstage.

Only a few were spared the ordeal which began in the dawn of April 18, 1906—Lillian Nordica, who journeyed only as far as Chicago; Heinrich Knote, the German tenor, and Lina Abarbanell, the Irving Place ingenue who had been the first Hänsel; as well as the property man, Philip Crispano, recovering from an appendectomy, and Conried himself, who had turned back to New York from Chicago in disgust at Midwest indifference, leaving Ernest Goerlitz in charge. Goerlitz, whom Grau had brought in as accountant in 1898, was that indispensable man, omniscient in detail, efficient to the fingertips, who sits at the heart of an opera company, always a lieutenant, seldom a captain. His coolness and resourcefulness in the three days and nights of horror to come undoubtedly saved the 300 members of the opera company from personal tragedy. Their loss in nervous strain and material possessions imposed hardship enough.

The engagement began tepidly for all the anticipation. Apparently the magnificent pillars and golden lions of Solomon's throne room could not compensate for the intrinsic musical and dramatic weaknesses of

Goldmark's *Queen of Sheba.* "Opera Crowd Cold" read a headline next day. Caruso's Don José rekindled enthusiasm the second night, although the chubby tenor would not learn for months that one gushing lady critic wanted to rechristen *Carmen* in the hero's favor. Fremstad's gypsy was termed "dutchy."

Next morning, when the San Andreas Fault split open along its 270-mile trail, the West's most glamorous metropolis toppled into ruins, soon licked by insatiable tongues of flame. The opera company was but a microcosm of the terror and heroism of the stricken city. Legends grew like thickets around their misadventures, not revealed in any measure until their exhausted return to New York, and then so contradictory that one could pick and choose one's own truth from the torrent of newspaper interviews. Caruso was seen in many strange circumstances, most of which he branded as false in his own account for the London *Sketch,* principally the contention that he sat on his valise in the street in front of the Palace Hotel and wept. His faithful valet Martino rescued three small trunkfuls of possessions, which later they bundled onto a cart to make the perilous trip to the Oakland Ferry, and from which the tenor was able to outfit several of his less fortunate comrades regardless of differences in size. He never once relinquished his hold on a huge framed portrait of Teddy Roosevelt which the President had given him in Washington. He had been overheard by Arnold Genthe, whose photographic record provided a poignant documentary of the holocaust and its aftermath, to mutter: " 'Ell of a place! 'Ell of a place! I never come back here!" And he never did.

Although everyone contributed a bit of color to the patchwork narrative, as told in this author's *Opera Caravan,* most memorable were Olive Fremstad, distributing long-stemmed roses to sufferers in a small park near her hotel; and Plançon, with his beard turning green for lack of daily dye (at least according to Scotti), and screaming with fright at the unwanted attentions of a cow, who insisted on licking his face while he dozed in a vacant lot. Emma Eames flicked the beast away with her handkerchief. Eames, moving coolly through the horror and uncertainty, recorded the experience in her autobiography, *Some Memoirs and Reflections* (the fullest account by any of the singers). Since only a few moments were available to shop for toothbrushes and other necessaries in Los Angeles, it is astonishing to realize how many of the ladies resisted trepidation long enough to pin on their elaborate hats. Sembrich appeared in a feathered toque in the photograph taken in the Chicago railroad station when one section of the rescue train paused there. She was supposed to have lost $40,000 in jewels and costumes, but Eames wrote that Sembrich carried her jewels with her from the hotel. Much later, Maria Jeritza remembered seeing in Sembrich's New York apartment a "curious misshapen lump" in which gold and silver and many colors appeared, and the outline of a watch was visible. Sembrich explained that it was some of her valuables oxidized by the fire. Louise Homer was the only missing singer; the ordeal had overwhelmed her. Her husband, Sidney Homer, took her off the train in Chicago to recover in a hospital.

Conried immediately sent Goerlitz back to make good his promise of refunds. In what was probably the largest such operation in theatre history, Goerlitz paid every applicant unquestioningly, with the result that San Franciscans, also put on their honor, did not abuse it. Still, the sum of $120,000 (less only the tiny amount taken in for two performances), plus the huge outlay for new scenery and costumes, put Conried into the red for the first time to the amount of some $84,000.

The manager's depreciating health caused great concern to the directors and became a matter of public speculation increasingly over the summer of 1906 and at the beginning of the season. The press was not disposed to take Conried's part in any controversy. He had attempted to dictate to the critics in his first year, going so far as to invade their sanctorum for unwelcome lectures. In spite of the involvement of Caruso, the most popular figure of all, the papers seized gleefully upon an incident just before the opening of the season and made a Roman holiday of it. The exuberant tenor was accused of making improper advances to a woman in the Central Park monkey house. She had him arrested. Conried, already uncertain on his legs, had to stand for long hours in the crowded courtroom; the injury to his physique equaled the embarrassment to his dignity and that of his prime star. Caruso protested his innocence throughout; in any case, if there had been a sly pinch, entirely within the realm of permissibility for any attentive Italian, the verdict of guilty and the imposition of a fine seemed a high price to pay. Caruso and Conried pondered deeply about the effect on the singer's career. They need not have worried. The ovation that greeted Rodolfo when the curtain went up on *La Bohème* on November 28 (Caruso's fans had had to wait twenty-four hours, since this was the occasion for Farrar's debut and Caruso appeared only on the second night) left no doubt where the public's affection lay. Never during the remainder of Caruso's life did this devotion swerve. Sobbing in his dressing room afterward, he resolved soberly to justify it. The more serious side of his nature took hold at that moment, his biographer avowed. But as his fortunes ascended, his manager's waned.

Now in 1906 arrived what Krehbiel called "a flowering of the old obsession that if one operatic establishment flourishes in a community there must be room for two." Already Conried had sensed the coming rivalry when he snapped at a reporter who asked him about replacements for the scenery lost in San Francisco: "I am not Oscar Hammerstein and cannot have these things done without time!" It is true that Hammerstein often put out opera houses as if he had merely run them up on his sewing machine, and he usually opened them while the plaster was still wet and the paint apt to rub off on white kid gloves. The new Manhattan was no exception, although it would have suited Oscar better to open earlier than December 3. He often contrived to infuriate his rivals by deliberately choosing to open on the same date. The advance hullabaloo for the impresario had been of unprecedented volume, carefully masterminded by Hammerstein himself and by the wiliest of all press agents, William J. Guard. *I Puritani* was the inaugural opera, a stranger to the Met since its opening season, one which Caruso no longer sang but which suited Bonci agreeably. No one else really mattered in this beginning of what was to be blown up as a "duel of tenors," although many favorable comments came out for the conductor, Cleofonte Campanini, who had appeared as a novice in the Met's first season.

Hammerstein was out for blood. Credited as no grudge holder, he nevertheless cherished an enmity for Conried that can be only partly explained by their earlier brushes of temperament. As Vincent Sheean says: "It was something more than the arrogance and bad behavior of the young matinee idol Conried had once been. It was more than the jealousy of one opera manager for another. No doubt Hammerstein felt, when Conried's appointment to the Metropolitan was announced, that this was a brilliant example of fate's perverseness and injustice," and he continued to "see the hairy hand of Conried" in any of his misfortunes as long as the latter lived.

Still, Hammerstein could never have endured domination by a board of financiers. He made the point clear by minimizing the position of society in his new opera house, where the boxes could not be seen by the general audience. He hammered it in by his speech after the final curtain, seemingly directed straight at Box 13, where sat Mr. and Mrs. Otto H. Kahn, when he said: "The responsibility is all mine. I have no board of directors, nobody to tell me what I should and should not do."

This fierce independence, added to his other failings, helped to betray him ultimately, but for the moment Oscar I sunned himself in the press' goodwill and the delight of his audiences. Although he soon ran into trouble, chiefly by having no replacements for an incompetent coloratura until Melba should arrive, and for the distinguished baritone Maurice Renaud who immediately lost his voice, he surmounted one crisis after another until the Metropolitan could not but help "feel the breeze," as Sheean put it. He even triumphed over his enemy by producing *Bohème* for Melba in spite of Conried's claim to sole rights, backed up in this instance by the Ricordi monopoly. Ricordi applied for an injunction against Hammerstein but was refused, whereupon he resorted to forbidding Hammerstein access to any scores. Oscar managed to secure a copy so mutilated that the publisher believed no performance possible from it, but Campanini knew the opera so thoroughly that he reconstructed it, even to the individual parts. (Campanini refused to conduct, however, probably not wishing to incur the enmity of the powerful publisher.) Legal or illegal, the disputed work came to Thirty-fourth Street and Eighth Avenue on March 1, 1907.

Conried had counted on Puccini to side with him in the *Bohème* dispute, but the astute composer maintained neutrality. He had been invited by Conried (at a salary of $8,000) to supervise the Metropolitan premieres of his *Manon Lescaut* and *Madama Butterfly*, but arrived only at six P.M. on the date of the former's performance, January 18, 1907. Even though ship-weary, he made the eight-o'clock curtain and gave every evidence of pleasure at the performance and the ovations accorded him. Throughout the five weeks he spent in New York, he remained outwardly courteous, seemingly amused and gratified by the attention and money showered on him (one autograph hunter paid him $500 for scribbling the opening bars of Musetta's Waltz, according to his biographer Morris Carner). He refused to be drawn out by the press except for a few compliments to American girls in plays (notably *Girl of the Golden West*) and some polite remarks about the singers in his operas. But he wrote to a friend that he had had all he wanted of America after a month. "At the opera all is well, and *Madama Butterfly* was excellent, but lacked the poetry I put into it. The rehearsals were too hurried, and the woman [Farrar] was not what she ought to have been. Also as regards your *god* [Caruso], *entre nous* I make you a present of him—he won't learn anything, he's lazy and he's too pleased with himself—all the same, his voice is magnificent."

This dispraise of its twin idols, Farrar and Caruso, would have constituted heresy even to the strictest New York critics, most of whom found *Butterfly* irresistible, even though Krehbiel's moral sense would not allow approval of the "carnality" of the story. Oddly enough, Puccini liked *Manon Lescaut* better, though the local men thought Lina Cavalieri not quite up to the part. Caruso and Scotti appeared in both new operas and won the public at least.

This season that should have been Conried's finest, what with *Salome,* the Puccini festival, and the arrival of Farrar, marked instead the acceleration of his downfall. Earlier he had attempted to save money in all the wrong ways—cutting the size of the orchestra, skimping on conductors and stage directors, allowing the chorus to become slipshod and the stage management (a phase that should have commanded his affectionate attention) to lapse in efficiency. A bridge had fallen in a *Carmen* performance of January 7, 1905, injuring several members of the chorus, and a falling counterweight weighing several hundred pounds had narrowly escaped the tenor Albert Saléza in *Roméo et Juliette* a month later. These were the first links of bad luck that eventually forged themselves into the chain of the manager's destiny. In 1907 he could look back on others: the earthquake, the chorus strike that brought the first rumbles of troublesome union relations, the blue law that threatened to obliterate an effort to make something qualitative out of Sunday concerts, the failure of Chaliapin to deliver income and prestige, the panic of 1907, and now, above all, the inroads of Hammerstein. The ailing manager could not even take comfort in the project that had grown to be his chief obsession: erection of a repertory theatre that would also do for light opera. Although this dream was made manifest, Conried never saw it. Even his satisfaction in the successes of *Parsifal* and *Madama Butterfly* had been dimmed by the cheeky Henry W. Savage, who chased—or some-times preceded—him all along the road with productions in English that many considered superior.

By January 1908, the report leaked out that the directors were already in touch with Giulio Gatti-Casazza of La Scala, and with the Scala's brightest figure, Arturo Toscanini. Efforts to secure the latter had doubt-less been put forth even earlier, as Campanini's luster increased and the Metropolitan's Arturo Vigna's dulled. Rodolfo Ferrari, who took over the Italian works in 1907–8, made little improvent. Still the Metropoli-tan's Rawlins L. Cottenet, in Europe during the early months, denied all rumors of negotiations in Milan. For their own sakes, Gatti-Casazza and Toscanini joined the chorus of innocence. But no doubt exists that the matter had already been settled. The hopes of Conried's champions were dashed when on February 12 the announcement of his resignation came formally out of a board meeting.

Regardless of private feelings, the stockholders, impersonally closing ranks against the public, blandly presented Conried with a framed testi-monial and an eighteen-inch-tall silver cup at his final jamboree on March 24. His final season closed, appropriately, with *Götterdämmerung*. Still undaunted, according to his son, he went to Europe, busy with plans and inventions to secure a future life. But it was too late. He died in Meran, in the Austrian Tirol, on April 27, 1909. Like Leopold Damrosch, that other German before him, Conried was the recipient of an elaborate public funeral in the Opera House on May 13, with the stage set for the second act of *Falstaff*, and in the center a catafalque seven feet high, banked in flowers. At its head stood a bronze bust of the impresario. Four thousand yards of black crepe draped the proscenium. Among the artists in the solemn musical program were three Americans who thought highly of Conried: Marie Rappold, Louise Homer, and Robert Blass. He was laid to rest in a mausoleum that cost $7,000.

If financial returns for his five-year efforts had formed the only criterion, Conried could not have complained. In addition to his $20,000 annual salary, he had pocketed an equal amount each year from the "manager's benefits," in which practically all his roster donated its ser-vices in his behalf. Furthermore, he got half of the first three years' profit of $300,000 (the final two years showed a deficit). His son, Richard Genée, stated in Montrose J. Moses' biography that his father died intestate, yet the papers of the day reported that his will had been probated at a gross of $455,031. Whatever the correct legal status, about half of this sum probably remained after his debts were paid. His widow sued the Metropolitan Opera and Real Estate Company for $75,000, alleging breach of contract, and received $58,000. A claim against Otto Kahn of $25,375 was also settled. Conried's library and the costumes and scenery of the Irving Place Theatre were bought by August Luchow. William K. Vanderbilt bought for $90,000 Conried's investment in the Conried Opera Company (the title the Met board allowed him). The Met profited by his death to the extent of $150,000 in life insurance.

A radical change had sprung from the dissolution of the Conried Opera Company. From now on, no manager would own shares or take any part of possible profits. He would be simply an employee of the new entity known as the Metropolitan Opera Company, which, with the Metropolitan Opera and Real Estate Company, looked toward a future in which opera might just possibly be produced without the necessity of making money.

12

A HOUSE DIVIDED

Can two walk together, except they be agreed?

—Amos 3:3

The regime that was to endure longest in Metropolitan history began in deep dichotomy. With a view to minimizing the hazards of Gatti-Casazza's job, Otto Kahn had suppressed any mention of the virtual mutiny that had greeted the announcement of the hiring of the two Italians. Toscanini's autocratic reputation had become well known, whereas Gatti's lay only in deeds. He seldom issued a pronunciamento or proclaimed a philosophy. His very silence hung ominously over the heads of the singers, who firstly dreaded change, like any other human beings, and then feared the new Italian broom and the implications that Conried's well-founded German repertoire would be swept into the dustbin. Toscanini's fast-growing *réclame* as a Wagner conductor was completely discounted, in spite of reassurances from the Metropolitan's board.

To forestall the objections that began to arise, the directors placed Andreas Dippel, the versatile German tenor, in harness with Gatti, qualifying him as Administrative Manager, but in reality leaving the lines of command between him and the General Manager blurred and all too capable of being misinterpreted.

Into the frame of confusion and distrust that clouded the season of 1908–9 stepped unwittingly the man with a deep font of patience—Giulio Gatti-Casazza. Arriving for a preliminary inspection on May 1, 1908, he was required without delay to draw upon that reservoir. The *Lusitania* paused at Quarantine and was boarded by Charles Henry Meltzer, who had gone back to the critic's desk at the *American* after his short service with Conried as press agent. Meltzer let it be known in superior fashion that he spoke with Gatti in pure Tuscan dialect. He was impressed with the tall man's self-control no less than by his simple and unforced dignity. "Women might call him handsome," with his moustache and rather small beard, under which the writer detected somehow a chin "that sug-

173

gests will without obstinacy." He was, as the French say, "somebody."

On the pier, they were joined by Meltzer's successor as press agent, Ralph Edmunds, and by Andreas Dippel, whom Gatti met for the first time. After checking him in at the Netherlands Hotel, they took Gatti to the opera house, putting its best foot forward by introducing him into the director's box while a Firemen's Benefit performance was in progress. Thus he saw the auditorium first. As luck would have it, Eames was at the moment singing "A Greeting to Spring." After greeting the prima donna in her box, the new general manager was taken to Dippel's office—as tiny and cramped as his own at La Scala, and so missed Anna Held rendering "I Just Can't Make My Eyes Behave," and Marie Desser in a flame-colored dress as the "Fireman's Bride."

Faced with a barrage of questions ranging from serious to impertinent, Gatti remained calm, spoke in French, displayed a saving sense of humor, reminded at least one reporter of Edouard de Reszke, admitted that he was not married (although he had been engaged to coloratura Maria Barrientos, whom later he engaged for the Met), professed to be a staunch Wagnerian, said he liked all moderns, including Strauss, Debussy, and Charpentier, complained that the Met had stolen all of Italy's artists already, but that his country would furnish an entirely new chorus (while Dippel paralleled with a German group); and was confident that Toscanini would work harmoniously with Gustav Mahler (Toscanini had agreed that if there had to be another conductor, he would prefer a good one to a mediocrity).

The auditorium, Gatti said, arranged its seats far better than La Scala's, where the only good ones were in the boxes, and at the same time, there were too many boxes. Furthermore, although he hadn't inspected the stage and "machinery," it couldn't be worse than La Scala's, which had been installed in the reign of Maria Theresa.

In a visit to Otto Kahn's Morristown, New Jersey, estate, Gatti told a different story. He admitted that the backstage conditions left him aghast. While the auditorium pleased him generally, the Orchestra and side seats were too close to the stage, and the standees too close to the Orchestra Circle, breathing disagreeably down seated patrons' necks. Kahn soothed his new manager by promising him a new house in "two or three years." It was not the banker's fault that it would take more than half a century and another determined manager to make his words good.

Another development unknown to Gatti was made public on the day of his arrival—Boston had a new opera house a-building, and the Met was invited to trade with Henry Russell's company, now in formation. Russell, the son of the man who wrote the music for "Woodman, Spare That Tree," "A Life on the Ocean Wave," and eight hundred other ditties, had brought a touring company to the United States as early as 1905, calling it the San Carlo after the Naples house that had first inspired him to seek an impresario's career. A flamboyant personality with a persuasive tongue and an undoubted gift for choosing singers and repertoire, Russell had caught the fancy of the Boston merchant prince Eben D. Jordan, who guaranteed him the house and who had now become allied with Kahn in the latter's burgeoning dream of empire. The New York *Herald* quoted Russell as saying, "Opera will now become the same serious, impersonal institution here as it is in Italy, France and Germany." (How could this vain, pretentious man dub "impersonal" a structure built on such temperamental personalities as his own and Gatti-Casazza's, not to speak of the stars under them, and the rugged individualists Jordan and Kahn!) The somewhat less than total cooperation between the two companies (Boston's would open on November 8, 1909, and endure for five years only) is told in this author's *Boston Opera Company*. Russell signed his contract with Dippel, but later established cordial relations with Gatti; the latter found Boston an outlet for occasional perplexities, such as giving his own wife enough roles to sing outside his own company.

Gatti sailed back to Italy, leaving New York to worry about other matters than the opera house. Headlines day after day spoke of "The Met," but in reference either to the new Metropolitan Life Insurance tower at Madison Square or the Metropolitan Street Railway, not the opera. Thomas Fortune Ryan, the speculator whose grandson would marry one of Otto Kahn's daughters, had allegedly garnered double profits from a "paper" railroad which he later sold to W. C. Whitney for the "Met." Other forms of transportation offered news: Brooklyn rejoiced in a new subway, which August Belmont helped to dedicate; and Alfred Gwynne Vanderbilt scandalized German papers by "accepting fares like a common cabby" as he drove his drag Meteor behind four gallant grays in a coaching trial from London to Brighton. Louis Blériot would take his flying machine from Calais to Dover in the following summer.

As mid-November arrived, signs of a world still peaceful appeared in a full-page panegyric to Kaiser Wilhelm and his foreign ambassadors as "Forces That Work Against War in Europe." Agitation grew among "preservationists" to save Stanford White's Madison Square Garden from demolition, not by any means the first of such crusades for landmarks nor the last. Economists pointed out how our luxuries help pay our bills, the revenues from fashion, the growing cosmetics industry, and tobacco going far to balance the economy. This came a little too late to save the Bradley-Martins and James Hazen Hyde from expatriation.

At the opera house real trouble was brewing. Distrusting the Italian management, several important singers flocked to their colleague, Dippel; waving the banner of rebellion in the forefront, the pert Geraldine Farrar enlisted four colleagues who seemed, oddly enough, the least likely to suffer under a fine Italian hand: Eames and Sembrich, who were in any case almost ready to hand in their coronets and retire gracefully, and the reigning gentlemen, Caruso and Scotti. In a letter dated two days after the American premiere of D'Albert's *Tiefland* on November 23, 1908, which had been Dippel's entire responsibility and could by great indulgence be called only a modest success, the quintet urged the claims of Dippel. On December 2 the board replied, under the signature of Otto Kahn and two other members. Within a mass of diplomatic verbiage, the gist stood out, clarion clear: "It is not possible to administer an organization like the Metropolitan under two heads, and it was never intended that it should be so administered."

Dippel himself received the news simultaneously and it was made public on December 7. However, he was allowed to stay on in a subordinate capacity for another season, until 1910.

Meanwhile, Farrar was left clinging almost alone on her high limb, deserted by the men, who treated the whole thing as a mistake and, as she said, "disclaimed offense with fervor," and virtually repudiated by the "tactful" silence of Sembrich. Eames "stood pat," wrote Farrar, "and never bent the knee. Why should she? She was always quite frank in her disapproval of the new regime." (She never welcomed a new manager and had been equally vehement against Conried, it will be remembered.) Miss Farrar concluded defiantly, "I assumed all responsibility."

It is doubly difficult to understand why Caruso should have signed the manifesto of rebellion, for he had previously enjoyed most cordial relationships with both Gatti and Toscanini. Gatti, hearing him at the Lirico in Milan in 1898, had tried to get him for La Scala in 1899, but Caruso was already booked in Petrograd. True, his debut at La Scala as Rodolfo when he finally arrived in 1900 had not gone particularly well, but any unfortunate memories were wiped out by his overwhelming success in a poor vehicle—Mascagni's *Le Maschere.* Then when Gatti revived Donizetti's sprightly *Elisir d'Amore* as a replacement for *Le Maschere,* an unmistakable furor kindled for the tenor. He sang Faust to Chaliapin's towering Mefisto in Boito's *Mefistofele,* and the next season returned for further kudos in the premiere of Franchetti's *Germania.* Toscanini had embraced him after *Elisir,* exclaiming: "By God! If this Neapolitan continues to sing as he does, he will make the whole world talk about him!"

But Caruso had just enjoyed his most triumphant season at the last of Conried's reign. Superstitious fear of a change partially influenced him, without doubt. As if to give life to his forebodings, the season of 1908–9 brought a crisis, the worst since he had become a mature artist. He was forced by illness to miss twenty-one performances and sailed for Europe immediately at the close of the season, obliging Gatti to borrow Giovanni Zenatello from Hammerstein for the tour. Needless to say, neither his early gesture of insubordination nor his defection were held against him. In the fall of 1909 he arrived light in heart, all the omens favorable. And by the time he had sung *Elisir* in 1916, Gatti told him: "You must truly have drunk of that elixir because your voice and your art have preserved the charm and the resources of that memorable night at the Scala."

For her thoughtless eruption, Farrar was never quite forgiven, although Gatti never openly showed resentment.

The horse show authorities revealed sense by opening a week ahead of the opera, on November 9. Oscar Hammerstein, too, jumped the gun with a week that included *Tosca* (Conried's passing had freed the Ricordi items for him) with Maria Labia, Zenatello, and Renaud; *Thaïs* with Garden; *Samson et Dalila* with Gerville-Réache, Dalmorès, and Dufranne; and Tetrazzini's first *Barber of Seville.* The Basilio was Andrés de Segurola, who had spent the season of 1901–2 in the Met and on tour with Grau, facts that seemed to be forgotten by Hammerstein. He would rejoin the Met in 1909.

Once more, as it had five times in the past, the Metropolitan "opened" out of town. On November 14, Farrar traveled over the bridge to inaugurate the new Brooklyn Academy of Music by singing "The Star-Spangled Banner" and then joining Caruso, Didur, and a new baritone, Jean Noté, in *Faust,* conducted by another newcomer, Francesco Spetrino (a Viennese in spite of his name and a protégé of Mahler's). The *New York Times,* condescending to cover the event, believed that "the heart of every Brooklynite must have been particularly joyous." This first "subway series" inaugurated a custom that was to endure until 1937, although its box-office intake was never again matched.

Two nights later, the real opening brought a new stir of excitement and what many sensed to be the unfolding of fresh pages in the opera's history. The "brilliant and strenuous" performance of *Aida* seemed to Aldrich of the *Times* to stem from the pit, galvanized by Toscanini, "a dominating power, a man of potent authority, a musician of infinite resource." Henderson in the *Sun* put his stamp on the new era; Krehbiel marked Toscanini as "in the best sense an artist, an interpreter, a recreator"; the *Herald* approved his promptness ("not three minutes after the announced hour" did he raise his baton); and even Finck yielded, after remarking that the Met had been used to the authority of German conductors, which Italians did not usually possess. Toscanini was an exception, he granted, "one of the most masterful ever heard here." He further marveled at this first display of that miraculous memory which permitted the banishment of a score.

Only one spectre supped at the feast. Reginald de Koven, in his second period as critic for the *World* and with all but three of his famous operettas in the past, waxed peevish with disappointment in Toscanini. He had liked others previously as well, if not better. The slim Italian's mannerisms and extravagant gestures annoyed him; Toscanini was lacking in plasticity, temperament (!), and poetic feeling; was too tense, too high pitched.

The *World* critic gave his banner headline to the new soprano, Emmy Destinn (née Kittl), and, indeed, others joined in praise of the

Czech soprano's voice of "great power, body and vibrant quality," as Aldrich said. For eight seasons, until mid-war, she would glorify the Met with one of the finest voices in a human throat. Her appetite for work was insatiable. Even after absorbing Aida, Tosca, Nedda, Santuzza, Gioconda, Butterfly, La Wally, Mistress Ford (*Falstaff*), Ricke (*Germania*), and Puccini's Girl, among Italian heroines, and the German Marta (*Tiefland*), Marie (*Bartered Bride*), Elsa, and Elisabeth (and even a Gerhilde in a Philadelphia substitution), she complained in Boston that the Metropolitan didn't give her enough to do. So she added Pamina, Amelia (*Ballo in Maschera*), Leonora (*Trovatore*), Valentine (*Huguenots*), and only tapped her reservoir of eighty roles by one fifth. Her name was closely associated with that of the strapping Algerian baritone Dinh Gilly, who came to be known as "La Forza del Destinn." Gilly made his debut in *Werther* at the Metropolitan's "annex," the New Theatre, in 1909 and remained until 1914, when he returned to Europe and became a prisoner of war in Austria. Destinn is supposed to have engaged in some undercover work for her country. A photograph in Francis Robinson's *Caruso: His Life in Pictures* shows the tenor playfully bestowing his blessing on Destinn and Gilly, "about the only blessing," Robinson remarks, "this union ever got."

Additional thrills for that opening-night audience of 1908 were provided by the new chorus and orchestra, by the rich tones of Louise Homer, the superb intensity of Antonio Scotti, and, to be expected, the glorious outpourings of Enrico Caruso. The tenor, in fact, rose to the occasion with a more prodigal expenditure of his resources than ever and a more insistent dwelling on the highest tones, the *Times* commented. The new scenery drew a few derogatory remarks but pleased Finck, who had found Conried's Viennese investiture "too gorgeous." The *Post* critic also liked the two white horses that drew Radames' triumphal chariot, though obviously the horses weren't happy. "But what do they know about Italian opera?" Finck asked.

This critic beamed at "the restoration of real German opera" when *Die Walküre* was produced the second night, November 18, with Gadski, Fremstad, Homer, and three newcomers, Matja von Niessen-Stone, who remained two seasons, Erik Schmedes (a "good" Siegmund), and Fritz Feinhals ("one of the greatest" Wotans), who lasted only one. Finck's "bravo" to Dippel for securing them was wasted. Allen Hinckley, the agreeable American bass, showed more staying power. Everything was harmonious on the stage, Finck thought, remembering the days when Hertz would protest crude staging and be told to shut up. The elevator orchestra pit, which had cost $22,000, was worth it. Hertz's *Parsifal, Meistersinger, Tannhäuser,* and *Siegfried* and Mahler's *Tristan* brought comfort to this Wagnerian, who was even persuaded by Toscanini's incandescent *Götterdämmerung* that the Teuton gods still had a life on Broadway. (It was at a *Götterdämmerung* rehearsal that the conductor's prodigious memory was revealed, when he corrected a note in a player's part that had always been wrong.) Toscanini did not reveal the possible depths of his Wagnerian conceptions in the six remaining seasons he allowed to the Met. Taking up *Tristan* and *Meistersinger* in his second year, he remained faithful to these alone, conducting several performances of each except in 1912–13, when he yielded the master's comic opera to Hertz, and in 1913–14, giving up one *Tristan* because of an injured hand.

But as the first season wore on and Gatti's hand could be seen emerging with the sceptre, early doubts that had been partially allayed by the general high excellence of most performances rose again as he paraded as novelties two early and feeble Italian works, Puccini's *Le Villi* and Catalani's *La Wally.* No matter how deep Italy's or Toscanini's regard for Catalani (one of his daughters is named Wally), nor how difficult the wags found rhyming "Villi-Wally" with "shilly-shally," were these to be the only novelties (apart from the gloomy *Tiefland* and the gay *Bartered Bride,* both of German stamp)? Uneasiness persisted in spite of brilliant revivals of *Manon, Falstaff,* and *Figaro.* Although ameliorated from time to time in Gatti's long reign by occasional high spots in repertoire and more than occasional avalanches of singing talent, those who feared the Italian's overbalance in favor of his native opera could point to the record and say, "I told you so." Undoubtedly Gatti's close ties with the house of Ricordi had much to do with it, for he accepted most of the constant spate of inferior works flowing out of Italy for the sake of producing the surefire hits in tie-in agreements. In the end, the Italians triumphed over the Americans two to one, and slightly more than that in the case of the French and Germans.

Gatti's fortunes began to brighten at the end of the marathon season of 1909–10, the year that contained more grand opera than had ever been heard before—or since—in the United States. The race began on

November 8, 1909, with the simultaneous openings of the new Boston Opera Company (*Gioconda*), the Manhattan Company (*Hérodiade*), the Metropolitan's Brooklyn season of twenty performances (*Manon*), and the New Theatre's drama series (*Antony and Cleopatra*). On November 9, the Met season of twenty-five Philadelphia performances was launched with *Aida,* followed by a November 11 matinee of *Madama Butterfly.* On November 12, Baltimore's series of twenty began with *Tannhäuser.* Then on November 15, not content with opening the House with *Gioconda,* the Met sent its German team to Brooklyn with *Tannhäuser.* On November 16, the operatic section of the New Theatre opened with *Werther* and the Met favored Philadelphia with *Bohème.* During this week, Oscar Hammerstein launched his second season in his new Philadelphia Opera House. Counting additional productions in Boston (seven) and at the Manhattan (six), but not the New Theatre dramas, the record mounted to twenty-four operatic performances in nine days!

Something had to give. The strain of a season that never let up told at its weakest links—Hammerstein and the New Theatre. The latter, an idealistic project that began with Conried's dream of a repertoire theatre mixed with operetta, was brought to fruition by Kahn and two dozen or so faithful cohorts, and ended by becoming Gatti-Casazza's nightmare. The handsome structure on Central Park West and Sixty-second Street, designed by Carrère and Hastings (who had redecorated the opera house in 1903) was plagued from the first by one contretemps after another in the building, and by its location too far uptown and westward. Worst of all, its acoustics boomed—"one resounding echo." For the forty performers of opera in its first season (plus the dramas that shared the eighteen weeks) the cost of three and one quarter million seems excessive. Of this, Kahn shared at least a third of the burden. "It is a pretty expensive privilege nowadays to rank as a protector of the arts," he wrote Henry Russell later, when the New Theatre had been sadly abandoned to musicals and renamed the Century. In her biography of Kahn, Mary Jane Matz quotes him as perceiving the real reasons for its failure: that "every project conceived by the rich for the rich was doomed to die of anemia; the support of the people was the lifeblood it lacked." It took the Metropolitan itself another two decades to realize this.

Of the nineteen operas produced in 1909–10 at the New Theatre, only four were unique to it: Paër's *Maestro di Capella,* Lecocq's *Fille de Madame Angot,* Lortzing's *Zar und Zimmermann,* and Bruneau's *Attaque du Moulin*—all a cut above what Krehbiel dubbed "the bastard spawn of the theatres called comic opera." The other fifteen works were shared with the parent house, including Massenet's *Werther* and Auber's *Fra Diavolo* (both with the exquisite French tenor Edmond Clément), Flotow's *Alessandro Stradella* (with the imposing new tenor Leo Slezak, who had made his debut as Otello on the second night of the home season), and the American *Pipe of Desire.* None of these lasted beyond the season.

The expansion of out-of-town forays was entirely Dippel's idea. He called it "fighting Hammerstein with fire." Urged on by the gleeful prodding of daily papers, the crafty Oscar had been engaging in ever-wider fantasies, including the new Philadelphia house, beachheads in Baltimore, Washington, Brooklyn, and Pittsburgh, the threat of a new opera house in Chicago and a virtual shutout in Boston, where the new house was not yet complete and Hammerstein beat Gatti—or rather Dippel— to the only other opera roof, the old Boston Theatre. The Metropolitan was better able to survive. Hammerstein's balloon burst on April 28, 1910, when, after alarums and excursions of sensational proportions, his interests were bought out by the Metropolitan for $1,200,000, not including the Manhattan house. He had put himself in debt in Philadelphia to Edward T. Stotesbury, a Morgan partner, who also had a determining foot in the Metropolitan's Philadelphia camp. Stotesbury and his wife so forsook the stereotype of Quaker City conservatism as to take over the Bellevue-Stratford Hotel for a party in early days of World War I, transforming one salon for sentiment's sake into Venice (where they had spent their honeymoon) and another into an inn in the Tirol. Mr. Stotesbury could afford the obligations of the opera; he had spent half a million on this jamboree and lived in a 145-room, 14-elevator mansion, White Marsh.

Hammerstein was enjoined not to produce opera in New York, Boston, Philadelphia, or Chicago for ten years. He immediately had a fling at comic opera in the Manhattan and built a new opera house in London; then tried yet again by building a new house on Lexington Avenue, but his days were numbered. Stotesbury promptly renamed his

Philadelphia house the Metropolitan, and that company moved from the flawless old Academy of Music for a few years. Of more importance, a new Chicago company arose out of Hammerstein's ashes, containing most of his properties and many of his singers, as well as the conductor he had alienated, Cleofonte Campanini, who became musical director. At last the proper place opened for Dippel. With the Met's blessing, he was sent to the Windy City as general manager, representing also three Met board members who meant to keep their fingers on every operatic pulse in the land—Kahn, Vanderbilt, and Mackay. The company was named Chicago-Philadelphia when in Chicago, Philadelphia-Chicago in annual visits to the Quaker City. The Met even opened its doors magnanimously for spring pilgrimages until 1914–15 (when the company disbanded for a year because of the war), but the sharp successes of Mary Garden and company in a fresh repertoire soon rested like a stone in Gatti's digestive system. The operas hewed close to the French line, with several novelties added: Victor Herbert's *Natoma,* Jean Noguès' *Quo Vadis,* and Wolf-Ferrari's *Secret of Suzanne* in 1911; Wolf-Ferrari's *Gioielli della Madonna* in 1912; Zandonai's *Conchita,* and Kienzl's *Kuhreigen,* given in French as *Le Ranz des Vaches* in 1913; and Février's *Monna Vanna* (which had so scandalized Boston) in 1914. The visits were discontinued in 1915, when the Philadelphia's role as "annex" was dropped, but in 1917–18, Campanini, finding his home stand altogether too short for financial comfort, brought some of his familiar singers and a new coloratura, Amelita Galli-Curci, to Hammerstein's Lexington house in direct competition with the Met.

Kahn cherished grandiose schemes until the First World War dealt the last blow to a structure already crumbling. The disastrous double tours of the spring of 1910 and the New Theatre fiasco, for which separate French and German rosters and orchestras had swollen the payroll beyond bounds, still left the godfather of the Met sanguine. When Gatti urged him to an overseas junket in the spring, Kahn acquiesced immediately. Gatti had yielded sooner than most European-born impresarios to the craving to go back and show off their accomplishments (Russell was to take the Boston Company to Paris in 1914 and Rudolf Bing to pilot the Metropolitan thither again in 1966). Kahn's ambitions chimed in perfectly, for his domain could just as well be extended to the Old

World. As Krehbiel said: "Shall we not between St. Denis and St. George compound an opera company, half American half Italian, that shall go to Constantinople and take the Turk by the beard?"

With singers, chorus, ballet, and technicians, the company that boarded the S.S. *George Washington* and the *Kaiser Wilhelm II* mounted to more than 200. The Châtelet Theatre, which reminded Edward Seidle, technical director, and Frederick Hosli, chief machinist, of a dilapidated old barn, had to be put in order in short time for the opening of the season with a public dress rehearsal of *Aida* on May 19. Toscanini, Destinn, Caruso, and Homer triumphed even over a demonstration said to have been incited by a disgruntled French singer, Marie Delna. Although several critics, a minority, came to carp, at least one accepted soothing salve (in financial guise) from Press Agent William J. Guard (Hammerstein's chief legacy to the Met) and changed his tune. Nineteen performances in the Châtelet were divided between *Aida, Otello, Falstaff, Manon Lescaut, Cavalleria,* and *Pagliacci,* and a gala in the Opéra itself (for the benefit of the survivors of the sunken submarine *Pluviose*), when the German language was heard for the first time in the hallowed Gallic halls as Fremstad and Burrian sang the second act of *Tristan.* In the Puccini *Manon,* new to Paris, they had expected to hear Lina Cavalieri, but the illness (or indifference) of that lady brought about the debut of a winsome girl who would loom large in the Met's future—Lucrezia Bori. The story of her "discovery" and triumph—as well as the other excitements of the month—is told in the author's *Opera Caravan.*

It was not unforeseen that Gatti-Casazza's first ukase, when he assumed complete control in 1911, would be: "No more touring." To stay home and consolidate his reduced forces seemed an utterly desirable prospect, soon reinforced by the advent of the war. Attempts to "nationalize" the company were not resumed until the mid-twenties; then once again curbed by the depression, touring did not occupy the energies of the troupe to any appreciable extent until the effects of World War II wore off.

When Gatti began to exercise full authority—emerging "Lord of the field," as he expressed it—affairs smoothed out into a well-oiled and steadily operating machine for a few years. He reformed Conried's casting system, which he sarcastically dubbed "marvelous." Conried's repertoire and casts had been made up every Monday for the following week in the presence of certain important singers and their husbands, wives, mothers, brothers, sisters, or agents, who cluttered up conferences with internecine squabbling. Gatti soon hung up the "not welcome" sign, and eventually concocted casts in his own mind, alone and farther in advance.

When he took up "this species of dictatorship," the Met's cupboard was bare. He refurbished it with a set of black figures. Gatti's secret lay perhaps in offering such a multitude of goods, the shoddy with the silk, that customers bought the lot wholesale—it is a notable fact that subscriptions climbed. The nest egg of a million or so became sucked dry with depression, but its very existence proved the justification of Gatti's motto, passed on to him by the shrewd old Verdi: "The theatre is intended to be full, and not empty." To which Gatti added the saying of an Italian philosopher, Vincenzo Gioberti: "Blessed be mathematics, which has the good fortune to admit of no dilettantes."

On the side visible to the public, the presence of William J. Guard added immense distinction. The press chief, set in the midst of seeming chaos in the tiny cubicle to the left of the Thirty-ninth Street officials' entrance, was at once the aristocrat and the businessman. He looked more like an artist than any singer or conductor, with his slender frame and face, the waggling goatee, the spats, Windsor tie in red, pink, black, or plaid according to mood, the pink striped shirts, the flowing cape and top hat. As he strode down the corridors on opening nights, he was "easily the most noticeable figure" in the House, said Olin Downes affectionately. Kind to the tyro, unforgiving to the fake, Billy Guard cast an air of civilized Bohemia over his realm, spiced with the wit of his native Limerick, until his death in 1932. The reins of the press department fell into no such distinguished hands again until the advent of Francis Robinson many years later. Guard's assistant, Frank Wenker, who boasted Neuchatel as a birthplace, held the job for a while, succeeded by professional public relations experts, notably two handsome ladies, Constance Hope and Margaret Carson. Billy Guard sorted well with Hammerstein and Gatti; it is impossible to imagine him in any later constellation.

Gatti's pattern became established: one world premiere per season after the initial two in 1910–11—Puccini's *Girl* and Humperdinck's *Goose Girl* (*Königskinder*), in which Farrar made an indelible impression for the sweetness and delicacy of her role and the flock of live geese she trained and herded on stage even on tour.

The General Manager began his commendable but not always canny search for American works immediately, even instituting a $10,000 prize which was duly won by Horatio Parker, whose *Mona* achieved performance in 1911–12 and never again. Similar fates met the first native piece ever to grace the Met—Frederick Converse's *Pipe of Desire,* and every other until Deems Taylor's *King's Henchman* and *Peter Ibbetson,* which lingered a few seasons. Most had largely American casts. *Mona* enlisted Homer, Rita Fornia (née Newman), Riccardo Martin (née Richard), Herbert Witherspoon (a prized acquisition of 1908–9), William Hinshaw, Putnam Griswold (who died untimely), and Basil Ruysdael (who turned to radio for a later career).

In 1912–13 it was Walter Damrosch's *Cyrano de Bergerac,* with Alda, Martin, and Amato; in 1913–14 Victor Herbert's *Madeleine,* with Alda, Leonora Sparkes, Paul Althouse, and the comical bass of earlier years, Antonio Pini-Corsi. Hertz conducted the first two; Polacco the third. By 1914–15 the American vein petered out and Gatti turned for novelty to Giordano's *Madame Sans-Gêne,* in which Farrar disported herself as the lively laundress and Amato portrayed the Little Corporal, with Toscanini in the pit. In 1915–16 Enrique Granados arrived for the world premiere of his sketchy but colorful *Goyescas,* a journey that ended tragically when his returning ship was torpedoed in the English Channel by a German submarine. World premieres at the Met were also torpedoed for a couple of seasons, though Gatti managed, as he had several times previously, to give first American hearings of several European efforts. The most notable was Gluck's *Iphigénie en Tauride* (given in the Richard Strauss revamping as *Iphigenia auf Tauris*), with the Germans Melanie Kurt, Johannes Sembach, and Curt Braun.

Gatti honestly tried to justify the Gluck panel on the proscenium. Both ambitious and unrewarded was the introduction of *Armide* as the opening for 1910–11, in which the heroine (Fremstad) monopolized the stage to such an extent that the two gentlemen, Caruso and Amato, lounged about in their dressing rooms for hours, bored and restless. A revival of *Orfeo* the same season brought together that famous team, buxom Louise Homer and lissome Alma Gluck.

He fared better with other revivals of older material and with certain works that were leaving the experimental category and gaining acceptance: *Boris, Les Contes d'Hoffmann, Rosenkavalier, Elektra*—and eventually *Salome—Eugene Onegin, Louise, Prince Igor, Coq d'Or,* and the Czechish works which were inevitably sung in German—*Jenufa* and *Schwanda*. The less common Russians also appeared: *Sadko, Fair at Sorochinsk, Snegurochka;* while his introduction of *Pelléas et Mélisande* bespoke his own championship of the work that had bored the Milanese. Most sensational was Massenet's *Thaïs,* which caused Krehbiel to remember Mary Garden mournfully. "A vaulting spirit such as Miss Farrar's," said the *Tribune* critic, who was by now slightly disenchanted with America's most beloved diva, "would never rest content with a mere water-color courtesan—nor even one by Watteau—she must attempt at least a Titian."

Out of thirty or so Italian works have remained only Puccini's *Girl, Triptych,* and *Turandot,* and Montemezzi's *L'Amore dei Tre Re,* with a few possibly viable entries by Wolf-Ferrari.

Little else has survived of any nationality. French items such as Dukas' *Ariane et Barbe Bleue,* Ravel's *L'Heure Espagnole,* Massenet's *Don Quichotte* and the savage *Navarraise,* Rabaud's *Mârouf,* and Gounod's *Mireille* are occasionally revived under other roofs, but where are the realms of the two Kings, *Lahore* and *Ys* or the Queen *Fiamette* or the bohemian raptures of *Louise's* successor, *Julien?* German works like *Königskinder* and later *Tote Stadt* and *Violanta,* mounted solely to show off Geraldine Farrar or Maria Jeritza, will probably never surround other prima donnas in America. The two von Suppé operettas put on for Jeritza, *Boccaccio* and *Donna Juanita,* just possibly stand a better chance. But who hears, now, let alone pronounces, *Der Widerspenstigen Zähmung,* Goetz's idea of *The Taming of the Shrew?* By some sort of shuddering consensus, the worst examples of American, French, and German remain only as bad dreams: Seymour's *In the Pasha's Garden,* Albert Wolff's *L'Oiseau Bleu* (to Maeterlinck's whimsical play), and Weiss's *Polish Jew (Der Polnische Jude)* (which as a play was a favorite of Henry Irving).

In those years before the war, Gatti's grievous losses were Eames, Sembrich, Fremstad, Mahler, Hertz, and Toscanini. It is saddening to realize that, except for Mahler, none of them was necessary. Sembrich, to be sure, had aged, but no one would admit it at the glorious farewell given to her in the House and at a private dinner, in which even the critics joined in feting her to the skies. Eames could have sung a little longer with charm and dignity—she *did* sing at the Boston Opera in 1911–12. Hertz conducted the San Francisco Symphony for fifteen years thereafter. But the deepest regret must be felt for Fremstad and Toscanini. The mystery of the fiery conductor's sudden break in 1915 has never been plumbed. Gatti unconvincingly attributes it to the conductor's patriotic wish to be in wartime Italy. "Money!" unhesitatingly said Bruno Zirato, Caruso's secretary at the time. Lack of rehearsals, insists Toscanini's son, Walter. It is true that Toscanini was refused what he considered minimum rehearsal time. That the directors would have let him go for lack of a salary raise seems incredible, since Gatti doubtless would have urged them to yield anything he asked, at least in Zirato's view, although others believe that the General Manager had by now succumbed to the universal attitude of penny-pinching. A personal rift (gossips attributed it to rivalry over Farrar) appeared between the two, not to be healed until 1932, when Toscanini had already returned to become entrenched in the New York Philharmonic-Symphony. He abdicated the opera throne quietly after a disastrous substitution of second-rate singers for key posts in *Carmen* and a final routine *Iris*. In the chorus of dismay over the news that he would not return, a curious note of denigration appeared under the signature of W. J. Henderson in the *Sun*. Toscanini would not be missed, Henderson thought. After all, his conducting "was appreciated by few." It seemed almost as if Reginald de Koven had slipped into the *Sun* columns from the *World*.

Artur Bodanzky, destined to give sturdy service in the German wing for two dozen years, succeeded Hertz in 1915, making his debut in *Götterdämmerung*, with Melanie Kurt as Brünnhilde. Polacco and a second-stringer, Gaetano Bavagnoli, succeeded but did not supplant Toscanini.

Blood had always been bad between Fremstad and Johanna Gadski; indeed, it flowed openly in one curtain call, when Fremstad-Sieglinde insisted that Gadski-Brünnhilde had purposely dragged her (Sieglinde's) arm across the nails on Brünnhilde's breastplate. The furious American allowed the blood to stream in taking further curtain calls, and "by some legerdemain," wrote Mary Watkins Cushing in *The Rainbow Bridge,* saw to it that Gadski's long sleeve got in the way. Other jealousies paled in the feud with Gadski. But this need not have driven Fremstad from the Metropolitan's stage. More influential was the deep misunderstanding between the prima donna ("difficult, very difficult," murmured Gatti about her) and the manager (who played "a devious political game"). Fremstad believed that Gatti allowed the name of Melanie Kurt to creep out as her successor, while giving Gadski more rein. She herself forced the decision; her pride would allow no less. But it was a bitter loss to her and to the American public, which rallied violently in her behalf when her departure became known. The final insult, oddly enough confirmed by Gatti's first wife as intentional, placed Fremstad in her least favorite role, Elsa, for her operatic farewell, with a routine Sunday night concert as the finality. At the same time, Gadski was given the *Tristan* Fremstad asked for on the last Saturday night. No amount of retribution —and the curtain blow was soon to fall in more unhappy circumstances on her rival—could sweeten the aftermath for Fremstad. The remainder of her story can be summed up in her own words, spoken once to a reporter: "I spring into life when the curtain rises, and when it falls, I might as well die. The world I exist in between performances is the strange one, alien, dark, confused!" In that land where Tristan asked Isolde to follow, *"Dem Land . . . der Sonne Licht nicht scheint . . . das Wunderreich der Nacht,"* this Isolde dwelt in shadow for thirty-seven years. Then her heart stilled, and she was buried in Wisconsin in peaceful obscurity.

Among the dozen newcomers who mattered, two of Gatti's choice led all the rest—alphabetically, at least. Pasquale Amato, the excellent Italian baritone, who with two lapses would continue to endear himself to the Metropolitan audiences until 1933, headed the roster until Paul Althouse, the American tenor, supplanted him in 1912. Frances Alda remained at the van of the "Female Artists" almost constantly until she retired in 1930, being supplanted in 1919 and again in 1923 by Merle Alcock, the young American. What the Metropolitan company found more difficult to cope with was Alda's position as First Lady. After two years of grave yet impassioned courtship by Gatti, Alda agreed to marry him on April 3, 1910, perhaps because she felt "for the first time in my life, alone," after an operation for ruptured appendix and a slow convalescence. The red-haired—and hot-tempered—New Zealander and the morose, dignified Italian made a strange pair. The differences in their ages and temperaments, working in the backstage ferment of the big opera house, ensured a rocky road, no matter how true the love. The title of her memoirs, *Men, Women and Tenors*, bespeaks the freedom and occasional malice—if not invariable accuracy—of her revelations.

Overhearing a conversation at a dress rehearsal between Kahn and Henry Russell, she burst in upon them as Kahn was saying: "As the director's wife, it is much better that Alda should not sing here next season." The soprano gave Kahn the shock of his life, retorting before he had time to catch his breath: "I suppose it would be all right if I were his mistress instead of his wife. I resign right now!"

Her absence from the Met for a year was noted. During that time she sang in Boston, but not as often as Gatti would have wished. Philip Hale, writing in the *Herald* after Alda's first appearance that season (in *Mefistofele*), noted: "Where goes Gatti, there goes she. Generous are the operatic fates that watch over her."

Alda remained entrenched until 1929, her red hair, resonant voice, and startling figure dominating the halls wherein she trod as the boss's wife. (So enormous was her upper structure that it seemingly did not diminish even when she was lying down, said Ziegler's daughter.) Whatever her gifts, and they were not inconsiderable, she aroused almost more fear and distrust than admiration, for her tongue was sharpened to produce a wound as often as a witticism. In 1929 she divorced Gatti and the next year he married Rosina Galli, the petite ballerina. Alda's departure coincided with that season, 1929–30. She had very little to do in those last months—a couple of Manon Lescauts and a Mimi in *Bohème*, the role she claimed as her greatest success. She sang it often with Caruso.

Bohème became the vehicle for Caruso's wildest pranks. He retrieved and displayed Alda's pantaloons, shed behind a sofa when a button gave way; filled Colline's hat with flour (or, some say, water), and sewed up the pockets of the *vecchia zimarra* so that the philosopher couldn't get his books in; inspired Scotti to squirt seltzer into Mimi's face as she bent over to warm herself at the fire; inserted bits of string, paper, nails, and buttons into the snow that fell from the propman's bucket onto the despairing heroine, and filled a wine glass with ink. Philadelphia was the scene of most of these shenanigans; being out of town on even so short a junket always let Caruso's high spirits loose. One performance broke up when the three men, Caruso (Rodolfo), Scotti (Marcello), and De Segurola (Colline), their backs to Mimi (Alda), suddenly turned and revealed bland faces each sporting a monocle. (De Segurola's was the only genuine article; he wore it almost always.) The climax of the high jinks arrived when the dying Mimi tossed on a shaky bed from which the front castors had been removed. The jokers paid a fine of $100 each with no regrets.

Alda doesn't say, but this shambles was probably not the performance (spotted by Philadelphia critic Max de Schauensee as December 23, 1913) at which Caruso pulled his famous stunt of singing *"Vecchia zimarra"* for the hoarse De Segurola, the one and only time he assumed a bass role, although he repeated it for souvenir phonograph records. No one past the footlights perceived the substitution except the shocked conductor, Giorgio Polacco.

Two additional newcomers in Gatti's first years proved pillars of strength. Margarete Matzenauer's developing versatility was not apparent at her debut as Amneris in Toscanini's 1911 opening night, although the voice issuing from the imposing body was one of superb quality, rich and dark, and genuinely artistic. She sang other mezzo roles— Brangäne, Waltraute, Ortrud, Hate (*Armide*), Orfeo, and Erda before revealing viable upper reaches in Kundry, which she undertook as a replacement for Fremstad—her first anywhere. This led to later exploits in the soprano register.

Giuseppe de Luca began a term lasting almost a quarter of a century when he sang the Figaro of *Barbiere* on November 25, 1915. He was recognized as "able," "competent," and all those other descriptions that show a lack of real enthusiasm on the part of a critic, but won his way to the pedestal reserved only for "Grand Old" examples of the species.

In his sixth year, Gatti experienced the evil of a practice that lent itself all too amiably to chicanery, governing the sale of tickets to the opera and theatre in the first part of the century. In the case of opera subscriptions it led to open scandal. When Frederick Rullman came to the assistance of Maurice Grau, the manager had shown his gratitude by allowing Rullman the libretto concession and, even more important, the privilege of buying blocks of tickets at a discount (it was said to be 15 percent) for resale at whatever the market would bear. Other agencies also flourished on this scheme, although the opera was beginning to rely more and more on its own box office. It was Tyson and Company who eventually had to face the law.

In the summer of 1913, this firm bought $157,000 worth of tickets, many for subscribers who were accustomed to order opera tickets on this basis from agencies, using them also to obtain theatre tickets at speculation prices. The head of Tyson, Richard J. Hartman, then used the tickets he had bought as collateral for a loan from the Metropolitan Trust Company, paid the opera with the proceeds, and bought more tickets. When the opera opening drew near, one third of the subscribers could not get their tickets; Hartman had not redeemed them and the trust company would not relinquish them. The pandemonium spread in several different directions, with the Met disclaiming the use Tyson had made of its subscription circular (although plain as day was the direction to correspond with that agency); the trust company offered bona fide subscribers the privilege of buying their tickets over again at a small discount (meanwhile the price had gone up from $5 to $6 for the "fashionable" seats); Tyson dug up enough money to redeem tickets for a week and somehow or other most of the first-nighters did not have to miss the glory of the November 17 *La Gioconda*. The twenty-six customers who had paid double got a refund. But in spite of the unhealthy odor of these transactions, the Met continued to use agencies for several years, until at last its own subscription office was set up. The speculators' business was not reformed by law until 1919, and even long after that, the service charges rose to whatever the customer could pay.

The events of July, 1914, in Sarajevo inevitably caused temblors under Thirty-ninth and Broadway, New York. Gatti's immediate problem was to rescue a few of his singers, notably Albert Reiss, whose unique talents were wanted for the Humperdinck Witch, the Wagner David and Mime, the Mussorgsky Simpleton, and a clutch of what, in his hands, could hardly be called "secondary" roles. He was plucked out of a concentration camp in France and stayed in America till after the war. Dinh Gilly could not be liberated. Several German singers arrived safely for their debuts—Johannes Sembach, Melanie Kurt, and Elisabeth Schumann (the adorable Sophie, Musetta, and Papagena of this one season, after which she returned to Germany, then enjoyed European acclaim until the late thirties, when she settled in New York).

Once he had his artists, Gatti faced another dilemma: What to do with all of them? He could not very well extend his own season, and two former avenues of exchange had been shut off when both Chicago and Boston opera directorates turned their faces to the wall. (The exchange with Boston had turned out rather one-sided: Gatti sent many more hostages than he received. Little lasting impression had been made on New York by Alice Nielsen, George Baklanoff, Lydia Lipkowska, Florencio Constantino, Maria Claessens, Elvira Leveroni, Giovanni Polese, and Edward Lankow, no matter what their importance to the Hub.) So Gatti found his jigsaw puzzle more vexatious than usual.

The question of giving German opera did not become acute until later. Toscanini went ahead with *Euryanthe,* which Krehbiel pronounced "almost ineffable," and which involved two Americans in the midst of a clump of Germans: Arthur Middleton, a new baritone; and Mabel Garrison, a delectable soprano. The title role was sung by the beautiful, blond Frieda Hempel, who had made her debut in December, 1912, after a trying summer in which she won a libel suit against the Berlin newspaper that had accused her of participating in an "orgy" in order to win a decoration from Leopold, King of the Belgians. Hempel had become a mainstay for her Mozart roles as well as her Olympia (*Contes d'Hoffmann*) and a half dozen conventional coloratura flights. The *Rosenkavalier* and *Fidelio* were still welcome for a while; the Wagnerian gods remained in their Metropolitan Valhalla; *Tristan* lingered unchallenged; and a new Hans Sachs in the person of the distinguished American Clarence Whitehill added what excitement could be summoned up for the German repertoire in 1916–17.

Thus matters stood, not too easily, while the calm ran before the storm. The lightning bolt that cleaved a world in two struck in the middle of an otherwise innocuous performance—the fourth of six—of Reginald de Koven's *Canterbury Pilgrims* on April 2, 1917. The work had already outlived its welcome; it reflected the management's "self-imposed duty" to native talent, but possessed not a serious moment, and though full of life and humor and gay tunes, sent the tone of the grand opera house too far in the direction of outright popularity. (That this estimation came from the pages of the *World* he had formerly tracked with his own opinions cannot have pleased the composer. The criticism was unsigned, but De Koven must have known his successor.) On the day of this relatively minor occurrence at Thirty-ninth and Broadway, other signs of the times carried more weight: a bomb had been found in a courthouse, and President Wilson had appealed to the railroads not to strike. New York Jews went on record as wild with joy over the success of the Russian revolution.

Plenty of warning should have prepared for the zero hour. As early as March 2, the opera audience had risen shouting to its feet as "La Marseillaise" rang out in a performance of *Madame Sans-Gêne*. For days the perfidy of Germany had been spread out for all to see; the contemptuous decision to wage unrestricted submarine war and the sinking of American vessels brought a climax. For days the President exhorted Congress to watchful preparedness until on March 26 he succeeded in calling out a militia of 20,000 and priming the Navy to a wartime basis. "We are being forced into war," he announced two days later. "Every obstacle removed," the actual declaration became a foregone matter. On April 1 a screaming *World* banner head added fuel: "America's Duty to Civilization Is to Declare War on Germany!"

Congress met on April 2 for the purpose of fulfilling that very duty. Senator Henry Cabot Lodge knocked down a pacifist. Ignace Paderewski predicted liberty for his native Poland. On April 3 the *Times* reported that "patriotism took hold of the Metropolitan Opera House last night and shook it until the auditorium fairly rang."

The actual moment of the declaration had been 8:35 P.M. but the Met found time to work it in only just before the fourth-act curtain of De Koven's opera. As Bodanzky (carefully and all too casually called a "Hungarian") entered the pit, tension rose. His arms lifted high, he gave the signal and the orchestra began the national anthem. Springing to its collective feet, the audience sang as no audience had sung before. Many applauded. "We are all one now," they seemed to feel and utter.

Suddenly to the front of Iselin's box—Number 15—pushed a man whom all quickly recognized. He was James W. Gerard, recently recalled as Ambassador to Germany. In a ringing voice he called for three cheers for President Wilson. There was a moment of hesitation. Then from (almost) 3,500 throats came the roar of approbation. Hardly had it died when someone in J. P. Morgan's center box sang out: "Three cheers for Ambassador Gerard!"

Several moments later the curtain rose on the scene where the King decrees that Chaucer (Sembach) does not have to wed the scheming Alisoun, the Wife of Bath (Margarete Ober) but may remain faithful to his Prioress (Edith Mason). It was the presidential, not the kingly, verdict that turned Alisoun white and faint. The records indicate that Ober sang the remaining two performances—one closed the season—but they were her last at the Metropolitan. Before the season had opened in 1917, she, together with Kurt, Sembach, Braun, and Goritz, were notified they were *personae non gratae*. Ober had openly avowed her enmity; this largely determined a negative verdict in her suit against the company. Goritz had also spoken too loudly—had even been accused, although no proof exists, of singing a macabre ditty in praise of the sinking of the *Lusitania*. This was alleged to have been part of the entertainment at a party celebrating the event, at which Mme. Gadski and her husband, Captain Hans Tauscher, were hosts. Tauscher had been accused in 1916 of plotting to blow up the Welland Canal, but was acquitted. Gadski thus uttered her final Metropolitan note in the *Tristan "Liebestod"* of April 13. Considering that she sang successfully in Covent Garden for four more seasons and toured the United States in concert and with the German Grand Opera until 1931, it seems unlikely that W. J. Henderson remained entirely unprejudiced when he wrote that she had been dismissed because of the "deterioration of her voice and art."

The April day that blackened the world deeply affected the tiny microcosm of the lyric and dramatic theatre. All up and down Broadway the same wild scenes scarred playwrights' creations (not all works of art, to be sure). It was star time on the Great White Way; ruefully we scan the list of the three dozen theatres, marveling nostalgically at the lustrous names: Maude Adams, Laurette Taylor, George Arliss, William Collier, William Gillette, and Jane Cowl (fragile and sentimental in *Lilac Time*). At the Ziegfeld "Midnight Frolic," Will Rogers no doubt found a few words to say. From the Forty-Fourth Street Theatre, a sobered audience filed out after the movie *Joan the Woman* (whose heroine was listed simply as "Farrar"), returning from the Maid's medieval conflicts to the twentieth century. America was at war. No one, not even those glamorous creatures in the theatres and opera house, not even those flickering shadows on the screen, could escape.

Congress delayed a few days while debate raged in both houses. The solemn declaration of war came forth on April 6. It happened to be Good Friday, and the Metropolitan provided ironic comment by its choice of opera: Wagner's compassionate *Parsifal*.

13

RECONSTRUCTION

Look, my friend, in politics as in the theatre, one must not act on the basis of absolute canons, but on reasoned expectability—what is not right today becomes right tomorrow.

—GATTI-CASAZZA,
in a letter to Bruno Zirato

One year, seven months, and nine days after the tumultous April scene in the Metropolitan's gilded auditorium, pandemonium broke loose again. This time jubilation took the place of grimness. The Armistice had been signed! The war had ended!

These glad tidings coincided with the opening of the Metropolitan's thirty-fourth season and Gatti-Casazza's eleventh. The crowds jammed Times Square and access to the opera house became difficult, almost impossible. Still the Parquet and upper balconies were jammed and a goodly number of boxholders took their places in time for the second-act curtain of *Samson et Dalila* (how fortunate Gatti had decided on a French opera!). Their early demeanor was quiet in contrast to that 1917 occasion, the *World* commented. But excitement grew as plump Pierre Monteux, the suave and knowledgeable Frenchman, waddled into the pit and gave the signal for the curtain to rise.

What shouts! What joy! It seemed "something bigger than ever before pervaded the opera house at a season's premiere. It drove deep into the hearts and souls of the audience—good fellowship, friendliness and brotherliness reigned!" concluded the *World*. Flags of the Allies in brilliant colors belled out across the stage, punctuating the mass of talented humanity gathered there. The entire company assembled, with Caruso in the center of the front line, holding aloft the Italian flag. Louise Homer bore the Stars and Stripes, Léon Rothier and the new baritone Robert Couzinou shared the French Tricolor. In the absence of a British subject, Paolo Ananian, the Hebrew Messenger of the cast, waved the Union Jack.

One national anthem followed the other, until the lights dimmed and spotlights simultaneously found the Belgian banner on the stage and the Belgian Minister to the United States in a box. Baron de Cartier de

Marchienne acknowledged proudly *"La Brabançonne,"* the anthem of his country.

At the opening of the 1917 season, America's close brush with the spectre of war had dimmed Society's glitter to the mere glow of a single tiara winking from the center box on the head of Mrs. Pierpont Hamilton. Most *grandes dames* "eschewed a display of 'ice,' " reported *Town Topics,* although Mrs. Harry Payne Whitney seemed to be having a little trouble with her long diamond chain, which became involved, together with her peacock feather fan, in her fervent applause for Caruso's Radames and debutante Claudia Muzio's Aida. Verdi's opera was decidedly not to the taste of Cyril Hatch, however, for prying glasses discovered him napping in the back of the Vanderbilt box, where his wife acted as hostess without (oh, scandalous!) gloves.

After a great deal of fussing in the back of the box, Mabel Gerry came forward to see and be seen, "having heard that there would be many changes in the little red-velvet bon-bon boxes." But she was reassured until her glasses reached Box 22, where Edward R. Stettinius and his Isabel held forth, the lady backed up against Mrs. Ogden Mills. "My heart nearly lost a beat," said the reporter, "every time the large black feather fan waved by Mrs. S. came near upsetting Mrs. Mills' coiffure. Still, I can picture the imperturbable Teenie, with perfect *sang froid,* saying merely, 'Ogden, hand me the reserve transformation.' "

Knitting needles had clicked all over the house, but *Town Topics* found it impossible to imagine the Parterre bringing half-finished sweaters to the show. "Fancy Mrs. Mills or Mrs. Twombly knitting away at some woolly garment with fortunes in jewels glistening about their heads and throats!"

Now that the Armistice had really arrived, on the exact date of the Metropolitan's 1918 opening, all classes from top to bottom threw dignity to the winds, reported *Town Topics,* "and were as hilarious as college boys on holiday." The first member of the Morgan family to reach the Opera House was Mrs. Herbert Satterlee, who progressed through the corridor exclaiming, "Oh, happy day! Happy day!" Morgan himself was so joyful that he shook hands with everyone, even the ticket taker at Thirty-ninth Street. Although many Parterre occupants were customarily late—and "who cared whether Mrs. Spondulicks got there in time to show her diamonds before the curtain went up?"—the members of Society who had arrived joined in vociferously. "Mrs. F. K. Pendleton, in Mrs. Ogden Goelet's box (No. 1), flung out her long, white-gloved arms wildly and sang 'The Star-Spangled Banner' in a voice that caused even the chorus on the stage to look up." She would have loved to let everyone know that her husband was a grandson of Francis Scott Key. Other singers were Mrs. John S. Rogers, in the Juilliard box (No. 2) with Mrs. Willie Greenough and Mrs. Joseph Earle Stevens, a Tuxedo crony. Flora Payne Whitney nearly fell out of her box. Mrs. William J. Schieffelin and her daughter and little Mrs. Fred Osborn sang, laughed, and cheered like three little maids from school.

Of course, reminded the writer, some of the box parties maintained the restraint expected of celebrities in public, no matter how great the provocation. Mrs. Twombly and her sister, Mrs. William Douglas Sloane, keeping up Vanderbilt standards, were enthusiastic, but only to a gentle degree. Mrs. Jimmie Burden, the most temperamental Sloane daughter, made up for this coolness, however. During intermission, she leaned over and had a lively talk with Elbert H. Gary. This was mentioned because it marked the first social intercourse between the two boxes. The velvet-covered bars between boxes, so long symbols of sharp social divisions and differences, were not of any account that Monday night.

All eyes and opera glasses were focused on Box 20, where Mrs. Enrico Caruso was hostess in Mrs. Ogden Mills's domain. Dorothy Benjamin had married the tenor on August 20, and all the maids and matrons who had been saying, "Oh, Caruso, why did you do so?" now had to admit that his bride looked stunning, "with her curly short hair framing her childish face, wearing a white satin gown with a large bunch of gardenias thrust into her girdle."

Mrs. George Jay Gould, who "looked even more nymphlike than last season, wore a violet gown and carried a large feather fan to match. She often talked to George F. Baker in the next box. . . . When Governor [Charles S.] Whitman burst into the Gould box and interrupted Baker's chat, the elderly financier registered displeasure and it was not long before the Governor beat a hasty retreat." But then, he had just been succeeded by the "uncouth" Alfred E. Smith and should perhaps be punished for losing. Mrs. Edward T. Stotesbury from Philadelphia was a "terrible disappointment"—hardly any jewels. Only a rope of pearls reaching below the waist and a diamond hair ornament. Mrs. Gould's egg-sized pearls far outshone the Quaker City matron's.

"Sonny" [Cornelius Vanderbilt] Whitney, now a lieutenant in the aviation forces, as *Town Topics* quaintly put it, arrived with the family, then ducked out "for an ice cream soda or something" and hadn't returned by the last curtain. The reporter speculated that the opera was not Sonny's idea of a celebration.

Society suffered its customary schizophrenia in being drawn both to the opera and the Horse Show. Ambassador Gerard and Reginald Vanderbilt were seen at Madison Square Garden; Mrs. E. H. Harriman, emulating Mrs. Paran Stevens of yore, registered her name in both spots.

The Metropolitan's single war year had proved more difficult for Gatti than his whole previous experience combined, including his ten years at La Scala and the first five at Ferrara. In spite of reassurances from critics and several board members, Gatti entertained a premonition that tolerance for German operas would melt away in the first heat of battle. He was proved right one week before plans had to be announced. In the hasty rearrangement, the company became "half American," the chief additions in this branch being Rosa Ponselle, Ruth Miller, May Peterson, Thomas Chalmers, Rafaelo Diaz (whose specialty was the cruelly high *tessitura* of the Astrologer in *Le Coq d'Or*), and Morgan Kingston. "Foreigners" included Hipólito Lazaro (who hit a high D at his debut in *Rigoletto*), José Mardones (another Spaniard, who had given five years of excellent service to the Boston Opera), Julia Claussen, the vivid Swedish contralto, and Florence Easton (really an Englishwoman who was brought up in Canada, and whose enormous versatility remained at the service of the Metropolitan for twelve years).

The return of two tenors caused little comment, for Riccardo Martin, the genuinely capable American, always had the misfortune to be in the same opera house with first Caruso and later both Caruso and Martinelli (and was said by Henry T. Finck to be *persona non grata* with the Metropolitan anyway), while John McCormack's unique command of the Mozart style found vent in America only in two performances as Don Ottavio in the Boston Opera's *Don Giovanni,* though he sang Rodolfo and other conventional heroes.

Gatti's 1917 acquisition of a new scenic designer had no war significance, for the Viennese Joseph Urban had been in the United States since 1912. He had made his first American splash with stunning sets for the Boston Opera—a *Pelléas et Mélisande* and *Tristan und Isolde* that were practically duplicated at the Met, *Contes d'Hoffmann, Louise, Gioielli della Madonna,* and many others. The disbandment of Russell's company in 1914 left Urban adrift, but not for long. He exercised his stage talents for Ziegfeld's *Follies* and other Broadway productions and his architectural genius for many luxurious homes in Florida and (notably) the late Ziegfeld Theatre in New York, then was summoned to the Met. His first display there was a *Faust* "of great beauty"; the same season he did settings for *Saint Elizabeth,* Liszt's staged oratorio, and a revival of *Le Prophète,* a triple play of new scenic standards. His greatest contribution was using light as a generator for color, sprinkled on in a pointillist fashion. Until his death in 1933 he contributed more than forty investitures to Gatti's repertoire, his last being the massive single set for *Elektra,* which was replaced only in 1966. His *Tristan* endured until the unworthy Otto substitutes of 1959; his *Parsifal* of 1920 replaced the dubious delights of the first postwar performance, which boasted what the *Sun* called "gold outhouses and pink bushes from the cover of a seed catalogue." Urban's atmospheric and lofty scenes gave way only in 1955 to Leo Kerz's slide projections. His initial *Faust* lasted until 1951.

Newcomers to the postwar repertoire included the innocuous *St. Elizabeth* (in English), Mascagni's *Lodoletta,* with Farrar (only once) and Caruso, and—several shades better—Rabaud's *Marouf.* Rimsky-Korsakoff's endearing *Coq d'Or* made the first of many Met appearances in a version that ranked the singers on side benches while the ballet, led by Gatti's new wife, took over the action. This and other coloratura specimens were introduced for the Spanish Maria Barrientos. Gatti's former fiancée had made her debut as Lucia in 1915–16. Frieda Hempel, a German, sang in Italian *The Daughter of the Regiment,* written originally in French, as another novel reconstruction.

Gatti resumed his practice of giving world premieres of American works, combining Charles W. Cadman's Indian opera, *Shanewis,* with H. F. Gilbert's ballet, *The Dance in Place Congo,* and a repetition of Leoni's *Oracolo,* thus, as Irving Kolodin remarked, "offering a prismatic sequence of red men, black men, and yellow men."

The end of the war did not necessarily restore German opera immediately to the bosoms of Gatti and his board of directors. (Perhaps believing that the American public, not knowing Weber's *Oberon* very well, would not realize that its composer had the honor of being crowned the father of German romantic opera, Gatti did not hesitate to retain it in December, 1918. It was, in any case, sung in English.) But even without Wagner, Strauss, & Co., the first postwar season shone with a certain splendor, embracing the world premiere of Puccini's *Triptych* on December 14, 1918 (a similar showcase for two American works, Breil's *Legend* and Hugo's *Temple Dancer* could be considered wasted), the first New York performance in French of Gounod's *Mireille* (with scenes made from somewhat mediocre designs by Victor Maurel), and the introduction into the opera calendar proper of Stravinsky's ballet *Petrouchka,* one of Monteux's many notable accomplishments. Hanging it as a pendant to—of all things—*Traviata* provided one of those incongruities with which Met annals are studded; the ballet ran in better company with Ricci's little *Crispino e la Comare,* seen for the first time in the House. *Petrouchka* had been a cog in the pinwheel of the Diaghilev Ballet Russe that had arrived in America after harrowing European experiences and occupied the Metropolitan boards for a spring season in 1915–16, to Otto Kahn's satisfaction. The great Nijinsky himself had danced two performances of Stravinsky's amusing ballet, among the few he vouchsafed eager American audiences.

Puccini's rather ill-assorted three operas-in-tandem allowed practically the entire American-Italian axis to parade in more or less satisfactory roles. The grisly *Il Tabarro* featured a new baritone, Luigi Montesanto, and a new tenor, Giulio Crimi, but allowed little scope for the soprano who later became the darling of Chicago, though never properly appreciated in New York—Claudia Muzio. *Suor Angelica* demanded an all-female cast, with Geraldine Farrar the hapless heroine. *Gianni Schicchi* was the hit of the night—"uproarious" in at least two critics' estimates. The chief figure, the rogue of the title, offered delicious opportunities for a baritone who had by now become a fixture in the Metropolitan's considerations—Giuseppe de Luca.

Hard feelings toward our conquered enemy did not abate—and then only partially—until 1919–20, when the Metropolitan cautiously ventured the (now) least controversial work of Wagner's—*Parsifal.* But to salve the feelings of those to whom the aggressors' language still struck harshly on the ear, English was the coin of the day. The translation by the esteemed Henry E. Krehbiel did little to advance the project artistically, however. The leading singers matched role for role—except for the Guileless Fool himself—with those who had participated in the fateful afternoon of April 6, 1917, when war was screamed through the streets outside. Chosen to ease the prodigal Teuton back into the fold was an American tenor, Orville Harrold, who had come to Gatti via vaudeville and Oscar Hammerstein, had made his debut as Leopold in the 1919 revival of *La Juive,* and would play opposite Farrar in *Louise* and Jeritza in *Die Tote Stadt,* as well as in many more conventional parts. Margarete Matzenauer, the Junoesque Hungarian contralto, and Clarence Whitehill, the dignified American bass, were the carry-overs, along with Conductor Bodanzky, who could now be freely labeled Viennese. Johannes Sembach would return—the only German of those dismissed to do so—the following year to take over some performances, but still in English, along with Florence Easton.

Although tolerance had arrived, if only by default, audiences could not bring themselves to care for a gesture by the German outcasts, Ober, Goritz, Braun, and Weil among them, who tried a season at the Lexington Theatre in October, 1919. Perhaps it was not tactful of Weil to end the opening concert with the Sachs manifesto on German art. Even conversion to English couldn't save the venture.

Sembach, Matzenauer, Whitehill, and Robert Blass (an American who had returned after a decade) made up the core of the English-singing team to ease *Tristan* and *Isolde* and *Lohengrin* back into circulation in 1920–21. Variations on the theme included the sumptuous Matzenauer singing her first Isolde in the House. She had practiced earlier with the Boston Opera in ideal circumstances. Her Tristan there had been her own husband, Edoardo Ferrari-Fontana, and under her royal robes she was carrying his child. (The tenor had created Avito in *L'Amore dei Tre Re.* Gatti summoned him for this role in 1913–14, but although he ranked as Italy's top Wagnerian, did not allow him a *Tristan,* probably because, although he had tried desperately to sing it in German in Boston, habit proved too much for him in the third act.) Two beautiful Americans, Jeanne Gordon of the class of 1919–20 and Marion Telva of 1920–21, alternated as Brangäne, while William Gustafson, the American bass who had also been Titurel the year before, took over from Blass as King

Marke and King Henry. Harrold and Morgan Kingston both had a chance at the Swan Knight, and Claussen showed a powerful Ortrud, no matter what the language. On March 6, Bodanzky daringly slipped in the "Prize Song" from *Meistersinger* in a Wagner concert—but still in English.

The native tongue still echoed from the stage in 1921–22 for the first *Lohengrin* and all the *Parsifals,* but *Tristan* was allowed to revert (with the same singers showing their adaptability) and *Die Walküre* made a triumphant return in *Urtext.* Maria Jeritza had come to delight her growing body of adherents, and when Korngold's *Tote Stadt* was introduced to America in her behalf, no question about language arose. She sang Elsa and Sieglinde in the mother tongue as well and nobody thought any more about the problem. Patrons could now worry about the increase in ticket prices to $7 at top and $1.50 for the cheapest seats. Furthermore, it was infinitely more vexatious not to be able to order a real drink in intermissions. The advent of Prohibition wiped out remembrances of all other noble experiments.

Still, although *Tannhäuser* soon joined the procession, caution kept that most German of German operas, *Die Meistersinger,* from possible contamination of the audience until 1923, when *Siegfried* also returned. But it was the usual difficulties of production, casting, and popularity that held the first and last segments of the *Ring* off until 1924. By now all segregating labels had been rinsed off, and *The Polish Jew* was remembered only for its dismal failure, not necessarily of any nationality. Weiss's feeble effort, in which Gatti went as far as could be expected in American chauvinism by engaging a full-blooded (if South American) Indian for the leading role, earned only scorn as "the deadliest soporific ever administered" in New York. Chief Caupolican lingered on the following season, only to sing the "Toreador Song" at a Sunday concert but never to assume the matador's toga in performance, and to enact a Brooklyn Tonio, but never to replace in New York the seasoned De Luca, the relatively new Giuseppe Danise, or bull-voiced Titta Ruffo, who had been a sensation in Chicago and in Europe, and finally reached the Met at the age of fifty-five.

In the first postwar season a new star had risen in the American firmament. Rosa Ponselle had made her debut in the Metropolitan's first *Forza del Destino* on November 15, 1918.

All the versions of this Horatio Alger story translated to the distaff side agree that Rosa was born in Meriden, Connecticut, that her real name was Ponzillo, and that she and her sister Carmela went the minor-league vaudeville route with tidy success, finally achieving Keith's Palace in New York. Bruno Zirato, arranging a benefit bazaar for widows of Italian soldiers who had died in the Allied cause, booked the sister act for the smaller theatre in Grand Central Palace. In order to fill the larger auditorium, Caruso was suggested as a performer. The tenor promised to do everything but sing and donated two small statues for auctioning. About this time, William Thorner, a former associate of the De Reszkes, had been persuaded to take Rosa on as a pupil. The lines all converged at the Metropolitan at an audition in which the soprano fainted. She was allowed to come back, and sang so divinely that Gatti was moved to entrust her with his important Verdi revival. Caruso promised to partner her. The voice that James Huneker called "vocal gold" went on to enrich such roles as Rachel in *La Juive* (her first opening night and with Caruso in the fateful season of 1920–21), Elizabeth in *Don Carlos,* and in various revivals of Verdi, Rossini (*William Tell*), Meyerbeer (*L'Africaine*), and Spontini (*La Vestale,* another opening night in 1926, this time with the stentorian Giacomo Lauri-Volpi and the new bass, Ezio Pinza). Her Donna Anna set a mark for Mozart singers. Her Violetta astounded critics who thought her incapable of the first-act fireworks, although London liked her really better than New York in this role. Ponselle's Norma, above all, became the ideal for Bellini's florid Druid. Finally, her Carmen created a controversy that followed her into an untimely retirement.

Ponselle's nervousness and superstition amounted to pathology. She would walk around the theatre several times before daring to enter. Her dismay at finding thirteen at table rose to panic. Gatti would resort to a roundabout tactic to get her into the House and ready to sing: knowing that she could be persuaded by Mrs. Earle Lewis (wife of the box-office treasurer), Gatti would call Lewis and say: "Please ask your wife to call Rosa—you know why." Stories about her retirement clustered as thickly as those about her beginnings. Francis Robinson, the present press chief, has heard that she walked across town with Edward Johnson in his second season (1936–37), begging all the way for a revival of *Adriana Lecouvreur*. At his reiterated "No," she promised not to return. That promise she kept. Meanwhile, she had become "Mrs. Baltimore," having married

Carle A. Jackson, son of the mayor, on December 13, 1936. This offered
enough reason to quit the opera house and she used it. Still, the rumors
persisted that her mixed reception as Bizet's Gypsy had soured her attitude. A story was also put about in limited circles by her secretary that
she had offended the management by pushing her sister too hard. Carmela
had indeed joined the roster for one period of four years, another of five,
and had managed to repeat the famous sister act at a higher level by
singing Laura to Rosa's Gioconda in 1932. Whether Henderson's remark
that "they made the fire fly" in their duet was meant as a compliment is
not clear. Rosa continued to thrive in Baltimore, if not as a matron, at
least as an opera teacher and scout, Lady Bountiful. Without the chilling
finger of stage fright at her spine, she produced a phonograph record of
superlative beauty in 1955, and another still later.

Gatti's Great Divide concurred with the middle of his regime. Two
more brilliant as well as more sorrowful seasons than 1920–21 and 1921–22
hardly have occurred in a modern opera house. As in the relay race, when
one runner hands his responsibility over to another, so should one generation of opera singers pass on the torch. It doesn't always work that way,
however. With Proteus in Shakespeare's *Two Gentlemen of Verona,*
opera fans seldom say:

> "As one nail by strength drives out another,
> So the remembrance of my former love
> Is by a newer object quite forgotten."

On the contrary, they are loyal to the objects of their affection even unto
death—and after.

So came the question to Gatti: "Who will take Caruso's place?"
And, a little later: "And Farrar's?"

The greatest tenor in the world celebrated his twenty-fifth anniversary in opera on March 22, 1919, taking the lead in scenes from three
favorite operas: *L'Elisir d'Amore,* which Conried had introduced for him
and Sembrich in his first season (Barrientos sang Adina now; Scotti was
again the Belcore); *Pagliacci,* in whose clown costume Caruso had become
the very symbol of opera (Muzio, De Luca, the comprimario tenor Angelo
Bada, and the new Danish-American baritone Reinald Werrenrath, who
had just made his debut as Silvio, surrounded the central figure) and
Le Prophète, whose John of Leyden had been one of the roles to show
his deepening maturity as artist (with Matzenauer, Diaz, Mardones, and

The exterior of the Yellow-Brick Brewery, ugly even when it was new, as seen in 1884
Opera News

On August 27, 1892, 10,000 watched the fire that burned out the Metropolitan's interior.
Opera News

The proscenium in the auditorium of the Old House, beautiful from the first; golden, glamorous and mourned as irreplaceable by many
Alexander Georges, *Opera News*

The Old Met—its viscera exposed by the wreckers—dies of internal injuries.
Erika Davidson, *Opera News*

J. P. Morgan, plutocrat in excelsis,
cynosure in the Met Golden Horseshoe

The Mrs. Astor, who ruled Society at
the nod of her proud, bewigged head

Mrs. O. H. P. Belmont, who made too
many enemies to be Queen of Society

Mrs. Cornelius Vanderbilt, symbol of
Grand Opera until her death in 1953

Lillian Nordica as Selika
Opera News

Emma Calvé as Carmen
Metropolitan Opera Archives

Emma Eames as Juliette
Metropolitan Opera Archives

Nellie Melba as Ophélie
Opera News

Jean de Reszke, the sun around whom prima donnas of the Golden Age lovingly revolved, is seen as Tristan.

Heinrich Conried, successor to Maurice
Grau as General Manager of the Opera

Giulio Gatti-Casazza and former star
Marcella Sembrich at a backstage gala

Carlo Edwards, *Opera News*

Edward Johnson, top-hatted and ready to
wish his performers traditional "luck"

Metropolitan Opera Archives

Rudolf Bing greets receptionist Winifred
Short in the vestibule of the Old House.

Opera News

Financier Morgan's sword of moralistic disapproval slays the notorious *Salome*.

Olive Fremstad played Salome only once before the Strauss opera was withdrawn.
Metropolitan Opera Archives

Involved in *Peter Ibbetson,* from the left: Wilhelm von Wymetal, director; Joseph Urban, set designer; Deems Taylor, composer; Tullio Serafin, conductor
Carlo Edwards, Opera News

Giullio Setti rehearses an early Metropolitan chorus.
Metropolitan Opera Archives

Conductors Arturo Toscanini and
Giorgio Polacco in consultation
Opera News

Conductor Fritz Stiedry, a colleague of Set
Svanholm, at the tenor's debut as Siegfried
Metropolitan Opera Archives

Rehearsing for *Salome:*
Fritz Reiner, conductor;
Ljuba Welitch, heroine
Opera News

Bruno Walter with (left)
Zinka Milanov, Ezio Pinza
and Herbert Janssen (right)
Metropolitan Opera Archives

In good company, left to right: Edward
Ziegler, administrator; the bass Feodor
Chaliapin; William J. Guard, press chief
Opera News

Bing beams at Rosalina, Steber, and
Adele, Munsel, at a gala *Fledermaus*.
Opera News

Lauritz Melchior and Helen
Traubel, rebels at the Met,
enjoy offstage conviviality.
Opera News

Curtain calls for *Périchole,* from
the left: Theodor Uppman, Paquillo;
Teresa Stratas in the title role,
and Cyril Ritchard as the Viceroy
Beth Bergman

Rosa Ponselle in *Forza*
Mishkin

Geraldine Farrar as Juliette
Dupont, *Metropolitan Opera Archives*

Maria Jeritza as Octavian
White

Enrico Caruso as the Duke
Metropolitan Opera Archives

Elisabeth Rethberg in
La Campana Sommersa

Lawrence Tibbett as Ford
Carlo Edwards

Lotte Lehmann as the Marschallin
Apeda, *Opera News*

Risë Stevens as Octavian
Bender, *Metropolitan Opera Archives*

Jan Peerce as Edgardo
Metropolitan Opera Archives

Marian Anderson as Ulrica
Metropolitan Opera Archives

Kirsten Flagstad as Isolde

Leonard Warren in the fatal
Forza
Sedge Leblang, *Opera News*

Alfred Hertz claims the conductor's right
to place *Walküre* singers: Johanna Gadski,
Brünnhilde, and Olive Fremstad, Sieglinde.
Brown Brothers

Composer Italo Montemezzi
coaches *Amore* lovers Grace
Moore and Charles Kullman.
Larry Gordon, *Opera News*

Peter Brook (right) directs
Robert Merrill, Victoria de
los Angeles, Nicola Rossi-
Lemeni, Thelma Votipka, Jussi
Björling in *Faust* rehearsal.
Sedge Leblang, *Opera News*

Composer Gian-Carlo Menotti
gives *Last Savage* pointers to
the George London (in cage)
and Roberta Peters as Osie
Hawkins and others look on.
Vernon Smith, *Opera News*

Frances Alda in farewell as her colleagues fete her; from the left: Antonio Scotti, Lucrezia Bori, Pavel Ludikar, Lawrence Tibbett, and Beniamino Gigli.

Opera News

The gilded tin cup is out. Hoping to fill it are, from the left, Grete Stückgold, Göta Ljungberg, Queena Mario, Anna Case, Giovanni Martinelli, Frieda Hempel, Louis D'Angelo, and Cecil Arden. At front, Désiré Defrère accepts cash from Fritzi Scheff.

Metropolitan Opera Archives

Guild business: Mrs. August Belmont and Opera President George A. Sloan

Opera News

Lily Pons and Milton Cross celebrate the 25th anniversary of broadcasting.

Opera News

Met royalty: Franco Corelli and Renata Tebaldi
Erika Davidson, *Opera News*

Francis Robinson gallantly escorts
Maria Callas at Met's Paris visit.
Jack Nisberg, *Opera News*

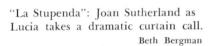

"La Stupenda": Joan Sutherland as
Lucia takes a dramatic curtain call.
Beth Bergman

Queen of Met, Princess of China:
Birgit Nilsson in Turandot finery
John Ardoin, *Opera News*

Mona, by Horatio Parker, the first American opera commissioned by Met, produced in 1910. The singers are, from the left, Riccardo Martin, Louise Homer, Rita Fornia, and Albert Reiss. The bear is genuine.

Metropolitan Opera Archives

Mourning Becomes Electra, by Levy, latest American opera commissioned. The singers: John Reardon, Marie Collier, John Macurdy, Evelyn Lear. Boris Aronson's "decayed" sets contrast with *Mona's* primitiveness.

Gary Renaud, *Opera News*

Leontyne Price as Cleopatra in the
Barber opera that opened the Lincoln
Center House. At her feet lies her
slain lover Antony (Justino Diaz).

Gary Renaud, *Opera News*

Cesare Siepi as Don Giovanni

Beth Bergman

Anna Moffo as Violetta

Cecil Beaton, *Opera News*

James McCracken as Otello

Hertha Ramme, *Opera News*

The Merry Wives make sport in Zeffirelli's *Falstaff*. From
left to right: Rosalind Elias as Meg Page, Judith Raskin as Nanetta,
Regina Resnik as Dame Quickly, and Gabriella Tucci as Alice Ford

Beth Bergman

Marc Chagall's brilliant sets for *Zauberflöte* almost overwhelm
the music and singers. Visible are Nicolai Gedda and Jerome Hines.

Gary Renaud, *Opera News*

Another of the nine new productions in the first Lincoln Center
season: Rudolf Heinrich's "abstract, booby-trapped" *Elektra*

Beth Bergman, *Opera News*

The impressive north façade of the new Lincoln Center Metropolitan, 451 feet long—like a forty-seven-story building laid on its side— dominating Lincoln Center Plaza; photogenic, especially at night.

Bob Serating, Lincoln Center for the Performing Arts

"Twilight settled serenely" as the VIP's stately pageant advanced: John D. Rockefeller III, Mrs. Lyndon B. Johnson, Mrs. Ferdinand E. Marcos and President Marcos of the Philippines, and Lauder Greenway.

Vernon Smith, *Opera News*

the durable Carl Schlegel, the Matthison of the Meyerbeer revival the previous season). The conductors, in order, were Gennaro Papi, already and old faithful dating from 1916; Roberto Moranzoni, who had made his American debut with the Boston Opera in 1910, and Artur Bodanzky.

The flag of the City of New York was presented by Police Commissioner Richard Enright to Caruso, who clutched its staff desperately through the ceremony that followed. Otto Kahn spoke feelingly, ending with a banker's tribute: "You have managed even . . . a gracious word in giving through the painful process of paying an income tax in six figures." Geraldine Farrar kissed her colleague on the cheek. Then he saw his gifts—from the directors, the thirty-five boxholders, and boxholders in Brooklyn and Philadelphia, from his fellow artists (a platinum watch set with 218 diamonds and 61 square-cut sapphires), from Gatti (a gold medal), from the various opera departments, and the Victor Talking Machine Company.

Artists seldom survive their quarter-century jubilee very long. It was a sobering thought for everyone. Was Gatti thinking, consciously or not, of new nails when he engaged Beniamino Gigli for 1920–21? To Mario Chamlee, the new American tenor, and the personable Charles Hackett, who had arrived in 1918, fell some of Caruso's roles while he was busy with *La Juive, Manon Lescaut, Le Prophète, Forza, Ballo in Maschera* (for Havana), and the lighter *Elisir* and *Marta*. Few would have nominated Gigli a Crown Prince at his debut as Faust in Boito's *Mefistofele* on November 26, 1920. Nor was there considerable talk about Giovanni Martinelli, Gounod's Faust that year and already a steady contender for seven seasons. Gigli's creamy voice (which stretched high enough to detonate the galleries) gradually became the Met's asset most nearly approximating gold. Martinelli could claim silver, but in a more reliable market. But for the moment, the King still had the corner on all the precious metal.

The season began dramatically with Caruso's Eléazar, repeated from 1919–20. He did not please everyone. *Elisir* brought an even darker reception. In *Samson,* Caruso was still not singing like Caruso. All his superstitions aroused, the tenor fell into melancholia and summoned Gatti with the intention of resigning. A friend urged him to cast everything into the balance with the *Samson* on December 3. This was a gamble Caruso won. But five days later, as he emitted the high A in Canio's

Vesti la giubba, the note cracked and the clown stumbled, clutching his side where an excruciating pain had struck. He finished the performance strapped in adhesive. The next call was to Brooklyn, the *Elisir* of December 11 that will live in the annals of despair. The harrowing tale of the bloody handkerchiefs and towels, the final agreement to give up, the announcement before the curtain to the shocked audience by William J. Guard belong in the blackest letters in the Metropolitan's book. Still, if common sense and better doctoring had been resorted to, if the conscientious artist could have been persuaded to rest, more lustrous years might have been added to the golden ones. But he persisted: a *Forza* and a *Samson,* although he gave in on December 22 and canceled an *Elisir.* Christmas Eve dawned. Gatti called. "You have always decided about everything . . . you must do so now." *"Padrone* [Caruso's name for his chief], I will sing."

Mrs. Caruso relates in her little book how when he left for the theatre she set about preparing a surprise for him. A beautiful crèche stood in the fireplace; the supper table lured with special Neapolitan Christmas Eve eels prepared in five different ways, with hot and cold octopus and "all kinds of little fishes fried in oil and dried. I didn't find any of these dishes very good," the American girl confided frankly.

"When Enrico returned I met him at the door. Although his eyes were eager, his face was the color of clay, as if the blood below had turned gray. He was touched by the crèche, amused by the supper, and glad to see his friends, but he didn't join in their laughter with his usual exuberance." The doctor who had so incompetently handled the whole affair was there too—"the only time he was welcome," commented Mrs. Caruso, "because he took a fishbone out of my throat."

After everyone had gone, she asked Enrico how he had sung. "They liked, but my side hurt—not strong but much." With the exception of the day when their daughter was born, this was the only performance Dorothy Caruso had missed—and it was his last.

The world followed with concern the almost fatal hours in its beloved idol's next months, his temporary convalescence, and the bitter day, August 2, 1921, when at last he died in Naples, where he had been born. The long series of wrong diagnoses, his own stubborn reluctance to give in to illness, and a final abscess on the lung when doctors were unavailable completed the tragic story.

Before twilight had set in, America's favorite tenor had opened the season of 1919–20 singing Cavaradossi with America's favorite soprano as Tosca—the last of their rare appearances as a team. Not only had their repertoires diverged from earlier days, but Gatti-Casazza had found it financially inexpedient to head any bill with the names "Farrar" and "Caruso" when separately they drew so powerfully. Two full houses are always better than one, thought Gatti, remembering Verdi's admonition.

La Geraldine, the "delight of gods and men," had the opera house pretty much her own way after her conquest of Toscanini, if their working relationship could be put on such a one-sided basis. Flare-ups and reconciliations between two of the hottest tempers in the opera house occurred frequently. The story that has gained currency in almost every account (and which of course must be repeated here whether or not one suspects it is apocryphal and is slightly wearied at the thin ring of its coin) supposedly originated at the first *Butterfly* rehearsal. Farrar resisted discipline with the remark, directed straight over the footlights at Toscanini: "But, Maestro, I am the star." Toscanini is supposed to have replied: *"Signorina,* there are no stars except in the heavens." That touched it off.

"I have never seen Vesuvius in action," wrote the soprano, "but probably no more inflammable combustion takes place in its venerable interior than in the person of this musical Napoleon, when the wild mood is upon him."

Still, they fulfilled their function of making glorious music together. Their real professional reconciliation—and probably personal as well— occurred at an "exciting *Butterfly*" in Chicago (April 15, 1909, with Zenatello and Scotti), when the Maestro came before the curtain with the artists, an unusual gesture for him. "I knew by his warm handclasp that our sad differences were at an end," said Farrar thankfully.

Another version of the story hints at the alleged closer personal relationship between the two. Farrar is supposed to have said haughtily, "Sir, in my field I am a star!" and the Maestro to have replied, "I will keep your secret."

Radiant, entertaining, witty, fascinating to men and women, young and old alike, the pet of the backstage crew as well as of audiences, vitally handsome and with a smile so ravishing that hearts lost a beat and stumbled to catch up—this American Beauty ruled the Metropolitan hothouse, seldom baring thorns. It is not recorded that she desired any role she did not get (except perhaps Elisabeth) but she was persuaded to accept "repertoire" choices against her better judgment. She "bodied forth" (as the stuffier critics liked to say) a Carmen that entranced many in the fall of 1914 but did not convince the *Times*. Farrar's decision to follow in the footsteps of the all-conquering Calvé and the "vulgar" Maria Gay (with whom, as Micaela, she had competed for José's love in 1908) was reached on shipboard, in the company of Toscanini, Caruso, and Amato; they rehearsed all the way across. The strain of the war, doubly distressing to her because of her affection for the German opera and its patrons, led to a partial breakdown in which she underwent a throat operation—the horrid bugaboo of any singer. During her period of convalescence, almost voiceless, Hollywood became a refuge. There was no talking—let alone singing—to be done there. She made ten movies, Jesse Lasky, Samuel Goldwyn (then Goldfish, she notes), and Cecil B. de Mille allowing her to cut her beautiful teeth on two minor roles before sinking them into the juicy one of Carmen. Her favorite was that same *Joan the Woman* that played in New York when war was declared. In spite of its differences, distractions, and emoluments, the film capital held an inner core of bitterness for Farrar as the place of meeting with Lou Tellegen, the handsome, vain former leading man of Sarah Bernhardt whom she married and later divorced after a few stormy years. She had not been brought up "to be good material for tandem going," she admitted through her "Mother's" portion of her life narrative.

Trailing clouds of Hollywood glory to the opera house, Farrar, while retaining almost complete domination of the more conventional Tosca, Madama Butterfly, and Marguerite, and the newly acquired Carmen and Thaïs, began to concentrate more and more energy on the novelties provided by the management, most of which only she could spice to palatability. Charpentier's *Julien* (1913–14) in no way rose to greater heights than *Louise,* to which it was a sequel. Farrar called it "a wild and confusing hodge-podge." She had five small parts in which she sang about two phrases each "and undressed more and more until the degradation of the last act." Her apparition as a lost soul, in drunken dishevelment, led some critics to suggest Carmen for her, to her disgust at the comparison. In a diverting aftermath, Caruso took out his Julien costume, powder-blue suit with velvet lapels, enormous blue felt hat, flowing cape, and

Windsor tie, to wear in his first call on his ladylove, Dorothy Benjamin, "so that you will remember me." Gorgeous costumes gave Farrar her chief joy in the trifling *Reine Fiammette* of Leroux (1918–19). She relinquished Mascagni's *Lodoletta* to Easton after the premiere (1917–18) because Gatti wouldn't hold a second performance for her when she was struck with bronchitis. Giordano's *Madame Sans-Gêne*, which Gatti had seen fit to retain each season from its first in 1914–15, provided comedy La Geraldine liked. *Suor Angelica* in Puccini's trio (1918–19) allowed her a most becoming nun's costume.

When she ran into direct competition with Mary Garden or Mary's remembrance, as in *Thaïs* or the *Louise* that Gatti finally put on the stage in 1920–21, Geraldine always seemed a little uneasy. Garden had sealed the memories of *Louise* in a Chicago season the previous year at the Lexington; "an apotheosis," Huneker dubbed it. Now Finck could say about Farrar's Louise that "Melba and Patti never saw the day when from the dramatic point of view they were anything but the merest amateurs and tyros compared with Geraldine Farrar, supreme mistress of facial expressions and eloquent actions." Only Calvé and Renaud ever equaled her in this gift. With his addition, "her Louise far surpasses in charm and sympathetic qualities that of her predecessor," the heroine could be content to ignore other less ecstatic estimates, and dismiss as petty some criticisms of her costumes. She had dressed the poor seamstress very well indeed, so elaborately that doubts were expressed in certain quarters about Louise's virtue even before she ran away from home. Orville Harrold was her not very dramatic lover, but her parents, the American Whitehill and the French Louise Bérat, made up for any weakness by the subtlety and passion of their characterizations. The huge cast was complete, down to the Nightwalker (Rafaelo Diaz) Hammerstein had omitted.

After Leoncavallo's *Zaza*, which played a determining part in her last years at the Met, but one novelty remained to Farrar between *Louise* and the curt announcement of January 18, 1922, that heralded her retirement. This was *La Navarraise*, Massenet's thoroughly atypical bit of blood and tears which Calvé had galvanized in 1895–96 and Garden had introduced to Chicago. Though Francis Robinson dubbed it "a piece of tripe" in his book about Caruso, several contemporaries enjoyed it, even if Farrar did not measure up to Calvé's tragic power in Krehbiel's memory.

If any nail at all pushed Farrar out—and no evidence but gossip remains to prove that her departure had any other cause but her long-stated determination to retire at forty—it was the shining, sharp-pointed Maria Jeritza. The scent of a putative prima donna feud draws hornets from afar. Whatever the truth buried deep in the hearts of both the dazzling dark-haired American and the coruscating Viennese blonde, the season in which they both participated gave off fireworks every day on the hour. The like of such a span may never come again. It opened with enough excitement for any operagoer—the arrival of Amelita Galli-Curci, who had aroused such a storm that the heavens shuddered when she appeared at the Lexington with the Chicago company in 1918. It was a "not since" occasion—this time Melba acting as the basis for comparison. Cries for Galli-Curci's presence in New York had hardly abated. Frieda Hempel had departed from the Met the next season—not cause and effect, and not unnoticed and not unmourned. After that, the coloratura trunk had contained Barrientos, Toti dal Monte (one season), and Garrison, all of them now gone. It was time for a blazing star. The fire that had preceded Galli-Curci's debut did not fizzle out, but the temperature lowered a few degrees as three years later she sang admirably —if nervously—as Violetta, a role she had often done in New York. Memories backstage and out front of the beloved tenor's opening nights and sad thoughts that this marked the first gap since 1906 could not have failed to affect all the singers, although Beniamino Gigli seemed imperturbable, and even acted with a little more conviction than usual.

Galli-Curci hardly gathered momentum in her first season. *Lucia* came three nights later, followed by Farrar's *Tosca*. The tinder was laid at the Saturday matinee. Jeritza made her debut in Korngold's *Tote Stadt (The Dead City)*, and because of its novelty and the fact that an *echt deutsche* opera had at last penetrated the censorship, at least as much space and thought were devoted to the opera as to the new soprano. Farrar sang three times in the days that followed—*Louise, Butterfly,* and *Navarraise*— to the blonde's one repeat of *Dead City*. Then the flint was struck and the conflagration soared. Jeritza was given a *Tosca* and sang *"Vissi d'arte"* lying flat on her stomach! "Sensation" was the mildest word the press could think of.

Krehbiel may be cited as an example. The venerable *Tribune* man so forgot his usual caution as to write: "The revelation . . . came like an

avalanche which swept thousands into a frenzied demonstration of enthusiasm. We cannot recall a similar scene in all the history of the opera
house, which has witnessed many a great artistic triumph. It was not
applause; it was an emotional tumult; a tempest." And a good deal more
to that effect, with personal triumphs catalogued and lingered over.

How could such explosions help but affect Farrar, no matter what her
original intentions? She avowed no rivalry existed, but her description of
the earthshaking event carries its sting: "Little note was taken of her
handsome presence and brilliant soprano [oh, yes, m'dear; much note was
taken] . . . the 'clou' of the performance lay in a pose of unashamed
abandon on the floor. . . . I obtained no view of any expressive pantomime
on her pretty face [the claws are unsheathed], while I was surprised by
the questionable flaunting of a well-cushioned and obvious posterior
[the claws sink in]."

After the announcement that shook her coterie to its foundations,
Farrar made one "last" appearance after another, encompassing portions
of her repertoire long discarded. Then she also planned the "last last"
shrewdly—no public eulogies from Management or Board of Directors,
no farewell supper and "patronizing addresses." Just Farrar alone with
her colleagues and her public. "They had loved me. And to them I
wanted to address those last words."

Because of this concern with her listeners, it seems apropos to quote
one of them who kept a close and loving record. After Jeritza's Tosca, he
had penned this bit of wishful thinking: "The reviewers having a good
time, but such a pace cannot keep up." Of Farrar's third-act Mimi, resur-
rected after eleven years for a benefit, what but *"Addio senza rancor?"* Of
her Manon: *"Nulle voix n'a de plus de doux accents/ Nul regard plus de
charme avec plus de tendresse."* After a special matinee performance of
Carmen, she refused to make a speech but made a "grand exit in open
automobile, wearing her beautiful last-act costume and scattering flowers"
—a prelude to the final event in this stirring spring. Every performance
brought carloads of flowers, mounting hysteria.

At the *Butterfly* in late March, "an exceedingly emotional scene"
the Cio-Cio-San stepped before the curtain in an unrehearsed (at least
by the management) speech, asking of her devoted public what role they
would prefer for her finale. The shout rose unanimously: *"Tosca!"* The
heroine acknowledged that the management would have something to say

about that. Indeed, Gatti did. Once more, as in the case of Fremstad, he deliberately dealt a slap to a beautiful and imperious lady. Quietly he assigned her *Zaza.* Equally reserved, Farrar made her plans.

She was allotted one more *Tosca,* her third to Jeritza's six. Among her floral tributes was a large nosegay from which, at the release of a spring, a live pigeon fluttered out across the footlights, attached to a ribbon which Miss Farrar drew back until the symbol of peace rested upon her fore- finger as she took myriad curtain calls. What Mme. Jeritza thought of this is not known. She insisted in her rather bland autobiography, *Sunlight and Song,* that she and Farrar had never had any discussion or disagree- ment about this juicy bone of contention, and that she was convinced Farrar had had nothing to do personally with the storm of criticism and antagonism that greeted the news when she was to sing a "so-called Farrar role."

The great day approached at last. *Zaza* it would be. When she had first burst upon the eyes and eardrums as the tempestuous music-hall star on January 16, 1920, everyone had agreed that this was indeed the role she had been searching for, however meretricious the opera itself. "Zaza in the role of Geraldine Farrar is a sensation," is the way Huneker put it. "She positively melts or thrills. There is only one role. She is Zaza. Zaza is Farrar."

The departing prima donna made the most of it, lingering deliciously on the disrobing scene that had so scandalized the conventional elements of the audience as well as a few moralistic critics. Oscar Thompson, a staff member of *Musical America* who had not yet succeeded his idol, William J. Henderson, on the *Sun,* called it "inartistic and unnecessary." (He later became a devotee of Jeritza.)

Farrar herself has admitted that she did everything she could think of to contribute to the character of the *demimondaine* Zaza. "But the idea of raising the skirt to perfume the panties with an atomizer came from [David] Belasco," she confided. In Atlanta, the only city except nearby Brooklyn and Philadelphia to witness the gay opera, Farrar frankly hinted to the gentlemen of the Atlanta Festival board that seats on the left side of the house might be preferable. The split-second, "now you see it, now you don't" baring of the beautiful back, accompanied by rather shivery music as Zaza's lover runs his hands along her spine, took place on the left side of a divided stage. This and the sentimental colloquy with a child, the daughter of her lover, played by tiny Ada Quintina (who was the most enchanting Trouble in *Butterfly* the Met has ever known), were the high spots of the opera proper (proper?).

But every moment was a high spot in that last performance on the afternoon of April 22, 1922. Such a day has never been seen at the opera house. Apotheosis for the darling of the opera stage, and for the crowd of screaming, weeping young girls out front. Anticipating the fanatic crowds for Frank Sinatra, Elvis Presley, and the Beatles were the famous 500 gerryflappers, a term coined by W. J. Henderson. "What is a gerry-flapper?" he asked. "Simply a girl about the flapper age who has created in her own half-baked mind a goddess which she names Geraldine Farrar." As the hushed reverence gave way to squeals and screams of delight, the afternoon climbed on to its climax. Oh, ecstasy! Oh, glory! The flowers could hardly be borne. They arrived in baskets, in sheaves, in a quantity that filled the lobbies and were thrown from all over the house. It was the last great demonstration of its sort—Jeritza, it will be noted, had asked for a rule against this floral marksmanship as being too dangerous, and got it.

When the last curtain had fallen, back to that tiny dressing room trouped dozens and dozens of hoarse, breathless admirers—many of the 500 had gone back after *Carmen*—to receive gifts and mementos of their goddess. Now they conveyed to her a special *costume de gala* made by their own hands so that she could leave her stage trappings behind her forever. She had already given away many belongings; in a later auction, she divested herself of every reminder of the theatre; her beautiful effects were scattered to the four corners of her kingdom.

Then out into Fortieth Street with its milling crowd, borne from the Seventh Avenue scenic bay on the shoulders of Phil Crispano, property chief, and Charlie Metterhouse, a stagehand. Once in her car, draped in a huge silken flag, surrounded by flowers and pennants, showered by con-fetti and posies, she was caught for a half hour in an impenetrable mob of cheering, groaning, weeping, and laughing humanity. Finally the car was pushed out to Broadway and was free.

Farrar had more than hinted in her vivacious speech at the very end that she would be entering a new phase of her career, with the help of a certain David Belasco. There were also intimations that she would return to the old opera house. But neither came true. Concertize she did,

and she took a disastrous swing around the country in her own production of *Carmen* as well as joining Scotti in an ambitious tour venture
that brought the baritone to near ruin. Finally she acted as a charming
mistress of ceremonies on the radio series that conveyed the Metropolitan
opera to the millions across the land. It was even her privilege to draw
Gatti-Casazza to the studio for his farewell.

When the incense had cleared from the season, it was perceived that
a good many other exciting things had happened besides the battle of the
prima donnas and Galli-Curci's advent. Chaliapin had come back and
enthralled a great many by his powerful Boris, albeit sung in Russian
against a solid wall of Italian. Titta Ruffo had made his debut as Figaro
in Rossini's opera, and would continue to regale his admirers for eight
seasons. And Mozart's *Così Fan Tutte,* which had waited in the wings
132 years, came to America for the first time on March 22, 1922. It was
thought to be a delicious morsel. The Met did itself proud with clever
sets by Urban. The cast seemed almost worthy of Mozart: Florence Easton
as Fiordiligi; Frances Peralta (who had sung with Rabinoff's Boston
company and in Chicago, as well as with the Scotti company, and had
made her debut in *Mefistofele* in 1920) as Dorabella (later sung by
mezzos); George Meader and Giuseppe de Luca as the two lovers; Bori, an
ideal soubrette, as Despina; and Didur as Alfonso. The public perhaps
did not realize that Meader's somewhat limited vocal equipment (later
to be used for glorious stuttering fun in *The Bartered Bride*), had forced
the omission of the two tenor arias.

With Rimsky-Korsakoff's *Snegurochka,* Boris Anisfield continued the
colorful designs that had begun with Albert Wolff's *Blue Bird* in 1919.
(This adaptation of the Maeterlinck play introduced a composer-conductor
for only the second time, preceded by Luigi Mancinelli and his *Ero e
Leandro.*) Wolff's *Oiseau* fluttered out the door on feeble wings after two
seasons; he lingered on for another. In this third term, he gave up
several French operas, which were assumed by the long-lived (fifteen
seasons) Louis Hasselmans. Two other novelties, Catalani's *Loreley* and
Lalo's *Roi d'Ys,* left no wake behind them.

The excitement generated in another part of town was almost
eclipsed by the Met's fireworks, but down at the Manhattan Opera House,
Mary Garden was also announcing her retirement—only from New York,
however. After Campanini's death in 1919, the directors of the Chicago

Opera Association decided to take a chance with "Our Mary." She immediately assumed the title of "directa" and proceeded to lose $1,110,000 for Harold McCormick in one season. Content to rest on these laurels, she retired to become a mere member of the company; and the Chicago touring maps excluded the East. In this valedictory season, New Yorkers —those who could be spared from Thirty-ninth Street—were treated to her Mélisande, Louise, Thaïs, Le Jongleur, Monna Vanna, and Fiora in *L'Amore dei Tre Re,* in which her three kings were Edward Johnson, George Baklanoff, and Virgilio Lazzari. One delightful novelty was Sergei Prokofiev's *Love for Three Oranges* (in French), not to be seen again hereabouts for more than thirty years. The crowning irony of the times was a benefit production of *Salome* for a most unexpected charity—one headed by Anne Morgan, whose sister and father had made the Metropolitan too hot to hold the grisly dancer in 1906.

14

GATTI WAXES...

I gat me men singers and women singers. . . . So I was great.

—Ecclesiastes 2:8–9

Before the catastrophe of 1929, the seven years of prosperity brought a brilliantly shifting scene on which many new faces appeared at the Metropolitan, some to remain while others left no more than the powdery dust of a moth's wing. Caruso and Farrar were not forgotten, but the public fancy could still be tickled with Jeritza as Elisabeth, Thaïs, Fedora, Maliella (*Jewels of the Madonna*) Jenufa, the elaborately gowned Turandot, the long-legged Boccaccio, and René (von Suppé's *Donna Juanita*), as well as Carmen (whose tradition she violated by wearing an auburn wig instead of a dark one), and of course the Tosca. On January 30, 1928, she once more made history by *not* falling flat on her stomach to sing *"Vissi d'arte."* The "blonde bombshell" kept her public until her retirement in 1932, a year after her original benefactor, Otto H. Kahn, had become inactive, partly because of failing health, partly from disillusion with the opera. William J. Henderson, the last of his critical generation, at first admired Jeritza's "amazing prodigality of tone" as Turandot, but later fussed at her as a "screaming scold."

Her departure coincided with Gigli's. The chubby tenor, in the dozen seasons since his engagement, had advanced to prime place, living up to Richard Aldrich's prediction in the *Times* that he would be a valuable accession, though still inclined to "sing to the audience" and to "cultivate the high note and make whatever there is to be made out of it in the way of applause." The beauty of his voice was appreciated in *L'Africaine* and many other roles he dominated. His place was filled for a few years by Tito Schipa of the velvet voice, one of the excellent legacies from the Chicago Opera, which suspended after the Insull debacle in 1932.

Tenors of various brands and standards graced the decade, lacking the tenor that neither Gigli nor Martinelli ever quite became. Giacomo Lauri-Volpi sang a good many lyric roles before the more strenuous

Calaf (*Turandot*) and Arnold (*Guillaume Tell.*) One of his most distinguished moments was as Ponselle's Pollione in the starry revival of *Norma* on November 16, 1927. Armand Tokatyan began many years of devoted service in 1922, taking, along with conventional parts, perhaps more than his share of flimsy novelties. One exception was Puccini's *Rondine,* in which he proved himself a ripe comedian in a part written originally for baritone, and holding his own with Lucrezia Bori, Gigli, and Editha Fleischer, a soprano whose ten years in varied roles from 1926 earned her one of the rare "indispensable" tags. Tokatyan was once cited for extreme gallantry in the face of disaster. As Don José, he killed his Carmen, the enterprising and attractive Canadian contralto Jeanne Gordon, who fell with her feet toward the audience. Her fancy last-act costume was unfortunately built on a crinoline, which proceeded to follow its own law of dynamics. The contrite lover now spared everyone some lively embarrassment by dropping quickly onto the ballooning skirt and corralling its mischievous hoop for the few short measures that remained. A murderer, yes, but this Don José was also a gentleman!

Among the new tenors was Miguel Fleta, a Spaniard who created Calaf at *Turandot*'s premiere in Milan on April 25, 1926. Gatti hired him in 1923 for *Tosca,* Mascagni's *Amico Fritz, Carmen,* and *Contes d'Hoffmann,* but did not entrust him with Calaf in 1926, assigning the part to Lauri-Volpi. Martin Oehman, a Swede respected highly at home, found little to do in one New York season, thus repeating the fate of another distinguished compatriot, John Forsell, who had not been appropriately cast in 1910 and went back to Stockholm to become head of the Royal Opera. Swedish men avoided the Met thereafter for many years although three women found welcome in this period: the artistic lyric soprano Marie Sundelius (1916), the vivacious contralto Julia Claussen (1917), and the tall, powerfully voiced Karin Branzell, who made her debut as Fricka in 1923 and helped to restore eloquence to Valhalla during more than twenty years in the House.

Frederick Jagel in 1927, Richard Crooks in 1932, and Charles Hackett in 1933 represented Gatti's last investments in American tenors, all of them excellent in French and Italian operas and Jagel registering exceptional longevity—until 1950. It speaks well for the Brooklyn-born Jagel's versatility that he added Herod in *Salome* in his penultimate season, and for his training that he was able to rush to the theatre to replace the ailing Martinelli in 1938, when the latter suffered an attack of food poisoning after *Celeste Aida* and the curtain had to come down during a broadcast matinee. Jagel was not around, however, when Martinelli braved the jinx that clung to *La Juive* after Caruso's tragedy, and sang one splendid Eléazar in 1924 before the curse caught up with him in the form of a bout of typhoid fever. The opera was postponed until his return two months later.

The omens clustered joyously around the debut of still another possessor of the bright voice when Edward Johnson appeared for the first time as Avito in Montemezzi's *Amore dei Tre Re* on November 16, the third night of the 1922–23 season. He had aready impressed New York in this role with the Chicago company at the Lexington Theatre in 1920. The piece had been restored to the Met in 1917 for Caruso and Claudia Muzio, after earlier performances starring Bori and Ferrari-Fontana. Martinelli and Easton had been other and perhaps less inspired lovers in the interval when Bori remained away because of vocal cords that would not obey her; in 1920 she returned to a loving public and to Fiora opposite a somewhat lukewarm Gigli. (Ponselle later enjoyed Fiora's woes, even to the extent of an opening night.)

Johnson at once became a favorite partner to Bori in many musical ventures, although the rumors of romance that inevitably followed such a companionship were impatiently—and rightly—dismissed. The tenor had emerged from a background that most immediately concerned three acclaimed seasons in Chicago. Reaching farther into his past, one found him in opera companies all over Europe from 1912 under the name of Edoardo di Giovanni. He sang *Parsifal* at La Scala among other feats. Still farther back, he had made his stage debut in Oscar Straus's *Waltz Dream* in New York in 1908 under his baptized name, resuming it only when he joined the Chicago company. The Italian disguise was a commonplace in those days when Anglo-Saxon names carried little promise of talent or glamour to European sensibilities. Born in Guelph, Ontario, Johnson became an American citizen coincidentally with his Met debut.

He was warmly received from the first, Aldrich dubbing him in the *Times* "a tenor who is something more than a voice, who is an artistic personality." Gatti valued his new acquisition, as had Chicago's Campanini and Mary Garden, for his ability to create difficult (and usually unrewarding) roles in Italian and French novelties, in a goodly number of which he buried his talents. But he also benefited from a variety of more coventional roles right away, with a wide range of complementary females: Des Grieux (Puccini) and Faust with Alda; Cavaradossi with Jeritza; Canio with Rethberg and Nina Morgana; Pinkerton and José with Easton; Dimitri with Matzenauer and Flora Perini, and Roméo with Queena Mario. Later he would present the ideal figure in a number of American ventures, notably Deems Taylor's *King's Henchman* and *Peter Ibbetson*. With the advent of this handsome and ardent protagonist who possessed exactly the right "physique," Gatti was able at last in 1924 to launch annual excursions into an opera close to his heart and tastes— Debussy's *Pelléas et Mélisande*. "Memorable" was Lawrence Gilman's word for the hero. The *Tribune* critic spoke of Johnson's rare intelligence, insight, art as a singer and actor, and commented that he "struck the right balance between the gravity, the simplicity, the aloofness and reserve that are essential to the character, and the sense of passion under difficult restraint." Furthermore, "it was a delight to hear the voice part . . . so beautifully and so eloquently delivered." Johnson and Bori proved irresistible to *Pelléas* devotees for the rest of Gatti's tenure, each year performing twice in what came to be almost a ritual. Bori still suffered in a way from comparisons with the only other Mélisande seen in New York, yet for many held her own against Mary Garden in a truly touching incarnation. For the first eight years, Clarence Whitehill completed the triangle as Golaud; when the American baritone (a noble Sachs and Wotan as well as esteemed in more than a dozen other roles in several languages) left in the debacle that attended salary cutting and reputation slashing in 1932, Ezio Pinza took his place for the remaining three years under Gatti.

Pinza had not been the only low voice to titillate the audiences of the decade. Chaliapin's return in 1922 electrified listeners waiting for sensation by his incomparable Boris (sung in Russian, with an Italian-singing family, court, and populace), a Mefistofele that had gained in majesty what it lost in exaggeration, a striking Don Quichotte and a King Philip II (*Don Carlo,* introduced with Adamo Didur two seasons previously). Ever the monarch no matter what role he played, the mighty Russian stepped to the footlights after a superb rendition of *"Ella giammai m'amo"* and commanded the shaken Gennaro Papi to do it all over again. The no-encore rule had been in effect since 1902, but rules meant nothing to Chaliapin, who got away with the same insubordination yet another time in *Don Carlo* and later in *Faust*. This prompted W. J. Henderson to remember the clever dodge used by Sembrich and Eames to repeat the Letter Duet in *Nozze di Figaro*. The former simply pretended to spill ink all over the first letter so that another had to be written (and sung) immediately.

It is no wonder that Chaliapin, the Méphistophélès of the November 30, 1923, *Faust,* thrust into shadow the Valentin, a gawky young American whom Krehbiel judged as possessing a voice as "light-waisted as his physique." The distinctly odd aspect of the performance was the empathy of the choristers for the newcomer. Knowing that he had plunged into the part with little knowledge and less rehearsal, they prompted him in his aria and stage business from behind tables, in treetops, and anywhere they could hide and throw him a line, as Francis Robinson described the unique event many years later. Still, Lawrence Tibbett had to wait yet a while in the wings of his carreer. He had made his debut also under the shade of Chaliapin, the Russian's magnificent Boris commanding all attention, while the American strode through the scenery chanting a few phrases under a concealing cowl as Rangoni, a Jesuit— the lowest name on the bill that November 24 matinee. Other bits came his way in his first season, the juiciest being Silvio in *Pagliacci*. Then after a Schlemil in *Contes d'Hoffmann,* another Valentin (which he knew by now), and several minor skirmishes came the explosion that catapulted Tibbett into grand orbit.

It has become one of the treasured legends of the House, that *Falstaff* of January 2, 1925. The American owed his position as Ford to the illness of a new Spanish baritone, Vincente Ballester, who sang little before the *Falstaff* and after, working out his contract with Sunday night concerts, those repositories of antiques and new goods, the olla-podrida of opera. Tibbett was likewise thrown into a half dozen of these, but allowed to show pieces of the repertoire that spelled "future"—the "Evening Star" from *Tannhäuser,* the *"Eri tu"* from *Ballo,* on which he had cracked at his first Met audition, and Mussorgsky's "Song of the Flea," which he appropriated from Chaliapin.

Even at the *Falstaff* dress rehearsal, the young baritone impressed the critics and the "inside" audience with his earnestness and the quality of his voice. Nevertheless, it was marked as Antonio Scotti's evening. The

admired Scarpia, Tonio, Don Giovanni, Rigoletto, Iago; the polished
actor, great gentleman, and beloved colleague had celebrated his silver
anniversary with the Metropolitan just a year before, on January 1, 1924.
Now Verdi's last masterpiece was revived for him, for the first time since
he had sung it in Gatti's initial two seasons.

Scotti's was the lion's share of applause, of that there could be no
doubt. But perhaps sensing destiny, the young Tibbett had "set himself
and let go" all he had, "tearing out my heart in the second-act aria"—
that consummate expression of tumultuous and gripping jealousy, unrivaled, as Oscar Thompson remarked, in modern opera, perhaps in all
opera. Even so, there was no disposition by the stage manager to let
Tibbett come out alone, until the demonstration arising in the audience
made it plain that they wanted to acclaim a new star. Tibbett had already reached his dressing room up two stairways when he was pulled
back to "show himself alone before the yellow curtains," as Lawrence
Gilman put it. "The audience split the roof." The noise and duration
almost matched the ovation that greeted Jean de Reszke's return in 1900,
but not quite, according to Tom Bull, the veteran doorman who kept a
record of such things.

Newspapers next day did not allow this extraordinary occasion to go
unnoticed; so it was that Tibbett set the first firm block in the edifice
that was to become an American institution, the most illustrious career
for a native male in Metropolitan history. It would be gratifying to
record that Tibbett's fortunes changed immediately, but there was still
a season of minor chores to be threshed out. And even when he sang Ford
once again and was allowed solo bows, the enthusiasm reached no point
as high as at first. The next season added little of substance. Gatti applied
to Tibbett his practice of easing new singers into novelties that might or
might not endure, casting him as Ramiro in Ravel's frothy *L'Heure
Espagnole* and allowing him to replace the huge-voiced Titta Ruffo after
the premiere of Giordano's *Cena della Buffa* (or *The Jest,* the title of Sem
Benelli's play in which John and Lionel Barrymore had recently starred).
In one Sunday concert his choice was Iago's "Credo," a straw pointing
ahead, although another selection, Tchaikovsky's "Why?" might indicate
a certain impatience with the slowness of his progress. Not only Scotti,
but the genial and artistically formidable Giuseppe de Luca, the trusted
Giuseppe Danise, Mario Basiola, and Ruffo among them had pretty well

carved up the bread-and-butter baritone roles as well as the added jam of Gerard, Iago, Falstaff, Carlo (*Forza*), Barnaba, Michele, Manfredo, Mercutio, Gianni Schicchi, Golaud, and, the four roles in *Hoffmann*. Tibbett eventually made a virtually complete conquest of this repertoire, as well as the Sheriff in *Fanciulla del West* that enabled him to emulate his California father, though not to the extent of real life, in which that sheriff had been killed by outlaws. Meanwhile, he was presented with two occasions that not only added to his stature but added to that of native opera. He was assigned King Eadgar in *The King's Henchman,* which had its world premiere on February 17, 1927, and he made the most of a final aria that the librettist Edna St. Vincent Millay insisted on restoring after conductor (Serafin) and stage director (Von Wymetal) had cut it. "Tibbett's enunciation of some of Miss Millay's best lines materially heightened the effect," approved Olin Downes in the *Times.* (This vivacious writer had come from the Boston *Post* to take over the nation's top music-critic job in 1924.) Tibbett almost automatically became first candidate for the lead in any American opera from then on; he graced Taylor's second, *Peter Ibbetson* (which had sixteen performances in four seasons after its 1931 premiere), and made a tour de force of Louis Gruenberg's *Emperor Jones* (ten performances between 1932 and 1934), but even his growing distinction could not save the misbegotten *In the Pasha's Garden* (1934), by John Lawrence Seymour, or the ambitious score by Howard Hanson to Richard Stokes's story called *Merry Mount* (1933).

The second opportunity for Tibbett was Verdi's *Simon Boccanegra,* an early score revised, which the Met produced for the first time in America on January 28, 1932, with a stunning cast. In addition to Tibbett in the name part, Pinza and Martinelli, the baritone Claudio Frigerio (in the role of Paolo that would later serve as a springboard for the American Leonard Warren), and the winsome soprano Maria Müller basked in almost universal critical approval.

Tibbett by now had ventured to that bourn from which few opera singers returned unchanged—Hollywood. It seemed to have done him only good. Henderson wrote that he had learned "much about dress, facial expression and gesture," had achieved one of the signal artistic successes of his career with Boccanegra, and in fact, "is now one of the best actors on the operatic stage."

Through the years leading to his command of Iago and other pinnacles of the lyric stage, including the Fat Knight Falstaff himself, Tibbett ventured but little into the Germanic realm. His constant testing of "The Evening Star" in concert at last brought him the impersonation of the whole character of Wolfram in *Tannhäuser,* but beyond that, and an early unsatisfactory Kothner, he achieved only a scene in English as Hans Sachs at a Walter Damrosch anniversary concert in 1935. Neither was he a Mozartean. He won opening nights in 1932 with *Simon Boccanegra,* then in successive years with *Peter Ibbetson, Aida,* and *La Traviata,* in 1938 with *Otello,* and the next year with *Boccanegra* again.

Gatti had inaugurated the practice of hiring singers for only a half season on the theory that changes of cast would entice more customers into the House. With a ceiling of $1,000 on fees imposed as an economy measure, the expensive songbirds had to seek other sources of revenue in the mass media—movies and radio—and most of all in concert tours, where fees rose to all the traffic would bear. This bustling world outside of opera caught up early with Tibbett; he was the all-American radio hero, made several films, and was badgered to fill concert dates. Wholly a product of United States training and with a career labeled "Made at Home," Tibbett particularly relished his first professional trip to Europe in 1937, when he sang Iago, Rigoletto, and Scarpia in several capitals and was warmly welcomed in concerts, expressing surprise that in Scandinavia men as well as women can be the targets for posy-throwing. Tall, virile, and purely American, he captivated a public that enjoyed his specialities, "De Glory Road," arias from *Porgy and Bess,* and, yes, "The Flea," as much as Americans had.

He was royally received in a literal sense, too, obeying a summons from King Gustav V to his summer residence in Båstad, where at seventy-nine the monarch still played tennis. While the singer filled another engagement, Mrs. Tibbett (the former Jane Marston Burgard, whom Tibbett had married in 1932 after divorcing his first wife) learned that a silk topper was *de rigueur* for confronting a king. She appealed to the concierge of Stockholm's Grand Hotel, who produced one as if by magic, although the exact head size had to be left untranslated from American to Swedish. The Tibbetts were reduced to hysteria when the hat sank down even over the baritone's Clark Gable-ish ears, coming to rest on his broad shoulders. At the last minute, the concierge found another, obviously smaller, and the couple set out for the south in haste. To their horror, the topper really topped, perching high and dry on the mortified baritone's cranium. He resorted to carrying it, but the moment arrived when, both hands occupied, he had to don it. And *Life* magazine cameras chose that moment to flash.

More congenial was the party after Tibbett's concert in the outdoor Stockholm park, Tivoli, when he was entertained by Jussi Björling (who would arrive at the Metropolitan the following year), and numbers of other singers and admirers in the restaurant dedicated to the poet Karl M. Bellmann. The entire company rose to greet his entrance with applause, then, one after another, singers sang toasts to the evening's star. When a portly gentleman got to his feet, the whisper went around, "Martin Oehman"—the tenor who had witnessed Tibbett's first triumph in his own brief year at the Met. The American, touched and gratified, responded with resonant words and a spiritual, and the merriment went on until after the early northern dawn.

Tibbett's silver anniversary was celebrated on January 21, 1949, at a performance of Britten's *Peter Grimes,* in which he sang Captain Balstrode. His opera career ended with that of his old friend, Edward Johnson, in 1950. The baritone's vitality had outlet for a while in the presidency of the soloists' union he helped to found in 1936—AGMA— and in abortive projects for Broadway musicals. Even before retirement his unique talent had become tarnished, possibly by the effect of his reckless private life on an already untrustworthy vocal method. But his death in 1960 brought an evaluation of his real contribution. His valedictory properly belongs to his last role, the one in which he made his final appearance on March 24, 1950, as Prince Khovansky in Mussorgsky's *Khovanshchina,* in the words of Olin Downes: "The greatest male singer among Americans whom the Metropolitan has advanced in its past quarter of a century."

Ezio Pinza started at the top and stayed there. From the opening night *La Vestale* in 1926, when the distinguished group around him consisted of Ponselle, Lauri-Volpi, De Luca, Matzenauer, and D'Angelo, the devastatingly handsome bass, as alluring to feminine susceptibilities behind scenes as in the audience, never lacked for a public or for glowing words he could clip, if he wished, and insert intact in advertisements. This first appearance brought a few from Gilman—"imposing figure, excellent voice, sings with brains and discretion." The critic added, "High priests are usually the dullest animals in the operatic herd [emulating Philip Hale of Boston, who collected "operatic bores" with glee]. Mr. Pinza made this one much more than tolerable."

After this brilliant debut, Pinza went on for twenty-two seasons to create one distinctive portrait after another in fifty operas. Perhaps his most famous, although largely controversial, was the Mozart libertine, Don Giovanni. Metropolitan managers since Grau have been bedeviled for producing too little Mozart; finding the "perfect" cast for *Giovanni* has often seemed impossible. Pinza's first immersal in the clear streams of Mozart's music must have given him a chill; Gilman wrote that he lacked practically everything necessary: elegance, grace, adroitness, magnetic charm. That he grew to cultivate all these except perhaps elegance (and the magnetism was still tagged "animal") was eventually conceded. At least he was *the* Don of the thirties and forties. John Brownlee, the personable Australian who arrived on Thirty-ninth Street via France and Glyndebourne, and who had sung the Don at the English festival that to American record collectors represented a prototype, got to repeat it here only twice. *Don Giovanni,* instead of a staple, became a preciosity like *Pelléas et Mélisande* soon after Gatti admitted it in 1929 for the first time since Conried's day. Around the central figure the casts were as shifting sands: the list of Annas stretched from Rethberg, Ponselle, Giannini, and Milanov to Bampton, Kirk, and Resnik; the Elviras dropped from Steber and Novotna to plateaus below; Sayao enriched Zerlina in an otherwise arid list; the Ottavios fared well with the Americans—Crooks, Hackett, Melton, and Kullman—and perhaps better with Schipa; while Virgilio Lazzari's comic Leporello gave way to the even more comic Salvatore Baccaloni.

The Figaro, which most critics liked better than Giovanni, lay in Pinza's future after Gatti's departure, as did the Boris and other towering figures. Always the diligent worker, the bass did not scorn the smaller roles that completed an ensemble, bringing to them "a true stellar touch," as Max de Schauensee said. His departure in 1948 for a glamorous role in the Rodgers and Hammerstein *South Pacific* opposite Mary Martin, where he made a popular hit out of "Some Enchanted Evening," brought him new luster and bereaved the opera house of a true *basso cantante* for a few years.

Pinza the man made headlines almost as frequently as Pinza the artist, and on front pages, moreover. His detention on Ellis Island as an enemy alien at the entrance of America into World War II proved to be the result of an act of spite by another singer who later admitted it. His romance with an opera soprano which brought divorce to both—but not marriage to each other—kept some sore memories alive for a while. Pure Italian male that he was, he considered all femininity his province to pinch a little, pull a little, and occasionally besiege seriously. (Ironically, he admitted to a colleague—male—that making love on stage was the most difficult bit of acting he had to do.) One aristocratic soprano from Central Europe, titled, patrician, and beautiful, and slim to boot, invariably crossed her arms over her bosom when the bass approached, greeting him coolly from a safe distance. His second marriage, to a charming young dancer, showed him in still another light—the devoted family man. Most Italians do like to settle down, even though the spark still kindles behind the eyes.

Clustered around these giants in Gatti's last years were other men, including the fine baritones Richard Bonelli, who came from Chicago in 1932 and remained many seasons, John Charles Thomas, who lent his mellifluous voice and rudimentary acting to one of Gatti's seasons and several of his successor's. Pavel Ludikar came from Czechoslovakia for a half dozen years. And George Cehanovsky began in 1926 that inestimable service to roles of all colors, stripes, and languages that has concluded only as this is written, an unparalleled record of forty years.

On the distaff side, the most sterling acquisition in a good many of Gatti's years was Elisabeth Rethberg in 1922 (who after her retirement in 1942 became Mrs. George Cehanovsky). The comely soprano could sing in any language, seemingly, and Gatti took advantage of this talent as well as her silvery voice, musicianship, and good looks to place her as Aida, Nedda, Sieglinde, and Sophie in her very first season. She went on to a solid career, and was designated at a high point of her life as possessing "the perfect voice." Other 1922 classmates were the distinguished contralto Sigrid Onegin and the less brilliant Ina Bourskaya; the piquant Queena Mario (née Helen Tillotson), who slenderly graced a number of roles, making an endearing Gretel; and a long-lasting Russian soprano, Thalia Sabanieeva.

All other claims to the coloratura crown were set aside at the advent

of the diminutive Frenchwoman who was to mount the throne and remain firmly there with a fixative compounded of talent, charm, and a
tiny mailed fist, until a time to leave of her own choosing—Miss Lily Pons.
Before that reign—set the beginning of it as January 3, 1931—several
contenders jostled for space. Toti dal Monte, who accompanied Melba on
a tour of Australia, lit few sparks in her single season, 1924–25; similarly
Elvira de Hidalgo (later famous as the teacher of Maria Callas) aroused
little excitement in her return after more than a dozen years. For a reception the like of which had never been witnessed before, it remained for
a seemingly simple little maid from Kansas City, Missouri, to take the
town apart. Marion Talley's story is not all razzmatazz, for her voice was
lovely, though not truly a *voix d'or,* as the French say, pointed out W. J.
Henderson, and she had a pretty doll's face and was but eighteen—time
to learn, if she had cared to. But she had little imagination and no flair,
and was oppressed by an albatross family. The rootin'-tootin' delegation
on a special train from Kansas City for her debut on February 27, 1926,
the fact that her father, a telegraph operator, was allowed to sit in the
wings and send out gushing reports, the high voice and the glamour
role (Gilda) allotted her (companioned by Lauri-Volpi, De Luca, Mardones, and Alcock, with Serafin to conduct) heated the press to boiling
point, especially when the packed audience ("packed" in two senses) went
crazy. Her additional appearances in this and the following year were
heavily sold. Only nearing the end, when her "Hymn to the Sun" in
Coq d'Or received no applause whatever (an unheard-of occurrence),
was it brought home to her that her welcome had been withdrawn. In
the meantime, she had reaped an all-time high of one third of a million
dollars on concert tours cannily exploited by Francis C. Coppicus, one-
time secretary to Gatti-Casazza and now a high-powered concert manager.
Music critics remained immune from the start. Henderson had particularly cutting things to say, the most damaging that her production was
all wrong and that she showed not a trace of musical instinct or intelligence. In 1929 Miss Talley went "back to the farm" and a checkered personal career that led her eventually to Hollywood.

　　Lily Pons, in comparison, crept onto the scene on mouse feet.
"Discovered" by Maria Gay and Giovanni Zenatello, the colorful singing
couple who had retired into a prosperous teaching career, Pons later
found it necessary to repudiate them and face the inevitable lawsuit. In

spite of Gatti's precautions—once burned by whoopla, he wanted no more—some inkling of her quality had leaked out, and she was not unheralded. The "foretaste of full-fledged virtuosity" seen by Downes in her *Lucia* Mad Scene became more than a promise; Lily was the Met's golden girl for a good long time. Even when her breath grew shorter and a special conductor (Pietro Cimara) was tacitly told off to conduct for her, she retained all her charm in the well-shaped vessel that was her body—one of the first to prove that a huge cage is not always necessary to hold a singing bird. She dared a *Lakmé* costume that left off at the delicate rib cage and resumed at the hips.

Pons' personal style is a byword: her pink dress makes others pale; her train is the few inches longer—or shorter—that spells chic in the absolute; her jewels glisten against skin that is still young—or at least can be cunningly made up to appear so. The voice, she says today, is better than it ever was because she has time to rest. She left the Metropolitan finally in 1961, after years containing only a few scattered performances each, but hers is still the voice that cuts through others in any ceremony. Divorcing her merchant husband in 1933, she married the popular conductor André Kostelanetz in 1938, a match that seemed bizarre but that lasted longer than anyone expected. One of her most typically Gallic traits is thrift; a maid once told of patched underwear, and her gorgeous gowns are often "run up" by a "little dressmaker" in Cannes.

Of all the Americans to join Gatti's latter-day parade, Grace Moore made the biggest splash. The successor of Farrar, she was the forerunner of Maria Callas in that species, prima donna, which commands at once adulation and loathing, obeisance and calumny, and above all, publicity, publicity, publicity. Headlines to Miss Moore brought more nourishment than bread, more intoxication than champagne. She once told a colleague that she had made her career on bad notices.

With a determination that outweighed even her naturally beautiful voice and peach-blossom skin, Moore achieved the opera stage after flirtations with Broadway (*Hitchy-Koo* and the *Music Box Review*) and jaunts over France, where she fitted appropriately into the Elsa Maxwell-Elsie de Wolf crowd—what came to be called "Café Society," and later, the "Jet Set." "A person whose name gets into the papers is to Grace an important person . . . she knows the real thing when she sees it, but sometimes seems to prefer the counterfeit," wrote Charles O'Connell in a devastatingly candid book, *The Other Side of the Record,* which broke all the rules by telling tales on people before they had been dead ten years and undoubtedly contributed to his loss of the post as music director for RCA Victor.

Meeting Otto Kahn socially in Europe, Moore secured money, encouragement, and advice from the philanthropist; then after two disastrous auditions at the Met, bet him $100 she would enter those sacred portals before two years were out. She made it, with a prettily sung, if not flawless, Mimi, on February 7, 1928, about which mostly cordial words were said. Gatti gave her Johnson, Scotti, and Fleischer to work with. Her audience, doubtless infected by "Talley fever," as a large contingent of Tennesseans sparked enough applause to bring twenty-eight curtain calls for the debutante, also had the example of Mary Lewis, a beauteous musical comedy star who had preceded Grace to the opera three seasons before. The great Farrar days seemed to have come again, but with one difference: Moore "had the capacity but not the willingness to work where music is concerned," as O'Connell brutally put it. Still, she cut a wide swath in the operatic world as well as in Hollywood (her films were a notch better than most; *One Night of Love* even created a worldwide sensation), the concert circuit, the Lido, and the Riviera. At the Met for her to observe were Bori and Ponselle as Fiora, and the former as Louise and Manon, roles Moore would later make popular successes. She studied Fiora and Louise with their composers. But she found all by herself the formula for being an opera singer—one part each of natural gifts, artistry, glowing good nature, grim will, and complete sham.

Coaxing Kahn to remember that he had prescribed European experience for her before her Met debut, she received his blessing to try France before returning for a second New York season, and lined up Bordeaux and the Paris Opéra Comique for *Manon.* Not her Des Grieux, but later to be her Metropolitan Roméo and to see his name linked romantically with hers, Georges Thill came to witness her Bordeaux debut and slyly told her that her obsequious reception had been motivated not by her talent but by the rumor that she was the mistress of America's richest tycoon. Pretending to be horrified, she was secretly tickled. Another courtesan, Giulietta in *Contes d'Hoffmann* as well as the modest Marguerite came her way at the Met, but it was as Tosca (who worshiped art and love) and Louise (who worshiped Paris and love) that her fans like to remember her.

This full-blown American made no secret that outside of singing her chief interest was love, in which she wrote she had always been "perfectly normal, happy, and enormously successful." In her autobiography, *You're Only Human Once,* she mentions "three of the richest men in the world," and a charming Frenchman, while giving full credit to her husband, the handsome Spaniard Valentin Parera. Apparently the romance had gone out of at least one tenor, for in 1937–38, when they were making the French film, *Louise,* she spoke disparagingly of Thill's "bay window."

At least one of the rich men was no figment of fiction. He had, it seems, given her the magnificent jewels she wore one night at a Cannes Casino gala where she sang. After making fairly heavy weather of *"In quelle trine morbide,"* she came back to her table, panting, and turned to the young man next to her, insisting he undo her necklace of diamonds and emeralds. "It's much too tight," she claimed. "You'll have to add another emerald to it," she carelessly threw over her shoulder at the "very rich man" at her right. Dorothy Parker, whose forked tongue had deflated many an egotistic bubble, tried now to prick her friend Grace. "You ought to get something to go with your face," she suggested. "Steel? Ice?"

Grace Moore caused Edward Ziegler the only spell of naïveté his daughter can remember. He refused to believe in the soprano's lust for life—or, rather, vice versa—because, as he plaintively said, "She never made a pass at me, and I'm not that unattractive!"

Moore sang on nearly to the last of the Johnson reign, coming and going almost at will. She never had quite the Farrar public, nor the privilege of retiring gracefully in the manner of that prima donna, or like Bori, whom she admired for doing so. Sadly, her life, which she boasted really began when the curtain went down, was taken from her in flaming tragedy in a plane crash in Copenhagen in 1947. She was on her way to tour Sweden, and the King had sent the Crown Prince to escort her. She probably would have enjoyed the eight-column headline reporting her death, her friends commented, in trying to console her personal representative, Jean Dalrymple, and would have liked the billing that put her name over the Crown Prince's. She died a happy woman because she had achieved what she wanted no matter what anyone thought of her. She had fun and, like Louise, she didn't regret a moment of it.

Other American girls penetrated Gatti's roster before and after Farrar and Fremstad and Ponselle. Memory recalls Anna Case, who came in 1909, created for America the *Boris* Feodor and the *Rosenkavalier* Sophie, and then retired after she married the tycoon Clarence Mackay. Others were the flexible-voiced Bernice de Pasquali, who succeeded Sembrich in repertoire but not in reputation, and who was supplanted by the more gifted Mabel Garrison; Edith Mason, who played an in-and-out game with both Chicago and New York as well as with her two marriages to Giorgio Polacco, the conductor in both companies; Margaret Halstead, a tall Venus and Giulietta, who also sang Ortrud; Frances Peralta, a delightful Dorabella among other leads; Nannette Guilford, the "baby prima donna"; Leonora Corona, a Texan, whose flaming hair atop a large head attracted as much attention as a svelte body and voluptuous big voice not too well disciplined as Leonora, Donna Anna (substituting for Ponselle), Tosca, and Gioconda. Nina Morgana, who married Caruso's secretary, Bruno Zirato, had an honored place in the company from 1919 until Gatti's departure.

Among darker voices were Marion Telva, the Dame Quickly who shared curtain calls with Scotti and Tibbett and whose vibrant contributions also included the ideal Adalgisa to Ponselle's Norma; Merle Alcock, who had almost every role she wanted in seven seasons, but had to wait for Carmen in other cities after 1929; Sophie Braslau, a darkly handsome girl entrusted with many novelties, chiefly Cadman's *Shanewis*; Florence Wickham, Alice Gentle (who changed her name from "True"), and Kathleen Howard. Carrying an import that endures to this day is Rose Bampton, who raised her voice from contralto to sing Sieglinde and Donna Anna, married the conductor Wilfred Pelletier after his divorce from Queena Mario, and teaches in New York. Louise Homer stayed honorably until 1930. The hard-working Doris Doe was active for twenty-six years, until 1947. Gladys Swarthout, who made her debut as La Cieca in 1929 and scored a hit in Rimsky-Korsakoff's *Sadko* the same season, went on to become the company's vivid Carmen. With her late husband, Frank Chapman, Swarthout has belonged to a little group of Met graduates who still attend operas, make opening nights glamorous, and take active interest in Met affairs.

Gatti honestly tried to give Americans their chance. But the balance of trade had not quite reached equilibrium. For every Tibbett there were still a Scotti and a De Luca, for every Ponselle a Rethberg and a Jeritza, for every Moore a Bori, for every Johnson a Gigli and a Lauri-Volpi, for every Whitehill a Schorr. Few Americans really penetrated the extremes of the coloratura and the heroic German.

Gatti's last and likely most precious find came in his final year. The emergence of Kirsten Flagstad seemed like a miracle. The lady from Norway not only brought new life to Valhalla, but in many minds she was thought to be the savior of the Met. Kahn had heard her sing Tosca in Oslo as early as 1929, and even in that role (which she never took at the Met), he knew he wanted her. But she ignored the letter of Eric Semon, the European agent. Oscar Thompson, writing in *Musical America,* carried rapturous tales after he heard her Isolde in Norway in 1932. He was gratified to utter a big loud "I told you so!" when she made her startling debut as Sieglinde at the February 2 broadcast matinee in 1935, her voice recalling to him "the summer landscape of that vast mountainous plateau between Oslo and Bergen: a voice of crystal clarity at the top; of warm glow, as of the play of sunlight on snow, in the middle; of dark, opaque, blue-gray shadows below. Variable as was the tonal color," he hastened to add, "this was not at the expense of a unified scale." Radio listeners at home gasped as the pure, powerful tones pulsed through their living rooms.

Flagstad's Isolde four days later brought out the full panoply of critical acclaim, together with the realization that here was a treasure indeed. Audiences went wild and became Wagnerites overnight; singers braced up to the new challenge and performed better; Bodanzky seemed fired with new incentives. This was the occasion to dust off the best words: "radiant, transcendent, poignant, sensitive, eloquent, communicative, supreme!" Both the *Walküre* and *Götterdämmerung* Brünnhildes followed with scarcely a drawn breath (Siegfried's Warrior Maid waited a couple of seasons, as the Norse maid missed one turn by indisposition and other sopranos had temporary priority); Elisabeth and Elsa crowded on the scene and she learned Kundry virtually overnight. She made twenty-three appearances at home and on tour that first season. The next brought *Fidelio* and the next *Der Fliegende Holländer.* So, when on December 23, 1936, fifty years and two days since the first *Tristan* at the Met, Henderson was inspired to compare all the Isoldes of the half century, Flagstad ranked high, beside Nordica, a peerless vocal achievement.

In the light of later events, it seems incredible that Flagstad should have thought of retiring even before she came to America. She was almost forty and had behind her a career of twenty years, encompassing every-thing—even operetta—but the Wagner *Ring* and *Parsifal*. She was hap-pily married to a wealthy industrialist and longed for family life. After only one season in America, she proclaimed the end again, repeating her vow to this writer in Copenhagen in the summer of 1936. The idea grew to a phobia, although she did not, like Patti, engage in prolonged fare-well seasons until later.

Perhaps because Gatti did not consider too much what would happen after he left the helm, he made no provision to renew the one-year con-tract he had given this dark mare, thus bequeathing confusion to the next regime, which had to fight for its new sensation against the claims of con-cert tours and San Francisco Opera appearances. Right from the begin-ning, contract and business arrangements got snarled among the singer herself, her husband, who was prone to act unilaterally, her accompanist Edwin McArthur (revealing the tangles in his *Personal Memoire* of 1965), her concert management, and the Metropolitan administration. The pub-lic knew nothing of this and continued to idolize the glorious voice. German opera had come back (and in its own language) even before the official welcome on February 10, 1923, of Siegfried Wagner himself. The master's son conducted the Metropolitan orchestra in a benefit for the restoration of Bayreuth. All wounds were healed as they played two of Siegfried's own pieces and Liszt's *"Les Préludes"* (in deference to Cosima?), and the American Clarence Whitehill sang Wotan's *"Abschied."*

The first complete *Ring*—if a body from which bits and pieces had been freely hacked can be called complete—was ventured in 1924–25. The roster blossomed with such names as Paul Bender, Michael Bohnen, who shared many bass roles; Ivar Andresen and Ludwig Hofmann came later, and Emmanuel List, a notable Ochs and an enduring singer, ar-rived in 1933. William Gustafson, an American, also played bass roles. Friedrich Schorr, who became the beloved Sachs of his generation, began a long career in 1923, adding many other roles; Gustav Schützendorf also filled a good number of baritone spots.

Tenors did not settle down so comfortably for a few years. After Lauritz Melchior arrived in 1925 and overcame several handicaps—he rehearsed in the midst of the ballyhoo over Talley, and he had to free

himself from awkwardness and the constricting effects of his early baritone days—Wagnerians began to wonder what they had thought they liked
about his predecessors and other incumbents: Johannes Sembach, Curt
Taucher, Rudolf Laubenthal, and Walter Kirchhoff. Ernest Newman, a
guest critic on the *Evening Post,* wondered why Taucher should be here
at all. In 1925 he was the victim of one of those freak accidents that
should not happen in a well-regulated opera house: he fell twenty-five
feet through an open trapdoor—but returned to finish the performance
(Siegfried).

A new crop of tenors brought Hans Clemens, acceptable as David
and in other lighter parts; Max Lorenz (who only much later etched a
searing portrait of Herod), and Gustaf de Loor.

To complement this male galaxy, Gatti had Rethberg and Jeritza
for the less strenuous Wagner efforts, and Easton for these as well as an
occasional Brünnhilde. Easton, in fact, could sing everything and did—
the last mistress of many styles. To these were added Maria Müller in
1924 and in 1927 the buxom blonde, Grete Stückgold (a swashbuckling
Octavian as well as a Wagnerian). It was always good policy to let a newcomer sniff around the edges of the roles of the incumbents—it kept
everyone on their toes. Dorothee Manski also came along in 1927, one of
the most versatile and agreeable ladies, cited by Ziegler's daughter as one
of those "without whoms," the cheerful indispensables, during her fourteen seasons. She could even supply a high note or two from the wings to
help out a colleague. (Manski headed the caravan to Indiana University
that eventually became a Metropolitan annex.) Editha Fleischer, another
dependable, made Siegfried's Forest Bird less like a cluck than most. The
contralto department was also well serviced with Branzell, Claussen,
and Matzenauer, all of whom stretched their magnificent ranges occasionally to a soprano role. The indestructible Schumann-Heink returned
twice in the decade to display her utter vocal mastery and knowledge as
the eternal Earth Mother, Erda.

As could be expected, it was the big guns, the Brünnhildes, Isoldes,
Leonores, and Kundrys that made the trouble, motivating the accession
of large voices that seemed to have either too much or too little experience—usually the former. Nanny Larsen-Todsen headed the procession in 1924, followed in 1927 by Gertrude Kappel, who persisted into

the next regime and was considered a decided improvement. Hers were the heavy chores, even to an Ortrud and an Elektra, which Gilman thought missed the composer's intent by a thousand miles, "a distracted Wagner heroine wandering in an alien land." Nevertheless, she and the opera had considerable success with the public.

Elisabeth Ohms, a Dutch soprano of great reputation, was one of those just past her prime in 1929. Göta Ljungberg, the tall birch tree from Sweden (1931), left an impression of awkwardness and angularity. Her name was corrupted by insensitive Americans to "Junebug." Her Salome revealed to Gilman little intensity and less Ljungberg—at least seven more veils would have had to be removed. By 1934, the competition with Flagstad, Lehmann, and Kappel left her on the sidelines, as it also extinguished Anny Konetzni.

Two superlative artists, Frida Leider and Maria Olszewska, finally brought up at the doors of the bashful Metropolitan—largely by reason of the preoccupation of Mr. Insull in foreign parts, said Gilman, referring to the Chicago financier who had "done a bunk'" to Paris after the collapse of his three-billion-dollar utilities kingdom, which left opera in Chicago almost dead. Not for the first time New York uttered suspicions that the Metropolitan had not been entirely honest in claiming that all the good singers had been seen and heard on Broadway. Here were two notable exceptions—an Isolde and a Brangäne who struck fire. Both provided many months of sheer delight—and some discomfort, for "they should have been here long since," ran the familiar complaint.

Another of the late-comers who did her best to make up for lost time by giving incandescent hours to the Metropolitan was Lotte Lehman, whose Sieglinde, Elsa, and above all, whose Marschallin entranced a following for ten years. After her retirement, which led not to inactivity but to passing on her wisdom to young singers as a sort of benevolent elder stateswoman, she said that perhaps her favorite role—certainly one of the most difficult—was the Leonore in *Fidelio* that she never was allowed to sing at the Met.

That German opera is not entirely without humor (leaving aside the intentional jocosity of *Meistersinger* and smaller comic pieces) is a theory only occasionally proved. Spears may fly on their wire over Parsifal's head and light bridges descend into view to reveal an animated card game by

electricians in the Grail Scene, but seldom are protagonists involved in
so protracted a bit of unintended hilarity as vexed Barbara Kemp and
Curt Taucher in one *Tristan* performance in the twenties. The German
soprano, as the wife of Max von Schillings, had made a successful debut
in his thriller, *Mona Lisa,* on March 1, 1923, striking Krehbiel (in his
last *Tribune* review before his death on March 23) as bearing a great
resemblance to the original Gioconda without the smile. Kemp was a
remarkable singing actress, who was even called a Teutonic Mary Garden,
but she did not fit into the Metropolitan frame. The Isolde in April
would have proved any actor's undoing. In a praiseworthy attempt to
keep Urban's fairly new scenery and props in condition, a propman had
repainted the cup from which the incipient lovers would drink. The
paint—green, it was—had not quite dried. As Isolde drained the potion
and Tristan snatched the cup from her, hands began to show green on
palms. Neither actor had the gumption to refrain for once from the
agonized gestures of that scene—the hands pressed over beating hearts,
feverish foreheads and cheeks—and the final frenetic embrace. When
Tristan and Isolde broke apart at Brangäne's insistence, it could be
observed that both resembled badly streaked park benches. Kemp bowed
out after another *Mona Lisa* the following season, complaining about
the amount of work and paucity of rehearsal. Gatti said she was nervous.
Little wonder.

Since Toscanini's departure in 1915, the Italian operas had been
directed more or less efficiently by Polacco, Papi, Bellezza, and Moranzoni, with assists from Giuseppe Bamboschek, Pietro Cimara, Giuseppe
Sturani, and others. Tullio Serafin's decade began in 1924 with an *Aida*
that made the faithful believe the good old Toscanini days had returned.
Serafin grew tired, however—as most conductors did, what with the
punishing schedule and rehearsal shortages. Pierre Monteux and Albert
Wolff gave way to Louis Hasselmans for French works, with Wilfred
Pelletier occasionally taking the week-night baton as well as shepherding
most of the Sunday-night concerts. Richard Hageman stayed some seasons from 1912, mostly behind scenes, but returned as a composer (*Caponsacchi*) after Gatti had left. The concertmaster Pierre Henrotte presided
over a concert or two now and then.

More systematic planning seemed to imbue the German department,
where there was an unquestioned chief in Artur Bodanzky and two com-

petent assistants, Karl Riedel and Paul Eisler. Then in 1929 Bodanzky announced that he was leaving to conduct for the Friends of Music. To the critics it was bitter news that Gatti couldn't seem to find the money for Bruno Walter or the taste for Otto Klemperer, both of whom had proved available for orchestra engagements in this country. Clemens Krauss, too, had been here as a symphonic leader. Rejecting still other possibilities, such as Erich Kleiber and Leo Blech, Gatti engaged instead an unknown from German provincial theatres, though born a Pole—Joseph Rosenstock. He made his debut with a *Meistersinger* on October 30, 1929. Such a blast at any one man's capabilities—or lack of them—has seldom been launched at first hearing in New York and continued at second, third, and fourth. His *Meistersinger* was at best "conservative"; his *Rosenkavalier* somnolent (though the placid cast was somewhat responsible); his *Walküre* and repeats of the others brought no balm. Soon it was plain that Rosenstock "must go." His "nervous breakdown" seemed altogether justifiable.

To the surprise of everybody, Bodanzky came hustling back, his new castles in cloudland having evaporated. Rosenstock crept off to Germany, where he had barely time to lick his wounds when Hitler propelled a number of artists out of their usual haunts. After a few years, the conductor seasoned himself all over again in Japan, spent a summer or two at Aspen, Colorado, and came back to New York to vindicate himself as few have managed to do, first in command at the New York City Opera, then to return to conduct *Tristan* and *Elektra* at the Met in 1960.

Meanwhile, no gap whatsoever appearing in his annual record at the Met, Bodanzky followed through into the next regime, as well liked as ever except by a few who felt he could have improved the orchestral playing in all those years. The days of conductor domination (what might be called a return to the Toscanini principle) awaited Walter, Beecham, Szell, Busch, Stiedry, and Reiner, some years ahead.

15

... AND WANES

The decision to leave the Metropolitan Opera to its own devices
marked the highest point on the chart of society hysteria.

—CORNELIUS VANDERBILT IV, *Farewell to Fifth Avenue*

One of the ponderable ironies of the Metropolitan's long history of
ups and downs is that the regime that began under permission to lose
money showed a profit every year for a while and at the end of twenty
years wound up with a nest egg of a million dollars. Gatti-Casazza's
surplus on the books was built up steadily from the season in which
he got rid forever of Andreas Dippel, the New Theatre, Hammerstein,
the double touring company, and the Paris trip (although the last as
well as the Hammerstein payoff came directly out of Otto Kahn's pocket,
it was said). That same season, 1909–10, racked up a loss of $200,000.
The profit for 1910–11 was slightly under $35,000. Though five figures
shrank to four ($1,500 or so) in 1914–15, the black figures mounted again
immediately until the 1927 high of $144,378. "Gatti should be hired for
life!" concluded Lawrence Gilman, who had succeeded Henry E.
Krehbiel on the *Tribune* at the latter's death in 1923.

The aura of satisfaction around management and board was not
even punctured by the loss of $300,000 on New York seasons and tours of
Diaghilev's Ballet Russe in 1916, a controversial affair whose effects
are still felt. Kahn pushed the "educational" tours with all his might—
personal, prestigious, and financial—while Gatti both deplored and
sabotaged, and Vaslav Nijinsky, the mercurial dancer (who did not arrive when expected and then was constantly "indisposed") made everyone's life miserable with his vacillations and crochets. The 1916 spring
season in the House, during which Gatti fumingly sent the opera company for an unprofitable month to Boston, went passably, although a
January season in the New Theatre (now named the Century) had
somewhat taken the edge off. Then a repeat in the fall brought disaster.
Kahn told friends he had underwritten the venture, but Gatti leaves

the point ambiguous. Whatever the truth of the ballet hassle, the results were soon swallowed up in prosperity.

How could these profits have mounted in an enterprise notorious for producing deficits? Even if, as Geraldine Farrar claimed, Gatti kept two sets of books, one to show the directors and the other for the discouragement of the singer asking for a raise, the million-dollar reserve fund was a solid fact. Scholars of the day attribute its existence to the low union demands and to an ever more restrictive policy against new mountings for old operas. The directors did not care to refute Gatti's contention that there was no use to concoct expensive new settings when at any moment a new opera house might be ready. In this, Gatti was still relying on the promise made him in 1908 by Kahn. A new home had been Kahn's dream since 1903, when he joined the board. Now, twenty-one years later, its realization seemed possible.

Without the slightest encouragement from his board and the box-holders, Mrs. Matz, his biographer, notes, the financier went ahead on his own, purchasing a plot 500 by 500 by 200 feet, bounded by Fifty-sixth and Fifty-seventh streets and Ninth Avenue, and negotiating a loan of $1,700,000 from the Metropolitan Life Insurance Company for beginning construction. It was a grievous mistake for this irresistible force to underestimate the resistance of an immovable body. He was immediately slapped down in a manner distinguished for cold rudeness and disregard of fact, which enraged the public and inspired the press to open cynicism. A letter signed by R. Fulton Cutting, chairman of the board of the Metropolitan Opera and Real Estate Company, was widely reprinted:

If the music lovers of New York want a new opera house they are entitled to have one and the trustees of the present property will certainly not oppose any obstacle or competition to such a project. They are not, however, of the opinion that the present house is antiquated or that its site is undesirable. It is producing opera more superbly than anywhere else in the world. The acoustic properties of its auditorium are unsurpassed. . . . If it is desirable that the building should be replaced by one larger and more scientifically equipped, I presume the company of which Mr. Kahn is chairman will undertake the project.

Outwardly ignoring this rebuff, as he had ignored others (for example, it was not until 1917 that the chief benefactor of the Met had been allowed to buy a box, so rooted was anti-Semitism among the Old

Guard), Kahn went on to line up as much approval as possible—William K. Vanderbilt, Clarence Mackay, Paul Cravath, George Eastman, Henry and Cornelius V. Whitney, Henry Rogers Winthrop, and some new board members: Vincent Astor, Edward S. Harkness, Robert L. Gerry, E. Roland Harriman, and Frederick Potts Moore. Kahn published the details of his plan, which included increasing seat capacity to 4,500 and improving sight lines, the reduction of Parterre boxes to thirty, and, most disagreeable to the opposition, a system of leasing, rather than owning, boxes.

The *World* applauded his intentions in a "Social Primer," thus:

> K is for Kahn who is doing his best
> To give ultra-exclusives a kick in the chest.
> He'd deny them the privilege, so 'twould appear,
> Of ruling the roost from the gilded parterre.

Grudging approval was finally given to Kahn, with one major compromise—the boxholders would continue ownership—and two architects were appointed: the conservative Benjamin Wister Morris (whose most apposite achievements were the Morgan Memorial in Hartford and J. Pierpont's Library Annex), and the more progressive Joseph Urban. Needless to say, their ideas veered sharply. By the sheerest chance, during a visit to the architect's studio, Urban's designs were spotted by Deems Taylor, who, as a favorite of Kahn, had been commissioned to write *The King's Henchman* the year before. "Mr. Deemus," as Gatti always called him, was editor of *Musical America* at the time. He published the designs, emphasizing that they were not "official." Nevertheless, the Real Estate Company and Morris took offense. The situation became more confused when a group of die-hards including Morgan, Cutting, Cornelius N. Bliss, and others virtually repudiated Kahn by looking for another site. Such an unlikely spot as 110th Street facing Central Park (and backing on Harlem) was favored by John Erskine and others; Fifty-ninth Street and Central Park South was mentioned, as well as the location of the New (now Century) Theatre on Central Park West. Kahn held on till the last minute to his mortgage on the Fifty-seventh Street property, then gave up in despair, taking a loss of $1,600,000. More bitter to him was the abandonment of an ideal: "the solemn obligation of a semi-public institution such as the Metropolitan to provide amply and generously for music lovers of small or modest means." The calamitous October of 1929 put a stop to any thoughts he may still have cherished about a new home for the Metropolitan. He lost interest to the extent of giving up his position on the board to Paul D. Cravath, his lawyer and longtime associate, who proceeded to deny all of Kahn's principles. Another attempt to move the opera company out of its barnaclelike encrustations had occurred in 1928, when John D. Rockefeller, Jr., offered the opera a place in what became Rockefeller Center. Kahn was said not to be in on this proposition. Rockefeller eventually found himself holding the same short stick that Kahn had grasped, except that no personal financial loss was involved. Rockefeller built his Center in spite of the depression, ostensibly for the opera, while the Met waited for what it considered a fair price—$13 million—for its land and the old building. The unreality of this price seems obvious. It was to be suspected that the powers were dragging their feet. Furthermore, they cannot have approved Rockefeller's proviso that the boxholders pay him rent after their theatre was built. Mrs. Cornelius Vanderbilt had been the *dea ex machina* to ruin Kahn's dream house. Would she agree to Rockefeller's? Obviously not. It was Cravath who spread butter on the dry bread offered the public as explanation for the refusal to move: "I should not feel very disappointed if we had to stay on in the old house. It has associations and traditions which attach audiences to it." The old-timers settled back with a sigh of comfort. They could still roost in "their miserable building with a collection of foolish boxes in which ladies expose their diamonds, chests, and boredom, and old gentlemen sleep," according to a disrespectful observer. And they could point with smug satisfaction to the inadequacies of the Center Theatre in Rockefeller Center—abominable acoustics, production space almost as cramped as the Met's, and with no more expansion possibilities, and a cavernous auditorium. Beautiful as it was, the theatre proved good for movies only, and lacking the wholesale glamour of its larger sister, Radio City Music Hall, languished and died. The rest of the huge building over it was propped up while its corner was replaced by a bank. One cannot do more than speculate what a real opera architect might have accomplished on the site.

To all but a few, Gatti-Casazza remained the mystery man throughout his entire twenty-seven years at the Met. In the opera house his dominion remained unflawed; his unheralded, almost ghostly appearance upon any scene of trouble or potential trouble suggested that his portly body was borne on wings or actually teleported. He never raised his voice, and is said seldom to have uttered a syllable of English, although it was an open secret that he both spoke and understood it very well. So he controlled his interlocutors and suppliants by forcing many of them into Italian. French he would tolerate, but just. The big, brown, sad eyes, the graying beard, the sloping façade which grew more and more convex every year, the thumbs hooked into vest pockets, the immaculate linen, the broad-brimmed hat, and polished shoes—this is the closest to a perfect picture of an opera impresario New York has ever seen.

One man in his establishment knew him comparatively well. Edward Ziegler had been engaged by Otto Kahn in 1916 as "administrative secretary," a position created for him and expanding to take in any duties chosen by or thrust upon him. His bias at first was purely artistic, as he had been for almost two decades a music critic, as assistant, then successor, to James Gibbons Huneker on *Town Topics* and assistant to the great man on the *Sun*; later on his own with several papers and magazines and eventually the *Herald* (1908–16). Huneker remained his god; a large inscribed photograph stood on Ziegler's dresser until his death, recalls his daughter, Suzanne (Mrs. Charles Gleaves). Huneker had met the young Baltimorean in the late nineties. Ziegler often saved his principal when Huneker was too lazy or preoccupied to hand in copy. Huneker dedicated the collection of essays, *Unicorns* (1917) to Ziegler and gave Ned good advice when the younger man had publicly attacked his colleagues:

"Don't, my boy, start in life quarreling with your own bread. It's bad form, besides it will prove a serious bar to your advancement." [And counseling him on style] "If you leave your books and theories and get to dealing with concrete facts, your style will become more robust, more red-blooded, more readable. . . . Not too harsh, not so bitter; use the dagger, not dynamite." [And, later] "Don't write with grave pauses, profound smirks and all the pompous, silly, mean little reservations, attenuations, paraphrases and involutions of your contemporaries. Far better an honest staccato phrase than a wilderness of sostenutos."

If it is true, as administrators in the succeeding hierarchy insisted, that Gatti "ran his office from scraps of paper in his pocket and [his secretary] Luigi Villa's memory," the unsuspecting Ziegler was thrust unprepared into a jungle he tried desperately to clear. His first apprehension of his job as "art" expanded perforce into the business of maintaining a polyglot opera company; he taught himself through happenstance and survived by expedient. His shrewdness as a financial expert became a byword. He sold the Met's endorsement of the Knabe piano for $15,000, rode herd on the profits from artists' phonograph records, and allowed the opera to be heard on the new invention, radio, for a consideration ($173,000 in 1931, the first year, according to Irving Kolodin). The singers still paid tribute to the opera for their concert tours, a practice instituted by Grau and carried on by Conried, who actually arranged appearances for Nordica or Eames or Plançon (who complained bitterly about being sent around the country in a trunk) or Caruso. The habit of taking commissions for outside engagements was broken only when the soloists' union, the American Guild of Musical Artists, was organized in 1936.

A small man with a firm mouth and cool eyes behind rimless glasses, as taciturn as Gatti and moving as quietly, Ziegler came to be the spinal cord of the nebulous structure. No detail of administrative or financial operations escaped him. He arranged repertoire, scouted for new talent in Europe in the summer, and arranged the spring tours, turning up personally in Brooklyn and Philadelphia. To these manifold duties he added that of liaison with his former colleagues, the critics, who, it must be said, did not always receive him gracefully. He maintained a friendship with Lawrence Gilman, however.

Gatti, secretive in one respect with his assistant as in almost everything with everyone else, never told Ziegler what the opening night's opera was to be until too late to matter to the press. If Ziegler didn't know, he couldn't give it away by even a facial expression (if he can be imagined betraying one). Gatti's system continued to be one of playing his casts close to his chest. A singer would often find out his roles for a week ahead only by consulting the newspaper listings.

All Ziegler's—as Gatti's—instincts forbade fraternizing with the artists outside of work hours. Mrs. Gleaves remembers only Florence Easton and Richard Crooks, whom the Zieglers met at mutual friends' homes, and Bodanzky, the conductor, and Joseph Urban, the designer, as frequent intimate guests. To Ziegler, Gatti showed a friendly cordiality seldom conceded to others. The two men enjoyed each other's company, even though Ziegler ruined his perfectly good French by bastardizing it to such mixtures as *"Lui est bono"* and similar mutilations. They never, never ventured into English, and Gatti knew no German, which was Ziegler's next best tongue. So night after night, when the Zieglers lived at Sixty-third and Park and the Gatti-Casazzas on West Fifty-eighth, the two men would wander back and forth, accompanying each other home several times, not willing to cut short a good story. Gatti's legendary wit found vent in these sessions.

After Toscanini had flung out of the opera house never to return, Ziegler was delegated one summer to scout the European theatres for ideas on lighting equipment, the Metropolitan having decided that some backstage reform was necessary. Milan's La Scala had just spent a fortune on a new light board, so this house was a prime target for Ziegler, accompanied by his daughter. Giving as an excuse that the Met schedule included *Andrea Chénier,* the opera holding forth at La Scala, the Zieglers inspected backstage arrangements closely. Afterward they were received cordially by Toscanini at Lake Como, "although he might not have been so nice if he knew of our snooping," confessed Mrs. Gleaves.

Both Gatti and Ziegler adored Wagner. When their particular passion, *Meistersinger,* was on stage, it was more than one's ears could bear to go near the director's box, Number 48, where the two men would be singing along, not so *sotto voce,* and in tone and pitch somewhat less than ideal. Otto Kahn also cherished fervent feelings for Wagner, especially *Tristan,* although it was his habit to miss as much of King Marke's second-act soliloquy as possible. Mary Jane Matz pictured him in *Opera News* as emerging into the icy wind of a winter's night, folding his opera cloak about him, pulling on white gloves, and clapping a top hat on his head, then striding up Broadway to Forty-second Street to watch a movie or an act or two of vaudeville or burlesque until time to slip into the directors' box for Isolde's *"Liebestod."* Ocassionally he would gather up a handful of lounging critics from the press room to go along on the excursion.

Meanwhile, the opera was at the top of a steep, swift slide into real trouble. The first loss in twenty years—almost $15,000 at the end of the 1929–30 season—pointed the way down. Income had slipped and would continue to recede, a million at a time, and losses mounted until at the end of 1931–32 they approached shiveringly close to half a million.

The opera had become the last recourse for Society, as Joseph Lilly noted in the *World-Telegram*. Where else could they go to show off? Still, several boxes remained unsold. The price was $150,000 to the "right family." Vincent Astor seldom showed up, but the cachet of the opera box was still a strong pull for the Goelets and Mrs. R. T. Wilson (Grace Vanderbilt's father had passed on, but her mother remained faithful), the Myron Taylors, George Bakers, H. Edward Manvilles, and the "Tony" Biddles. After all, the Horse Show had been taken over by professionals.

Professionalism became the watchword of journalism as well. Helen Worden, who became a distinguished reporter for the *World-Telegram* in the field of crime and later was married to John Erskine, began to write of Society as humans instead of dummy figures at this juncture. Her columns in the *Evening World* were regarded with respect tinged with a slight fear. Cholly Knickerbocker (Maury Paul) had learned to check his facts more carefully since his debut as a gossipmonger, when he thought he had discovered who was present in the opera boxes by examining the venerable names on brass plaques attached to the doors. Mrs. Stuyvesant Fish remarked that he had opened half the graves in Woodlawn Cemetery by his account next day.

Even in these perilous times, Barclay Beekman of the *Mirror* scolded the Parterre for not dressing more brilliantly, but a slow trend would soon appear, the return of the more courtly dress appropriate for opera, although only a few tiaras twinkled.

But it became increasingly clear that drastic measures were imperative. Cravath scouted bankruptcy or a move to a less expensive theatre. Cutting expenses was an obvious expedient—but how? A reorganization came first, a reshaping that changed the Metropolitan Opera Company into an association without obligations or property. Moving into the void, the new corporation structure took along all its old ballast and shibboleths. Gatti was still allowed to pursue his now tired and cynical course; his salary came down a few notches but still exceeded $40,000. Serafin also continued to draw a high fee, but singers had to accept a 10 percent cut, while signing at the same time a protest against the conduct of Beniamino

Gigli, who had refused the cut. The tenor became a *cause célèbre* and left the opera after 1932.

The slogan "Save the Metropolitan" crept into public notice for the first time. Just how to achieve this laudable end was not at first clear. The old backers were highly in favor of the rescue—if someone else would do it. They shed their responsibility as easily as their artistic pretensions.

Only a few public protests greeted their abdication, after one gesture that provided a guarantee fund of $250,000 spread among the two groups, the new Metropolitan Association and the old Real Estate Company— their first contribution since Gatti began to make money. There were whimpers about not having received dividends all these years, but they had forgotten their agreement to waive profit. As quoted by Irving Kolodin, the surprising statement, "It was the artists who saved the opera," came from Artur Bodanzky, who thus sounded the first note in what was to become the chorus celebrating the "democratization of the Metropolitan." This meant a "broadening of the base" (a favorite phrase in those days) so that everybody was invited to become a patron. In addition to taking their cuts, the artists joined committees to raise funds, and the campaign began in earnest at a radio broadcast on February 25, 1933. Bori, Johnson, and Tibbett, the great trio that had sung together in the American operas, now talked a new refrain: "Give! Give! Give!"

The part of the Wall Street male and his Fifth Avenue or Park Avenue female (Park had come into favor after World War I, when commerce had crept up the lower limbs of Fifth and into its very vitals) was viewed with contempt by the black sheep of the Vanderbilt clan, Cornelius IV, in his *Farewell to Fifth Avenue.*

Commenting on the abdication, he said, "I do not have the name of the person first to stumble across the brilliant idea of letting the masses finance entertainment for the upper classes, but I do know the suggestion was received with the most enthusiasm in the houses of the boxholders." He heard many expressions of this attitude: "If they like opera, let them pay." "Now that we don't dare display our jewelry in public, why continue to support those Wops?" "Let them remove the breadlines from the vicinity of the Metropolitan first. Fancy my driving past that mob wearing my emeralds!" And the clincher: "Subscribe for 1933–34? Why, the Soviets may be here by then!"

This bitter scion concluded:

> The money spent on their champagne and lunch would have financed the whole season. [Instead], the boxholders made gracious appeals to shoemakers and tailors on the radio. . . . Few events in modern history were as disgusting and revealing in their boundless hypocrisy as that "Save the Met" drive conducted by millionaires among paupers. [To see] Mrs. —— in her silver foxes and pearls *et al.,* addressing sales girls at R. H. Macy's, begging them to come to the aid of the unemployed!

Vanderbilt was one of them and could say it. Otherwise the pious relinquishment of privilege was accepted without outcry, even with approval in some parts. But like Boston's Eben D. Jordan and Chicago's Harold McCormick before them, the suppliants discovered that when you have underwritten a cultural adventure all by yourself and have excluded the public from any deeper participation than buying tickets, it takes pull on a million strings instead of any one or a dozen to draw that kind of support. So the hat-passing continued. When receipts from an opera ball and sundry benefits and a grant from the Carnegie Corporation were added, the first emergency of 1933–34 was coated over with a thin and temporary film of security.

From the shadows of the near past a new source of revenue now appeared. Augustus D. Juilliard, longtime occupant of Box 2, loved the Metropolitan and provided for it in his will when he died in 1919. (Mrs. August Belmont, who occupied Box 4 next to him, credited him with more faithful attendance than any other boxholder. His fatal attack, indeed, occurred during a performance.) It was said that before his death, Juilliard had asked Gatti what would be most useful, and had been told that the opera needed a warehouse to store old scenery. "If Mr. Gatti had asked for new scenery, perhaps he might have got it," wrote John Erskine in *My Life in Music* some time later. But the textile tycoon had no interest in preserving old rags and tatters. Erskine, author and musician, and in due time president of the Juilliard School of Music, which received the greater part of Juilliard's bequest for music, became a very big cog in the Metropolitan's wheel when Juilliard's thoughtfulness was remembered in the crisis.

Kahn had turned down the proposed benefaction in 1924, fearing to upset the "normal" course of the opera programs. Spoken or unspoken within its provisions lay a strong bias toward American artists and works. Gatti probably felt he was doing as well as could be expected by both. Kahn himself could not be accused of slighting Americans. He had commissioned Deems Taylor to write two full-length works, and just before the emergency Howard Hanson had received the green light for *Merry Mount.* But this observance was considered merely "token" by the trustees of the Juilliard Foundation. They agreed, however, to "see the Met through" on the following conditions: educational opportunities— attending rehearsals, etc.—for properly qualified students; a supplementary season of *opéra comique* to draw in a larger audience; introduction of modern stage methods; production of the Hanson work; lowering of salaries.

This manifesto carried to the ears of Lucrezia Bori and Cornelius N. Bliss, heads of the fund-raising committee, the implication that the Juilliard Foundation would contribute a king's share of the fund, vitiating the drive. Infuriated, they confronted Erskine with this accusation. Their dismay mounted when they learned that "seeing the Met through" meant only $50,000, one sixth of the amount needed. (The next season it was $40,000.)

Meanwhile, economy measures had to be applied in the only way that suggested itself—shortening the season. The initial reaction to Johnson's suggestion that a moratorium on all performances be imposed for one season (euphemism for closing) was horror. Twenty-four weeks had become a "norm," with as many as forty-seven works (novelties expensively produced, then relegated to the warehouse, plus chestnuts pulled out year after year until to poke a finger at them invited collapse). Eight weeks were sheared off in the depression season of 1932–33. One other expedient could now be resorted to: because of the new status as a "tax-exempt educational" institution, ticket prices were cut from their all-time high of an $8.25 top to $6.50, the association losing a dollar, the subscriber saving seventy-five cents on the transaction. Single seats sold for $7.

The shortest season since Conried's fifteen weeks in 1903–4 showed a loss of more than a third of a million, although the lower prices had pulled in more customers. But the next one clipped off still another

week and, though slightly sweeter in operating loss, brought the bitter
realization that the old House would creak its last while violating a
dozen building codes if more than half a million was not spent immediately on propping it up. The strain on the fund raisers was relieved
by a mortgage of $600,000. Behind the scenes the operating company
(Association) and the Real Estate board engaged in their habitual tug
of war. The death of Otto Kahn in March 1934 had but put a period
to the waning days of his power, leaving an ill-assorted group of lawyers
and businessmen to tackle the problems brought to their doorstep by
depression and their own boredom.

One of the more foolish actions of the directorate had been to pro-
pose a merger with the New York Philharmonic-Symphony, itself on
financial reefs. Carnegie Hall, of whose congenial auditorium the orchestra was chief tenant, remained in constant danger of the wrecker's
ball even then, so the Met was proposed as the joint home of the two
organizations. Even though Bruno Walter, arriving for an engagement
with the orchestra, boldly opined that the idea had no merit, a still
higher court was sought. Bruno Zirato, by this time associate manager
of the orchestra, was sent on a mission to sound out Toscanini in Italy.
He returned with a flat No in three parts: one, the Met was no good
for concerts acoustically (a pronouncement that later champions of saving the House might ponder); two, the Philharmonic would have to cur-
tail its repertoire; three, the Philharmonic standards would be lowered.
The first was enough to quash the project, while if anyone cherished
in secret the hope that Toscanini might thus be brought back into the
opera fold, the Maestro's son Walter poured immediate cold water on
the dreamers with an unqualified negative. The plan was dropped and
the two noble examples of New York's cultural life went separate ways,
each with its own begging bowl. The ground was too shallow and too
tortured just then to receive any seed that might sprout into a future
cultural center.

Now Juilliard support was sought in earnest. Allen Wardwell, counsel for the Metropolitan Opera and Real Estate Company and later
president of the Association, had long been an official at the music
school. Over a cocktail with John Erskine at the Century Club, he confessed that the board was about ready to close the doors of the Metropolitan and no "moratorium" about it. "They want to leave their baby

on the Juilliard doorstep," Erskine quoted him as saying. He pressed Erskine to make good on a previous statement that a different management might succeed. Erskine replied in a long letter that outlined salient points, more stringent than before. To get three times the first grant, or $150,000 (plus $100,000 the next year) involved radical changes—in fact, the writer urged planning as though a new company were being started. With a reasonable expectation of taking in about a million, the budget ought to be set at that, putting the personnel on a Procrustean salary bed after fixed charges had been taken out and letting go those who didn't like it. Otherwise the gist covered these points:

The subscription must be hiked by at least 10 percent. The main season should run fourteen or fifteen weeks, with a supplementary season of six months for which air conditioning was a must, as well as a reduced stage size, lower prices, lower salaries, more young Americans, all operas in English (novelties to be tried out first at the Juilliard). This season would be managed by Edward Johnson. Skeleton companies might be sent out as a package to cooperate with small local companies (an idea that has fascinated producers ever since but never quite worked out successfully). Any profit should be split three ways between improvement of equipment, increase of salaries, and lowering of admission prices.

In control of this new plan was to be an Opera Management Committee, which eventually coalesced to include Bori, Bliss, Wardwell, and Johnson, with Erskine as chairman. Furthermore, Erskine, Ernest Hutcheson, and two other representatives of the Juilliard Foundation would be elected to the Metropolitan board. The choice of Herbert Witherspoon to succeed Gatti was practically mandatory, with Ziegler retained as business manager.

Witherspoon, the former bass, qualified for an administrative job by reason of a year's experience in Chicago, where he had instituted a policy "that above everything else opera should be first-class entertainment," according to Ronald Davis in *Opera in Chicago*. This was in 1931–32, when people needed cheering up.

Mrs. Witherspoon tells the story of her husband's appointment. One day in October 1934 Erskine brought a bulging briefcase to lunch with Witherspoon, while Mrs. Witherspoon lunched in another room with Jane (Mrs. Lawrence) Tibbett. Erskine came in to the women empty-handed, saying: "I've just dumped the Metropolitan Opera in Herbert's lap." She, said Mrs. Witherspoon, had "married Herbert [the same year] on the conditon he never accept this job."

Gatti arrived in November to a *fait accompli,* enough similar to the circumstances in which he had accepted office twenty-six years previously to make any manager think long thoughts. His time had already run out. Kahn's support had meant more to him than perhaps he acknowledged. And his marriage to the tiny ballerina, Rosina Galli, in 1930, after his 1929 divorce from Frances Alda, was said not to set well with the directors. Doors were closing behind him. Erskine states that his actual resignation was triggered by a demand for an auditing sheet by David Sarnoff, a recently elected board member, who had hired an "efficiency expert" to go over the opera's affairs. These were misty indeed. The report got about that there had been no audit since Gatti's first days. Exaggerated or not, it seemed a fact that, no matter how operations had been conducted, the board had taken little interest until the reserve fund dried up.

The new broom at least tried to reach into little pockets where inefficiency or worse had loosened discipline or conduct. Some time-honored if not necessarily honorable practices could be recognized if not always scotched. It was seen to be a conflict of interest that any employee of the Met should also act as a personal representative for artists. Perhaps it would be possible to obviate the necessity for an American artist to go to Europe and come back as a client of a European agent, in order that the latter might get his commission. There were mutterings about dispensing with the claque; there had been such mutterings before but they always died away as distant thunder with no lightning preceding. (The generalissimo of New York's hired applauders was still to be seen in the Fortieth Street corridor long after. American singers sometimes made the mistake—in those good old days—of believing that they could function without this artificial help.)

Reconstruction of the inner scaffolding of the company meant an overhauling of the chorus, which had been allowed to fray away into ineptitude, according to an observer from the housecleaning squad. Giulio Setti, chorus master since Gatti's early days, had once upon a time earned from Krehbiel praise for bringing the chorus to a "truly marvelous unity of effectiveness" in *Prince Igor.* That was 1916–17. Twenty years had taken their erosive toll.

Many a bitter pill lurked in this new dose of Juilliard vitamins, but Witherspoon possessed a firm yet persuasive manner and generally got his way. From October to May he toiled in the little office in the Metropolitan Studio Building while downstairs Gatti saw his last season through. On March 19 practically every singer in the roster joined in complimenting the departing boss in one of those customary galas, from which $15,000 accrued. Gatti promptly turned it over to the emergency fund. On March 31 another jamboree ended with the third of a series of Surprise Parties. The first unbuttoned benefit had provided icing on the cake commemorating Gatti's twenty-fifth anniversary on February 26, 1933. Beatrice Lillie devastated the 1935 audience by singing the first act of *Carmen* in several known and some unknown languages, while her colleagues tried to keep straight faces and clear French.

A beauteous trio consisting of Lily Pons, Helen Jepson, and Gladys Swarthout made history by a convincing rendition of "Minnie the Moocher," and Pons in tights hefted Melchior in an acrobatic stunt (assisted by a stout wire attached to the tenor's harness, to be sure). Gatti for once appeared stoically in his box, while on the stage his double (the bass Emanuel List, cunningly made up) appeared to take applause. The General Manager at last agreed to an interview with Joseph Alsop and supposedly "told all." At least he spelled out the Fremstad story from his point of view, repeating how "difficult" he had found her.

In the box with Gatti appeared his old friend-enemy, Toscanini, all now in amity. Gatti had made up, said Bruno Zirato, after a concert of the Maestro's. They were pictured together with Farrar at a luncheon to celebrate the reunion.

A miniature Post-Season in 1935 brought Flagstad to sing one Isolde and two Kundrys, after which Gatti could consider his term at an end. At the end of April, he boarded the *Rex* the night before sailing, "very downcast," his wife reported. The next day, two hundred friends stormed on board to give him a champagne farewell. There were tears and broken speeches by Rosa Ponselle and other favorites, who must have felt their future insecure. Back at the House, the third Opera Ball, a glamorous means of fund raising, made the auditorium ring with "A Pageant of the Old South" on May 2.

On May 10, Witherspoon finished a conference with Ziegler and Lewis preparatory to a board meeting, crossed Secretary Villa's office, and then paused, laughing, on the threshold to the corner office, long ago "interior-decorated" by Frances Alda for Gatti, and now his. Mrs. Witherspoon awaited him there. Suddenly he sank to the floor, dead. In the dreadful days that followed, Erskine quickly installed Johnson in the post that, it was said, Gatti had wished for him. The planning went on apace.

But now a new element entered the confused situation, one that would materially influence the destiny of Johnson and the opera itself. The Metropolitan Opera Guild was organized by Mrs. August Belmont and Lucrezia Bori, with Mrs. Witherspoon as director, and the seat of power shifted imperceptibly from the Union Club to the Colony.

16

ONE THIRD OF A REGIME

We are *not* a training school!

—Edward Johnson,
at the beginning of his fifteen-year tenure

Herbert Witherspoon was said to be signing contracts just before his death. This does not jibe with the statement of an official that Flagstad's was practically the only contract under seal at that moment. The confusion was understandable. Under strong Juilliard pressure, Witherspoon had arranged for a number of young Americans to join the roster; these were revealed one or two at a time as Johnson confirmed them. What shocked the public—or rather, the press, which made the facts public—was that the quartet of singers which soon was labeled the Big Four had not been reengaged. Johnson protested all along that "negotiations were in constant progress," but the stories continued to appear: Pons, Ponselle, Lehmann, and Tibbett had not signed. Holdouts, they were called. Tibbett's manager, Lawrence Evans, asserted that the popular baritone could not squeeze out enough time to pursue the real money-making phases of his career—radio, films, and concerts. Fees at the opera house remained notoriously low. In addition, the old agreement initiated under Grau provided commissions to the opera management for concerts sung by its artists. Tibbett complained that these commissions overbalanced fees—in other words, he was paying the opera more than they paid him. He proposed to take off even more weeks. As for Johnson, he was said to be "peeved" at the time consumed in these extracurricular affairs. Still, he could not control the time of his singers.

This bone of contention raised itself into the Great Divide over which the Metropolitan's fortune's slid. It became increasingly difficult to complete the jigsaw puzzle when important pieces insisted on absenting themselves at vital times in order to "make a living." And the cachet of the Met's name from here on would be increasingly misused as a

256

talisman for singers working as little as possible to justify it or singers possibly not deserving it.

As abuses always bring strong countermeasures, the solo artist caught in between the demands of his operatic and concert careers took up a vantage point outside both and attempted to solve his dilemma by organizing a union. The single most important idea in the musical world at the time was said to have been conceived on a golf course in New Jersey, between shots by Lawrence Tibbett, Gladys Swarthout, and her husband Frank Chapman. Later Tibbett met with Jascha Heifetz, the reigning monarch of the concert realm, and the American Guild of Musical Artists (AGMA) was born. Current Metropolitan members present at the first meeting on March 11, 1936, included Queena Mario, Swarthout, Tibbett, Richard Bonelli, Charles Hackett, Frederick Jagel, and Mario Chamlee; former star Alma Gluck, future member James Melton, and several instrumentalists completed the nucleus. The infant union soon joined Associated Actors and Artistes of America, known as the Four A's, which was affiliated with the American Federation of Labor. By its charter in 1937, AGMA got jurisdiction over concert, recital, oratorio, and grand opera, merging with the Grand Opera Artists Association, which had held the charter for the operatic field. The next spring saw their absorption of the Grand Opera Choral Alliance. On July 27, AGMA signed its first agreement with the Metropolitan. Concert agreements and clarification of jurisdiction with Actors' Equity and Chorus Equity followed.

An eighteen-month struggle, bitter in implication and fact, eventually established the lines between AGMA and the powerful American Federation of Musicians. Each agreed not to object to their members' enrollment with the other, but AGMA remained the sole collective bargaining agency for all solo concert artists, relinquishing jurisdiction over accompanists, conductors, composers, arrangers, instrumental groups, and orchestras, but reserving independence for piano accompanists on tour with solo artists. Thus matters stood in 1941. AGMA's later gains paralleled the emergency situations which arose one after the other.

At the beginning, Johnson laboriously compiled his roster, worrying simultaneously about young Americans and the Big Four. It could not have been the threat of Josephine Antoine that brought Pons back into the fold, as one newspaper claimed. Lily was too sure of herself for that kind of jealousy. Antoine, a pert and pretty blonde from Denver, one of the first Juilliard graduates to put "Metropolitan" to her name, sang Pons's roles, to be sure, but not when Pons wanted them, although Antoine remained fifteen years in competition with old and new coloratura contenders.

The Big Four were soon reinstated, but with Lehmann on a guest basis on Ponselle on the strength—or, as it turned out, weakness—of one role, her erratic Carmen. Lehmann, vexed at Flagstad's accession to a role she considered her own property (Frida Leider had previously usurped her in Chicago as well), refused to sing Leonore in *Fidelio*. But she allowed her name to remain on the roster in an unbroken line for eight years.

As Johnson signed more and more Americans and prepared to scout Europe for additional material, he was heard to utter a rebuttal to Leonard Liebling in the *American,* who charged that there were "some headshakings at the [Juilliard] running things."

"We are not a training school!" snapped the new General Manager. One observer questioned: "Did he have his fingers crossed behind his back?" Perhaps it only seemed that the new native blood carried Juilliard corpuscles exclusively.

The most durable and virile ran in the veins of Charles Kullman, Yale graduate, German trained, who began a career both long and distinguished, although promise seemed greater than delivery in his first season's Faust, Alfredo, Duke of Mantua, and Don José. Of longer experience after her departure from academe was Dusolina Giannini, who in fact never gained in her native land the *réclame* bestowed warmly in Germany, especially for Carmen. For six seasons she persisted, but the diminishing returns pained her genuine admirers, who remained loyal even after she retired. Julius Huehn, a giant who grew from little bassbaritone roles to big ones, was deflected for a time by the war. Susanne Fisher was a Butterfly, Marguerite, Nedda, Manon, and Micaela of new stamp, who had in her past datebook three seasons in Berlin and two in Paris.

Making debuts in the regular season, and therefore presumably ready to carry on at a top—or at least medium—level were Hilda Burke, whose husband Désiré Defrère was again placed on the roster as a baritone after an earlier season (1914–15) and would go on at indefatigable length as stage director and stage manager; Helen Olheim, a pretty mezzo-soprano who had been trained at the Eastman School in Rochester, for a change; and Joseph Bentonelli, a tenor who Italianized his last name (from Benton) but not his first (to Giuseppe). Thelma Votipka, the beloved "Tippy," came into Johnson's first opening night as Flora in *La Traviata* and remained to assume the crown as Queen of the Comprimarias, a worthy successor to the Mathilde (always called "the little") Bauermeister, indispensable until 1906 and never really replaced until Tippy's advent.

A dozen or so additional natives were saved for the Spring Season, out of which all but the unlucky Emily Hardy carried over to the next winter. Several even became fixtures: Norman Cordon, a hearty bass from North Carolina; Anna Kaskas, a vivid blonde Lithuanian mezzo; George Rasely, an admirable light tenor who stuttered superbly in *Bartered Bride*; John Gurney, a lanky bass; Natalie Bodanskaya, who soon shortened her name to Bodanya; Lucielle Browning, who seldom saw *her* name spelled correctly; Maxine Stellman and Wilfred Engelman. Sydney Rayner figured the next season in an important lady's debut when he turned up as Des Grieux instead of the ailing Richard Crooks, with whom the enchanting Bidu Sayao had rehearsed. Rosa Tentoni made an impression as Santuzza and Aida, but lasted only two seasons. Her husband Joseph Royer also spent two years in the House.

Some heavy European weight fell into the scales to try to even up with the Americans. Physically the gain was on the men's side, with the huge Arthur Carron, an English protégé of Florence Easton, whose great success as Canio inspired the management to the rather unsuccessful attempt to mold him into a *Heldentenor*. René Maison, a six-foot Belgian, began a long and admired career with Walther, José, and Lohengrin just to show his bilingual command, and went on confidently to French or German as the case might be in many interesting roles—Samson, Des Grieux, Julien, Erik (*Flying Dutchman*), and Herod. A good-sized baritone, Carlo Morelli, came from Chile and remained a few seasons.

Three widely different women generated excitement in 1935. Marjorie Lawrence, slim, blonde, vivacious Australian, launched the procession of debutantes with her Brünnhilde in *Walküre* on the second night, and won from the *Times* the right to a substantial place in the House. Her experience at the Paris Opéra told in such roles as Rachel in *La Juive,* while her Wagnerian Valkyrie had youth, strength, and "a commandingly dramatic temperament" in its favor. She electrified the audience (and no doubt the stagehands as well) by leaping on the back of the beast Grane to ride triumphantly offstage from *Götterdämmerung*'s shambles, not actually mounting Siegfried's pyre but giving the impression that she could if she would. When this vigorous and beautiful woman was stricken with polio in 1941 the world mourned, then rejoiced at the courage and willpower that restored Lawrence to health and even some opera performances, though she had to be wheeled on and off and was forced to remain seated on stage.

Gertrud Pålson-Wettergren brought from Sweden two attributes not commonly ascribed to the North: a flaming temperament that could turn into temper and a dark beauty that flouted accepted ideas about blonde Scandinavians. Called in to a *Carmen* that Ponselle had to relinquish, Wettergren sang her role in Swedish and further upset colleagues and audience by casting a shoe into the orchestra pit while attempting to kick a soldier. By next season she had been persuaded to learn the part in French (as well as Dalila). Her best-sung role remained Amneris, however. She might have stayed past 1938 had she not bitten the General Manager's lip in an excess of New Year's gaiety during one of the blithe parties that annually celebrated the Lawrence Tibbetts' wedding anniversary.

Bruna Castagna arrived with a great deal of experience, but in an opera company from the other side of the tracks—the Hippodrome at Forty-fourth and Sixth Avenue. The management did not give her a chance to compete in *Carmen* until the Spring Season, but she later shared the Gypsy with Wettergren and finally had it all to herself briefly before dividing with Swarthout and eventually yielding to Lily Djanel and Irra Petina, all of whom she could outsing if not outact. Her Amneris often kindled fire, even in her last year, 1945.

Not content with these additions, Johnson summoned five favorites to return for at least one season: Grace Moore, Florence Easton, Edith Mason, Mario Chamlee, and John Charles Thomas. In addition to Flagstad, Pons, Ponselle, and Lehmann, he managed contracts with eight familiar sopranos: Bori, Fleischer, Jepson, Kappel, Manski, Mario, Rethberg, and Eidé Norena (a personable Norwegian who had been in Chicago). Also reengaged were the mezzos Bampton, Bourskaya, Branzell, Doe, Flexer, Halstead, Leonard, Meisle, and Swarthout. Nine tenors signed again: Althouse, Clemens, Crooks, Hackett, Jagel, Martinelli, Melchior, Tokatyan, and Nino Martini (who had brought a light voice and an ingratiating personality in 1933, and whose success in films and radio enhanced his popularity). In addition to Tibbett, the males with darker voices included the well-liked Bonelli, D'Angelo, Hofmann, Lazzari, List, Pinza, Schorr, and Rothier. When the 1935-36 comprimario and bit singers were added, the stunning total of fifty-four men and fifty-one women was reached—the largest roster in Metropolitan history to date. Important names missing were Ljungberg, Morgana, Müller, Olszewska, De Luca, Schipa, and Schützendorf.

What could a manager be expected to do with these 105 singers in nineteen weeks (including the three in spring) and spread over thirty-one operas—eighteen fewer than Gatti's list at flood tide? Exactly what Johnson did: shift casts rapidly and often disconcertingly. There were a few exceptions in this season of musical chairs. Part of the German repertoire stayed fairly stable, with, for example, Flagstad as the only Isolde and Leonore (*Fidelio*), Melchior the only Tannhäuser, Maison the only Walther, and Clemens the only David. A few other roles also were the exclusive property of Manski and Schorr, while Fleischer and Mario kept Hänsel and Gretel to themselves.

The French-Italian wing also revealed a few consistencies, with Pinza the sole Méphistophélès and Lothario, Bonelli the only Valentin, Lescaut, and Di Luna, Pons keeping Lakmé, Rethberg the *Trovatore* Leonora, and Bori sharing Mignon and *Rondine*'s heroine with no one. Five *Gianni Schicchis* changed the title role from Tibbett to Huehn. But the oddest bit of steadfastness occurred in the role usually tossed from lyric soprano to soubrette and back again: Musetta. The young American Helen Gleason (in her last of four seasons) clung to the Parisian coquette through six *Bohèmes*, while four Mimis and four Rodolfos revolved around her. Morelli sang all the Marcellos.

Traffic in and out of star dressing rooms occasionally became embarrassing, echoing a fracas of Jeritza's latter years. The stars then sent their maids ahead to put up personal decor. Jules Judels, glorified callboy since 1891–92 and taleteller of first magnitude, vouched for the color schemes: Jeritza's gold, Bori's blue, Leonora Corona's orchid. The temptation to stay on and entertain one's friends could be indulged at night, but on matinee days, comings and goings collided. Bori, finding Jeritza still ensconced in her own chintzes one Saturday, took herself and *her* decor to the mezzo's room at right angles in the corridor and remained there ever after. She would have agreed with the actress whom Francis Robinson quoted as saying: "Where I am is center stage." Fortunately, Bori's operas seldom called for a star mezzo.

Variety of impersonations seemed indeed to be the *sine qua non*. A persistent operagoer to both winter and spring seasons could have compared six Neddas, five Don Josés, three Carmens, four Micaelas, an equal number of Escamillos and Dukes, three Rigolettos, four Gildas and Maddelenas, and three Sparafuciles. Only one Wagner role boasted four protagonists: the undecided Venus, portrayed twice by Halstead and once each by Wettergren, Kappel, and Branzell.

The Spring Season brought the closest approximation of novelty that Johnson offered, with no casting shifts: *Bartered Bride* and *Orfeo*. Both had been heard in the House, but not previously in English. Both provided the best showcases for the new ballet unit with George Balanchine at its head. Effective folk ballets were tacked on Smetana's charming work after the first performance, while *Orfeo*'s characters, sung by Anna Kaskas, Jeanne Pengelly, and Maxine Stellman, were mimed by Lew Christensen, William Dollar, and Daphne Vane in a production that seemed not so much choreographed as overwrought. Balanchine remained for three seasons, then went the way of all dancing feet up until then— out. *The Bartered Bride* endured for a while in its colloquial English ("I've got a honey with lots of money" causing some heartburning among purists), but *Orfeo* suffered the customary spotty fate of the Gluck operas.

When the audits had cleared and Johnson could draw a breath, it was a breath of relief. He had survived without overbalancing the Juilliard budget requirements, while mounting new productions of *La Traviata* and *Die Walküre* to silence at least partially the critics of the senile scenery. He lost twenty-three from the roster, no important men but a half dozen women who would be missed, chief among them Lucrezia Bori. Easton's Brünnhilde on February 29 enabled her to shout farewell with a hearty *"Ho-Jo-To-Ho!"* Moore absented herself for a season; Kappel and Mason forever. The versatile Fleischer would be hard to replace.

Johnson hired thirteen new men and the same number of women, bringing the total to 112, another record-breaker. To take on some of the waning Ponselle's previous duties came Gina Cigna from Italy; for her, *Gioconda* and *Norma* scenery was once more stacked on Seventh Avenue. A contralto of true Wagnerian opulence hailed from Sweden in the person of Kerstin Thorborg, who made her debut beside her sister Scandinavian when Flagstad was honored on opening night with *Walküre*. Thorborg shared with Branzell the weighty roles and took the part of Mary when *Der Fliegende Holländer* brought Flagstad's first Senta.

Bidu Sayao, although her voice seemed tiny at first, soon demonstrated that focus beats force, and impressed her gentle and subtle characterizations of Manon, Mimi, and Violetta on a public ever increasing in affection for this graceful Brazilian. A competent Frenchwoman, Vina Bovy, played all four roles in *Contes d'Hoffmann* (Olympia, Giulietta, Antonia, and Stella) for the first time in America, to match Tibbett's assumption of the four baritone roles, the latter a first time at the Met, although Maurice Renaud had accomplished it for Hammerstein and Chicago (where it was fairly common practice) and Vanni Marcoux for Boston. De Luca had sung three of the roles for a couple of seasons in the twenties, but they were divided up again. Bovy scored a better success than several of the sopranos who took one part or another, although Jepson's Giulietta showed the progress made by this tall blonde American.

Other excitement on the distaff side had to wait for the Spring Season, when the Wagner potential was recognized in the voice of St. Louis–born Helen Traubel, although Damrosch's *Man Without a Country* (in its world premiere) could have been sheared away from around her without much loss.

Johnson counted a great deal on four baritones: John Brownlee, who lived up to expectations; Donald Dickson, a young American who preferred radio after two seasons; Thomas L. Thomas, the rich-voiced Welshman (first winner of the Auditions of the Air, who didn't show off well between opera walls); and Robert Weede, who never had a sustained chance. The high tenor, Karl Laufkötter, would prove useful as David and Mime.

The General Manager felt justified in planning a second supplementary season, but engaged an executive to replace him. Lee Pattison was a pianist whose chief fame had come with Guy Maier as a two-piano team. At this juncture he was serving as the head of the New York City

Works Progress Administration. This and his term at the summer school at Juilliard were his only qualifications for an opera post. His usefulness to the Met was never entirely proved.

Mugginess of the auditorium as Spring rolled around provided enough alibi for dropping the pendant season, at least for a few years. The second venture had brought little of interest beyond the world premiere of Damrosch's opera and a revival of Rabaud's *Mârouf*. Richard Hageman's *Caponsacchi* had been designed for Spring but found a place in the regular lists and soured some of the favor with which the new management was beginning to be regarded. The advent of the Russian-Canadian Jennie Tourel as Mignon and Carmen presaged dimly what the mezzo's stature as an artist—chiefly in concerts—was to become. Ruby Mercer, who would later win admiration as a radio interviewer of opera personalities, repeated her Marguerite and Nedda of the previous Spring. Marguerite Daum, who appeared briefly as the inevitable Musetta, was not around the following year to portray the flighty heroine of Gian-Carlo Menotti's *Amelia Goes to the Ball*, whom she had embodied in its premieres in Philadelphia and New York. Amelia was taken over at the Met by the insouciant Savoyard, Muriel Dickson, whose bright presence and immaculate diction did wonders for the credibility of her other English roles, Marie in *Bartered Bride* and Caroline in Cimarosa's *Secret Marriage*. When these three operas were dropped almost immediately, Dickson was left high and dry except for an occasional Musetta (of course!) but still on the roster. Agnes Davis' brief brush with Elsa, and Myron Taylor's with Nolan in Damrosch's opera, led to a life of concerts and eventual teaching. The two met again at the University of Indiana.

Instead of his frittering process, Johnson might have taken the example of the Philadelphia Orchestra in 1934-35 and lost money in grand fashion by giving virtually perfect grand opera. A third-of-a-million deficit wiped out for many years any idea that this distinguished body of instrumentalists would again descend to the pit, but they had the satisfaction of public acclaim for *Falstaff, Iphigenia in Aulis, Die Meistersinger, Carmen, Rosenkavalier, Tristan und Isolde, Pelléas et Mélisande, Boris,* Stravinsky's *Mavra* with *Hänsel und Gretel, Le Nozze di Figaro,* and Shostakovich's sensational *Lady Macbeth from Mzensk,* conducted by Fritz Reiner or Alexander Smallens, designed by Norman Bel Geddes and others and directed in several cases by Herbert Graf. Philadelphia did not miss the Met at all—this was the first season it had been absent in forty years. But the Met missed the significance and quality of the Philadelphia experiment. It was not quite enough to hire Herbert Graf out of the wreckage, because his talent soon became bogged down in the "system." This system, which Johnson was later to refer to airily as "discipline" and still later to recall as "tradition," was really no system at all. Each season seemed to shape up by an ever-constricting formula. A genuine desire to delve into the richer and less frequented troves of the repertoire was often invalidated by inappropriate casting. No decidely firm ground plan for advancement shaped up. The fallibility of the slipshod structure was not recognized for a few seasons, but signposts cropped up. Although the Spring Seasons were abandoned, singers of the caliber engaged for what Mrs. Belmont significantly called the Junior Company came in anyway, sometimes through the Auditions, which chased aspirants merrily along until 1946 under the sponsorship of the Sherwin-Williams Paint Company. Occasionally it seemed that newcomers got in by default. As if to prove his earlier contention that the venerable Met had not set up classrooms, they often bypassed proper instruction and pitched these untried young ones directly into roles they were not by any stretch of the imagination ready for. What resulted was a kind of creeping blight that ate away at the record, which, to be sure, showed occasional splendor as well.

If the lesser lights could have been allowed to work their way up more slowly in a genuine training school such as Conried's, the Auditions would have fully justified the consideration paid them, for they cast up such lasting effulgences as Leonard Warren, Eleanor Steber, Margaret Harshaw, Regina Resnik, and Robert Merrill. Patrice Munsel, the second "baby of the Met" (although Nannette Guilford had been forgotten), was also Audition-spawned. Hugh Thompson came off the airways to be useful, first as a baritone, then as a stage director.

Of these, Warren developed most slowly, but with a glorious voice in his favor, so that his first crudities of acting were overlooked. After a Sunday night concert and his stage debut as Paolo Albani in *Boccanegra* on January 13, 1939, he was allowed to work on Ford, the character that had sent Tibbett up rocketlike, but not to play it against Tibbett's Falstaff. The latter had no intention of allowing history to repeat itself. Warren himself ascended to the Fat Knight, as well as other Tibbett roles, including Boccanegra. Not exactly an intellect, Warren contained in his big body all the sinews of prima donna-ism and exerted them frequently in treatment of colleagues and in trying to get his own way against conductors and stage directors. His tragic death on stage in 1960 in the midst of a performance of *Forza del Destino* brought to historians the memory of the collapse of Castelmary sixty-three years before. Warren was stricken at the zenith of a notable career. Francis Robinson, press chief, was working in his tiny office when the public address loudspeaker that carried the opera to all corners of the administration suddenly became still. Robinson rushed into the auditorium, then backstage. "It was as if a great tree had been felled," he said.

Among those who aroused attention during the Auditions competition but received a contract separately was the puissant Risë Stevens, glitteringly handsome in "trouser roles," especially the snowy-clad silver-aureoled Octavian, in which she made her debut with the company in Philadelphia on November 22, 1938. After her first appearance in the House as Mignon, she became the idol of constant visitors. Her Carmen topped a long series of individually treated roles. An appealing part in a film with Bing Crosby piled up national fandom for this Juilliard graduate, who had shown the sense to work in Europe before taking the route from Claremont Avenue and 122d Street to Broadway and Thirty-ninth. During this useful hiatus, she acquired an attractive Hungarian actor for a husband; Walter Surovy has since filled the role of shrewd business guide to his wife. Stevens is the second Metropolitan feminine star to manage an opera company: Flagstad stood at the head of the Oslo house for several years, while this American of Norwegian ancestry joined her own establishment as co-manager of the National Company later organized.

Like threads of gold through the motley tapestry ran the performances of half a dozen Europeans during these few years before World War II again scattered the jigsaw pieces. Zinka Milanov and Jussi Björling seemed heaven sent. Those two ravishing voices, each perfect in its way (although Milanov displayed variables, nothing could match her tone floated on seemingly endless breath when she was "in voice"), soon built up loyal followings for whom they could do no wrong. It is true that they seldom gave cause for complaint, although to the end of his days Alec Templeton, the pianist who possessed the keenest ear of his time, insisted that "Jussi sings sharp." Whatever you might think of this, it was better than singing flat. Björling once told Max Rudolf that when he was singing really well, his voice did not seem to be in his body at all, but to float in the air about a foot in front of him. Despite a lovable, boyish personality, Jussi's personal problems, which a devoted wife, a deeply concerned management, the opera administrations of New York and Stockholm, and a fanatic public could not assuage, rendered him undependable. Stockholm put the tenor on a guest basis as early as 1937 and philosophically took him when they could get him. Absent from the Met during the war years, he returned to unabated adulation in 1945 and went on to sing in Mr. Bing's opening-night *Don Carlo,* influenced temporarily at least to unbend a trifle and very nearly act a role as well as sing it under the clever direction of the Shakespearean Margaret Webster. His fans never quite decided which they preferred: his Verdi, his Puccini, or the French roles in which he excelled. His death after a heart attack in 1960 impoverished the music world.

Milanov came from Zagreb after study with her legendary countrywoman, Milka Ternina, by way of Vienna and Salzburg, where she was chosen for the Verdi Requiem by Toscanini. (The Maestro later insisted on this "dramatic" voice for Gilda in a huge benefit in Madison Square Garden, a feat she accomplished without a tremor.) She too was absent for a war year and three later seasons. Max Rudolf narrates that her manager Jack Adams came to Bing in his "observation" year with the news that Milanov was now better than ever, and took Bing and Rudolf to Hartford to hear her in *Forza* to prove it. Grown into a full-fledged prima donna, she returned triumphantly as Santuzza and went on to fix her own retirement date in 1966.

Of a different stripe but comparable vitality was the soprano who sparked the revival of Strauss's *Elektra* in 1937. No other singer, said Olin Downes, could bring to the title part the "intensity, majesty and dramatic power" of Rosa Pauly, or a voice "so magnificently adequate to the music." Having found the perfect Elektra, the management abandoned the opera after two seasons and left this dark Hungarian with nothing but Venus and Ortrud, decidedly not her dishes. She never got to sing her other famous Strauss role, Salome, as Marjorie Lawrence commanded it in the two seasons *Elektra* was being given. Johnson never thought of reviving *Die Aegyptische Helena* for her, or giving *Wozzeck.*

Her Chrysothemis was the Viennese-born Irene Jessner, who had made her debut as Hänsel the previous year. Jessner displayed a versatility not altogether believable—or perhaps wise?—during three years in which she added Desdemona, Elisabeth, Elvira, Eva, Gutrune, Euridice, Ortlinde, Elsa, Tosca, the First Flower Maiden, Sieglinde, Marschallin, and Amelia in *Boccanegra*—a mixed bag indeed. Until 1952 she continued to switch on one current after another to generally creditable, if not world-shaking, effect.

Herbert Janssen's truly beautiful baritone voice was added in 1938, but his value lessened as he became increasingly a prey to illness. Following him around lugubriously through the corridors with nurselike watchfulness, his wife added no joy to his aura. He also departed in 1952.

Beniamino Gigli's return in 1938 provided uncommon interest. Still the practiced singer, the tenor first gave out ravishing sounds in several roles, reaped publicity and horny-handed applause to his heart's delight, then returned to Italy with ill tidings of the House that had sheltered him. Somewhat the reverse procedure was followed by Grete Stückgold, who had breathed fire when she was not reengaged in 1935, branding the Met as a "dying social tradition," but now helped it come alive again with a Marschallin and an Elisabeth.

Opera began to suffer almost immediately from the conflict in Europe that began on September 1, 1939. Not only was "luxury money" scarcer, but several doors were slammed on European talent. A good many singers were already in the United States, including two from whom Johnson expected—and received—great performances: the elegant and beautiful Jarmila Novotna, a Czech baroness, and the virile and musical Alexander Kipnis, a Russian bass. Another of fine caliber to arrive in time for a February debut was Licia Albanese. George Cathelet slipped through the ban to sing Pelléas; Walter Olitzki, a good Beckmesser, also got here, as did Hilde Reggiani, another coloratura discovery of Pons's mentors, Gay and Zenatello.

A new French tenor from above the border came out of the Auditions. Raoul Jobin made the first of many appearances in 1939, lit no soaring fires, but stayed, with a few intermissions, as long as Johnson.

Europeans who failed to show up were several who had been given only a year to prove themselves: Maria Caniglia, Marisa Morel, Lina Amaro, Mafalda Favero, Galliano Masini, Hans Hermann Nissen, Herbert Alsen, and Erich Witte. Among the Americans hired to fill the gaps, lasting quality appeared in the baritone Mack Harrell, an Auditions winner. He was one of those seemingly all-too-typical Americans whose beauty of voice was not accompanied by a theatrical temperament. He gradually learned his trade and gave some pleasurable performances, but turned increasingly to concert work.

The crazy-quilt season (patches of silk and velvet scattered among cotton and burlap) brought moments of pure delight, among them the return performances of Giuseppe de Luca. The first five notes of his Germont aria "made the pulses beat because of the beauty and art of the song," wrote Olin Downes. The baritone was fifty-four, a living example of the highest art as he followed with Marcello, Rigoletto, and a farewell Figaro in *Barbiere*.

The tenor yarn that belongs to this period attaches not to Björling, to the inimitable Alessio di Paolis, who began his series of imperishable portraits in 1938, nor to Carl Hartmann, the *Heldentenor*, whose Tristans, Siegfrieds, and Tannhäusers brought less in realization than expectation. The tenor of tenors just then was the handsome Pole Jan Kiepura. He once startled a press gathering by opening his arms wide and demanding: "How do you want me?" When it eventuated that he meant which roles should be recommended for him (without consulting Johnson), and someone foolishly murmured, "Perhaps *Pelléas et Mélisande*," he asked in all seriousness: "Is there a good tenor part?"

He made his debut in *Bohème* with Sayao and a new baritone, Carlo Tagliabue. Another performance found him opposite Grace Moore. Upstaging her outrageously, he continued with each melting phrase to slide the chair in which she would have to sit farther and farther from center. You didn't treat Grace that way more than once. The next time the American Mimi advanced, fainting, to the table, and Rodolfo solicitously tried to place her off-center, the chair didn't budge. Grace was liked backstage. The carpenter had obligingly nailed the chair to the floor. Such vengeance is doubly sweet scored on a tenor.

17

JOHNSON'S NEW DEMOCRACY

The ladies: Bless 'em! Whose bright eyes rain influence.

—JOHN MILTON

Johnson plunged into the sea of troubles that threatened to inundate the Metropolitan Opera buoyed up by what was probably the first women's opera auxiliary in the world. America had become familiar with the symphony orchestra committee of women workers, dozens of them even now cropping up in the wake of the Works Progress Administration units that were busy keeping orchestras alive all over the country. This depression-spawned government support with its "made work" hardly entered into the Metropolitan Opera's consciousness. Any serious thought of federal subsidy of opera waited a long time in America, all the while it was settled fact in Europe. For this generation at least, the Met preferred to keep its subsidy under the heading of "private enterprise."

The combination of feminine forces focused on the opera became irresistible. Mrs. August Belmont, the appealing Eleanor Robson, whom August Belmont took off the stage in 1910 for a life of yachting, horses, and all the panoply of Society at its prewar apogee, came back into the limelight as a selfless organizer of benefits and a worker for the Red Cross. On a governing body after the war, Cornelius N. Bliss was her admiring colleague. Her ability to raise Red Cross funds precipitated Eleanor Belmont into a Metropolitan Opera board meeting in May 1933, which was "almost as difficult as an opening night in the theatre," she wrote in her autobiography *The Fabric of Memory*. "Mixed company on boards was far from a familiar sight at that time, and when I slipped into a chair, several of the directors looked solemnly uncomfortable."

Although she did not speak up immediately, "she was at her best talking," recalled John Erskine. "Whatever she said was so much music."

As a member of the executive committee, she proposed in 1935 a plan for a membership organization, thinking of "closer association with glamorous artists," attendance at rehearsals, and a channel through which tickets might be purchased. "Putting together piece by piece a mosaic of various ingredients," she was authorized to go ahead.

"Democratization of the opera had begun!" she underlined in her autobiography.

Although still somewhat skeptical, the board advanced $50,000. Mrs. Belmont decided to invest in a national group of honorary sponsors before braving the public eye. She soon listed 200, headed by President Franklin D. Roosevelt, governors of nine states, and Mayor Fiorello LaGuardia of New York. The first of many "At Homes" launched the campaign, which resulted in 2,000 members the first year and the gift of a drastically needed cyclorama. Eager to tell its story even more widely, the Metropolitan Opera Guild launched a *Bulletin* in May 1936, which rapidly turned into the highly informative and rapidly expanding *Opera News,* with Mrs. John DeWitt Peltz as its first editor.

Mrs. Herbert Witherspoon, still happy to be associated with the Met even after her husband's tragic death, was immediately drawn into active participation as the Guild's director. It gave her deep satisfaction to carry out her husband's ideas of reaching far into other communities for broader support and to substitute subscribers for handouts.

"The Met had for so many years been a citadel for the few," she said. "Now we could begin to look on it as a national institution."

Lucrezia Bori, third of the Guild's three graces and long the darling of the Met itself, waited until then to retire from performing life, thus fulfilling a desire that had possessed her since 1933. She sang her last in the House on March 29, 1936, "surrounded by her friends in the company and with a warm air of sentiment and affection pervading the ceremonies," reported W. J. Henderson. Her own contributions were scenes from *La Traviata* and *Manon*. Mimi was her final role on the stage, sung before an adoring Baltimore audience on April 2.

Bori, who always managed effortlessly to appear chic offstage in any given era, no matter how extreme the styles, brought not only a dazzling personality to the board, but the experience of a performer as well as a clear appreciation of reality. She knew well what it was to take responsibility, having supported a doting—and typically restrictive—family for many years. As a great Spanish lady (many tired jokes followed the revelation that her family name had been Borja), she was subjected to strict chaperonage, at first by father, later by brother. Her disposition seemed not at all soured by this. She cast a natural radiance over the opera's auxiliary functions for the rest of her life, still the *"toute jeune fille"* Gabriel Fauré had called her in Paris in 1910, still beloved by everyone except possibly Frances Alda, that notorious hater of sopranos (except perhaps Mary Garden and Flagstad). Alda wrote in her autobiography just about the time of Bori's retirement that her Mélisande, in rendering the phrase, *"Il fait froid ici,"* sounded "like a schoolgirl who steps out of bed without her slippers." Furthermore, Alda had seemed to get the greatest pleasure out of calling Bori "Mother" when she played Nannetta to Bori's Mistress Ford in *Falstaff.*

After the first year, the Guild grew by geometric progression. Numberless new productions have borne its "courtesy" mark (it was not the Guild's fault that the $165,000 they raised for new Ring sets by Lee Simonson proved inappropriate and too clumsy to tour comfortably); thousands of school children make annual pilgrimages to the opera by virtue of low-priced tickets on which the Guild absorbs the difference; the Guild's own "Opera News on the Air" takes over a broadcast intermission regularly for interviews and instruction made palatable by men and women of distinction.

As the opera's perplexities increased, the Guild reached out to help in the two ways that counted most—money and subscribers. At the end of a decade, the performing company was buttressed round with auxiliary comforts on which it had grown to depend heavily. From Guild membership which had increased twelvefold to 24,000 (with several classes of dues up to $100), a substantial check passed to the management each year, amounting to $30,000 at its tenth anniversary. Its contributions to new productions climbed to more than $175,000. Mrs. Belmont cunningly pointed out to the membership that each one could take pride in individual contributions—perhaps to one bit of fantasy in Richard Rychtarik's setting for *Magic Flute,* the eerie staircase in *Lucia* (also by Rychtarik), or the thrilling assemblage of the populace in *Meistersinger* (the second-scene, third-act set had been borrowed from Chicago). The Guild had bought nearly $600,000 worth of tickets for resale. It had paid for thirty-two student matinees witnessed by 100,000 youngsters. Scholarships for additional training of young singers had come partly from the sale of swatches from the old curtain, replaced in 1940 after thirty-five years.

In addition to the cyclorama, the stage had been improved by new tormentor borders for the proscenium and the buffet lounge sported a new crystal chandelier. *Opera News* had expanded and was flourishing. Guild branches had been set up in several other cities. Things were on the march indeed, with the ladies in the van. They never asked for anything in return, John Erskine admitted, but their influence became pervasive. After all, they showed a great deal more imagination—and just plain gumption—in these touchy times. The men—or at least some of them—remained timid or uncommitted. Paul D. Cravath, the lawyer who had, as chairman of the board, appointed Mrs. Belmont to the executive committee, always seemed more at home in his efforts to improve the condition of the Negroes than in the labyrinthine affairs of the opera, where, one of his follow board members suggested, he was apt to hedge quite a while before taking action, then to act unilaterally. One of his preoccupations at the time was building an artificial brook on his estate in Long Island at the cost of $75,000. His best gift to the opera was his daughter, Mrs. William Francis Gibbs, who with her naval architect husband persuaded Cravath to learn at least a little something about music by attending the Layman's Music Courses laid on brilliantly by Olga Samaroff Stokowski for just such high-echelon amateurs as Cravath, and attached for quite some time to the Guild's own program. Mrs. Gibbs has been a faithful opera lover from the first.

As she first cast about for ideas, Mrs. Belmont consulted Lauder Greenway, a Yale graduate who had taught English at his Alma Mater, then become successively assistant secretary and secretary to the Metropolitan Museum of Art. He suggested a collection of memorabilia. The result of suggesting anything to Mrs. Belmont is rather like volunteering in the army. You get the job. Greenway, who had been devoted to opera all his life, soon found himself inextricably bound to the Met, first as a member, then a vice-president, and in 1948 president of the Guild, succeeding Mrs. Belmont, who assumed the title of founder and president emeritus with a citation from Archibald MacLeish which called her "Artist in art and artist in life." Bori was made honorary chairman.

Greenway was elected to the Metropolitan Association while still on Navy duty in the Pacific in World War II, and became successively President and Chairman of the Board, relinquishing his Guild presidency to Langdon van Norden in 1954–55. He then entered on a wider sphere of influence, although perhaps less intimate. "I really knew more details about operations in the Guild," he said. "After all, the directors employed a manager to deal with singers. And if I wanted to applaud, I'd sit somewhere else than in the directors' box, for George Sloan, chairman of the executive committee, thought applause from that particular spot might be prejudicial."

Greenway's generosity, warmth, taste, and humor bestow a tone of both elegance and practicality on the opera's functions. He may be said to be typical of the new board members who work seriously and strenuously for the Met, reminiscent of Otto Kahn but without his omnipotence.

Another who presided as an *éminence grise* over Mrs. Belmont's early efforts was the "Kentucky Colonel," the eccentric and wise Joseph M. Hartfield, who took as his premise the invulnerability of the Met. "It must never close," he reiterated. Senior partner in White and Case, the law firm of Lowell Wadmond (who also belongs to the breed of working directors and has served as president), Hartfield attended meetings religiously, removing his broad-brimmed hat and sitting with his feet tucked under him because they could not reach the floor (he was but four feet tall). A bachelor, he never used anyone's first name and was the soul of courtesy, modesty, and good judgment. Mrs. Belmont had known him on the Red Cross War Council.

It is hard to discipline people who have become used to calling you "Eddie." Catapulted into his new position as General Manager of the Metropolitan Opera, Edward Johnson was not allowed to forget altogether that he had been "one of us," a colleague of those he now had to dismiss or reengage, and, if retained, choose repertoire for, call on the carpet for insubordination and, most important, grant or refuse a raise in salary or fee. Johnson was not a no-sayer by nature. He liked everyone—or almost everyone—and would promise anything or everything, one of his former associates recalled with bitter sweetness, leaving someone else to adjust or placate. "You could hardly get a definite Yes or Nay out of Eddie. He was charming, charming at all costs—too damned charming!"

The two areas in which Johnson shone—knowledge of singers and choice of conductors—partly made up for his weakness in managerial competence, but did not in the end serve as determining factors. Johnson knew singers. As a rule, he selected well; if left to his own artistic conscience, he might have discriminated more carefully between the genuine but unformed new talent and the predestined duds. But expedients were thrust upon him, originally by the Juilliard directive, then by the war, both committing him to a policy of Americans first. The union prescription finally solidified this position, whether for weal or woe cannot even yet be determined.

Once engaged, the newcomer tended to blossom under the General Manager's consideration. The wise word delivered as if especially tailored for one's needs alone—and no doubt sincerely so; the solicitous visit to the dressing room for a *"Hals und Beinbruch"* ("May you break your neck and back!") or *"In bocca al lupo!"* ("May you be eaten by a wolf!") or the simple obscenity *"Merde!"* which forms the odd reverse of the coin of theatrical good wishes in three languages (you must never wish anyone out-and-out good luck); and after the performance, the pat on the shoulder, the kiss on the cheek, the warm word, and the radiant smile— it made a singer feel good.

After all, the boss had been there; he knew. And Johnson reinforced the original fountain of performing authority in the opera house by hiring conductors who in some measure restored musical vitality reminiscent of the better days of Seidl, Mahler, and Toscanini. He placed in the pit such good influences as Erich Leinsdorf (1937–45, with one year's absence for war service); Bruno Walter (a six-year tenure beginning in 1940); Sir Thomas Beecham (who lent his wit and style to three seasons from 1941); Fritz Busch (four seasons from 1945); Stiedry, the second Fritz (appearing for the first of many seasons in 1946); and Reiner, the third Fritz (who began his five-year reign in 1948–49). The Russian Emil Cooper came in 1943 after appearances with the New Opera Company in New York (Stiedry was also a "graduate").

Of less importance, a new spokesman in the seldom-lauded Giuseppe Antonicelli, the experienced hands of Cesare Sodero, Fausto Cleva, and Pietro Cimara carried on in the Italian wing; many opportunities were made for Max Rudolf, Paul Breisach, and Wilfred Pelletier in a varied repertoire, and Louis Fourestier took over French works in 1946 for two years, never very brilliantly.

Tristan seemed irresistible to conductors as different as Beecham, Busch, and Jonel Perlea, a slight, bearded gentleman who delighted critics in Johnson's last year but seemed not to impress the incoming management. His *Rigoletto, Carmen,* and *Traviata* were exemplary, but *Tristan* was scaled down to chamber-music caliber, exquisitely played. Perlea afterward found a respected place in New York educational circles.

In a repertoire of comparatively "connoisseur" works such as late Verdi, Wagner, Mozart, Richard Strauss, Debussy, and several Russians, eight of the leaders shaped much that was magnificent in these years. Their attainments thoroughly refuted Maurice Grau's argument that "people don't buy tickets to see the back of a man's head."

That Johnson turned out the perfect public relations man was no accident. He conceived this to be his role from the beginning: to "keep in touch with the public," as he stated in *Opera News.* One must come out of the ivory tower. The image was flawless. Particularly in the cities of the tours (which persisted even through the second World War and gained momentum thereafter), Johnson was virtually worshiped, and along with him his assistants, Edward Ziegler and Frank St. Leger.

"When you saw these three stride arm in arm across the lobby, their silk hats and patent leather pumps glistening, their white ties crisp and immaculate, the tails of their coats dancing behind them, you knew the Met had come to town," said John Rosenfield of the Dallas *Morning News.* When the most gregarious boss the Metropolitan had ever known left his post, his collection of trophies included "keys to a dozen cities, a Confederate bond and flag (from Atlanta of course) and innumerable scrolls testifying to his popularity," wrote this author in *Opera Caravan.*

In the core of administration, Johnson inherited Edward Ziegler as well as Earle R. Lewis, in spite of the rumor that Witherspoon had intended dispensing with both. Ziegler (who was never called "Eddie," although "Ned" came easily to intimates, remained as chief no-man to the General Manager. Their relationship was expressed, perhaps unwittingly, by a caption on a cover photograph of *Opera News,* calling Ziegler the "head" and Johnson the "front" of the Metropolitan Opera.

Lewis had advanced from box-office clerk as assistant to Max Hirsch in 1909 to treasurer a year later. The sound of pennies dropping in the till was the only music he recognized, as he boasted of not knowing one note from another and of never having sat through a performance. Still, he did not require musical knowledge to spot potential success or failure for any singer or production. His contact with the public, as intimate as the brass bars of the box-office window would permit, was his stock-in-trade. He never forgot anything. And he grew to have such a hypnotic effect on ticket buyers that, as his daughter Marjorie said, "I've seen difficult customers go away with the same inferior location they had complained of in the first place. It was all there was, but Father made them like it"—at least for the moment, until it was too late and the poor fellow sat miserably behind his pole. The inadequacies of the House affected this department as grievously as backstage. All anyone could do was grin and bear it—and make a skit out of Lewis' persuasive powers at a testimonial dinner tendered him along with Johnson and Ziegler a few years after the triumvirate had become firmly welded. Lewis remained as long as Johnson, then retired to Atlanta, his family, and the golf course. Spanning two regimes, he expressed sentiments that echoed a general impression around the House: "Gatti-Casazza was a benevolent despot. For him I felt the reverence of a son; for Edward Johnson the affection of a friend."

But Johnson's most faithful buffer, the man whom he came to rely on and entrust with the untying of knots, was Frank St. Leger, whom he had known as accompanist, coach, and friend, first in Florence and then in Chicago. Of Irish descent, though born in India, St. Leger showed all the volatility attributed to his race as well as many of the talents. In 1912 he met Nellie Melba in Australia and toured five years with "that remarkable woman." Then Cleofonte Campanini called him to Chicago, where he divided time with Covent Garden, working summertimes with Lucien Muratore at Eze in northern Italy or Edward Johnson in Florence. After the Chicago collapse, he conducted with the American Opera Company for three years, associated with such future Metropolitan singers as Kullman, Olheim, Votipka, Gurney, and Engelman. The restored opera house in the Rocky Mountain gold town of Central City, Colorado, occupied him in 1934. He was ready to sign a contract for the Met with Witherspoon when the latter died. Rather hurt that Johnson did not at once send for him, St. Leger put in time at radio and various coaching jobs until in 1939 Johnson finally approached him.

"Eddie had lots of convictions but not always courage," recalled his long-time colleague. "He spent thirty minutes chasing around the bush before he slapped me on the shoulder and said: 'Frankie, how'd you like to come to us for a hundred and ten dollars a week?' I joined Local Eight-O-Two like a shot, and there I was."

Pelléas et Mélisande was supposed to be St. Leger's specialty; he had prepared it in Chicago with Mary Garden. At the Met he shared the fate of all assistant conductors: preparation but seldom performance. Leinsdorf presided over the Debussy work that season and the next.

Typical of the insouciant atmosphere of the management was St. Leger's first assignment. In Philadelphia to accompany Maxine Stellman at a Guild luncheon, he was asked by Earle Lewis if he had his Sunday concert program ready. He hadn't even been notified of the concert. Now only a few hours intervened. Obviously no rehearsal time had been scheduled. So as to draw on works already rehearsed, St. Leger chose the first scene from *Tannhäuser*, secured Arthur Carron for the title role, then cast about for a Venus.

"Get Helen Traubel," suggested Johnson. The St. Louis soprano had made her debut in Damrosch's *Man Without a Country* in the Spring Season of 1936–37 and had sung again when the opera was transferred to the next regular season, but for a reason never clearly understood, Johnson was reluctant to put her on permanently. St. Leger followed his injunction without knowing that Traubel had already turned down the part (in the whole opera). Whether this bit of devious dealing was meant as revenge, St. Leger never knew, but the buck-passing didn't work. "She gave that fantastic laugh of hers and replied that she didn't even have a contract." Her entry as a full-fledged star over Johnson's objections came about soon after. Olin Downes and Oscar Thompson must have reassured the General Manager. The former spoke of Traubel's "glorious voice, fresh and warm in color, brilliant and capable of meeting fully the dramatic climaxes of the music." The latter said simply that the new soprano "took her place worthily beside the Brünnhilde of Flagstad." *Time* magazine noted that "the debutasters trooped in droves," and *Variety* dubbed her "the year's new box-office personality." She was presented to the public in the role she had held out for so stubbornly: Sieglinde.

Receiving the rebuff from Traubel that Johnson undoubtedly knew would be forthcoming, St. Leger finally secured Dorothee Manski, the logical choice in the first place, as she had sung Venus only two days previously. St. Leger conducted three more concerts that season. Then in 1941 he was called on to fill in for Gennaro Papi, who died on the morning of a scheduled *Traviata* matinee. The death in 1940 of Giuseppe

Sturani, the veteran of Hammerstein, Chicago, and Met experience, had left vacant the position of musical secretary he had held since 1927. St. Leger seemed the logical one to slip into the tiny cubicle next to Johnson's corner office at Thirty-ninth and Seventh Avenue.

"I could find hardly a piece of paper to go on," recalled St. Leger. "As in the Gatti days, Sturani and Luigi Villa relied on their fabulous memories. I swear that I was the first one to draw up a real budget—that is, to try to determine in advance how much would be needed for various operations and then stick to it. This seemed next to impossible sometimes. The auditing department would tell me it was none of my business. And Ziegler, bless him! would wag his pencil at me and say, 'You spent eight thousand dollars more on the chorus than last year. Tell Cleva [then chorus master] to cut down on rehearsals.' "

Among the ideals of management Johnson started out with was the plan to differentiate sharply between artistic and business matters, as Chicago had done with Giorgio Polacco and Herbert Johnson. But at the Met the two kept overlapping. The post of administrative secretary fell to Eric T. Clarke in 1940–41. The tall, rangy Englishman had directed the Eastman Theatre in Rochester, New York, bringing the Met there for the first time; he also managed the Rochester Philharmonic. Among other later musical posts, he was managing director of the National Music League, a nonprofit artists' management in New York, working with Harold Vincent Milligan, organist and choirmaster at Riverside Church, and afterward assistant to Henry Souvaine in the production of the intermission features of the Met's Saturday broadcasts. Clarke soon departed the Met to serve with the Occupation Forces in Germany. Julius F. Seebach replaced him and also took over some of the duties of Edward Ziegler, who lay seriously ill for two years before his death in 1947. Seebach had been a singer, business administrator, and program director or assistant with Station WOR and the Columbia Broadcasting System. His first action at the Met was to reorganize the rental system of the studios and apartments at a saving of $100,000 for the Met. But his service was cut short by a tempting offer of program direction from CBS.

"Seebach was a great businessman," said St. Leger. "He wanted the budgets on the nose—not just roughly two hundred thousand for the artists and a fifteen percent contingency fund. We tried to make some sense out of it. But it was tricky when, for example, George Szell demanded twenty-one hours of rehearsal for his debut *Salome* in December 1942. And the royalties we had to pay! Oh, well, we amortized both over two years. Szell asked for only nine hours the second time. Or the year we had to talk the Guild out of Prokofiev's *War and Peace*. It would have spread over two evenings if not cut. And what that would have done to my 'popularity chart'!" These charts were St. Leger's way of showing graphically which operas paid off and which didn't. He kept them for four years. Although it seemed a foregone conclusion that the "ABC" of popularity (*Aida, Bohème,* and *Carmen*) would rise to fever height, some surprising facts came to light with other operas, and provided guideposts for repertoire choice.

It seemed a little silly to St. Leger that when they finally turned a profit of about $5,000, by scrimping on production costs and by the circumstance that the unions had favored a *status quo,* this was spent on a brochure.

Max Rudolf, who had been introduced by Szell in 1945–46 as an assistant, and paralleled St. Leger's experience by taking over more and more administrative duties, watched the shifting events with sympathy for both sides when Johnson finally gave way to Bing. To Rudolf, an old friend from Germany, Bing confessed frankly that he could not afford to keep St. Leger on—a man older than he who knew so much more about the scene. In this embarrassing situation, St. Leger "behaved marvelously," said Rudolf. "He did all the dirty work—sixteen hours a day of it. I have always thought that Johnson originally turned to him to escape the supervision of those two old-timers, Ziegler and Lewis. All the last year, he would remind Frank that he was working for him, Eddie." St. Leger left with his chief, taking a job at Twentieth Century-Fox, and later joining the Indiana University faculty as coach.

Johnson needed fortifying in another quarter as well. He developed a reluctance to approach the board, said St. Leger. George Sloan and Charles Spofford and Lauder Greenway remained agreeable and charming, but Johnson began to fear them. The saying was current about this time that the Metropolitan got its chief exercise by jumping from crisis to crisis. Two major emergencies, one financial, the other martial, loomed on the horizon when the company was just groggily recovering from the depression and Johnson had barely found his footing. He had in fact completed only four seasons when the first calamity threatened.

During the summer of 1939, the Metropolitan Opera and Real Estate Company, whose interest in what went on in the Opera House had gradually ossified, proposed to get out from under and sell the property to produce revenue instead of opera. Once before a similar threat from the same unfeeling kind of source had produced a rescue squad. Now it had to be done all over again.

This time, the Association was determined to buy out the real estate group, which grudgingly accepted Cornelius Bliss's offer of a half million cash, transfer of the $470,000 mortgage of 1934–35, and a million dollars' worth of bonds. However exorbitant this sum might seem to the Association in view of the fact that the real estate folk had had constant and lucrative jurisdiction over their boxes, and that, most of them having died anyway, their estates ought to do the generous thing by the sister group, some fierce dissent arose from a third of the stockholders, who went to court to get more money. Robert Goelet, who had stubbornly resisted Kahn's influence, the Clews estate, the current Iselin, Elbridge T. Gerry, and Mary W. Harriman were the names that the Met might have liked to brand infamous. A newcomer, Frazier Jelke, had only recently bought Harold Vanderbilt's box for $200,000 and might be forgiven a little peevishness, but the others had for so long been dignified, however undeservedly, as "patrons." They eventually lost their suit.

George Sloan, the Guild, AGMA, and countless workers held out the tin cup once more to the public, both local and in the vast reaches of "radioland." They asked a million, only half in cash. It seemed the better part of caution to build up a reserve. Every cranny of politics, show business, education, and the art world was invaded in the cause. Irving Berlin had introduced a ditty, "The Met Must Go On," into his revue, *As Thousands Cheer,* in the drive of 1933; now the blossoming medium of television came to the aid of the campaign, the dapper young announcer, Gene Hamilton, inserting plugs all through the very first TV performance by Met forces: a scene from *Pagliacci* with Hilda Burke, Armand Tokatyan, Richard Bonelli, George Cehanovsky, and Alessio de Paolis, plus several arias and ensembles, with Frank St. Leger conducting.

As in the earlier campaign, radio response once again saved the day, to the tune of $327,000; a third of a million was raised by the Guild, and other contributions came from fifteen foundations (Carnegie gave $50,000 and Juilliard $70,000), businessmen, the subscribers themselves, Association directors, members of the company (both artistic and technical) and out-of-town groups. Even labor participated to the extent of several thousand dollars. The grand total: $1,040,000. At last the House belonged for the first time to the company that produced opera in it.

With the new ownership came a renovation of the House. Although they may have read in their newspapers or in *Opera News* that the Old Lady of Broadway had undergone a face-lifting in the summer of 1940, the audience that thronged in for the opening night on December 2 gasped with pleasure and surprise at the reality. The whole auditorium shone softly gold, with the new unbroken horseshoe of the Grand Tier now backed by rows of comfortable seats like those in the Orchestra, instead of the boxes segregating spindly chairs. As eyes followed the lyric curve from one side of the proscenium to the other, the central feature elicited ohs and ahs. Glistening in its hundreds of square feet of chastely designed brocade (woven on the same looms as its predecessor), the golden curtain dominated the huge chamber. Probably for the first and last time, an inanimate piece of cloth was applauded to the echo. And when its folds drew swiftly up to reveal the first of the elaborate new settings by Mstislav Dobujinsky for *Un Ballo in Maschera,* eyes followed its graceful sweep until it was looped to its final place as frame for the stage.

The public at large could enjoy the fresh bright colors and peer at the mysterious bank of four windows dead center in the new Grand Tier, wondering at their functional appearance in so gaudy a setting until they realized that this was the new home of the broadcasting crew headed by the announcer who was to remain a fixture as long, and beyond, its own existence—Milton Cross. They had formerly occupied Box 44 on the side. What the public would not see was the new Opera Guild Room that had been cunningly constructed from the former ladies' parlor added to a small pressroom just opposite the Guild box. Space for a new ladies' room had been found a little farther along the corridor, a top slice off a storage room.

To hunt and perhaps to find yet another little cubbyhole yet unsuspected in the queerly shaped building provided constant adventure for John Boardman, English engineer, who had come to America to inspect concrete reinforcements of new buildings in San Francisco after the fire and had roamed widely in his profession ever since. As early as 1934 he had tapped here and there to discover a hollow sound that denotes empty space. The elevator shafts proved fruitful. He had to be careful which walls he tore out, of course. "You never knew when you might be stopped from piercing a wall or changing a level," he said.

Before anything new could be undertaken, the auditorium had to be cleaned. Two trucks were required to remove the dirt. Sadly, no stray diamonds turned up, although one ten-cent ring caused momentary agitation. The new façade of the Grand Tier involved burning away the original steel "scallops," making casts of the old design, then clay models and elastic gelatin molds that would fit the curve. Finally a new steel border of twenty-four-foot plates was welded together and the new ornament applied. The tinting had to match the antique finish of the rest of the auditorium. It was a beautiful job. Furthermore, it yielded thirty new seats to mount to 500 that could be sold for $5 as a median between the Orchestra at $7 and the Dress Circle at $4.

In the working part of the House, new comforts and conveniences prevailed—improved water systems and fixtures in dressing rooms and studios, thousands of feet of cable to control movable units of scenery, movable lights on metal towers, a new ventilating system for the stuffy box-office cubicle, fresh paint everywhere in the offices. New carpeting to the amount of 45,000 square feet blossomed on corridors and floors; 6,000 square feet of lumber was installed as flooring for roof stage and wardrobe rooms. Even a painters' strike of five weeks did not daunt Boardman, who had provided for emergencies. No other building commanded more affection from him than the old opera house with its idiosyncrasies and weaknesses as well as its unique advantages, he told *Opera News*. The improvements should stand up at least seven years, which for builders as well as humans seems to be the magic number.

Now, for the first time, control of the boxes passed from individuals to the company. Only Mrs. Cornelius Vanderbilt retained her Number 3 for the entire season; others were split up into that ritual of Odds and Evens, Mondays through Saturday matinees. It was significant that Mrs. Vanderbilt turned her back squarely on the new occupant of Box 1, Mrs. Harrison Williams (destined for a long life at the head of the Best-Dressed List. Her costume was sheer white chiffon with long sleeves, intricately embroidered in sequins). Although it was probably not intentional, remarked Barclay Beekman in the *Mirror*, it served as the chief topic of intermission gossip. What Mrs. Vanderbilt thought of Ganna Walska across the chasm in Box 4 is not recorded. The Polish dilettante sported a plumed headdress suggesting Henry of Navarre, and was draped in sables and three emerald necklaces.

"The old guard sells out but doesn't surrender," was the way Nancy Randolph described in the *American* the sprinkling of Astors, Vanderbilts, Cuttings, Goelets, Wetmores, and Whitneys still visible among the new order of Society, although a "socially significant minority stood in bed," wrote James Whittaker in the *Mirror*, "letting almost anybody with a few hundred loose dollars supplant them on the Big Night." Cholly Knickerbocker (he had progressed through social consciousness to what amounted to social conscience) wrote bitterly that "opera had been saved for people with $75 seats, raising a barrier few could hurdle." It was the first time he'd heard of *hoi polloi* giving the rich what they wanted but wouldn't pay for. "One glance at Mrs. [George Washington] Kavanaugh and you know instinctively she definitely couldn't be one of 'the people' for whom the opera had been saved—or was she?" Only five years before, this Cholly dubbed Mrs. K. the "authentic" Met opener and delightedly described her cloth-of-gold gown, her full-length ermine cape, the dozens of diamond bracelets and the "two rocks, each four times bigger than the Kohinoor," which dangled from her ears. A six-inch-tall diamond tiara sat on her butter-yellow hair. "She was got up like the Queen of Sheba." She wore all her sparklers to the 1941 opening, after America had entered the war, even though others around her had dimmed their diamonds. Then the lady whose millions had come from beer kegs became a caricature.

Conspicuously missing was Mrs. Huntington Astor (divorced from Vincent and not yet married to Lytle Hull), who, as she later confessed, "never cared much for singing." She had joined the Hungarian pianist, Yolanda Mero Irion, in working for the Musicians' Emergency Fund, a charity to which she has remained faithful, and had worked hard to fill Madison Square Garden for an Ice Follies benefit the same evening as the Met opening. They drew the John Jacob Astors, many of the Old Guard, and most of the younger crowd. The New Opera Company, which opened a year later, was also under Musicians' Emergency sponsorship. Mrs. Hull went on to become the Great Lady of the New York Philharmonic, more congenial to her than the opera.

Others absent were Harrimans, Gerrys, Bakers, and Clewses. But the most telling gap in the Old Guard line occurred at the center of the circle, where J. P. Morgan and his family had reigned so long. Now, at least for Mondays, the new IBM dynasty appeared in the person of Thomas J. Watson. The Watsons' guests were Mr. and Mrs. André Kostelanetz. The beautiful Lily Pons was not singing, Cholly Knickerbocker noted, but she was working. "Her press agent is at her elbow directing her everywhere. . . . Then like vultures . . . the cameramen move on to the next eligible female, Mrs. Lawrence Tibbett." Next day, Cholly's story would mention Mrs. Tibbett but not Miss Pons. Miss P. was strictly musical; Mrs. T. was musical *and* social.

Still, even with the changing times, it was a distinguished gathering, there were acres of chinchilla to prove it, the *Times* said wistfully. The *Tribune* was glad to note Mrs. Howard Cullman in a "dream dress" of white net; Mrs. Cornelius Dresselhuys (in Vincent Astor's Box 7) in white velvet with ostrich plumes; Mrs. Byron C. Foy, who earned from Cholly the appellation of Society's Clothes Horse, in a full-skirted purple velvet gown; and Kitty Carlisle (singer and wife of Moss Hart) in demure pinky-beige net. Simon Simone represented the movie set in blue satin. But, the reporter sadly concluded, "there was hardly a rotogravure in the lot, unless you could rip off a few extra feathers and flounces, eliminate pounds of jewelry and tear pompous corsages at least in half."

Symptomatically, the impression of motley in the auditorium perhaps allowed clearer focus on the stage. And, indeed, "The show stole the show!" exclaimed Whittaker in the *Mirror*. "The spotlight veers from the boxes to the opera at long last."

What drew attention was the splendid performance of the restaged *Ballo in Maschera* with Milanov, Björling, Thorborg, and a new Hungarian baritone, Alexander Sved. So effective was the show that Miles Kastendieck wrote in the Brooklyn *Eagle* that the Met had "not only withdrawn somewhat from the star system, but had moved into the realm of modern theatre"—a consummation honored rather more in the breach than in the reality of what followed. For after an uneasy year, America itself was drawn into the war and many gains were wiped out.

18

STARS AND "STARS AND STRIPES"

So proudly we hailed . . .

—Francis Scott Key,
"The Star-Spangled Banner"

During the last peacetime season the balance between American singers and outlanders evened up. The returning tenors, Bruno Landi and Tito Schipa, were added to the buffo bass, Salvatore Baccaloni, rich in voice and comic mannerisms, magnetically individual in *Don Pasquale* and *La Fille du Régiment,* the two sopranos, Stella Roman and Norina Greco, and Alexander Sved, who later returned to Hungary and was never heard from again. The half dozen new natives included another couple of baritones, who, with Sved, endeavored to fill the place left by Lawrence Tibbett, struggling with strained vocal cords for half a season. They were Arthur Kent, brother of the polished musical comedy star Alfred Drake (their family name was Caputo), who began a career that ended almost immediately with war service, and Frank Valentino, who had at least twenty years ahead of him. Another baritone, Emery Darcy, lifted his voice to realms as ambitious as Parsifal and Siegmund. Josephine Tuminia proved a coloratura bird of passage. But most important was the advent of Eleanor Steber. The soprano was not plunged immediately in over her head, although her debut as Sophie on December 7, 1940, was trying enough without having a strange Marschallin, Maria Husser from Chicago, Lehmann being indisposed. The West Virginia beauty went on through small parts to the Marschallin herself, to the heights and depths of Mozart's Fiordiligi, Constanza, Pamina, Countess, Elvira, and Anna, and to many roles in the lyric realm. There are admirers who rate her the greatest dramatic soprano of the times; others who will settle for lyric supremacy. Retaining her beauty, a matter of glowing skin, dancing blue eyes, and a dimpled smile, Steber was fond of the pleasures of the table and allowed herself for a while to wax in figure, but somehow manages to shed pounds as if they were costume padding when necessity requires. Her vitality is unimpaired. Not long ago she was capable, after an enormous dinner, of singing *Tosca* all the way through with Philadelphia critic Max de Schauensee doing all the other roles and accompanying at the piano.

America's entry into the war in December 1941 occurred a fortnight after the season had opened with *Le Nozze di Figaro*—which provided a typical case of critical words being swallowed whole. Johnson's production of 1939 after a hiatus of twenty-one years aroused screams of anger and pain at "tradition violated." The chief trouble seemed to be Ezio Pinza's nonchalant stroll to the footlights and placing of one foot on the prompter's box as he sang his last-act aria. But gibes soon turned to doting praise. And if ever a cast seemed "ideal," though few used the word, this one deserved the label—Pinza, Rethberg as the Countess, Sayao as Susanna, Risë Stevens as Cherubino, Brownlee as the Count, Lazzari or Baccaloni as Bartolo, Petina as Marcellina, and De Paolis, Rasely, D'Angelo, and Marita Farrell. Their list should have been embroidered on a sampler headed "Mozart Bless Our Metropolitan—for Once."

America's war status further limited the influx of European performers until in 1944-45 no new singers or conductors whatever penetrated the embargo. The importance of the steadily accumulating native forces thus assumed new dimensions; the fifteen newcomers that season all claimed the American language as their birthright, and they joined the twenty-two native men and the same number of women already in the fold for a total of fifty-nine, as against twenty-eight European men and eighteen European women—many of these already, or in the process of being, naturalized. Johnson's last decade, in fact, saw seventy singers come fresh with the home brand, although one seventh lasted only one season and more than one tenth faded after two. But it must be said that the policy instituted by Juilliard pressure and carried on by the management's own wishes saved the Metropolitan in one of its most potentially dangerous periods.

That a Lower East Side New York Jewish boy named Jacob Pinkus Perelmuth could grow to be thought by a great many connoisseurs to be the finest Italian singer of his day is one of those American rags-to-riches sagas that can happen even in the opera house. Someone picked the stage name of Jan Peerce for him, and he graduated from what is known as a sideman in a dance band (his instrument, the more aristocratic violin)

to be the featured singer in Radio City Music Hall, the gaudiest movie
palace in the metropolis, in 1933. Not until 1938 did he make his operatic
debut, a *Rigoletto* Duke in Philadelphia. Then a New York recital
brought him closer to what was to be his real home, the Metropolitan.
Even with his slim experience, the House audience for the *Traviata* at the
matinee on November 29, 1941, and the millions of radio listeners
recognized a beautiful voice when they heard it. Ettore Panizza conducted.
Gennaro Papi had died that morning, but few knew. Peerce sang like
the professional he was. As his experience increased, the lyric roles he
assumed became more polished, and his superb voice production enables
him to fill the House amply. After twenty-five years, both quality and
quantity remain.

The Metropolitan couldn't send Brünnhilde's flying horse Grane to
bring a replacement for Lotte Lehmann when that soprano fell ill just
before a December 6 *Walküre,* so it was fortunate that Astrid Varnay
could be found right there in town, learning her role in Gian Carlo
Menotti's *Island God,* scheduled for its premiere on February 20, and
planning for her debut as Elsa on January 9. Varnay, the child of Hungarian parents, had been born in Stockholm, where her father was a stage
director at the opera. Her mother left him and brought the child to
America, teaching her singing and coaching her in roles until she was
twenty-three in this year of 1941. She had never appeared on any
stage when Johnson asked this favor of her. The furor she created for
her noble vocalism and her uncanny stage poise as Sieglinde almost overshadowed Traubel's beautiful singing as Brünnhilde, but she had to share
headlines evoked by action on a wider stage the next day, December 7,
the Day of Infamy, when the Japanese attacked Pearl Harbor.

Varnay pulled another bouquet of flowers out of the air when she
stepped in for Traubel six days after the first feat, singing Brünnhilde
this time to the lovely Sieglinde of Rose Bampton. A purely sung Elsa
and a glowing Elisabeth in January rather took the surprise out of her
appearance in Menotti's opera at last, but then the opera itself offered
little excitement. (Menotti learned from his failure with this static piece
and never again composed a work that lacked drama altogether.)

Eleven years later, in December 1952, this intrepid Wagnerian needed
Grane more than ever when only thirty-two hours in advance she was
summoned from Dallas to replace Traubel once again—this time as the

Götterdämmerung Brünnhilde, which she had never sung at the Met. Even modern aircraft almost failed; Varnay was grounded at Memphis, but managed to get another flight and arrived at the House at six P. M., with just enough time for a piano rehearsal with Conductor Stiedry, into costume, and on stage. These rescue operations, thrilling as they were, were no help to a singer's constitution. Varnay, furthermore, is an intensely hard worker. As she mounted to Wagnerian heights, her voice lost some freshness, but she gained in dramatic power until her Isolde became a young, supple, and flaming heroine; her Elektra and Salome also showed gripping force and poignancy. In 1944, she married the Metropolitan assistant conductor Herman Weigert, with whom she had coached, and after his death in 1955 chose to live and work in Europe, hurt at Bing's preference for Harshaw, then Nilsson.

Among the stalwarts, Margaret Harshaw, a debutante of 1942–43 by way of the Auditions, and Regina Resnik in 1944–45 suffered from overambitious casting. Harshaw was plunged into roles for which she had hardly been prepared by life as a Philadelphia telephone operator and a brief period of study. She wove her own fate somewhat better than that of the gods at her debut as a Norn and was soon—too soon?—singing Dame Quickly, Azucena, Amneris, Geneviève, and La Cieca; then she moved to the rich Wagnerian pastures with Erda and other dark roles, some of which were thrust upon her without breathing space. Fortunately her physique proved husky enough to take it; in fact, she ascended to the soprano realm in 1950 as Senta, then sang her first Brünnhilde *(Götterdämmerung)* in February 1952, and used the Philadelphia Civic Opera as a tryout for Isolde on March 13. She went on from strength to strength until she joined the Metropolitan enclave at Indiana University in 1964.

Resnik traced an opposite path, from dramatic soprano down. Forced into a *Trovatore* by Milanov's illness, three days before her scheduled debut as Santuzza on December 9, 1944, she undertook another Leonore shortly afterward—Beethoven's, and in a clumsy English translation that made it harder as well as seeming to violate the spirit of the work. *Tosca,* the unrewarding strenuosities of Bernard Rogers' *Warrior,* and the more grateful but difficult Ellen of Britten's *Peter Grimes,* plus the altitudinous demands of both of Giovanni's Donnas, could well have ruined her originally shining voice had she not taken herself in hand and become a powerful mezzo, impressing her Carmen on audiences' sensibilities in world capitals. A Sieglinde in Bayreuth preceded this metamorphosis.

On Resnik's return in 1955 to her second Alma Mater (she had come to the Met from the City Opera) she took rather tentative steps as Marina in *Boris* and Laura in *Gioconda,* while the almost mute Baroness in Samuel Barber's *Vanessa* in the spring of 1958 showed that she was a superb actress. Carmen (Stevens' almost exclusive property since the 1951 revival) came Resnik's way first at a student matinee in 1958. She had been preceded by Stevens, Rosalind Elias, Jean Madeira (also later quite a celebrity abroad in the role), Blanche Thebom, and the sophomore Belan Amparan. Steadily the ripples of Resnik's career widened to admit Herodias, Orlofsky in *Fledermaus,* Magdalena in *Meistersinger,* Ulrica, Czipra in *Gypsy Baron,* Geneviève, Amneris, Marcellina, and Klytemnestra. Her Dame Quickly and *Pique Dame* Countess are recent acquisitions. Europe still calls for as much time as she can give.

Although he is said to have known only the roles he "stood up in" (De Brétigny and Silvio) in 1942, Walter Cassel learned fast. Physically and in the tone of his voice he brought a haunting reminder of the younger Tibbett. After three seasons at the Met, this tall baritone became one of the City Opera mainstays, turning in one excellent performance after another. He came back to the Met in 1955 for Scarpia and Mandryka (*Arabella*) and has added roles and reputation since.

A product of radio, where he was one of the original Revelers Quartet, James Melton spent five years in the opera house after his debut in 1942. His best role was Tamino in *Magic Flute,* although unlike another Irish tenor, John McCormack, he never achieved Mozartean perfection in spite of a lyric, flexible voice. Accustomed to running his own affairs, and very much the golden boy of the Met's broadcast sponsors, the Texas Company (for whom he did a successful radio show), Melton scoffed at direction and presented his own image in almost every characterization. He provided one of the tenor yarns of the decade. In his later television show, he once yielded to the insistence of his director that he turn his back to the camera while his soprano, Dorothy Warenskjold, was singing her part of the *Butterfly* duet. Watching the kinescope a few days later, the star put his hand affectionately on the director's shoulder. "Never do that to me again, buddy mine, y'understand?" he said through bared teeth. To stay "his," the director had to agree. Melton's Metropolitan career ended with Bing.

Since it seems fated that every generation should produce a Talley-like phenomenon, Patrice Munsel filled the bill with as much promise and more performance than the Kansas City nightingale of 1925 when she was discovered by Auditions in 1943. Barely seventeen, the Spokane prodigy launched into the coloratura stratosphere before she had learned to breathe even mountain air—a victim of the philosophy that Met audiences will be glad to hear any fresh talent. How much of this policy was determined by Juilliard influence and how much by management's growing *laissez-faire* cannot be sorted out, but the result in Munsel's case was near vocal disaster, while audiences became increasingly conditioned to acceptance of mediocrity as the norm. Not that Munsel was a mediocre performer, far from it; but starting at the top left her nowhere to go but down. When her voice descended to the lyric stratum, she showed a charming style as Zerlina, and even essayed a Mimi, although soubrettish roles proved to be her forte. She followed up a perfect embodiment of Adele in *Fledermaus* with the title role in *La Perichole* and Despina in *Così fan tutte*—pert, sparkling, witty, alluring; then exited from the grand portals to "show biz" in which her winning personality and chic gained her star status among television boys and girls and provided her with such healthy leading roles as the Merry Widow.

In 1944, Jan Peerce was joined at the Met by his brother-in-law, Richard Tucker (Reuben Ticker). Tucker had been a highly paid cantor, and the beauty of his voice, backed by excellent technique, added to the dimensions of the tenor wing. He gives off an aura compounded of a rather humorless dignity, profound religious feeling, and a businesslike approach to his career. Peerce's enormous jollity covers serious artistic and equally religious viewpoints. With Robert Merrill, who followed the two tenors to the Met in 1945–46, Peerce projects that fast-talking blend of affection and insult that is particularly Jewish yet universally appreciated. They, with the addition of a brash new boy from Texas, the baritone William Walker, are old hands at informal television appearances, which have acquainted millions with the more picturesque as well as the human side of grand opera. Peerce bears the distinction of having been chosen for four of Arturo Toscanini's broadcast operas—*Bohème,*

Fidelio, Traviata, and *Masked Ball*; Merrill sang in the latter two, and Tucker was the Radames in *Aida.* The tenors command the cream of their repertoires, which occasionally overlap. It is not true, as often stated, that Peerce and Tucker became brothers-in-law by marrying sisters. Tucker married Peerce's sister, to be sure, but Peerce married the sister of Sidney Kaye (Kalmanovich), the protean boniface of the Russian Tea Room on West Fifty-seventh Street, where all these in-laws frequently gather, along with luminaries of what is glibly called, all in one breath, "stage-screen-radio-television."

Merrill (Moishe Miller) has revealed his progress from a Brooklyn Jewish background (in a singularly frank story written by the experienced Sanford Dody) through odd jobs and odder friends, in movie houses, and over the "borscht circuit" (upstate New York resorts peopled by serious pleasure seekers of the same faith). An Auditions winner, he made his Met debut in the role that would continue to show him off best: Germont in *La Traviata,* which called for little acting but depended on the kind of lustrous vocalism Merrill has always had on tap. Tucker was the Alfredo, Albanese the Violetta, Sodero conducted. Without any very perceptive idea of the parts he was playing (except perhaps the antic barber Figaro), this baritone rose very high until he came up against a blank wall in the unrelaxed regime of Bing. The shock to the carefree Merrill when told he was in breach of contract because he had chosen to skip the tour in favor of becoming a Hollywood neophyte sobered him decisively. "I had sung my swan song at the Met, and I was rewarded with the biggest turkey in Hollywood history," he recalled ruefully. After a painful interlude, he promised to be a good boy thereafter and was reinstated. Merrill's brief marriage to Roberta Peters (Peterman) made headlines for the world and heartaches for both singers. Their divorce left each free to find more congenial mates.

When contralto Karin Branzell retired in 1944, she remarked that she hoped she had made a place for a young American. Blanche Thebom might have been fashioned to order. Of Scandinavian descent, with a figure beautifully proportioned and well carried, her regular features crowned by a braid of dark hair that could be unwound to reach her ankles, Thebom came onto the stage as a personage from the first. Like Stevens, she had been put into a Philadelphia debut (Brangäne), then made her entry into the House as Fricka in *Walküre,* replacing another statuesque Swede, Kerstin Thorborg. Many of Thorborg's roles fell to Thebom, first in the year the former was absent, 1946–47, and after she retired in 1950. Thebom brought a strong, individual voice and great beauty and style to her impersonations, even when as Baba the Turk in Stravinsky's *Rake's Progress* her face was partially eclipsed by a beard.

Also of lasting star quality to come on the scene in this period, Dorothy Kirsten, a New Jersey girl, entered under the wing of Grace Moore, who had paid her expenses for a year of study in Italy. This and further European toil, in addition to several seasons with the Chicago Civic Opera, the New York City Opera, and a half dozen others, gave the handsome golden girl a self-assurance rare among her compatriots. *Opera News* opined that "by the very set of her chin, you always knew she would arrive." She went on to probe much of Moore's repertoire, including the relatively arcane Louise and Fiora. Her temperament always seemed a little bridled for these and other hot-blooded ladies such as Tosca, but she has been a convincing, even poignant Mimi, Butterfly, Marguerite, and Violetta. Kirsten provided one of the most startling moments in opera when, in Act III of the production of *La Fanciulla del West* in 1961-62, she had to replace a suddenly voiceless Leontyne Price, and Minnie turned blond.

A new source of performers became available in the early forties, after the twin seasons of the New Opera Company which had been founded by Mrs. Yolanda Irion and Mrs. Huntington Astor. December 1941 had marked its debut with considerable éclat. Its repertoire included such exotica as Verdi's *Macbeth,* Tchaikovsky's *Pique Dame,* Mussorgsky's *Fair at Sorochinsk,* and a long-running adaptation of *Fledermaus* called *Rosalinda*. Three conductors made pre-Met appearances: Fritz Busch, Emil Cooper, and Fritz Stiedry; several singers were recruited, chiefly Florence Kirk and Martha Lipton. Kirk was pronounced by *Opera News* to possess "a bit of the mantle of greatness, something of the dignity, high seriousness and smoldering fire of an operatic prima donna in the grand manner." That Johnson believed in her was evident from the roles she took on. Donna Anna (which she had sung at the Colon in Buenos Aires and in Mexico with Beecham) headed the parade, but the "smoldering fire" rather fizzled out after four seasons.

Lipton, whose previous experience had been mainly in concerts and a City Opera *Martha,* never rose to white heat, but burned her talent with a steadier flame. She made her debut as Siébel at the 1944 opening night. A voice of velvet, sparkling eyes in a pretty face, the earnestness of a good worker, and the American girl's ability to walk unscathed through a milieu teeming with sophistication distinguished Lipton's seventeen years at the Metropolitan, after which she moved to Indiana University.

Beginning an uninterrupted service in 1946 was a young Californian who looked more like basketball material than grand opera. Six foot seven, Jerome Hines soon made his way by his prepossessing person, his splendid voice, and his willingness to work. This kind of eager vessel always got filled to overflowing by a management that thought less of long-range planning and caution for the stamina of its stars than of their immediate and often haphazard display. Fortunately Hines stood up under it, and even gloated a bit about his swift accumulation of roles— fifteen in four seasons, six of them in a single span. In the succeeding regime he sang both Philip and the Grand Inquisitor in *Don Carlo,* Sarastro, Pimenn, and finally the pinnacle of a bass's ambition, Boris and Don Giovanni. Wotan in *Rheingold* and *Walküre* were included in the total that rose to thirty-seven by 1965. Because of his exemplary character and the unfailing smoothness of his voice, one found it less possible to believe in the menace of his Méphistophélès, Giovanni, Inquisitor, or Sparafucile than in the goodness of his Sarastro, Pimenn, Dossife, Arkel, Guardiano, or other kings and priests. Jerry's sincere religious beliefs recall those of René Maison, who used to pray fervently before singing Parsifal. He has written a sacred "opera," *I Am the Way,* which has been sung—by him and others—in many appropriate places. His less reverent fellows occasionally comment on this aspect of his makeup. As the Met plane took off safely for the 1966 trip to Paris, a stentorian voice was heard from midships intoning: "Thank *you,* Jerry Hines!"

From both New Opera and City Opera experience came Eugene Conley in 1949 to sing lyric tenor roles and to remain until 1956, one of his most prized accomplishments being the creation of the strenuous part of Tom in Stravinsky's *Rake's Progress.* Others who had roles to fill throughout many autumns and springs belong in the record book: Frances Greer, a pretty soprano Auditions winner who left in 1950; Nadine Conner, a lyric soprano from California, who retired only in 1961; Brian Sullivan, the resolute tenor who sang Narraboth to Welitch's

Salome and Admetus to Flagstad's Alceste, and in many other honorable spots including the title role of *Peter Grimes.*

Still on the active list at this writing are the vivacious baritone Frank Guarrera and the superlative character tenor Paul Franke, both of whom first stepped on the Met stage in 1948. Guarrera, a Philadelphian of Italian descent, won the Auditions and an appearance with Toscanini at La Scala at one blow, singing Ford's Monologue from *Falstaff.* His debut as Escamillo was followed by the expected repertoire, rising as high as Boccanegra. An assured stage presence and handsome figure contribute to his artistic equipment. Of Franke's sixty-five parts, only a few can be singled out: the waspish Captain in *Wozzeck,* Shuisky and the Fool in *Boris,* David and Eisenstein, a long road upward from his debut as a Youth in *L'Amore dei Tre Re.* Also present are the personable baritone Clifford Harvuot, consistently busy since 1946, and the bass-baritone Lawrence Davidson, who entered the same year and has been absent only in the mid-sixties.

To many listeners, several transients in Johnson's last decade may ring a certain chime: the handsome Southern baritone Lansing Hatfield; Mona Paulee, an Auditions winner alongside Hatfield (both came to prefer the Broadway stage); pretty Paula Lenchner, who preferred Europe; Irene Jordan, who made a career in concert opera and in other houses; Inge Manski, the attractive daughter of the former mainstay, Dorothee Manski; and Mimi Benzell and Lois Hunt, who transferred to a wider world of concerts and mass media.

Of the large American legacy left for Bing, ten were subtracted, partly by his choice, partly by theirs, among them the comely Polyna Stoska, a Worcester girl of Baltic descent, who had created a furor as the *Ariadne* Composer at City Opera before joining the Met in 1947. Broadway offered her a remarkable opportunity that same season as the bitter wife in Weill's *Street Scene,* considered by Olin Downes as "the most important step toward significant American opera yet encountered in the musical theatre." Norman Cordon had left the big House to play the jealous husband. Stoska's silvery voice became strained in the difficult role of Susanna in *Khovanshchina* after she had sung Ellen in *Peter Grimes,* Donna Elvira, Freia, Eva, Elisabeth, and the *Figaro* Countess, to all of which she brought artistry. Her departure, along with Claramae Turner,

marked an example of conspicuous waste by the Metropolitan. Turner
went on to a very satisfactory career based on the New York City Opera
and also in Europe.

To apply the term "permanent" to certain situations and faithful
servants is tempting, particularly when Atlanta and Osie Hawkins are
concerned. To the Georgia city, most lavish hostess of the spring tours,
came the young Alabaman who bombarded the opera management until
he won a place. After his debut as Donner in 1942, he sang many roles,
then graduated to executive stage manager. That stentorian voice can be
heard above even carpenters' poundings and orchestra babble. Osie
quickly learned the ritual of curtain calls, as previously outlined by
Désiré Defrère, whose long career paralleled his own.

Opera News printed the rules: Every solo singer must take at least
one call, alone or with others; if his part is small—one aria—just after
the act. Principals come last; the final bow goes to the lady unless her
part is overshadowed as in the last act of *Boris.* In *Tristan,* Isolde,
Brangäne, Tristan, and Kurvenal must appear after the first act; after
Act II the order is Marke, Brangäne, Tristan, Isolde; then all four, then
the first two, then the last two in any number of joint appearances. After
Act III Kurvenal first, then Tristan, then Isolde.

Carmen, Act III, is a knotty problem. Carmen should come last, but
Micaela invariably gets more applause than anyone. "Nothing should
be improvised," the old master concluded. "Even between such passionate
lovers as Tristan and Isolde or Lohengrin and Elsa, misunderstandings
will arise if curtain calls are not properly arranged."

It would be a mistake to think of these Americans, grouped here to
make a point, as occupying a watertight compartment. Their true value
is in their ability to mix with Europeans without fear or favor. In the war
years a few highly treasured individuals arrived from overseas, including
the versatile Martial Singher (who encompassed Pelléas and the four
Hoffmann villains among more conventional assignments and went on to
become an adviser to the French wing); the evergreen tenor, Kurt Baum;
bass-baritone Gerhard Pechner; and the hardy perennial Lorenzo Alvary,
who sings bass-baritone roles in all languages but his native Hungarian,
produces opera and runs a popular radio interview show. Jacques
Gérard arrived in 1942 for French roles; Frederick Lechner the next year
for German ones. Ella Flesch hardly lived up to her Vienna and Munich

reputation; she was thrust suddenly into a substitution for Lily Djanel as Salome, then sang with varying success Santuzza, Tosca, and Sieglinde. Infinitely more satisfactory was her Ariadne with the New York City Opera.

Before she became a well-loved member of the Met family in 1942, the Viennese-born Herta Glaz had sung widely in this country. The mezzo served the Thirty-ninth Street House in almost all the roles that can be named on the fingers of several hands until she turned to teaching in 1956. Rosa Bok might have had a brilliant career, in spite of a shaky start as Queen of the Night in 1941, if it had not been for an injury when the cart tipped over in *Coq d'Or*.

With channels to Europe open slightly again, three Swedes slipped through, the already beloved Björling together with Torsten Ralf and Joel Berglund. Ralf filled Wagner tenor roles (except Tristan and the Siegfrieds) to the critics' satisfaction until 1948; soon afterward he succumbed to a fatal illness. Berglund's sympathetic Sachs and Kurvenal as well as his rich-toned Wanderer and Wotan made him a favorite with the public too. After 1949 he took over the directorship of the Stockholm Opera.

In the same open season of 1946–47, an Italian baritone, Giacomo Vaghi, arrived via South America, and a South American baritone, the Chilean Ramon Vinay, arrived via the New York City Opera. Vinay, an enormous man with a handsome dark countenance, became so well known as a tenor that his early baritone range was forgotten until much later. He undertook Otello on twenty minutes' notice when Ralf was ill, and became famous in the role.

In 1946 three Hungarians, two Swedes, one Italian, one Frenchwoman, and one Yugoslavian crossed to New York. Sharing Magyar origins were the excellent tenor artist, Leslie Chabay, and the two basses, Deszo Ernster and Mihaly Szekely. Ernster stayed around in kingly roles almost without interruption until 1964; Szekely, more beautiful in voice and equally impressive in stature, returned to Hungary and disappeared from sight. The French lady was Renée Mazella, the Yugoslav was Daniza Ilitsch, one Swede was the pretty soprano Hjördis Schymberg—none of them long for this opera world. The Italian and Swedish tenors were the prize catches. Ferruccio Tagliavini, tenor to his pudgy fingertips, came heralded by phonograph records. His voice seemed smaller in the House, but of lovely quality and lift. His wife, Pia Tassinari, joined him one season but did not match her record reputation. Tagliavini contributed to the gaiety of nations by becoming the object of a paternity suit which added to, if it did not uplift, opera publicity. He sang his Edgardos, Rodolfos, *et al.* in diminishing numbers until 1954.

Set Svanholm remained the better value. Olin Downes wrote of the Swede's debut as the young Siegfried on November 15, 1946, that the new *Heldentenor* was "not only an exceptionally gifted singer, but also a sound musician who sings his part accurately as it is written; he can also by his appearance create illusion." Svanholm was the fully rounded artist, capable of portraying the corrupt Herod and the weak Aegisthus as well as the boyish Siegfried and the saintly Parsifal. He never stopped seeking the inwardness of his roles, especially Tristan. As he delved into meanings and interpretations, he resembled Olive Fremstad, who painstakingly thought out every moment of a part, particularly Isolde, according to her biographer, Mary Watkins Cushing. Svanholm's short stature, which induced him to wear the clumsy built-up shoes he called "Carmen Mirandas" after the South American's Wedgies, occasionally militated against complete illusion, especially when his Brünnhilde or Isolde was Traubel. But with Flagstad or Varnay the stage vibrated with the truth and beauty of their interpretations. Svanholm was wont to watch Flagstad's immolation from Siegfried's bier through half-closed eyes, glorying, he said, in the soaring voice which rivaled the flames. These two completed the trio who took on opera management after splendid singing careers; Svanholm succeeded Berglund in Stockholm in 1956 and Flagstad became director of the Oslo Opera in 1959. The hero maid preceded her Siegfried to Valhalla in 1962; he followed in 1964.

Several Italian imports in Johnson's last three years did well for themselves. Giuseppe di Stefano seemed the most promising, a tenor with a beautiful lift to a lyric voice, but all too indifferent to characterization of any role. The audience and the prompter vied successfully for his attention against the soprano beside him. Chicago and San Francisco took him from New York, while his European reputation mounted and his records sold everywhere. Giuseppe Valdengo similarly concentrated more on his big baritone voice than on any verisimilitude in character. Italo Tajo never came very close to rivalry with Pinza in the two seasons after that idol departed for the Broadway stage. Nor could Melchiorre

Luise, good as he was in buffo parts, banish from memory the even more corpulent and popular Salvatore Baccaloni. "Superb" seemed the consensus about Cloe Elmo, a contralto with sumptuous voice and vivid presence, but she had only two seasons to show them.

Central Europe fared better. Paul Schoeffler, the experienced Sachs, Giovanni, and Scarpia, would play those and other roles many times; the aging but still fresh-voiced Erna Berger had two seasons singing Sophie, Queen of the Night, and Gilda brilliantly; Peter Klein likewise remained a brace of seasons for David, Valzacchi, and other parts. Lubomir Vichegonov came from Bulgaria in 1948 and remained as Lubin Vichey, singing bass kings and priests until 1956, when he took over for a few years the concert management that had been handling his affairs.

The sensation of the decade, what Francis Robinson called without qualification "the greatest night in the Opera House," occurred on February 4, 1949, when Ljuba Welitsch made her debut as Salome and Fritz Reiner presided in the pit for the first time. For weeks the fiery Bulgarian had been a cynosure in the House and outside; in an interview she claimed to love men and money in that order; she was said to have dyed her swirling mop of hair that flaming red expressly for Salome. Her powder-puff skin, quantities of it often on display, her temperament, matching her tresses, her silvery voice with its steel edge—all aroused uncommon excitement.

The *Salome* setting by Donald Oenslager harked back to 1934, when the ban dating from 1907 had first been lifted; Herbert Graf drew on his staging plan for 1938, the second revival. Herbert Janssen was scheduled for Jokanaan but was replaced by Berglund at the first performance; Max Lorenz had not sung Herod since 1934; his alternate, Frederick Jagel, had performed it at the New York City Opera recently. Most of the others were new: Thorborg as Herodias, alternating with Harshaw; Sullivan as Narraboth.

Complete illusion waited upon performance, for the plump soprano, her unruly hair roached back like a slavey's, went through rehearsals in a plaid suit, first wearing galoshes on the drafty stage, then changing to the silver Wedgies, almost as awkward, she would actually wear. Minutes after Johnson, elegant in white tie, tails, and top hat, stood on stage for his last-minute inspection, the curtain went up and the spell of a searingly great performance gripped the packed auditorium. Ninety minutes later pandemonium greeted a new star. Welitch (she soon dropped the "s") took the tigress' share of the ovation, but Reiner deserved the lion's. He was the last of the grand leaders who gave Johnson's regime a good name.

Conductors are often as fertile a source of merriment, intentionally or otherwise, as tenors. Sir Thomas Beecham's opinion of the male singers with lofty voices but low I.Q.'s were often eccentrically expressed, as when he saw James Melton in a rather fussy costume for *Traviata*. "Who is the gentleman jockey?" he inquired blandly. Needless to say, this story was passed on gleefully—by another tenor. Chapters have been written to extol Beecham's wit; legendary have become the tales of the failure of one suspender at one orchestra concert, the fall off the podium at another ("Podiums are designed as part of a conspiracy to get rid of conductors") and his verbal scalping of the ladies' auxiliaries that surround American musical institutions with cotton batting. One of the anecdotes in Alan Wagner's *Prima Donnas and Other Wild Beasts* credited Beecham with urging the Covent Garden orchestra to play loud enough to drown out the singers "in the public interest." Perhaps his most famous remark concerned the misbehavior of an animal on the stage: "A distressing spectacle, but gad! what a critic!"

Italo Montemezzi, invited to conduct his own *Amore dei Tre Re,* crossed poniards with Grace Moore in a manner recalling the old Farrar-Toscanini duel. Charles Kullman, who with Montemezzi and Moore sang Avito both in San Francisco the previous fall and in New York that winter of 1940–41, watched from the Met wings as Moore rehearsed the famous lift-and-carry scene with Pinza. As the bass hoisted his murdered daughter-in-law to his shoulder and staggered away from the footlights, Moore came alive and, face upside down and reddening, screamed in high soprano register, "This is too damned slow!"

Montemezzi rapped for silence, leaving the bass reeling under his squirming load and addressing all and sundry about him: "Who wrote this anyway?"

Moore was particularly anxious to succeed in this part and did indeed win praise for her singing, but her action left something to be desired. At least one ludicrous moment resulted. As she mounted the parapet to wave to her departing husband, she tossed from her shoulders the red velvet cape, gold-trimmed and bejeweled, onto the steep flight of steps behind her. It looked quite garishly dramatic there. But when her lover entered and she wanted to run to his arms, she was forced to pick her way cautiously down over the slippery velvet folds and somehow the first fine rapture got lost.

Emil Cooper, who waddled into the roster especially for *Pelléas*, which he had conducted for Mary Garden in Chicago, became more communicative to the public in Russian works that came later—*Boris, Coq d'Or,* and *Khovanshchina*. But he made himself less understandable to colleagues, mumbling in an accent that never became comprehensible. Tibor Kozma, the conductor who prepared the last of these works for him—and whose Hungarian accent held its own terrors, although he used and demanded precise English speech and diction and harbored a fierce devotion to opera in English—unraveled a few Cooperisms.

"Dere iss moosik wat iss heesy 'n' dere iss mossik wat iss hon-eesy," the chubby little Russian said gravely one day. "Diss moosik [*"Abscheulicher!"* from *Fidelio*] iss hon-eesy." The soprano thought so too, but overcame the difficulties. After figuring that out, this one should be "heesy":

"Vy you honoppy?" he asked a colleague, who didn't understand. "You know 'oppy," Cooper said impatiently. "Vell, you *hon*oppy." His companion, indeed, admitted to being miserable.

19

A YEAR OF SCHIZOPHRENIA

Off with the old! On with the new!

Why did Edward Johnson quit? Managers before and after him have not considered fifteen years too much. His fifteen undoubtedly had left their mark on him and he was tired. He had been dissuaded from retiring once before, then, as one informant put it: "He resigned once too often." Managers don't possess that built-in alarm that tells a singer when the voice is failing, allowing time to make a graceful exit before it is too late.

Johnson began to lose control at the moment when he tossed out a few impulsive words that changed the current of thought around the House. Visiting him one day in the midst of the usual turmoil was a slim greyhound of a man who had come over from England to investigate possibilities for American performances of the Glyndebourne Opera, of which he was general manager. His old-time colleague, the conductor Fritz Stiedry, had introduced Rudolf Bing to Johnson as a courtesy. Johnson turned away from a plaguey telephone call and half-laughingly said to his visitor: "How would you like this job?"

This was tantamount to the challenge issued by the mother who left her three children alone with the admonishment: "Don't put any beans up your noses." Everyone, including Bing himself, began to think about an operatic version of beans and noses. Johnson's jest—for undoubtedly he meant it so—turned into reality sooner than anyone could have expected. George A. Sloan, chairman of the board, approached Bing tentatively, then promised after only two days that something definite would happen within six weeks. While talks were going on among the board, Mrs. Belmont went to Europe, a trip that caused considerable misunderstanding. She visited with Mrs. Otto Kahn (who died shortly afterward) and with an unknown Englishwoman. They apparently let the board know they approved of Bing. He was summoned to appear in May 1949 and given a contract for a three-year term beginning June 1, 1950. Meanwhile, in an effort to smooth the takeover, he was asked to spend the season of 1949–50 as a paid "observer," watching Johnson's wheels go round. As a practical measure this had many advantages. But it was the worst possible move to ensure smoothness. Personalities had been left out of account. It was a year of schizophrenia, old and new sniffing at each other's heels in mutual distrust.

How early Johnson began to repent his hasty opening of the exit door cannot be determined, but as the 1949 tour began, he expressed himself several times. For his successor, the singers Tibbett, Melchior, Brownlee, and Bonelli were said to be in the running. Laszlo Halasz, director of the New York City Opera, was discussed. But St. Leger seemed the Johnson favorite. Johnson sent him on a scouting trip to Europe as a fortification of his reputation.

Max Rudolf, watching the events of the tour with concern, saw signs of the General Manager's unrest as early as Atlanta. Frank Daniels, the veteran reporter for the Atlanta *Journal*, asked Johnson who his successor would be. "Oh, anybody," exclaimed Johnson. "Kullman. Brownlee." (The latter was thought to have society backing.)

Nerves were rasped almost to the breaking point by the murder of John Garris, the young character tenor, in Atlanta the night of the company's departure. His body was discovered in an alley the following morning. Rudolf was dispatched back from Memphis to handle the affair from the company viewpoint, while a police lieutenant followed the troupe to other tour cities and made their lives miserable and their performances shaky by his constant surveillance. It was all to no avail. "From recent guarded statements by another member of the Atlanta police," this writer said in *Opera Caravan* in 1955, "one can infer a belief in the guilt of an early suspect, a vagrant. But the trail grew cold long ago. The case remains in the books as 'unsolved.' "

To this grim atmosphere was added the letdown of a second season in Los Angeles that did not hold up to the previous one. Merely because *Peter Grimes* drew crowds the first time as a novelty did not guarantee success for a repetition; Johnson should have known better. The certainty grew that this 3,000-mile trek would be the Met's last.

To break the news to St. Leger, arriving from Europe, that Bing had been chosen fell to Rudolf. Johnson confirmed it: "The board is sold on Bing."

Although he began his work in a little office in the Met studio building at 1425 Broadway, the upcoming manager's presence began to be felt throughout the building. His wiry figure hurrying down corridors, his unsmiling face seen in the management box (it was perhaps a trifle tactless of him to sit there instead of in comparative obscurity), his thin nose pointing ever forward, his air of inscrutability that both alienated and intrigued—everyone knew very soon that the new boss was there and that he was critical of the old.

Johnson's smile grew a little strained, notably in confrontations with newspapermen, who no longer seemed so friendly. Standing stiff-legged with his arms folded across his chest in a typical pose, the General Manager rolled his "r's" even more crisply than usual, the blue eyes sparked, the white hair (he had put aside the black dye bottle along with the tenor scores) seemed to bristle with an electric charge.

Bing, too, suffered from the onslaught of the fourth estate. His first encounter was unfortunate. A dossier had been sent out from the House at the time of his engagement, but on a weekend, so that no check could be made. Two glaring mistakes called for retraction, both attributing to him posts higher than those he occupied, first in Darmstadt and Berlin, then in Glyndebourne. His open letter to the press corrected the "promotions," but lost him the friendship of Carl Ebert, whose place at Glyndebourne he seemed to have usurped. Rumors had piled up to the effect that he had already engaged Flagstad to return in spite of the objection of many Americans; and that he would throw out Italian opera and American singers. Smarting under the necessity to counter this animosity, Bing persuaded the board—much against Johnson's will—to allow him a press conference on February 1, 1950.

Helen Traubel beat him to the starting post. She announced on January 28 that she would no longer sing at the Met. Her contract had not been renewed, although many younger singers had already been favored. Two days later, Melchior joined the rebellion. Max Rudolf has listed the sequence of events. Bing had told Melchior that he wanted to conclude contracts first with those who would give many continuous weeks to the opera. Svanholm, Björling, and Tucker had agreed. Warren, whom Bing heartily wanted, had claimed to be upset by the delay, but an agreement had been reached "out of court." The key to the situation rested in the fact that all three of the dissidents, Traubel, Melchior, and Warren, used the same concert manager, James A. Davidson, whose ideas

of publicity verged on belligerency. The news of Warren's signing got
to the other two. On Saturday evening, Kleinchen (Melchior's diminutive
and vivacious wife, who ran her huge husband's affairs with a finger of
iron), phoned Max Rudolf. If Bing didn't offer a contract by Monday
morning, his biggest *Heldentenor* would not return. Max pointed out
that Bing wanted Melchior but this was not the right way to do things.
"Don't force an ultimatum," he counseled softly. Kleinchen was adamant.
So was Bing.

"I will not be dictated to," he declared, adding to his public statement the pronunciamento that became famous: "No doubt I shall make
mistakes, but I can assure you that I will attempt to run this House—
unmoved by promises or threats—on the principle of quality alone."

With poise and good nature and an offhand wit that astonished and
delighted the more sardonic of his listeners in his first press conference,
Bing disposed of the amenities, which included a disclaimer of criticism
directed toward the current mangement, and got on to future prospects.
These soon shaped up as a master blueprint, springing from a diagnosis
that reached far under the surface. "He is ready to employ all necessary
surgical measures," remarked Cecil Smith in *Musical America*. "The policies of the Metropolitan, it often seems, have 'just growed.' After years
of habituation, artists and public alike have learned to take for granted
an atmosphere of artistic nihilism that is actually unique in the operatic
world."

In order to bring the Metropolitan up by its bootstraps, Bing proposed internal reforms that included a rehearsal schedule sure to step on
the concert bookings of those birds of passage who alighted at Thirty-
ninth Street barely long enough to acquire the Met label which would
improve their concert market.

He planned, he said, "an ensemble of stars, not comets."

A shudder ran through the building when he suggested that even
the top singers might like to audition for him, as he had not been able
to hear them all in performance. But the rumor that he would dismiss
50 percent of the personnel was a mere canard. "Apart from murder,"
he added, "there is hardly any crime I am not suspected of." Also nonsense was the accusation that he would cut the repertoire to three operas,
and those German. Wagner, he acknowledged, commanded a public,
and furthermore the Met still owned the *Ring* sets of Lee Simonson that

had been used for a cycle only once. Some wear had to be got from them. Otherwise, the Teutonic load would not be overbearing. Bing's own preferences—his ten "favorites," as outlined for Howard Taubman in *The New York Times Magazine,* bore out his lack of Germanic bias: *Rosenkavalier, Fidelio,* and *Wozzeck* were listed, but no Wagner, and the balance included three Verdi works (*Otello, Don Carlo,* and *Aida*), Puccini's *La Bohème,* Mozart's *Nozze di Figaro,* Bizet's *Carmen,* and Mussorgsky's *Boris.* The inclusion of *Wozzeck* puzzled many. Berg's "masterpiece" (as it became reverently labeled) had been given under the auspices of the League of Composers with Stokowski conducting in 1931 —and at the Metropolitan. It soon became a kind of symbol of sought-after modernity, brought up incessantly at high-level meetings by some progressive director or other, but not penetrating to performance until 1958, and that a year or so after the New York City Opera had undertaken it. But then, after all, as Lauder Greenway said of the "production" committee of the board, when confronted with suggestions for new ventures, "there are always so many reasons not to give any one work." (Greenway himself would like to see again Dukas' *Ariane et Barbe Bleue,* Respighi's *Campana Sommersa,* and Pizzetti's *Fra Gherardo,* but acknowledges such revivals are unlikely.)

Refurbishing the chestnuts was to become fixed policy, and along with it an emphasis on the visual part of production. This rejuvenation, Bing thought, would bring new interest from audiences. Further to inspire attention, he planned to cut all eighteen-week subscription series into two of nine each.

Yes, it was true that Flagstad would return. He was firmly convinced that as a great artist she belonged at the Metropolitan and he decided that political passions must not affect his judgment in artistic matters. He himself had had every reason to fear and hate the Nazis, having been driven from Germany by them, but, he told Taubman, "I would have felt myself a coward if I had let my personal feelings influence the artistic position of the Metropolitan." Bruno Walter, himself a refugee from Hitlerism, would return to conduct *Fidelio* for Flagstad. What was never brought out in the heated discussions that followed was the availability of the singer in Johnson's last years and the fact that the political situation had not influenced that manager's decision against her, but rather the *cause célèbre* that had been created over her insistence that her accompanist Edwin McArthur conduct for her—otherwise no tour, she threatened. This was considered insubordination. The word "blackmail" was not uttered but quivered in the air. Flagstad's action is still spoken of indignantly by survivors of the experience. John Erskine wrote that the company could have only one general manager, implying that Flagstad was not that one. McArthur tells his side—and Flagstad's—in his unusually candid *Personal Memoir*. The chief political reaction to the soprano's reengagement in 1950 was the resignation of Morton Baum from the board. This shrewd lawyer thereafter devoted himself exclusively to the City Center.

Meanwhile, Bing's tentative list of singers who would return did not include Melchior. The tenor went on to his farewell Lohengrin on February 2, 1950, the night after the press conference, at which Johnson, who had previously called him "an old boat," repented and publicly hugged the tenor as far as he could reach around him. Traubel and her husband negotiated a contract that called for parallel appearances with Flagstad: the usual Wagner and a new role, the Marschallin for Traubel; *Fidelio* was restored for Flagstad. It was later that the touchy American again made trouble by announcing her allegiance to nightclubs. Bing called Kurt Weinhold, by now her manager in Columbia Artists. Weinhold admitted his star's whim with some trepidation; it might affect her concert schedule too. All right, said Bing, but she must not appear at all in such places before the Met season, nor for four weeks after her last performance—in other words, no night-clubbing before February. Traubel once again sought justice in the newspapers with information some considered inaccurate. Bing once more put his slender foot down. Traubel appeared no more on Thirty-ninth Street after her Isolde at the matinee on March 21, 1953. Other media claimed her and she was seen jovially kidding Jimmy Durante by millions of television addicts. She had added one new fashion note—costumes that were more appropriate to Hollywood than Valhalla or Cornwall. They had indeed been designed by the cinema's Adrian.

With the passing of both Traubel and Melchior, some semblance of discipline returned to Wagnerian performances. Both had scorned the humdrum business of rehearsals, and the lady went so far as to command Stiedry to her apartment to do work that properly belonged in the opera house. Melchior had relapsed from the momentary shot of adrenaline supplied by the presence of Svanholm and even the aging Lorenz. He actually refused orchestra rehearsals now and then. The result showed in that no performance of Traubel's was free of errors, according to Max Rudolf, while Melchior could at least be trusted always to make the same mistakes.

After all, it was always possible for a manager to deal with this kind of dereliction, as when a great lady suggested that her understudy do the rehearsal.

"Very well, but the understudy does the performance too!" was the rejoinder.

But Bing did not always get his way straight down the line. Another malcontent appeared, with vague threats to start a splinter group in the Radio City Center Theatre in case the Italian repertoire was slighted. Licia Albanese, assured that Bing was no Germanophile, stayed around, but still wanted roles that Bing thought not to her advantage. Max Rudolf spent many hours trying to convince the soprano's hardheaded husband, Joseph Gimma, a Wall Street grandee and high official in the Republican Party, that Tosca should not be added to Albanese's Butterflys, Mimis, Manons, Marguerites, and Violettas, but reluctantly gave in. She got her Toscas in 1952. "I am happy now," she said. "I was unhappy before." In San Francisco, where she could do no wrong, they even allowed her a Donna Anna in 1955.

Johnson's formal farewell took the form of a *Tosca,* followed by a pageant and ceremony in which the entire company participated. Lucrezia Bori, in her former Violetta costume, did the honors, along with Giovanni Martinelli, as Otello (he had retired in 1946), and Friedrich Schorr (his retirement was in 1943). John Brownlee showed that suavity as master of ceremonies that was to attain prominence the next season when he assumed the winglike cape of the Bat. The hero of the evening pointed a few words to the audience (and possibly toward his successor, who, however, was not present by reason of not having been invited, it was "reliably" said). The gist was that "one is not born a general manager—one learns the hard way, by making mistakes and correcting them." Johnson's admission of "trial and error" as his basis for running the opera house plainly and painfully clarified what Kolodin defined as an axiom: "A new man can always see the faults of his predecessors; what he cannot see, after a few years, are his own."

The *Tosca* performance established rowdiness as a norm. Welitch tore through it like a tornado, roughing up Tagliavini's hair, choking him with an ostensibly loving arm, and making it difficult for him to sing in various other intimate ways, then turning on Tibbett to toss furniture at his living body and kicks at his corpse. (Her relish for a good romp reasserted itself once more when as Musetta—one of the more inspired bits of casting of her final season, 1951–52—she rode her Marcello piggyback offstage.)

Schoeffler had been intended for Scarpia, but was ill. He took the part at an April 4 performance also dedicated to the manager, as its proceeds were turned over to an Edward Johnson Memorial Fund. This came in the midst of the customary Post Season, which for a number of years had run through a week, usually comprising a pair of *Parsifal* performances and occasionally an overflow student matinee. Long ago it had ceased any pretext as Mrs. Belmont's "Junior Company."

The nervous strain of that final season mounted to a terrific pressure. Performers suffered along with management. The only novelty was Mussorgsky's *Khovanshchina*, an interesting experiment although doomed not to be repeated. Sets of the previous *Boris* were patched up. *Manon Lescaut* received a viable new production. *Meistersinger* felt the tremors most heavily, although from natural causes. Harshaw failed after one act and Glaz stepped in; at the next performance, the reliable Svanholm had to bow out, leaving Walther in the last two acts to Kullman; at a third, Janssen gave way to Schoeffler. When Traubel couldn't sing Brünnhilde, the wife of a new baritone, Ferdinand Frantz, was called in, so that Helena Braun appeared as a daughter to her real husband.

Johnson got out on the Spring Tour of 1950 before he openly indicated his doubts in an interview with the Cleveland *Press* quoted by Kolodin. He "expressed anxiety" over Bing's policies—"overpublicized," he thought them, in a revealing phrase. He hoped that Bing would become better acquainted with America. Then he might think twice before thrusting such an unworthy presentation as *Die Fledermaus* on the opera house. "Bing's plan to offer it some twenty-odd times has prompted Johnson to call it joshingly *Fleder-mice*," wrote the interviewer. (The new manager was doubtless ignorant of the fuss stirred up by Conried's use of the lively operetta as his own benefit forty-six years previously, and probably wouldn't have cared, anyway.)

In the fall of 1950, John Erskine's book, *My Life in Music,* appeared, casting a cat in the dovecote. He complained that "the women" chose Mr. Bing and that he, for one, was not notified of the appointment until it was practically a *fait accompli.*

Mrs. Belmont indignantly rebutted his facts as well as his opinions in a discussion of "errors of omission and commission" in *Opera News* for November 27. Erskine was simply not accurate, she stated, and did less than justice even to himself. "He does not reveal the necessary detachment to the historical approach," she continued, and his "blinkers completely block any point of view not his own." As for the choice of a manager, Erskine was in error: it was not true that she had selected Bing; the men did. She had merely been requested to secure some supplementary information. The Opera Guild had nothing—repeat, *nothing*— to do with his engagement. It had always operated under the strict policy of noninterference with management.

Further dissension with Erskine's point of view about American opera and the contributions of various board members was beside the point. Mrs. Belmont felt betrayed and hurt, as a personal letter to Erskine's wife, Helen Worden, indicated. Womanlike, Mrs. Belmont had the last word. Erskine died in 1951 without a public riposte.

Johnson's friends remained fiercely loyal to him in the trying decade that separated his departure from the Met and his death in 1959. He had in later years devoted himself to the opera department of Toronto University, seldom appearing below the border. There are many who prefer to remember him as a singer—although one of the Metropolitan staff found his own memories slightly abraded, thinking of days when the strains of *"Ridi Pagliaccio"* more than once penetrated to his cubbyhole, indicating that the General Manager was impressing some visitor with the former glories of his recorded voice.

It is kinder to remember that the singer was illustrious indeed, and to commend him for submerging the artist in the administrator, if such was his choice. We can be sorry that a projected *Pelléas et Mélisande* in Bori's last year had to be put away for this reason but recall the happy partnership that went before. In 1955 he told this writer that he had decided to make the clean break when he recalled how Mary Garden as manager had cast herself as protégée.

Johnson never remarried after the death of his wife just before his

Met debut. It was an achievement she had prayed for, ever since their days in Europe when he was singing as Edoardo di Giovanni. She was a distinguished Portuguese, Beatrix Maria Ferreira da Veiga d'Arneiro, and her presence would have lent tone to the tenor's New York career. He remained the eligible widower, devoted to his daughter, Firenze (named for the meeting place of her parents), and the probable despair of many a marriageable lady.

It may lighten the canvas to leave him with an amusing insight into the tenor mind, which, it seems, is not altogether different from the prima donna mind. Blanche Witherspoon, a famous cook and hostess, found her dinner table dominated one evening by a discussion of costumes—opera costumes, of course, and European opera costumes. Which were the most beautiful? "Mine from Rome," insisted one disputant. "No, mine from Paris!" argued a second. "Mine, mine from Vienna!" the third chimed in. The argument, which began to include various triumphs in which those costumes had played a part, ranged through the entire evening, while the other guests watched and listened incredulously. The three were Charles Hackett, Paul Althouse, and Edward Johnson—all tenors.

But perhaps it is even more fitting to give Johnson a send-off in the words of a former associate who never quite accustomed himself to the brisker and brusquer regimen around him since. "Eddie was never rude," mourned this worthy. "He was a gentleman."

20

PASSWORD: "PROFESSIONAL"

All things must change; to something new, to something strange.

—HENRY WADSWORTH LONGFELLOW, *Kéramos*

The time had come for the pendulum to swing, as it always had, from the performer-manager to the professional. The alternation had been unbroken at the Metropolitan Opera House beginning with the professional Abbey. It ran: Abbey to Damrosch (and Stanton) to Grau to Conried to Gatti to Johnson to Bing. Rudolf Bing took over in the acceleration of the space age, and just as science had advanced faster in the second quarter of the twentieth century than in all previous eras laid end to end, so the Metropolitan leaped forward into new conceptions to keep pace with a new kind of life.

The differences hardly showed at first, although Bing let it be known that he intended to run a tight ship. He was not allowed to jettison some ballast he must have considered dead weight, but began immediately to shore up the internal structure of the company and to impose discipline on staff and artists alike. The insistence on punctuality and obedience to the rules met with some grumbling but did result in some neater performances.

Behind the scenes, doors were locked that had always swung open to denizens who love to haunt an opera house and consider they have the right to do so, possibly from previous acquaintance with a functionary or a singer, or merely because they admire the operation or some individual part of it and have been around long enough to become familiar to doormen and ushers. Or they have been at one time or another a member of the press, "working" (either steady or employed on *ad hoc* business), or fringe staff. Sentries were posted to keep these out, and changed frequently so that no one would become too friendly. Appointments had to be firmly set before Winifred Short would reach under her desk in the drafty Thirty-ninth Street vestibule and press the buzzer that opened the door to backstage, offices, and auditorium. The

312

artist himself was required to leave names at the door if any congratulatory company wanted to visit a dressing room after a performance.

The visual element of the stage took a bound upward into the promised quality from Bing's first-night production, Verdi's *Don Carlo,* with a transfusion from the legitimate theatre in the person of Margaret Webster as stage director. This Shakespearean instilled the idea that singers could act even in such unlikely material as Jussi Björling and Robert Merrill, while Delia Rigal, Jerome Hines, Fedora Barbieri, and Cesare Siepi took naturally to it.

Other adventures of this nature followed, not always as successful, but a distinct earnest of Bing's determination to improve the looks and action of the Met's shabby stage—in effect, a genuine revolution. As in all such sweeping reforms, newness alone doesn't carry a watertight guarantee of quality. Yet Bing's master blueprint, lying plain and clear after his first fifteen years, paid off in physical aspects at least: castle walls no longer wave in the breeze or shed flecks of paint at every touch; costume colors are clean and fresh; platforms hold fewer splinters to menace the unwary.

In the Old House, Bing went through the repertoire to the extent of fifty-six works, counting at least three new productions each season (except for the strike-plagued 1961–62, when only *Ballo* was redone, and the season of 1965–66, with *Faust* and *Queen of Spades* the only newcomers). Five had to be done over again even in this span. Rolf Gérard's *Aida* of Bing's second season gave way to Robert O'Hearn's in 1963. Charles Elson's 1953 unit set for *Don Giovanni,* a cumbersome, curving ramp that reminded the irreverent of a traffic cloverleaf, was replaced by Eugene Berman's impressive but excessively detailed Seville only four seasons later. Gérard's *Faust* of 1953, which put Méphistophélès in top hat and tails (staged erratically by Peter Brook, the London wonder), was succeeded by the French Jacques Dupont's in 1965, in turn not altogether innocent of mixing styles between abstraction and realism, and leaning heavily on symbolism. Some superb crowd scenes directed by Jean Louis Barrault and reminiscent of Breughel redeemed this production. The other replacements were for the Heavenly Twins. Horace Armistead overdesigned *Cavalleria Rusticana* and underdid *Pagliacci* in Bing's first year; the controversial sets were scrapped in favor of Gérard's in 1958.

Theatrical designers have not been uniformly successful, even when they had gained opera experience before working for the Met. Harry Horner's *Magic Flute,* using a few slide projections by Leo Kerz, had its day and gave way to Marc Chagall's in 1967. Kerz's projections for *Parsifal,* unveiled in 1955, were still current ten years later. Oliver Smith, swamped with demands for Broadway and ballet designs, turned about and swamped the Met's *Traviata* with two mammoth staircases, the one in Flora's "palace" occupying so much space that the farandole had to be danced on a supper table. By contrast, the second-act summerhouse would barely hold one occupant. This production, young by Met standards—ten years—was shelved in favor of Cecil Beaton's, with only one staircase. The point about staircases is that directors have to make the actors play to and on them. Gérard's in the first act of *Carmen* offered irresistible temptation—or compulsion—to Tyrone Guthrie, so that characters ran busily up and down, posing at intervals, and Risë Stevens as the Gypsy was carried up and down by stalwart citizens of Seville.

Smith also joined forces with Motley (Elizabeth Montgomery), one of the most respected designers and costumers for Broadway, Britain, and points between, for the fussiest fiasco in a decade, the *Martha* of 1960, which Bing's old boss, Carl Ebert, had the misfortune to direct, and which earned from *Time* magazine the subtitle, "The Last Rose of Flotow." What Irving Kolodin in the *Saturday Review* called the "cheap, illiterate, vulgar English libretto" didn't help. Its author asked that her name be removed, but Kolodin thought it didn't matter whether she was Ann Ronell or "Ann Onymous." Ebert veered from "valid realization of sentimental moments" to heavy, stilted comic ones. Even Flotow's charming old tunes didn't compensate. Motley's *Trovatore* the previous year had been unremarkable as opera sets go; many did not realize that the old ones had been replaced.

Esteban Frances' *Ernani,* chided by Paul Henry Lang in the *Herald Tribune* for the blindingly sequined costume of Carlos, which would "suffice for all the road signs from here to Charlemagne's tomb," will probably still hold the stage and the dazzled eye if *Ernani* is revived, while the prospect of watching intimate laundry flap from a line in Count Almaviva's noble palace seems unending as long as Oliver Messel's otherwise rather commonplace settings for *Le Nozze di Figaro* remain.

Messel's vast experience in English opera, theatre, and ballet should have produced something more viable, too, than the *Ariadne auf Naxos* of 1962, although Strauss's split-level opera is notoriously hard to design. But both, as well as Gérard's *Così fan tutte,* might have seemed more satisfactory if they had been tailored for the Met in the first place, instead of being merely let out from original Glyndeborne designs.

Ita Maximowa's luridly colored *Ballo* of 1961 was followed by the *Manon* that shares with *Martha* the honors for a booby prize. This olla-podrida involved a French composer, Polish designer, German director, American conductor, and three Italian-American principals—only the Russian-Swedish Nicolai Gedda approximated a French style, and he was soon relieved by an American, while a Hungarian took over the baritone role. This kind of mixture need not be poisonous, but some evil alchemy operated, the more noticeable in a season that sparkled with Zeffirelli's *Falstaff* and Montresor's *Last Savage,* and also boasted a good *Aida.*

Rolf Gérard has received the most commissions among the stable of designers, his total being fifteen, plus a revised *Rosenkavalier* and a ballet, *Les Sylphides.* Bing's first curtain rose on his *Don Carlo.* His *Eugene Onegin* (for which Peter Brook returned as director) and *Hoffmann* were most ambitious; *Bohème* the most atmospheric; *Fledermaus* perhaps the most successful. *Tannhäuser* and *Sonnambula* must rank low in the scale.

Eugene Berman, the noted Russian painter, has provided five substantial mountings, of which perhaps the *Rigoletto* of Bing's second year is most gratifying, although suffering a last-act change of style from High Renaissance to a kind of surrealism, with jagged, broken structures of red brick monopolizing the dreary landscape and reducing Sparafucile's tavern to ridiculously tiny proportions. There is hardly room for the Duke to turn around in the upstairs chamber, let alone lie down. No wonder he left early. Either the awkwardness of the set or the squeamishness of the director (Herbert Graf) brought a violation of the principle of leaving the "fourth wall" open to spectators when, as Gilda was about to be murdered, a curtain was drawn across this opening, invariably producing a momentary shock.

Olin Downes of the *Times* allowed himself to describe Berman's *Forza del Destino* of 1952 as "going off with a Bing!" After a charming

Barbiere di Siviglia, Berman completed his Metropolitan rounds with *Don Giovanni* and *Otello.* All four "grand operas" were staged by the well-seasoned Graf.

Between the advent, at Bing's halfway mark, of José Quintero, moving spirit of New York's Circle in the Square, to restage *Cav-Pag,* and Margaret Webster's first opera venture in 1950, five additional nonopera directors tried their hand at opera, grand or comic: Garson Kanin, Tyrone Guthrie, Alfred Lunt, Joseph Mankiewicz, and Cyril Ritchard. Kanin was responsible for *Fledermaus,* most enduring of the three operettas that have gone far to prove Bing's contention that customers like a little icing on their cake, especially at holiday time. Kanin, who brought his inimitable cheekiness to the shenanigans in Johann Strauss's name, worked with the colloquial libretto of Howard Dietz. Offenbach's *Périchole,* introduced a few years later, also reveals signs of persisting, but Strauss's *Gypsy Baron,* faintly remembered as the controversial benefit for Manager Heinrich Conried years before, was a crashing bore, even with a cast that included the actor Walter Slezak, son of the Met's former gigantic tenor and himself acutely conscious of his heritage and his own comedic talents. All three had fancy decor by Gérard; the two latter moved under the fine Australian hand of Ritchard, who had been introduced in *Barbiere di Siviglia* in 1953–54 with a "fresh and joyous version, bubbling over with high spirits," according to Louis Biancolli of the *World-Telegram and The Sun.* The saucy actor-director of sophisticated theatre and musical comedy found opera so congenial that he returned for *Les Contes d'Hoffmann* two years later and in *La Périchole* even made his singing (!) debut as the amorous Viceroy of Peru. *Le Nozze di Figaro* was also entrusted to Ritchard in the same year as his *Gypsy Baron,* 1959–60. Both were rapped as being even too comic.

Towering over six feet, the British Tyrone Guthrie arrived in Bing's second year for *Carmen,* a choreographic effort that reaped as many Nays as Yeas from the critics. Guthrie was too much occupied elsewhere to give Bing his services again until the equivocal *Traviata* of 1957. Alfred Lunt instilled grace into the 1951 *Così fan tutte.* A recruit from Hollywood in this period was Joseph Mankiewicz, who lent many telling touches to the *Bohème,* which was sung both in Italian and English. The vernacular version by Howard Dietz didn't catch on and was soon abandoned; so was the staging detail that had Mimi and Rodolfo remaining in the studio at the end of the first act with the obvious intent of consummating their relationship before joining the Christmas Eve merriment at the Café Momus.

Bing's reliance on the sister media for both direction and design has continued intermittently. Webster returned for her third duty, the *Simon Boccanegra* designed by Frederick Fox, famous on Broadway for more than 200 shows and in television for color spectaculars. Fox had already accommodated Bing with a grandiloquent *Andrea Chénier* and a revision of *Tosca*.

Without question, the greatest excitement in Bing's stewardship was kindled by the *Falstaff* of 1963–64, both designed and directed by that Italian whirlwind, Franco Zeffirelli, who had astonished New York with his earthy, realistic Old Vic production of *Romeo and Juliet* and brought some of the same robustness to Verdi's Shakespeare. Although not of the same powerful caliber, Beni Montresor's bewitching fantasies for Menotti's *Last Savage* further enhanced the season. Montresor, who designed films in Italy, later fashioned theatre productions as well; his first operas were for Menotti's Spoleto Festival and Glyndebourne. The year 1963–64 also brought the new *Aida* of Robert O'Hearn and Nathaniel Merrill, the Americans who had come to the Met with *Elisir d'Amore* (and its diverting balloon landing for Dr. Dulcamara) in 1960. Merrill's directing experience had been solely in opera (Tanglewood, Boston University, Hamburg, Wiesbaden, Glyndebourne, assistant, then full title at the Met), but O'Hearn began in the theatre. His first opera was *Falstaff* for Sarah Caldwell in Boston, followed by Stravinsky's *Rake's Progress,* when he joined Merrill. The two have since worked well together for the Met in *Meistersinger* and *Samson et Dalila. Meistersinger* was especially praised, although some observers objected to the switch to a kind of stylization in the third act, when the Nuremberg maidens, all dancing about in anachronistic accordion-pleated skirts, disturbed the authenticity previously shown. O'Hearn and Merrill have occasionally split up, as when the former's *Queen of Spades* was directed by Henry Butler, originally a protégé of Gian-Carlo Menotti, and the latter directed *Adriana Lecouvreur* with C. M. Cristini's sets to sketches by Camillo Paravicini.

Motohiro Nagasaka's authentic and delicate *Madama Butterfly* in 1957–58 elicited approval from even the most jaded viewers, while his sets were matched by the meticulous staging of Yoshio Aoyama, Kabuki

expert before he undertook opera. Aoyama (with Merrill) also lent cre-
dence to Cecil Beaton's riotously colored *Turandot* a few seasons later.

It is interesting to note that while legitimate theatre directors whizzed
around him like pinwheels, Graf remained at the core of the Met's staging, receiving as many commissions for new productions (twelve) as the
other two next in line combined—the young Nathaniel Merrill with
seven and the veteran Dino Yannopoulos with five. Taken all in all, this
part of the operation has remained conservative in spite of the splashiness
of the occasional outsider.

Bolstering this element of familiarity were two European dyed-in-
opera imports: Carl Ebert and Günther Rennert. In addition to the
frivolous *Martha* and the languishing *Ariadne*, Ebert's chores included
the supervision of *Così* for one year only and the somber *Macbeth*. None
rewarded him, and he returned to California. Rennert drew a dud in
Manon and won hardly more *réclame* for *Nabucco* (the first at the Met,
with bargain-basement designs by Teo Otto and Wolfgang Roth), *Ballo*,
and the recent *Salome*, with its turgid scenery dominated by projected
slides devised by Rudolf Heinrich. Margherita Wallmann's inauspicious
debut as director of the heavy *Lucia* production by Attilio Colonello that
opened 1964 earned for her the backstage nickname of "Dr. Strangeglove"
because she never removed her hand coverings.

Considering Bing's avowal that the Metropolitan is a museum like
its sister and namesake uptown, it is perhaps unfair to criticize the opera
curator for neglect of newborn works. "With an unsubsidized company,
the public is always right," he declared. "And that public loves what it
knows—it is inalterably conservative. Europe can afford to do things the
public doesn't necessarily want—it is an age-old tradition in Germany,
for example—but we cannot afford to antagonize subscribers to that extent, no matter how heavily we may be subscribed at any one time. Subscribers are not ours till death do us part. They can get a divorce any
time."

In spite of this conservatism, the air of sheer daring does hang over
Bing's years, because of the sweeping changes in all decor. Only one pre-
Bing setting went along when the Met left the Old House—*Manon
Lescaut*. Bing achieved his primary purpose: truckloads of bright drops,
clean furniture, and fresh costumes. Asked to recall his favorites among
fifty-six new mountings, he reverts instantly to his very first *Don Carlo*,

then skips to the *Faust* that inaugurated the last year in the old House. It is rather saddening to sum up the outright production triumphs, less than half the total: *Falstaff, Fledermaus, Périchole, Turandot, Last Savage, Bohème,* and *Butterfly,* and add the partial successes: *Meistersinger, Aida, Forza, Rigoletto, Giovanni, Samson, Otello,* and *Barbiere*—an astonishingly uneven tablature of taste for so much time, effort, talent, and money.

But it must be said for Bing that once a setting is under way, he has never withdrawn it, even though he may regret his initial commission. In fact, he could not commit so arbitrary a gesture in the face of costs and the relentless pressure of deadlines. "Only Felsenstein in East Berlin could get away with such a thing," he commented. Once a design is in the works, Bing is stuck with it.

A few single efforts remain in the mind: the *Alcestis* design and direction in 1960–61 by Michael Manuel, who had previously worked as executive stage manager and became co-manager with Risë Stevens of the Met's National Company; the earlier *Don Pasquale,* in which Wolfgang Roth first used a revolving stage, inserted somehow in the Met's old inner workings; the Gérard *Arabella* of 1955, marking the first appearance in New York of this appealing Strauss heroine. Some oddities also cropped up: the *Boris* of 1953, partly lifted by Mstislav Dobujinsky from his *Khovanshchina* production for Johnson's last season; the skimpy trees in Gérard's *Faust* and Otto's semi-abstract *Tristan* as opposed to the monster ash in Lee Simonson's *Walküre. Tristan* remains with us, unfortunately for other aspects of the design as well, but Bing promised sorely needed new *Ring* trappings, beginning in 1967.

Productions were required during these fifteen years for only four actual novelties, of which the Met could claim as absolutely original only one—Samuel Barber's *Vanessa,* ushered to stage in 1957–58, designed by Cecil Beaton in Northern Gothic and perceptively directed by Barber's librettist, Gian Carlo Menotti. The latter's own *Last Savage* came to America in 1963–64 after its lukewarm premiere in Paris; similarly Stravinsky's *Rake's Progress,* in Armistead's trappings, reached the Met's stage in 1952–53 after its initial showing in Venice. Engaging George Balanchine to direct the *Rake* led to no firm conclusions on the advisability of a choreographer taking over the dramatic stage. To the Met's board of directors, which had haggled over it for years, Berg's *Wozzeck* (designed by Caspar Neher) seemed a novelty, although its world premiere occurred in 1925 and it had already been given in New York by Leopold Stokowski and the Philadelphia Orchestra in 1931 (and in the Met itself!) and by the New York City Opera in 1952.

The General Manager's results with conductors are as perplexing as his stage ventures. The list of the great and near great he has hired reads like a *Who's Who of the Baton,* yet the overall impression is not of musical scintillance but rather of patchwork.

From Bing's beginning, Fritz Reiner, Fritz Stiedry, and Bruno Walter were retained, Alberto Erede and Fausto Cleva engaged. Erede stayed only five years, too short a period considering his fire and verve and his ability to hold a performance together, plus the fact that the singers liked him. Cleva, the former chorus master who got the bulk of his pit experience elsewhere, remained to become the inevitable *routinier,* always dependable, increasingly uninspiring.

Eugene Ormandy's presence as guest to lead *Fledermaus* resulted from Bing's decision not to let Reiner do it, prompted by a conflicting record contract. The two Hungarians were always at each other's throats during Ormandy's early days with the Philadelphia Orchestra and Reiner's as head of Curtis Institute in that city (Reiner was also a proud guest conductor in many centers and shared the Philadelphia Orchestra's brief but glorious opera season before Ormandy arrived). Each had attained superiority—Reiner at the opera, Ormandy with the orchestra—at this time, so they could stand to be in the same House without actual bloodshed; nevertheless, the private mutterings turned fairly sulfurous. Ormandy returned for one more season, but after that, *Fledermaus* fell to another Hungarian, Tibor Kozma, and to various other batons until the expert, Franz Allers, symphonically trained but with unique Broadway experience in Lerner and Loewe shows, took over the operetta department at Thirty-ninth Street in 1963.

When Reiner left in 1953 to return to the comparatively peaceful symphonic world in Chicago, some of the luster went out of the orchestra he had trained with his infallible technique. The men may have squirmed under his whiplash discipline, but they played for him. All his performances were not as glowing as some, for Reiner was subject to fits of boredom (notably in *Don Giovanni*), as if the gods wearied for a spell of their own omnipotence and chose not to give off sparks. Nevertheless, when he felt in the mood, his *Salome, Rosenkavalier, Tristan,* and *Elektra* raised unforgettable standards. Bing gave him no chance to repeat the flawless *Falstaff* of Johnson's penultimate year. In 1963–64, in ill-health, Reiner was slated to return for *Götterdämmerung,* but suffered a fatal heart attack during rehearsals.

Stiedry, a friend of Bing's from prewar Germany, stayed on until 1958 with his massive authority, but growing hard of hearing and gradually slowing down until his Wagnerian nights kept stage and orchestra managers in nervous perspiration as their stopwatch hands circled on toward midnight and union overtime. Walter returned for scattered seasons before his death in 1962. He was "the heart and soul" of the *Magic Flute* in 1955–56, according to Irving Kolodin in the *Saturday Review.* And George Szell came back for a *Tannhäuser* revival in 1953, appearing for only four performances before he resigned in a blaze of publicity, proclaiming darkly that he did not approve of the way things were handled on Thirty-ninth Street. It was quite obvious that he had no control of his casts and assumed that he would preside over a new production of *Tannhäuser.* Without the authority he considered due him, he was having no more of the Bing monarchy.

The grand old man Pierre Monteux opened the 1953–54 season with *Faust* and stayed another couple of years to demonstrate his complete mastery of music and men in *Pelléas, Orfeo ed Euridice, Les Contes d'Hoffmann,* and the more conventional French operas. In the middle of his final season, his repertoire was assumed by the assistant conductors Kurt Adler (also chorus master) and Martin Rich. For Monteux's admirers this was too little and almost too late, although the magical *Maître* could have gone on awhile; he died only in 1964 at ninety.

Two men arrived in 1954 with enormous prestige and potentiality for the Met: Rudolf Kempe, from Dresden and Munich, and Dimitri Mitropoulos from Carnegie Hall, where he was the New York Philharmonic's presiding genius. Kempe, making his New York debut with *Tannhäuser* and continuing with *Arabella* and *Tristan,* then adding *Meistersinger* and *Rosenkavalier* in his second season, was considered a true man of the theatre but had no chance to deepen the good impression. Illness kept him away for a time, and he has been too busy in

Europe since, notably in London and at Bayreuth, where he conducted Wolfgang Wagner's new *Ring* production.

Mitropoulos, brought to the House for *Salome*, was immediately hailed for his flaming way with the score—urging "sonorities and waves of sound from his crew that were downright blistering in their heat," wrote Jay Harrison in the *Herald Tribune*. He also did a "finely balanced" *Ballo*, according to Paul Henry Lang, once conducting the Verdi work the very next afternoon after the Strauss. Orchestra conductors often indulge in this tandem performance, although usually with the same program; with two difficult operas it was a test of endurance. The Greek Maestro's ensuing duties were *Tosca, Boris, Manon Lescaut, Ernani, Butterfly, Carmen,* and *Walküre,* not all equally brilliant. In fact, his *Ernani* was dubbed erratic. He opened the 1957–58 season with *Eugene Onegin* (one of Bing's unfathomable choices for this gala occasion) and added the world premiere of *Vanessa* and the mirthful *Gianni Schicchi* to accompany *Salome*; launched 1958–59 with *Tosca,* two nights later did *Boris* and added *Cav-Pag.* Then in 1959 a heart attack prevented him from leading the first Metropolitan *Macbeth* and his only new production was the *Simon Boccanegra* (the next to last appearance of Leonard Warren). Mitropoulos planned to return for the elaborate *Turandot* on February 24, 1961, a benefit for the Opera Guild. On November 2, 1960, just before a rehearsal of Mahler's Third Symphony at La Scala, wrote Gerald Fitzgerald in *Opera News,* Mitropoulos likened himself to "an old automobile that still works. After about ten minutes he stopped conducting, and, before anyone could reach him, toppled from the podium; he died on the way to the hospital."

At the opera house, where one of his previous revivals, *Boris Godunov,* was being conducted by Erich Leinsdorf, the news saddened and dismayed everyone, not least the orchestra men, who had given him rare devotion. The management rallied and quickly approached Leopold Stokowski, who had conducted only a few works at the New York City Center since his *Wozzeck* in 1931. The splendidly tailored Maestro, his famous aureole of blond hair thinned and whitened, created a sensation when he hobbled into the pit on crutches. His gameness after surgery on a broken hip won as much sympathy as his continuing mastery won admiration. He vitalized the Puccini work one season, led a few performances in a second, then withdrew. With constant changes of cast under Kurt Adler, the excellent production went downhill fast. In 1964 a revival under Cleva was similarly checkered with cast replacements.

What happened to *Turandot* is fairly typical, an example of the restlessness and uncertainty that pervade the orchestra pit. Another case is Georg Solti, one of those enkindling Hungarians who came to the Met after a rich experience in Europe—Salzburg with Toscanini, Munich, Frankfort, Glyndebourne, Edinburgh, and London—then American orchestras and two opera houses, San Francisco and Chicago. Arriving in New York in 1960, he led *Tannhäuser* (soon taken over by Ignace Strasfogel), was absent the next season, and returned in 1962 to conduct *Boris, Tristan,* and *Otello,* a repertoire and performance that led many to believe another Szell was in our midst. In the following year he was given *Aida, Don Carlo,* and the Verdi Requiem and thereafter disappeared from the Met, to take over the musical direction of Covent Garden and engage in such fascinating pursuits as producing Schönberg's *Moses and Aaron.*

Ernest Ansermet was called in for a single experience with a "non-opera," Manuel de Falla's *Atlantida,* the Met's contribution to the opening of Philharmonic Hall in Lincoln Center in 1962. The distinguished leader of many European orchestras, notably the Suisse-Romande, contributed *Pelléas et Mélisande* in an unprecedented five performances in the House, but has never exhibited his superb talent since.

Leonard Bernstein was wooed away from the New York Philharmonic and presided for one season over the greatest success of the decade, the *Falstaff* of 1963–64. But this all-round virtuoso, darling of many worlds including the jet set, Broadway, and television, has not squeezed the Met again into his tight schedule, though he found time for the Vienna State Opera. Also out of the American symphonic realm came William Steinberg, one of the world's most expert, for a single season while he was on sabbatical leave from the Pittsburgh Symphony. His assignments were *Walküre, Aida,* and *Vanessa.* Brought up in Europe, he had not been confined to the "wing" system, and had led many diverse matters in San Francisco. The tendency to stray over national lines is becoming more usual at the Met, although less comfortably, perhaps, with Georges Prêtre, who has a way with his native French repertoire (*Samson* and *Faust*) but is less masterful in *Tristan, Trovatore,* or *Parsifal.* Before him, the excellently schooled Frenchman Jean Morel, who had registered well in San Francisco and at the New York City Opera, cut across boundaries twice, with *Butterfly* and *Orfeo,* and was appreciated in *Périchole,* away from the limited French territory in his six seasons.

The Austrian Karl Böhm, as authoritative as a volcano, illumined Wagner, Mozart, and Strauss, as well as *Fidelio,* in a half dozen seasons from 1957. Joseph Rosenstock's vindication in 1960 led to a steady succession of assignments in the German kingdom. Erich Leinsdorf piled up successful years before going to the Boston Symphony in 1962. One conductor who never really got the appreciation he deserved also left the House in which he had so faithfully served as Bing's lieutenant from the first—Max Rudolf, whose departure for Cincinnati and its orchestra in 1958 left a gap in both the administration and the pit.

Bing has not been unwilling to engage young conducting talent. Three exponents have produced a great deal of interest and some excitement. The senior in service is Thomas Schippers; the latest recruit, Zubin Mehta; the middle one, since departed, Loren Maazel. A grown-up prodigy, volatile and mettlesome, Maazel did not settle down in 1962. He was accused by interested parties of paying more attention to the orchestra than to the singers, but his *Rosenkavalier* and *Don Giovanni* were absorbing if a bit shaky. Reengaged for *Magic Flute* the next season, he suffered an accident and could not return; later he was claimed as musical director of the West Berlin Opera. Mehta, who came from India by way of the Los Angeles Philharmonic, plunged into Metropolitan affairs with a fiery *Aida* in 1965 and made a place for himself.

Schippers has become the golden boy on the conductors' staff, receiving choice assignments all the way from his debut in 1955 with *Don Pasquale* to *Queen of Spades* in 1965. It is an indication of the management's capricious treatment of conductors that after Mehta's success with *Aida* and Schippers' with *Otello* the assignments were reversed, giving neither time to consolidate his gains.

A protégé of Gian-Carlo Menotti, whose *Consul, Amahl,* and *Saint of Bleecker Street* he conducted, Schippers has done everything "first" and "youngest." He was the youngest American ever to conduct at the Met; the first American to lead an opening night *(Nabucco* in 1960), the first American to conduct the Met in Paris *(Barbiere* in 1966). He fills most duties capably, many brilliantly, having a real flair for instilling fire and *brio* into the early Verdi works such as *Ernani.* Among his European stands are La Scala, Bayreuth, and annual appearances at Menotti's fashionable Festival of Two Worlds at Spoleto, Italy, where he is artistic director. Tall and boyishly handsome, he deserves a place among what society writers call the Beautiful People by his marriage to the highly social Nonie Phipps, a cousin by marriage of Mrs. Ogden Phipps.

Meanwhile, back at the House the Italians continue to grind it out. Cleva leads the way, followed for a few seasons by the lesser practitioners, Nino Verchi and Nello Santi. The advent in 1965 of Francesco Molinari-Pradelli, who has been welcomed in all the major opera houses of the world (including San Francisco), lends brilliance to the scene. Presiding over *Ballo, Rigoletto,* and *Andrea Chénier,* he relinquished *Rigoletto* to another Italian newcomer, Lamberto Gardelli, who stepped in to spell Cleva during the latter's illness in 1965. Joan Sutherland brought a Swiss along in 1961, Silvio Varviso, who conducted her *Lucia* and *Sonnambula* and was allowed excursions into *Magic Flute* and *Ariadne,* but departed after 1965–66 to direct the Stockholm Royal Opera.

The roster differentiates between "conductors," "associates," and "assistants," currently placing another two, Kurt Adler and George Schick, among the first; Jan Behr, Ignace Strasfogel, and Martin Rich in the second; and nine names, plus a prompter, in the third. Adler is the former chorus master; Schick, a veteran of wide experience and competence. The others have risen from the ranks, and do an honorable job of preparation, coaching, and supervising myriad details of a performance. But no matter what their talents, they are too often sent to the pit to carry on a series of performances originally shaped by the conductor. The lapse in tautness, efficiency, and mastery is almost invariable. Occasionally one will flame out, as Behr did, and hold out the hope that he may climb into the upper bracket. But the power of inertia is too strong and these takeovers seldom scale the peaks. When one subscription audience hears Mehta or Böhm or Molinari-Pradelli and another draws one of the lesser lights, and both are paying $15.50 top, the latter crowd may well feel cheated. Without mastery on the podium, an opera performance is meaningless. The deterioration in production values when a director has departed after one season is perhaps not so noticeable to unsophisticated audiences, but it contributes almost equally to the suspicion that screws are loose somewhere. It should be possible to bring the original stage director back for the first of a repeat series just to tighten up lighting cues, singers' actions, and crowd movements. "Production by" one man and "Staged by" another appears too often in the Met's programs. Bringing back the original conductor is more difficult when he has passed on to new works or even out of the Met's domain. The only solution to this problem is to keep enough masters around and keep them happy. While this picture may improve in the future, the management has not yet become a champion of these imperious ones. Bing's Golden Age of Conductors has yet to dawn.

21

HOW MANY CROWNS?

I hate the word "star."

—RUDOLF BING,
in a TV interview

Rudolf Bing assumed office on the campaign promise to do away with the star system, echoing the sentiments of others before him, notably Damrosch, Conried, Witherspoon, and Johnson. None fully lived up to the pledge; only Leopold Damrosch achieved a temporary homogeneous ensemble. Conried found Caruso to be the key to popularity. Witherspoon's reign was too short to count, but Johnson carried on the idea, although he inherited from Gatti-Casazza such luminaries as Tibbett, Pons, Flagstad, Melchior, and Pinza, and eventually added Milanov, Traubel, Stevens, and Björling on his own. All these gentlemen learned the hard way that the public continued to dote on the prima donna of either sex and stubbornly held on to the belief that grand opera connoted, was even synonymous with, the star image. To paraphrase a *New York Times* critic's recent dictum: "It don't mean a thing if the singers can't sing."

Bing has apparently absorbed this prickly truth at last, although in a recent television interview he blurted out his opinion of the word "star." He was asked what he would substitute. "A superb artistic personality who can catch an audience both off and on stage," he offered. It seemed like a lot of words to replace one. But he added the distinction: "A star is rarely an artist."

The General Manager has not of course freed himself from bondage to the singing voice—what opera boss could? Opera exists to be sung—a truism. And in spite of his efforts and his impatience, at least six great ladies of opera should be indispensable to him, whatever the definition of their qualities: Maria Callas, Renata Tebaldi, Birgit Nilsson, Joan Sutherland, Leontyne Price, and Eileen Farrell. He has yielded to temperamental demands from most of them, but the public knows only his spectacular clashes with Callas.

327

Two gentlemen—or shall we call them tenors?—have also asked for and got concessions far beyond the bounds of reasonableness: Mario del Monaco and Franco Corelli. Neither will sing in the same house with the other, so a manager must choose between them. The Met *had* Del Monaco; it *has* Corelli. There are rumors that the former would be willing to relax a bit and return to New York, sharing the billing of *primo tenore,* but the latter will not hear of it.

One exception to this imperious attitude is furnished by the Met's star bass, Cesare Siepi, who seems to get along equably; if he incurs any rifts with management, they never appear. Furthermore, he has even reneged on opera in favor of musical comedy (unsuccessfully) and been welcomed back cordially, and held his own against the newest bass sensation, Nicola Ghiarov.

On a plateau slightly below, several "superb artistic personalities" function distinctively; many call them stars, but their fuel is not the stuff that projects them into the stratosphere—among them Régine Crespin, Leonie Rysanek, Victoria de los Angeles, Lisa Della Casa, Christa Ludwig, Rita Gorr, Nicolai Gedda, Jon Vickers, and Sandor Konya, as well as a few newcomers. These are truly international ones, who sing everywhere and in many languages and almost always with superior art. Bing makes his seasons mainly out of their services, together with the topflight Americans and dozens of good and useful others. But that half dozen or so are even greater than stars—they are the blazing suns of the day. Bing cannot do without them; no manager can. The season would pass superlatives that contained them all. But it is safe to bet that will never happen here, chiefly because Callas will probably never come back—nor will Farrell.

Callas is a very special case. In 1945–46, as an intense, overweight, black-eyed Greek-American, she auditioned for Johnson at the request of her countryman, Nicola Moscona, who had already had seven years of admirable service as a leading bass. (Moscona had refused the girl's request that he impose on Toscanini for an audition.) Callas' Metropolitan hearing was thought good enough to produce a contract, but one she felt bound to refuse. It meant singing *Fidelio* in English and *Madama Butterfly*, the kind of incongruous casting that Johnson (among others) seemed prone to. Leonore eventually was taken by Regina Resnik, while Cio-Cio-San was left to the more appropriate Licia Albanese. Thus it happened that Maria Callas did not come to New York for another ten years, in which, to put it mildly, a great many things happened to both the Met and herself.

In his sixth season, Bing visited behind scenes at Chicago's Lyric Opera with contract in hand and lips pursed to kiss the hand of his new prize, now known as *La Divina* in Milan and elsewhere. With him as prime minister was Francis Robinson. This was after a *Trovatore* in her second season for Carol Fox. A few nights later, after her final performance, the diva encountered a battery of process servers, bent on redressing alleged wrongs done to her "original" benefactors, Edward Bagarozy, brother of the *World-Telegram* critic Robert Bagar, and his wife, Louise Caselotti. (The Bagarozys had assumed management and teacher duties, respectively, under a signed contract giving them 10 percent of the lady's earnings.) Callas, slimmed down sensationally and no longer averse to simulating the petite Japanese, was still in her *Butterfly* kimono. To plunge from the heights of exaltation at the audience's frenetic farewells to the dark cavern of legal indignity affected Maria as if a waterfall had suddenly landed in the red-hot crater of Vesuvius. The photographers on hand got what was probably the ugliest picture of Callas ever published—a raging Erinys, eyes blazing, wide mouth open over clenched teeth. Such E's in alt had never been heard in any role.

The incident, for which she blamed the Chicago management, made only more portentous her engagement by the Metropolitan. Her debut as Norma on opening night of 1956 brought back to Broadway some of the glamour that had been missing too long. Her colleagues, Fedora Barbieri, Del Monaco, and Siepi, even dared Bing's wrath by slyly leaving Norma alone to take solo bows, recently interdicted. New York was not ready to swallow Callas whole, however. An article in *Time* before her debut had shown up her feud with her mother and various other flaws. Temperament can be forgiven a diva, but not repudiation of her mother. Moreover, quite a few Met patrons thought she hadn't even sung very well.

Four additional impersonations of the Bellini priestess, an equal number of Lucias, and two Toscas completed her initial stand. She encountered no competition as Norma, nor could the substitution of Dolores Wilson as Lucia on one night when the diva pleaded illness dim her luster, although long after her departure, Lily Pons came back to her own fandom, singing the mad Lucy twice. *Tosca* was later sung by five others, including Tebaldi, the only prima donna who could lay claim to a pedestal as lofty as Callas'. But the battle of the divas, so fearfully and deliciously anticipated, never came off. Bing was too canny to permit them both in the House at the same time; only Carol Fox seems to have got away with that double exposure. The two reigning queens had even appeared back to back in the daring Chicago season of 1955, alternating as Elvira in *Puritani* and Aida, Leonora in *Trovatore* and Mimi on succeeding nights.

Still, Fox couldn't control her prima donnas offstage. Callas attended Tebaldi's debut in *grande toilette,* and somehow managed to lose a diamond bracelet during the third act of *Aida* as her rival agonized over losing her country. For appreciable moments, the audience didn't know which action to follow, Tebaldi behind the footlights or Callas behind a flashlight.

The New York situation was further complicated by the presence of Zinka Milanov, who never considered herself a whit less worthy of attention than the other two. When either rival sang, she had a habit of strolling down the aisles to a front seat just as an act was about to begin, drawing attention from her loyal coterie. Indulgence in this bit of arrogance at Callas' debut drew a rebuke from Tebaldi in a magazine article. Milanov sailed serenely through both the Callas and Tebaldi sectors that season, happy with her *Trovatore, Aida, Gioconda, Cavalleria,* and a new *Ernani.* After all, Callas hadn't rated a new production. *Lucia* was in tatters and *Norma* on the downhill, past its "revision." Tebaldi was also soothed by a specially designed *Traviata.* It was no wonder that the imperious Callas chafed for a fresh setting by her third season. Bing's proposal of *Macbeth* seemed ideal until Callas learned she would have to alternate this dark, dramatically taxing role too closely with the lighter but equally strenuous Violetta. On her arrival in America in 1958, she let out a queen-size grumble. Bing, who is not to be bested at this kind of dialogue, compromised only to the extent of offering Lucia instead of Violetta, ignoring the fact that the pitiful Bride of Lammermoor is even more of a vocal contrast with Lady Macbeth, though both are murderesses in their way. In any case, Callas was understandably sick of the *Lucia* sets. There seems to have ensued a certain amount of shillying and shallying on the diva's part; she was profitably busy with a concert tour and a few gold-plated appearances in Dallas, where Carol Fox's estranged partner, Lawrence Kelley, made a great pet of the prima donna. She was starring—and no nonsense about it—in *Traviata* and *Medea,* mounted lavishly for her (but as diverse as the roles Bing had proposed).

"In Dallas we are doing Art," remarked Callas smugly. (In New York they were doing an opening *Tosca* with Tebaldi.) Then in Dallas, as they were rehearsing *Medea,* Bing wired to know the lady's contractual intentions—by ten the next morning, please. Too absorbed with *Medea,* she didn't answer. The telegram that arrived in midafternoon, together with Bing's statement to the press, left no loophole—Callas was out. And the Met, "grateful for her artistry for two seasons . . . is nevertheless also grateful that the association is ended." (Rysanek would make her debut as Lady Macbeth, Bing announced simultaneously, showing that he had given the matter some previous thought. But Rysanek's repertoire didn't include the other Callas roles.)

Maria got through *Medea* in fine, furious style, taking out her spleen on the doubly unfortunate Creon and Jason, then exploded into print. "All those lousy *Traviata*s [Bing] made me do without rehearsals, without even knowing my partners. . . . Is that Art?"

This was only another in the chain of opera houses she had "burned behind her," as Bing noted. She had canceled Edinburgh, Vienna, Rome, and San Francisco. She would walk out of La Scala. As *Musical America* put it in an editorial: "It is clear that she is an all but impossible lady to deal with on a business basis. It is equally clear that she is one of the most incandescent, and therefore most fascinating, artistic personalities to be visited upon this glamour-starved generation."

Callas had already taken her place beside baseball heroes and denizens of the so-called jet set as object of attention on several continents, whether adored or abominated. But where could she sing now?

She was by virtue of her front-page magnetism a celebrity in the widest sense, one of the "hottest properties" in show business, which is somewhat different in range and objective from mere opera. She toured that 1958 season in concerts, accepted an invitation to sing Bellini's *Pirata* in concert form with the American Opera Society in Carnegie Hall, took time to visit in the limelight with her onetime enemy, now turned sycophant, the columnist party-giver Elsa Maxwell, and prophesied solemnly that she would always win out "until God kisses my voice." Paris justified this prediction by overwhelming her with adulation at a gala concert, and the Paris Opéra joined London's Covent Garden and Dallas, which still burningly wanted her. She patched up several rifts, but because she loathed the advance plans that opera managements find mandatory, there was always an aura of uneasiness about her schedules until she was actually in the house.

Whatever kept the prima donna in the public eye, she created an image that fascinated and at the same time repelled—a passionate, arrogant woman who disliked her own mother and imperiously wrecked a household for her own desires. That this household consisted of possibly the richest man on the Continent and his beautiful young wife added the touches of opulence and sinning expected by hungry readers of the sensational press. Aristotle Onassis had appeared on the Callas scene many times before the cataclysm of 1959. He was Greece's most fabulous citizen; they even called him Ulysses. He practically bossed Monte Carlo and Monaco (until Prince Rainier bought him out in 1967); his yacht *Cristina* sheltered more priceless paintings than many a gallery. Maria's 1959 cruise on the *Cristina* precipitated a crisis with her husband of ten years, businessman Battista Meneghini, who had supported and managed his wife through the tortuous channels of her opera career, shrewdly but not always diplomatically. Their separation was made fact that same year, after Tina Onassis had already slipped away for a divorce and subsequent remarriage to the Marquess of Blandford. Still, Maria vowed, as she appeared on the arm of the Greek shipping magnate, that they were but "the best of friends." As if to emphasize the call of Greek to Greek, she later renounced her American citizenship in favor of her ancestors; this made divorce from the Italian possible.

The astonishing fact about Maria Callas is that in America she achieved a nonpareil position with a minimum of singing. By actual count, her operatic appearances total forty-two in eight roles and six seasons; her concerts number about a dozen, plus the *Pirata* with the American Opera Society. The opera count breaks down as follows: thirteen in two Chicago seasons—two each of *Norma, Traviata,* and *Lucia* in 1954; two each of *Puritani* and *Trovatore,* three of *Butterfly* in 1955; twenty-one in three Met seasons—five of *Norma,* four of *Lucia,* two of *Tosca* in 1956–57, and one *Norma* in Philadelphia; two each of *Traviata* and *Tosca,* three of *Lucia* in 1957–58, and the two sold-out gala *Toscas* in 1964–65. Dallas enjoyed a splendid concert in 1957, two *Traviatas* and two *Medeas* in 1958, and two *Lucias* and two *Medeas* in 1959. When this paltry outlay is compared with her Scala record of 157 performances of twenty roles in seven seasons, it is possible to complain that America did not hear the best or most of Callas. Recordings help fill the void, of course, as recordings are apt to do in these high-fidelity days, when the platter takes the place of the person. Reputations are now made in advance—Callas helped set the pattern— and sometimes not lived up to. The perfection of a disc that has taken advantage of electronic science to amputate bad notes and splice in good ones often makes live performances seem shabby. Artists suffer from critics who judge on this basis even more than from fans who admit no flaws in their idols, whether from the living presence or the vinyl disc.

Callas had everything to gain by physical presence (although many of her recordings are triumphs) and so had her audiences. "To see her at work on the stage is to revise upward all previous standards of operatic acting, at least in this generation," wrote Alan Rich in the *Herald Tribune* after the *Tosca* that returned her in excitement and amity to the Met in 1965. "Her every bodily movement conveyed some idea about the woman Tosca, and in the end it was a woman who dominated the stage; not an operatic personality."

Rich concluded that a Callas mystique did not actually exist (on this point he would meet a stubborn resistance from Callas-ites), but that the mystique "is in the nature of opera itself, and it devolves onto Callas merely because she is the total embodiment of the operatic ideal." One is forced to the opinion that Bing is derelict in his duty to the public for not setting aside any and every obstacle and problem in order to bring Callas to the American public. It is sad to come to the conclusion that Bing's dismissal marked the dividing line in Callas' active career. She sang little in public after that, and now is virtually retired at forty-five.

Whatever the limitations of voice as instrument—and Callas always showed flaws that increased with the years and inactivity—no other acting singer (preferable to "singing actress") of our times deserves this

absolute, "total embodiment of the operatic ideal"—not even her closest
rival, the soprano of beauty in voice, face, figure, and, some say, disposition: Renata Tebaldi.

If Callas is dubbed—at least by management—as the "Bad Girl of
Opera," the public thinks of Tebaldi as the "Good Girl." The contrast
is between sun and storm, say a few who profess to know them both. Not
many will admit, of course, to being intimates in both camps—the schism
is too deep. Tebaldi's disciples speak in hushed tones of "the Other
One," never calling Callas by name. Callas fans hardly mention Tebaldi
at all. Tebaldi's calm exterior suppresses emotion that seldom breaks out;
the most severe disturbance occurred after her mother's death. The
mother had been companion, adviser, the only visible object of Renata's
affection. (Comparison to Callas' attitude toward her mother was inevitable.) Tebaldi's loss unnerved her so grievously that Bing allowed her
a season's sabbatical, a dispensation that dispels the old adage that for a
trouper the show must go on no matter what happens. It is difficult to
imagine another singer wresting such a concession from the General
Manager. Her singularly open life has closed a bit since her freedom from
parental observation; she seems happier and, after a slight slip, is singing
better than ever.

Tebaldi in her earlier seasons possessed one of the truly beautiful
and evenly produced voices of the age, though a little short of top range.
Occasionally it could be raised to sharpness when she dictated tempi to a
conductor—a scene seldom witnessed by an outsider, and reminiscent
of the Farrar-Toscanini episode except that this soprano got away with
it. As for her acting, if one is tempted now and then to chide her for
stiffness and compare her inflexible torso to a redwood tree, it should
be remembered that she was afflicted with polio—another reason for her
dependence on her mother—and has valiantly conquered that crippling
disease. She wanted very much to sing Alice Ford in the 1965 *Falstaff*, it
was said, but couldn't manage the complicated arrangement of steps in
Zeffirelli's setting. Her deep piety is thoroughly mixed with the kind of
primitive superstition common to many opera singers, particularly
Italians, who cherish amulets and tokens of every description.

She flouted authority by showing up late for a new production of
Simon Boccanegra in 1959–60 and then sang only two of six performances;
but her strongest display of pique occurred when, after Bing promised

her a revival of *Adriana Lecouvreur,* he canceled the whole 1961–62 season because of an orchestra strike. After the season had been saved, it was too late to mount Cilèa's opera, the General Manager decided. Tebaldi refused to come at all. The next season she demanded and got the part, but defected after six of the ten scheduled performances, vocal insecurities pursuing her. Licia Albanese took over, her first try at the role and without even a piano rehearsal; she sang three times. Mary Curtis-Verna, an American who made a virtue of substitutions, earned a halo for the final performance of the season. Tebaldi has since made a strong vocal comeback.

No one has expressed Tebaldi's magnetism better than Francis Robinson. "She is a complete, extraordinary individual," said the Press Chief, "with a hold on the public that has nothing to do with her singing —hers is a virginal appeal; they worship her as the Virgin Mary, with her clear skin, blue eyes and unclouded brow."

Birgit Nilsson, the statuesque Princess of the North, has come to mean to opera very nearly what Kirsten Flagstad once meant. A great Wagnerian singer will always enthrall a public. In her native Stockholm, Nilsson is allowed a comprehensive repertoire, as are all singers on their home ground. The big voices flex themselves for lyric expression; type-casting is not nearly as prevalent as in New York. But this handsome, wholesome Swede has been allowed to break bonds as few Wagnerians before her: She may sing *Aida* and *Ballo* if she wishes—and she does— although she is not invariably superior in romantic roles. *Salome* and *Elektra* are not *verboten,* nor *Turandot,* nor *Tosca,* that piece of dramatic expression every prima donna craves. Nilsson was the first at the Met to encompass the extremes of both Venus and Elisabeth in one evening of *Tannhäuser,* the historic date being March 19, 1966. Such versatility is good for us if only to jounce us out of a rut, although it is not commended by the sopranos upon whose territory Nilsson encroaches.

Joan Sutherland's phenomenal voice, laden with silver and pathos, has put her at the pinnacle. Fortunately, New York has heard her at her prime. She made her debut in the fluttering old rags of the Met's *Lammermoor* in 1961. This shabbiness was at last remedied by 1964, but *Lucia* came as a poor third for *Norma,* which had been planned to show off Sutherland for the first time in the role in a major opera house, and for *Puritani,* her second choice. The lady decided that the Druid still demanded too much even for her amazing vocal technique and the Met was afraid *Puritani* would not draw even with Sutherland. Since her debut we have been regaled additionally with only the tall Australian's Amazonian Amina in *Sonnambula* in 1962 and a Violetta in 1963. She took a year to tour her native land with her own company, and returned to the Met in 1966–67 for Donna Anna and more Lucias. She will be absent in 1967–68 because, it is believed, Bing was piqued at her refusal to tour *I Puritani,* a longed-for revival since canceled.

The customers would like more of the five-foot-eight phenomenon with the four-foot crop of flaming hair—"*La Stupenda,*" as Venice dubbed her. They hunger to hear her Queen of the Night, *Puritani, Alcina, Huguenots, Daughter of the Regiment*—oh, anything, anything! Sutherland comes as a package deal now, with her husband, Richard Bonynge, engaged as conductor wherever she goes. One is reminded of Patti's insistence on the engagement of her tenor-husband, Nicolini, as well as a more recent example. It is ironic to remember that one of Bing's closest associates vowed that "Rudi would never have permitted Flagstad to bring McArthur with her," as Johnson had finally done, yet had to admit that Bing had given in to Sutherland. She must have the man who encouraged her to abandon *Aida* and Wagner and take to the heights, adding ornaments and frills to the plain vocal line as she went, in conformity with older baroque habits. Fortunately, Bonynge's talent has matured.

Two American women can mount thrones alongside this foreign quartet: Leontyne Price and Eileen Farrell. It is a deep satisfaction to Bing that Price is considered one of the greatest *prime donne* ever to illumine Metropolitan rolls, even though her quality was recognized throughout the world before her debut as Leonora in *Trovatore* in 1961. She emerged first at two prominent educational centers in the East—Tanglewood and the Juilliard School, singing Ariadne at the former and Mistress Ford at the latter. Europe hailed her in *Porgy and Bess* with her (then) husband, William Warfield. In 1955 Samuel Chotzinoff of the NBC-TV Opera daringly cast her as Tosca, which aroused a wave of controversy and served to make her known the length and breadth of her own country. In 1957 she graced the San Francisco *Dialogues of the Carmelites,* later was Chicago's Liu and Thaïs (an even more venturesome bit of casting), and soon was blazing an opera trail through Europe.

All bars come down before a talent like this one. Her scope is boundless at the Met—Donna Anna to Butterfly, Minnie to Aida, Tosca to Elvira (*Ernani*), Amelia (*Ballo*) to Fiordiligi, Tatyana to the Verdi Requiem, and more to come.

Eileen Farrell has presented unusual difficulties. It took a good many years to get her onto the opera stage at all, even though her radio and concert public screamed nonstop. A buxom, hearty, plainspoken Irish-American, Farrell fought a weight problem and ingrained laziness along with apparent indifference of Metropolitan officials to her drawing power. She finally appeared as Santuzza in Florida, then Kurt Herbert Adler persuaded her to make her San Francisco debut in *Trovatore* in 1956. Two years later he mounted *Medea* for her and in 1959 cast her as Ariadne. She vouchsafed to Chicago her splendid Gioconda, then finally gratified starved Met patrons with Alcestis in 1960, the role Flagstad had chosen for her farewell, and evoked favorable comparisons; the same year she also gave a rousing performance of "Ocean, Thou Mighty Monster" from *Oberon* at a gala benefit for the Employees Welfare Fund. Opening night of 1962 was hers with Maddalena in *Chénier* and she was chosen as Isabella in the Met's contribution, Falla's *Atlantida,* to Philharmonic Hall opening ceremonies. Her other roles were Gioconda, Santuzza, and Leonora (*Forza*). The twin Farrell mysteries continue to perplex her followers: why she sings so little opera and why no Wagner at all, when the voice is custom-made. She remained on the Met roster until 1966–67; whether her infrequent appearances are by her own choice is moot. Whosesoever the decision, New York is deprived of one of the greatest voices of the age.

Every one of the feminine star sextet, plus Del Monaco, sang elsewhere in America before descending on Thirty-ninth Street—in Chicago or San Francisco or both. In fact, of the crowned heads, only Franco Corelli is pure Bing from the start. Not one attribute of tenordom is absent from Corelli's makeup. He is self-taught and self-assured to the point of sublimity. He demands the attention reserved exclusively for *prime donne* and permissively taught children. If he chooses, he will take off on a high D-flat where none exists in a score—even in so serious a work as *Don Carlo*—and get away without reprimand from Bing. He will, it is said, not show up for rehearsals à la Patti, but then not realize that a cut has been opened, leaving him stranded and mumbling.

Stunningly handsome, he is careful about the view he presents to the audience—only rarely does a director get him to turn his back as in *Turandot*. Feminine hearts flutter at any angle whatsoever he shows them, whether any character is registered or not—more often not. His long legs are as shapely as Siepi's and a little more youthfully fleshed; the figure is slim and outlined like a divinity in his better costumes; the bodily movement shows it off rather than any inwardly generated emotion. It is painful to be close to a television screen when he and Tebaldi contort their faces and grasp each other's hands in an effort to betray tender passion.

The voice—ah, the voice!

Big, loud, manly, with a bleat that leads uncharitable Italians to call it *"voce di caprino,"* a very unflattering comparison with some of the lesser attractions of a goat. It is hardly nuanced, but often charged with warmth. Both he and Del Monaco honestly tried to reduce and refine their enormous output of sound; sometimes Corelli succeeds, having learned that a pianissimo can garner almost as much applause as a fortissimo.

His jealousy of colleagues' success rivals or even surpasses Del Monaco's. The tenor story of the period belongs to the latter, however. Del Monaco's turbulent spirit had not yet been quelled when on one spring tour Max Rudolf discovered a poster on a pillar in the Peabody Hotel in Memphis, Tennessee, one second before the tenor followed him into the lobby. Rudolf's sleight of hand in turning the card wrong side out saved the season. Del Monaco would not have sung that night—or probably any other—if he had noticed that his billing lacked a fraction of an inch in type size of matching the soprano's. He carried a pocket ruler to measure for himself. On one unluckier occasion, he threatened Rudolf with a raised chair in his powerful arms and was saved from committing assault only by the arrival of a husky callboy. He sang that night too, but the curtain waited several minutes while he simmered down to cooing noises from his wife, Rudolf, and sundry other pacifiers.

Singers' fees have always been a cause for amazement to the public, which cannot seem to understand why a fellow or girl should get thousands of dollars for standing up there and uttering a song or two. More sophisticated operagoers know that a genuinely fine singer will have spent the years of training expected of any profession; that the instrument is the singer's own body and subject to every ill wind; and with the best of luck the active span of a working life is short and encrusted with perils. So let them gather their cachets while they may (and pay their high income taxes).

The nonprofit-making opera company summons cogent reasons for not allowing singers' pay to mount exorbitantly. One retrenchment took place in the beginning of Grau's regime; another cut down the soloists' budget in 1932 under Gatti. When Bing arrived, the top fee paid to those who work on the "per-performance" basis was said to be $1,000, no matter what the name or fame. (The per-week contingent has been regulated by the union AGMA since Johnson's time.)

The advent of Callas broke the overhead barrier, it is reliably said. Chicago's pressures in the fifties also helped. Fees for Callas and a few others went up to $1,500, then to $1,750 during the Callas-Tebaldi period. Nilsson and Sutherland may have begun at that figure. Corelli came in at a new high—$2,750. Because of the demand for their glitter, a thousand or more probably has been added to the checks of Tebaldi, Sutherland, and the other crown wearers. The top price at present writing has been quoted at $4,000. Outside of the Met, Corelli commands $10,000 for, say, a southern *Aida,* and Sutherland can get $8,000 for herself, $2,000 for Bonynge for a provincial *Traviata.*

We still have to go only a thousand more before climbing to Patti's heights. This regal personage sang nowhere for less than $5,000 (although it will be remembered that she *reduced* the amount for the pleasure of having her husband perform with her—just the opposite procedure to Sutherland's).

In an inflationary period, it seems only natural that this item of the budget should be escalated along with everything else. What makes it hard on the management, however, is that the high-bracket folk no longer pay for themselves at the box office. It makes no difference whether a $1,750 tenor or a doubly expensive Corelli struts the stage; the subscription avalanche has overwhelmed the operation to the saturation point. No longer can any singer be considered a top draw except in the number of customers turned away. The end result may play into Bing's calculations: The stars may be allowed to swing into other orbits and leave the Met leveled out but fully subscribed—at least for a while.

22

SOME WERE METEORITES

The night shows stars and women in a better light.

—Lord Byron, *Don Juan*

Rudolf Bing's aspiration to an "ensemble system," which he later modified to an "ensemble of stars," sometimes is thwarted by what actually happens on the Metropolitan Opera stage. The General Manager all too frequently winds up with neither star nor ensemble. Rare is that happy night when all of "Heaven's eyes" sing together in Heaven.

Bing's attitude toward singers seems as arbitrary and inspired by prejudice as that of most other managers, and he is sometimes less shrewd in anticipating public reaction than many. He is of course beset by the built-in difficulties of a mixed operation that veers between the *stagione* and repertoire systems. The first, practiced largely in Italy, gives a run to a single opera of as many performances as the traffic will bear (keeping the cast intact if possible), then drops it for the next work. The second displays a different opera every night. The American practice leans less to *stagione* (an Italian word meaning literally "season") and more to repertoire, but with occasional modifications. For example, Bing's plan for the 1966–67 season introduced four new productions repeated with casts nearly intact over the first half of the season, adding one or more revivals at intervals. But there is still a different opera every night.

There are two ways of hiring singers: one is to set the repertoire and try to find singers to fit; the other is to get singers and let repertoire fall where it may. Bing would like to adhere to the former plan, but finds it necessary to compromise because of the outside pressure to present reigning stars. So he ends up with a sort of star system in spite of himself. And audiences hear many singers in familiar roles and play the old game of comparing their virtues and faults. But then, as Irving Kolodin says in the new edition of his history of the Metropolitan, there is nothing wrong with the star system if you use some system in hiring the stars.

The number of singers who have come and gone in Bing's seventeen years greatly outranks those who have come and stayed. Newcomers have averaged about nineteen a season. It must seem to Bing (as to others before him) that the public demands fresh voices and unfamiliar faces constantly; there has never been a Met season when a few hitherto unknown names didn't turn up on the list—even when only a few or none of the old ones departed. Bing has engaged in this reinforcement procedure rather less than Gatti, rather more than Johnson; we must remember, however, that the latter's freedom was hampered by war and depression, which deeply affected the Met's operations. Circumstances in the other opera houses of the world seem to play a lesser part in Bing's calculations than might be expected, as new operas and singers crop up steadily on the Continent and in England, but never cross the Atlantic to the Met. Furthermore, Bing—and his European scouts—often exhibit questionable taste in the choice of some European singers, considering what they have to pick from. Really great ones escape entirely sometimes or come to the sacred New York portals with their bills of lading marked "Past Prime."

Opera buffs in New York frequently torture themselves with a parlor game: casting from among Metropolitan absentees. They want Rita Streich as Queen of the Night, Zerbinetta and Sophie (she sang the last two in San Francisco); Leyla Gencer from La Scala in Norma, and perhaps some old Verdi and late Prokofiev. She was the one who stepped in for Callas as Lucia in San Francisco and also sang *Francesca da Rimini,* Elisabetta (*Carlos*), and Manon. They wanted Anita Cerquetti in almost anything in her heyday (she was Chicago's Amelia and Elisabetta).

New Yorkers would have given a good deal to see and hear Sena Jurinac in Mozart and Strauss. She was scheduled for the Met (Vanessa and Mimi) in 1957–58 but never made it because of illness; then in 1961, when the season was canceled in advance, she had made other plans before the emergency was settled. San Francisco, however, welcomed her as the Composer, Donna Anna, Butterfly, and Eva. All of America may feel deprived at not experiencing what even one supposedly impartial dictionary called "the finest Octavian of the century," though she has since dropped that role in favor of the Marschallin.

Perhaps New Yorkers don't miss Nan Merriman as Dorabella, but those who heard the comely mezzo in San Francisco or England or La Scala or with Toscanini in *Falstaff* and *Otello* or even in a Town Hall recital wish her back in costume. Too late; she has retired. Neither is it much use to argue now about Margarethe Klose: the great German mezzo was in San Francisco for a single season's Klytemnestra, Brangäne, and Fricka in 1953, but she too has retired.

The most famous *Fidelio* Leonore in Europe, Gré Brouwenstijn, should have given New York a chance to wrestle with some odd spelling (along with Finnish, Yugoslavian, and other alphabet twisters) in addition to an arresting personality and voice. San Francisco saw her as Leonore and Amelia; Chicago as Jenufa and Sieglinde.

The might-have-been game continues: Why does Marilyn Horne, the favorite sidekick of Joan Sutherland, matching the soprano run for run and trill for trill, sing elsewhere but not at the Metropolitan? We know that Boris Christoff was engaged for New York in 1950 and was forbidden entrance for political reasons; still, he sang later in Chicago, San Francisco, and Boston. What is the excuse for the absence of Dietrich Fischer-Dieskau, who has dignified any number of opera houses all over the world—except America's? As recently as 1965 the crafty Carol Fox bagged Elena Suliotis, now considered the "new Callas," and not only because she is a Greek. Will she be allowed to wear out —like Cerquetti—before New York knows her?

Even some promising Met Auditions material has been allowed to make its way in other houses—witness Claire Watson, accepted at La Scala, Glyndebourne, Salzburg, and Munich; Arlene Saunders, whose career began at the City Opera and has flourished in Hamburg (she sang with the Met on tour as Eva and Rosalinda in *Fledermaus*); Richard Cassilly, a City Opera leading tenor; Saramae Endich, whose European experience and concert expertise brought her back to a City Opera debut; the late James Pease, with a parallel career; and Shirley Verrett, the beautiful girl who has found favor in Covent Garden, La Scala, Spoleto, and even at the Moscow Bolshoi. It might have been argued that some of these voices are not "big" enough for the Met, but many smaller ones are regularly employed.

The list of the illustrious who made their debuts in San Francisco or Chicago instead of New York is startling. Carol Fox in Chicago and Kurt Herbert Adler in San Francisco seize every opportunity to score over Bing. Consensus points to Elisabeth Schwarzkopf as the most glaring sin of omission. The golden beauty was in this hemisphere as early as 1953, singing concerts; she made her opera debut in San Francisco in 1955 as the Marschallin, also singing Donna Elvira. Returning there almost every season, she sang the Countess in *Capriccio* in 1963, which Adler mounted especially for her without any guarantee that the public would walk over the red carpet to hear Strauss's last opera. In 1959 Chicago produced raves for her Fiordiligi, and in other seasons she showed one or both American cities a triumphant Mistress Ford, Marie (*Bartered Bride*), and Countess Almaviva. New Yorkers had to be content with her records, a larger-than-life film of *Der Rosenkavalier,* occasional concerts, and Handel's *Hercules* and *Julius Caesar* (Cleopatra) in concert form. When at last the Met curtain opened on the inevitable Marschallin on October 13, 1964, Schwarzkopf already had to handle her voice carefully, although her impersonation retained much radiance. Devotees wept in mingled joy and pain. She sang eight *Rosenkavalier*s, then came back in 1965 for Donna Elvira, but managed only one performance because of "vocal difficulties." With Schwarzkopf, it was clearly a case of too little too late.

Italy's magnificent singing actor Tito Gobbi sang and acted in San Francisco as early as 1948. Gobbi liked Chicago too, giving Fox the benefit of all the "regular" baritone roles as well as Michele in *Tabarro,* Renato in *Ballo,* Rance in *Fanciulla,* Gérard in *Chénier,* Michonnet in *Adriana,* De Siriex in *Fedora,* Verdi's lesser-known Nabucco, and the crowning Iago and Falstaff—this through 1965, while sparing for the Met two seasons beginning in 1955 and a third, 1958–59. His poise and skill, as befits the master of ninety roles, impressed everyone. But the Met already had its own baritones to think of in Gobbi's roles—Warren, Merrill, London, Guarrera, Bastianini, Cassel, Singher, Valentino, and a few others—so Gobbi got no more than one Rigoletto, two Scarpias, and one Iago. Small wonder he preferred Chicago, where he was even allowed to stage *Boccanegra* and *Otello* as well as star in them. He came again to the Met in 1963 and at last in 1966 was allowed to display his fabulous Falstaff three times—with Iago for 1967.

The record of delayed debuts contains a further quantity of stardust: Leonie Rysanek, Inge Borkh, Régine Crespin, Rita Gorr, Giulietta Simionato, Alfredo Kraus, Geraint Evans, Pilar Lorengar. . . . Rysanek in a veiled voice unveiled a San Francisco Senta and Sieglinde before becoming firmly fixed in New York's firmament. She is an exponent of a vocal type Bing seems to favor, probably because of his middle-European background, where the ear possibly becomes attuned to the covered voice. In New York Rysanek has been asked too often to do the Verdi roles not as well suited for her as, say, Senta or Elsa. Borkh began on the West Coast in 1953 with Elektra, Turandot, Sieglinde, Salome, Senta, Leonore (*Fidelio*), Lady Macbeth, and Elsa before consigning Salome and Sieglinde (only) to the Met in 1957, then returning in 1960 as Elektra. Crespin, though a Frenchwoman, has never sung French opera in New York after beginning with a Chicago Tosca, but fully dramatized many roles at the Met—the Marschallin, Amelia, Senta, Elsa, Kundry, and Tosca since 1962. She was absent in 1966–67, apparently preferring the full-scale *Troyens* of Berlioz that San Francisco staged for her, but will return in 1967–68 for Tosca and Senta, as well as the *Walküre* Brünnhilde, which she has been doing with von Karajan in Salzburg. Rita Gorr, a Belgian, made Chicagoans sit up in excitement at her American debut as Dalila in 1962, then appeared first in New York the same fall as Amneris, later adding Azucena, Santuzza, Dalila, and Waltraute. Her mammoth voice, rather rough on occasion, does not ring in New York's ear as pleasantly as more refined organs, but her lusty stage presence galvanizes an audience.

Occasionally a favorite is engaged in New York both late and for the wrong reasons. Such was the fate of Simionato, the renowned contralto, who was "discovered" by Adler in 1953, Fox in 1954. Bing had invited her for the same year she appeared in Chicago, but it was said that she suffered a broken heart, which led to a broken contract. She did not come to New York until 1959, and then had only the Azucenas and Santuzzas that demonstrated about one tenth of her talent. Concert-opera audiences were luckier to experience a few roles at which she shone—the Jane Seymour of Donizetti's *Anna Bolena* and even Gluck's Orfeo, but never had a chance at her Adalgisa, which Chicago paired with Callas as Norma. Chicago, with its more flexible repertoire in shorter seasons, allowed Simionato Preziosilla, Laura, Eboli, Dame Quickly, and even Carmen, in addition to Azucena and Santuzza. Many of these were also the roles of Ebe Stignani, who had sung in San Francisco in Johnson's time and had been invited to the Met just as war intervened. The big-voiced mezzo and Johnson never got together on a contract; Bing evidently considered her passée.

Two charming Spaniards, Pilar Lorengar and Alfredo Kraus, are recent models of the "New-York-last" school. Both could be found in San Francisco or Chicago the season before they enchanted the Met, the soprano with Donna Elvira and Mistress Ford, the tenor with the Duke and Don Ottavio. The Met will probably never give Kraus the lead in *Favorita,* one of his Chicago roles. Geraint Evans, the Welshman, was San Francisco's Kothner, Music Master (*Ariadne*), Kezal, Wozzeck, Leporello, and Beckmesser long before captivating New York with his Falstaff and later appearances as Figaro and Leporello.

So it goes and continues to go. To those who, for whatever reason, have been valued elsewhere before becoming New York regulars, must be added (alphabetically) Carlo Bergonzi, Walter Berry, Anselmo Colzani, Mirella Freni, Nicolai Ghiaurov, Sandor Konya, Gianni Raimondi, Nicola Rossi-Lemeni, Cesare Valletti, and Jon Vickers, as well as many Americans of first magnitude.

In the light of the qualities and reputation of this galaxy, Bing's recent comment, quoted in *Time,* does not apply: "Let them learn elsewhere—Chicago, San Francisco, Boston. They should sing here only at their peak. I came after a long climb, they can too."

A few of those who have fired a single shot in America's greatest opera house are not less distinguished. There was good reason (political) why Galina Vishnevskaya flashed only momentarily across our skies; we had to be content with an Aida sung four times and a single Butterfly (one honest listener swore that Pinkerton offered vodka to Sharpless instead of "wheeskee" on the occasion). It is harder to understand why the endearing Irmgard Seefried, a European partner to Schwarzkopf in many Mozartean and Straussian adventures, should come to New York only in 1953 for only five Susannas. (Bing wanted her in 1956, to be sure, for Bruno Walter's *Magic Flute,* but she refused to sing Pamina in English.) Seefried did better by Chicago with two seasons and three roles, Zerlina, Marzelline, and the Composer in *Ariadne,* and San Francisco heard her as recently as 1964 in *Rosenkavalier* with Schwarzkopf.

Christel Goltz, justly celebrated overseas for the more than 120 roles she is said to "possess," was allowed only one in New York, Salome, in 1954–55. To wait until 1964 to introduce Gerard Souzay to Thirty-ninth

Street, when he had already sung concerts here and had appeared as Orfeo in the City Opera's adventurous mounting of Monteverdi's classic, seems afterthought or accident, for he sang exactly once at the Met as Count Almaviva after Hermann Prey, Gabriel Bacquier, and William Dooley. Helga Pilarczyk, specializing in contemporary roles, didn't show up until she acted as a substitute for Teresa Stich-Randall in three performances of *Wozzeck,* and was at a disadvantage singing in English.

No matter what happens to American immigration laws, the melting pot continues to boil at the Metropolitan and contains an amazing lot of mediocrities, who often return to the obscurity from which they came. Or, unfortunately, they stay. The chorus of an old song ran something like this: "The Rumanians, the Bulgarians, the Armenians, and the Greeks," to show the ingredients thrown into the pot. It seems sometimes as if Bing visited a different country every season in rotation and came away with whatever was there without regard for an overall European— or American—yardstick. Various nationals have arrived in little clusters from time to time. No one minds if they come straight from the crown jewels of each land, but some of them are frankly paste.

A trio of dubious Rumanians provides a case in point: the baritone Nicolae Herlea, whose name has since vanished from the roster, the mezzo Elena Cernei, and a tortured tenor of passage, Ion Piso. The Bulgarian-Yugoslavian-Czechoslovakian corridor is kept open; through it have passed from Bulgaria the tenor Dimiter Uzunov and the soprano Raina Kabaivanska (in the last season downtown she sang Elisabetta, Manon Lescaut, and Mistress Ford). Sopranos like Milanov don't arrive any more from Yugoslavia, and two mezzos hardly make the weight: Ruza Pospinov—her chief roles, Ulrica, Maddalena, and Madelon (*Chénier*), and the lady with the practically unpronounceable name, Biserka Cvejic, who hails from a town called Split. Miss Cvejic made her debut in 1961 as Amneris and has been around ever since, singing steadily (or unsteadily) in multiple performances as Azucena, Amneris, Eboli, and Dalila. Between the one and the other Yugoslav, it is possible to wonder what is happening to a girl named Nell Rankin, an American who comes in now and then to do a few performances of one or two of those operas. Also Mignon Dunn is right there and worthy. Applied chauvinism is not the answer, because another American, Irene Dalis, gets all these roles and more, in preference to Rankin and Dunn.

As for Czechoslovakia, the Iron Curtain has lifted for the soprano Ludmilla Dvorakova, who was reengaged for 1966–67 on the strength of three unexceptional *Fidelios* the previous season. Hungary, which used to be generous with dark voices, chiefly male, has skimped of late with only one baritone, Vladimir Ruzdak, a two-season man of little impact.

The frozen North of Finland has sent along, in addition to the tenor who filled in for Wolfgang Windgassen in the latter's unexpected absence (his staccato name is Pekka Nuotio), the handsome but stolid bass Kim Borg, often miscast in baritone roles, and the soprano Anita Välkki, who shared Kundry with Crespin and sang Venus on two occasions in 1965–66. She had previously been a Brünnhilde, Senta, and Turandot, all competent rather than compelling.

New York has even heard a singer from Greece, but only one, the baritone Kostas Paskalis, who stirred Glyndebourne with his Macbeth. He was engaged in midseason of 1964–65 for a single Don Carlo in *Forza,* then was supposed to return but didn't. These all constitute the fringes of questionable immigration in recent years, aside from the Italians, Germans, and occasional French we are accustomed to.

Of higher gem content were the Spaniards, three of whom arrived in 1965–66, including Lorengar and Kraus, with the ravishing Montserrat Caballé leading the way. She had already shown her scintillant facets in Donizetti's *Lucrezia Borgia* and *Roberto Devereux* with the American Opera Society. Her single Met Marguerite hardly did her justice. She had more to give and gain in Philadelphia's *Chénier,* Hartford's *Trovatore,* Dallas's *Traviata,* and Pittsburgh's *Bohème.*

South America has yielded little of late except the fine tenor Luigi Alva, although Delia Rigal, certain of beauty if not always of voice, made her debut in Bing's opening *Don Carlo* and stayed a half dozen years, while the tall, dark, and handsome Chilean, Ramon Vinay, has spent more than a dozen intermittently, enlarging repertoire and reputation and even reverting to his original baritone roles and basso buffo.

As for the German wing—containing more Scandinavians and Hungarians than actual Germans—Bing's first season betrayed an uncertainty that brought ten brief candles for a single span: the Swede Sven Nilsson, a Daland and King Marke; Fritz Krenn and the Hungarian Endre Koreh, who sang nothing but Baron Ochs, each in a season; Günther Treptow, not deeply appreciated as a *Heldentenor;* Alois Pernerstorfer, who spent more time singing Sparafucile than German roles and was not liked in either; the aging Elisabeth Höngen, a magnificent, raddled Herodias and Klytemnestra in a well-Straussed season; Walburga Wegner, engaged for Chrysothemis and Eva; the Swede Sigurd Björling, an impressive Telramund, Rangoni, Kurvenal, and Amfortas, who didn't feel at home in America; Josef Greindl, a King Henry and Pogner; and Hilde Zadek, an Israeli, whose Eva, Anna, Aida, and Elsa made no lasting impression. Two were luckier and gave better service for two seasons: Erich Kunz, an extremely lively Leporello, Beckmesser, and Faninal; and Richard Holm, an engaging David. Hans Hopf scarcely filled (except physically) Walther's big boots, Lohengrin's silver armor, Tannhäuser's robes, or Siegfried's bearskin through several seasons.

The heroic German tenor poses eternal problems; Bing seems to have run into consistent trouble with this distinctive and disturbing category. Before the departure of Set Svanholm in 1956, Treptow, Bernd Aldenhoff (hack actors with poor, worn voices), and even Vinay had been put into the mold as alternates to the powerful Swede.

Europe's most celebrated, Wolfgang Windgassen, tried New York in the 1956–57 *Ring*; many liked him, but his reengagement was not scheduled until 1966. He didn't arrive. Bing called him "in breach of contract" when he appeared in good health elsewhere on days he claimed to be too ill to rehearse here. The rumors flew one way and another: the tenor was dissatisfied with his fee (still not as large as an Italian's); he was accustomed to new productions and thought *Tannhäuser* would be freshly set for him; he shared the majority distaste for the old *Ring* sets. At any rate, only his replacement, the Finn Nuotio, and the unlovable Ticho Parly appeared on the 1966–67 roster, although the Americans James King, Jess Thomas, and James McCracken could be in the grooming stall for *Heldentenors*.

Whether it is a shortage in this breed or an indifference to the heavier Wagner, the complete *Ring* cycle has had only two go-arounds in ten years, 1956–57 and 1961–62. Liebl remained faithfully at Bing's disposal from 1958, a saccharine lyric tenor, not for the robust roles. Vinay has taken several *Ring* parts. Through 1966, Bing's Lohengrin has been in turn Brian Sullivan, the strapping American; Sandor Konya, the Hungarian with the ringing tones (sometimes vulgarized with the Italianate sob); Jess Thomas, the American with European polish; and

Arturo Sergi, the American with the Italian name who sings Alfredo, the Duke, and the more lyric Wagner and goes the Italian heroic limit with Otello. Vickers' Wagner so far is confined to Erik and Siegmund; McCracken continues to decline to strain his voice beyond the Verdi Moor.

Some sable-voiced males have left deeper impressions in the Wagner-Strauss (and occasionally Beethoven-Berg) axis. Hans Hotter, the towering baritone, carried over his artistry in portrait-singing from an incomparable Dutchman to a matchless Grand Inquisitor with Wagnerian stops between in Bing's first four seasons. (Hotter was known as a "wet" singer; a fine spray shot into the air in front of him at his every exhalation. Svanholm possessed the same peculiarity. Woe to the Senta before her Dutchman or Elsa faced with such a Lohengrin! Astrid Varnay, kneeling before her Knight after the line: "My shield, my angel, my protector," used to add *sotto voce* to Svanholm, "Make it an umbrella!")

Hermann Uhde, a peerless artist, enriched several Met seasons until his untimely death, making his debut as Telramund (1955–56) and going on to other Wagner roles, including an unforgettable Amfortas, and broadening his scope and our experience by his Wozzeck, Orestes, and Grand Inquisitor, as well as Scarpia. (He was the first Chief of Police slim enough to wear Scotti's costumes.) Like the good trooper, the perfect repertoire man, Uhde even sang the minor role of Melot in a season crowded with more important assignments. He was probably the first to play his own worst enemy in a single performance, taking on both Amfortas and Klingsor.

Otto Edelmann will be remembered chiefly for his Ochs and Hans Sachs in the last half of the fifties; he returned in 1961 to pursue his placid course until 1966, adding Rocco in *Fidelio*. On one occasion, when he fell ill after two acts of *Walküre*, Randolph Symonette, a West Indian baritone, took over the Wotan and failed in turn. Edelmann was summoned back midway in Act III by Erich Leinsdorf, who cut several pages, yet left the suffering god to deal with his farewell to his erring daughter.

Other names from the period may be recalled: Kurt Böhme (no relation to the conductor Karl Böhm), a Pogner, Fafner, and Hagen; Josef Metternich, who uncomfortably inhabited the Italian realms as Renato, Don Carlo (*Forza*), Di Luna, and Tonio more than the German, with Wolfram and Amfortas in three seasons. Karl Dönch came as Beckmesser, sang the Doctor in *Wozzeck,* went away, came back as Beckmesser, went away again, and again was to come back as Beckmesser in 1966–67. Marko Rothmüller, at present one of the Indiana University enclave, sang roles including Kothner but was never allowed the Wozzeck in which he scored at Covent Garden and the New York City Opera. The superb Gottlob Frick was with us so briefly that the full qualities of the bass in his few appearances as Fafner, Hunding, and Hagen in 1961–62 could hardly be tasted. Yet the less celebrated Ernst Wiemann is still on the roster after five seasons in bass roles. Paul Schoeffler, a favorite of the House since before Bing's regime, appeared as late as 1964–65 as a memorable Sachs—in his sixty-eighth year.

Women of German birth have been fewer and usually on the high-soprano level as the more dramatic parts go to Scandinavians and other Middle Europeans. Hilde Gueden, the pretty Viennese with the curling smile, provided pretty singing and some that even transcended prettiness in such diverse matters as Gilda, Sophie, Zdenka (*Arabella*), Zerlina, Anne in Stravinsky's *Rake's Progress,* and Rosalinda during Bing's first decade. Anneliese Rothenburg, a cherished Viennese Sophie, impressed Americans as well, also as Zdenka in a half dozen seasons. Lisa Della Casa has been steadily in the Met's orbit since 1953, her beautiful face and elegant figure adding to the pleasure with which she has been greeted as Arabella, Octavian, as well as the Marschallin, diverse Mozart roles, and the more conventional Elsa, Eva, Mimi, and Cio-Cio-San. Exceptions to the lyric-coloratura rule were the Bayreuth-bred Martha Mödl and the Munich stalwart Marianne Schech, both of whom sang in the *Ring* cycle of 1956–57 and returned intermittently. Nilsson occupied by then the important niche, while on the plateau below Rysanek and Loevberg merely perched. It was enough to send Mödl in retreat to Europe, where eventually she returned to mezzo status.

The Italians have kept up a steadier flow, particularly tenors, who either wear out fast or are thrown out. Opera houses can never seem to get enough of this breed. Not counting the Olympians (Del Monaco and Corelli) and the half dozen or so comprimarios, the "leading" tenor list numbers eighteen since Bing took hold, averaging more than one a year. This of course is no way to assay the situation; rather should the lasting qualities of the high-voiced males be judged. But the temptation to print the list is irresistible—it trips so mellifluously off the tongue, no matter what the owners' voices sounded like. So in no particular order, here they are:

Giuseppe di Stefano	Gino Penno	Giuseppe Prandelli
Flaviano Labo	Giuseppe Campora	Cesare Valletti
Eugenio Fernandi	Mario Ortica	Primo Zambruno
Gianni Poggi	Carlo Bergonzi	Bruno Prevedi
Daniele Barione	Giuseppe Zampieri	Ferruccio Tagliavini
Dino Formichini	Gaetano Bardini	Gianni Raimondi

They should be set to music!

What matter that some of them sang only once; that others contain in their throats a beautiful vocal organ but in their heads no ability to read music? From the eighteen, several deserve Hall of Fame status: Di Stefano, Valletti, Bergonzi, and perhaps the newcomers Prevedi and Raimondi. Two fresh young provincial voices were required by Bing to sing roles too heavy for them—Barione and Fernandi. Tagliavini of course made his reputation earlier and returned merely for a short period to see if the claque still existed.

Baritones sound equally tuneful but less impressive numerically: Ettore Bastianini, Mario Sereni, Anselmo Colzani made substantial careers; Renato Capecchi stayed too briefly; others will not be missed. Basses roll out sonorously but briefly: Cesare Siepi, Fernando Corena, Nicola Rossi-Lemeni, Bonaldo Giaiotti. One baritone, Enzo Sordello, may be mentioned for the trouble he stirred up. After a tangle with Callas about who should hold a high note longer, he departed in clouds of derogatory publicity; it was not the soprano who got him dismissed, however, but the conductor, Cleva. One bass not listed could qualify as a pacifier, since he was hired for the sole purpose of keeping a more illustrious landsman—a tenor—from being lonesome in this strange country full of barbarians who don't speak Italian.

Italian women are far fewer, oddly enough. In the past fifteen years, only Herva Nelli (who boasted Toscanini's favor) and Antonietta Stella (an attractive and large-voiced Aida, Butterfly, and Elisabetta among other heroines from 1956 to 1960) have left memories. Stella departed in a huff, fired, it was said, because she refused to go on tour and demanded solo bows. Gabriella Tucci arrived in 1960 and has made a warm place for herself with Butterfly, Violetta, Mimi, and Alice Ford. She was out of place, however, as Marguerite. Renata Scotto came to New York in 1965, although she had sung years earlier in Chicago. An excellent singer and musician, she overcomes illusorily the handicap of a dumpy figure in a gamut from Puccini to the Lucias. The frail beauty and tenderness of Mirella Freni's Mimi early in the 1965 season and her delicious Adina assured her of a return and of New York's devotion.

The French visitors are fewer and farther between, obviously because of Bing's neglect of their repertoire. (He is only following Metropolitan precedent.) With an all-around artist such as Crespin, this does not matter. Jane Rhodes (Gallic in spite of her anglo-Saxon name) showed brilliance but eccentricity as Carmen (once) and Salome. Two light French (Canadian) tenors have graced the roster a year or two apiece: Leopold Simoneau, a Chicago favorite for Ottavio, Nemorino, and Ferrando, but allowed the first-named only a few times by Bing; and Richard Verreau, who sang in *Manon* and *Faust* a few times. Gabriel Bacquier, a baritone of wide European experience and also known in Miami, Chicago, and with the American Opera Society of New York, performed two roles he would or could not do at the Met: the title part in Menotti's *Last Savage,* which he created, but in French at its world premiere; and Orfeo, which is conventionally given to contraltos. Bing engaged him for Scarpia, Count Almaviva, and the High Priest in *Samson*.

For whatever reason, few singers filter through from the British Isles. But we have been privileged to witness the artistry of the Welshman Geraint Evans and the Scottish Murray Dickie, our chief David from 1962 to 1965. David Ward, another Scot, has sung Sarastro, the Dutchman, and Hunding. There is only one Englishman, Michael Langdon, a one-shot Ochs of 1964, but not an Irishman in the place!

The Scandinavian tradition has persisted with Nilsson and Ingrid Bjöner, the latter a Junoesque Norwegian who arrived in 1961 for Elsa and Gutrune, Ariadne and Donna Anna, and has remained. Two gracious and charming Swedish ladies have come and gone in the past half dozen years: Elisabeth Söderström, a lyric soprano of high spirits and multiple talents, and Kerstin Meyer, a slim mezzo whose Carmen didn't travel well, but who succeeded with Orfeo, less so vocally with the Composer. Perhaps the great line wore a bit thin in two previous seasons with the Elsa,

Eva, Fidelio, and Sieglinde of Aase Nordmo Loevberg, who followed Flagstad and preceded Nilsson without seriously rivaling either.

Bing inherited about three dozen Americans from Johnson, among whom Kirsten, Madeira, Resnik, Thebom, Peerce, Tucker, Guarrera, Merrill, and Hines remain at this writing, while Steber and Harshaw have departed. The General Manager added his own natives, of whom Roberta Peters, Lucine Amara, and Mildred Miller stay, while Margaret Roggero had a tidy mezzo career until 1962. Peters' debut was a 1950 wonder. Called in on the advice of Max Rudolf, who assured Bing she was ready after years of persistent study but no stage experience, the girl delivered a highly professional and sweetly sung Zerlina in place of Nadine Conner. Her star quality has been well established by diligence as well as talent. Amara, with a lovely lyric voice, has occasionally been pushed into dramatic roles that do not suit her, and was assigned only Mimi and Ellen in *Peter Grimes,* in 1966–67.

Bing has also made the most of the supporting-cast people without whom an opera can never (or hardly ever) be put on. Thelma Votipka, the beloved Tippy, who not only could sing anything but also teach others how, retired only in 1963 after twenty-eight years. Steady and reliable, and constantly occupied, are Clifford Harvuot, Paul Franke, and the newest buffo tenor, Andrea Velis. They all look back reverently at Alessio de Paolis and George Cehanovsky, the inseparable and inimitable tenor-baritone team for more than a quarter of a century.

The mainstream is fed by the Auditions. Recent winners were Justino Diaz, handsome Puerto Rican bass; George Shirley, tenor; Martina Arroyo and Teresa Stratas, sopranos; and Ezio Flagello, bass, all of whom have gone quickly to the top. Earlier gainers of contracts were the sopranos Heidi Krall and Carlotta Ordassy, the bass Louis Sgarro, and the tenor Charles Anthony, who considered it presumptuous to use his real name, Caruso (although a later Italian with the first name of Mariano gives old-timers a momentary *frisson* at glimpsing that hallowed surname in such characters as the Spy in *Chénier* and Cassio in *Otello*).

The auditions for the Metropolitan National Company turned up masses of talent. But there are still a good many young ones from California or Indiana, Louisiana or Maine, who cannot breach the American wall and seek experience in Europe, even if subconsciously they mean to use Europe as a lever against the Met's doors. When they do come home in triumph, there is a double ration of joy—for them and for us. Sour grapes change to sweetest wine to welcome a James McCracken (who left the Met as a bit-player and returned as Otello), a James King, an Evelyn Lear, a Thomas Stewart. Jess Thomas came to New York after European kudos (he had been a winner of San Francisco auditions and was received first and properly by the Golden Gate). The comely mezzo Mildred Miller belongs in this company, which could well be expected to say, "I told you so."

To Bing's credit is his steady employment of the Negro voice since his fifth season, when he introduced Marian Anderson and Robert McFerrin. Shirley and Arroyo followed, although the latter soon took off for greener European pastures, to return triumphantly as Aida, and establishing her place in *Don Carlo, Butterfly,* and *Trovatore.* Mattiwilda Dobbs's first role in 1956–57 was Gilda; it was also her last in 1963–64. In between she sang Olympia, Lucia, and other altitudinous parts. Gloria Davy, a famous Bess in the Gershwin opera, sang Aida, Nedda, Pamina, and Leonora in *Trovatore* during four seasons, then married in Europe. In a single season (1965–66), three beautiful girls were introduced: Grace Bumbry, Reri Grist, and Felicia Weathers; all bore European cachets and firm American reputations to boot. Leontyne Price's unassailable position has already been noted.

American names have their own good sound (sometimes with the trace of an accent): the sopranos Anna Moffo, Gianna d'Angelo, Mary Costa; the mezzos Rosalind Elias, Belan Amparan, Helen Vanni; the tenors William Olvis, Andrea Velis; the baritones Morley Meredith (a Canadian), Sherrill Milnes, William Dooley; the basses Giorgio Tozzi, Raymond Michalski. All these ring chimes of achievement throughout the first seventeen years of Bing's stewardship. The percentage of Americans is high; not so high as is generally quoted, but impressive. The General Manager has admitted that the Met cannot get along without them.

The most profitable supply pool has been the New York City Opera. Since 1944, this valiant troupe under Julius Rudel has stretched its shoestring to the breaking point but gallantly survives. It continues to turn out a covey of ambitious, passionately earnest, and often greatly gifted singers who can also look attractive while they give some indication of knowing what a character feels and does. Among earlier important

graduates were Regina Resnik and Dorothy Kirsten; Walter Cassel cut
his teeth at the Met but learned his trade at City Center before going
back as a leading baritone; Theodor Uppman is one of the few baritones
to sing both Pelléas and Paquillo; Frances Yeend came over for Chrysothemis; Brenda Lewis went out on the ill-fated *Fledermaus* tour that
scarred Bing's second year, then stayed in the House for Venus, Elvira,
Musetta, Salome, Marie in *Wozzeck,* and additional Rosalindas. Norman
Kelley played character tenor parts several seasons in both companies and
continues in Rudel's good graces. Other transfers have been the sopranos
Virginia MacWatters, Jean Fenn, and Laurel Hurley, the mezzo Mignon
Dunn, the baritone Sherrill Milnes, and the bass Norman Scott.

Several young ones have won Met Auditions or scholarships but
found work first with the City Opera: the fast-rising Shirley Verrett,
Janis Martin, Spiro Malas, and Ron Bottcher (who joined the Met in
1966). Loren Driscoll is another new Met face (handsome) and voice
(tenor) who has gleaned both City Opera and European polish. The
tenor wing was further bolstered a few years ago by the stalwarts John
Alexander and Barry Morell; Cornel MacNeil, John Macurdy, and
Donald Gramm have proved their right to a place among the larger
House's deep voices; the versatile John Reardon now bears the number
of stars beside his name in the City Opera roster that signify "on loan
from the Met." Other prizes captured from the younger company are
Beverly Bower and Judith Raskin, the latter a charming Susanna, Nan-
nette, Marzelline, and Sophie, who virtually stole the show in the NBC-
TV documentary on the Met's Paris trip, which should have been retitled:
"Judy Goes to Paris."

It is difficult to assign any one opera company to Phyllis Curtin, for
this soprano has made her way all over the world. Gifted with beauty,
a soaring voice, and musicianship that allows her to conquer the most
difficult contemporary as well as pure classical works, Curtin sang for
many seasons with the City Opera in roles as widely separate as Constanza, Violetta, Salome, and Susannah (in Carlyle Floyd's piece by the
same name), then graced the Met for a single Fiordiligi in 1961–62.
Rudel made no better use of her that fall; it was her own loyalty to Floyd
that put her into the one real turkey the composer has turned out: *The
Passion of Jonathan Wade.* Thereafter, Curtin was off on her travels, to
return to the Met in 1966 for Violetta, Eva, and Rosalinda.

Rudel has kept exclusive a nucleus of fine singers (and has his fingers constantly crossed). Decidedly Met-worthy are Beverly Sills, who can do some of the prettiest, supplest, and loftiest coloratura singing in a generation; Norman Treigle, the expressive bass-baritone who has filled characters from the hypocritical Reverend Olin Blitch in *Susannah* to the overt Don Giovanni; Beverly Wolff, a mezzo of charm and vocal excellence; Patricia Brooks, an able and musical lyric-coloratura. Other names come to mind—Frances Bible, whose qualifications for the Met were never in doubt but who never showed her superb Octavian there; Chester Ludgin, an enormous baritone with a good voice—but it is useless to list names for Bing's benefit. That gentleman knows the field very well—either he or one of his scouts shows up at every important debut— and he does his own casting.

23

SEVENTEEN YEARS IS AN EPOCH

It all works out somehow. The curtain goes up and stays up.

—Francis Robinson

What has been learned of Bing—the manager and the man—in seventeen years? Soon after his arrival, in the midst of the whirlpools created by his dynamic presence and individualistic character, he realized, as Howard Taubman wrote in *The New York Times*, that he would be presiding over "a temple of temperament as well as of art," and that he would deal with "a public with as many grandstand managers and second-guessers as a major league ball club." H. I. Phillips, celebrated columnist of the *World-Telegram and Sun,* called him a courageous man and asked what vitamins he was taking. "You are opening yourself as a target for knife throwers, harpoon tossers, rock heavers and amalgamated needle guilds," added H.I.P. "You will be blamed for everything from . . . poor parking arrangements, flashlight burns, laryngitis, the ten-cent subway fare, high taxes and the New Deal. . . . Luck be with you—also the Red Cross. . . . Keep up your health and accident insurance."

H.I.P.'s crystal ball did not lie. Very early, Bing remarked that "if I had known the operatic facts of life in America, I would have asked twice the salary."

Impresarios are usually mystery men to the public and often to their colleagues. Even the gregarious Johnson grew a protective shell of remoteness and deviousness—the remark made often about him today is that no one really knew what he was thinking. This is true of Bing to a certain extent: no one is said to know him really. But he often lets someone in on his current state of mind. Taubman states an early instance: When Bing asked for information and got the reply, "I can't help you," he looked vaguely around him and murmured, "I'm afraid *no one* can help me." He cannot resist the quick riposte, the "topper," no matter what it may cost him later. Martin Mayer reported in *The New York Times*

Magazine in the midsixties that a loyal associate cited as Bing's chief
weakness: "He talks."

His ready tongue can flay an artist's sensibilities (one christened him
"Mr. Vindictive-of-all-time"). The story Eleanor Steber tells is a case in
point. In 1962, after singing a dress rehearsal of *Don Giovanni* full voice
over a cold because it was a treat for the Guild, the soprano found her
voice drying up at the Christmas Day performance and made an error in
"Non mi dir." In the second performance, nervousness assailed her as the
trying moment approached, and she felt her throat closing. In order not
to repeat her mistake, she interpolated a short scale passage at the crucial
point and got through the aria. The young conductor didn't appreciate
her effort. He stormed backstage to Bing, who had not spoken to Steber
since the first mishap.

"Eddie Johnson would have been right there in the wings the first
time, knowing the psychological blocks a singer is subject to and the
value of consolation and encouragement from the boss," Steber said.
"Instead, Bing waited until the end of the season to speak to me, then said
that as long as I couldn't do *Don Giovanni,* he had nothing for me. I was
out two seasons. Then he had to call me to replace Kirsten in *Fanciulla*
in January 1966. I suppose I was a fool to do it. But he would have had to
cancel.

"All the camaraderie backstage was gone, particularly since Max
Rudolf left," the soprano concluded.

Bing's wit can also be turned on himself. It's funnier that way. No one
can resist the tale, even if it is apocryphal, of the photograph of Maria
Callas smiling triumphantly after her 1958 *Tosca,* with Mr. Bing's head
in profile, his lips barely touching her forehead. It was supposed to bear
the inscription: "Darling! You're fired!"

It's a very old joke to Bing nowadays. A few profess to find even
more amusing Bing's rejoinder to the remark: "Callas is her own worst
enemy." "Not while I'm alive!" the General Manager is supposed to have
snapped.

He was lean as a whippet when he first came ("his face looks as if it
had been slammed between two doors!" Helen Worden Erskine, reporter-
author, quotes one of his more caustic observers as saying; Steber compares him to a profile on a Roman coin). Still, he seems to get thinner
every year, a manifest impossibility. When this writer solicitously re-

marked on his apparent loss of weight in his second season, he retorted: "Wishful thinking!"

His sense of the theatrical was revealed in a gesture in his first year. Pitying the would-be standees who bore the long vigil on the Broadway sidewalk and around the corner, sometimes for several days before opening, Bing rushed hot coffee to them (and was of course photographed in the act), a custom that became ritual and was discontinued only much later.

Bing's never-desiccating well of antic fun showed as early as 1950, when, after the curtain had fallen on the hilarious jail scene of the Christmas time *Fledermaus,* it rose again to reveal three baggy, frenetic charwomen (as the British would say), brandishing their mops at the audience between swipes at the floor and admonishing them to go home. It took a few minutes to identify the new General Manager and Assistants Francis Robinson and Reginald Allen under the shapeless rags and fright wigs. The genuine champagne in the glasses at New Year's Eve *Fledermaus* routs became traditional. And Prince Orlofsky's ballroom was once the scene of an all-star olio (as in Conried's day), when famous singers did turns, one of them a series of verses both in tribute to and ribbing of Bing. One example:

> The operas that must be your choice
> If you like plays that sing
> Are solely dependent on one voice—
> The voice of Rudolf Bing!

Bing shows himself to possess a streak all ham and a yard wide. He loves to wave a stick over an orchestra and has done so on several occasions—notably a Guild jamboree as *Kapellmeister* for "The Star-Spangled Banner" and at least once on tour of the *Faust* stage band. "Between you and me," he remarked, "conducting is not as hard as all that." Made in jest, this comment may reveal a deep belief in the fallibility of the man in the pit.

His *lèse-majesté* toward himself showed up at the dress rehearsal of the 1965 *Faust,* when a steamy, un-air-conditioned House created hell for the spectators long before the hero was required to take up residence there. Bing in shirt sleeves, perspiring as heavily as his nature will allow, was a sight for mortals. He also favors such informal attire on hot summer days, when he makes his usual walk to the opera from the Essex

House on West Fifty-eighth Street, where he lives with his Russian wife Nina (a former ballerina)—what hours he is away from the "factory."

This small iconoclastic gesture is only part of a larger attitude, what Martin Mayer shrewdly spotted as the "aristocratic Socialist," a type "bred originally in Central Europe, and now at home in England," but to Americans "almost incomprehensible and pretty thoroughly unsympathetic—they have been brought up to see all the hypocrisy and none of the virtue in the fellow who honestly loves mankind and honestly can't stand his neighbors." In the spring of 1953, President Truman signed a bill granting permanent residence to Bing and his wife, with the privilege of applying for citizenship after five years. The Bings never have taken advantage of this eligibility; they remain British subjects and Bing is perhaps most proud of his order, Commander of the British Empire, granted in 1956. "I am still a guest here," he reminds anyone who mentions American politics.

The press has never got on cozy terms with Bing. At his very first interview, he showed his point of view to a *Herald Tribune* representative who had said: "I'm supposed to ask tactless questions." Bing's immediate reply: "And I to give evasive answers!" After two full-dress press conferences, with Scotch and gin laid on, he merely invited the press to an intermission broadcast and announced his plans "in a single omnibus gesture," wrote Cecil Smith in *Worlds of Music*. "His personal relations with the press had been taken care of in the first two years. . . . He is a past master at budgeting both his time and his affability, as no doubt he needs to be."

At the end of a rocky decade and a half, his attitude seemed for a short time to be changing. There were those who claimed to see a conscious softening of the image, believing that Herman Krawitz had assumed the posture of a no-man, so that Bing could relax. He has been known to take five steps away from a conversation to shake hands with a reporter, to cross a theatre floor to brief a *Times* man, and even to go so far as to call in critic after critic for individual chats. But these were artificial gestures, prompted by the gentle urging of his own press department. Since then he has suffered a renewed onslaught of slings and arrows and has reverted to his position of armed indifference.

"I didn't know there was any press," he said wryly—one of those outrageous exaggerations that contain more than an ounce of truth.

"Don't you read what they write about you?" he was asked.

"Not if it goes beyond one page," he answered. "Oh, when I was younger, I did care what they wrote. Now I've given up."

After a few sulfurous remarks about the current crop of critics, comparing them unfavorably with even the recent past, he concluded: "The critical profession should be licensed!"

When *Opera News* later quoted this injudicious remark, it drew blood from Harold Schonberg, who had assumed the role of Bing's archenemy by then. In a Sunday *Times* article which rehashed the *Opera News* rehash of the responsibilities and privileges of critics, Schonberg suggested that some day we might get around to licensing opera impresarios. The air has not cleared since then. It will not help materially to smooth relations between these two forces to note that Bing's autobiography, under contract for four years but not yet begun, will probably not come out until Bing is well away. "I would not want to encounter a certain critic," he gave as a reason for not publishing yet.

Gleefully Bing seized the opportunity afforded by Schonberg's vacation and an invitation to take over the *Times*'s Sunday column to interview himself. He asked all the right questions and got all the right answers. But his review of the critic-versus-opera situation is not likely to win over his absent critical host—on the contrary, one remark may only deepen the rift. He wrote: "Apparently I did not realize that many of them [critics] have no trace of a sense of humor (God save us from Mr. Schonberg's humorous pieces—I'd rather have his standard vicious ones). . . ."

But John Gutman will not admit that Bing has changed essentially. He has always been aloof, and it's better to remain that way. Gutman calls it a defense mechanism.

Are there any differences then? Gutman liked to believe that everyone laughed more, but this was before the agony at the new House wiped the smiles even off administrative faces. He also cited an "inside" joke that never fails to get a reaction. When, in a casting meeting in Bob Herman's office, someone howls in dismay, "This tenor is impossible!" someone else is sure to reply, "But it's a *Wiener schnitzel*." It seems that a Viennese aristocrat dining in his favorite restaurant was told by the waiter that he was going to enjoy his *Wiener schnitzel*. When the customer protested that he hadn't even looked at the menu yet, the waiter replied

sorrowfully, "Yes, Herr Baron. But the only thing we have today is
Wiener schnitzel." It is a sad fact of operatic life that the menu often
contains a *Wiener schnitzel* or two.

What about the kind of scandal that always seems to hover about an
international opera house? The present and possible occupants of the
"casting couch"? The soprano (married) who runs off with the auditor
(also married) or with the bass, baritone, or tenor (all benedicts)? The
paternity suits slapped on prominent singers by unknowns desiring to be
equally prominent? Or, more recently, the tall tenor who can't read
the English on his big fluffy bath towels which says: "Stolen from
Hotel——"? Is there less scandal than before because everybody's so busy?
Gutman answers: "Nobody's too busy for scandal. But I think we handle
it quite well."

As an organizer, Bing is unsurpassed by any previous incumbent. He
had plenty of administrative experience as branch manager of the John
Lewis department store chain in London during the war years when opera
in Britain had become vestigial, but never lost sight of his true calling,
and professed to like best the store's hairdressing department because "its
atmosphere of irrational hysterics reminds me of opera." When he came
to the Met, it was inevitable that he would try to reduce (or perhaps one
should say, raise) the company's unwieldy, temperamental mass to a
smoothly functioning machine.

When his contract expires in 1970, he will have run a twenty-year
course. Is that enough? According to indications at the moment of writing,
it may be.

"I'll be sixty-eight then," he said in a kind of disbelief. The idea of
trying to match Gatti's twenty-seven years appalls him, but no one can
predict how he will react after twenty, when the moment of truth arrives.
Has he considered a successor? The coincidence of Leonard Bernstein's
resignation from the New York Philharmonic's musical directorship to be
effective in 1969 had simply not occurred to Bing. "Why in the world
should Bernstein want this job?" he queried in amazement.

Opera management is almost invariably dictatorship and not consensus, Bing agrees, quoting the old joke about the camel being a horse
designed by a committee. A possible exception was Johnson's troika,
although his successor disagrees, maintaining that Johnson was *the* general
manager, just as he, Bing, is. Bing's operational team, honed down to

sharp efficiency and welded into harmony over the years, seems stronger and more solid than ever. He paid them the compliment of saying he had little doubt they could run the opera without him—whether true or not, we are not likely ever to find out. He can delegate authority, but not without knowing every detail of what his assistants are doing.

"It's good to know, when you feel like a little boy who may make a mistake, that a father is there to back you up," admitted one of the assistants. Bing looked distressed at this imputation of a father image to him, but reiterated his responsibility down to (his favorite example) the third Orphan in *Rosenkavalier*. He will take the blame for an assistant's mistake. He knows he is going to get it anyway, since the name Bing stands for and is synonymous with the institution and all its doings.

"If things go right, it's the team; if they go wrong, it's me," he remarks philosophically. He wins loyalty by the principle practiced by former President Harry S. Truman, who kept prominently on his desk a sign reading, "The Buck Stops Here."

Three of his present close associates preceded him into the House. It is practically unheard of to keep on your predecessor's lieutenants, but two proved to be unexpectedly congenial, and the third, Max Rudolf, was an old acquaintance. Rudolf gravitated from conducting to the administrative side as Bing gave him more and more chores. Francis Robinson, who came in 1945 as an experienced road man with Sol Hurok, soon found his niche in the House. For a period he held two jobs, both box-office treasurer and press chief, relinquishing the former as complications set in. This suave gentleman, as opera-struck as he had been stage-struck in the years he worked as roadman for Katherine Cornell and others, makes the cheerful liaison between the all-too-often cruel outside world and the inner workings. One hectic evening, when Bing scurried through the corridors vainly seeking a physician to attend a ballet member who had collapsed, and Robinson scurried after him, the Press Chief was heard to mutter: Why didn't I take a job with the Equitable and have a nice home and wife and family in New Jersey?" A few moments later he admitted he would have hated every moment of it and belonged exactly where he was.

Reginald Allen, whose passion for the lives and works of Gilbert and Sullivan cannot be hidden long in any conversation, succeeded Jules Seebach as business manager the year before Bing's advent, having reaped

this kind of experience as manager of the Philadelphia Orchestra after
service on its board and special promotion work for Stokowski's productions of *Wozzeck* and *Sacre du Printemps*. After a spell as executive director of operations at Lincoln Center, Allen has returned as special assistant to the President of the Association and to the General Manager.

John Gutman completed Bing's cabinet. They had known each other
in the twenties in Darmstadt, then later in Berlin and London. Gutman
likes to jest about their early relationship; as a critic he could afford to
"tell Bing how lousy his productions were." But not after 1950. The two
men met in London even before Bing had been called by Carl Ebert to
manage the Glyndebourne Festival. Both were adrift—"We had nothing
to do, so where could we get money for drinks?" Bing chose the department store and eventually the Edinburgh Festival; Gutman came to
America in 1938. His experiences were more varied. His first job was as
a paint salesman in Harlem at $12 a week; later the Office of War Infor-
mation employed him for five years as a linguist. He also struggled for a
while as a secretary in a big corporation where the boss never told him
which of five letterheads to use when he said, "Take a letter," and no one
bothered to pay him for several weeks. During these indecisive times he
wrote the adaptation of Haydn's opera *The Man in the Moon,* which
Max Leavitt produced in the ambitious little Lemonade Opera in a
downtown church basement. It got such good notices that even the vice-
president of Gutman's company read them. His only comment was, "Did
you write it on company time?"

From these lean years and unsatisfactory milieus Bing summoned
Gutman. In Gutman's house Bing ate his first New York dinner. It was
thirteen years since they had met. The host greeted his friend: "If you
don't ask where my belly came from, I won't ask where your hair went."

These four men—Gutman, Rudolf, Allen, and Robinson—helped in
Bing's rough transitional period. But immediately beneath them, the
ground dropped sharply away. Today around the buzzing hive of the
opera house they pause now and then to recall their sense of shock
when they realized they didn't have enough help at submanagement level.
Early in 1954, Anthony A. Bliss, who had recently joined the board,
approached Richard Aldrich and his theatrical production office for
help. Aldrich sent him Herman Krawitz.

The moment management appeared on the stage with a newly hired technician the stagehands threatened a strike. On a Monday morning, with *Tannhäuser* in the offing for the night, they called out pickets and stopped work for ten hours, returning to see the opera through but refusing to touch an afternoon dress rehearsal for the next day's *Norma,* which was to be a benefit for the Guild. "We decided to set up the stage ourselves," Bliss remembers. Newspaper legmen and photographers flocked with glee to let the public in on Bing, Bliss, Allen, Gutman, and the Opera Association's lawyer, Lincoln Lauterstein, in shirt sleeves, rustling props, staggering under flats, and pulling lines. Bing, as befitted the headman, manipulated the curtain and let them have such a fast one that it nearly caught Zinka Milanov, the Norma, and Fedora Barbieri, the Adalgisa. As he wiped his brow, the General Manager breathed in relief: "Well, nobody's dead!"

Fortunately, Richard Walsh, president of the International Alliance of Theatrical Stagehands, considered the strike unauthorized. The Met had the right, he affirmed, to investigate the efficiency of its own operations. He allowed six weeks' grace for negotiations to resume. (These had been going on for fourteen months and had become deadlocked over a 2 percent raise, retroactive, as all pay was generally agreed to be when workers went on past contract expiration date.) The overdue contract was signed at last.

Bing was enormously impressed with young Krawitz and put him immediately into the place vacated by Horace Armistead, from which he has risen to be an assistant manager.

Robert Herman, the musical son of a beloved baseball player and coach, "Babe" Herman, found his way to New York via the tutelage of Carl Ebert in California. Bing was delighted with this protégé of his old boss. Herman began as an assistant stage manager, then became artistic administrator, succeeding Rudolf in 1958. This tall young man also learned fast; today he is largely responsible for performance and rehearsal scheduling, what Reginald Allen calls a cubic chessboard, with games going on simultaneously in three dimensions—the twentieth-century successor to the simpler jigsaw puzzle. Herman also sits in on union matters, winning a compliment from Hy Faine, executive secretary of AGMA, who says Herman "does his homework and knows every detail of the matters in hand." His title is now assistant manager, along with Gutman, Robinson, and Krawitz. Assistants to them were appointed in relative abundance as soon as possible. Now active are Paul Jaretzki, who had spent some time in the New York City Opera administration, and is now the Met's assistant artistic administrator; Glen Sauls, a general assistant; two Krawitz lieutenants, Charles Riecker, who infinitely prefers life around an opera house to a bank, and Michael Bronson. Frank Paola remained in that double job known as company manager and musical secretary; he is an experienced jigsaw puzzler.

"How did Johnson, Ziegler, and St. Leger do it all by themselves?" one or another of today's management will pause to wonder in odd moments.

As the magnitude and complexity of the opera machine grow, the problems keep pace. Dealing with the thirteen unions that govern the personnel outside the executive's tent is a full-time year-round headache. Bing's first encounter was with AGMA. He compromised on a few singers he had meant to drop, but got $100,000 from the board for Social Security and unemployment benefits for the first time. Later, severance pay was provided for and in the early sixties converted to pensions. One of the first issues was the size of the chorus. Through Gatti's time there were two big groups, one Italian, one German. In the forties the number was cut to ninety-six, the minimum specified in AGMA's contract, and the character homogenized. The Met didn't take kindly to the large minimum and proposed seventy-eight, the number the Met's Robert Herman says is employed full time, with extras available for mass movements, as AGMA insists. In these enlightened times, the rights of choristers as of principals—and at last, of dancers—are thoroughly safeguarded —a far cry from the Conried days when (in January 1906) the chorus struck briefly for pay higher than $20 a week and a berth to sleep in on tour! That emergency brought Caruso and other principals to step in and sketch out the chorus parts, and an opera *sans* chorus was substituted for one using a large group. Today, a similar rebellion would take the whole company out. Along with the principals (called "artists" in the contracts), the chorus and ballet are ringed round with protection in money, time, insurance, vacations, conditions of employment, and grievances; management is also protected from insubordination, tardiness, and infractions of the rules.

In the AGMA contracts is a little paragraph that is designed to do away with the kind of practice known as "kickbacks," a word barely whispered in opera corridors. Several *ancien régime* characters (who shall, of course, remain nameless) were deemed guilty of this nest-feathering, and cynics maintain that, like sex, it will always be with us. However, the paragraph reads in part: "No person who occupies a paid supervisory or a paid executive position . . . with [the] Association or . . . with AGMA shall be permitted to act as a manager, agent or personal representative of any Artist . . . or receive any fee, commission or other consideration of any kind. . . ." In fact, says John Gutman, the assistant conductor who coaches a newcomer in a part nowadays (and singers are required to know their roles better than in the days when they got by at their engagement with one or two arias and boned up hastily on the rest) now is paid by the Association.

Bing's second brush with a union was the stagehand emergency in 1953–54, which climaxed a season that Howard Taubman thought might well have driven the General Manager to join the Foreign Legion or politics for a little peace. Local 802, the powerful unit of the American Federation of Musicians, which controls the orchestra, was playing without a contract; Traubel left in a short burst of rocket fire, followed by George Szell's equally explosive departure; a fuss arose with the publisher Ricordi over royalty payments on *Simon Boccanegra,* causing *Cav-Pag*'s hasty substitution; Blanche Thebom duplicated Eleanor Steber's 1951 feat of singing twice in one day: Fricka at a matinee and Amneris as a replacement for Fedora Barbieri at night. Everyone survived, but Taubman felt the Met was living dangerously.

But Bing's most crucial moments on Thirty-ninth Street came in August before the season of 1961–62, when he actually—and many thought arbitrarily and unnecessarily—canceled operations because the festering dispute with Local 802 finally burst open. President Kennedy's Secretary of Labor, Arthur Goldberg, stepped in to settle things, but the *giubilo* was *immenso* only for the time being, because the orchestra got no raise. (Ironically, this very year was singled out in advance by a Dallas correspondent as the beginning of Bing's Golden Age because of the advent of Price, Nilsson, Farrell, and Corelli.) Another hassle occurred in 1964, when the Goldberg contract expired. No new one was signed, and from that time, discontent simmered up to the time of the opening of the new House on September 16, 1966. All other unions had settled as of that date, and all were brought into concurrence, with simultaneous expiration dates to facilitate orderly negotiations—all but the musicians. These recurring hairbreadth escapes wear on everybody's nerves. Bing expressed himself publicly, as quoted by Martin Mayer: "I can't tell the American people how to handle their union situation, but this business of a bloody battle every year is such a *bore!*"

Bing gets along with the opera auxiliaries, the Guild and National Council, accepting them as facts of life, although they startled him at first. "I was afraid," he admitted. He was "slightly nonplused by people —mostly women—getting together in helpful groups the way we do in America," remarked Mrs. Herbert Witherspoon with some amusement (she had returned as Guild director a few years before Bing's advent). "It was a different pattern from any he had been accustomed to." But both sides soon "put it on the line," and Bing proved easier to deal with than Johnson. "He likes people not to have too many embellishments," as Mrs. Witherspoon put it. His bluntness was refreshing; so was his sly sense of humor. He has to all intents and purposes suppressed any fundamental dislike for interference in his operations when it comes to dealing with these two powerful groups, and is even able to say of late that he has little "personally" to do with them.

The Guild has had only two directors since Mrs. Witherspoon departed to try concert management in the West—both of them in Bing's regime: the polished Richard P. Leach and the petite Harriet (Mrs. Heywood) Gilpatric. In the spring of 1967, the Guild got its sixth president, Michael V. Forrestal, son of the late James V. Forrestal, the Secretary of Defense. Only forty, Mr. Forrestal is of the new, vigorous breed that the opera and its auxiliaries are seeking. Previous presidents were Mrs. Belmont, Mrs. William Francis Gibbs, Mrs. Joseph R. Truesdale, Lauder Greenway, and Langdon Van Norden (who held the record for longevity in the post—fourteen years).

The National Council was organized in 1952, an aggregation of wealthy and socially prominent men and women from many parts of the country who have been induced by national cultural pride and the winsome Mrs. Belmont to form a united front at the highest level. Their dues are $500 per annum ($250 for associate members); many large donations also come from their membership or solicitation. In addition to a production fund, their good works include sponsorship of a Central

Opera Service, which endeavors to act as a clearinghouse for opera producers and devotees throughout the United States, and the Auditions, which have increased in scope and vitality through organization on a regional basis. Howard J. Hook, Jr., a Princeton graduate who spent several years studying lieder singing with Ria Ginster in Europe, came home to find a larger duty awaiting him, joined the Council, and soon became chairman of the Auditions.

The gain to the Met in young talent is obvious, but equally important is the emphasis on human values and on the concept of community relationship to opera, Hook believes. The Auditions provide scholarships from $50 to $5,000, depending on the need—"anything to further a promising career," says Hook. The singers are constantly reheard to check progress. Hook cited such singers as Joan Marsh and Veronica Tyler, winners of the 1966 Tchaikovsky competition in Moscow, as recipients of help. Auditions for the National Company also were conducted by Hook's committees.

A change in the structure of the Auditions came about in 1967. The former pattern was a step-by-step progress to finals, with one or two contract awards and a half dozen or so scholarships ranging up to $2,000. Now semifinalists in the spring will each receive $2,000 to prepare for the finals six months later, one month under auspices and training of the Met itself. The final winner will receive a possible contract and $2,500 award. This makes sense, Hook belives, as it channels careers toward the Met and ensures adequate preparation. The administration grumbled a bit because it meant extra work, but whether they like it or not, this is an important aspect of their future—at least until possible government sponsorship.

The Council's total contribution to the parent company was $100,000 in 1965–66; the Opera Guild reached $488,000, of which $14,000 was earmarked for the National Company.

Bing also gets along with his board, although in the early days there was some talk that he and George Sloan, president of the Association, "made each others' lives miserable" for a few years. This could possibly be attributed to the board's timidity after long, lean years of depression and war, when the idea of spending rather than saving sent shivers down the spines of bankers and lawyers. Bing's boldness has paid off in winning almost complete autonomy. Bliss and Lauder Greenway and the active members of an almost totally committed board understand his ambition and have been proud to foster it. From the beginning he let them know that he expected them to find money for him. Furthermore, he announced firmly that the board has "never once interfered in artistic matters, such as asking me to engage any performer."

The word "deficit" became taboo. When the Federal Government delayed year after year in rebating the 10 percent admissions tax, Bing coolly asked his subscribers to make up the amount and double it by contributing 20 percent of their subscription fees. Gasps, shudders, and shrugs to the contrary, the opera was richer by $125,000 immediately. Though the tax was eventually taken off, the tithe continues (and has even been doubled in a later emergency).

An enclave within the House itself has always seemed to be a fly in the amber for Bing. The Metropolitan Opera Club had its origin as a Vaudeville Club, installed in the rebuilding after the 1892 fire. Considerably less decorous than its successor, the Vaudeville Club held forth on the opera's dark nights—Tuesday, Thursday, and Saturday—and entertained many a lively lass and uproarious skit in the large room off the Grand Tier it has always occupied. As the operation of the opera changed and enlarged, the club changed with it, later becoming known for its restrictiveness. White tie was—and is—*de rigueur* for evening; ladies are invited for Saturday matinees but are not allowed to keep their hats on; no one is permitted to lean forward, as this obstructs the view in the club box at the extreme left side of the auditorium. Of late years, the club has turned to raising money for the opera by holding an annual gala ball, but Bing still chafes, it is said, over his lack of control of the block of seats on Mondays, Wednesdays, Fridays, and Saturday matinees. However, it is doubtless apocryphal that at the annual dinner given in his honor the General Manager begins his greetings thus: "I am always happy to see again the same damned faces!"

The Saturday afternoon broadcasts, which have grown to such popular proportions that Milton Cross is possibly better known to millions of listeners than Bing, at first plagued the latter by their demands and their virtual autonomy under the sponsorship of the Texas Company, which has already celebrated its silver anniversary as benefactor. But Bing seems resigned, as indeed it is felt he must be considering the value received in money as well as recognition, and even takes to the air himself on state occasions. The production of the famous intermission features, the Opera News on the Air and the Opera Quiz, has been the successful operation for many years of Geraldine Souvaine, who succeeded her late husband Henry in the post.

Over a period of four or five years, a new space-time relationship was envisaged, differing from Einstein's but equally radical, since it foresaw year-round activity. The unions continuously pressed for fifty-two weeks of employment, but to achieve this revolutionary time extension required new space, and space that could be air-conditioned. So Bing and his board began in 1955 to work for a new opera house, and in ten years achieved at last what Otto Kahn, alone against the world, could not. The ferment had never ceased, however. Plans were advanced and rejected; sites offered, considered, rejected. Mayor Fiorello LaGuardia was keenly interested in a performing-arts center with the Met at its core; when his proposal came to nothing, he concentrated on the Mecca Temple on West Fifty-fifth Street and saw it transformed into the New York City Center of Music and Drama, which bred its own ballet, opera, musical comedy, and drama troupes. After a study between 1948 and 1950, Robert Moses, Chairman of the Triborough Bridge and Tunnel Authority, offered the Met the Columbus Circle site where the Coliseum now stands; when that fell through, the Lincoln Center area came into focus.

The New York Philharmonic was seeking a new home because of the threatened razing of Carnegie Hall, so the opera and orchestra boards got together and the idea of the center was born. (The ultimate salvation of Carnegie Hall in 1960 came too late to affect the Philharmonic, which in any case was merely a tenant of the old hall.)

John D. Rockefeller III entered the picture in the summer of 1955, renewing the twenty-year-old interest of his family in providing a home for the opera. The locale shifted uptown from Rockefeller Center. With the celerity that accompanies the plans of big men, Lincoln Center for the Performing Arts developed apace, drawing in the Juilliard School of Music, the music division of the New York Public Library, and a repertory theatre company. Rockefeller employed Wallace K. Harrison of the firm that had designed the midtown complex known as Radio City or Rockefeller Center, and set off with the architect and Herbert Graf (who had made intensive studies of the physical plants of opera houses) to scout Europe. Herman Krawitz went too, determined to find out "what not to do," since this new house was to be specifically tailored for its occupant and not merely thrown together on general principles.

The figure of $40 million danced before the eyes of the gentlemen and ladies concerned, and fund-raising campaigns began immediately. When various emergencies arose—an underground water system treacherously appeared and was promptly named Lake Bing, and costs mounted, as costs always do—the budget finally stood at $45.7 million. Beyond this no one wanted to go, although an extra effort would have avoided some compromises that made the building less than perfect—chopping off ten feet on either side and thus cramping office space needlessly; cutting thirty-five feet from the length, compressing the interior even further; moving rehearsal rooms from upstairs to the cellars. Many of the workers, in new quarters as cramped as the old, wondered why they had been asked to take the trouble to outline their particular space needs. The Met was forced to compromise on yet another point when the Lincoln Center authorities and architects balked at the opera's desire to route traffic right by its front door for patrons' convenience in inclement weather. All this was locked in by 1962; from then on there could be no change, even though little provision had been made for the growth of the operation itself through the addition of the Studio and touring companies and other outlets. Eventually the Guild and *Opera News* offices, which had been settled in the studio portion of the old House, had to find space in a building a few blocks away from Lincoln Center.

The Studio and touring companies were designed as long-range undertakings. The first is the pet project of John Gutman, who can boast that it is the only element of the Met's activities that has never lost a penny. This young and sprightly group takes an opera such as *Così fan Tutte* to schools, charging a fee of $750. It has been giving one hundred performances a year, and may double that in the future, says Gutman. A new concert group is expected to add to studio success. Solvency is not owed entirely to box office, however, for overhead is paid by the Lincoln Center Educational Fund, an endowment that operates solely for the purpose of extending to youth the activities of the Center's components.

The touring group—The Metropolitan Opera National Company, to give it its full and preferred title—was Reginald Allen's baby.

In a surprise move, the popular singer Risë Stevens was selected to be co-manager, along with the former executive stage manager, Michael Manuel. Its untimely amputation as an economy measure after its second season must be reckoned as one of the tragedies of the Met's new incarnation. Winning its way rapidly as a thoroughly rehearsed, freshly voiced, colorfully costumed and accoutred group in a repertoire that says what it has to say, old and new, with sparkle, the company had begun to achieve two of its objectives as outlined by Allen: providing full employment for young artists and a quality product without stars for cities that have never seen opera as well as those who had had a few performances top-heavy with imported stars (almost always from the Met). The third original objective was almost always overlooked, Allen believes. This was the hope of stimulating audiences all over the country to the point where they are conditioned to like opera and keep on importing it year after year, with the eventual result of creating regional companies that could serve and interchange with several states. "We were looking for spin-offs," Bliss commented on this aspect of the National Company.

The gloom at the sudden order to disband permeated backstage at the New York City Center where the company went through its paces in a January-February season. A potential miracle waited in the wings, but did not show itself until February 9, 1967, a few days before the end of the run. Mrs. DeWitt Wallace, who with her husband is co-chairman of the *Reader's Digest* and a generous benefactor to good causes, offered $1 million to save the young company. The gracious gift startled everyone and perplexed the Met for a while, because it could not use the money for any other purpose, badly as such a substantial sum was needed. Ultimately, plans were set afoot to try to redeem the vital junior adjunct for the season of 1968–69.

In spite of the discouragement, they gave some smart performances at City Center. New York had not been particularly kind the previous season, but this visit brought vindication. Notoriously hard-boiled Chicago and Los Angeles furnished "wonderfully quotable" reviews, said Allen, and the Washington *Post*'s critic, Paul Hume, also joined in to make the parent company feel proud of its offspring. Washington claimed a godfather's concern, for the John F. Kennedy Center for the Performing Arts put up $400,000 from income on capital investment (for the first season only). However, that didn't automatically predispose a stringent critic like Hume in its favor. Still, the real surprise was Mexico, which can eviscerate a performance it doesn't approve. The young troupe came away not only unscathed but flattered.

The National Company was conceived in a philosophy of deficit, as opposed to the genesis of the *Fledermaus* touring company of 1952, which originated in terms of profit-making, explained Allen. This latter, incidentally, was not the failure everyone thought it—"We didn't lose our shirts. We merely pulled the string after twenty-two instead of thirty-two weeks. We got involved in Red Channels [that bible of the witch-hunters of Senator McCarthy's time], our tenor, Donald Dame, died suddenly on the road, and we were up against a Hurok company playing the same work."

The year-round concept brought the summer months into focus for the first time. Various sorties were devised to keep everyone busy—in 1965 the Met took over Lewisohn Stadium, which had drawn thousands to stone benches and uncomfortable folding chairs to hear symphonic music since 1918, under the guiding hand and admonitory voice of Mrs. "Minnie" Guggenheimer. A second season followed. Now the Stadium will be razed for the development program of the City University of New York, on one of whose campuses it stands, and the Met has discontinued its uptown operation. In its place Bing was able to take advantage of the new enthusiasm for mass culture in New York City by accepting the offer of Mayor Lindsay's special administrator August Heckscher to play in the parks of the five boroughs during June and July 1967. Nine performances with first-rate casts drew huge crowds, already accustomed to equally high-class entertainment such as the New York Philharmonic and the Shakespeare festivals.

Other junkets were added: a week in Paris, and an exchange with the Newport Jazz Festival that took opera-in-concert to Rhode Island and brought jazz to the Stadium and prompted John Gutman to offer the festival director, George Wein, his own theme song: *"Wien, Wien, nur Du allein . . ."*

In the summer of 1967, the Newport season was expanded to a Verdi Festival from August 17 through August 26 under the Met's own auspices with generous support from Gov. John H. Chafee, the state of Rhode Island, and Mrs. Claiborne Pell, wife of the Rhode Island senator. Concert performances of *Macbeth, Rigoletto, La Traviata, Il Trovatore,*

I Vespri Siciliani (not even in the Met's repertoire and performed only once before in this country, by Thomas Scherman's Concert Opera), *Otello,* and *Aida* enlisted top Met singers designed to entertain the fashionable resort enormously.

Intensive planning and lively imagination went into this festival, which both sides hope to make permanent. Such attractions as recorded concerts of old Verdi operas in the gardens of the Elms, one of the Newport Preservation Society's showcases, and chamber music in both the Elms and Marble House (the gaudy palace built by Mrs. W. K. Vanderbilt and also an acquisition of the Preservation Society), and the complete songs of Verdi, performed for the first time in history as a unit, are highlights. Others are a scene from Virgil Thomson's *Byron,* libretto by Jack Larson, the opera most recently commissioned by the Met, and the American premiere of the English Malcolm Williamson's *Happy Prince,* sung by the Barrington Boys Choir and Met soloists, the latter a part of the program for children and young people that the Met hopes will lay a firm foundation for the future.

Virtually every executive of the company planned to give a talk on every aspect of the mammoth operation in seminars and workshops during daily Opera Bazaars. Old films that have operatic flavor round out the ambitious program. Glen Sauls was the chief administrator.*

Still other streams had to be panned for gold. "The times are different," said Bliss. "We have no Otto Kahn today." Without burdening the reader with bookkeeping, a glimpse of the final year before Lincoln

---

* At the end of ten days crammed with fifty-five events, both sides expressed a desire to continue, even though the Met will lose almost a quarter million dollars. Inimical weather hampered the entire operation, the last two operas being forced indoors, courtesy of the Navy, which offered a drill hall not quite commodious enough to contain even ticket holders, but obviating the use of the outdoor amplification system which very nearly scuttled artistic pretensions. Highlights of the seven Verdi operas were the expressive Macbeth of Kostas Paskalis, the impressive debut as Rigoletto of the English baritone Peter Glossop (who returned as Iago when Tito Gobbi canceled), the drama and pathos of Gabriella Tucci's Violetta and Leonora, the sweetly sung Alfredo of George Shirley, the welkin-storming of James McCracken's Manrico, and Renata Tebaldi's sensitive Desdemona. Roberta Peters, Grace Bumbry, Martina Arroyo, Virginia Zeani, Eugenio Fernandi, Jon Vickers, and Richard Tucker also had their moments. But even more important as an augur for the future was the revelation of the young talent that remains submerged in an ordinary season: the excellent singing and attractive presence of Nancy Williams, Lilian Sukis, Karan Armstrong, Joann Grillo, Gene Boucher, and Russell Christopher; the vivacious and charming company that clusters in John Gutman's Studio; and the competence and enthusiasm of the usually least appreciated segment of the roster—the young maestros and accompanists. Not only did the seasoned George Schick, Ignace Strasfogel, and Jan Behr win their place in the sun (or fog), but John Ryan, Louise Sherman, Lawrence Smith, Marshall Williamson, and David Stivender (the latter responsible for the stunning presentation of the Verdi songs) were constantly and rewardingly in view. The ballet had its night, ending uproariously with a takeoff on every dance cliché, and orchestra members played chamber music brilliantly. These peripheral events, held in the Breakers as well as the other two mansions, proved to be the real jewels, a possible nucleus for a festival structure.

Center proves enlightening. Not counting the National Company, the regular tour, and the summer Stadium, the expense budget was $8,441,-000. Box-office intake from twenty subscription series, single sales, and benefits amounted to almost $6,700,000. The resulting gap of approximately $1¾ million had to be closed. Almost a million was raised by a recently formed Development Committee under Mrs. Lewis W. Douglas with Ione Page as executive. This comprised a Patron's list, individually solicited, with a minimum contribution of $1,000, and a Corporate Patron's body, whose minimum is $2,500. A thriving segment of industry showed concrete interest, sometimes to the extent of six figures, as in the case of the $110,000 advanced by the American Export and Isbrandtsen Lines for a new production of *Aida* in 1963–64. Another transportation agency, Eastern Air Lines, gave $25,000. The list grows encouragingly. Most recent was the gift of $500,000 from Eastern Air Lines to pay for the new production of Wagner's *Ring* cycle, to be spread over four seasons. The new climate of industry sponsorship for the arts was reflected by Floyd D. Hall, president of Eastern, who called the half million the "largest single ongoing commitment" of his company to a nonbusiness cause.

An additional $400,000 was raised for the production and opera house funds. Very few of the new investitures in Bing's regime have had to be absorbed by the general budget; most are gifts from individuals (prominent among them Mrs. John D. Rockefeller, Jr., Mrs. Albert Lasker, John Newberry, Francis Goelet, Mrs. Izaak Walton Killam of Montreal), several foundations, and the Guild.

When Bing came, the total budget hovered around $2 million. After seventeen years, the estimated figure for 1966–67 was closer to $15 million —not including the new House. Recent developments have blown this up alarmingly. The financial organism has proliferated to such an extent that a full-time director has been appointed, William H. Hadley, a former executive of Standard Oil of New Jersey and, significantly, in addition a graduate of engineering, business, and law schools and a bond assistant to Secretary of the Treasury Henry L. Morgenthau, Jr., before World War II. So, as it moved into its glossy new home, the Metropolitan Opera could at last claim to be Big Business, but didn't like the prospect very much.

24

ADDIO—CON RANCORE

"The Queen is dead. Long live the Queen!" Rudolf Bing used these timeworn words and made them ring movingly true.

—Life magazine

The two wings of the gold curtain came down slowly, slowly, gradually shutting away the sight of the entire company massed on stage. In its front ranks, waving, weeping, or barely controlling themselves, were the stars who had sung the Old Met out with a gala program and a final *"Auld Lang Syne"* on April 16, 1966. The audience stood, all over the House, and waved back, tears and sobs mingling with the applause and shouting of farewells. It was 1:30 in the morning, but the crowd seemed loath to go. The dedication of the performance on stage, when the entire roster, almost without exception, had sung or danced their valedictory with eight current and three former conductors in the pit, the nostalgic welcome for three dozen great ones of the past, and the delirious greeting of friends and colleagues in the jammed corridors and public rooms had held back the tide of sorrow for five hours. Now a somber shadow seemed to have fallen with the curtain, and everyone departed with final looks over the shoulder at the beautiful-ugly temple that had held so many memories and now harbored so many ghosts.

That Rudolf Bing struck exactly the right note in his curtain speech was admitted even by those who had considered him callous in his willingness to trade the shabby old building for an up-to-date one. "This is a farewell and every farewell hurts," he paraphrased Juliet, adding, "fortunately it is a good-bye to brick and mortar only and not to friends. A building is replaceable. Friends are not. . . . I would like to feel that [your support] was meant for the company rather than for a building. The company goes on. . . . The Queen is dead. Long live the Queen!"

Lauder Greenway, chairman of the board, was equally felicitous in his choice of words: "Thoughts throng upon us too deep for human tears. . . . It is a matter of farewell and hail."

"Singularly graceful and well-turned phrases," commented *Variety*. "Impeccably decent" were the officials about the issue of saving the House, an issue that had arisen a month or so previously in a belated rush of sentiment. But the very reticence, continued *Variety*, "contributed a certain sense of pregnancy to the unmentioned campaign."

If the management believed that its own attitude would be mirrored by all the performers, however, it was due for a rude shock at the outset. Leopold Stokowski had just conducted what was perhaps the best-sung "Star-Spangled Banner" ever to rise to the ornate ceiling and followed this whole-throated community sing by a rousing performance of the *Tannhäuser* March, "Entrance of the Guests." Turning to the audience, the Maestro uttered a few words that opened wide a Pandora's box of troubles for the Met.

"What a beautiful house!" he exclaimed. (Rustle of surprise; applause.) "What splendid acoustics!" (Ripple of laughter.) "Help us save this magnificent building! (Thunderous applause from a few sections; stunned quiet from others.) The reaction of Bing to this gratuitous contribution raised speculation everywhere. Joseph X. Dever of the *Journal-American* claimed a direct quote from the Met's "able, iron-clad manager." Bing snapped: "It was rude. He was invited to conduct, not to make a speech." (Footnote: The *Times* inexplicably considered Stokowski "rather funny.")

When quiet had been restored, the program, what *Variety* headlined as the "World's Slowest Vaude," got under way and proceeded down a long road. In order to get everyone in, there were two sextets: from *Lucia* (Moffo, Ordassy, Sergi, Anthony, Diaz, Walker), and the Triumphal Scene from *Aida* (Curtis-Verna, Madeira, Baum, Sereni, Macurdy, Scott), in costume and with a ballet display; three quintets: *Carmen* (including Thelma Votipka, recently retired, and George Cehanovsky, just about to, with Resnik, Baldwin, and Franke); *Magic Flute* (Pracht, Grillo, Kriese, Shirley, Uppman); *Vanessa* (Steber, Thebom, Dunn, Alexander, Harvuot). Oddly enough, no quartets were needed, but four trios absorbed a dozen singers: *Forza* (Delia Rigal returned to substitute for the ailing Amara, with Peerce and Tozzi); *Cosi fan tutte* (Stratas, Miller, Guarrera); *Rosenkavalier* (Caballé, Raskin, Elias), and inevitably the Final Trio from *Faust,* which had opened the first season as well as the last in the Old House (Tucci, Gedda, Hines). Duets roused wild enthusiasm: *Otello*

(McCracken, Colzani); *Manon Lescaut* (Tebaldi, Corelli); *Gioconda* (Crespin, Cvejic), and *Andrea Chénier* (Milanov, Tucker). The last kindled frantic ovations for Milanov (who had officially retired a few nights before) that took some indignant shushing to close off.

Singing alone were Robert Merrill, Cesare Siepi, Jon Vickers, Leontyne Price, and Sandor Konya. Also singled out was Fernando Corena, who burst into the unfamiliar *"Heil diesem Hause"* from Cornelius' *Barber of Bagdad,* the reason soon revealed in a salute in several languages to "this House." Birgit Nilsson heroically sang Brünnhilde's entire Immolation Scene, proudly wearing across her bosom the golden wreath that had been presented to her namesake Christine Nilsson (no relation) eighty-two and a half years before.

Roberta Peters suffered the handicap of singing right in front of Lily Pons, who had claimed her own voice was as good as ever and expressed chagrin at not being invited to use it. Dorothy Kirsten also competed with Pons, but not vocally; her pale pink taffeta *robe de style* faded before Lily's vivid rose gown. Licia Albanese seized the occasion of her solo appearance singing *"Un bel di,"* dressed in a contemporary adaptation of a geisha kimono in rich tangerine obi cloth, to kneel gracefully and kiss the hallowed floor (or at least to transfer the caress from her lips by her fingers). Many applauded the diva for this seemingly spontaneous gesture, which must have been meticulously rehearsed.

Almost more enthralling to the audience was the presence of three dozen former favorites on stage in a semicircle behind the performers. The women were escorted in by the graceful boys of the ballet in white tie and tails, and each given a bouquet; the men made it under their own steam and minus nosegays. From the more recent past, those who had departed after Bing's arrival, were Bidu Sayao, Risë Stevens, Lily Pons, Patrice Munsel, Martha Lipton, Vilma Georgiou, Herta Glaz, John Brownlee, Eugene Conley, Charles Kullman, and Nicola Moscona. The Junoesque Karin Branzell, who retired in 1951, appeared in an honor box but not on stage; neither would Gladys Swarthout show herself except in the audience. Marian Anderson belonged entirely to Bing's regime.

Of earlier vintage were the conductors Giuseppe Bamboschek and Wilfred Pelletier; the latter's wife, Rose Bampton; the baritone Richard Bonelli; and a cluster of tenors—Mario Chamlee (who died the following November 13), Richard Crooks, Frederick Jagel, Raoul Jobin, and the

snowy-haired Giovanni Martinelli, who watched with transparent emotion and mouthed along as the younger McCracken sang the role
Martinelli loved best—Otello. (A half dozen European tenors couldn't
come; Lauritz Melchior wouldn't.) Marjorie Lawrence beamed from the
wheelchair that had confined her since her attack of polio in 1942, but
which has not crippled her spirit. Lotte Lehmann, *"Geliebte Lotte,"*
won cheers as she appeared, all silver from hair to gown, vital as ever.
Looking frail and tired when she arrived, Elisabeth Rethberg bloomed
under the genuineness of her welcome. Also warmly greeted were the
"Baby" Nanette Guilford, still a charmer; Helen Jepson, now an ash
blonde; Ruth Miller, the wife of Chamlee; Nina Morgana, the wife of
Bruno Zirato; Irra Petina, the vivacious Russian; and Stella Roman, who
departed in 1950. Special applause arose for Edith Mason, who had
not sung in the House since 1936; even anteceding this soprano was
another, Anna Case, who retired in 1920 after her marriage to Clarence
Mackay. Her delight in feeling the stage beneath her feet affected her
much as the smell of battle rouses an old warrior. She lavished curtsies
and smiles and waves in a miniature ovation all her own.

The newspapers reacted to this gallimaufry of sight, sound, tears, and
smiles in their own typical way. The half dozen New York dailies then
existing provided a spread of opinion and individuality; the long ordeal
had not yet begun that was to compress three into one under the awkward
title of *World Journal Tribune* (and the eventual death even of this hy-
brid, leaving New York bereft of all but the *Times, News,* and *Post*). In
true *Times* fashion, all the facts and lists and programs were presented
in full and correctly; a historical résumé dominated one page after
the conventional front-page audience photo and story. Harold Schonberg and Charlotte Curtis shared another page for critical review and
"background social story." Miss Curtis described the audience as "hundreds of formally dressed aristocrats, tycoons, bankers, nabobs, diplomats,
moguls, grandes dames, fashion plates and other notable over-achievers,"
a list she fancied so much that she was to repeat it almost word for word in
reporting the gala opening of the New House. But why should she not use
precious words twice when such an authority as Mrs. Cornelius Vanderbilt Whitney wore the same tiara to both events? (Neither was caught
in the repetition.)

One *Herald Tribune* story by Herbert Kupferberg featured the final

Bohème matinee, quoting Mimi's remark that she was *"bella come un tramonto"* ("beautiful as a sunset") to sum up the twilight of Thirty-ninth Street. Louis Biancolli's imaginary colloquy between Verdi, Mozart, Puccini, and Wagner marked his own farewell; he retired from the *World-Telegram and Sun* before its own sunset. The *Journal-American* spread itself handsomely, but over two days. One full page of nostalgia under the head "Farewell to the Met" bore a box that confused the non-sports reader by its laconic pronouncement: "Mets: 1 down—161 to go."

Society Editor Devers agreed with Miss Curtis that no opening night could compare with this "goodbye to the Grand Old Lady." He cited names to prove it: Belmont, Astor, Whitney, Vanderbilt, Aldrich, Donahue, Rockefeller, Houghton, Kennedy, Lasker—then added diplomats and the show-business contingent and remarked the absence of first-nighter Hope Hampton.

To assign credit for the last note sung gave reporters a little trouble: for the record, it was not Méphistophélès' *"Jugée"* ("Condemned") but the chorus' *"Resuscité"* (referring to the Saviour and thus not applicable to the House, as some partisans tried to make it).

As the lights went out at last, the Old Lady seemed to settle onto her bones with a creak and a sigh. All color ebbed out of the dull red carpets. Cherubs high above flung down flakes of gilt paint to shimmer in the feeble rays of the single work light on stage. The darkness was uneasy with despair and promise. Although the living creature was leaving its home, the shell would not be abandoned until after three and a half weeks of occupancy by the Bolshoi Ballet, making the anticlimax of the morning after all the more distressing. For weeks, the costumers, electricians, propmen, business officers, rehearsal chiefs, secretaries, studio occupants had been clearing out racks, chests, cubbyholes, corners, desks, closets, and corridors, moving to the rhythm of a chant as poignant as any spiritual: "We're weeping but we're packing!"

In the Thirty-ninth Street entrance, receptionists and switchboard genii Winifred Short and Mary Colligan treasured their gift from J. William Fisher, a Met board member from Marshalltown, Iowa—a miniature gilded dustpan and broom, "For taking some of the old dirt to the new home," the way a transplanted national brings along to his new land a handful of his old earth.

On April 17, the House stood the more forlorn for having been the scene of a wild treasure hunt, now bearing "the depressing look of a living room the morning after a big party," said the *Times*. "Many Met patrons, especially those at the Gala, have been saving the Met recently by taking little bits of it home with them. . . . How disappointing the artifacts filched by the souvenir hunters must look in broad daylight."

Ever since 1958, "polite requests for the theatre's decorations started coming in," wrote Bill Cunningham in the Chicago *Tribune*. Now "the dowager Metropolitan is staging a sentimental striptease of near hysterical proportions. . . . The sentimentality (or acquisitiveness) of America is showing. . . . Is it love or larceny? It seems people afraid of not getting a souvenir have no conscience about stealing one."

The problem of salvaging was breaking everyone's heart, concluded Cunningham, "especially when they think of the unsentimental hammers of the wrecking crew." It was this crew that had the last word, as matters turned out.

The curtain came down almost immediately after the ballet's visit— literally down, not merely lowered. Before it was conveyed to the American Drapery and Carpet Company for what the *Times* called "the unkindest cut of all," Leontyne Price took a pair of shears and sliced off the first of 45,000 $2\frac{1}{4}$-by-$3\frac{1}{4}$-inch swatches which accompanied an RCA-Victor album nostalgically recalling opening nights at the Met. For this privilege RCA paid a $10,000 advance and royalties.

But further demolition was almost immediately postponed. While the building grew dingier on the outside and drearier on the inside, a battle raged over its fate that turned into the most hairbreadth cliff-hanger since *The Perils of Pauline*. Committees to Save the Old Met fought the Met management, sometimes winning, sometimes losing, in an on-again, off-again tug of war that lasted until after Christmas.

25

GIANTS CAN STUMBLE

There is no doubt about it. The Metropolitan stumbled.

—RUDOLPH BING,
in a letter to the Vienna *Express,* June 22, 1966

The Metropolitan's second visit to Paris in early summer 1966 wrote no glorious chapter in its annals; still, apart from prejudice, the little season in the little Théâtre de l'Odéon was not without merit. The real trouble lay in the original conception. Paris got chamber opera when it expected—unreasonably, to be sure, considering the known restrictions—the grand variety. Until the Moment of Truth, both sides persisted in their opposing dream worlds, the Met wearing blinders of self-justification after accepting the inevitable conditions; Paris, preparing its welcome after fifty-six years of anticipation with burning jealousy, feverish curiosity, and perhaps a bit of shame, wrote Jan Maguire in the Paris *Herald Tribune.* There is little doubt that into the official diplomatic, artistic, social, and critical audiences infiltrated professional "aginners," motivated by what Mr. Maguire called "green-eyed frenzy."

The error in judgment was admitted by Bing in that rarest of documents, a public apology addressed to a newspaper. The Vienna *Express* had done Bing the "unaccustomed" honor, it seems, of asking about events before reporting. His letter ran:

Probably it was a mistake, my mistake, to come to Paris after more than fifty years with works like *The Barber of Seville* and *The Marriage of Figaro.* When I received Jean-Louis Barrault's invitation . . . I had to decide: accept with the smallest works we could find (the delightful old theatre has a stage the size of [a pocket handkerchief] and an orchestra pit which could barely accommodate thirty-eight musicians) or wait until we could come with *Aida* and *Turandot* [which would have been the right thing, he confessed later]—most likely another fifty years.

Such big guns would have upped the budget beyond the capacity of any private support. America's lack of government subsidy thus provided

383

the string plucked by Bing in advance and even more loudly in the after-math. "We have no kind of subsidy," he wrote to Vienna, "and the Met could not finance such a venture out of its own funds. . . . Some noble friends of the Met and France provided the funds." The amount made public was $140,000; the "noble friends" remained anonymous. It was rumored that three principal donors bore the brunt; one of these is suspected to be Mrs. Lillian Phipps, wealthy cousin-in-law of Conductor Thomas Schippers. The Met board was not called upon at all; in fact, a minority was said to have disapproved the venture and afterward ad-mitted regret at being right.

America crying poor was a new experience for France, and gave the carpers another peg on which to hang their spite. Out of the smugness of their governmental umbrella, they undoubtedly relished the spectacle of the United States' greatest performing musical institution passing the tin cup. Bing took the occasion in his letter and in an interview with *News-week* to add that while at least three illustrious European opera com-panies would be sent to the 1967 Montreal Exposition, the Met, "only 400 miles away," couldn't go.

Once the miniature framework had been accepted, the choice of the two works could be rationalized in that they were both based on plays by Pierre Augustin Caron de Beaumarchais. No anniversary in round num-bers could be conjured up, but something "historical" might be made of Beaumarchais' sympathy with the American Revolutionists. On paper this looked fine. In actuality, Beaumarchais proved a flimsy reed, fit only for passing official notice. What counted was that chamber opera is not exactly the Met's forte, while the French consider they have done this sort of thing rather well, at the Opéra-Comique fifty years ago, more recently at the Aix-en-Provence Festival. Cruel comparisons could be made—and were. "A peepshow," wrote Maguire. "A cocktail cracker thrown to a hungry lion."

These two New York productions, smart and sprightly as they ap-peared when pristine (although there was no universal approval for the Mozart work even then), have blurred slightly around the edges, subject to the natural tendency of singers to play while the director's away. They simply didn't get the brushing up they needed, although *Barbiere* went on tour and was performed at the matinee on the day of departure with the Paris cast excepting Figaro (Robert Merrill) and Almaviva (Luigi

Alva, who took the place of the scheduled George Shirley). Schippers conducted these performances, so was routined. But *Nozze* (as the Mozart opera will hereinafter be designated) had not been in the repertoire for a year. Erich Leinsdorf, who was summoned from the Boston Symphony to preside, had little rehearsal opportunity. The justification for bringing him in out of left field became plain as he demonstrated his ability to make an "instant" performance.

Jean-Louis Barrault, who had staged the 1965 revival of *Faust,* and his wife Madeleine Renaud had endeared themselves to the Met management while in America. "I succumbed to Barrault's charm and to Paris' beauty," confessed Bing. The distinguished French couple were in charge of the tenth season of the Théâtre des Nations, which each spring brings to Paris representatives from other world capitals—in 1966 theatrical companies from Italy, the Soviet Union, Poland, Germany, and the United States (notably the Living Theatre in the controversial *The Brig*). The heated air of scandal still hung over the Place de l'Odéon when the Met arrived—police riot squads had left it not long before after quelling nightly disturbances over Jean Genêt's sensational *Les Paravents* (The Screens). The outside of the building still bore scars from identified flying objects, while intervening weeks of Italian and Russian theatre troupes had not rid the premises of latent turbulence. The spoors of boos and hisses lay in the Rococo carvings and red plush of the ancient auditorium, ready to be revived at the slightest encouragement. Some Parisians acknowledged that it had been "a booing season." Georges Auric, general administrator of the national theatres, had been forced to withdraw the conductor and a mezzo-soprano from a gala production of *Don Carlos* at the Opéra only a short time previously, while Tito Gobbi, learning of the disturbance, declined to subject himself to possible disorder, so a replacement had to be found.

Into this charged atmosphere the Metropolitan fell like a blindfolded wayfarer who misses a step on a footbridge over a ravine.

Unprecedented and shattering, the Met was booed—*"Des 'hou-hou' s'élévaient dans la salle,"* as the expression goes. And at one of the first performances, which made the newspapers and created damage that could not be publicly repaired. Not enough consolation was to be found in the eventual warm reception by later audiences and in the apology of one responsible critic for the behavior of a "handful of *énergumènes* [fa-

natics]," quoting Henri Sauguet, celebrated composer, as saying that such
grossièreté (rudeness) against foreign artists was inadmissible. Sauguet
had leaped to his feet after the first *Nozze,* shaking his fist at the demon-
strators and shouting: "Down with the public! I will never compose
another note for you!"

The unfortunate thing about hindsight is that you can't possess it in
advance—without clairvoyance. Omens both good and evil could have
been discerned, possibly, before the trip, but once signed and sealed, the
company started down a one-way road. Going on in advance were Bing,
John Gutman (just out of hospital but necessary as translator and general
troubleshooter—Bing does not speak French fluently though he pronounces well, says an expert), Press Chief Francis Robinson, Herman
Krawitz, and his assistant technician, Charles Riecker (who had prepared
logistic details for six months and is idiomatically fluent in French),
Master Mechanic Louis Edson and Chief Electrician Rudolph Kuntner.
The scenery, costumes, props, and electrical equipment for *Nozze* went
by ship in April; those for *Barbiere* (fifty tons' worth) were picked up by
cargo plane in Detroit, the final tour city, while 130 company members
followed in a chartered Air France jet.

Kaleidoscopic memories of the flight remain, a surrealistic mixture.
On board were singers (except for Peters, Merrill, Siepi, Alva, and
Corena, who found their way individually, as did Conductors Schippers
and Leinsdorf); twenty-five choristers and eight dancers, men and women;
and the orchestra of thirty-eight—a small, small orchestra indeed, but
looking very formidable as they ranged three by three on either side of
the aisle, randomly dressed from business suits to colored sweaters or
T-shirts, mostly unsmiling. Many orchestra men find little to smile at
anyway, and these were undoubtedly exhausted. One could spot Cyril
Ritchard, Bob Herman and his assistant Paul Jaretzki, Frank Paola,
Henry A. Fischer (assistant comptroller), Felix Eyle (orchestra manager),
Associate Conductors Jan Behr and Ignace Strasfogel; Prompter William
Weibel, Apprentice Conductors Millard Altman and Giulio di Nunzio,
Stage Directors Patrick Tavernia and Bodo Igesz, also a half-dozen back-
stage chiefs. Add a couple of dozen spouses and companions; one well-
behaved baby (belonging to Assistant Concertmaster Stanley Ritchie and
his pretty, redheaded wife); the NBC-TV crew and critics from the *New
York Times, Newsweek,* and *Opera News,* and the pilgrims' noses counted

to 162. The arrival in a high wind found those resilient opera stars as fresh and ready for cameras and greetings from Bing, Gutman, and Robinson as if they had arisen from ten hours' sleep instead of the fitful upright dozing between sumptuous meals and a premature dawn. Theirs is a peculiar vitality, necessary for their profession, very attractive and utterly infuriating to weaker vessels. Scattered to their various hotels, mostly on the Left Bank near the theatre, the *Barbiere* cast could look forward to more than two dozen blissful hours to rest or explore the city. Leinsdorf called a *Nozze* rehearsal next day, at which Corena, Gladys Kriese, and Andrea Velis had to appear, being in both casts. Thereafter few free moments appeared, for in addition to performances, most signed up for a trip to Versailles on Thursday and a tour of the Opéra building on Saturday (when a few unreconstructed individuals were heard to murmur: "*This* is what an opera house should be!"). The ceiling by Chagall in the rich and glamorous old auditorium seemed as incongruous as, although less disturbing than, the overhead abstract splashes of color by André Masson in the Odéon.

Paris was at her most beautiful, the Seine sparkling, the tall trees nobly green, the parks bright with flowers, the air clear and hot (until a cloudy Sunday), the ocher and gray streets opening to vista after vista—and at her most crowded and noisiest. Construction of a new parkway messed up Right Bank streets. Special shops drew the women; men sought targets for their cameras. Most indefatigable of photographers was James Hosmer, the lanky flutist; Julian Tivin left his bass fiddle in the theatre as he won the medal for most persistent sightseeing.

But Paris would not attune certain habits to Americans. Eating a good dinner became the number-one problem, for no restuarant thought of serving that meal until seven, when conscientious performers had to be in the theatre. Many a fellow grew tired of ham sandwiches (on long, crisp-crusted rolls). A gourmet lunch was the only solution until one restaurant, just opposite the Odéon on the rue Corneille, took pity and received Metropolitan patrons at five thirty.

The old building where the Americans spent most of their waking hours has suffered the reputation of a hard-luck theatre. Completed in 1782, it twice burned and was reconstructed; housed the Théâtre Français twice, but was closed once because of a play that displeased the authorities; and witnessed a score of failures after it had been rechristened the

Odéon in 1797. After the fire of 1818, which did not affect the exterior with its magnificent portico of eight Doric columns, Louis XVIII ordered it rebuilt. To justify its name, which means "a place where one sings," one incarnation at least provided music when the Italian Opera held forth there in the reign of Louis Philippe. A restoration in 1875 and the current refurbishing left it in excellent condition.

Once inside the stage door, opening from the rue Vaugirard opposite the Jardin du Luxembourg, one might as well be in a private house, served from floor to floor by narrow, red-carpeted circular staircases. Even in the section between stage and auditorium, occupied by offices and dressing rooms, the ambiance of the theatre is lacking. Bing, hurrying by on his way from the office of Barrault's assistant, Gilles Bernard—Bing never walks; he strides, his body bent forward from the hips to balance his heels in motion—muttered to himself (but obviously for the benefit of anyone in earshot) one of his amusing *ad libs:* "There must be a stage here somewhere!"

A sign in six languages showed him where, as if he didn't know.

In the house proper, wandering through the halls lined with water colors and prints and photographs of scenes and actors, pushing through velvet-padded swinging doors and up uncarpeted stairs with handrailings of wood as soft and smooth as satin, one came to the top gallery, where on hard benches customers could sit and peer through a chicken-wire barrier at the scene below. Seats in the orchestra (with their affixed *strapontins,* folding stools that torture their occupants but increase the capacity by almost one hundred), and the lower boxes were still sheltered under protective canvas, thrown aside here and there as the invaders made further inroads. The rehearsal had got under way and all was not happy. Edson and Kuntner in particular were encountering the language barrier. "It's murder!" vowed the lighting expert as he watched a French electrician climb up a twenty-foot wooden ladder to adjust a spotlight. Charles Riecker claimed never to have experienced a more amiable working relationship than with the French administration and technicians, but he possessed the gift of tongues.

The *Barbiere* rehearsal left everyone praying for the truth of the saying: "Disastrous rehearsal, good performance." It ended in near panic, with eight seconds to go before midnight and overtime. Bing almost laughed, but not quite, when someone said to him: "Agony without the ecstasy." Kind words, even for getting through on time, were waved away with superstitious horror.

Next day the *Nozze* dress rehearsal went better, although the stage-hands kept to their own perplexing schedule—perplexing at least to management. The timing of their lunch break didn't jibe with the Americans' ideas. "I'm laughing through my tears," confided Bing. "We're really the civilized nation—we eat sandwiches while we work."

The "covers"—Jeannette Scovotti, Jean Fenn, Gene Boucher—wandered about, singing softly with their principals, but knowing in their hearts no one would get sick. At the interval, Cherubino and the Count and Countess ran across the big square in costume and sipped coffee at an outdoor café, bombarded by cameras. Corena was let go early as he had to sing in *Barbiere* that night; Lorenzo Alvary, placed as Antonio the gardener, finished Corena's Bartolo as well as his own part. Bing congratulated Stratas, the Cherubino, on her precise, heel-clicking bow, then turned to the assemblage and called out: "Let's be of good cheer; we have a rough day."

How rough—and for how many days—no one could foresee.

On the opening night, from across the Place de l'Odéon, where they had dined as guests of Mrs. Ogden Phipps at the Meditérranée, American and French dignitaries made their way leisurely to the theatre, into the little foyer, and up the steps flanked by the honor guard. An American could recognize Lauder Greenway with Mrs. John Barry Ryan (daughter of Otto Kahn, who had financed the Met's first visit to Paris in 1910), Mrs. Frederick Weyerhauser of the Met's National Council, Mrs. Kenyon Boocock of the Guild, Howard Hook, and Mrs. Lillian Phipps. Mrs. Gould, the second wife of the late George Gould, son of the original holder of Box 2 at the Met, is even better known in Europe than America by virtue of her great benefactions, which include the restoration of Versailles. Accompanying them was Mrs. Estée Lauder, head of a well-known cosmetics firm.

But the cynosure lay not with these, nor with such dignitaries as Premier Georges Pompidou and his wife, Ambassador and Mrs. Charles Bohlen, Mme. Hervé Alphand, wife of France's former Ambassador to the United States (in a creation from the couture house she now represents), M. and Mme. Barrault, M. and Mme. Georges Auric, nor with Minister of State Louis Joxe. More sought after than any of these, the tall, divinely cool, exquisitely *soignée* Maria Callas was the evening's darling, solicitously escorted by Francis Robinson, arousing a wave of delighted comment where'er she walked. Joy and complacence gave way to dismay, however, when, after Roberta Peters had concluded her second-act aria with a note less than perfect, a coarse shout came from high in a balcony: "*Brava,* Callas!"

Shocked ears could not credit it. Disbelieving whispers and nervous titters washed as far as the forward orchestra seat occupied by the prima donna. In the dark house, the *France Soir* reporter could not possibly have seen her smiling under dark glasses and thus attributing to her a sense of revenge for her "*mésaventures au Met,*" which had "closed its doors to her." He was also slightly behind the times. Those doors had been propped wide open of late.

When at least two of next day's papers carried first-page photographs of La Diva with various French VIP's—none from the Met—and over one the headline, "*La Callas Fut la Plus Applaudie,*" with the addition, "although she didn't sing," chagrin was deepened. Everyone disavowed inviting her, until the buck passed to its final destination. Mr. Bing had invited her, it seemed, and Mr. Bing had been heard to say that it was his second-biggest mistake. The first was left unrevealed—until, perhaps, the letter to Vienna?

Detailed reviews were delayed until late afternoon or even another day, so the company picked itself up and steeled itself for *Nozze.* Although this performance was demonstrably superior to *Barbiere,* the reception became even more devastating. The little coterie that perched in an upper tier apparently did not care for the style and voice of Lucine Amara as the Countess and let her know it in a chilling barrage of boos after "*Porgi amor.*" Something about John Reardon's Count—chiefly his voice, but incredibly, also his youth—also irritated these vocalists, who let go their spleen whenever the baritone uttered. "They knew the terror," remarked *Paris Soir,* not with sympathy. The contrasting ovations to everyone else—notably Stratas as Cherubino—showed up the insult more plainly, as had the previous night's hurrah for the male singers. Most shocking to Americans (who are not used to this sort of thing) was the shout that arose when Leinsdorf, who had previously been acclaimed—and justly—for the brilliance and style of his tiny orchestra, attempted to draw Amara and Reardon back for a bow. Deeply offended at the demonstration, the conductor refused to appear before the curtain in any subsequent performance, even at the finale, when never was heard a discouraging word.

The irrepressible Cyril Ritchard, who had made a unique target as director for both operas, took his share of lashes for action that seemed to some captious Parisians perhaps too comic. He indulged in a small revenge. Blowing kisses right and left with solemn irony while the noise rose and fell, he launched a small kick toward the monster just as the curtain came down. Hardly anyone noticed, but it afforded him a bit of satisfaction.

Scenery and costumes for both operas were destined to disappoint Paris, which notoriously prefers its operas gorgeous to look at no matter how they are sung or played. Paris' own addition to eye appeal was never more evident than in productions running concurrently in the two big houses. *Les Contes d'Hoffmann* at the Opéra Comique boasted elaborate scenery and large, gilded, fantastic figures of clowns and animals crossing the stage on a moving belt, clumsy choreography, and indifferent singing and orchestra playing. No hissing greeted the baritone who broke conclusively with his high note in the "Diamant" aria, but then the audience may have contained a large number of Americans. It is a measure of the way the state operas are run that the same man (Jacques Mars) was required to sing the Grand Inquisitor in the Opéra's *Don Carlos* the very next night (incidentally, he sang it far better than Dapertutto). Other singing fell even to the level of mediocrity, but a bit of a boo for Elisabetta was quickly hushed. The scenery entranced—it was conceived by Jacques Dupont of the Met's latest *Faust* and forthcoming *Carmen*.

The note of Paris' artistic inadequacy had been sounded in Harold Schonberg's first dispatch after *Barbiere:* "Of the world's major opera houses, the two in Paris . . . occupy a low position in the international world. The French know this as well as anybody else." Bing later echoed this more pungently: "So Peters had a bad night. Paris has had a bad century."

A letter to the Paris *Herald Tribune* chastised the French for comparing the Met to the "sorry, second-rate performances at the Opéra Comique," while another to the *Times* suggested that the booers were motivated by nationalism.

Very few remembered the circumstances of the Met's earlier visit, when the sheer weight of *Aida, Otello, Falstaff,* and *Manon Lescaut,* plus the caliber of the singers—Fremstad, Scotti, Bori, and Amato, in addition to Caruso, Homer, and Destinn—and the genius of Toscanini soon won over the inimical portion of the audiences in the huge old Châtelet (now done over and housing a musical comedy). The sumptuous settings pleased everyone in 1910. Comparisons between the two Met incursions break down at every point except for the hard core of Parisian objectors.

Backstage after the first—and fatal—*Nozze,* the beleaguered ones were surrounded by consolatory colleagues and friends. When told that fifty-six years ago such giants as Toscanini, Caruso, *et al.* had been on the receiving end of just such brickbats, Amara smiled gamely through tears and professed herself proud to be in such company. (What was not generally known was that she had barely recovered from a serious illness.) Reardon was equally stoic. Both had to sing twice more, and did, like good troupers. Still, apprehension hung in the air until the last note was utttered Sunday night, when pandemonium of the right sort soothed abraded egos. It had been noticeable that Leinsdorf had not allowed a bit of breathing space after *"Porgi amor,"* just in case. And in spite of the suggestion of Stage Manager Osie Hawkins that only ensemble curtain calls be permitted, solo bows remained. It was reliably said that at least two gentlemen objected to passing up individual glory.

The impact of the newspaper reviews hit hard. The good words— and many appeared—were driven out by the bad. Cotte in *France-Soir* apparently shot poisoned arrows out of a miraculously refilling quiver, complaining that Schippers led the "Marseillaise" like a goosestep; suggesting that Peters risked another Pearl Harbor with each note; saying that the productions "so lacked in invention that one would hesitate to present them in the provinces." Even Clarendon in *Figaro,* who deplored Parisian bad manners and excoriated the booers as possessing only the erudition gained from discs—*"soi-disant connaisseurs"*—reiterated his own objections each time in case he should be thought a traitor. In fact, he "hemmed and hawed in an ecstasy of confusion until praise and blame became indistinguishable," wrote Hubert Saal in *Newsweek.*

How much of the Parisians' discontent lay in what Bing called an "anti-American, anti-Vietnam" spirit will never be known. Barrault, in an engaging curtain speech, had referred to the theatre, flying the American flag alongside the French tricolor, as "the fifty-first state," but as

Time remarked, "not everybody was ready to join the Union." Rather oddly, Barrault never publicly attempted to stem the critical tide. Perhaps he thought it would be useless.

Amity backstage grew as the outside atmosphere heated up. At the very last, on Sunday midnight, the French working crew leisurely enjoyed a supper of salami, bread, cheese, and red wine set up festively in the "green room" as a grateful gesture of the Met. Then Americans and French, buddies to the end, finally finished loading onto huge trucks the cargo destined to be transported by ship and wound up toasting each other into the early hours of the morning in a café across the street.

Possibly the damaging effect could have been countered, partly written off as prejudiced, had it not been that the most colorful phrases were gleefully picked up in New York. The Met possibly felt unlucky to be in the midst of a newspaper strike when only the *Times* held forth and the *Times* could very well be inimical, as it had proved in the past, to Bing and all his works. Schonberg had written complimentary phrases in his first dispatch about *Barbiere,* praising the settings, the acoustics, which made the small orchestra sound "luminous and elegant," along with mild reservations, and concluded that "on the whole, the performance was well received." His tone changed next day to agreement with the French line. And frequent references to the disillusion of the Paris "intellectuals" in a Sunday article renewed and deepened his previous whip strokes and raised the temperature in the air-cooled beehive in Lincoln Center.

Bing's occasional rash gesture, rising through a crack in the imperturbable façade, always startles onlookers. The Vienna letter, in spite of its air of frankness and humility, contains this sentence: "I always thought it a sign of greatness that when giants stumble, the dwarfs enjoy themselves. Let them have their fun." Neither the French nor the American press (both of which are inferred) could be expected to enjoy being called dwarfs.

26

"CULTURAL SUPEREVENT"

The gaiety, the splendor, the excitement of this evening are really over-whelming. One cannot help but feel that it is the beginning of another "Golden Age" in the history of the Metropolitan.

—Mrs. Lyndon B. Johnson, in a letter to Anthony A. Bliss

Five months to the day from the tearful farewell downtown, the world premiere of Samuel Barber's *Antony and Cleopatra* in the new Metropolitan Opera House in Lincoln Center on September 16, 1966, was perhaps "the single biggest theatrical event in all of human history," wrote Shana Alexander in *Life,* ". . . nothing less than the cultural super-event of the culture center of the culture capital of the civilized world."

"Never had a social event in New York exploded with such excite-ment," affirmed *Time,* gallantly carrying on the tradition that every successive opening night deserves to outrank all its predecessors. This one certainly came closest to any in memory as unique. For preliminary "flourishes and fanfaronade," *Newsweek*'s Hubert Saal had to hark back to Giuseppe Verdi's creation of *Aida* to celebrate the opening of the Suez Canal, and quoted one blasé matron who regressed even farther: "This is quite possibly the greatest social event since the Nativity."

Every element that could add a spark to the pleasurable delirium was there: an almost insupportable anticipation, the glittering new House, the promise of a spectacular new opera, and the conflux of humanity, "dressed, jewelled and coiffed to the teeth," in the picturesque language of Suzy Knickerbocker, the *World Journal Tribune*'s girl guide. Headed by the First Lady of the Land, "in floating white chiffon by Stropoulos, a nifty hairdo and a smile that wouldn't quit," hundreds of tycoons, aristo-crats, etc., etc., reported by Charlotte Curtis in the *Times* (repeating the list from the Farewell), created high-class traffic jams and opulent bottle-necks as they stared at each other—"all the goodies of the world of the rich, the celebrated and the social," added Suzy.

Keeping cameramen, reporters, and Secret Service minions on the *qui vive* were innumerable foreign dignitaries: President Ferdinand E. Marcos and the First Lady of the Philippines; Federal Minister for Foreign Affairs Tonck-Sorinj of Austria (which donated $160,000 toward the cost of the twenty-eight starry chandeliers) and his wife; Vice Chancellor Erich Mende of West Germany (donor of the largest amount, $2,500,000) and his wife, and ambassadors and consuls general from all over and *their* wives, and the United Nations Secretary-General U Thant. Not to be outdone, the United States offered, in addition to Mrs. Johnson, Secretary of Housing and Urban Development Robert C. Weaver, Secretary of Defense Robert McNamara, United Nations Ambassador Arthur Goldberg, White House Cultural Adviser Roger L. Stevens, Senators Edward and Robert Kennedy, Jacob Javits, and J. W. Fulbright, Governor Nelson A. Rockefeller, Mayor John B. Lindsay (all with wives), and many more.

Social figures with founders' names who had rather neglected the Met of late made a special effort to show themselves, notably Mr. and Mrs. Cornelius Vanderbilt Whitney, Mr. and Mrs. Alfred Gwynne Vanderbilt, Mr. and Mrs. John R. Drexel, as well as Mrs. Lytle Hull, the former wife of the late Vincent Astor. The present Mrs. Astor had been more faithful. Suavely gowned, heavily jeweled (in Mrs. Whitney's case topped by the same tiara of the Austrian Empress that she wore to the Farewell, boasting almost 2,000 diamonds), they appeared before the multitude in the suffocatingly crowded corridors only long enough to reach the new Met's luxurious retreats for the VIP's—the Grand Tier Restaurant (approximating the old Sherry's), the Opera Club, its door heavily guarded, and the Board Room (named for Cornelius N. Bliss, father of the then president of the Association), under even stricter security as the dining room of the Very Exalted Indeed.

Distinguished members of the musical world were not lacking, among them the heads of opera houses in London, Vienna, Munich, Hamburg, and Geneva. Others who could afford the tariff, which mounted as high as $250 for an orchestra seat, swelled the total to 3,800, producing a record gross, $400,000—more than a dozen times the usual Met gala sellout. But this seems quite in order for an opera house that took more than a hundred times $400,000 to build—almost forty times the cost of the old House.

Boxholders were in residence on a one-time basis, as is usual for Bing's opening nights. Most of them had not even had the say about choosing their own guests above the four seats allotted them, but had found the honor guests billeted on them. This necessary but highhanded requisition led to a few odd boxfellows. One of the wealthiest women in America, a constant opera patron, did not object to an ambassador, but raised the golden roof a few inches at the presence of what she considered a climber and got the unwelcome person transferred somewhere else at the last moment, although the name still appeared in that box in the program. (With a reticence unmatched since the original season, the programs contained no listing of regular boxholders, nor would this information be forthcoming in the future, it was said officially. Even in the more communicative programs of the past, certain names had been suppressed at the wish of the boxholder.)

"Reaching for the pinnacle of social position, many of the new industrialists dipped into their millions to help build the new opera house and were thus assured of seats with the surviving first families," wrote Bill Cunningham in the Chicago *Tribune*. "Annenberg, Haupt, Neff, Wrightsman, Cummings, Revson will go down in history as the new ambitious society that socially invaded the boxes of two Astors, two Mellons, one Whitney, and a distant Vanderbilt. All opera glasses were focused on the historical social battle. . . . Social historians will forever refer to these occupants . . . as the new elite." New York was consumed by the social integration gossip.

The Chicago Nathan Cummingses, who brought boxes of their product (chocolate Sara Lee cookies) with them for opera-viewing snacks, shared a box with Mr. and Mrs. Owen Cheatham. Mrs. Cheatham is the owner of most of the incomparable and audacious jewels of Salvador Dali, and wore a prized 500-carat amethyst. The *Tribune* reporter noted that Dame Alicia Markova, director of the Met's ballet, left a box in exasperation at the whispered comments on the love life of one singer after another.

Prominent among the flashier elite was Mrs. Laura Johnson, widow of a department store tycoon, whom Cunningham called "this generation's Molly Brown." She was escorted by a Cartier officer, friendly but also watchful of the blazing jewels she had borrowed from his firm. "I pinned my own emerald-and-diamond drop earrings on my silk underpanties in case of a fainting spell," she was heard to relate.

This bit of daring marked the farthest limit of outrageous behavior, quite a difference from several of the pre-Bing openings when anything might happen. Most notorious was the dowager Mrs. Frank C. Henderson (Betty), who, as Francis Robinson put it picturesquely in *Opera News,* "hoisted an aged gam on a table in Sherry's and demanded of the gleeful throng, 'What's Marlene got that I haven't?'" That was in 1947. The "era of the showoffs dates from 1939," wrote Robinson, "when Richard Knight stood on his head on the sidewalk outside the Broadway entrance for the benefit of press photographers. For the next ten years, the clowns and cutups took over."

Outlandish costumes have always been in evidence on opening nights, usually on the forms of professional models, but sometimes worn for fun. The Lincoln Center launching was no exception. Most startling was the wife of the singer Jess Thomas, who sported a trim figure sheathed in black and hung with dozens of gold chains resembling the bead curtains in the new State Theatre. The *Post's* society editors quoted Bing as exclaiming, "My God, she thinks she's an Egyptian empress."

Excitement began to build as early as six P.M., when spectators trickled onto the great stone plain of Lincoln Center Plaza, soon to be confined behind police barriers, remaining good-natured and admiring, often openmouthed, the procession that passed by. Alighting from black limousines and colored taxis at the access road to the Plaza off Columbus Avenue, the elegant women and their escorts found a broad and gleaming red carpet to lead them past the central fountain and up the treacherous shallow steps before the opera's gleaming façade.

"It was fun," said the *Times* man simply. In even a finer night than the one described by his predecessor in Chapter Three of this book, the twilight settled serenely as voices mingled and were lost in the play of the fountain, and flashbulbs hardly pierced the sunset glow. From a phalanx of their own stepped Rudolf Bing, John D. Rockefeller III, Anthony Bliss, Lauder Greenway, and other officials to greet honored guests in the open air. Mrs. Johnson was late, but warmth still lingered in the sky as the *Opera News* photographer got the stunning shot of a half dozen VIP's and surrounding *élégants* that appears in this volume.

Stars shone through the tears in the eyes of Mrs. John Barry Ryan (Margaret Kahn), who told Bill Cunningham: "I feel just like a little girl who has realized her father's greatest dream." Otto Kahn should have been there, but he had died thirty-two years before, frustrated in his many attempts to put a new home around the opera company he loved.

To the sorrow of all in the inner circle, one dignified white head was absent. Mrs. August Belmont, so closely woven into the fabric of the opera that a great portion of its warp seemed to be gone, was ill. Her health improved later in the season, but not to be at this milestone celebration of the company for which she had worked so faithfully was a bitter disappointment.

Outside the building, the confusion attending the first opening in 1883 was markedly lacking, but once inside, the swirling eddies of dressed-up humanity clotted on the spiral staircase, hiding its marble treads and crimson carpet, packing tightly the space behind the narrow steel or broad wood railings that offered magnificent observation points. Diners in the public restaurant uninventively named "The Top of the Met" got the best view of all as they stepped to their front railing, for beneath them lay the whole lobby, before them the leaded glass panels of the five great arches reflecting the crystal chandeliers and revealing the colorfully lighted Plaza with the two sister buildings at either side and beyond, the darkening profile of the city.

By almost universal consent, this sixth-floor aerie contains the most agreeable art works of the House: semicircular murals of diners even gayer than New York's, painted by that master of French whimsy, Raoul Dufy, for the Anouilh play, *Ring Around the Moon,* and presented by the producer Gilbert Miller. The two murals by Marc Chagall had been much more in the news, but many patrons openly or secretly echoed the opinion of the *Times* art critic, John Canaday, that no matter how charming the floating figures done in red on one side, lemon-yellow on the other, it was all pretty much *vieux jeu.* The only unobstructed, full view of them is from the Plaza, although the arch glass leads arbitrarily cut them into patchwork. On the Grand Tier the space is too narrow to get a perspective, even by the most acute neck-craning. That they were an afterthought is painfully apparent, commissioned when a drastic alteration of the plans resulted in these two blank unfunctioning spaces. Chagall, when he first saw his murals in place, wanted them lower, but they were already fixed to the cement.

Other art works in the building are decidedly conventional, pleasing to a conservative like Winthrop Sargeant of the *New Yorker,* who used the word "junk" to describe the sculpture and other "avant-garde stuff that clutter the State Theatre and Philharmonic Hall," but "pointless" to Canaday. They include three statues by Aristide Maillol (two presented by the Henry L. and Grace Doherty Charitable Foundation, which also gave the Chagalls) and a "Kneeling Woman" by Wilhelm Lehmbruck (not to be confused with Maillol's kneeling woman, which is subtitled "Monument to Debussy"). The statue was the visible symbol of the enormous German gift.

Lehmbruck's son, a noted German architect, who came over for the celebration, expressed himself as gratified at the reception of his father's work, but privately voiced some doubts about the Center's general architectural scheme. To him, as to many other observers, the three important buildings look as if a knife had sliced them off flat at the top. The Met in particular suffers from this lack of soaring spirit, the arches seeming to be squashed down by the shallow topping.

In the auditorium the most puzzling piece of all adorns the top of the proscenium, an abstract free-form sculpture by Mary Callery which reminds the irreverent of a pair of brass handcuffs or a broken dog collar or even a gilded chasity belt. For the rest, the opera-house art consists of the paintings and sculptures of prominent opera figures moved from the Old House, plus a bust of Mozart donated by the Austrian government and the City of Salzburg. These line the walls of the Founders' Hall (reception corridors on the Concourse or lower level). The museum that was to house them wound up on the cutting-room floor in a final frenzy of economizing.

Most of the 171 donors of more than $100,000 did not specify where their money was to go, but thirty-seven did. Only a few of these were for art. Two names originally associated with the Met appear prominently: Harold S. Vanderbilt, whose $750,000 helped to build the Family Circle (a nice democratic touch), and the family of Robert Walton Goelet, who gave half a million toward construction of the grand staircase (a regal gesture). Operagoers are reminded of these and other gifts by plaques of various sizes all through the House, and in the Book of Friends.

A few center steps down lead to the Orchestra section, the entrance kept too dark for either elated spirits or easy recognition of friends. The entrance doors are bottlenecks, particularly with the new rule that no admission is allowed after the music starts. Everyone hurries to get in at the same time, resulting in a subway rush, well-bred but annoying. This rule caused considerable fuss at first, especially when the hour-plus length of the first act of *Don Giovanni* found more than 200 late-comers caught outside. Even more drastic was the experience of those who were tardy for *Elektra* with its single act. The only recourse is a closed-circuit television screen in a narrow corridor. New Yorkers, who struggle with their own tendency to be late and then with the increasing traffic and parking problems, will probably continue to be irked. But the boon to those in their seats who are not disturbed is incalculable.

The full effect of the auditorium chamber is not immediately apparent at Orchestra, Grand Tier, or Dress Circle levels because of the overhang, although it bursts on the sight of boxholders and the Balcony and Family Circle, which are continuous. One of the best features of the House is the openness and comfort of the higher tiers, which also offer more advantageous standing room and a service bar all to themselves. On other levels, the overhang must be cleared to see the ceiling, with its golden circles which suggest to some a cluster of flowers with the blazing chandeliers for stamens—"scalloped lily pads," said Sargeant—and to others, less poetic but more up to date, a set of overlapping flying saucers.

Each curved box front is faced with a custard-creamy scallop which stands out rather too boldly, but as a subscriber was heard to say, "nothing that a little dirt won't improve." Several details continue to cause controversy, notably the brilliant narrow panels of lights on alternating boxes, like cheap brooches. The whole effect resembles "illuminated brassieres," one light-minded critic suggested. It has been whispered that Mrs. Belmont offered $50,000 to remove them, but they persisted through the season. Given time, enough money, and constant complaint, these matters of interior decor can be dealt with.

The House, inside and out, is decidedly photogenic. By some trick of color film, in order to keep purple out of the red carpeting, a preponderance of yellow creeps in so that the stark white of the staircases and other marble is softened to gold. The effect is resplendent.

In spite of considerable dissension from architects and architectural and art critics, the opinion crystallized during the season that the House is a good place for grand opera. By some optical illusion, the auditorium seems much shallower than in the Old House, so that audiences feel closer to the stage and singers believe they do not have to force their voices. Even the detractors of the architect, Wallace K. Harrison, who was also responsible for the decor in the auditorium, had to admit that he was victorious in the most mysterious realm of all, and in this case the most precarious—acoustics.

Everyone walked on tiptoe and whispered behind hands when this touchy subject was broached. Big Sister Philharmonic Hall had suffered a million-dollar goof in its sound properties, and Little Sister State Theatre still has plague spots in spite of New York City Opera officials' assertions that they play to universally happy ears. If acoustics in the Met had gone sour, the whole $45.7 million would be considered a waste, the more so because the listenableness in the Old House grew steadily more admirable as sentiment encroached on reality and acoustics became part of the myth surrounding the virtues of Thirty-ninth Street.

Cannily, the management tried it out at a sneak preview for a student matinee on April 11—the first actual performance in the new House. The children were deposited in Lincoln Center without warning and enjoyed the whole adventure, although not understanding its seriousness. A small invited group—the press had sworn to withhold comment on the one particular in question—joined the management and crew in breath-holding, finger-gnawing, and hair-tugging as the first act of *La Fanciulla del West* proceeded, after a little target practice before the curtain—acoustical properties, it seems, are validly tested by shooting off guns harmlessly at an audience. Jubilation grew as the hours passed. No doubt existed: the Met was a "sound" success. "After it was all over, we burst into fine cold sweat and went absolutely limp with relief," one technician confessed.

There is current an acoustical joke, now that this property is so good that it may be joked about. One listener asks another: "Could you hear Nilsson and Corelli from where you sit?" (As if the two loudest voices in the company could be unheard anywhere!)

When it became known that Harrison had compromised every bit of decor—matchstick relief on the inner proscenium, perforated rosewood walls, and other seemingly odd details—in favor of acoustical value, some objectors were willing to settle for everything except the junk jewelry. Harrison was a blissful man on opening night, toasted and feted by the Rockefellers and others who had selected him from their previous knowledge of his accomplishments for Rockefeller Center and other mammoth undertakings. He was made to feel that his function had been fulfilled.

Criticism, small or large, no longer mattered. The building was up. It would work. Yet an architectural purist, quoted by Josh Greenfield in a *New York Times Magazine* estimate, cited his taste as "dismal," and another admitted that while Harrison satisfied his clients, this "only reflects the alarmingly high illiteracy rate of the public in architectural terms." He was undaunted, having been guided by an opera house committee all the way and presumably making them happy.

That the House is a perfect plant for producing opera (once its machinery works) cannot be denied. "The Elaborately Practical Theatre," Martin Mayer called it in *Opera News.* "The new stage," he continued, "will restore to opera that special magic of spectacle which was how the whole thing started—and which the movies temporarily stole."

Statistics can be staggering. Herman Krawitz has described it all in a guidebook published in June 1967. The exterior is 451 feet long, 234 wide at the stage house, tapering to 175 at the front façade. The favorite graphic illustration was to imagine a forty-seven-story building lying on its side. The stage is in every way larger, higher, deeper than the old one. For example, the distance between the curtain line to the back wall of the stage is only 8 feet longer (80 against 72), but that 72 was frozen. The ultimate back wall here is 146 feet away, or practically at Amsterdam Avenue. The width of the proscenium opening is only 4 inches larger than the 53 feet 8 inches of the old one, however. Increase is not necessary at this point. The height to the rigging loft was 89 feet 6 inches; it is now 110 feet. The depth under the stage was 27 feet; it is now 44. There are three other stages the same size as the one in use, so that scenes can be set up on any one and moved into place (presumably; some of the machinery has not yet been made tractable). The old orchestra pit contained 1,000 square feet; the new, 2,385, yet accommodating the same number of players. And so it goes. As for the rehearsal rooms, workshops, electric plant, carpentershops, paint bridge, and all the means of actually manufacturing a grand opera, "We have a factory here," said President Anthony Bliss.

The new Met is run like a factory. The part the public will never see is the heartbeat, the lungs, the corporeal body of the House. Through its cement-lined corridors pass hundreds of men and women, scurrying on their mysterious rounds, learning at last their destinations without leaving a paper trail. It is still dungeonlike, an official admitted, adding that there was hope of making the backstage area more congenial.

"It is natural that the company should not feel at home for a while," resumed Bliss. "I know that at first every time I went there, I got lost. It will take quite a while to acquire atmosphere. It's just a question of time."

Time—and money. It was a question of both as the House began to operate. More things went wrong than anyone could have anticipated, so strong is the present-day faith in the omnipotence of machinery. First, the fifty-eight-foot turntable stuck; the scenery for *Antony and Cleopatra* was too heavy for it. No repairs were possible until season's end, so the next most complicated production, *Die Frau ohne Schatten,* had to be revised by Nathaniel Merrill to go "up, down, right, left, backwards, forwards. Any direction but around," remarked Raymond Ericson in the *Times.* And the premiere, the last of four planned for a single opening splash within one week (at elevated prices) had to be postponed. Elevators jammed, trap doors yawned unclosable. Intermission time at the first *Frau* stretched to forty-five minutes, at a subsequent performance, to an hour and five minutes. Time, in this case, spelled money as it raced into overtime; time and money indeed were inextricably twined during the first agonizing month, when the smooth production was rare, and on into the season. It recalled to this observer the remark caught *en passant* from Alfred Hubay, House manager, scurrying through the corridor in the old House at its farewell and questioned about the new prospects: "You push buttons. You push and push and nothing works." He meant to be sardonic, but it turned out to be too painfully true.

But mechanical bugs can be put right; there is no limit to the skill and ingenuity of man. It is the human relationships that often cause more irritation and anguish. "One Hundred Men and Bing" played out their drama on an open stage in the late summer. The orchestra, never satisfied with Secretary of Labor Arthur Goldberg's insistence on the status quo in 1961, had seen two years go by without renewing their contract. In September 1964, they turned down a five-year offer, then didn't report for work one evening. City and state mediators patched that one up, but two autumns later, the alarming news went out that an orchestra strike was called coincidentally with the Lincoln Center opening. Out of consideration for the enormous intake of the first "first night," and also, it is hoped, for a certain fitness of things, the men agreed to play for *Antony,* but that was all. The House would go dark immediately after its opening. Even if an agreement could be reached by the fateful September 16, the three additional "premieres" would have to be postponed—*Frau* had already been advanced; now *Gioconda* and *Traviata* hung in the balance. As these had high price tags attached too, the first week looked to be a shambles, although eventually all new productions were given. What the delay and difficulties did to the budget was best expressed by one official who prophesied that five years of running full speed ahead would barely see recovery. This was a body blow, as indeed two more months would show.

Cynics never admitted that the orchestra's contemporary cry of "Wolf" meant what it portended. Accustomed to many false alarms, one viewer nudged a companion as, at the end of the second intermission of *Antony,* Bing stepped before the curtain. "Here it comes," whispered this prophet, as the General Manager began to speak what John Molleson of the *World Journal Tribune* called the most triumphant third-act prelude since *Lohengrin*: "The dispute with the musicians is settled. The strike is over. The season is secure. The years of frustration, animosity, and unpleasantness depart, and I welcome this fine orchestra back as friends."

To the entire audience and the reporters, this struck the dramatic note lacking in the stage proceedings. *Antony and Cleopatra* was rated as one of the biggest and costliest flops in operatic history, even though showing what Harriett Johnson called in the *Post* the "ultimate in pageantry" and providing for John Chapman of the *News* an "eye-popper, one other gaudy night," to quote the original author of the libretto. Schonberg of the *Times* found quite a few words for it: "Big, grand, impressive, vulgar; a Swinburnian melange of sad, bad, mad, glad; rich and also nouveau riche; desperately aiming for the bigger and the better . . . [proceeding] with the enthusiasm of a group of children around an Erector set." A huge Sphinx that wandered all over the lot (unable to circle because of the turntable failure), reminding the *New Yorker* of a lost locomotive; metal pipes in ranks that looked to more than one critic like brilliant Venetian blinds shimmering in rainbow lights; a veritable menagerie including one small camel; and a junior pyramid that opened up to show Romans—in which Leontyne Price got stuck in rehearsal for a few unpleasant moments—all added to the confusion if not to the enjoyment. Egyptian costumes, especially Price's regal robes, hung so massively on the human frame as to burden freedom of action. Rosalind Elias and Belén Amparán, as the Queen's attendants, also suffered from this overstuffing. The Romans—Justino Diaz as Antony, Jess Thomas as Caesar, Ezio Flagello as Enobarbus, and Mary Ellen Pracht as Octavia—were less dressed and happier.

Other press comments hit sorer marks. Hubert Saal in *Newsweek* made do with the word "disaster," claiming that Franco Zeffirelli's "artless" libretto was originally at fault. "Shakespeare cannot survive the battering of switched lines and shrunken, displaced scenes." But the author must bear some of the guilt. What singer in this world could get out such a mouthful as "Antony, leave thy lascivious wassails"?

Barber's music found few champions. Even though most writers granted a few telling moments, Shana Alexander summed it up tersely in *Life*: "Did Zeffirelli overwhelm or did Barber underwhelm?"

If a TV special program sponsored by the Bell Telephone Company could have been seen immediately after instead of at several months' distance, public sympathy might have been enlisted and the blow softened. It was clearly shown that Zeffirelli had made demands no House in the world could meet; the trouble and dismay clearly appeared on administrative faces as one impossibility piled on another. Seeing the opera on film also presented something of a solution—*Antony* would make a gorgeous movie, with Barber's music taking its rightful place as incidental. Camera cuts would relieve much of the confusion and monotony; close-ups gave the singers a needed advantage over the orchestra.

The most emotional moment all evening came with the audience's dedicated singing of "The Star-Spangled Banner" under Thomas Schippers' baton, while the liveliest occurred "when a kicky, twitchy frieze of fifty press photographers, or *operazzi*" (Shana Alexander adapting the word for the press pack in the film *La Dolce Vita*) scrambled onstage from under the curtain, raising a spontaneous guffaw from the elegant House.

The finest evening in Metropolitan history, regardless of the failure of an honorable gesture to the American artist in choosing composer, cast, and conductor, lasted for many minutes after curtain fall, as guests, invited or otherwise, streamed to the Grand Tier for a party given by Mayor John V. Lindsay. (Host in name only, the charming Mayor experienced a few bad moments when his right to accept private contributions for public affairs came into question.) Waves of champagne washed from the carpeted foyer to the wide outdoor promenade. Then, as the merrymakers wandered away, the Lincoln Center Plaza and the city played the final roles, lights winking out in the small hours of the glamorous night.

27

THE HOUSE THAT HATED TO DIE

The Old Met, mercy killing or murder?

—JOSEPH X. DEVER, *World Journal Tribune*

The old House came down at last. But not for nine months, and not until emotions on both sides had deepened into enmity. Loudly vocal individuals, exacerbated by frustration and spurred on by the noise of the bandwagon, cast Rudolf Bing and all his minions as villains, heartless and arrogant. The General Manager retorted with the appellation, "amateurs and politicians," which somehow was taken to mean "amateur politician" as applied to Sen. Robert F. Kennedy, a mistake that caused wry amusement in several quarters.

Thus the campaign engendered more heat than light, more hysteria than reason, more sentimentality than sense. As the target of bitter recriminations in public and private, the Met, having previously ignored a feeble salvage attempt from a few individuals led by a Westchester County partisan, thought—perhaps mistakenly—that reticence should be the defense against this attack as well. Its dignified silence was broken only later by Bing's comments in two radio broadcasts, ranging from the plaintive to the acrid, and Anthony Bliss's rather dry presentation of facts in a radio panel whose opposing members overwhelmed him with passionate arguments that displayed an abysmal ignorance of actual conditions.

The seesaw had risen in favor of the Old Met group on June 24, 1966, when a bill introduced in the New York State Legislature more than a month earlier was signed by Gov. Nelson A. Rockefeller. It granted a reprieve of 180 days to allow for raising a sum that varied in the telling from $8 million to $15 million as recompense for the Met in place of the $250,000 expected in annual rental from Keystone Associates, purchaser of the property, who intended to build a business structure there. Keystone was to be guaranteed $200,000 damages, which the saviors had to raise immediately, in case their fund drive fell through.

407

Two lower courts subsequently found this legislation unconstitutional and were upheld on December 30, 1966, by the New York State Court of Appeals on the grounds that it "constituted an unreasonable interference with property rights" (majority decision written by Associate Judge Kenneth B. Keating). But no official wanted to seem hardhearted in the face of aroused public sentiment. Still, as the headlines changed daily from hope to despair and back again, a note of cautious cynicism began to appear, and at last the word "politics" was injected.

Legal decisions had never daunted the saviors, who had indeed enlisted political help, notably from New York Senators Robert F. Kennedy and Jacob K. Javits. Former Mayor Robert F. Wagner had his say. And an appeal was made to the White House. In their haste to get the good news before the public, the saviors misinterpreted Roger Stevens, cultural adviser to President Johnson, as "being certain that the Administration will give any reasonable proposal serious and prompt consideration," his words appearing in a large advertisement in the *Times* of January 12. Stevens pointed out subsequently that it was the city and state's responsibility to ask for use of eminent domain, and that any money would have to come from Congress, which hadn't even been approached.

Meanwhile, Keating had relented to the extent of a twenty-four-hour reprieve from the deadline of January 9. Another bill had been introduced in the New York State Legislature providing for New York City to acquire the House by condemnation and then lease it to the Old Opera House Organization, a body to be formed by provisions in the bill. This brought Mayor John V. Lindsay into sharp focus. His City Council voted for home rule, although Martin Sleeper in the *World Journal Tribune* wrote that "six Democratic councilmen are still nursing badly twisted arms after reluctantly casting their votes to help save the Old Met," and exposing Lindsay's real reason for a certain underlying coolness toward the project—the probable cost to the city, now estimated at a minimum of $25 million. Governor Rockefeller now backed up his fellow Republican (he had been "caught out in left field," a Met official said of his signing of the original bill). Now both Democrats and Republicans could blame each other. Senator Kennedy waxed especially sorrowful in chiding Lindsay and Rockefeller, as professed art lovers, for standing by and permitting "the destruction of this historic building."

The Met (now forced to call itself "New," although it had threatened to enjoin the "Old" from any use at all of the titles "Met" or "Metropolitan"), was constrained to state its own case in a public advertisement in the *Times* of January 11. The inability to borrow needed money on its impounded property, added to its other misfortunes, had placed the operating company in jeopardy. The champions of the old House headed their advertisement next day, "Save Both Mets." But the signatories bore the insurgent stamp.

Nelson Rockefeller again came under fire on January 23, even after demolition had started, in an advertisement signed by his brother Laurance, and purporting to be chastisement for ignoring his own (Temporary Hudson River Valley) commission's report on "Historic Sites and Buildings," in which the Met was allegedly listed for preservation. Laurance promptly denounced the advertisement as "deliberately misleading," explaining through a spokesman to the *Times* that "almost all of the material . . . is from a consultant's report and the commission did not formally adopt the report." While his name was at the bottom, "he did not prepare, insert, or approve of it." The Old Met committee was revealed as the financial source, but no names were given.

Who were these "amateurs and politicians" who fought so quixotically for a lost cause? The composition of successive committees changed considerably, although a few zealots remained constant. These latter included Joseph Gimma, the husband of Licia Albanese, who had once before threatened to break away when the incoming Bing's intentions toward the soprano were not clear. Having paid her respects dramatically to the stage at the gala farewell, Albanese once again commanded attention by dressing in her Butterfly costume and singing *"Un bel di"* in the shell of the old structure "in almost total darkness," wrote one evening-paper columnist tearfully.

The January 12 advertisement had been signed by ten names, including Mrs. Nathan Cummings, wife of the Sara Lee bakery tycoon; Mrs. William Randolph Hearst, Sr.; Frederick R. Mann, Philadelphian; Mrs. William Paley, socialite wife of the CBS board chairman; and Frederick W. Richmond, who had been instrumental in saving Carnegie Hall. Mrs. David Brockman, who had displayed enthusiastic ignorance in one broadcast, was called the campaign's Joan of Arc by one columnist. Although names were never made public, the rumor grew that dis-

gruntled would-be boxholders, lost in the shuffle at Lincoln Center because of the smaller number of boxes, hastened to the rebellion, reversing
the trend that sent Academy of Music rejects to the Met in the first place.

Leopold Stokowski, who had started the rumpus, dropped out of
sight, but the parade of celebrities increased, many of them only casually
in touch with operatic affairs—actors, authors, producers—although a
few, such as the actress Peggy Wood, cherished genuine sentiment for the
golden cavern where they had spent happy evenings. Several retired
singers, headed by Giovanni Martinelli, no longer had anything to lose.
Members of the current roster, of course, could not appear publicly
rebellious no matter what their private feelings. A few journalists signed
up, Irving Kolodin among them. He had always been fearless in his
criticism of the Metropolitan in any aspect.

The accession late in the day of the capricious millionaire, Huntington Hartford, spelled the beginning of the end to the sharp-eyed. Though
friends credit him with worthy intentions, his past performance should
have given the rebels pause. Few of his pretentious art schemes had enjoyed long lives: he had disposed of his art colony, his magazine (*Show*),
and his New York art gallery. He was said to have put up half (or all)
of the $200,000 required as security for Keystone, and even was supposed
to have raised several millions, the exact amount never divulged.

Hartford became the symbol of the saviors, three despairing photographs of him appearing in the *World Journal Tribune* as demolition
began. He was quoted as saying, "This is going to give America a black
eye for years to come." Then he was ordered out of the building by a
foreman of the wrecking crew. "It was the only time the suave arts patron
had been thrown out of the Met," the reporter John Molleson added.
Hartford was not listed as a subscriber to the 1966–67 season in the new
House, as might be expected.

Time ran out on January 17 at three P.M. A conscientious and law-
abiding buildings' commissioner had at last granted the wrecking permit.
The sound of wreckers' hammers echoed from the roof, crowbars began
to pry at the secrets of dimmed footlights, marble water fountains were
dragged from their moorings, and the interior of the dusty old auditorium, struck with mortal chill, disintegrated.

The news reached Bliss at 4:15 P.M. in his Rockefeller Center office
through a phone call from Henry Lauterstein, the Met's lawyer. The

Association President listened quietly, then expressed what became the official line, no less sincere for being characteristically low in key: "Mixed emotions." He added that he hoped none of the Met people would be there to be photographed. He needn't have worried. They were too busy uptown.

The grim shell, no longer even describable as the Yellow Brick Brewery of 1883, lingered for a while, surrounded by scaffolding which barely concealed its shame. At last, even the most fanatic of the saviors disappeared, those who had scrawled pitiful graffiti on the protective walls and handed out bulletins crammed with indignation and misinformation.

Like a defiant old beldam, the building squatted for a few months, a prey to fires and a hostess to rats as big as a tabloid newspaper, according to John Molleson in the *World Journal Tribune*. After the wreckers closed down their chilly Thirty-ninth Street corner, where bits and pieces torn out of the viscera of the House commanded unrealistic prices from sentimental scavengers, the structure seemed to reject human beings. The caretaker shivered inside his plywood cubicle, finally becoming used to the dank wind that swung doors open eerily. A kind of black humor began to go around, centering on opera phantoms and probable life below decks. "That's where Judge Crater went," one joker insisted.

Yet the speculation continued. Was the House really necessary for visiting opera troupes? Would restoration really have cost only $200,000, as one architect claimed? In spite of the seven hundred obstructed-view seats and the impossibility of seeing dancers' feet from the front of the Orchestra, was it really a good ballet house? Were the acoustics actually perfect and not spotty, as dissidents insisted? And contrary to Arturo Toscanini's negative verdict many years ago, could orchestras give concerts from the stage satisfactorily?

We shall never know the answers now. The matter became academic as the great brick walls tumbled and the Old Metropolitan Opera House died from internal injuries.

28

NEW INCARNATION

The Age of Miracles is forever here!

—THOMAS CARLYLE, *Heroes and Hero-Worship*

The move into the New House signaled the most turbulent season in the Met's entire history. It generated the sort of controversy not always good for an institution's image, but also produced many rewarding moments that should not be forgotten. The elements of strife perhaps outbalanced the achievements, for the call to the miracle makers went out sooner than anyone had expected. On November 12, 1966, the new Finance Chief, William H. Hadley, expressed the need succinctly: "We are like a family that moved from a cottage into a castle. The upkeep of the castle has proven staggering."

This was the apologia for raising ticket prices in midseason, an unprecedented hike that left the public aghast. Single seats went up almost 20 percent as of December 12, with the top $13 raised to $15.50 and corresponding lifts at all levels except for the lowest ticket of $2.50 and standing room ($2.50 in the Orchestra, $1.50 in the Family Circle), which remained the same. Subscribers were asked to contribute another 20 percent, which increased the overload to nearly 40 percent of their original subscription price.

While the official statement mentioned only the unforeseen expenses of technical failures, overtime, and the costly musicians' strike, George S. Moore, treasurer of the Association, emphasized the stalemate over the Old House. The Met could not use the equity in the building as the desperately needed basis for a loan.

Added to the overtime problem incurred after the season opened was the lateness of the move, a fact either not known or forgotten by the public. Anthony Bliss revealed that the New House had been promised for January 1, but was not entirely ready until midsummer, necessitating overtime piled on overtime. "The whole company—dancers, singers,

412

musicians—would sometimes be working here until three in the morning," said Bliss.

Consequently the budget for the season had gone up from the estimated $14 million to $19.7 million, a gap that could not be closed by the expected intake of $13,100,000 (or more than 66 percent) from box office, rentals, and broadcast rights.

"We just made a mistake," Mr. Moore admitted. "We miscalculated," added Rudolf Bing.

Mr. Hadley, obviously a budget and plus-cost man, next applied the shears to the National Company. A "finance engineer" (efficiency expert) was called in; very soon, subterranean rumbles began to come to the surface, seeming to threaten the senior company's annual spring tour. "The cities will simply have to dig up more money," is the way one harassed official put it.

To the layman the behind-the-scenes costs may seem inexplicable, but as the *Times* pointed out, perhaps the easiest way to understand is to compare the cost of getting the curtain up on each performance and the highest possible box-office intake for that performance. Roughly it works out like this at the former scale: Cost, $60,000 (compare with Abbey's original high of $5,000 in 1883); intake, $34,000. In the first few months of 1967, the new prices raised the over-all box-office intake from single-seat sales to about $200,000, with an additional half million in voluntary contributions from fourteen thousand subscribers.

On March 3, 1967, the result of long hours of deliberation was announced: an emergency campaign for $3 million. The operating deficit of $6,600,000 would be half made up by contributions already budgeted; the public was asked to chip in once again, on a scale commensurate with the inflated economy.

On April 11 the news that Moore had been elected president to succeed Bliss roused considerable speculation. The *Times* listed three factors that contributed to the shift in leaders: labor relations, the ballet, and the National Company. Bliss was felt to be too soft on all three. Confronted with the charge that the new regime meant curtailment in addition to the *fait accompli* of the National Company's dissolution, Moore denied it firmly. "Nobody wants to trim—not one iota," he declared. "There is no doubt but that the company is economically viable. Before this year's emergencies we never missed our budget by more than 1 percent—better than the bank!" (Moore is president of the First National City Bank and knows whereof he speaks.)

But the new president admitted that there would be economies, citing as soft spots the numerous unnecessary stage changes, entailing extra stage hands, in such an opera as *Antony and Cleopatra,* which cost a half million to produce.

Although the board promises to continue on the principle of hands off artistic decisions, Moore feels that once the finances are seen to be on an even keel again, "We may start being a little braver." A Verdi man himself (as well as a Republican and a Yale graduate), the banker obviously prefers favorite operas to unknown ones, and brands as ridiculous the practice of a composer "to write music up to the last minute." (Mozart would have had a bad time at the new Metropolitan.)

Moore's accession means that business is in the saddle now that the Met itself has qualified as Big Business; the lawyers are giving way before the men of action. It goes without saying that the ballet will get shorter shrift than ever before; it has always been a stepchild in spite of the presence of glamorous names, including Dame Alicia Markova. As for the National Company, Moore suggested that he had a "hunch" it would be revived—but completely under the wing of the parent company. "We are not used to being associated with failures," proclaimed this eminently successful individual.

On July 12 another upset added to the sense of crisis. The Soviet Government, which has sent attractions here since 1958 under the management of Sol Hurok, canceled the entire ten-week tour of a group that was to have appeared at the Met for two weeks. No reasons were given, but the Soviets have not hesitated previously to use their cultural "ambassadors" as political pawns, and the world situation found Soviet-American relations not at their happiest just then. Hurok had engaged the Met for four weeks, but the troupe had already postponed its opening date by a fortnight. The responsibility for the rent fell *presumably* on the impresario, although Herman Krawitz hoped to "minimize his costs."

Filled with the company's own activities, the opera's home is no longer open to the commencements, old guard military and civic receptions, benefits for orphan asylums, Lambs' Gambols, fencing drills, monster balls, and sundry other extracurricular events that sprinkled

the Old House records. Soloists, bands, orchestra, and other opera companies had also hired the old auditorium on many an occasion. But the
available rental time in the New House is scarce enough in summer,
practically nonexistent during the season. Hurok's imports had been
counted on to absorb most of the slack.

Meanwhile the season had progressed with its highs and lows. The
dissension over the most elaborate production of all, *Die Frau ohne
Schatten,* sparked excitement. One had only to turn to two pages in the
World Journal Tribune to run into conflict between Alan Rich, who,
believing the opera itself to be ponderous and pretentious, thought the
sets also ponderous and "alien in color and design and shape to the
language of the opera," while Miles Kastendieck approved thoroughly.
Harold Schonberg, calling the *Frau* a "super-opera," granted that the
Met had given it a "super-production, one certainly unparalleled in
American opera history . . . even if it has gone overboard in unnecessary
stage effects. Those backstage gadgets must be hard to resist," the *Times*
critic suspected. He further opined that Robert O'Hearn as designer
"walks just the right line between Godhead and humanity . . . it is hard
to see how it could have been approached any other way."

The huge cast was almost universally inspired, with superlative performances turned in by Christa Ludwig as the Dyer's Wife and her
husband Walter Berry making his debut as Barak. Only slightly less
magnificent were Leonie Rysanek as the Empress, James King as the
Emperor, and Irene Dalis as the Nurse. To Karl Böhm in the pit went
the audience's wildest approval for his electrifying evocation of Strauss's
most inward meanings and most outward show. His ovation would have
been the first genuine outbreak of approval had not the first subscription
week intervened, bringing a *Turandot* that held its own and set the
audience cheering for its beauty and the ringing vocalism of Birgit
Nilsson and Franco Corelli. (In the unfathomable processes of planning
opera at least two seasons in advance, the *Frau* was not scheduled to return in 1967–68 to capitalize on its success, because, it was said, the same
cast and conductor could not be assembled.)

The other two productions designed for opening week but now
placed on whatever night could be found for them were less contentious,
although Cecil Beaton's *Traviata* got some stinging words for its gloomy
bedroom scene à la Charles Addams. Alfred Lunt's direction reverted to

the primitive, with old-fashioned gestures and emotings. Anna Moffo repeated her most famous role. Beni Montresor's *Gioconda* was more successful, lavish in spectacle and color, with a handsome ship for Enzo. Renata Tebaldi and Franco Corelli won the triumphs expected of them.

Strauss's *Elektra,* next in line for redressing, was again a bone of contention, for Rudolf Heinrich's "booby-trapped" set went "abstract and symbolic for this most realistic of operas, so that his whole approach becomes questionable," wrote Kastendieck. The broken ground at various levels, treacherously raked, and the overhead panel cracked into four jagged parts resembled lava, he thought, while Harriett Johnson of the *Post* compared them to coal. They became luminous and changed colors under the light projections that Heinrich favored also in his *Salome,* and thus added mood, albeit artificially. The set cramped Herbert Graf's attempt at drama, so that much of the significant action, such as Aegisthus' murder by Orestes, was lost. Nilsson sang magnificently, although her "beauty-parlor appearance" (Kastendieck) scarely fitted the libretto's description of her as a king's daughter in rags. Klytemnestra, too, was far too elegant in her red robes, while Regina Resnik's face, once out from under one of the stylized masks the designer thought appropriate to Greek tragedy, showed fresh color and no lines, much less the haggard decadence that had distinguished many of her predecessors, notably Elisabeth Hoengen, or more recently Jean Madeira. Rysanek's Chrysothemis was similarly stylish in accordion-pleated panels. Whatever the authenticity of these and other costumes of early Greece, the effect seemed anachronistic with the symbolism of the settings.

The new staging for *Lohengrin,* designed by the Master's grandson, Wieland Wagner, just before his untimely death in Munich on October 16, 1966, was carried out by his assistant Peter Lehmann in presumably authoritative fashion and seen for the first time on December 8. As if the opera were not static enough, with characters all too difficult to make human, Wagner's stained-glass bowl of somber blue (reminding American antique-lovers of nothing so much as a Tiffany lampshade) brought the action virtually to a standstill and made the characters seem automatons. The chorus was ranged along semicircular platforms, only their mouths moving, their bodies clothed identically. There was of course no realistic river, swan, or dove. The two birds materialized as huge light projections on the bowl, while Lohengrin and the little prince were elevated into sight from behind the platforms, as if from lower rather than more angelic realms. There was one moment of passionate movement in the bridal scene where Elsa tried to cajole Lohengrin's secret out of him, but otherwise the principals stood around with nothing much to do. The costumes looked unfinished: the men wore no headgear, leaving the King and Telramund merely ordinary mortals and Lohengrin (with a wavy blond wig) a tall Boy Scout. Elsa never changed her dress, a misfitting white affair that looked crumpled after the first ten minutes. The singers all behaved well under the circumstances, especially Ingrid Bjoner as Elsa, Sandor Konya and later James King as Lohengrin, Christa Ludwig or Nell Rankin as Ortrud, Walter Berry as Telramund. Böhm's conducting provided the liveliest element.

Britten's *Peter Grimes,* which came along on January 20, provided the *succès d'estime* of the nine new productions, finally achieving "the stature it should have had all these years," according to Kastendieck, who dubbed it "powerful." The decor was by Tanya Moisiewitsch, who will be remembered for her extraordinary masked production of the Canadian Stratford Festival's *Oedipus* a decade ago. The brilliant Colin Davis, "the kind of dynamic conductor the Met can use," said Kastendieck, made his Metropolitan debut. He had previously been heard in America with the London Symphony and as guest with other orchestras. Tyrone Guthrie succeeded notably in getting the singers to act their parts, Kastendieck thought. Of these singers, Jon Vickers was a superb Grimes, Geraint Evans a virile Captain Balstrode, and Raymond Michalski a manly Swallow. Among the women, Jean Madeira etched a searing portrait of Mrs. Sedley, but Lucine Amara, suffering from a cold, hardly coped with the intensities of Ellen. The production was not listed for 1967–68.

The long-awaited *Zauberflöte* with its Chagall decor burst forth on February 19, its spinning colors, vibrant and pervading, all but swamping Mozart, in Schonberg's opinion. This made for "an extremely wearing evening" for the *Times* critic. Rich of the *World Journal Tribune* also thought the artist "an intruder," not necessarily unwelcome, but "pouring onto the stage such a smothering flood of love that the love-object becomes drained of its own life's breath." Others were not so unkind. This writer, for example, found the Chagall investiture more exciting than the fairy-tale fantasies of Beni Montresor at the City Opera. *Zauberflöte,* sung in German (a procedure still debatable where comedy is concerned) enlisted two casts, one all-American, one mixed. First nighters, all excellent, included Pilar Lorengar, Lucia Popp (Czechoslovak soprano making her debut satisfactorily as Queen of the Night), Nicolai Gedda, and Hermann Prey, with the Americans Jerome Hines and Paul Franke, and the Canadian Morley Meredith. (Fritz Wunderlich, the gifted young German tenor, had been slated for Tamino, but the shocking news of his death from a fall came even before the loss of Wieland Wagner, another tragic upset for the management.) The other cast featured Judith Raskin, Roberta Peters, George Shirley, Theodor Uppman, John Macurdy, Andrea Velis, and Walter Cassel. The practice of casting three uncertain boy sopranos as the genii must be deplored in so large an auditorium. They sounded better, however, over the air. The top musical value in the performances was the new conductor, Josef Krips, a man of authority, acclaimed as a Mozart stylist.

To leave Marvin David Levy's *Mourning Becomes Electra* until last of the new mountings may have been a matter of expediency but it also turned out to be a dramatic climax of the first order, leaving a trail of excitement and controversy in the air as the season closed. The critics were not willing to acknowledge that the young composer's first full-length stage piece was music of high order. Schonberg called it "background music and yet not background music . . . neither very modern . . . nor very conservative [with] plenty of melody, but the melody does not sing or say anything . . . heightened recitative." Kastendieck also found the score ambivalent. But the staging by Michael Cacoyannis brought to the opera the robustness of his film *Zorba the Greek,* and distilled the power of Aeschylus through Eugene O'Neill and the expert librettist, Henry Butler, into what "became one of the most dramatic experiences ever staged at the Metropolitan," wrote Kastendieck. "That the drama of O'Neill upstaged the composer came as no surprise," he added. Equally potent elements in this later-season triumph were the marvelously decayed sets by Broadway's Boris Aronson, evocative of the incest and madness that were played before them. The singers were no less powerful. In debuts, the Australian Marie Collier as Christine (Clytemnestra) and the gifted American Evelyn Lear as Lavinia (Electra) brought to the Met a new vibrance and a dynamism hitherto lacking. John Reardon as Orin (Orestes), Sherrill Milnes as Adam Brant (Aegisthus), and John Macurdy (Agamemnon) also rose to fever pitch. Smaller roles were no less in keeping: Lilian Sukis, Ron Bottcher, and Raymond Michalski. Zubin Mehta whipped the score out of the pit.

Holdovers from the previous repertoire were carefully chosen to display the hospitality of the new stage. All but *Butterfly* and *Bohème* contained elements of grandeur. After *Turandot, Aida* transplanted best—in fact, brought a fresh inauguration "like a second baptism in the waters of the Nile," wrote Raymond Ericson in the *Times,* referring back to the unfortunate *Antony.* "The more orthodox rite . . . made the place legitimate." The "lusty one-year-old *Faust*" of Dupont and Barrault, as Kastendieck described it, "aligns itself neatly with the latest productions."

The substantial scenery as well as the musical values of *Rigoletto, Lucia, Don Giovanni, Otello, Queen of Spades,* and *Meistersinger* made their transfer highly acceptable, while *Trovatore* and *Tristan* carried their problems right along with them. The oldest Bing production to be retained, his first-year *Fledermaus,* seemed quite at home bringing New Year's Eve cheer across the footlights. Kitty Carlisle, the versatile actress, sang Prince Orlofsky for the first time.

This winter was also marked by the death of two great singing actresses. One, Mary Garden, sang in the old Metropolitan, but never with the company, yet her portrait has been placed in the "museum" at the new opera house. She died on January 3. The other, Geraldine Farrar, died on March 18, 1967, as Milton Cross announced at the end of a *Traviata* broadcast. The management of the Met made no public tribute to the soprano who had led their roster for sixteen years, appearing with Caruso and Toscanini on many memorable nights.

For his second season in the New House, Bing planned to add five new productions and coast on six of 1966–67. He thought well enough of the Beaton-Lunt *Traviata* to put it in the opening slot on September 18, but with different casting—Montserrat Caballé, Richard Tucker and Cornell MacNeil instead of Anna Moffo, Bruno Prevedi and Robert Merrill—Fausto Cleva as conductor. Repetition of such fancy business as the four "opening nights" was rejected out of hand; those ten days that shook the Met were best forgotten. Instead, two solid subscription weeks have been added, bringing the season to thirty-one.

To ease the burden on the central budget, four new productions are benefits for the Guild, which means that the auxiliaries girded for almost double their previous efforts. Gounod's *Roméo et Juliette* was scheduled

for the second night of the season, September 19, and the other three have
been scheduled at fairly regular intervals thereafter. They are to be *Die
Walküre* on November 21, *Carmen* on December 15, and Verdi's early
Luisa Miller on February 8. Material aid came from Mrs. John D.
Rockefeller, Jr., for *Roméo, Carmen,* and *Luisa Miller. Hänsel und
Gretel,* sponsored by the Gramma Fisher Foundation of Marshalltown,
Iowa, is set for November 1. The first segment of the new *Ring,* entrusted
to Herbert von Karajan as part of a three-year plan to restore all four
music dramas, brings uncommon excitement, the high-powered Karajan
being due to appear as producer as well as conductor, with the all-
important casting, as always, by "mutual consent." In other words, Bing
had his say. Agreement rested (although reportedly not without a conflict
of wills in one case) on Nilsson for Brünnhilde, Ludwig for Fricka, Jon
Vickers for Siegmund, Thomas Stewart for Wotan, and Gundula Jano-
witz (scheduled for Bing's Pamina in 1966–67 but released as a favor to
Karajan) for Sieglinde with Crespin, Rysanek, and Berry in later performances. The scenic designs were in the hands of Günther Schneider-
Siemssen, who did *Carmen* and *Boris* for Karajan at Salzburg. The replacements for Lee Simonson's sets have been perhaps more eagerly
awaited than any other single upheaval at the Met.

The other novelties seem slight by comparison, although some
new casting promised fresh interest, including Mirella Freni and Franco
Corelli as the star-crossed Juliet and Romeo, and John Reardon as the
feckless Mercutio. A new director, Paul Emile Deiber, from the Comédie
Française, joins designer Gérard and conductor Molinari-Pradelli. *Hänsel
und Gretel* was assigned to the behind-scenes team of O'Hearn and
Merrill, with a new pair of stage siblings, Rosalind Elias and Teresa
Stratas, and Franz Allers as conductor. The captivating fairy tale had
waited twenty years in the Met's wings. *Carmen,* another collaboration
between Barrault and Dupont after their successful *Faust,* promised
Grace Bumbry as the Gypsy girl, Nicolai Gedda as her Dragoon, Jean-
nette Pilou a debutante Micaela, and Justino Diaz as Escamillo, with
Zubin Mehta in the pit. *Luisa Miller* was to feature Caballé, Tucker,
Giorgio Tozzi, Ezio Flagello, and Sherrill Milnes (who made even the
Lohengrin Herald vocally exciting), offering Verdi's old melodies with
Cleva conducting.

After the initial splurge, no new operas of any nationality were contemplated, although Virgil Thomson has been commissioned (with funds from the Ford and Koussevitzky Foundations) for a possible production of an opera on Lord Byron, with a libretto by Jack Larson. (An earlier Ford commission to Marc Blitzstein for an opera on the story of Sacco and Vanzetti, which brought the fury of conservative groups to the Met's door, was abandoned after the tragic slaying of the composer in 1964.) *Mourning Becomes Electra* was penciled in for repetition even before its premiere. Also held over are the new *Gioconda, Lohengrin, Elektra* and *Die Zauberflöte*. But in order to give other works a chance to preen in new surroundings, many 1966–67 successes retire temporarily (only *Butterfly* and *Aida* remain) to make room for *Forza del Destino* (with Leontyne Price singing her first Leonora), *Falstaff* (with Fedora Barbieri as Dame Quickly), *Nozze di Figaro* (with Pilar Lorengar, Mirella Freni, Teresa Berganza in a long-awaited debut as Cherubino, Cesare Siepi, and a new Finnish baritone, Tom Krause, as the Count.) Others to parade in the Met's second Lincoln Center season are *Manon Lescaut, Tosca, Der Fliegende Holländer, L'Elisir d'Amore, Un Ballo in Maschera,* and a revival of *Martha* for the holiday treat.

In spite of the marvels of the new building, life in the computer age in an arts center is not without its disadvantages. The Met has reached a new plateau on which its footing is still somewhat uncertain. A pleasant devil-may-care rakishness has all but disappeared: life is real, life is earnest on Lincoln Center Plaza and the Establishment is a hard fact of that life.

The Met of course forms its own Establishment, with a fixed hierarchy and an attitude that seems to say you are either for it or agin' it, with no middle ground. Prolonged or too pointed criticism may earn you the status of "an enemy of the House," a phrase that falls quite unselfconsciously from the lips of many in the upper reaches of management and sponsorship.

Framing this image is a superior Establishment—Lincoln Center itself, with John D. Rockefeller III as chairman of the board, and William Schuman, the former head of the Juilliard School of Music. A composer of stature, and a brilliant and attractive personality, he was blamed in the press for the attempt to hire Herman Krawitz away from the Met for the Center's Repertory Company when it was changing management amid considerable hullaballoo in 1966. Bing instantly charged "piracy," and Krawitz remained at the opera. There has been no overt sceptre-wielding since; each component remains autonomous in direction and programming—at least, that is the ideal.

"Autonomy is basic to the health of the Center," Schuman avowed. To the charge of "institutionalization" brought by critics, Schuman replied that he believed in "institutionalizing art while freeing the artist." In other words, the Center aims to give the artist a frame, a home. "Without such a frame, an artist is like a professor without a university," he maintained. "The trick is to keep the 'establishment' hospitable to new ideas. It is quite understandable to wish to preserve the past, but we must try to instill the same excitement into this process as into stimulating new ventures."

Admitting that ideal status has not been achieved, Schuman still expressed the wonder that the Center was working as well as it did after only ten years in the planning and considering that it wasn't all finished yet. Fresh responsibility had been aroused among the Lincoln Center Council, made up of representatives of each constituent who, during the first hectic year of the Met's occupancy, had been meeting once a month instead of four times a year as formerly. Schuman insisted that success depends on the faithfulness with which the Center's philosophy is carried out and the reasonableness of the men who direct it. "Most of all, we need dynamic leadership," he emphasized.

Perhaps the critics and observers in New York have been too close to get a perspective on Lincoln Center. One day they will realize, Schuman thinks, that here is a man-made wonder as great as the United Nations or St. Mark's in Venice.

"With a statue of Dante across the street, the suggestion has been made that we are an Inferno. But I prefer to believe that the integrity of Lincoln Center is epitomized by the image of Lincoln himself. No, there is no statue of the Great Liberator, but don't think we aren't offered one at least weekly."

Schuman maintained that the function of the Center, in addition to providing the framework and centralizing physical services, is a three-way coordination, two aspects of which concern the opera. The first is in education. Under the former Juilliard Dean Mark Schubart, the Center works as the cultural agency of the New York State Department of Education in a plan that is already highly developed, maintaining high professional standards in the materials it prepares for teachers and in the performances it presents to thousands of schoolchildren. The Met's Studio, as John Gutman has boasted, is enormously successful. But it is a truism, as Schuman remarked, that good news is no news. "Impeccable management is of no interest to the press," he commented.

The second function of the Center in aid of its components is the Festival idea, built up under Schuyler Chapin for its introduction in the summer of 1967. The Philharmonic's part was a widely spread contemporary program; the opera listed ten open performances freed from subscription. Two performances each of four of the new productions were on display—*Traviata, Lohengrin, Gioconda,* and *Zauberflöte*—with *Ballo* added.

The Hamburg Opera came for a short visit after appearing at Montreal Expo 67, allowing New York to see Günther Schuller's *Visitation,* the American work which had scored brilliantly in its Hamburg premiere. New York critics and a portion of the public disagreed, finding the work musically weak and dramatically foolish, with that kind of overstatement that Germans admire but Americans tend to laugh at. The cast was universally fine, including Felicia Weathers, the vibrant Negro soprano who had been practically wasted in the Met's *Queen of Spades,* the only role Bing picked in 1965–66 out of her impressive repertoire. Respect if not affection greeted Hindemith's *Mathis der Maler;* Klebe's *Jakobovsky and the Colonel* aroused applause from those who could understand the drama, but left one wondering why the composer had bothered to set music to the delightful play. The undoubted successes of the brief season were Janáček's *Jenufa,* Stravinsky's *Rake's Progress,* staged by Menotti, and Berg's *Lulu* (the latter with Anneliese Rothenberger, stunning in the title role). Rolf Liebermann's gifted company (including the Americans McHenry Boatwright, Jeanette Scovotti, and Richard Cassilly as well as Weathers) held out a lesson for all to read in their perfection of ensemble and excellence of individual acting. The staging (if not invariably the scenery) was a joy to watch.

When the festival was all over—it included a Czech film program, an Indian sitar concert, and a play as well as orchestral concerts and opera— the deficit was lower than expected, only $700,000. "Lincoln Center assumed the entire risk of underwriting," said President William Schuman. Visits from the Bolshoi and Rome Operas are projected for 1968.

The third function of the Center concerns films and chamber music, the locale of which will be the new Alice Tully Hall in the Juilliard School building.

Critics of the new complex have not been idle. Perhaps the most vitriolic was George P. Elliott, who wrote a piece in the *New York Times Magazine* entitled "A Center in Search of a Role" that could not have failed to infuriate everyone in the travertine halls of Lincoln Center. They must have felt it entirely unjust that the poet-novelist-critic quoted Robert Brustein, controversial drama critic of the *New Republic* and Dean of the Yale School of Drama: "Lincoln Center is what America produces instead of art." There was no comfort in the qualification that Brustein's and Elliott's darts were not directed at the individual components of the center, but at the "architectural totality and the idea of a functioning monument."

The conviction was expressed some years ago by John D. Rockefeller, III with a new perspective (most of his family's benefaction had been directed previously to other channels) that "the arts are not for a privileged few but for the many, that their place is not on the periphery of society but at its center." His statement will be emblazoned on a dedicatory plaque in Lincoln Center. But a belief is growing that "the many" cannot afford Lincoln Center, as was evidenced in storms of letters to editors, radio programs, and in other protests after the Met's opening. The rise in already prohibitive ticket prices further confirmed this attitude. It was summed up rather neatly in one of the couplets in a sardonic Christmas greeting from a concert manager and his public-relations-expert wife, which made a good many comments on the state of culture and arts centers in our burgeoning artistic life:

> "What matter that none but the rich can get seats,
> If only we've plenty of sweet Yuletide treats."

But there is no immediate way out of the subscription bind that increasingly constricts the organisms of Lincoln Center, as indeed all performing-arts organizations dependent on both the public and a supporting body in the background. While the Met and the Philharmonic have recognized this fact of life almost from their beginnings, the New York City Opera and Ballet have only resorted to it because of their move to the State Theatre. Their subscription series have succeeded beyond their wildest dreams. Both can plaster little red "Sold Out" signs on most of their *affiches*. And one City Opera official breathed in awe: "We had to *return* more than $250,000 [in the Fall of 1967]!"

Sudden affluence puts these two groups in the same category as the Met so far as the occasional visitors are concerned. These seem to have grown in numbers and in the propensity to write furious letters to the newspapers. The Met protested at the beginning of its 1966–67 season that it could offer from 450 to 900 seats at the window for each performance, but these included everything out of subscription—a number put aside for the Guild, which operates its own ticket bureau for members and has been having comparable trouble, as well as a few for possible high-level emergencies. At the time ticket prices were raised, all mail order business was closed out.

So there are never enough tickets. The couple who would like their occasional Night at the Opera find the going rough. They would have had to try five weeks ahead, standing in a line of which only the first hundred or so can be assured of getting in the House at all, to sit or stand. The new streamlined process of ticket buying at the window has some advantages, however. If you get there in time (and that usually means a dawn patrol at the very latest and, in case of a great attraction, perhaps a thirty-six hour wait) you can buy a seat or standing room. A whole new system of S.R. has been instituted at the suggestion of Alfred Hubay, box-office chief. The plush-covered rails back of the Orchestra and in the Family Circle are all numbered, just like tickets. No more pushing and shoving and stealing of place.

"Social orders have been rent asunder by the new system," wrote Alan Rich in the *World Journal Tribune*. The management had come to resent the *soi-disant* power of this coterie, he continued. Bing tried twice to banish them altogether, but the resulting howl shattered nerves in the entire garment district around the Old House. Now he has at last reduced them to some kind of order. But the resentment is on the other foot. Bing received only the coolest welcome, the insult of complete silence, as he made his customary inspection of the line the day before opening.

Because of the heavy subscription, it might seem that Bing could slip in an increasing number of novelties for his captive audience. The nine in the first Lincoln Center season set something of a record—even for European houses—and probably will never again be equaled by the Met itself.

But as Bing has said, subscribers cannot necessarily be counted upon ad infinitum. It is even conceivable that the waiting list, which has been reduced to some 7,000 from 12,000 according to Clare Moroney, subscripiton secretary, by the enlarged accommodations in the New House, might wear out some time.

"Furthermore, the House itself will not be the same novelty, not quite as new the second year . . . or the third," added Bing.

"We are dependent on many influences. Just consider what happens to us—and to all entertainment—when the stock market goes down. The public must realize that opera lives by its subscription. But this is a game we can't win. If we are sold out, people write those letters to newspapers and make loud noises in the box-office line. If we didn't sell out, the loud noises would come from the board of directors."

Other vexations have appeared since the Met's move to its new home. One is being ignored publicly for a while, but provides many private needle pricks. This is the competition of the New York City Opera. "Competition" is not a word Bing likes to emphasize. Indeed, almost everyone agrees that there is room for both organizations; interestingly enough, their audiences differ widely, except for the fringe of buffs who must see all the opera in town. But Julius Rudel has an irritating way of coming up with, say, Handel's *Julius Caesar,* directed by Tito Capabianco, ten days after the Met's opening with the Barber-Zeffirelli *Antony and Cleopatra,* and garnering all the good critical words withheld from the Met. The City Opera *Traviata,* rather commonplace, full of clutter and nonoperatic style, still outranked (in the press view) the Met's. Rudel got his *Magic Flute* in first, with designs and direction by Beni Montresor (who thus might be considered a traitor, though he had already done the Met's new *Gioconda*). The *Times* found the City *Flute* "relaxed and charming," leaving what the Met feared might be the taste of anticlimax for Chagall's elaborate and fanciful dressing, although the five months' interval allowed the public to approach it freshly.

"It seems as if everything they do is right and everything we do is wrong," said Bing in a moment of frustration. The comparison between

Traviatas was particularly irritating. If this is typical American championship of the underdog, Bing wants none of it. All too often it appears that
the press motto is "Love Rudel, Hate Rudy."

What friends of both institutions refuse to acknowledge as a feud
really goes back a considerable way, when the City Opera began to feel its
oats but on several occasions was not able to afford them. In one emergency, the Met offered to take over the younger company and operate it
as an adjunct, a kind of *opéra comique*. Morton Baum and Newbold
Morris redoubled their efforts for the troupe in the old Mecca Temple
and got enough money and public interest to save the situation and go
on from there. "Instead of settling for some consideration as the second
opera company in New York," Rudel remarked, "we have become 'the
other company' "—quoting Martin Bernheimer in *Opera* magazine.

Their move to Lincoln Center became inevitable; every circumstance
dictated it. When the New York State Theatre was built with $15 million
of state and $12 million of city money for the immediate purpose of
participation in the New York World's Fair of 1964 and 1965, the state
leased the theatre to Lincoln Center. The City Center won control of the
theatre (as they contended had been the original intent of the law) only
after a fight with Lincoln Center that the *Times* described as "acri-
monious." Rockefeller eventually gave way gracefully, and Rudel's troupe
took over in February 1966. (One ironic result was that the Met's National
Company had to go to City Center for its second—and last—New York
season).

Rudel, in his own way as deep a mystery man as Bing, summed up
his attitude in the program of the following autumn season in an article
headed "Jostling the Establishment." "I sometimes believe," he wrote,
"that the New York City Opera had to be invented to be the thorn in the
side of the staid and stuffy Opera." He admitted that their success brought
the possibility of danger—they may "be considered part of the Establishment" themselves, and need a little jostling in turn.

The Met may perhaps feel that such jostling was the last thing wanted
in this year of *Sturm und Drang*, but the elder and younger sisters are
side by side—or rather at right angles—in the new supermarket of culture,
and must learn to live with each other. Although one could possibly wish
a meeting of the minds and assortment of repertoire, it is perhaps not

unfortunate that an occasional clash occurs. The worst did not happen when, as predicted, they both performed the same opera (*Traviata*) on the same night. Both houses were sold out.

The real problem was the traffic, for enough taxis are never seen with their "free" lights on, some buses don't run late enough, the parking space underneath is insufficient (1,700 or so places) and that on the streets practically nonexistent, while the subways remain dreary and far between. When, one night, the Met had its stylish new *Elektra* with an early curtain, Philharmonic Hall housed Thomas Scherman's concert performance of Janáček's *Jenufa,* which let out after eleven, and the City Opera was giving its *Traviata,* the advantages of staggered curtain time, although unplanned, could be seen.

One *Random House Dictionary* definition of the word miracle is: "A wonderful or surpassing example of some quality." The Metropolitan Opera has counted for its life on such surpassing examples from its own personnel and from its public time after time. Occasionally it seems as if the other property of the word, a supernatural agency, has been evoked. A miracle intervened at the very first to preserve an inappropriate opera house with an inartistic sponsorship past financial flurries and the near fatality of fire. Wonderful examples of the public's loyalty have bejeweled every decade since the turn of the century. In its newest emergency, this kind of miracle is what's wanted. But the thousands of supporters have the right to hope for something miraculous as well—the artistic development that has not invariably kept pace with new concepts of opera-house management and opera production. It may be too late to retreat from the jet age, which hurtles singers from continent to continent faster than the sound of their own voices without the breathing space formerly provided by lovely, leisurely nine-day ship crossings. It is probably also past time for any but one-man rule of the opera, and that man as knowledgeable in business as in art. The miracle would be a man whose taste matches his ability and ambition. It is hard to imagine any previous impresario coping with the intricacies of present-day opera management. Rudolf Bing has been shaped by events, but he has also had a hand in shaping them to his will. The Metropolitan today is largely his creation. What awaits his successor is in the realm of speculation—and of additional miracles.

SELECTED BIBLIOGRAPHY

Alda, Frances, *Men, Women, and Tenors,* Houghton-Mifflin, Boston, 1937.

Amory, Cleveland, *Who Killed Society?,* Harper, New York, 1960.

Beebe, Lucius, *The Big Spenders,* Doubleday, New York, 1966.

Belmont, Eleanor Robeson, *The Fabric of Memory,* Farrar, Straus, New York, 1957.

Bispham, David, *A Quaker Singer's Recollections,* Macmillan, New York, 1920.

Brown, Eve, *Champagne Cholly,* Dutton, New York, 1947.

Brown, Henry Collins, *New York in the Elegant Eighties,* Valentine's Manual, 1927.

—————— *In the Golden Nineties,* Valentine's Manual, 1928.

Carner, Morris, *Puccini,* Knopf, New York, 1959.

Caruso, Dorothy, *Enrico Caruso: His Life and Death,* Simon & Schuster, New York, 1945.

Clews, Henry, *Twenty-Eight Years in Wall Street,* Irving Publishing Company, New York, 1887–1888.

Cushing, Mary Watkins, *Rainbow Bridge,* Putnam, New York, 1954.

Dalrymple, Jean, *September's Child,* Dodd, Mead, New York, 1963.

Damrosch, Walter, *My Musical Life,* Scribner's, New York, 1923.

Depew, Chauncey M., *My Memories of Eighty Years,* Scribner's, New York, 1922.

Eames, Emma, *Some Memories and Reflections,* D. Appleton, New York, 1927.

Eliot, Elizabeth, *Heiresses and Coronets,* Obolensky, New York, 1959.

Erskine, John, *My Life in Music,* Morrow, New York, 1950.

Farrar, Geraldine, *Such Sweet Compulsion,* Greystone Press, New York, 1938.

—————— *The Story of an American Singer,* Houghton, Boston, 1916.

Finck, Henry T., *Success in Music and How It Is Won,* Scribner's, New York, 1909.

—————— *My Adventures in the Golden Age of Music,* Funk & Wagnalls, New York, 1926.

Gatti-Casazza, Giulio, *Memories of the Opera,* Scribner's, New York, 1941.

Gerber, Aimé, and Heylbut, Rose, *Backstage at the Opera,* Crowell, New York, 1937.

Glackens, Ira, *Yankee Diva,* Taplinger, New York, 1963.

Holbrook, Stewart H., *The Age of the Moguls,* Doubleday, New York, 1953.

Hoyt, Edwin Palmer, *The Vanderbilts and Their Fortunes,* Doubleday, New York, 1962.

Huneker, James, *Letters,* New York, 1922.

Jeritza, Maria, *Sunlight and Song,* D. Appleton, New York, 1924.

Key, Pierre V. R., and Zirato, Bruno, *Enrico Caruso,* Little, Brown, Boston, 1922.

Kolodin, Irving, *The Story of the Metropolitan Opera: 1883–1950,* Knopf, New York, 1953 (later edition, 1966).

Lehmann, Lilli, *My Path Through Life,* Putnam, New York, 1914.

Lehr, Elizabeth, *King Lehr and the Gilded Age,* Lippincott, Philadelphia, 1935.

Leiser, Clara, *Jean de Reszke and the Great Days of Opera*, Minton Balch, New York, 1934.

Lundberg, Ferdinand, *America's Sixty Families*, Vanguard Press, New York, 1937.

Mahler, Alma (Werfel), *Gustav Mahler*, Viking Press, New York, 1946.

——— *And the Bridge Is Love*, Harcourt, Brace, New York, 1958.

Martin, Frederick Townsend, *The Passing of the Idle Rich*, Doubleday, Page, New York, 1911.

——— *Things I Remember*, John Lane, 1913.

Matz, Mary Jane, *The Many Lives of Otto Kahn*, Macmillan, New York, 1963.

McAllister, Ward, *Society As I Have Found It*, Cassell, New York, 1890.

McArthur, Edwin, *Flagstad: A Personal Memoir*, Knopf, New York, 1964.

Moore, Grace, *You're Only Human Once*, Doubleday, New York, 1944.

Moses, Montrose J., *Heinrich Conried*, Crowell, New York, 1916.

Murphy, Agnes, *Melba*, Doubleday, Page, New York, 1909.

Myers, Gustavus, *The History of Great American Fortunes*, Modern Library, New York, 1936.

O'Connell, Charles, *The Other Side of the Record*, Knopf, New York, 1947.

O'Connor, Harvey, *The Astors*, Knopf, New York, 1941.

Pulitzer, Ralph, *New York Society on Parade*, Harper, New York, 1910.

Robinson, Francis, *The Life of Caruso in Pictures*, Studio, Viking (T. Y. Crowell), New York, 1957.

Saarinen, Aline, *The Proud Possessors*, Random House, New York, 1958.

Satterlee, Herbert, *J. Pierpont Morgan*, Macmillan, New York, 1939.

Schwab, Arnold T., *James Gibbons Huneker*, Stanford University Press, Stanford, 1963.

Seltsam, William, *Metropolitan Opera Annals*, Wilson, New York, 1947 (supplement, 1957).

Sheean, Vincent, *Oscar Hammerstein*, Simon & Schuster, New York, 1956.

Townley, Lady Susan, *The Indiscretions of Lady Susan*, D. Appleton, New York, 1922.

Untermeyer, Jean Starr, *Private Collection*, Knopf, New York, 1965.

Vanderbilt, Cornelius, Jr., *Farewell to Fifth Avenue*, Simon & Schuster, New York, 1935.

——— *Queen of the Golden Age*, McGraw-Hill, New York, 1956.

Wecter, Dixon, *The Saga of American Society*, Scribner's, New York, 1937.

Wharton, Edith, "After Holbein," in *Best Short Stories*, Scribner's, New York, 1958.

Winkler, John K., *Morgan, the Magnificent*, Vanguard Press, New York, 1930.

Worden, Helen, *Society Circus*, Covici, New York, 1936.

INDEX

ABC of popular operas (*Aida, Bohème, Carmen*), 280,

AGMA (American Guild of Musical Artists): agreement with Met, 257; and Bing, 366; eliminates commissions for singers' outside engagements, 245, 366–7; establishes jurisdiction, 257; and Faine, 365; and Herman, 365; organized, joins other unions, 257; and Tibbett, 226, 257; and weekly salaries, 339

Abarbanell, Lina, 165

Abbey, Henry Eugene, 45, 50, 52, 53, 57, 58, 59, 67, 70, 79, 96–7, 101, 103, 139, 312; benefit for, 58; benefit for daughter, 120; contract canceled after fire, 102; costs compared with Bing's, 413; dismissed by directors, 64–5; divorce, illness, death, 120; at 1883 opening, 45, 50, 55; financial difficulties, 62–5; "gambler" (Damrosch), 61; Mapleson on, 53–4; Mapleson rivalry on road, 62; *Music and Drama* on, 61; *Musical Courier* on, 98; opens in Chicago, 89; opens with *Roméo*, 90; opens with *Faust*, 90; orders costumes from Worth, 25; Park Theatre burns, 52; pirates personnel from Mapleson, 52–3; on power of money, 121; rents Met, 128; repertoire: 60, and casting, 90, 93–4; to return, 86–7; and scenery, 68; tour (1889–90) with Patti, Nordica, etc., 86, 96, 128

Abbey, Mrs. Henry E.: divorces Abbey, 120

Abbey and Grau: away during fire, 102; give opera in native languages, 97–8; new contract for, 99; and star system, 98; and novelties, 127

Abott (Abbot), Bessie, 151, 156

"*Abscheulicher!*" (*Fidelio*), 301

"*Abschied*" (*Walküre*), 235

Academy of Music (New York), 1, 7, 8, 22, 26–7, 50, 52–3, 65, 69, 71, 80, 121, 126, 410; rivalry with Met, 7, 53, 64, 84; sold to Gilmore and Tompkins, 84

Acoustics: at Center Theatre, 243; joke about, 401; at new Met, 401; at New Theatre, 181; at old Met, 62, 411; at Philharmonic Hall, 401; at State Theatre, 401; *Tribune* on, 49–50

Acté, Aino, 156

Actors Equity, and AGMA, 257

Adams, Henry Sherman: on Max Alvary, 78

Adams, Jack: and Milanov, 267

Adams, Maude, 195

Adams, Suzanne, 116, 140

Addams, Charles, 415

Adler, Kurt, 321, 323, 325

Adler, Kurt Herbert: and Bing, 342–3; and Farrell, 337; and Schwarzkopf, 343; and Simionato, 344

Adrian, makes Traubel costumes, 307

Adriana Lecouvreur (Cilèa), 158, 317, 343 (Chicago); Bing cancels, restores, 335; directed by Merrill, 317; Ponselle refused by Johnson, 205; sets by Cristini-Paravicini, 317

Aegyptische Helena, Die (R. Strauss), 267

Aeschylus, 418

Africana, L' (*L'Africaine*) (Meyerbeer), 92 (also Chicago), 97, 116 (French), 118, 126, 139, 205, 218

Age of the Moguls, The (Holbrook), 9, 15

Aida (Verdi), 93, 118, 135, 155, 181 (Philadelphia), 198, 238, 315, 319, 323–4, 330, 335–6, 339, 375 (Newport), 383, 419, 421; in ABC of popularity, 280; Aldrich, Henderson, Krehbiel on, 178; a Bing favorite, 306; directed by Merrill, 317; Ericson on, 419; Grau on, 136; opening 1908, 31, 178–9; opening, 225; in Paris, 184, 392; sets by Gérard, 313, by O'Hearn, 313, 317; and Suez Canal, 394; Toscanini broadcast of, 292; Triumphal Scene from, at Gala Farewell, 378

Aimée, 61, 118

Air France: Met to Paris with, 386

Aix-en-Provence Festival, and chamber opera, 384

Albanese, Licia, 268; dissension with Bing, 308; and husband Gimma, 308; kisses stage floor at Gala Farewell, 379; sings "*Un bel di*" in Old Met, 409. Roles: Adriana, 335; Butterfly, 308, 328; Donna Anna (San Francisco), Manon, Marguerite, Mimi, Tosca, 308; Violetta, 292, 308

Albani, Emma, 65, 86–7, 93, 96, 98

Alceste (*Alcestis*) (Gluck), direction, sets by Manuel, 319

Alcock, Merle, 189, 229, 233

Alda, Frances: and Boston Opera, 190; decorates Gatti's office, 255; described by Ziegler's

431

son on as manager, 310; Krehbiel on her Thaïs, 187; Mélisande compared to Bori's, 221; retires from New York, 216; success in New York, 183; and *Thaïs* dispute with Hammerstein, 159; values Johnson as singer, 220. Roles: Fiora, Jongleur, Louise, Mélisande, Monna Vanna, Salome, Thaïs (New York), 217; Mélisande (Chicago), 301; Salome (Hammerstein), 151–2

Gardner, Mrs. John: gives diamond to Melba, 112

Garris, John: murdered in Atlanta, 303

Garrison, Mabel, 193, 212, 233

Gary, Elbert H.: at 1918 opening, 199

Gates, John ("Bet-you-a-million"): and Morgan, 15

Gatti-Casazza, Giulio, 31, 156, 175, 203–4, 223, 227–9, 238, 255, 312, 327, 339, 341; and American operas, 186, 201, 250; and American singers, 230, 233–4, 250; approached by Met, 171; Armistice coincides with 11th opening, 197; and ballet losses, 240–1; borrows Zenatello, 177; and Boston Opera, 175; and Caruso, 177, 200; casting kept secret, 245; complains of House, 174; and conductors (German), 239; and Deems Taylor, 242, 250; described, 243–4; Dippel associate to, 173; divorces Alda, 190; and *Don Giovanni*, 227; downcast at farewell, 254; engaged to Barrientos, 174, 201; exchanges with Boston and Chicago ended, 193; farewell gala, 254; and Farrar, 200; Farrar on double bookkeeping, 241; final season, 253–4; financial acumen, 185; and Flagstad, 234–5; fortunes brighten, 180; and Fremstad, 189, 214, 254; and German opera, 201–4; Gilman on hiring for life of, 240; gives Caruso gold medal, 207; gives Farrar *Zaza* instead of *Tosca*, 214; and "Great Divide," 206; hires singers only half year, 225; interview with Alsop, 254; interviewed by Farrar on radio, 216; irked by Chicago successes in New York, 183; and Johnson as singer, 220; and Juilliard, 249; Kahn promises new House, 174–5, 241; and Kemp, 238; Lewis on, 277; loses Toscanini, singers, 187; marries Alda, 189; marries Galli, 190, 254; Meltzer on, 173–4; million-dollar nest egg, 240–1; and Moore, 230–1; and new singers, 191, 219; New Theatre a nightmare to, 181; novelties, 157, 180, 185–7, 201–2, 219, 223; on politics and theatre, 197; and Pons, 250; and Ponselle, 205; preliminary inspection in New York, 173–5; problem to replace Caruso and Farrar, 206–7; prohibits long tours, 184; quotes Verdi, Gioberti, 185; reforms Conried's casting system, 184–5; refuses to revive *Iris* for Eames, does so for Bori, 140; relies on memory, 279; repertoire of, 180,

185–7, 201–5; revives *Pelléas*, 221; and Ricordi, 180; rivalry with Hammerstein, 182; roster of, 180, 235–6, 261; and salary cut, 247; at La Scala, 171; sends Alda to Boston, 190; and Sturani, 279; and Tibbett, 223; and ticket scandals, 191–2; 25th anniversary of, 254; and Urban, 200–1; and Villa, 245, 279; and W. J. Guard, 185; and Wagner, 246; war problems, 192–5, 200; Witherspoon to succeed, 252; and world premieres, 185–6, 201; and Ziegler, 244–6

Gay, Maria, 141; and Carmen, 210; and Zenatello discover Pons, 229, 268

Gedda, Nicolai: and Bing, 328; at Gala Farewell, 378. Roles: José, 420; Tamino, 418

Gencer, Leyla, 341

Genêt, Jean: see *Paravents, Les*

Geneva Opera: director attends 1966 opening, 395

Genthe, Arnold: on Caruso and San Francisco earthquake, 166

Gentle, Alice (True), 233

George V, King of England, and Queen Mary: honored by Met in Toronto, 124

George Washington, S.S., 184

Georgiou, Vilma, 379

Gerard, Florence: see Abbey, Mrs. Henry

Gérard, Jacques, 296

Gerard, James W.: at Horse Show opening, 200; at Met for war declaration, 194–5

Gérard, Rolf: receives most commissions from Bing, 315; revises *Rosenkavalier*, 315. Sets for: *Aida, Cavalleria, Pagliacci*, 313; *Arabella*, 319; *Bohème, Così fan Tutte, Don Carlo, Eugene Onegin, Fledermaus, Sonnambula, Tannhäuser*, 315; *Carmen*, 214; *Faust*, 313, 319; *Gypsy Baron, Périchole*, 316; *Roméo*, 420; *Sylphides* (ballet), 315

Gerber, Aimé: begins as office boy, becomes paymaster, 122; on Conried's *Parsifal*, 148; on Grau's casts, 122

German Grand Opera: Gadski tours with, 195

German language: accepted again, 204

German opera, 143, 324; and Bing, 305–6; and Farrar, 210; finds home in America, 65; given in German by Abbey, 98; halcyon days end, 83–5; humor in, 237–8; "outcasts" in New York season, 203; restored slowly after war, 201–4, 235; returns briefly, 121; rumored to return, 99; saved temporarily for Met, 86; war problems with, 193, 200

German "outcasts": Ober, Braun, Weil give German opera at Lexington Theatre, New York, 203

German singers, 347, 350

Germania (Franchetti), 177, 179

Germania Theatre (New York): and Neuendorff, Hammerstein, 138

Johnson, Edward (*continued*)
toire of, 265; resents Bing, 304; retires, 280; Rosenfield on, 276; roster of, 257–8, 260–1, 262–3; Rudolf on, 280; and St. Leger, 276–9, 303; and *Salome*, 299; on split management, 279, 362; and star system, 327; and Steber, 358; sympathy for singers, 274–5; testimonial dinner for, 277; and Tibbett, 226; and tours, 276, 309; unable to control singers' time, 256; and unions, 275; weaknesses of, 274–5; and Wettergren, 260; and Ziegler, 276-7

Johnson, Firenze, 311

Johnson, Harriett (*Post*): on *Antony and Cleopatra*, 404; on *Elektra*, 416

Johnson, Herbert: as business manager of of Chicago Opera, 279

Johnson, Mrs. Laura: as flashy elite at 1966 opening, 396

Johnson, Lyndon B., 408

Johnson, Mrs. Lyndon B.: Met's new Golden Age (in letter to Bliss), 394; at opening of New House, 395, 397

Johnson, R. E., 141

Johnson Memorial Fund, Edward: benefit *Tosca* for, 309

Jomelli, Jeanne, 145

Jongleur de Notre Dame, Le (Massenet): by Chicago Opera in New York, 217

Jordan, Eben D., 249; builds Boston Opera House, 175; joins Kahn in international scheme, 175

Jordan, Irene, 295

Jörn, Carl, 157

Journal-American (New York), 378, 381

Journet, Marcel, 131–2, 151; first Titurel at Met, 149. Roles: Colline (Los Angeles, debut), King in *Aida* (San Francisco), 139

Journey in Other Worlds (Astor), 108

Judels, Jules, 261

Juilliard, A. D.: box occupied at 1918 opening, 199; boxholder in 1892, 105; fatal attack of, 249; as Met benefactor, 249; Mrs. Belmont on, 249

Juilliard Foundation, 251; American artists, operas favored by, 250, 256, 275, 287, 291; conditions of, for Met assistance, 250, 252, 254; Liebling on Met and, 257; representatives of, elected to Met board, 252

Juilliard School of Music, 252, 421, 424; graduates from, at Met, 258, 266; and Juilliard bequest, 249; to Lincoln Center, 371; Price studies at, 336; summer school of, 264

Juive, La (Halévy), 67 (in German), 68, 76, 203, 207, 220, 259; postponed for Martinelli, 220

Julien (Charpentier), 187, 210

Julien (character): Caruso wears costume of on visit to Dorothy Benjamin, 210–1

Julius Caesar (Handel), 343 (concert); 426 (N. Y. C. Opera, directed by Capabianco)

Jurinac, Sena, 342

Kabaivanska, Raina, 346

Kahn, Margaret: see Ryan, Mrs. John Barry

Kahn, Otto Herman, 274; attempts to build new House, 241–2, 371; backs Conried on *Salome*, 151; becomes Met board member, 143; Bliss on, 375; and daughter, 175, 397; death of, 251; demotes Dippel, 176; and Diaghilev ballet, 202, 240–1; disillusioned, 218, 243; and dream of empire, 175, 183–4; and Flagstad, 254; and Gatti-Casazza, 173–4, 253; and Gatti and Alda, 190; and Goelet, 281; illness of, 218; as Jeritza benefactor, 218; and Juilliard bequest, 250; Krehbiel on, 184; letter from Cutting to, 241; and love of *Tristan*, 246; Matz on, 241; as Moore benefactor, 231; and Mrs. Vanderbilt, 243; on need for people's support, 181; on New Theatre disappointment, 181; pays Hammerstein, 240; promises Gatti new House, 174–5, 241; directors refuse Met box to until 1917, 241–2; retires, 218, 243; sends Met to Paris, 183–4, 240, 389; sued by Mrs. Conried, 172; and Ziegler, 244

Kahn, Mrs. Otto H.: Mrs. Belmont visits, 302; death of, 302; with husband at Hammerstein opening, 169

Kaiser Wilhelm II (liner), 160, 184

Kalisch, Paul, 73, 93-4; marries Lehmann, 74; persecuted by Vianesi, 94; remains after German regime, 82

Kanin, Garson: directs *Fledermaus*, 316

Kansas City (Mo.): and Talley, 229, 291

Kappel, Gertrude, 236–7, 260. Roles: Elektra (Gilman on), Ortrud, 237; Venus, 262

Karajan, Herbert von, 344; for new *Ring*, 420; at Salzburg, 420

Kaschmann, Giuseppe: as Don Giovanni, 60

Kaskas, Anna, 259; as Orfeo, 262

Kastendieck, Miles (Brooklyn *Eagle*, *World Journal Tribune*): on *Ballo*, 285; on *Elektra*, 416; on *Faust*, 419; on *Frau ohne Schatten*, 415; on *Mourning Becomes Electra*, 418; on *Peter Grimes*, 417

Kavanaugh, Mrs. George Washington: Cholly Knickerbocker on, 284

Kaye, Sidney (Kalmanovich): Peerce marries sister of, 292; and Russian Tea Room, 292

Keating, Kenneth B.: and Old Met, 408

Keene, James R.: absent in 1892, 104; subscribes to Mann's *Fads and Fancies*, 30

Kelley, Lawrence: and Callas, 331

Kemlitz, Otto and Frau, 66

Kemp, Barbara: compared to Mary Garden, 238; contretemps in *Tristan*, 238; in husband's *Mona Lisa*, 238; Krehbiel on, 238

by, 61; tribute for concert tours eliminated by AGMA, 245; troubles, 246; Vanderbilt on Society's abandonment of, 240; war effect on, 200, 268, 280, 285, 287; youth program at Newport, 375; Ziegler's financial achievements for, 235; Ziegler "head," Johnson "front" of, 276; see also Broadway, Lincoln Center, Metropolitan Opera Association, Metropolitan Opera House, New York City, Thirty-ninth Street

Metropolitan Opera Co. administration (management): artistic and business functions overlap, 279; aspirants to post, 141–4; change in policy, 172; and Farrar, 213; fights Old Met Committee, 382; and Flagstad, 235; growing *laissez-faire* of, 291; Italian, distrusted by several singers, 176; and Juilliard, 291; longest regime begins in dichotomy, 173; need for submanagement personnel, 364–5; not possible under two heads, 176; policy on Americans saves Met, 287; professional versus performer as manager, 312; in seminars at Newport, 375; see also Abbey, Bing, Conried, Damrosch, Gatti-Casazza, Grau, Johnson, Witherspoon

Metropolitan Opera Co. ballet, 80; and Bliss, 413; headed by Balanchine, 262; by Markova, 396; at Newport, 375; in Paris, 386; stepchild, 414

Metropolitan Opera Co. casts: inappropriate, 265; many changes in, 261, 322–3; nearly intact, 340

Metropolitan Opera Co. chorus: and AGMA, 366; Gatti brings new Italian group, Dippel furnishes Germans, 174; injured in *Carmen*, 170; Krehbiel praises in *Prince Igor*, 253; to Paris, 386; slipshod, 170, 253; strikes, 170, 366

Metropolitan Opera Co. conductors: attainments, 276; and Bing, 320–6, 359; Conried skimps on, 170; and Johnson, 275, 300

Metropolitan Opera Co. Newport Festivals, 374–5; loss at, 375; younger personnel featured, 375

Metropolitan Opera Co. opening nights, 1, 19, 43–56, 84, 90 (1883); 108–110 (1893); 178–9, 181 (1908); 198 (1917); 197–9 (1918); 205 (1920); 212 (1921); 220, 225, 233, 259, 282–6 (1940); 287 (1941); 294 (1944); 313 (1950); 337 (1962); 394–406, 424 (1966); antics at, 397; in Brooklyn, 178; finest night in history, 405; Gatti keeps secret, 245; outlandish costumes at, 397; same night as Academy of Music, 27, as Horse Show, 27, 200

Metropolitan Opera Co. orchestra, 53, 61; conducted by Siegfried Wagner, 235; cut down by Conried, 170; and Goldberg settlement, 367, 403; Mahler praises, 163; members play chamber music at Newport, 375;

to Paris, 386; strike of, 335, 367, 403–4, 412; strike settled, 404

Metropolitan Opera Co. radio broadcasts: and Bing, 379–80; Farrar commentator for, 216; intermission features, 371; and Milton Cross, 282; response to saves fund drive, 281; sponsored by Texaco, 370; see also Opera News on the Air; Opera Quiz

Metropolitan Opera Co. repertoire, 80, 157, 180, 185–7; "connoisseur" works, 276; German, 163–4, 173, 179, 193, 261; neglect of French, 352; odd double bills, 202; see also Abbey, Bing, Conried, Gatti-Casazza, Grau, Johnson

Metropolitan Opera Co. roster, 145; French, 183; largest in history, 261, 262; see also the various nationalities of singers; Abbey, Bing, Conried, Gatti-Casazza, Grau, Johnson

Metropolitan Opera Co. singers: all (except Gigli) accept 10 percent cut, 247; many spend single season at Met, 345–6; top quality at Newport, 375; see also the various nationalities of singers

Metropolitan Opera Co. Spring (Post) Seasons, 254, 259, 260, 262–4, 278, 309; dropped for few years, 264–5; Mrs. Belmont calls "Junior Co.," 265, 309; Johnson as director of, 252; succeeded by Pattison, 263–4

Metropolitan Opera Co. stage directors, staging: in Bing regime, 313–320, 314–21; Conried skimps on, 170; Finck on, 180

Metropolitan Opera Co. stage management: lapse in efficiency, 170

Metropolitan Opera Co. student matinees, 272, 309; *Fanciulla* at, in first performance in New House, 401

Metropolitan Opera Co. subscribers, 339; Bing on, 318; and fund drive, 281; give extra contributions, 370, 412

Metropolitan Opera Co. subscriptions, 192, 376, 424–6; Bing divides series, 306; two weeks added in 1967–68, 419

Metropolitan Opera Co. Sunday concerts: 204, 278; Fremstad in farewell at, 189; called olla-podrida, 222; Pelletier conducts, 238; St. Leger conducts, 278; Tibbett at, 22; threatened by blue law, 170

Metropolitan Opera Co. tours, 181, 240, 389, 391–2; with Abbey, 62, 89; with Conried, 143, 165–7; with Damrosch, 70–1, 183; Dippel's expansion of, 182; double company, 181; *Fledermaus* on, 342; Gatti curtails, 184; with Herman Grau, 82–3; with Maurice Grau, 124, 130, 133; and Johnson, 276, 303, 309; to Paris, 1910, 183–4, 240, 272, 391–2; to Paris, 1966, 294, 374, 383–93 (booed, 385–6; French-American entente backstage, 388, 393; impact of reviews, 392–3; NBC documentary on, 355); Ziegler arranges, 245;

480 THE MIRACLE OF THE MET

Smetana, Bedřich, 262; see also *Verkaufte Braut, Die*
Smith, Alfred E., 199
Smith, Alva: see Vanderbilt, Mrs. William K. and Belmont, Mrs. O. H. P.
Smith, Cecil: on Bing and Met policies, 305; on Bing and press, 360
Smith, J. Henry, 142
Smith, Lawrence, 375
Smith, Oliver: sets for *Martha* (with Motley), *Traviata*, 314
Smith family (southern), 17
Smyth, Ethel, 134; see also *Wald, Der*
Snegurochka (Rimsky-Korsakov), 187; sets by Anisfeld, 216
Society: and Mrs. Belmont, 270; decrescendo after 1883 opening, 57; new order of, 284; see also New York Society
Society as I Have Found It (McAllister), 20
Sodero, Cesare, 275, 292
Söderström, Elisabeth, 352
Solti, Georg: takes over Covent Garden, 323; with Toscanini in Salzburg, other European and American engagements, 323. Conducts: *Aida, Boris, Don Carlo, Moses and Aaron* (London), *Otello, Tannhäuser, Tristan*, Verdi Requiem, 323
"Some Enchanted Evening" (*South Pacific*): Pinza sings, 227
Some Memoirs and Reflections (Eames), 166
"Song of the Flea" (Mussorgsky): sung by Chaliapin, 222; by Tibbett, 222-3, 225
Sonnambula (Bellini), 58, 61, 325, 336; sets by Gérard, 315
Sordello, Enzo: and Callas, 351
South American singers, 297, 347
South Pacific (Rodgers and Hammerstein): Pinza and Mary Martin in, 227
Souvaine, Henry: produces Met radio intermission features, 279, 371
Souvaine, Mrs. Henry (Geraldine): succeeds husband, 371
Souzay, Gérard, 345-6
Soviet Union: cancels tours, 414; sends theatre to Paris, 385
Spalding, Charles: and Melba, 113
Spanish singers, 345, 347
Sparafucile (character), 262, 315
Sparkes, Leonora, 186
Spetrino, Francesco: conducts Brooklyn *Faust* (debut), 178
Speyer, James: backs Conried on *Salome*, 151
Spofford, Charles: and Johnson, 280
Spokane, 291
Spoleto Festival, 317, 325, 342
Spontini, Gasparo: see *Fernand Cortez; Vestale, La*
stagione system: versus repertoire, 340
Stagno, Roberto, 59

Standard Oil Co. of N. J., 376
Stanton, Edmund C., 73, 86, 102, 134, 312; against Conried renting Met, 138; appointed Met secretary, 5; and novelties, 79-82; stockholders complain at his $15,000 salary, 121; succeeds Abbey as manager, 65, 71; and touring, 82-3; tribute to, 83-4
"Star-Spangled Banner, The": Bing conducts, 359; at Gala Farewell, 377; at 1918 opening, 199; at 1966 opening, 405; quoted, 286
star system, 91, 155-6; and Abbey and Grau, 98; and Bing, 327-39; Conried attempts to abolish, 139; Kastendieck says Met withdraws from, 285; Kolodin on, 340
State Theatre (Lincoln Center), 397; acoustics in, 401; art in, 399; built for World's Fair, 427; N. Y. C. Ballet in, 424-5; N. Y. C. Opera in, 424-5, 427
Staudigl, Joseph, 66
Steber, Eleanor, 286-7; Auditions winner, 265; on Bing's vindictiveness, 358; at Gala Farewell, 378; informal *Tosca*, 287; sings in *Così* and *Otello* same day, 367. Roles: Constanza, Countess (*Nozze di Figaro*), Donna Anna, Marschallin, Pamina, Sophie (debut), 286; Desdemona, 367; Donna Elvira, 227, 286; Fiordiligi, 286, 367
Steichen, Edward: describes J. P. Morgan, 16
Steinberg, William: from Pittsburgh Symphony, in San Francisco, 323. Conducts: *Aida, Vanessa, Walküre*, 323
Steinway, William: in Box 102, 7; leases Irving Place Theatre to Conried, 138
Stella, Antonietta, 351-2
Stellman, Maxine, 259, 262
Stengel, William: see Sembrich, Marcella
Stettinius, Mr. and Mrs. Edward R.: at 1917 opening, 198
Stevens, Paran, 27-8
Stevens, Mrs. Paran, 200; attends three openings, *Tribune* on, 27; position in Society of, 28
Stevens, Risë, 327; co-manager of Met National Co., 266; with Manuel, 319; engaged through Auditions, 266; in films, 266; at Gala Farewell, 379; married to Surovy, 266. Roles: Carmen, 266, 290, 314; Mignon, 266; Octavian, 266, 292 (debut, Philadelphia)
Stevens, Roger L., at 1966 opening, 395; and Old Met, 408
Stewart, Thomas, 354; to be Wotan (*Walküre*), 420
Stich-Randall, Teresa, 346
Stiedry, Fritz, 239, 289, 320-1; engaged by Johnson, 275; introduces Bing to Johnson, 302; slows down, 321; with New Opera Co., 275, 293; and Traubel, 307
Stignani, Ebe, 344-5
Stillman, James, 16

Williams, Nancy, 375
Williamson, Malcolm: see *Happy Prince, The*
Williamson, Marshall, 375
Willis, N. P.: on women in Society, 20
Wilson, Belle: married to Ogden Goelet, 8; see also Goelet, Mrs. Ogden
Wilson, Dolores: as Lucia, 329
Wilson, George W.: aspires to Met management, 141–2; and Carnegie and other Pittsburgh millionaires, 142–3; loses, returns to orchestra management, 144; relinquishes Met Pittsburgh management to Schlotterbeck, 146
Wilson, Grace: fascinates two Vanderbilts, 39; marries Cornelius Vanderbilt III, 8, 39; see also Vanderbilt, Mrs. Cornelius III
Wilson, Mrs. Orme (Caroline Astor): at opera with Mrs. Fish, 38
Wilson, R. T., 5, 7; absent from *Parsifal*, 150; death of, 247; in upper box, 6; moves to Parterre, 104
Wilson, Mrs. R. T.: faithful to opera, 247
Wilson, Woodrow: and war, 194
Wilson family, 17, 32, 39, 40
Windgassen, Wolfgang, 347; Bing says is in breach of contract, 348; in *Ring*, 348
Windsor Hotel (New York), 59
Winkler, John K.: describes J. P. Morgan, 15–6
Winthrop, Mrs. Buchanan: opera gown described, 26
Winthrop, Henry Rogers, 142; approves Kahn plan, 242; backs Conried on *Salome*, 151
Winthrop family, 3
Witherspoon, Herbert: as manager: 256, 278; in Chicago, 252; death of, 255; and star system, 327; to succeed Gatti, 252–3; at work, 254; as singer: 186
Witherspoon, Mrs. Herbert: on Bing versus Johnson, 368; director of Guild, 255, 271, 368; on husband's appointment, 252–3; at husband's death, 255; and tenors, 311
Witte, Erich, 268
Woerishoffer, Charles T.: in Box 11, 10; described by Clews, 10; missing in 1892, 104
Wolf-Ferrari, Ermanno, 187; see also *Gioielli della Madonna, I; Segreto di Susanna, Il*
Wolff, Albert, 216; second to conduct own opera at Met, 238; see also *Oiseau Bleu, L'*
Wolff, Beverly, 356
Wood, Peggy: and Old Met, 410
"Woodman Spare That Tree" (Russell), 175
Worden, Helen (*Evening World*): on Bing, 358; married to John Erskine, 247; on Mrs. Belmont and Erskine, 310; on Society, 247
World (New York), 54, 57–9, 60, 81, 90, 178; acquired by Pulitzer, 8; on *Canterbury Pilgrims*, 193–4; De Koven critic for, 103, 178, 188; on De Reszke brothers, 88; on draw-

backs in New House, 63; on "Duke's Grand Opera," 82; on fashion, 25; on fire at Met, 100, 102; on Franchetti, 81; installs first halftone equipment, 107; interviews Nilsson, 58–9; on Kahn, 242; on openings, (1883) 46, 49, 50–1; (1918) 197; on preparations for war, 194; on stockholders of Met, 84; on stockholders as delinquent, 102; on Vanderbilt ball, 23–5; warns Met may be sold, 103
World (New York *Evening*), 247
World Journal Tribune (New York), 394, 404, 415, 417, 425; merger, death of, 380; on Old Met, 408, 410–1
Worlds of Music (Smith), 360
World-Telegram (New York), 329; and *The Sun*, 316, 357, 381; Lilly on Society in, 247; Worden reporter for, 247
Works Progress Administration, 270
Worth (Paris): Abbey orders opera costumes from, 25; Mrs. Astor's robe by, 27; Nilsson's wardrobe by, 59; two gowns by at opera, 25
Wotan (character), 235
Wozzeck (Berg), 267, 295, 319, 346 (English), 350 (Covent Garden), 355; a Bing favorite, 306; given by League of Composers with Stokowski, 306, 320, 322, 364; Met controversy over, 306, 319; at N. Y. C. Opera, 306, 320, 350; sets by Neher, 319–20
Wright, J. Hood, 16
Wunderlich, Fritz: death of, 418
Wymetal, Wilhelm von: directs *King's Henchman*, 224

Yale School of Drama, 424
Yannopoulos, Dino, 318
Yeend, Frances, 355
You're Only Human Once (Moore), 232
Yugoslavian singers, 297, 346
Yurka, Blanche: in *Parsifal*, 145
Yznaga, Mrs. Fernando: at Vanderbilt ball, 24

Zadek, Hilde, 348
Zambruno, Primo, 351
Zampieri, Giuseppe, 351
Zandonai, Riccardo: see *Conchita; Francesca da Rimini*
Zar und Zimmermann (Lortzing): at New Theatre, 182
Zauberflöte, Die (Mozart), 72, 134, 290, 321, 324–5, 345, 417 (new, in German), 421; first time in German, then Italianized, 164; Grau's cast for, 135; Kolodin on, 321; at Lincoln Center Festival, 423; at N. Y. C. Opera (sets by Montresor), 417, 426; quintet from at Gala Farewell, 378; Rich on, 417; Schonberg on, 417; sets by Rychtarik, 272; sets by Horner, 314; sets by Chagall, 314, 417, 426; *Times* on, 426; two casts for, 418